HUNTINGTON LIBRARY PUBLICATIONS

MIDDLE-CLASS CULTURE
IN ELIZABETHAN ENGLAND

The University of North Carolina Press, Chapel Hill, N. C.; The Baker and Taylor Company, New York; Oxford University Press, London; Maruzen-Kabushiki-Kaisha, Tokyo; Edward Evans & Sons, Ltd., Shanghai; D. B. Centen's Wetenschappelijke Boekhandel, Amsterdam

MIDDLE-CLASS CULTURE
IN ELIZABETHAN ENGLAND

BY

LOUIS B. WRIGHT

Chapel Hill

The University of North Carolina Press

1935

To
F. B. W.

PREFACE

LIFE in Elizabethan England has been for the past hundred and fifty years the theme of a multitude of scholars. Zealous antiquarians of the eighteenth and early nineteenth centuries, bored vicars in dull parishes, Victorian ladies adoring Shakespeare, painstaking scholars—all have added to the heap of background books dealing with Shakespeare's England. Of books about Elizabethan life, the manners and customs of the time—culture in the broad sense—we have an abundance. But in all that welter of books, one subject has been comparatively neglected: the important matter of the average citizen's reading and thinking, his intellectual habits and cultural tastes. In the series of studies which make up this book, it has been my aim not to add to the growing list of works on manners and customs but to describe the intellectual background and interests of the literate common people, the rank and file who composed the great middle class. The composition of this middle class I have tried to make clear in the opening chapter.

The pigeonholing of society into compartments with descriptive labels like "middle class" is always unsatisfactory, and never more so than when discussing things of the mind, which heed no social barriers. Indistinct as the border lines of stratified society were becoming even in the sixteenth and seventeenth centuries, and diffused as were many of the ideas and intellectual interests of the day, there can be discerned nevertheless a large middle group in Elizabethan society whose preoccupation was trade and whose intellectual concerns were largely colored by the peculiarities of their place in the social order. Though we cannot separate social groups into elements as accurately as the chemist breaks a compound into its parts, nor can our generalizations about human phenomena take on the finality of scientific statements, we can analyze, at least roughly, the social compound and describe the characteristics that seem peculiar to certain elements. With due recognition of the dangers of oversimplification in social and intellectual history, I have attempted little more than a survey of the materials that reflect the mind of the middle class.

It may be well to point out that the concern of the present study is not merely with books written by middle-class authors, or works written exclusively for middle-class readers, but with the general literary background that influenced the thinking of this group. Some authors who reflect bourgeois characteristics were not themselves of that class. A case in point is Richard Brathwaite, a country gentleman, who became so saturated with the bourgeois ideology which was constantly becoming more influential in his time that his works not only appealed to middle-class readers but they give many clues to an understanding of middle-class thought.

For want of a better term, I have followed the conventional practice of using the word "Elizabethan" to describe the period beginning with the accession of Elizabeth and ending with the Puritan Revolution in the 1640's. Rapid and great as were the intellectual, social, and political changes taking place in England, there is a consistent and progressive development in the commercial group particularly which gives a fairly logical unity to a study of the middle class through this period.

So little study has been made of sixteenth- and seventeenth-century bourgeois backgrounds that it has been impracticable to present a neat and closely knit history of the intellectual life of the middle class. Rather it has been necessary to hew a way through a wilderness of contemporary books and pamphlets and to present in a series of chapters, each complete within itself, the materials which, it is hoped, will contribute to the understanding of the mental state of Elizabethan commoners and make possible the writing of a history of culture that does not neglect the mind of the average citizen in the English Renaissance.

Since each chapter is a separate unit, for the convenience of the reader I have made the first reference to an authority in the footnotes bibliographically complete in each chapter. The long titles of Elizabethan books have been shortened where the verbiage adds little to the description of the book. In some cases, where the additional matter seems to be of interest, the full title has been quoted in the footnotes, but no attempt has been made to give complete transcripts of title-pages, since to do so would have increased the bulk of the volume beyond the limits of the practical. Whenever the title has been quoted directly from the book, I have adhered in the first reference to the original spelling, punctuation, and initial capitalization, but I have not attempted to preserve type peculiarities, and I have corrected certain obvious misprints. The same statement applies to quoted passages from the texts, but here consistency has been impossible, for it has often been necessary to quote from reprints, some of which have modernized texts.

Portions of six chapters included in the present volume have been previously printed in periodical form, but they have undergone revision before their inclusion here. For permission to reprint this material, I am indebted to the editors of *Studies in Philology*, the *Journal of English and Germanic Philology*, the *Journal of Modern History*, the *Philological Quarterly*, and the *Library*.

The gathering of the material for this study was made possible by the award of a fellowship from the John Simon Guggenheim Memorial Foundation, followed by an appointment to the research staff of the Huntington Library. To the staffs of the British Museum, the Bodleian Library, and the Huntington Library I wish to express my appreciation of many courtesies. Of the Huntington Library staff, I wish to thank particularly Miss Mary Isabel Fry, assistant reference librarian, and Miss Helen Domine, of the catalogue department, for assistance in checking references and in proof reading; and Miss Edith Klotz, for help in the preparation of the manuscript. For valuable criticisms and suggestions, I am indebted to my former colleagues in the Department of English at the University of North Carolina, to Professors Howard Mumford Jones, Hardin Craig, and Godfrey Davies, to Mr. Merrill H. Crissey, and to my wife. But the greatest debt of all is owed to the late Professor Edwin Greenlaw and to Dr. Max Farrand, director of research at the Huntington Library. Professor Greenlaw's interest in the history of ideas and his zeal for research profoundly influenced all who were privileged to call themselves his students. Dr. Farrand's rare ability to impart to his colleagues some of his own enthusiasm for learning has been an unfailing source of inspiration. By his sympathetic encouragement, no less than by his penetrating criticism, the task of completing the present study has been furthered.

Louis B. Wright

The Huntington Library
San Marino, California
January 10, 1934

TABLE OF CONTENTS

PART I
THE BACKGROUND

I

THE MIDDLE CLASS

WE have created a conception of Elizabethan England as a land of dashing courtiers like Raleigh strewing coats in the mud for a queen to walk upon, of court intrigues, of maids of honor listening to sugared sonnets, of statesmen reading Spenser's *Faerie Queene* as a political document, of life spent in palaces or in high adventure on the Spanish Main. Of what the draper, the baker, the butcher, and their apprentices were reading and thinking we hear little.

But why consider the man in the street, dead these three hundred years? Perhaps he never read much, and thought less. If he did, what influence did it have? Why resurrect dead dullness? Is the taste of the average citizen of the present time not deplorable enough without unearthing the crudities of his ancestors?

We must remember, however, that the Elizabethan tradesman, the average citizen, was the backbone of progressive enterprise in England and the direct ancestor of a civilization soon to predominate on both sides of the Atlantic. His vigor and strength enabled England to take its place in the front rank of nations. As he pushed ahead, he developed new ideas of his own importance and bred an ambition for better things, material, spiritual, and intellectual. In the furtherance of his social ambitions, the Elizabethan business man evolved a philosophy of success, which emphasized thrift, honesty, industry, and godliness. Education, he found, was the key to advancement, and in the cultivation of his wits he foresaw the attainment of his ambitions. Substantial commoners, gathering strength in the sixteenth century, grew in intelligence and mental stature to become the power that was to conquer a new continent and make England great. The impetus gathered by the commercial classes swept England toward the Puritan

Revolution of the mid-seventeenth century and the Whig supremacy of the eighteenth. Naïve, awkward, and crude as were the Elizabethan citizen's first attempts to take his place among the learned or the gentle, he possessed a strength of mind and character which gave vitality to his thinking and enabled him to propagate his ideas so luxuriantly that they have survived in all their vigor to become the clichés of modern civilization. The cultural interests, then, of so virile a group as the Elizabethan middle class deserve attention, for in these interests we may find much that explains our own culture.

Elizabethan society may be roughly separated into three major divisions. The highest class consisted of the titled nobility, the landed gentry, and the more important members of the learned professions. The lowest class was composed of unskilled laborers, an illiterate peasantry, and those small artisans whose trades required little training and whose rewards were meager. Between these extremes was a great class of merchants, tradesfolk, and skilled craftsmen, a social group whose thoughts and interests centered in business profits. They made up the middle class, the bourgeoisie, the average men.

But the lines of distinction, even in the stratified society of the sixteenth and seventeenth centuries, were not distinct and mutually exclusive. The highest caste was eternally being recruited from the ranks of the rich merchants, and the lowest was always being swelled by economic derelicts. From both extremes the middle class absorbed new recruits. If the younger sons of the gentry regarded business as a refuge from the tyranny of primogeniture, poor youths, fresh from country toil, looked upon an apprenticeship in trade as the certain pathway to prosperity. If a rich merchant could aspire to a peerage or to lands and a coat of arms, many a daughter of a gentle house did not disdain a match with a tradesman who could offer her luxuries and the gaiety of the city. Professional men—preachers, lawyers, and physicians—frequently shared the ideals of the commercial group with which they were associated and from which, in many instances, they had come, and some of the yeomanry had much in common with the lower middle class. Nevertheless, despite the constant flux within the social order, the classes remained sufficiently independent of each other to be roughly distinguished, and preachers and lay writers constantly emphasized the necessity of the system of social degree.

The middle class developed a way of life, a code of ethics, and a set of ideals which gave distinctness to its qualities. While the improvident poor degenerated into wretched misery, and the extravagant nobility ruined themselves with lavish entertainment, the middle class cultivated the virtues of thrift. "Put money in thy purse" echoed in the ears of every tradesman. Courtiers might fawn upon favorites for patents and monopolies, but enterprising business men, by dint of their own exertions, acquired not only wealth but a spirit of sturdy independence. Though not averse to profiting by political expediency, merchants and tradesmen learned that honesty and industry were the most certain ways to success. Having realized that wealth could be won by their own endeavors and that money would exalt their positions, tradesmen grew ambitious for further improvement. The ideal of progress—if not the word—was cultivated by the middle class in their desire for the improvement of their lot here below. If poets wished to pine over the lost golden age, it was merely proof of the impractical nature of poets. The tradesman set about gilding the age to his own taste. The middle class found that trade was not a tarnishing, shameful thing, but something to be proud of. Like his American descendant, the self-made man of Elizabethan England did not hide his light under a bushel. Deloney and Dekker were fond of honest craftsmen who stood before kings and boasted of their labors. Thus many concepts of modern business life are traceable to the molding influence of Elizabethan bourgeois ideals. Utilitarianism was born of them and humanitarianism was a natural sequence. The materialistic dye which so deeply colors modern life was brewed in the cauldron of Elizabethan business by tradesmen who believed that money and possessions were the proof of success. Even Calvin's grim theology did not discourage man from gathering material possessions. Instead, it was twisted to the profit of acquisitive society, for bourgeois religion, despite all its smoke and hell-fire, did not put away the world, and business expediency influenced the ethics evolved by the middle class.

The emergence of a prosperous citizenry with virile ideas and a propelling ambition had tremendous influence, not only upon England but upon all Europe. Indeed, at least one historian has declared that the whole ferment of the Renaissance is traceable to the development of the middle class.[1] Whatever may have been the complex causes of the social and intellectual upheaval that changed Europe from a medieval to a modern world, certainly the rise of the citizenry went far toward working the metamorphosis. Tales of the glory of the great houses of Venice, Genoa, and Florence were brought to England to inspire merchant princes to emulate the grandeur of Italian traders, who had founded names for themselves and had poured their wealth into art and letters. The notion of the "Compleat Citizen," which dominated English bourgeois thinking in the seventeenth century and was transmitted to America to find an echo in Franklin, was not an English monopoly, but had been set forth in Florence in the fourteenth and fifteenth centuries and had passed to England to help crystallize ideas of conduct acceptable to tradesmen.[2] Throughout Europe from the fifteenth to the seventeenth century occurred a development in trade which multiplied the populations of cities and sent fleets of merchantmen to search the ports of the world for cargoes. Seamen and traders, meeting strange peoples and seeing new sights, helped to spread a curiosity about the world and stimulated the desire for further knowledge. In the transmission of ideas, the Renaissance trader was no less potent than the scholar.

Although commerce was altering the social complexion of most of Western Europe, with the possible exception of the Nether-

---

[1] A. F. Pollard, "The Advent of the Middle Class," in *Factors in Modern History* (London, 1907), pp. 39-40: "Nearly every movement of this period is a symptom of this middle-class development. The Renaissance represents its intellectual aspect; art, science, and letters had hitherto been ecclesiastical; the Renaissance is a secular, and sometimes even pagan revolt against this sacerdotal monopoly. The Reformation is its religious counterpart, the rebellion of the middle-class laity against the domination by the Church over the relations between God and man. Socially, we see rich burghers competing with feudal lords for rank and title. . . . Politically, this expansion shows itself in the development of the House of Commons at the expense of the House of Lords and of the monarchy."

[2] Werner Sombart, *The Quintessence of Capitalism*. Translated and edited from Sombart's *Der Bourgeois* (1913) by M. Epstein (New York, 1915), pp. 97, 103, 104, 113.

lands,[3] England felt the greatest transforming influence from the emergence of the middle class. The evolution had been gradual. The Elizabethan bourgeoisie did not spring full-grown from the head of some mercantile Jove, but its foundations had been laid in the slow commercial development of England since the thirteenth century, when the wool and cloth trade with Flanders and the wine trade with Bordeaux had started a business expansion which rapidly swelled in the sixteenth and seventeenth centuries until its ramifications approached in complexity modern commercialism.

Political changes favored the growth of the middle classes in England. The rise of the Tudors saw the ascent of a bourgeois dynasty. Henry VII may have had the habits of a usurious merchant, but his son enjoyed wealth with the abandon of any *nouveau riche* and stood not upon high birth for advisers, companions, or mistresses. Though the mythical ancestry of the Tudors went back to King Arthur, Queen Elizabeth had a nearer progenitor, a great-grandfather, who was a London merchant.[4] A shrewd intuition for the feelings of the common people was a source of Tudor strength completely lacking in the Stuarts. As the old feudal aristocracy, decimated by the Wars of the Roses, gave way to new houses recruited from wealthy merchants, it became increasingly easy for tradesmen to cross the line into the ranks of the gentry. Many of the great names of Elizabethan England had lowly origins. The Cecils and the Walsinghams were upstart gentry;[5] perhaps Burleigh's bourgeois heritage was responsible for his canny financial and economic policies, which lay behind much of Elizabethan strength. From Elizabeth, rich merchants and daring seamen in the service of trade won knighthoods, for her government honored business and awarded it the trappings of greatness.

The Stuarts found the middle class strongly entrenched, conscious of the power that an era of peace had brought, and far

---

[3] Indeed, the middle-class prosperity of the Netherlands in the early seventeenth century exerted considerable influence in suggesting democratic ideas to the English who traded with them. *See* G. P. Gooch, *English Democratic Ideas in the Seventeenth Century* (2d ed., Cambridge, 1927), p. 45.

[4] Pollard, *op. cit.*, p. 40.

[5] *Ibid.*

less inclined than formerly to submit to a God-sent sovereign. Though James scorned the multitude and had purple notions of the divinity that doth hedge a king, he too honored tradesmen—with knighthoods at £30 each. The English Solomon, fearful, it is said, of even the sight of a bare sword, kept his country out of war and encouraged peace abroad, thus enabling Englishmen to push further their trading ventures. As the momentum of business progress urged the nation on, the middle class grew in strength and power until it set in motion forces that swept a king to trial and execution. Although the conditions of life in their kingdom produced new economic and social ideas, the Stuarts clung to medieval notions of kingship; the failure of James and Charles to appreciate the changing temper of the times and to understand the mind of the citizenry toppled their house into the maelstrom of the Civil War. The democratization which the Tudors had turned to their purposes paved the way for the destruction of their less shrewd successors,[6] under whom common citizens, holding the national purse, presumed to dictate to royalty.

Economic changes of the sixteenth and early seventeenth centuries favored the development of industry and commerce, which absorbed the activities of an ever increasing proportion of the population. As the feudal agricultural system gave way to inclosures, farms and old corporate towns were depopulated,[7] and a floating group struggled to adjust themselves to new conditions. The result was the swelling of the population of London and a few other industrial and trade centers, the development of new industrial villages and towns, and the spread of a system of cottage industries.[8] The Statute of Apprentices of 1563 provided that all persons except gentlemen, scholars, and possessors of property must choose a trade from the crafts, the sea, or agriculture. Though it sought to prevent workers' wandering from one locality to another, it failed to stop their migration to industrial districts. The wool and cloth trade, which for centuries had been the core of English commerce, increased as England gradually

---

[6] R. H. Tawney, *Religion and the Rise of Capitalism* (London, 1929), pp. 176-77.

[7] *Idem, The Agrarian Problem in the Sixteenth Century* (London, 1912), pp. 265 ff.

[8] George Unwin, "Commerce and Coinage," in *Shakespeare's England* (Oxford, 1916), I, 326-27.

wrung more trade from foreign markets and improved its means of distribution abroad through the trading companies that were so important in the expansion of Elizabethan business.[9] As the demand for English cloth grew heavier, its production was stimulated by the increase in weaving in cottage and village. Since small manufacturers could not keep on hand a large supply of wool, there arose a class of middlemen who lived in the smaller towns and dealt in wool and cloth.[10] For the benefit of such local tradesmen, legislation was repeatedly demanded to prevent London merchants and foreign buyers from purchasing directly from the small manufacturers; but so strong was the insistence upon the village weaver's right to sell where he wished, that restrictions on his trade were finally abolished.[11] Not merely did the cloth trade expand and produce a host of related businesses, but such industries as iron founding, steel manufacture, the mining of coal, tin, lead, and gold, and a score of other industrial activities received new life in the later sixteenth and early seventeenth centuries. Thomas Sutton, founder of Charterhouse School, made a fortune in coal mining, and Bevis Bulmer succeeded so well with lead, tin, and gold that he won a knighthood and enlisted King James in a project for searching out gold in Scotland.[12] Projectors, ancestors of the modern high-pressure salesman, swarmed in London with innumerable schemes for new businesses and industries, and inventors boasted of new processes for smelting iron with pit coal, making nails with a slitting machine,[13] or even turning lead into gold. The romance or the tragedy of industrial development had begun, but such was the peculiar quality of Elizabethan industry that instead of centering business in the hands of a few great manufacturers with an army of slaves, as in the later Industrial Revolution, it multiplied the middle class.

---

[9] The development of the cloth trade was progressively upward, but, like all businesses, it had its periods of depression. For a discussion of the state of the trade at the beginning of the seventeenth century see Professor George Burton Hotchkiss' Introduction to his edition of John Wheeler's *A Treatise of Commerce, 1601* (New York, 1931).

[10] W. A. S. Hewins, *English Trade and Finance Chiefly in the Seventeenth Century* (London, 1892), p. 110.

[11] Unwin, *op. cit.*, p. 328.

[12] H. M. Robertson, "Sir Bevis Bulmer, A Large-Scale Speculator of Elizabethan and Jacobean Times," *Journal of Economic and Business History*, IV (1931-32), 99-120.

[13] Hewins, *op. cit.*, pp. 12 ff.

The industrial development of the sixteenth and seventeenth centuries had this quality which distinguishes it from modern industry: the individual craftsman was closer to the completion and distribution of the product of his labor, and the apprentice or journeyman might look forward to becoming a master craftsman, who could, if he wished, combine the functions of manufacturer and retail or wholesale distributor of his finished products. The division of labor had not yet become so complex that the skilled laborer felt that he was merely a cog in an industrial machine. On the contrary, the system encouraged the development of a strong bourgeois spirit, for even a cottage weaver might employ one or two apprentices and journeymen weavers, who in turn might look forward to setting up as independent workmen. Though many journeymen continued to work for wages, the progression from apprentice to independent manufacturer was steadily going on to increase the number of small masters. Since the apprentice of today was the master of tomorrow, he was exhorted to cultivate the qualities that would make him a substantial and successful business man when he won his freedom and set up for himself. Although something like the factory system was foreshadowed in a few industries, such as cloth manufacturing,[14] throughout the period the skilled craftsman could expect, provided he was industrious and thrifty, to become a manufacturer employing assistants to increase his output, and marketing directly his own handiwork. From the cottager with one apprentice to the employer of many journeymen, the economic points of view were similar. So overlapping were trades and

---

[14] A. P. Usher, *An Introduction to the Industrial History of England* (Boston and New York, 1920), p. 223. Leland describes a certain Stump, a clothier, who leased the Abbey of Malmesbury "to be full of looms and to weave cloth." He is later reported to have leased an abbey near Oxford, where he employed two thousand persons in weaving. Doubtless the number is greatly exaggerated. Deloney's description of Jack of Newbery's activities as a great manufacturer is well known. Professor Usher (pp. 216 ff.) also calls attention to another form of capitalistic enterprise in the clothing industry as early as the fifteenth century, the "putting-out system," by which clothiers put into the hands of cottagers wool to be woven. This method, suggestive of the modern sweatshop, helped, however, to foster the independent cottage industries. Furthermore, since the cottager was frequently paid in kind, he had, even under the putting-out system, a greater interest in the business of distribution than the modern victim of the sweatshop.

business occupations that they combined to produce a middle class relatively far more extensive than modern industrial society permits. One historian thus epitomizes the industrial and business ramifications that made for a relatively homogeneous social outlook:

At one end of the scale was the merchant, who would probably be a member of a trading company—the 'economic man' of the mercantilists—and at the other, the simple journeyman craftsman. But midway between these was a large class whose functions in the industrial system overlapped each other, and cannot easily be separated. We find (1) the master craftsman, with his journeymen and apprentices, purchasing his own raw material and selling the product to the dealer; (2) the master craftsman working up with the aid of journeymen and apprentices the raw material which was given out by the dealer; (3) the master craftsman acting also in the capacity of dealer; (4) the simple dealer in finished commodities; (5) the dealer, with craftsmen working on his own premises under his supervision; (6) women and children working independently for the dealer, or assisting the husband or father; (7) any of these combining his ordinary functions with a retail trade, and sometimes with agriculture.[15]

The business point of view extended even to farming; one of the stock complaints was directed against the land hunger of city merchants who bought up land and farmed it for profit,[16] ceasing to be, in the old manorial sense, "house-keepers" of the sort that had given employment to swarms of retainers and had dispensed hospitality to the countryside.

Although the widespread diffusion of industrial and commercial interests in Elizabethan England created a middle class who were not exclusively urban, yet as industry and trade tended more and more to concentrate in thickly populated areas, London and a few other towns became centers where large groups of citizens had an opportunity to develop an urban way of life and to taste the luxuries that further stimulated the pursuit of wealth and the acquisition of a set of social ideas prompted thereby. Port towns like Bristol, Plymouth, and Southampton grew into thriving marts. An industrial development prophetic of the future began

---

[15] Hewins, *op. cit.*, p. 97.
[16] Tawney, *The Agrarian Problem*, p. 192.

in Birmingham, Sheffield, Halifax, Leeds, Wakefield, Manchester, and many other towns and villages,[17] in which iron and cloth were the backbone of business. Even if foreign artisans—many of whom were brought in by the government—created intense animosity among native workers, they nevertheless taught Englishmen new trades and developed new industries which swelled the urban population. The manufacture of glass, paper, cutlery, and certain types of fabrics was improved by foreign immigrants, who settled in Canterbury, Sandwich, Norwich, Dover, and numerous other towns. Abundant as were the complaints in the sixteenth century about the decay of the old corporate towns, many new municipalities were laying the foundations for a commercial development that was soon to bring them size and prosperity.

Of all the urban developments of the sixteenth and seventeenth centuries, the growth of London was the most phenomenal and did the most to color the whole of Elizabethan civilization. In Chaucer's prime, London had a population of probably fewer than 50,000 inhabitants.[18] The population in 1563 has been estimated at 93,276; in 1580, 123,034; in 1593-95, 152,478; in 1605, 224,275; in 1622, 272,207; in 1634, 339,824. Since the population of the whole of England in 1600 was only about 4,460,000,[19] the importance of London in relation to the rest of the country is at once apparent, for the capital was many times the size of any other city in the realm. In less than three-quarters of a century London more than trebled in size, expanding from a provincial walled town into a cosmopolitan city stirring with business, surrounded by busy suburbs. With the gradual decline of Venice and Genoa and the fall of Antwerp in 1585, London became the economic capital of Europe, a banking center, the seat of merchant princes, a distributing point for foreign and

---

[17] Unwin, *op. cit.*, p. 326.

[18] Usher, *op. cit.*, p. 108. Professor Usher quotes the figures from C. Creighton, "The Population of Old London," *Blackwood's Magazine*, CXLIX, 484, 486, 495. These figures necessarily are more or less conjectural, but they give a reasonably close approximation of the size of London and the suburbs. A brief essay on the population of London in the early seventeenth century is to be found in F. P. Wilson, *The Plague in Shakespeare's London* (Oxford, 1927), pp. 209-15. Professor Wilson bases his estimates on the mortality bills, and estimates the population in 1612-14 at 250,256; 1620-22, 294,734; 1632-34, 317,097.

[19] Wilson, *op. cit.*, p. 215.

domestic goods. Its harbor teemed with ships whose tall masts astonished visitors. Its Royal Exchange, built by Sir Thomas Gresham in imitation of the Bourse at Antwerp, was the meeting place of traders from the ends of the earth. The gentry of England, who crowded to London to shine in the glory of the court, were followed by an army of tradesmen, great and small, who lived on the needs of the mighty. Cheapside, resplendent with shops, was a sight which travelers noted in their diaries. Rich silks from China, rare spices from the Indies, plate of hammered silver and gold, glassware from Venice, besides the endless array of articles of commoner use, filled the shops. The craftsmen, native and foreign, who plied their trades in and about the city were almost as varied in their occupations as the contents of the shops. Infinitely busy, London was forging ahead as the leading city of the world in commerce and industry.

From country cottages, from small villages, from other industrial and commercial towns, tradesmen and craftsmen poured into London. The ambition of every provincial apprentice was to go like Dick Whittington to London, where he might grow rich and become an alderman or even lord mayor. Nor were the provincial gentry averse to apprenticing one or more of their younger sons to London tradesmen. With the world of commerce open before them and with a keen ambition driving them to success, these new citizens of London acted like a leaven to keep the fermentation of progress eternally at work. The result of their effort was evident in the prosperity of the city and in their personal achievements. Many did rise to positions of honor and authority, and a survey of the aldermen, sheriffs, and the lord mayors of the late sixteenth and early seventeenth centuries shows that a majority of them were of provincial birth, often of humble parentage.[20] From all the counties of England came immigrants to settle in London and establish substantial families of industrious citizens. Though the plague might come like a holocaust to destroy the people, and though King James might pronounce a royal decree against crowding to the capital, the metropolis swelled until it burst its

---

[20] *See* A. B. Beaven, *The Aldermen of the City of London*, 2 vols. (London, 1908-13), and G. E. Cokayne, *Some Account of the Lord Mayors and Sheriffs of the City of London during the First Quarter of the Seventeenth Century* (London, 1897).

walls and overflowed into the suburbs, and approached the neighboring boroughs.

With the spread of commercial undertakings, the London citizenry, long famous for their sturdy independence, acquired new enterprise and daring. By the end of the sixteenth century trading companies were multiplying, and there were few citizens of even moderate means who did not have an interest in some of the ventures to the Indies, Russia, the Levant, or the New World. English ships pushed into strange ports and brought back stranger produce—sometimes to the disgust of the conservatives of the older generation, who looked askance at the traffic in luxuries that their fathers had got on without. As rumors of the profits from some of the trading ventures were bruited about and the appetites of investors were whetted, a rage of speculation swept England, until no scheme was too fantastic to find subscribers. The early seventeenth century was particularly favorable to promotion schemes, which drew into their nets high and low, rich and poor, without distinction of rank and degree. Subscribers to the joint stock of the East India Company in 1617 included "15 dukes and earls, 13 countesses and other titled ladies, 82 knights . . . , 18 widows and maiden ladies, 26 clergymen and physicians, 313 merchants, 214 tradesmen, 25 merchant strangers, and 248 without designation; total 954."[21] The scramble for profits was democratic. While dukes and earls, and even the sovereign, took an interest in these trading ventures, the direction, control, and chief support remained in the hands of citizens. Sir Thomas Smith, the greatest promoter of the time, was a successful merchant, by patrimony free of the Company of the Haberdashers and also of the Skinners. The imagination and daring of men like Smith laid the foundations of England's commercial and colonial expansion. No longer was the only highroad to glory found in the wars, for now the avenues of trade led plain men to riches and honor.

The reigns of Elizabeth and the first two Stuarts were generally prosperous, though there were periodic depressions when men

---

[21] Hewins, *op. cit.*, p. 59.

complained of the stagnation of business,[22] and the state, as is the manner of governments, tried panaceas and nostrums to stimulate industry. Despite the rise in prices brought about by the influx of Spanish silver and gold, the grinding poverty of the unskilled laboring classes (whose wages never caught up with the prices), and the monopolies and patents granted to court favorites, business flourished and the commercial population multiplied and waxed richer than it had ever been before. Prosperity brought with it new luxuries. Rich citizens strode in silk and velvet through the Royal Exchange, dined on rare dishes served in pewter or silver, and generally aped the manners of the gentry. So grandly did the wives of tradesmen dress that foreigners complained that they could not distinguish them from fine ladies. And all the while, preachers warned that, because of the unseemly extravagance and corruption of gold which the older generation had not known, the iniquitous country would be swept by pestilence and damned to perdition.

The love of luxuries, which the traffic of business placed in reach even of small tradesmen, had tremendous esthetic effects. As citizens of London and other towns could afford it, they tore down their old houses and built new and finer homes with chimneys and glass windows and carved stairways. No longer, as in the days of their fathers, were tradesmen content with rude furnishings and bare necessities. Now they hung their walls with painted cloths and tapestries and had their portraits painted. As they grew richer, they laid out gardens and dreamed of country estates. Although diligence and industry were cardinal points in the tradesman's creed, he took time for honest pleasures, of which music was a favorite. Unlike his modern descendant, who turns a mechanical gadget and listens to a broadcasting crooner, the Elizabethan tradesman sang himself, either at his work or in the evening with his household. Folk songs were mingled with newer forms like the popular madrigal, introduced from Italy. For the singing of madrigals, Nicholas Yonge, a lay clerk of St. Paul's, was accustomed to bring together at his

---

[22] For a discussion of the disruption in business caused by crises in such key businesses as the cloth trade, see Professor Hotchkiss' Introduction to Wheeler's *A Treatise of Commerce*.

house "a great number of gentlemen and merchants . . . for the exercise of music daily."[23] If so minded, the tradesman might play the lute, for even in barber shops he would find one provided for his convenience. With some misgivings, because the reforming preacher often railed at such frivolities, he might join in a dance with his friends and neighbors. The urban tradesman of the sixteenth and early seventeenth centuries was learning to cultivate the amenities of life, to enjoy the world about him, and to make it pleasanter for himself.

The danger of damnation, it is true, was ever being dinned into his ears, but the picture, created by critics of the Puritans, of a nation of solemn shopkeepers, singing psalms through their noses and praying raucously in public, is a caricature which has distorted later thinking about the Tudor and Stuart middle class. Violent hatred of the forms and ritual of the Established Church flared at intervals because these forms symbolized a clinging to an older faith which the majority of the citizenry had learned to fear and hate. Fanatical asceticism swept England in the 1640's, but these were years of upheaval and hysteria, the causes of which were far more complicated than the word "Puritan" connotes. Stained-glass windows were broken, images destroyed, and brasses from churches stolen, but there is evidence that Cavaliers and Roundheads alike were guilty of vandalism. Though it was a common sneer that all tradesmen were Puritans, it cannot be emphasized too strongly that only the minority were destructive ascetics, for the rank and file of the commercial classes were not stern haters of the pleasant and the beautiful. In the three-quarters of a century preceding the Puritan Revolution, they had learned to appreciate new luxuries, new comforts, and new pleasures. And with the development of their taste came the stirrings of a new interest in the fine arts, which manifested itself chiefly in the desire of burghers for houses comfortably furnished and handsomely adorned. "Great prouision of tapistrie, Turkie worke, pewter, brasse, fine linen, and thereto costlie cupboards of plate" filled the houses of "knights, gentlemen, merchantmen, and some other wealthie citizens," William Harrison asserts in the *Description*

---

[23] J. W. Hebel and Hoyt H. Hudson (eds.), *Poetry of the English Renaissance, 1509-1660* (New York, 1929), p. 981.

of England (1577),[24] and even "the inferiour artificers and manie farmers" had plate, napery, "tapistrie and silke hangings." As in literature, bourgeois taste in art inclined to the useful and the didactic. The wall motto, which has not yet completely vanished into the limbo of discarded furnishings, edified the citizenry, whom Nicholas Breton enjoins to

> Reade what is written on the painted cloth;
> Doe no man wrong, be good vnto the poore:
> Beware the Mouse, the Maggot, and the Moth;
> And euer haue an eye vnto the doore:
> Trust not a foole, a villaine, nor a whore.
> Goe neat, not gaie; and spend but as you spare:
> And turne the Colte to pasture with the Mare.[25]

Not every citizen could have possessed "fifteene faire Pictures . . . couered with Curtaines of greene silke, fringed with gold," which Deloney places in the wainscoted parlor of Jack of Newbery, the clothier, but every citizen would have approved the sentiments reflected in those pictures, all of which portrayed some hero who, from the station of laborer or tradesman, had "been aduanced to high estate and Princely dignities, by wisedome, learning and diligence."[26] Naïve though the artistic sense of Elizabethan commoners may have been, the esthetic consciousness of plain men and women was growing with a vigor stimulated by increasing wealth, which placed within reach of the multitude painted pictures, tapestries, and other handiwork of sundry native and foreign craftsmen skilled in the decorative arts.[27] No longer content with smoky hovels and crude furnishings, citizens seeking the

---

[24] F. J. Furnivall (ed.), *Harrison's Description of England*, Pt. I, New Shakespeare Society, Ser. 6, I (1877), p. 239.

[25] *No Whippinge, nor trippinge: but a kinde friendly Snippinge* (1601), sig. B 3.

[26] F. O. Mann (ed.), *The Works of Thomas Deloney* (Oxford, 1912), pp. 40-42.

[27] Picture shops were common in London. William Painter in his little book of aphorisms, *Chaucer new Painted* [*c.* 1623], alludes to the picture sellers who have their shops from Temple Bar to Charing Cross:

> "You curious Painters
>   and you Limmers all,
> From Temple-barre
>   along to Charing-crosse,
> That your gay pictures
>   hang out on the wall,

ornamental developed a taste for color and gorgeousness, which is reflected in all Elizabethan art, including literature.[28]

The immense activity of the business life of London stimulated also the intellects of its citizens. If for no other reason, self-interest demanded an increase in knowledge, and utilitarian considerations prompted a new search after information. It was profitable to be informed. Nimbler wits than the countryman needed in his struggle with the forces of nature or in his wrangling on market days were required of the city dweller by the exigencies of urban

> Goe take them downe,
> for they are all but drosse:
> For here are liuely
> pictures to behold,
> More worth then those
> that guilded are with gold."—Sig. A 4.

(The presumably unique copy of this book is preserved in the Huntington Library.)

Cheap pictures were exported from the Netherlands to England and sold in the shops of London and at fairs. In addition to these imported pictures, foreign artists, chiefly refugees from France and the Low Countries, did a thriving business in England. *See* Lionel Cust, "Painting, Sculpture, and Engraving," in *Shakespeare's England* (Oxford, 1916), II, 6-12, and the same author's "Foreign Artists of the Reformed Religion Working in London from about 1560 to 1660," *Proceedings of the Huguenot Society of London*, VII (1901-4), 45-82. Wealthy merchants and other citizens with sufficient means were fond of having their portraits painted. From the time of Holbein, the best painters, as well as the lesser artists, found among the citizenry a large part of their clientele. Portrait painting, however, was relatively expensive, but subject paintings on canvas, known technically as "painted cloths," were within the range of persons of moderate means. Shakespeare has many allusions to painted cloths, which he may have seen in his own home and in the homes of his friends. His grandfather, Robert Arden, enumerated in his will eleven painted cloths. The subjects of these paintings were frequently biblical or allegorical, and often included mottoes. For a statement of Shakespeare's interest in painting see Margaret Farrand Thorp, "Shakespeare and the Fine Arts," *Publications of the Modern Language Association*, XLVI (1931), 672-93.

Improvement in the taste of the multitude is one of the purposes which Richard Haydocke declares have led him to translate *A Tracte Containing The Artes of curious Paintinge Caruinge & Buildinge* by Giovanni Lomazzo (1598). In order that the artist may not be hampered by the bad taste "amongst the ordinarie sorte," Haydocke asserts in his introduction that he has "taken paines, to teach the one to iudge and the other to worke."

By the late sixteenth century, few houses of people of even moderate means were without at least some hangings of tapestry or "arras" work, and perhaps a few pictures painted on cloth or wooden panels.

[28] Professor Frederick Hard, "Spenser's 'Clothes of Arras and of Toure'," *Studies in Philology*, XXVII (1930), 162-85, provides an interesting account of the influence of tapestries on the work of Spenser.

competition. The cunning of the peasant gave way to the shrewdness of the business man. By constant association with his fellows,
the citizen's mind was sharpened until he was able to penetrate
new mysteries and grasp new ideas. As the goodliness of the world
seized him, his ambition was magnified, and he acquired new
desires and a way of life which led him to think in concrete
terms of practical matters, to become a utilitarian. But getting
and spending, establishing a reputation, founding a name respected in the community, and becoming perchance an alderman
or even lord mayor, were not the sole preoccupations of worthy
citizens, for some of the infinite curiosity that characterizes
the intellectual Renaissance filtered down even to tradesmen;
and unlettered men, more versed in the language of the market
place than in that of the university, began to speculate about the
universe and their relation to it. As a new physical world unfolded
before their eyes, their own intellectual horizons widened, until
it was no strange thing for plain citizens to think, talk, or read
about everything from predestination to the motions of the planets.
In the Renaissance, for the first time, books were useful to the
rank and file of commoners, and as the literacy of Englishmen
increased, ever more numerous became the books and pamphlets
prepared for the intelligence of the "mean sort of men." Even
stubborn learning gradually let down its bars of Latin until at
length stores of erudition were available in English, and an
Elizabethan apprentice might speak with more clerkly wisdom
than a scholar in a previous age. And it was in this period that
education came to be a goal desired of the generality of men. So
potent was the ferment which set the minds of the middle class
working that from their ranks came many of the writers, good
and bad, who contributed to Elizabethan literature. Doubtless
many a tradesman who sent his son to the university was not too
pleased when the youth turned out to be a Bohemian, who
rioted and wrote in London, but however that may be, many
a tradesman's son sought to make his way with his pen. George
Peele's father was a salter; Christopher Marlowe's, a cobbler;
Anthony Munday's, a draper; John Webster's, a merchant tailor;
Henry Chettle's, a dyer; Robert Herrick's, a goldsmith; Gabriel
Harvey's, a ropemaker; Joshua Sylvester's, a clothier; John

Donne's, an ironmonger ; Thomas Browne's, a mercer ; and many another had some connection with trade. A few skilled artisans like Thomas Deloney, the silk weaver, plied their pens in addition to the tools of their crafts. The busy world of trade, especially in London, woke men from the easy provincialism of the past and helped to set in motion the currents of activity that stimulated the desire, not merely for more and finer material possessions, but for better things in literature and learning.

The aristocracy of Elizabethan letters is a commonplace of criticism, but even if the poets themselves and the formal critics condemned the rabble rout and the rascal many, the tale of contemporary literary culture is not complete with the doings of the courtly writers. While the critics of letters united in agreeing that the common herd should not meddle with poetry, should not invade the sacred precincts of this mystical learning, the printing presses poured forth a flood of ballads, pamphlets, and books to entertain and instruct the average commoner who was without benefit of gentle or clerkly background. While great figures like Spenser, and many a lesser poet, wrote with one or both eyes on the court, scores of others spent their energies frankly for the plaudits of the multitude. While Shakespeare, unconsciously writing for all time, kept in his mind's eye the approval of lordly patrons of Blackfriars, Thomas Heywood and his kind catered to apprentices and shopkeepers who haunted the Red Bull. A vast literature, rich with reflections of the tastes of commonplace Englishmen, indicative of many developments in the future intellectual evolution, survives to reveal the outlook of the average citizen in a period when England was laying the foundations for Anglo-Saxon dominion in realms of mind and matter. Although these books, once pored over by tradesmen, their wives, their sons, and their daughters, now gather dust and are forgotten, they furnish an insight into the thinking of the middle class, without a knowledge of which a complete understanding of the age is impossible. From the surviving literature written for or by plain citizens, the following chapters attempt to make a start toward charting the way that leads to an interpretation of the intellectual awakening of the middle class.

II

THE CITIZEN'S PRIDE

NO characteristic is more significant of the quality of the Elizabethan middle class than the self-respecting pride of the citizenry in their own accomplishments and in the dignity of their position in the commonwealth. For even if merchants and tradesmen were understandably eager for titles of gentility and lands to support such honors, they did not scorn their connection with trade, and many a wealthy citizen who died in possession of a title was buried with both the pomp of heraldry and the ceremonies of a trade guild[1] without anyone's feeling the incongruity of knightly pennons waving over a deceased brother of, let us say, the Fishmongers. Though the tradesman might be awarded a knighthood, he retained a healthy regard for his vocation and did not despise the commerce that had made him. Sir Thomas Gresham remained, in spite of honors, a busy banker and trader; Sir Baptist Hickes, later Viscount Camden, continued to keep a shop after being knighted, though this indeed was regarded by the aldermen as something of a scandal.[2] This characteristic of prideful independence distinguishes the middle class throughout the period from the accession of Elizabeth to the culmination of middle-class power in the Commonwealth. Proud of their self-made success, proud of their material accomplishments, proud of their greatest city, London, the Elizabethan middle class developed a self-respect and a self-esteem that at times reached the proportions of smug self-satisfaction. Suffering from no complex of inferiority because of his business, the tradesman believed himself deserving of social recognition and frequently

---

[1] R. H. Gretton, *The English Middle Class* (London, 1919), p. 125.

[2] Cf. J. W. Burgon, *The Life and Times of Sir Thomas Gresham*, 2 vols. (London, 1839), I, 284-85.

plumed himself with the titles of a gentleman to the disgust of critical moralists like Philip Stubbes, who made the sarcastic comment in *The Anatomie of Abuses* (1583) that

now a daies euery Butcher, Shoomaker, Tayler, Cobler, and Husband-man, yea, euery Tinker, Pedler, and Swineheard, euery Artificer and other, gregarii ordinis, of the vilest sorte of men that bee, muste bee called by the vaine name of Maisters at euery woorde. But it is certaine, that no wise man, will intitle them, with any of these names, worshipfull and Maister (for thei are names and titles of dignitie, proper to the goodlie wise).   [Sigs. L 3v-L 4.]

Although the middle-class person who could afford it was ready enough to equip himself with the trappings of gentility, he as yet saw no necessity for eschewing his origin, and it was not until the social eclipse of the Restoration that wealthy members of the bourgeoisie began to ape the prodigality of courtiers and attempt to hide their connections with trade.[3]

The acquisitive habits of the middle class, which soon brought much aristocratic property into their possession, their self-assertive manners, and at times the arrogance of their wealthier representatives aroused the hostility of the older aristocracy and caused a feud which is well described by George Whetstone in *A Mirour For Magestrates Of Cyties . . . and . . . A Touchstone for the Time* (1584) in a passage deploring the prodigality that brings gentlemen into the clutches of greedy citizens who plunder them of their land. The hatred of the two groups, the author asserts, has come to such a pass that when a gentleman wishes "odiously [to] name a man" he calls him a "trimme merchaunt," to which tradesmen retort by calling "euery rascall A ioly Gentleman."[4] The greed of citizens in the acquisition of land and houses, some of which are turned into dicing resorts

---

[3] *Ibid.*, pp. 144-45.

[4] "I must here digresse from the prodigalitie of the gentleman, vnto the couetous-nesse and vsurie, I can not properly say of the Citizen, although he dwelleth in ye Citie: for the true Citizen (whereof London hath plentie) liueth vpon his trade, be he an aduenturer abroade, or a mechanicall crafts man at home. But these shames of good Citizens tradeth but to a dycing house . . . Among them there is such deceit coloured with such cleanly shifts, as many gentlemen are for a trifle shifted out of their liuings without hope of remedie. The extremitie of these mens dealings hath beene and is so cruell, as there is a naturall malice generally impressed in the hearts of the

further to plunder gaming gentlemen of their property, is a great evil, declares Whetstone, who suggests that merchants should employ their money in commerce and be forbidden to purchase land, "other than a garden for recreation."[5] This economic conflict, putting as it did the older gentry at the financial mercy of the commercial classes,[6] who were eager for the social distinction symbolized by the possession of land, is responsible for much of the ridicule heaped upon the latter by aristocratic writers. But since humility was not a prominent quality in the bourgeois temperament, the citizen did not submit blandly to attacks, and instead of being ashamed of his connection with trade, as might have been the case with a later social-climbing member of the middle class, he set out to prove that he was as good as anybody and to show also that the ideals he stood for were the backbone of the commonwealth. There appeared, therefore, throughout the later sixteenth and first half of the seventeenth centuries a considerable literature which had for its aim the expression of the middle-class satisfaction in its own position and good qualities. Furthermore, much of this literature was intended to instill a class pride into the minds of the apprentices who would soon occupy positions of importance in the world of trade.

Not only did writers from the ranks of the bourgeoisie defend

---

gentlemen of England towards the citizens of London, insomuch as if they odiously name a man, they foorthwith call him A trimme merchaunt. In like despight the Citizen calleth euery rascall A ioly Gentleman. And truely this mortall enuie betweene these two woorthie estates, was first engendred of the cruell vsage of couetous merchaunts, in hard bargaines gotten of Gentlemen, and nourished with malitious words and reuenges taken of both parties."—Sigs. I I-I IV.

[5] "If the magistrats surueide but these vile houses by honest conseruators, you should finde the painefull trauels of capital Magistrats much eased, many mens liues shalbe saued, Gentlemen shall haue more lande, and Citizens greater store of money : which mettal is the greatest strength of a Cittie, for where mony is not scarce, traficke is plentie, which chiefely supporteth al Cities. And therfore in many wel gouerned cōmon wealthes, Citizens (to the ende they should onely imploie their money in traficke) were forbidden to purchase lande, other than a garden for recreation. But to my purpose, these deuellish houses are causes that merchants haue so much lande, and Gentlemen so litle vertue."—Sig. K I.

[6] Professor R. H. Tawney, *Religion and the Rise of Capitalism* (London, 1929), p. 208, calls attention to the enmity between the aristocrats of the Restoration and the thrifty bourgeois class who soon had the former in economic subjection. This tendency was already beginning in the latter part of the sixteenth century. The plays of Middleton are filled with satirical allusions to the conflict, usually derogatory to the citizens.

the honor of tradesmen, but occasionally more aristocratic authors turned a hand in the same cause when for some reason they needed to curry favor with citizens. In fact, one of the most important defenses of the social position of tradesmen came from the pen of an indigent gentleman, Edmund Bolton, who was in the Marshalsea prison for debt in the year that he published *The Cities Advocate, In This Case Or Question of Honor and Armes: Whether Apprentiship extinguisheth Gentry?* (1629).[7] Doubtless hoping that his championship of the City would earn a patron who would rescue him from his creditors, Bolton presented a carefully reasoned defense of the right of the mercantile classes to claim coat armor and to aspire to equal rank with the military and clerical groups. The author in an address to the "Right Honorable" readers says he has consented to print his work "after tenne or twelue yeares from the first date of the accomplishment" because he wishes to refute

that pestilent error, which hauing some authority for it, and many iniurious partakers, layes vpon the hopefull, and honest estate of Apprentiship in London, the odious note of bondage, and the barbarous penaltie of losse of Gentry : to the great reproach of our Kingdomes policie, and to the manifold damage of the publike.

To strengthen his argument that the tradesman is worthy of being called a gentleman, he cites the authority of Roman precedent as well as the like opinion "of our Sages" who "did euer leaue the gates of Honor open to City-Arts, and to the mysteries of honest gaine, as fundamentall in Common-weale."[8]

The crux of the problem of the tradesman's right to aspire to

---

[7] *The Cities Advocate, In This Case Or Question of Honor and Armes; Whether Apprenticeship extinguisheth Gentry? Containing a cleare Refutation of the pernicious common errour affirming it, swallowed by Erasmus of Roterdam, Sir Thomas Smith in his Common-weale, Sir Iohn Fern in his Blazon, Raphe Broke Yorke Herald, and others. With the Copies or Transcripts of three Letters which gaue occasion of this worke* (1629). Another edition with a slightly altered title was published as late as 1675. (Cf. *Dictionary of National Biography, sub* Bolton.) Bolton proposed an elaborate history of London with detailed maps, but the project never materialized.

[8] "For, though the Schooles, and Camp, are most proper for Honor and Armes, yet the ancient wisedome, and the like ancient bounty of our Sages, did euer leaue the gates of Honor open to City-Arts, and to the mysteries of honest gaine, as fundamentall in Common-weale, and susceptiue of externall splendor : according to the most laudable examples of rising Rome, vnder her first Dictators, & Consuls."—Sigs. A 3ᵛ-A 4.

the ranks of the gentry was in the attitude to be taken toward apprenticeship. According to some views apprenticeship represented a servile station and disqualified the apprentice thereafter to take his place among people of gentle birth. It is to combat this view that Bolton writes in defense of the honor of apprenticeship, and it is this question which lends significance to the other literature glorifying apprenticeship. Bolton himself is careful to state that he does not include in his defense all the riffraff going under the name of apprentice, but only those who are worthy; and for these he appends an epistle to his work urging them to ways of sobriety, virtue, and loyalty to London.

Bolton claims that his treatise had been precipitated by certain letters, the first of which is from a citizen in behalf of his son who had complained of the affronts received because of his father's former apprenticeship. The father pleads that for his sake and that of hundreds like him Bolton clear the matter up. "I am confident," he writes, "that by hauing once beene an apprentice in London, I haue not lost to be a Gentleman of birth, nor my sonne." Indeed, he prays to be like some of the heroic citizens of London who have risen from the ranks of business to positions of honor.[9] Following this suggestion, Bolton points to the valiant and noble citizens who rose from apprenticeship to places of eminence. Throughout the treatise he praises London, exalts the discipline of apprentices, maintains the necessity of degree in the ranks of society, and encourages all to "honest industrie."

The social upset implied in Bolton's treatise had long been a subject of discussion. A half century before, William Harrison, enumerating in his *Description of England* (1577)[10] the classes in English society, mentions under "burgesses and citizens" that

In this place also are our merchants to be installed, as amongst the citizens (although they often change estate with gentlemen, as gentlemen doo with them, by a mutuall conuersion of the one into the other)

[9] ". . . yet shall I euer wish, and pray rather to resemble an heroicke Walworth, a noble Philpot, an happie Capel, that learned Sheriffe of London Mr. Fabian, or any other famous Worthies of this royall City, out of any whatsoeuer obscurest parentage, then that being descended of great Nobles, to fall by vice farre beneath the rancke of poorest Prentises."—Sig. A 4.

[10] F. J. Furnivall (ed.). Pt. 1, New Shakespeare Society, Ser. 6, I (1877), pp. 131-33. Cf. p. 128.

whose number is so increased in these our daies, that their onelie maintenance is the cause of the exceeding prices of forreine wares, . . .

Many yeomen and artificers by industry

do come to great welth, in somuch that manie of them are able and doo buie the lands of vnthriftie gentlemen, and often setting their sonnes to the schooles, to the vniuersities, and to the Ins of the court; or otherwise leauing them sufficient lands wherevpon they may liue without labour, doo make them by those means to become gentlemen: . . .

The nobility resulting from trade and the glory which comes to both tradesman and commonwealth from the former's activities were vigorously emphasized by Thomas Nash, author of *Quaternio Or A Fourefoll Way To A Happie Life; set forth in a Dialogue betweene a Countryman and a Citizen, a Divine and a Lawyer* (1633). The citizen, answering an objection from the countryman that the Neapolitan gentry and the old Romans despised trade, compares the honored magnificence of the Venetians, all of whom live by trade, with the despised poverty of the Neapolitans, and draws a parallel between English tradesmen and Venetian grandees. He has only contempt for the snobbish pride which holds, "contrary to the opinion of all *wise-men*," that the offspring of a marriage between a gentleman and the daughter of a tradesman "are but Gentlemen of the halfe bloud." Of a "cleane contrary opinion" are the Venetians and the Genoese,

who hold it an additament and encrease of honour, to deale in the way of Marchandise; . . . Vertue they account the chiefest Nobilitie; and suppose it never casts a better lustre, than when it shewes it selfe in men professing the trade of Marchandizing: to descend from the loynes of noble progenitors with *Catiline*, and to be a villaine; or with *Hermodius* to pull an ancient house vpon his head, and to be the last of it; or with *Salust* to relye wholy vpon dead mens bones, they accounted the greatest *dishonour:* but by good husbandry, and thriftie course of *Trading to raise themselues from meane estates*, and from Gentlemen of low degree, to be potent and mightie, (as *Cato* did in another course of life from a poore Cottage in *Tuscanie;*) that they held the chiefest glory. So that in the flourishing state of *Venice*, there is not a Gentleman of note or qualitie, but hath a stocke going in the trade of Marchandizing. It is true, I must confesse, there was a Law amongst the old *Romanes*, which did prohibit Senators and men in authoritie, to deale by way of Trade; but the reason of that was not because it was a disparagement for a great man to Trade, but because Senators were set apart for another end and purpose; that is, to looke to the affaires of the Common-wealth; and therefore they were not to busie them-selues about private matters. It is true likewise, it is a received opinion amongst the learned *Armorists* and *Heralds*, *Mercatura non competit viro generoso*, that it is a base & dishonorable part for any man of qualitie to deale by way of Marchandizing, but you must vnderstand it to be meant of Merchandizing in poore and meane Commodities, as in monopolizing of *Pinnes, Cards, and Glasses, or such poore Commodities*, not beseeming a Gentleman, or in exporting the bullion of the Kingdome, the iron and lead, the hydes and skins, the Corne and graine, and in stead of them to bring home leaues, Indian-weeds, feathers, drugs, and spices, Oranges and Lemmons, and the juice of grapes, and things of the like nature, rather hurtfull than profitable to the Common-wealth: but to adventure for the gold of *Ophyr*, and the vsefull and necessary Commodities of *Cyprus*, and *Persia* hath beene an imployment not vnworthy the adventure of *Drake*, of *Frobusher*, of *Candish*, and the noble spirits of former times. So that without doubt *Pegius* was in the right, when he affirmed, that it may well stand with the degree of Knight-hood, to deale in the way of trade and Marchandizing.   [Pp. 56-58.]

Not only do tradesmen enrich the commonwealth, but they leave behind them tangible evidences of their munificence in schools, colleges, almshouses, highways, and bridges; and, the citizen asks, if finally "for the good service we haue done to our Countries, we are honored with the degree of Knights, or Barons, or Viscounts, doe you thinke posteritie shall not reape the benefit of these things, though wee haue our originall from the Citie?"[11] So cogent is the citizen's reasoning that he convinces the countryman that "we may be Gentlemen and truely noble, though we take vpon vs the profession of Marchants, or any other mechanicall trade or occupation."[12]

A considerable body of dramatic and narrative literature de-veloped at the end of the sixteenth century and during the next few decades, exalting the merchant, and especially the valiant apprentice, who about this time aroused the bourgeois imagina-tion. Thomas Heywood's *The Four Prentices of London* (acted *c.*

---

[11] P. 59.   [12] P. 60.

1592) put characters on the stage who were becoming popular in ballads and pamphlets.[13] Dekker and Deloney represent the apprentice and his master in sympathetic and idealized pictures. Richard Johnson made national heroes out of apprentices and citizens in his *Nine Worthies of London* (1592). Johnson's Worthies, held up as examples for other apprentices to follow, were used by later chroniclers of apprentice-heroes. William Vallans, a tradesman, produced in 1615 a pamphlet typical of the kind appealing to the commonalty, consisting of several unrelated stories and bearing the title of *The Honourable Prentice: Or This Taylor is a man.*[14] It is significant that he emphasizes the apprentice story in the first phrase of the title. In *The Honourable Prentice* the author holds up for imitation the example of Sir John Hawkwood's bravery and daring in the Italian wars and, like a good business man, stresses his thrift in acquiring great wealth, which was conveyed to England after his death.[15] Vallans sincerely believed that citizens ought to chronicle their own glories, a sentiment which he expressed in certain verses in commendation of John Stow.[16] And precisely that was done in the literature commending the deeds of budding tradesmen, as an anonymous poet

[13] *See* a ballad printed in 1592, *The honours achieued in Ffrannce and Spaine by iiij prentises of London.* Cited by H. W. Willkom, *Über Richard Johnsons Seven Champions of Christendome* (Berlin diss., 1911), p. 15.

[14] *The Honourable Prentice: Or This Taylor is a man. Shewed in the life and death of Sir John Hawkewood, sometime Prentice of London: interlaced with the famous History of the noble Fitzwalter, Lord of Woodham in Essex, and of the poisoning of his faire Daughter; Also of the merry customes of Dunmow, where any one may freely haue a Gammon of Bacon, that repents not mariage in a yeere and a day. Whereunto is annexed the most lamentable murther of Robert Hall at the High Altar in Westminster Abbey* (1615).

[15] Cf. the anonymous prose tale of the later seventeenth century, set forth as solemnly as history to glorify the apprentice: *London's Glory, Or The History Of the Famous and Valiant London Prentice: Being an Account of his Parentage, Birth and Breeding, together with many brave and Heroick Exploits perform'd by him throughout the Course of his Life; tó the Honour of London, and the whole F[amous] Nation* [Temp. Car. II?]. The author concludes the tale, which recounts the adventures of one Aurelius, with the pious hope: "Thus Reader, have I revived this ancient Hostory [*sic*] of the famed *London* 'Prentice (or rich Merchant) which for many Years has layd in Obscurity; which no doubt will be a great encouragement to Youth, to be Virtuous and Valiant, and to those of elder Years, to hope by industry from a small beginning to rise to great Advance; and if both succeed, I have my Wish."

[16] Stow Papers in MSS Harley 367. Quoted by C. L. Kingsford (ed.), *A Survey of London by John Stow*, 2 vols. (Oxford, 1908), I, lxxxviii. *See* Chapter IX, *infra*, p. 311.

of the people indicates in *A Ballad in Praise of London 'Prentices, and What They Did at the Cockpit Playhouse, Shroue Tuesday, 1617*, which begins:

> The 'prentices of London long
> Have famous been in story,
> But now they are exceeding all
> Their chronicles of glory.[17]

It became conventional for popular writers, particularly in controversies, to flatter the apprentices in an effort to win their favor. Such an appeal is made by Esther Sowernam in *Ester hath hang'd Haman* (1617), a reply to the famous attack on women made in Joseph Swetnam's *The Araignment Of Lewd, Idle, Froward, and Vnconstant Women* (1615). She calls on the noble apprentices to defend women against such unchivalrous attacks:

You my worthy youths are the hope of Man-hoode, the principall poynt of Man-hoode is to defend, and what more man-like defence, then to defend the iust reputation of a woman. I know that you the Apprentises of this Citie are as forward to maintaine the good, as you are vehement to put downe the bad.   [Sigs. A 4-A 4ᵛ.]

Richard Johnson made a bid for apprentice favor in *A Crowne Garland of Golden Roses* (edition of 1631), in which he includes among other ballads of bourgeois appeal "A Song of Richard Whittington" and "The Story of Ill May-day . . . and how Queene Katherine begged the Liues of two thousand London Prentices." This ballad ends with fulsome praise of apprentice-glory:

> And when King Henry stood in neede
> of trusty souldiers at command,
> Those prentices prou'de men indeede,
> and feard no force of warlike band.
> For at the siedge of Tours in France
> they shewd them selues braue English men;

---

[17] Reprinted in part in Alfred H. Headley, *London in Literature* (London, 1920), pp. 72-74; also in Charles Mackay (ed.), *A Collection of Songs and Ballads Relative to the London Prentices and Trades*, Percy Society, Vol. I (1841). The latter collection has a number of ballads praising apprentices, but most of these are of a later date.

> At Bullein also did aduance
> S. Georges glorious Standard then.
> Let Turwen, Turney, and those townes
>   that good King Henry nobly wonne,
> Tell London prentices renownes,
>   and all the deedes by them there donne.[18]

Johnson has another ballad in this collection which praises the merchant class and flatters the tailors in particular : "A delightful Song of the four famous Feasts of England, the one of them ordained by King Henry the seuenth, to the honour of Merchant-Taylors, shewing how seuen Kings haue beene free of that Company, and now lastly graced with the loue of our renowned Prince Henry of Great Britaine."

The most complete summing up of the virtues of apprentices came in 1647, during the troublous times when the tradesman was becoming the ruling factor. It took the form of a long poem entitled, *The Honour Of London Apprentices.*[19] From time immemorial the valor and honor of apprentices have been conspicuous in the "eye of Christendome" and have been a further embellishment to the glory of London, the author maintains in a prose eulogy that prefaces the poem.[20] After emphasizing the loyalty of apprentices to each other and to the city, the author launches into the poem, which declares that no side can lose when supported by the valiant London apprentices, whose heroic deeds have shone

---

[18] Reprinted by J. P. Collier (ed.), *Broadside Black-Letter Ballads* (London, 1868), pp. 96 ff.

[19] *The Honour Of London Apprentices: Exemplified, In a briefe Historicall Narration; Containing many Heroicall actions done by (some in particular, the rest in generall) Prentices of the most renowned, and (in that regard) truly honourable City of London, both at home and abroad. In long, fore-past, present, and moderne times. Collected and published, by a Well-wisher to what himselfe once was, that is to say, a Prentice (and now a free Citizen) of the famous City of London* (1647).

[20] "This generall denomination, hath begoten admirable effects in all ages, as may be seen in our English Chronicle, and in Master *Strouds Survey of London,* where the honour of London Prentices in generall (and of some in perticular) is conspicious to the eye of Christendome, (I & further too) the valiant exploits and notable feats of armes achieved and done by London Prentices is so remarkable that from time to time the condition hath alwaies been an inseperable adjunct to an Heriditary Honour, which drawn in a line of this present age, hath Ilustrated with its beames, the glory of that honourable City, as the Seminary (or seede plot) of martiall Spirits as the Isue of my muse in Heroricall verse shall . . . declare . . ."—Preface.

throughout the world.[21] Some of the famous apprentices are
named, as, for example,

> . . . . one *William Man*
> On Fish-street-hill, a Vintner at the Swan,
> Did shew himself a perfect man (though young)
> For with a matchlesse force he laid along
> Five of the Rebels (bleeding) on the ground,
> Four slain (out-right) the fift with many a wound,
> Was carryed from the field : all men of might
> And eminence, for which he was dub'd Knight
> By the Black Prince, and Baron made of *Denbigh;* . . .

So it has been with brave hearts through the ages, the author
continues, even unto the recent troubles, in which the courage
of the apprentices was such that Parliament granted a petition
that they might be given one day's holiday in each month. The
poet now concludes with a warning to bawds that the virtuous
apprentices may tear down their houses, and adds :

> . . . . brave Prentices,
> Do utterly abhor such things as these.
> Adieu my noble hearts, judge not amisse
> Of him who to your honour publish'd this.

A picture of the apprentice as the future governor of the city is
given in a little book of characters, *The Wandering Jew telling
Fortunes to Englishmen* (1649). The old question of the honor of
apprentices comes up again, and the author asserts once more that
this bondage is not servitude but "a noble Bondage, a Bondage
with libertie," the discipline of which makes it possible for the apprentice to be fitted for the obligations and duties that will come to
him later in life. His place in society is an honorable one, and
from it he may proceed to some of the highest positions in the

---

[21]   "At home, abroad, in *Europe, Asia,* and
          Hot *Africa,* and *America* by land
          Or Sea, no action worth regard
          Was done, but *London* Prentices in it shar'd.
          The rayse of *London* Prentices did shine
          Among the Infidels in *Palestine,*
          When that renowned christian Champion nam'd,
          Godfrey of Bulloigne (through the world so fam'd)
          Went to the holy war (so called then) . . ."—Sig. A 2ᵛ.

municipal establishment.[22] Some of the early seventeenth-century apprentice literature was obviously inspirational, seeking to encourage the youth of the city to industry. Some is also obviously a part of that literature of growing pride in the position of the tradesman.

Unexpected praise of the merchant class is found in Richard Barckley's *A Discourse Of The Felicitie Of Man, or His Summum Bonum* (1598), a pious treatise edited by Thomas Heywood in 1631. Although perfect felicity cannot be found in the craft of merchandising, and although the merchant's life is full of trouble, yet it is one "which many wise men, as *Thales, Solon, Hippocrates* and others have exercised; and which nourisheth amitie and loue betweene Princes, transporting their commodities from one countrey to another; . . ."[23] Nicholas Breton, some of whose works have a strong bourgeois appeal, praises the merchant in the character of "A Worthy Merchant" in *The Good And The Badde, Or Descriptions of the Worthies, and Vnworthies of this Age* (1616):

. . . he is the life of Traffick, and the maintainer of Trade, the Sailers Master, and the Souldiers friend; hee is the exercise of the exchange, the honor of credit, the obseruation of Time, and the vnderstanding of thrift: his studie is number, his care his accounts, his comfort his Conscience, and his wealth his good Name: . . . out of his trauailes, he makes his discourses, and from his eye-obseruations, brings the Moddels of Architectures; he plants the earth with forraine fruits, and knowes at home what is good abroad: he is neat in apparell, modest in demeanure, dainty in dyet, and ciuill in his carriage. In summe, hee

---

[22] ". . . but it is a noble Bondage, a Bondage with libertie: if the Mr. holds one end of the staff, the Prentice fastens on the other. The Prentice is bound to serve his Master; and in the same Indentures the Master is tied to serve his Prentice with apparell, victualls, lodging, and all things necessary, and to teach him what himselfe (in his Art) knowes. . . .

"In the Musicke of City Government, a Prentice for a while practises onely the Gamoth on his fingers; but when he comes out of his yeers, is free, and weares a livery Gowne, hee then beares a voice in the Commonwealths Consort.

"London had never seene the face of a Lord Major, a Sheriffe, an Alderman, a Deputie, a Churchwarden, a Constable; but that they were all drawne by the picture of a Prentice: a Prentice comes to bee all these; and all these had never come to what they are, but by having beene a Prentice. A Prentice then being so brave a Spark, let us see what fire this will kindle when he appears." Reprinted by J. O. Halliwell-Phillipps in *Books of Characters* (London, 1857). *See* pp. 33-36.

[23] Edition of 1631, pp. 380-81.

is the Pillar of a City, the enricher of a Country, the furnisher of a Court, and the worthy seruant of a King. [P. 18.]

The unworthy merchant described in the next character is merely a charlatan of baubles, a dishonor to the city. More extended praise of the merchant class as the backbone of the state is given by Breton in *A Poste With A Packet of Mad Letters* (edition of 1633), in a letter "To my very good Cousin I. D.," commending him for apprenticing his son to a merchant. Breton calls trade a "noble Profession"; the merchant is a "royall fellow," who ought to be honored for his daring in foreign trade :

. . . shall the Merchant bee grudged his price of his Wares? what shall I say? who upholds the state of a Citie? or the Honour of a State vnder the King but the Merchant? who beautifieth a Court with Jewels and outward Ornaments? but the trauell of a Merchant? who beautifies the Gardens with sundry sorts of Fruits and Flowers, but the trauelling Merchant? . . . consider of the sweet ciuill manner of their liues : whose Houses more neate? whose wiues more modest? whose apparell more comely, whose diet more dainty? and whose cariage more commendable? valiant without quarrels, merie without madnesse, bountifull in their gifts, . . . and how many poore do they relieue at home? what Colledges? what Hospitals? what almshouses haue they builded? and in effect, what Cities haue they enlarged, and what Countries haue they enriched? . . . [Pp. 77-79.]

In short, the merchant is the sum of all the civic virtues. In another letter Breton advises the young man going to the university to study arithmetic so that he may enter trade and be a financial success.[24]

As one might expect from so staunch a believer in the virtues of mercantile ideals, Thomas Gainsford offers a stout defense of the merchant in *The Rich Cabinet Furnished with varietie Of Excellent discriptions* (1616). Although he disarms criticism by taking cognizance of some of the conventional faults of merchants, he hastens to offset these faults with greater virtues and assures us that the citizen is the foundation of stable government and of prosperity. Gainsford's character of the citizen maintains that

A Citizen is a professor of ciuilitie; and liuing in a glorious quiet,

---

[24] Pp. 66-68. Cf. Chapter III, *infra*, n. 92.

maketh the Common-wealth to flourish: and how-euer he is condemned for too much ease, yet cannot the souldier repulse the enemy,
or maintaine the warre, except the Merchant adde fuell to the fire. . . .

A Citizen, how-euer he may be noted for couetousnesse, and corruption in trading: yet vnder colour of priuat enriching himselfe, he
laboureth for the publique good. For abroad is nauigation maintained,
and the forraine kingdoms explored: and at home the Cities are
enlarged, the country supplied, the commerce of people maintained,
the streets filled, the houses adorned, the subiects encreased, & the
Prince honoured in the multitude of obedient seruitors. [Sigs. E 3-E 3ᵛ.]

Surely bourgeois praise could no better sum up the citizen's
place in the commonwealth. But Gainsford has still more to say.
He insists that however envious citizens are among themselves,
yet "will they vnite their forces for the publique good." Although
he condemns as undignified the citizens' aping of gentlemen,
Gainsford finds a sly satisfaction in the eagerness of gentlemen to
mend their fortunes by marriage with burghers:

. . . Citizens in times past did not marry beyond their degrees, nor
would a Gentleman make affinitie with a Burgesse: but wealth hath
taught vs now another lesson; and the Gentleman is glad to make his
younger sonne a tradsman, and match his best daughter with a rich
Citizen for estate and liuing.

In a further character of a merchant,[25] the author lauds him as
"a worthy comon-wealths man" who

is a ciuill and conuersable man, rich in money, delicate in apparell
dainty in diet, sumptuous in furniture, elloquent in discourse, secret in
his business, carefull in his losses, watchfull for his profit, and aboue
all, sparing in his lending of money. Merchant continuing his estate,
may setle his fortune, and augment his credit: but if he once turne
Gentleman before his time, hee is like a gamster that playes at a game
he knowes not for a great deale of money.

Citizens are put next to courtiers in the social order as Henry
Peacham arranges it in *Thalias Banquet* (1620), a collection of
epigrams. In the prefatory verses, the author invites to the banquet
first the courtiers and then the citizens:

---

[25] Sigs. N 1-N 2ᵛ. Gainsford cannot resist satirizing the thriftlessness and vanity
of the gentry in a character entitled "Gentry."—Sigs. H 5ᵛ-H 6.

> Citizens ye that were made
> As well for learning as for trade,
> Come braue spirits of the Realme, . . .

Lawrence Price's ballad *The Honest Age* (1632) praises trades-men above others for their honesty.[26] The deserving business man's honesty and upright dealings are described by Thomas Fuller in *The Holy State* (1642) in a character of "The good Merchant."[27] The worthy trader does not "export things of necessity, and . . . bring in forrein needlesse toyes," which make "a rich Merchant, and a poore Kingdome." Good merchants, however, are so useful in knitting one country to another and in maintaining peace and harmony that Fuller finds them very necessary to the body politic. Richard Flecknoe's "The Character Of An English Merchant, resident in forrain parts" in his *Miscellania* (1653) discovers in the merchant the representative of England's honor abroad:

Hee is one that goes abroad with a stock of Honour, as wel as mony to Traffick with, and manages either bravely, being a Master, and not a Slave to Wealth, and such a Master as Honours it by his commands, making it only serve to noble Ends. He neither sticks at triviall Expence nor gaine, nor anticipats poverty for fear of being poor (like those who kill themselves for fear of Death) nor accelerats it by vainglory of appearing Rich, (like those who guilde ruinous Palaces) but looke in his Ware-houses and Accounts, and you finde him a wealthy Merchant, looke in all the rest of his House, and you find him a Noble and Gallant minded Gentleman.

In brief, He neither starves the channell with Penuriousnesse, nor exhausts the Spring with Prodigallty, but as a particular Art to keep a bounteous stream still running, and the Fount still full,

So as we may well say of him in these miserable dead times, there is none lives but he; who whilst your greatest landed men are outed of all they have, as long as the Sea is open, or ships are stirring, is sure of his comings in.

To conclude then, we may well say of him, that he is the Honour of

---

[26] Hyder E. Rollins (ed.), *A Pepysian Garland* (Cambridge, 1922), pp. 406 ff. Professor Rollins suggests that Martin Parker was probably answering this ballad in his *Knavery in All Trades* (1632), which takes the opposite point of view. Cf. Chapter XII, *infra*, pp. 426-27.

[27] Pp. 113 ff.

8

his Nation abroad, and that therefore his Nation should be most unworthy and ungratefull, shud it not alwayes honour him.

[Pp. 132-33.]

The height of the London tradesman's self-glorification was reached in the elaborate lord mayor's shows which usually represented in some appropriate allegory the past deeds of the guild from which the lord mayor-elect had been chosen. Skillful writers were hired to heap flattery on the trade as well as on the personality of the newly chosen dignitary. Heywood, Dekker, Middleton, Webster, and other dramatists furnished pageants, but perhaps none was better equipped for the task of glorifying trades-men than Anthony Munday, who was both a draper and a pageant-maker. Typical of his own activities and of the *genre* was Munday's *Chrysalaneia: The Golden Fishing: Or, Honour of Fish-mongers. Applauding the aduancement of Mr. Iohn Leman, Alderman, to the dignitie of Lord Maior of London* (1616), a pageant which drew on the chronicle-histories for material to describe the bravery of fishmongers and goldsmiths at the taking of Jerusalem. Such a mixture of pious and valorous deeds was certain to delight the tradesmen-spectators, who were also once more reminded of the patriotic heroism of the Sir William Walworth, the fishmonger, who slew Wat Tyler, the rebel. Other pageants differed only in the variety and method of treating similar themes. Always Lord Mayor's Day was the occasion for vaunting the pride and satis-faction of tradesmen in their past, present, and future glory, for often the allegory predicted the continuing fame of London's citizens.

Next to praise of the citizens themselves came the glorification of the city of London. The pride of the citizenry was one reason for the popularity of city chronicles which perpetuated the fame of London and its institutions. Stow's *Survey of London* (1598), with its continuations, was a standard work of civic glorification. Robert Greene knew how to flatter the citizen and praise London when he wished to curry popular favor. His compilation of moral maxims designed for tradesmen, entitled *The Royal Exchange* (1590), contains a dedication to the Lord Mayor and officials of the city, filled with praise of London, which is exalted above Venice because of the civic pride, generosity, and bravery of its citizens, whose ships, harbored in the Thames, could match those of the strongest city in the world.[28] London is the perfect city, to be compared with the commonwealth of Plato, Greene further boasts in an address to the "right honourable Cittizens of the Cittie of London." The city is

famozed with great & auncient buildings, excelling for lawes executed with iustice, renowned for worthy Magistrates, & peopled with warlike Merchaunts, and politick Cittizens, I cannot but compare it to the imagined Common-wealth of *Plato*, and say, O fortunate Cittie for so famous Cittizens.

Like Greene, Thomas Johnson, the apothecary, finds London the most glorious city of a modern Eden. For no reason at all except a desire to sing the praises of his town and country, he inserts this passage in his *Cornucopiae, Or diuers secrets* (1596) :

What country in Europ comparable to England? what more wonderfull than London? wherein if it be considered? what aboūdance of fewell? what store of beefes what multitude of Cattell are occupied there daylie, it may seeme straunge from whence they haue it? What cittie in the world so populous, so merchantable, more rich, more stored with women of most amiable countenance and beautie, more ciueller in their attire? . . . what countrie more stored with fruit, with precious simples? what nation more firtile for honie, for tinne, for lead, for foule, for beasts and cattel, for swannes, for plentie of wooll, for clothing, for

---

[28] "For our Merchaunts and other Cittizens, though they generallie attaine not to that excesse of riches that the Venetians do, yet for the enlargement of the liberties of their Citie, they stand so much vppon their credits, as they grudge not to disburse any sum, eyther necessarie to their priuate *Poluteia*, or helpfull to the common profit of theyr Countrey. For religion they haue the Gospel, for iustice a seuere law executed with clemencie, beeing Merchaunts wyth theyr freendes and traffique fellowes, otherwise martiall minded souldiours, to resist the violence eyther of any priuate mutinie, or any common enemie, as valiant to attempt in wars as to counsaile in peace. And although Venice be a Cittie seated in the Ocean, and enuironed round about with the Sea, standing much vpon their Armado and Nauall fight, yet our Citizens of London, (her Maiesties royall fleete excepted) haue so many shyppes harboured within the Thames, as wyll not onelie match with all the Argoses, Galleyes, Galeons, and Pataches in Venice, but to encoūter by sea with the strongest Cittie in the whole world : Considering therefore, (right honourable and worshipful) the excellencie of thys Cittie, the honour of the Magistrates, the worshyp of the Merchaunts, and the generall worthines of all in one simpathie. I thought good, as the Italian presented his *Bursa Reale* to the Venetians, so to presume the patronage of this *Royall Exchange* vnto your Honour, . . ."—Dedication.

fish, for curious and costly hangings? Where more store of fine gold &
plentie of siluer? where more finer wittes, more profound and learned
men in all sciences? nay where so many, where so famous vniuersities
& schooles of learning? where more valiant and couragious souldiers?
where such succour ministred to strangers, to the distressed, to the
persecuted, to the afflicted? nay what countrie or nation in the worlde
is there at this presente that nourisheth so manie Aliens from all
parts of the world as England doth? We haue our mines, our quarries
for stones, our gems, our pretious stones and all other necessarie and
profitable things, our good God be blessed and praised therefore. Wee
are not troubled with poysoning Serpents, nor with fierce Lyons, or
with deuouring Tigers, Beares, Wolfes, Panthers or any such hurtfull
beastes as other nations are.   [Sigs. F 2-F 2v.]

Many tributes to the city are found in the works of Deloney,
Heywood, Dekker, and others. Sometimes praise and blame are
mixed, as in the works of Dekker, who is fond of enumerating the
sins of the city.[29] The pride of London brought condemnation
from some critics. Nashe, for example, in *Christs Teares Over
Ierusalem* finds that since the fall of Antwerp, Pride has come to
dwell in "riche London . . . the full-streamed wel-head."[30]

The more bourgeois writers, however, usually gave their meed
of praise fulsomely and uncritically. The author of *A Breefe
Discourse, declaring and approuing the necessarie and inuiolable maintenance of the laudable Customes of London* (1584) maintains that long
sanctioned customs of London should have the effect of law;
indeed, any objection to these customs comes from outsiders who
envy the wealth of the city : "This obiection made by the enuiers or
enimies of the wealth of London . . . rather deserueth a hisse
than a replye."[31] Civic pride is evident in the ballad literature and
in the popular pamphlets. In the anonymous *Pimlyco. Or, Runne
Red-Cap. Tis a mad world at Hogsdon* (1609),[32] a poem extolling the
virtues of the ale at Pimlico, a resort in Hogsdon, the author
inserts the following tribute to the metropolis :

---

[29] Dekker is directly concerned with the city in *The Wonderful Year, The Seven Deadly
Sins of London, Jests to Make You Merry, The Dead Term, The Gull's Hornbook,* and *A
Rod for Runaways.*

[30] R. B. McKerrow (ed.), *The Works of Thomas Nashe,* 5 vols. (London, 1904-10),
II, 81.

[31] Pp. 30-31.

[32] Reprinted by A. H. Bullen (ed.), *Antient Drolleries,* No. 2 (Oxford, 1891).

As thus they sat, and I them saw,
A Frame (as rare) mine eies did draw
(With wonder) to behold a farre,
The brightnes of the Kingdomes* Starre;   *London.
A thousand Steeples, Turrets, Towers,
(Lodgings, all fit for Emperours,)
Lifted their proud heads boue the Skie,
As if they had sole Soueraigntie,
Or'e all the Buildings in the Land,
And seem'd on Hilles of Gould to stand,
For the Suns Beames on them being shed,
They shewed like Mynes new burnished.
Upon the Left hand and the Right,
Two*Townes (like Citties) fed the Sight,   *Islington,
With pleasure and with admiration,   & Hogsdon.
For (as they stand) they beare proportion,
As to an Armie doe the Wings,
(The maine Battalion led by Kings.)[33]

Smug satisfaction with London as the most glorious city of the world is often the point of view of treatises by citizens.

The ideals and, unconsciously, the vanities of citizens are reflected in all the work of Richard Johnson, who is always ready to praise and encourage philanthropy glorifying London and its people. This he does in *The Pleasant Walkes of Moore-Fields. Being the guift of two Sisters, now beautified, to the continuing fame of*

---

[33] Sig. B 2. Cf. the reference to London in verses entitled "Londons Progresse" in Thomas Freeman's *Rubbe, And A great Cast. Epigrams* (1614), sig. B 3 :

"Why how now *Babel*, whither wilt thou build?
I see old *Holborne, Charing-crosse*, the *Strand*,
Are going to *St. Giles* his in the field ;
Saint *Katernes* she shakes *Wapping* by the hand :
And *Hoggesdon* will to *Hy-gate* ere't be long.
London is got a great way from the streame,
I thinke she meanes to goe to *Islington*,
To eate a messe of straw-berries and Creame.
The Citty's sure in Progresse I surmise,
Or going to reuell it in some disorder
Without the Walles, without the Liberties,
Where she need feare nor *Mayor* nor *Recorder*.
  Well, say she do ; 'twere pretty, but 'twere pitty
  A *Middlesex Bayliffe* should arrest the Citty."

this worthy Citty (1607).[34] But commendation of the two sisters' generosity is merely an excuse for advertising the increasing beauty, prosperity, and virtues of London since its foundation by Brute. Bearing a dedication commending the aldermen for laying out walks in Moorfields, it is a well-written prose dialogue between a country gentleman and a London citizen, in which the latter proves himself a true ancestor of the modern booster of the city beautiful. The gentleman is much impressed with the improvements pointed out by the citizen and frequently bursts out in a paean of praise:

All England may take example, at your London Citizens, who not onely seeke for their owne benefites, but striue to profit others, shewing themselues good common-wealths men, and as they be called the Fathers of the Citie, so be they cherishers of the poore and succourlesse. . . .

The Citizens I perceiue euer carried gallant mindes, and to this day (I see) they continually striue to beautifie this famous Citie, for what faire summer houses with loftie towers and turrets are here builded in these fields, and in other places, the suburbes of the Citie, not so much for vse and profite, as for shewe and pleasure, bewraying the noblenesse of their mindes.   [Sigs. A 4v-B 1.]

After expressing approval of London citizens' wives, who "resemble the verie modest Sabine Ladies of Italy," Johnson inserts a verse panegyric of "Londons Description."

London citizens, it is true, were unusually prone to boast uncritically of their municipal grandeur and national assets, but no less a person than Bishop Joseph Hall wrote a book to prove the virtues of remaining in England, without the contaminations of foreign travel. Why travel when England is perfect, he asks in *Quo vadis? A Iust Censure of Travell as it is commonly vndertaken by Gentlemen of our Nation* (1617):

God hath giuen vs a world of our owne, wherein there is nothing wanting to earthly contentment. Whither goe yee then, worthy Countrymen, or what seeke yee? Heere growes that wealth, which yee go but to spend abroad; Here is that sweet peace which the rest of the world

---

[34] Also reprinted by J. P. Collier (ed.), *Illustrations of Early English Popular Literature*, 4 vols. (London, 1864), Vol. II.

admires and enuies : Heere is that gracious, and well-tempered gouernment, which no nation vnder heauen may dare once offer to parallel :
Here all liberall Arts raigne and triumph : And for pleasure, either
our earth, or our sea yeelds vs all those dainties, which their natiue
Regions enioy but single. Lastly, heere Heauen stands open, which to
many other parts is barred on the out-side with ignorance or mis-
beleefe. And shall our wantonnes contemn all this bounty of God, &
carry vs to seek that, which we shall find no where but behind vs, but
within vs?   [Pp. 87-88.]

No modern real-estate advertiser could equal in hyperbole the
extravagancies of Thomas Gainsford in *The Glory Of England, Or
A True Description of many excellent prerogatiues and remarkeable blessings,
whereby She Triumpheth ouer all the Nations of the World: With a
iustifiable comparison betweene the eminent Kingdomes of the Earth, and
Herselfe; plainely manifesting the defects of them all in regard of her
sufficiencie and fulnesse of happinesse* (1618). After comparing England
with the kingdoms of the world, past and present, and finding
that she is "neerer the example of Canaans hapines, than any
other nation," Gainsford turns his attention to London. His
method is to contrast London with the chief foreign cities and
to show the former's superiority. Compared with London's grandeur, Paris is a village of hovels. Gainsford's language is that of the
real-estate promoter who glories in a "bigger and better" city.
Curiously enough, even the weather is much better than that of
Paris :

. . . instead of a beastly towne and dirty streets, you haue in *London*
those that be faire, beautifull, and cleanely kept : insteed of foggy mists
and clowds [!] : ill aire, flat situation, miry springs, and a kinde of
staining clay, you haue in *London* a sunne-shining and serene element
for the most part, a wholesome dwelling, stately ascension, and delicate
prospect : insteed of a shallow, narrow, and sometimes dangerous
riuer, bringing onely barges and boats with wood, coale, turff, and
such country prouision : you haue at *London* a riuer flowing twenty
foot, and full of stately ships, that flie to vs with marchandize from all
the ports of the world, the sight yeelding astonishment, and the vse
perpetuall comfort.   [Sigs. S 1-S 1ᵛ.]

This vein of boasting runs through the treatise. London Bridge
is the "firmest erected structure of that kinde of the Vniverse" ;

in London his Majesty has many palaces instead of merely one "Louure, newly graced with an extraordinary gallery"; the Guild Hall and the city churches are the finest in the world :

Insteed of obscure Churches, we haue first the goodliest heap of stones in the world, namely *Pauls;* next the curiousest fabricke in Europe, namely *Westminster* chapple, and generally all our Churches exceede for beauty, handsomnesse, and magnificent building . . .

London merchants are orderly and dignified, governed by a mayor "that keepeth a Princely house."

To conclude, if you looke on and in our *London* truly, as it is composed of men following trades & occupations, there is not such a city, such a gouernment, such a method of conuersation, such a vnity of good fellowship, such a glasse to see vnity and beauty in, such a treasury of wealth, such a store-house of all terrestriall blessings vnder the sunne.

In London are the best amusements at reasonable prices,

For with vs our riding of horses, musique, learning of all Arts and Sciences, dancing, fencing, seeing of commedies or interludes, ban-quets, masques, mummeries, turnaiments, shewes, lotteries, feasts, ordinarie meetings, and all the particulars of mans inuention to satiate delight, are easie expences, and a little iudgement with experience, will manage a very meane estate to wade through the current of pleasure, although it runne to voluptuousnesse.

Gainsford continues his comparison of London with all the famous cities of the world and ends his pamphlet with a summary of England's good qualities, from hospitality to the administration of justice.[35] He declares that he makes this praise of England not out of vainglory

---

[35] Extravagant praise of England is, of course, frequently encountered in Elizabethan literature, but some of the bourgeois statements are especially striking. See, for example, a passage in the preface to John Speed's *The Theatre Of The Empire Of Great Britaine* (1611). Apologizing for his presumption in venturing to undertake so great a work, Speed asserts that he would not have attempted it had not "the zeale of my countries glory so transported my senses." Describing England's almost celestial glories, the author further remarks of the country :
"Whose beautie and benefits, not a farre off, as Moses saw Canaan from Pisgah, but by my owne trauels through euery prouince of England and Wales mine eyes haue beheld : and whose Climate, Temperature, Plentie and Pleasures, make it to be as the very Eden of Europe (pardon me I pray if affection passe limits) for the store of corne in the champian, and of Pasturage in the lower Grounds, presseth the cart vnder the

but meerely I protest to affront some *humorists*, who as irresolute or ignorant thinke too slightly of our worth, and in my owne hearing haue presumed to match petty Princes with vs, against whom I dare maintaine, that if there were such occasion, the *Voluntaries* and idle disposed of our Country would goe in such troopes, and in such a manner, that we need neither pay customes for silkes out of *Florence, Genoa, Leuca,* or some other of their principall states of *Italy;* nor haue our store-houses empty of the marchandice of *India* or *China.*

One of the most blatant pieces of "booster" literature in the age, Gainsford's civic panegyric naturally delighted his readers. A reissue of the 1616 edition, with amplifications, appeared in 1619; another issue came out in 1620; and a "third edition newly revised" was published in 1622.[36]

sheaues to the barn, and filleth the coffers of their possessors. Neither are the faces of the Mountaines and Hils onely spread ouer with infinite heards and sorts of cattell, but their intralls also are in continuall trauell, and continually deliuered of their rich Progenies of Copper, Lead, and Iron, Marble, Cristall, Iet, Alablaster, yea the most wonder-working Loadstone; to say nothing either of Cannol and Sea-coale as rich for profit and as needfull for vse, or of the goodly Quarries of choisest stone, as necessary for strength, as estimable for beauty. Her Seas and Riuers so stored with Fish, and her Fels and Fens so replenished with wild foule, that they euen present themselues for ready prey to their takers; briefly, euery soile is so enriched with plenty and pleasures, as the inhabitants thinke there is no other Paradice in the earth but where they thēselues dwell."

Again, in "The Proeme" to that portion of the work designated as *The History Of Great Britaine* Speed comments:

"That this our Countrey and subiect of History deserueth the loue of her inhabitants, is witnessed euen by forraine writers themselues, who haue termed it the *Court of Queene Ceres,* the *Granary of the Westerne world,* the *fortunate Island,* the *Paradise of pleasure* and *Garden of God;* whose Typographicall descriptions for the whole Iland, and Geographical surueyes for the seuerall parts, exceed any other kingdome vnder the cope of Heauen; that onely excepted which was conquered and diuided by Josuah; And for fruitfulnes and temperature may be accounted another Canaan; watered with riuers that doe cleaue the earth, as the Prophet speaketh, and make the land as rich and beautiful, as was that of Aegypt. Our Kings for valour and Sanctity, ranked with the worthiest in the world, and our Nations originals, conquests, and continuance, tried by the touch of the best humane testimonies, leaue as faire a Lustre vpon the same stone, as doeth any other, and with any nation may easily contend (saith Lanquet) both for antiquity, and continuall inhabitants, from the first time that any of them can claime their originals."

[36] Another tradesman a quarter of a century later published almost as extravagant praise of his home town, in this case Shepton Mallet in Somerset. He was Richard Watts, author of a treatise on thrift, entitled *The Young Mans Looking Glass* (1641). To this work he appended "A Concise Poeme on the Scituation, Trading, &c. Of Shepton Mallet, in the County of Somerset." This little town is the Eden of England and of the world in Watts' description.

Londoners were as jealous as any modern chamber of commerce about their city's reputation for good health, but its frequent plagues gave apologists for the town considerable difficulty. Richard Milton in the great plague year of 1625 brought out *Londons Miserie. The Countryes Crueltie: with Gods Mercie,* in which he rebukes the country for its lack of hospitality toward Londoners and shows that, though plagues come from God's visitations upon sinners, London has been chastened and has repented. He is also careful to insist that the city suffers no worse from plague than any other place of dense population. Furthermore, London is famous for its charity and is deserving of the highest praise for its courage in time of pestilence. The implication is that London is as good a city in which to have the plague as one can find.

The Londoner's pride in his city was merely another manifestation of the middle-class pride in its own accomplishments, for London was essentially the creation of tradesmen. Although the court might reside in the curtilage of the city, the tone and quality of London were determined by Cheapside rather than Whitehall. A city of merchants and tradesmen, its commercial power and its pomp of bourgeois circumstance were already beginning to color the civilization of England.

The middle class of the sixteenth and seventeenth centuries, which was laying the foundation for the eventual transformation of England, showed no greater evidence of vitality and strength than in its proud realization of its own importance, its glorification of the dignity of trade, its insistence upon the valor, virtue, and worthiness of tradesmen. The literature which gives articulate expression to these ideas provides a significant revelation of a phase of the middle-class background that helps to explain much in bourgeois attitudes and development.

III

THE CONCERN OVER LEARNING[1]

NO phase of the middle-class background has greater cultural significance than the interest displayed by plain citizens in school learning from the mid-sixteenth to the mid-seventeenth century. When this period began, secular agencies had only recently assumed the major responsibility for education, which earlier had been almost entirely in the hands of the church ; when it ended, citizens of a commercial society, who had grown accustomed to the social obligation of providing adequate schools, were beginning to discuss the shortcomings of the educational structure and the means of remodeling it to meet the utilitarian needs of a practical world. If within this hundred years actual changes in the curricula and organization of the grammar schools, and even of the universities, were less noteworthy than one might expect, nevertheless the ground was being prepared for innovations that were to come later. Undoubtedly the educational demands of a large middle class exerted a powerful influence upon pedagogical theorists of the seventeenth century who set out to reform the schools. But between the secularization of education and the reform movement, there is roughly a century during which citizens placed an uncritical faith in the grammar schools and regarded with infinite respect the learning of the universities. Since the premium put upon learning throughout the Renaissance enhanced the value of education as a means of rising from low to high estate, the sensitiveness of the ordinary layman to the importance of schools was greatly stimulated. With Protestantism came another incentive to education, in the firm belief (which the Reformed faith encouraged) that learning would open the kingdom of God

[1] Much of the material in this chapter first appeared as an essay, "The Renaissance Middle-Class Concern over Learning," *Philological Quarterly*, IX (1930), 273-96.

to the faithful. With the rapid growth of an urban civilization there came also a more general realization of the prestige as well as the practical advantages that schooling bestowed, until there begins to be discernible the modern faith in education as a means to cure all social ills, to induce happiness, and to make mankind generally wiser, wealthier, and more godly. Elizabethan tradesmen, therefore, loosened their purse strings for the benefit of grammar schools and university scholarships and earnestly strove to see that their sons received as much learning as the choice of the youths' careers permitted.

If the eldest son had to leave the free grammar school early to begin his apprenticeship, perhaps his brother might finish and receive a scholarship at one of the universities, whence in due course he would emerge a learned preacher to bring honor to his parents. Even if a youth attended only the petty school, which was preparatory to entering the grammar school, he received the rudiments of education, acquiring there the ability to read and write as well as to cipher. It is safe to say that few middle-class parents allowed their children to grow up in complete ignorance of school learning.[2] The belief in the value of education and the importance of the schools was already becoming firmly ingrained as a dogma in burgher thinking.[3]

Even before the stimulus of the Renaissance had become diffused among all classes in England, commoners had found the schools a useful means of improving their lot, as the rise of many a prelate-statesman, not least of whom was Wolsey, can testify. Indeed, as early as the last decade of the fourteenth century the author of *Peres the Ploughmans Crede* had complained against the schools for advancing the sons of the lowly to high places in the church:

Now may every cobbler set his son to school, and every beggar's brat

---

[2] J. W. Adamson, "The Extent of Literacy in England in the Fifteenth and Sixteenth Centuries: Notes and Conjectures," *The Library*, 4th Ser., X (1929-30), 163-93. Mr. Adamson offers evidence that a large proportion of the population, including many of the more intelligent of the servant class, could read and write.

[3] Professor Hardin Craig, "A Contribution to the Theory of the English Renaissance," *Philological Quarterly*, VII (1928), 321-33, stresses the Renaissance belief in "the promise of unbelievably good things held out to those who acquired learning." Professor Craig does not refer particularly to the middle class, but this was precisely their point of view.

learn from the book, and become either a writer and dwell with a lord, or a false friar to serve the Devil. So that the beggar's brat becomes a bishop, to sit esteemed among the peers of the land, and lords' sons bow down to the good-for-nothings, knights bend to them and crouch full low, and this bishop's father a shoemaker, soiled with grease and his teeth as tattered as a saw with champing leather.[4]

Since poverty and low degree were no barriers to learning, the schools thus early became associated in the popular consciousness with opportunity, for they provided training that was both academic and practical.[5] With the commercial expansion of the fifteenth century, the demand increased for apprentices and assistants who could read, write, and keep accounts—fundamentals which they might learn in petty schools maintained as a part of numerous religious foundations because teaching, as well as praying, was the duty of many chantry priests who undertook the instruction of the community children.[6] Moreover, already in the fifteenth century wealthy tradesmen had begun to establish schools unattached to religious foundations, a habit which was to account for much of the later educational development.[7] The ordinary citizen's realization of the value of learning, clearly evident in the

---

[4] The quotation cited here is a modernization as given by J. W. Adamson, *A Short History of Education* (Cambridge, 1922), p. 76, from the original manuscript, dating from about 1394, edited by W. W. Skeat for the Early English Text Society, Orig. Ser., XXX (1867), ll. 744-53.

[5] The grammar schools, with their instruction in Latin, were originally intensely practical, since Latin was the entrance into all learning. *See* H. T. Mark, *An Outline of the History of Educational Theories in England* (London, 1899), p. 95.

[6] A. F. Leach, *English Schools at the Reformation, 1546-8* (London, 1896), *passim*, emphasizes the educational functions of the endowed chantries. It should be remembered, however, that keeping a school was often merely an incidental duty and was by no means a general practice.

[7] A. F. Leach, *The Schools of Medieval England* (London, 1915). Leach says (pp. 244 ff.) that the first school known to have been founded by a London citizen was that by William Sevenoaks, grocer, in 1432 at Sevenoaks. He thinks this is an indication of an antisacerdotal tendency beginning in education. The example of Sevenoaks was followed by others. John Abbott, mercer, founded a free school at Farthinghoe and made the Mercers' Company trustees. "He thus anticipated by sixty-seven years," Leach points out, "the supposed innovation of Colet in entrusting his new endowment for St. Paul's to the same Company." Among other merchant-founders at this time was Sir Edmund Shaa, goldsmith, who provided in 1487-88 for a priest to teach grammar, and to pray for his soul, at Stopford. In 1505 Sir Bartholomew Read, goldsmith, founded a school at Cromer.

period when feudalism was decaying and leaving to him additional social responsibilities,[8] was greatly sharpened in the succeeding years when further social, religious, and political changes increased both his obligations and his opportunities.

The social upheaval, begun in early Tudor times and continued throughout the sixteenth and seventeenth centuries, magnified the ambitions of commoners and thus made more acute their desires for the means with which to encompass their dreams. One of the most obvious of these means, of course, was learning, which gave an opportunity to even the poorest youth, provided he had sufficient capacity. To commissioners who wished to exclude "the ploughman's son" from the Cathedral School at Canterbury, Archbishop Cranmer replied by insisting that ability should be the basis of choice. ". . . if the gentleman's son be apt at learning, let him be admitted ; if not apt, let the poor man's child, being apt, enter his room."[9] This point of view was long to prevail and was to make the grammar schools and the universities the stepping-stones to preferment. Pious appreciation of the opportunity which school foundations give to the lowborn is the point of a comment by Abraham Fleming in *A Memoriall of the famous monuments and charitable almes deeds of the right worshipfull Maister William Lambe Esquire* (1580), apropos of the benevolence of this London citizen and cloth-worker :

And remembering that learning bringeth preferment, yea euen to them which are but basely borne, as it pleaseth God to moue him by his good and gratious spirite, he proued himselfe by testimonials of his

---

[8] W. H. Woodward, *Studies in Education during the Age of the Renaissance, 1400-1600* (Cambridge, 1924), p. 117, discusses the humanistic ideal of education as a discipline for the training of leaders, "in no way determined by birth or wealth, but by capacity. Yet its tendency was to set up a class, not narrow or professional in type, rather an educated upper-middle class, upon which were falling the responsibilities now slipping from a feudal society." Woodward goes on to say that the Renaissance "offered little in the way of educational hope to the people, except on condition that the individual rose out of his class to receive a training for a rank above it," but this was precisely the hope which permeated the middle class. Lesser tradesmen, who hoped to improve the positions of their families, found the schools a vehicle for advancement. Great merchants, equally desirous of social advancement, looked upon the universities and inns of court as the instruments which would transform their sons into influential servants of the state.

[9] Norman Wood, *The Reformation and English Education* (London, 1931), p. 26.

doings a louer of learning, and fauourer of euerie honest profession. For in the towne of Sutton Valens in Kent, this worshipfull Gentleman at his own costs and proper expences erected a Grammar schoole for the education of youth in the feare of God, in good maners, in knowledge and vnderstanding. [Sig. B 4ᵛ.]

The opportunity for the advancement of the humble but capable person is also emphasized by C. Thimelthorpe, author of *A Short Inuentory of certayne Idle Inuentions* (1581), in verses which declare that "by virtue of learning" even "the meanest man of all" may "to honor high" attain [sig. G 4].

The knowledge that through the doors of the schools his sons might pass to great rewards urged every father to try to give his children educational opportunities. Richard Mulcaster comments that "everyone desireth to have his children learned,"[10] and John Brinsley a little later in *A Consolation For Our Grammar Schooles* (1622) refers to the same desire:

. . . there is no man, hauing the nature of a wise father, who would not haue his child to haue some learning, howsoeuer he purpose to employ him afterward, and who to that end would not haue him so instructed, as whereby to get the best learning, in the shortest time, and with the least seueritie, or who will not giue almost double, if he may be assured to haue his child so trained vp. [P. 40.]

But it does not follow that every middle-class youth proceeding along the paths of formal education was a person of ability. Since the distinction conferred by learning was generally recognized, well-to-do fathers freely laid out their money to make it possible for their sons to attain at least the outward signs of education. Thus from the time of Henry VIII onward the universities—and the inns of court likewise—were crowded with wealthy students from the upper middle class, many of whom had come merely because it was fashionable to have the "cachet of a university training."[11] Many a new-made gentleman who had risen from trade by means of learning produced a son who became just such a fashionable drone in the schools. This type of youth provoked the sarcastic comment of Thomas Nashe: "Pride the peruerter of all Vertue, sitteth appareled in the Marchants spoiles, and ruine of yoong

---

[10] Foster Watson, *The Old Grammar Schools* (Cambridge, 1916), pp. 117-18.
[11] Wood, *op. cit.*, pp. 81-82.

Citizens : and scorneth learning, that gaue their vpstart Fathers, titles of gentry."[12] Though learning may have been contemned by an occasional *nouveau riche* youth like the one described by Nashe, its power to promote the tradesman to a better station made it almost a fetish with the middle class. The practical result of their faith was amply demonstrated by the able men of low birth who had come from the grammar schools and universities to serve the state with distinction. Even the bohemian world of literature, of which the average thrifty tradesman would not approve, was peopled by bright young men of humble parentage, who had received their background of learning in the free schools of the land. Shakespeare, Marlowe, Jonson, and their colleagues were the products of a school system within reach of any student capable of the discipline. Augmented desires for learning demanded increased opportunities, which became the object of much bourgeois beneficence throughout the period.

The religious impact of the Reformation was a factor of inestimable consequence in fostering the public concern over education during the formative years of the sixteenth century and later. One of the major objectives of the Reformers was a Bible in the vernacular so that every man could profit by the wisdom of the Scriptures. We may be sure that Protestant Englishmen who had been willing to shed their blood for a translated Bible would not achieve the privilege without practising the right to read the precious book. It therefore became a solemn duty to see that children learned at least enough to enable them to read and understand Holy Writ. An insistent cry went up throughout the sixteenth and seventeenth centuries for teaching which would produce *understanding* rather than mere memorizing by rote. When Puritanism added a new religious fervor, the importance of the schools loomed even larger, for the Puritans, with an insistence unknown before, urged the need of a learned ministry. Since the grammar schools, open to any youth of capacity regardless of financial and social standing, occupied a key position in the training of the clergy, the Puritans cherished and supported them, in addition to making it easy for worthy students to attend

---

[12] *Pierce Penilesse* (1592), edited by G. B. Harrison (London, 1924), p. 22.

the universities. Furthermore, the general feeling that the grammar schools inculcated good morals exercised a powerful influence in their favor. Hence, pious commoners struggled to send their sons, and sometimes even their daughters, not only to the petty schools, but also to the classical grammar schools where they might be instructed in the fundamentals of "good learning," a phrase constantly repeated in the documents of the time.

The acts of Henry VIII and Edward VI for the suppression of the chantries and the schools connected with them, plunged the educational system of England into chaos for a time, but the ultimate result was to place education in the hands of secular authority and to give the average citizen a keener sense of his duty to the schools. Without doubt the schools suffered for a while, and the sons of the poor and even of the moderately well-to-do found the door of opportunity through learning harder to enter than it had been previously. Although the number of schools was seriously diminished by the disestablishment of the religious foundations and not even the refounding of many of them by Henry and his son provided for all the needs formerly met by teaching priests,[13] some of the schools underwent a rejuvenation which enabled them to care for larger numbers of students and to give more earnest attention to instruction than had been given in chantry schools where priests were ignorant or lazy.[14] The very scarcity of schools had a beneficial effect in arousing the laity to their needs. From this time onward, town aldermen, trade guilds, and individual citizens took a more active part in the administration and foundation of schools. When Elizabeth came to the throne, the school movement was so strong that the Queen was content to leave the founding of schools to her subjects,[15] who fulfilled their duties so well that by the end of her reign the very number of schools equaled, if not surpassed, the numerous chantry foundations which had previously gone through

---

[13] For a recent discussion of the acts disestablishing the chantries, see Wood, *op. cit.*, pp. 20-27, 30-34.

[14] *Ibid.*, pp. 9-12.

[15] *Ibid.*, p. 49. Although some schools founded after 1558 bear the name of "Queen Elizabeth Grammar School," the title is generally one of courtesy.

4

the motions of providing instruction for the public.[16]

The founding of schools and the support of poor scholars at the universities became the fashion, and almost a religious obligation, during the reign of Elizabeth and her successors. Before Henry VIII destroyed the chantries, rich men, contemplating death, had found solace in the knowledge that if they furnished an endowment for a chantry, priests would for perpetuity intone prayers for their souls—and perchance teach the townsmen's children. Now all that was changed. No longer could a rich burgher provide for his soul's repose by endowing priests. But Protestantism, which destroyed the mass-priests, did not eradicate the notion that a good deed at death would argue for the deceased on the Day of Judgment. Barred from endowing chantries or giving his money to some monastery, the Renaissance man of wealth gradually began to bestow his largess on the schools. As the new conception of the dignity and virtue of learning, part of the Renaissance spirit, reached the level of the average citizen, he sought to show his civic piety by good works in the interest of learning. The necessity of providing for schools once administered as a matter of course by the church, the vague faith in the salvation accruing to the giver, and the development of the idea that education is the open sesame to all good things, both of the world and the spirit, produced a succession of educational philanthropists among the wealthy business men of the kingdom, especially among the merchants and tradesmen of London. Writers on education did what they could to stimulate the belief in the value of educational subventions. John Brinsley, for example, stressed the virtue which redounds to generous benefactors. A marginal note, written by him, pointedly observes that it is "The chiefest glory in earth to be aduancers of learning & piety,"[17] and he further amplifies his comment:

To this purpose if that heathen Orator could likewise say further, euen by the light of nature: *That to all who haue preserued, helped, or any way augmented the happinesse of their countrey, there is a most certaine place ordained in the heauens, where they shall enioy eternall happinesse;* how much

---

[16] A. Monroe Stowe, *English Grammar Schools in the Reign of Queen Elizabeth* (New York, 1908), p. 11.

[17] *A Consolation For Our Grammar Schooles,* p. 17.

more boldly may we Christians auouch the same, vpon certaine grounds
out of the word of God : That there is indeed a place of euerlasting
happinesse, and glorie prepared for all those, who in witnesse of their
loue & thankfulnesse to Iesus Christ, and to their countries, shall
employ their studies, and their wealth, to the greatest aduancement
of all heauenly learning, and vnto the vertuous education of youth,
the hope of the succeeding ages?

For the Renaissance, the grammar school was the entrance to "all
heauenly learning" and surely no more worthy undertaking could
be induced in the citizen than "the vertuous education of youth."

Elizabethan tradesmen who had grown rich in London often
showed a loyalty to their birthplaces by endowing a school or
making a contribution to the schools already existing. Nicholas
Carlisle lists more than fifty endowments by business men in the
sixteenth and early seventeenth centuries in his *Concise Description
of the Endowed Grammar Schools in England and Wales.*[18] The memory
of the village school where the benefactor had received his start
toward a successful career frequently prompted gifts which were
made as a mark of the giver's gratitude for the benefits received.
Bequests sometimes acknowledge such an indebtedness to the
schools and express the pious hope that the donor's gift may aid
other worthy youths to get ahead in the world. Education for
temporal success was strong in the Elizabethan consciousness. In
view of the popular belief that Elizabethan grammar schools furnished only pedantries of Latin, it is significant that hard-headed
merchants, remembering their schools as useful institutions, aided
in their multiplication. The good work of school founding had
proceeded so well that by 1577 William Harrison could say :

Besides these vniuersities, also there are great number of Grammer
schooles through out the realme, and those verie liberallie indued, for
the better reliefe of poor scholers, so that there are not manie corporat
townes now vnder the queenes dominion, that hain not one Gramar
schoole at the least, with a sufficient liuing for a maister and vsher
appointed to the same.[19]

---

[18] 2 vols. (London, 1818), *passim.*
[19] *Description of England*, Pt. I, edited by F. J. Furnivall, New Shakespeare Society,
Ser. 6, I (1877), p. 83.

The generosity of London citizens in matters of education caused honest John Stow, himself a merchant tailor, to write glowing praise of mercantile philanthropies in *A Survey of London* (1598), in which he gives a list of prominent benefactors. This list was increased by the authors of the continuations to Stow's work,[20] until in the edition of 1633 more than sixty tradesmen-benefactors of education are named. Although these were all Londoners, the schools they founded were scattered throughout England. The philanthropies mentioned by Stow and his successors are only a few of the bourgeois benefactions of the sixteenth and early seventeenth centuries. Since business men in other commercial towns besides London were following the same philanthropic impulses, schools which owed their beginning to the interest of citizens multiplied at a remarkable rate.[21]

Not only were individual citizens endowing grammar schools and loan funds at the universities, but the great trade guilds, as organizations and through their individual members, actively exerted themselves to foster learning, both elementary and advanced. With something of the same spirit that at times permeates the civic and so-called "service" groups of today, the guilds undertook to aid schools and to establish scholarships to such an extent that a friendly rivalry in these activities developed. The records of the great companies show that they contributed to the support of a large number of schools and kept many students in the universities.[22] A few examples from various guild records will

---

[20] Cf. the edition of 1633, brought up to date "by the study and labor of A.M. H.D. and others," pp. 86-112. Here in double columns one finds recorded the "Honour of Citizens, and worthiness both of men and women in the same," in their charities and philanthropies. A summary of Stow's remarks on this subject in the 1603 edition may be found in Watson's *The Old Grammar Schools*, pp. 46-48.

[21] The chapters on education in the *Victoria County Histories* give some indication of the development of the provincial schools in this period through the activities of business men. *See*, e.g., *A History of Gloucestershire* (London, 1907), II, 361 ff., which relates the interest of the local merchants in the Bristol Grammar School.

[22] *See* William Herbert, *The History of the Twelve Great Livery Companies of London*, 2 vols. (London, 1837), *passim*, under "Histories of the Separate Companies," where he gives summaries of their charitable activities. *See also* A. Monroe Stowe, *op. cit.*, pp. 32-33. For the attitude of the medieval guilds toward education, see "Medieval Gilds and Education," in *Studies in Economic History: The Collected Papers of George Unwin*, edited by R. H. Tawney (London, 1927), pp. 92-99.

illustrate the nature of their educational activities throughout this period.

Although trade guilds had shown an interest in schools before the sixteenth century,[23] early in that century they began to play a more prominent part in the encouragement of learning. So great was their reputation for probity, as well as for an intelligent interest in education, that John Colet could think of no better auspices for St. Paul's School than the Mercers' Company, whom he made governors of the school in 1509 because, as Erasmus said, "he had found less corruption in married citizens than in any others."[24] The statutes of the school stipulated that a group of surveyors, appointed from the company, should periodically visit the school to see that the children were being instructed in "not . . . only good literature, but allso good maners."[25] There is every indication that the Mercers conscientiously visited the school and gave it judicious attention during the years that followed. Colet's provision for a numerous body of surveyors, so that many individual members of the company might come in contact with the work of the school and make it their personal concern, proved a wise step in promoting the guild's pride in the institution.

Much later in its foundation but closely imitative of the Mercers' famous school at St. Paul's was the Merchant Taylors' School, established in 1561 through the generosity of Richard Hilles with Richard Mulcaster as its headmaster. The statutes of the school, which one of its early historians declared were dictated by "good sense, piety, and benevolence,"[26] were taken, in places, almost verbatim from the statutes of St. Paul's ;[27] they also made provision that members of the company should keep in close touch with the conduct of the school. The master and wardens of the Guild of Merchant Taylors kept in their own hands the admission of students, but it was specified that "children of all nations and countries indifferently" were to be eligible, provided that they be not

---

[23] *See* Leach, *English Schools at the Reformation*, pp. 34 ff.

[24] Quoted from Erasmus' *Letters* (ed. of 1642, Bk. XV, Letter 14, p. 705) by A. H. Johnson, *The History of the Worshipful Company of the Drapers of London*, 5 vols. (Oxford, 1914-22), III, 334.

[25] Carlisle, *op. cit.*, II, 71.

[26] *Ibid.*, p. 49.

[27] Stowe, *op. cit.*, pp. 72-73.

"dunces nor neglected of their parents," and that "they can say the Catechism in English or Latin, and read perfectly and write competently."[28] The purpose of the school is said in the statutes to be the "bringing up of children in good manners and literature."[29] The administration of this school, which numbered among its students many who were to become prominent in after life (not least of whom was Edmund Spenser) is a tribute to the sagacity and practical wisdom of a body of active business men of London.

Not only as a group but as individuals, the merchant tailors of London were liberal supporters of learning. Generosity to schools became a tradition in the guild, the records of which show a long succession of benefactions from the beginning of the sixteenth century onward. One of the earliest of the merchant-tailor founders of schools, Sir John Percyvale, in a bequest to his native town of Macclesfield in 1502 describes a condition which prompted many another tradesman to make a contribution to education. The need was great for a school, declares Sir John, because "God of His abundant grace doth send to the inhabitants copious plenty of children to whose learning and bringing forth in cunning and virtue right few teachers and schoolmasters are in this country [around Macclesfield], whereby many children for lack of such teaching fall to idleness and live dissolutely all their days."[30] Surely no better reason for a school could have recommended itself to a tradesman than the curbing of iniquity through the prevention of idleness, a cardinal sin according to bourgeois economy. Other early merchant tailors to found schools included Sir Stephen Jenyns, who established Wolverhampton Grammar School in 1508 for "instructing boys in good morals and literature,"[31] and Sir William Harper, to whom Bedford School owed its origin in 1552.[32]

But of all the merchant tailors the one best known as a benefactor of learning was Sir Thomas White, who founded in 1555 St. John's College, Oxford, which he dedicated "to the praise and honour of God, the Blessed Virgin Mary, and St. John Baptist

---

[28] C. M. Clode, *Memorials of the Guild of Merchant Taylors* (London, 1875), p. 404.

[29] *Ibid.*, p. 417.

[30] C. M. Clode, *Early History of the Guild of Merchant Taylors*, 2 vols. (London, 1888), II, 17-18.

[31] *Ibid.*, p. 34.

[32] *Ibid.*, p. 241.

(the patron saint of the Merchant Taylors' Company)" that it might become an instrument for "the learning of the sciences of holy divinity, philosophy, and good arts."[33] Sir Thomas was typical of the self-made men of the sixteenth century, having been born the son of a Hertfordshire clothier and apprenticed early to a London tradesman who gave him his first start in business. White's only formal schooling was obtained in the Reading Grammar School, which he later remembered with two scholarships. When his shop in Cornhill had brought him riches, White generously gave to educational causes, though he objected to the expense incidental to being made an alderman. Although he joined with Hilles in the establishment of the Merchant Taylors' School, White's name is now remembered chiefly because of his endowment of St. John's College, which from the day of its establishment became the object of philanthropy from many merchant tailors, who must have found St. John's emphasis on divinity pleasing to their sense of what was proper for a college. For example, Walter Fish in 1580 left funds to support "five poor studious scholars of St. John's College, Oxford, which should be most like to bend their studies to divinity."[34] John Vernon in 1615 provided for "four poor scholars, students in divinity in St. John's College, Oxford, 16 l. yearly viz., 4 l. a man, to be elected by the master, wardens and assistants [of the Guild of Merchant Taylors], to continue no longer than they should study divinity, and remain in the said college."[35] Other merchant tailors made similar bequests. Although not all insisted upon the study of divinity, the frequency with which merchants endowed prospective preachers suggests an unconscious subsidy, which must have colored the opinions of future ecclesiastics and have been a potent influence in the shaping of religious beliefs to comply with middle-class bias.

The gifts from members of the Guild of Merchant Taylors of London influenced educational progress not only in the metropolis but also in other parts of the kingdom. Typical of such benefactions were those of Richard Osmotherlaw, whose will in 1612 provided £10 yearly to "find a sufficient and learned schoolmaster

---

[33] *Dictionary of National Biography, sub* Sir Thomas White.
[34] Clode, *Memorials*, p. 291.
[35] *Ibid.*, p. 307.

to educate fifteen poor men's children, inhabiting within the towns of Langrigge and Bromefield,"[36] and of William Parker, who provided £20 yearly to employ an unmarried minister to teach "men children" of Great Bloxith and that neighborhood in Staffordshire "to read English, both printed and written-hand."[37] Evidence of a desire to imitate in the provinces the London Merchant Taylors' School is found in the will of John Harrison, a member of the London company, who left £500 in 1618 to establish a school "for educating children and youth in the grammar and rules of learning, forever, to be called 'The Merchant Tailors School, founded at the charges of John Harrison'" at Great Crosby in Lancashire.[38] The extent of the influence exerted by this single guild, collectively and individually, cannot be measured by statistics, which merely indicate the amount of its contributions and the number of schools founded or assisted; to appreciate fully its influence, one must also consider the moral effect upon popular education of the active interest and support of such practical and respected citizens as those who composed the Merchant Taylors' company.

Other trade guilds were not far behind the Merchant Taylors in their benefactions to education. As early as the last year of Edward VI's reign, the Haberdashers' Company took the lead for the moment in the encouragement of university training by proposing "to give £5 yearly towards finding of a poor scholar at the University, 'so that the rest of the twelue *Most Worshypful Companies* of the citie do the like.' The merchant tailors agreed the same day, and consequently all the rest."[39] Both secondary schools and university scholarships received much help from members of the various guilds in the century that followed.

Just as the Merchant Taylors made their London school a favorite charity, so the Company of Skinners interested themselves in Tunbridge Grammar School, founded in 1553 by Sir Andrew Judd, one of their members.[40] Thereafter loyal Skinners not only

[36] *Ibid.*, p. 302.   [37] *Ibid.*, p. 310.

[38] *Ibid.*, p. 314. Girls as well as boys seem to have been educated in this school.— *Ibid.*, p. 726.

[39] Herbert, *op. cit.*, I, 103 n.

[40] James Foster Wadmore, *Some Account of the Worshipful Company of Skinners of London* (London, 1902), pp. 225 ff.

gave money to the school but helped its students to the universities and contributed generally to educational undertakings. The example of generosity set by Sir Andrew Judd was followed by his daughter, Dame Alice Smythe, who in 1593 left £100 each to Oxford and Cambridge,[41] and by his grandson, Sir Thomas Smythe, who in 1619 gave funds to Tunbridge School and £10 to send a poor scholar from the school to one of the universities. The latter fund was increased in 1625 to provide for six scholars "who should principally study divinity."[42] Henry Fisher, who in 1562 aided John Wheland, student from Tunbridge School at Brasenose, Oxford, also provided a permanent endowment at Brasenose for a Tunbridge scholar.[43] Sir James Lancaster, citizen and skinner as well as picturesque trader and sea captain, in 1618 left £20 to the free school at Basingstoke, other funds for a petty schoolmaster, and adequate provision to aid three poor scholars in divinity at Oxford and Cambridge.[44]

The Company of Drapers, who seem to have kept a close watch on recipients of their benefactions, supported annually two scholars at Oxford and one at Cambridge, whom they supplied with books.[45] Since the encouragement of a learned ministry was the reason behind their gifts, they did not tolerate trifling on the part of holders of scholarships; their records reveal the dismissal of one student for poor scholarship and another for marrying and giving over the study of divinity.[46] A gift of £40 was made in 1617 by the Drapers, who joined the Mercers, the Goldsmiths, the Haberdashers, and the Skinners in complying with a request from the Archbishop of Canterbury for funds to help in establishing "public schools of disputation" at Oxford.[47] The philanthropic activities of individual drapers are illustrated by the founding of a school in 1593 at Barton in Staffordshire through the generosity of Thomas Russell,[48] and the creation of a fund in 1620 by Sir

[41] *Ibid.*, p. 207. [42] *Ibid.*, p. 217.
[43] *Ibid.*, pp. 202-3. [44] *Ibid.*, p. 212.
[45] A. H. Johnson, *op. cit.*, II, 161-62.
[46] *Ibid.*, pp. 161-62. In a note here Johnson observes that "the Jesuit Campion . . . was a Scholar of the Grocers' Company and Fellow of St. John's College at Oxford."
[47] *Ibid.*, III, 68-69.
[48] *Ibid.*, II, 162. The master in 1596 was reported "too vigorous." In 1618 the master was again complained of for beating pupils over the head. A new one was appointed at an increase in salary.—*Ibid.*, III, 113-14.

John Jolles "for the education of thirty-five boys of Stratford Le
Bow and Bromley 'in the fear of God and good manners.' They
were to learn to write and to cypher, grammar and the Latin
tongue."[49]

The Company of Ironmongers served as trustees for several educational funds. In 1571 a Mr. Carr left £500 to the Company to be
used for certain stipulated charities, which included the distribution of £7 10s. "Amongst five of the poorest scholars professing
divinity in the University of Oxford ; and the like sum to five poor
scholars of Cambridge."[50] William Chapman in 1579 left £200
to the Ironmongers to maintain yearly at Oriel College, Oxford,
"two poor scholars to study divinity there, until they should be of
the age of 30 years, when they should be displaced, and two other
poor scholars appointed in their room, and so on from time to
time."[51] Thomas Hallwood in 1622 left £400 to the Company to
provide for four scholars forever, two at Magdalen College, Oxford, and two at Christ's College, Cambridge, for three years each,
if they "should study and proceed for divinity."[52] Sir James Campbell, alderman and ironmonger, in 1641 provided £666 13s. 4d.
for a free school at Barking in Essex.[53]

The Guild of Saddlers, says their chronicler, "appear from a
very early date to have supported a number of poor Scholars at
the Universities." The company records show a payment on July
27, 1613, to Giles Rankin at St. John's, Oxford, "towards his
maintenance of his studie in good literature." On October 9, 1621,
the stipend of Thomas Akers, "being one of our Schollers," was
increased. Gifts of books were made to the scholars, who also
received a cash donation on graduation.[54] Other guilds made similar provisions for the encouragement of learning. The Pewterers
as a company maintained scholars at Cambridge, and perhaps at
Oxford.[55] The Cutlers' Company held trust funds for the educa-

---

[49] *Ibid.*, p. 114.

[50] John Nicholl, *Some Account of the Worshipful Company of Ironmongers* (London, 1851),
p. 472.

[51] *Ibid.*, p. 530.   [52] *Ibid.*, p. 542.   [53] *Ibid.*

[54] John W. Sherwell, *A Descriptive and Historical Account of the Guild of Saddlers of the
City of London*, 2 vols. (London, 1889), I, 77.

[55] Charles Welch, *History of the Worshipful Company of Pewterers of the City of London*,
2 vols. (London, 1902), I, 260, 277 ; II, 94.

tion of young men at each of the universities without respect to college.[56] Occasionally, when trust funds were not available, the trade guilds helped deserving youths from the company funds, as in the case of a certain Roger Smith sent to Cambridge in 1578 by the Haberdashers.[57] Few worthy students desirous of studying at the universities could have failed to find sympathetic patrons among the guild members of London.

The support of schools and the maintenance of scholarships throughout the sixteenth and seventeenth centuries remained a matter of fraternity pride among the worshipful companies of London. While certain guilds were more profuse in their outlay than others, and while some concentrated upon other forms of charity, it is clear that most of the trade organizations took seriously their obligations to foster learning. So important were the educational foundations in the trusteeship of the guilds that the administration of the funds must have been in some of the companies a responsible and complex duty. Occasionally the administration called for a coöperative effort on the part of more than one guild, for sometimes members of one made bequests to schools administered by another, as in the case of Henry Cloker, who left a fund in 1573 in the trust of the Company of Coopers for the upkeep of "the Schoole House at Ratcliffe, late erected by Nicholas Gibson, Grocer."[58] The results of guild management, over a long period of years, of schools like St. Paul's, the Merchant Taylors', Tunbridge, and many lesser foundations demonstrate the civic interest and sagacity of such organizations of citizens.

So important, indeed, had become the activities of London citizens in educational endeavors by the last quarter of the sixteenth century that governing authorities leaned heavily on their generosity, depending so much on private donations that at length Londoners were moved to make an official protest. When the Lords of the Council demanded in 1579-80 that the citizens of London provide a perpetual maintenance for a school at Barnet, the lord mayor objected on the grounds that a great burden of education and charity had already been assumed by the citizenry:

---

[56] *Idem, History of the Cutlers' Company of London*, 2 vols. (London, 1923), II, 169-70.
[57] E. H. Pearce, *Annals of Christ's Hospital* (2d ed., London, 1908), p. 68.
[58] Cuthbert Lake, *Notes on the Will of Henry Cloker, 1573* (London, 1924), p. 9.

"Besides the large number of scholars that were provided for in the Vniversities, both by the Companies and by particular Citizens, they likewise maintained sundry scholars at great charge."[59] Further obligations, the lord mayor maintains, would be onerous. But more annoying than the additional burden of expense was doubtless the evidence of a desire on the part of the Council to coerce citizens who had a strong sense of individualism and independence and preferred to give as they chose, not as authority decreed.

So ingrained had become the notion that schools were instruments of both profit and piety, which should be encouraged by every patriotic citizen, that soon after English colonies were established in America subscribers to colonial ventures began to consider methods of educating the children of the settlers and the native Indians. The Virginia Company of London received letters patent from King James in 1617 to solicit funds for the foundation of a college in Virginia for the education of both Indian and white children. Such generous response was made to the appeal for funds that by May, 1619, £1,500 had been collected and additional gifts, including a copy of the works of the Reverend William Perkins, were made a little later.[60] The project for the Indian college strongly appealed to Nicholas Ferrar, a wealthy member of the Skinners' Company, who had such a vision of educating the Indians in godliness and honest trades that in 1620 he left

£300 to the college in Virginia to be paid when there shall be ten of the infidels' children placed in it, and in the meantime twenty-four pounds by the yeare to be disbursed unto three discreete and godly men in the colonie, which shall honestly bring up three of the infidels' children in Christian religion and some good course to live by.[61]

Although the subsequent history of the school was disastrous, it came to naught through no lack of support from subscribers at home, most of whom were pious citizens.

---

[59] W. H. and H. C. Overall, *Analytical Index to the Series of Records Known as the Remembrancia* (London, 1878), p. 140.

[60] P. A. Bruce, *Institutional History of Virginia in the Seventeenth Century*, 2 vols. (New York, 1910), I, 362 ff.

[61] R. R. Sharpe, *London and the Kingdom*, 3 vols. (London, 1894), II, 48.

Further illustration of the concern of middle-class philanthropists for education may be seen in the benefactions to Christ's Hospital, Gresham College, Charterhouse, and Dulwich College or the College of God's Gift. The profitableness of instruction at Christ's Hospital was improved as a result of gifts in 1577 from Dame Mary Ramsay, wife of a wealthy merchant. She stipulated that her funds were to be used for the teaching of utilitarian subjects, such as commercial writing and bookkeeping. Later she provided an additional trust fund to keep four scholars and two fellows, chosen from Christ's Hospital, at Peterhouse, Cambridge.[62] Gresham College, founded by the merchant prince, Sir Thomas Gresham, on his death in 1579, through a trust fund administered by the Corporation of London and the Mercers' Company, became a great influence in the diffusion of learning among middle-class Londoners, as will appear later in this discussion. Although Thomas Sutton, who founded Charterhouse School in 1611, probably came of a landed family and apparently attained to some rank in the army, he soon turned his talents to business and became the richest commoner in England as a result of successful exploitation of the Durham coal fields.[63] With the practical judgment of a man of business he insisted that the master and usher of Charterhouse School should take care "to teach the scholars to cypher and cast an accompt, especially those that are less capable of learning and fittest to be put to trades."[64] The College of God's Gift at Dulwich owed its foundation in 1613 to the generosity of Edward Alleyn, partner of his father-in-law, Philip Henslowe, in various theatrical ventures. Though an actor, he was far from the bohemian blade that is the common conception of an Elizabethan player. Instead, he was a canny business man who got rich by shrewd investments, became a warden in his parish church, shared the points of view of his neighbor tradesmen in many respects, and lived to found a hospital and school which may have been suggested by Sutton's provisions for Charterhouse. These four institutions made a large contribution to the educational advantages of London, whose citizens already in the early seven-

---

[62] Pearce, *op. cit.*, p. 268.
[63] *Dictionary of National Biography*, *sub* Sutton.
[64] Adamson, *A Short History of Education*, p. 153.

teenth century were boasting of the eminence of the capital in its opportunities for learning.

By this time, indeed, London had become famous for its schools, which had been multiplying throughout the sixteenth century, largely, let it be emphasized, as a result of the intellectual awakening of the city's own inhabitants, until it is small wonder that they felt privileged to compare the opportunities of London with those of Oxford and Cambridge. A description of the diversity of educational facilities in the metropolis, and fulsome praise of its people for their beneficence, found expression in 1615 in Sir George Buck's *The Third Vniversitie Of England*.[65] With the zeal of a modern real-estate promoter, Buck elaborates upon the privileges open to residents of the city. Beginning with the schools of law and divinity, he continues an enumeration of "schools" of instruction in everything from poetry to swimming. Lectures in such practical subjects as arithmetic, geography, and navigation, which were being taught at Gresham College, receive the commendation of the author,[66] who praises Gresham for his wisdom and generosity and exhorts other citizens to remember by this "notable example to the rest of his qualitie the richer Marchants, and the more opulent Cittizens of London, the fauorites of Pluto and Mercury, to employ some good part of their great wealth in publike workes of necessarie or pious vse, or of ornament."[67] Richard Whittington is cited as an early example of merchant-philanthropist because of his establishment of "Whittington College . . . for the seruice of God, and the reliefe of the poore of this cittie, and for the good education of children," and his endowment of the library at Grey Friars, later Christ's Hospital. In similar fashion Buck praises the good work which "Alderman Knowles, and alderman Eyre, and some

[65] *The Third Vniversitie Of England. Or A Treatise Of The Foundations Of All The Colledges, Auncient Schooles Of Priviledge, And Of Houses Of Learning, And Liberall Arts, Within And About The Most Famous Cittie Of London. With A Briefe Report Of The Sciences, Arts, And Faculties Therein Professed, Studied, And Practised. Together with the Blazon of the Armes, and Ensignes thereunto belonging. Gathered faithfully out of the best Histories, Chronicles, Records, and Archiues, by G. B. Knight.* The British Museum Catalogue describes the treatise as "Pp. 958-988 of Stow's 'Annales.' " It first appeared in Edmund Howes's continuation of the *Annales* published in 1615.

[66] Pp. 980-81.

[67] To aid prospective philanthropists, Buck gives a list of needed public improvements. *See* p. 980.

few other rare Cittizens, vertuous and honorable minded Marchants have done [in] founding good Monuments, for the benefit and ornament of this Cittie."[68] Because the new business school at Christ's Hospital appeals to Buck's practical sense, he commends Lady Ramsay's generosity toward it : "Lately the good lady Ramsey founded there a Schoole for reading, writing, and Ciphring, to bee taught to poore children, for their better enabling to learne and exercise trades and occupations, whereunto they are apt or destinate."[69] Likewise, Thomas Sutton's new school, which offered similar training, meets his approval : "And nowe very lately Thomas Sutton, founder of the great new Hospitall in the Charter house, hath translated the Tenis Court to a Grammar Schoole . . . for 30 schollers poore mens children."[70] London was filled with schools which offered instruction in almost every useful subject, if we may believe Buck's account. Besides such conventional studies as law, medicine, and theology, Buck describes less orthodox subjects which made up the vast curriculum of his "third university," where one might study—among a number of other things—writing, bookkeeping, stenography (very useful for taking "a Sermon, Oration, Play, or any long speech"), modern languages (both European and oriental, useful for merchants), even dancing, self-defense, horsemanship, and artillery tactics. Finally the author adds, "I must not omit that the Art of Memorie is taught within this Vniuersitie of London."[71] The general conclusion is that the schools of London make that city the greatest and most useful university in the world for the education of anyone, whether tradesman or gentleman.

Buck's treatise reveals that by the early years of the seventeenth century utilitarian learning was making strong headway, and it also suggests that there was beginning to take shape the modern conception of a university as a place where all things, both learned and useful, might be taught. The progress in teaching practical subjects, as Buck shows, was powerfully influenced by the middle class.[72] While business men were frequently content to furnish the money for schools and let the pedagogues decide the curriculum,

---

[68] Pp. 981-82.   [69] P. 982.   [70] P. 983.   [71] P. 988.

[72] It is not the contention of the present writer, of course, that all utilitarian tendencies were a result of middle-class influence, but that this influence was extremely

some of these benefactors, even before the seventeenth century, had ideas of their own which shaped the objectives of their foundations. One of the best examples of the citizen-philanthropist who dictated the policies of his institution was Sir Thomas Gresham. While Gresham had stood before kings and had played an important rôle in the political and financial life of England, he remained in reality and spirit a merchant whose greatness did not divorce him from the social outlook of many a lesser business man. Although he had attended the university, he had also served his apprenticeship in trade and had made his way in the world of commerce by his own ingenuity and innate shrewdness. Hence, Gresham possessed as did few others the cultural and practical background which enabled him to prescribe a curriculum and a manner of instruction designed to be of maximum service to the intelligent citizen. Gresham College sought, not only to supply the deficiencies of the universities in some of the practical aspects of education,[73] but also to make certain elements of learning available to citizens who had not had the advantages of university lectures. These facts are made clear in a summary of Gresham's provisions for his college by Professor Foster Watson:

He endowed professorships in divinity, astronomy, music, geometry, law, medicine, and rhetoric. He urged in his directions to professors

---

important in bringing about changes in the policies of the schools. Sir Humphrey Gilbert in *Queene Elizabethes Achademy* (1572) [reprinted by the Early English Text Society, Extra Ser., VIII (1869)] had sought to bring the education of the gentleman into closer touch with realistic problems of life, and aristocratic education was making some progress in this direction. Indeed, Foster Watson in *The Beginnings of the Teaching of Modern Subjects in England* (London, 1909), p. xxi, maintains that aristocratic education was more favorable to the introduction of new ideas: ". . . the Grammar Schools, though more progressive than is ordinarily supposed, were relatively reactionary and conservative compared with the educational arrangements for the children of the nobility. The reason is not far to seek. The Grammar Schools were controlled largely by authority, which after the manner of authority, sought to economise energy by drifting into tradition. The education of the higher classes was as free as the winds. Subjects of direct usefulness or of social prestige could be chosen and could be pursued, often under favorable conditions." Watson somewhat overstates the case. While it is true that the grammar schools were conservative, the bourgeois interest in utilitarian and practical knowledge was paving the way for many changes in the curricula of the schools, as Watson himself later points out.

[73] The aridity of university training doubtless has been exaggerated, but while there is evidence of some interest in practical matters, especially at Cambridge from

that they should remember that the hearers of the lectures would be "merchants and other citizens," and therefore he says the lectures are not to be "read after the manner of the Universities, but let the reader cull out such heads of his subject as may best serve the good liking and capacity of the said auditory." The astronomy professor was to read "the principles of the sphere and the theoriques of the planets, and to explain the use of common instruments for the capacity of mariners," and was to apply "these things" to use by reading geography, and the art of navigation. The geometry professor was to lecture for one term on arithmetic; the next on theoretical geometry; and the third on practical geometry. In music "the lecture was to be read, the theoretic part for one half-hour or thereabouts, and the practical part by help of voices or instruments for the rest of the hour." It will thus be seen that Sir Thomas Gresham brought into useful study modern subjects not then taught in Grammar Schools, and but little in the Universities, that he required the subjects to be taught in English and not in Latin.[74]

Gresham's ideal was to provide a combination of humanistic and utilitarian learning brought to the level of the intelligent citizen's understanding. A precursor of modern university extension courses, Gresham College was the first of the great institutions devoted to popularizing learning for the benefit of the middle classes.

In his insistence on practical instruction in utilitarian subjects, Gresham was not a lone crusader in the sixteenth century. Richard

the late sixteenth century onward, the curriculum had not yet thrown off the shackles of scholasticism, and it must have seemed to a man of Gresham's practical sense wasteful of time. The provisions which he made for Gresham College show an effort to adapt those elements of university training which he believed most applicable to the problems of life. In regard to the universities in the early seventeenth century, J. Bass Mullinger comments: "The student of the history of science, who, amid these wearying strifes of theologians and that ceaseless reiteration of dogma which have so largely filled our pages, seeks to discern the signs of the growth of a more real knowledge and of the bestowal of the 'divinely-imparted gift of reason on that which should benefit the human race' is compelled reluctantly to admit that whatever Cambridge then achieved in this direction was the outcome of individual genius, rising superior to the prevailing influences of the culture that surrounded it."—*The University of Cambridge from the Royal Injunctions of 1535 to the Accession of Charles the First* (Cambridge, 1884), pp. 572-73.

[74] Watson, *The Beginnings of the Teaching of Modern Subjects in England*, p. xxxviii. Cf. W. H. Woodward, "English Universities, Schools, and Scholarship in the Sixteenth Century," *Cambridge History of English Literature*, III, 426-27. Woodward calls attention to some of the utilitarian purposes of Gresham College: "The professor of law was expressly directed to treat of contracts, monopolies, shipping, and the like."

Mulcaster, for example, the guiding spirit of the Merchant Taylors' School, was an educational realist who argued against the attempt to give a "literary" education to all students regardless of their fitness and aptitude. Although he insisted that everyone with the wit to profit therefrom should have the advantage of classical instruction, he conceded that many youths destined for trade might more profitably study practical subjects.[75] In similar fashion, while Christ's Hospital offered a background of cultural teaching,[76] the provision for vocational instruction, made possible by the generosity of a merchant's wife, was a recognition of a demand in education which, gathering force in the late sixteenth century, gained impetus in the seventeenth to culminate in the various projects for educational reform set forth by theorists in the middle of that century. Much of this impetus to utilitarian learning came from popular demand as well as from certain practices already becoming established as a part of middle-class training. Indeed, the utility of mercantile education was so well recognized that noblemen and gentlemen sometimes apprenticed their sons to merchants for the sake of their education in modern languages and practical affairs.[77]

The demands for the reformation of education in order that it might serve the practical ends of society became increasingly insistent during the seventeenth century. Through the diligence of the school founders of the sixteenth century, England was well

---

[75] *See* Foster Watson, ''Richard Mulcaster and his 'Elementarie,' '' *Educational Times*, January, 1893, and Woodward, *op. cit.*, pp. 436 ff.

[76] To add to the cultural advantages of Christ's Hospital, Robert Dove, a merchant tailor, in 1612 bequeathed funds for the teaching of music there. Anthony Nixon, who wrote *Londons Dove: Or A Memoriall of the life and death of Maister Robert Doue, Citizen and Marchant-Taylor of London* (1612), after praising Dove for other bequests to educational causes, mentions a provision in his will, ''Allowing sixteene pounds a yeere for euer, to Christs-Hospitall in London : to be imployed towards the vse and maintenance of a Schoolemaister, to traine vp and instruct tenne young Schollers, in the knowledge and learning of Musicke and Pricksong.''—Sig. D 3. The chief contribution of Christ's Hospital, however, was to utilitarian training. Pearce, *op. cit.*, p. 146, says of Christ's Hospital : ''Placed as it is in the midst of a commercial community, Christ's Hospital has from the first extended to its sons the benefit of a commercial education, and few schools have turned out better penmen than some of our 'Blues.' ''

[77] Watson, *The Beginnings of the Teaching of Modern Subjects in England*, p. xxxvii. Francis Osborn in *Advice to a Son* (1656), p. 59, explains the advantages of a gentleman's becoming a merchant.

provided with grammar schools, and the greatest need now was to bring the curriculum into closer relations with the problems of life. Even so good a classicist as John Brinsley, author of *Ludus Literarius or the Grammar Schoole* (1612), stressed the necessity of rationalizing the course of study so that pupils might "learne only such bookes and matters, as whereof they may have the best use, and that perpetually in all their learning, or in their whole life."[78] It was even believed in some quarters that England had too many grammar schools, which were unfitting their pupils for earning a livelihood. Young men in excessive numbers, it was said, were vainly seeking political preferment in the state, whereas they would have been much better off as apprentices and farmers if the schools had not educated them to despise such labors. These were Bacon's asserted reasons, whatever ulterior motives he may have had, for opposing Sutton's foundation of Charterhouse School. The critic of modern education who laments the multiplication of candidates for "white-collar jobs" will find Bacon's expressions in a letter to King James about the Charterhouse foundation strikingly modern in the problem stressed:

Concerning the advancement of learning, I do subscribe to the opinion of one of the wisest and greatest men of your kingdom, that, for grammar schools, there are already too many, and therefore, no providence to add where there is excess. For the great number of schools which are in your Highness's realm, doth cause a want, and likewise an overthrow; both of them inconvenient, and one of them dangerous; for by means thereof, they find want in the country and towns, both of servants for husbandry, and apprentices for trade; and on the other side, there being more scholars bred than the State can prefer and employ, and the active part of that life not bearing a proportion to the preparative, it must need fall out that many persons will be bred unfit for other vocations, and unprofitable for that in which they were bred up, which fill the realm full of indigent, idle and wanton people, who are but *materia rerum novarum*.[79]

Bacon, therefore, suggests that it would be better to use some of Sutton's money to increase the stipends of lecturers at the two

---

[78] J. W. Adamson, *Pioneers of Modern Education, 1600-1700* (Cambridge, 1905), p. 24.

[79] *Ibid.*, pp. 16-17. The entire letter is reprinted in James Spedding's *The Letters and the Life of Francis Bacon*, 7 vols. (London, 1861-72), IV, 249-54.

universities, "as well of the three professions, Divinity, Law, and Physic, as of the three heads of science, Philosophy, arts of speech, and the mathematics."

Education for the relief of man's estate, an expression given life by Bacon, became the concern of educational theorists of the seventeenth century. The extent to which Bacon himself influenced educational theory is a problem beyond the scope of the present study, but he clearly believed that schools should provide the training best suited to the pupil's aptitude and future station in life. To attain this end, schools should adapt their curricula to life as it is, not as it might be in a state of rhetoricians and grammarians. Bacon's ideal of learning as a useful instrument in the service of man, a doctrine implicit in the *Advancement of Learning* (1605) and the *New Atlantis* (1627), was more explicitly voiced by such reformers as Samuel Hartlib, John Dury, and William Petty, all of whom wrote under the influence of the great Czech theorist, Comenius, and to a lesser extent, of Bacon.[80] The outburst of criticism and suggestion voiced by these men was not a sudden phenomenon of the middle of the century but represented the accumulated effect of a movement which had been long growing not only among learned philosophers like Bacon but also in bourgeois thinking. It is significant that Hartlib, Dury, and Petty were in close touch with commercial life and the needs of commercial society.[81]

Comenius' proposals to organize learning into a great pansophia or encyclopedia of all knowledge aroused the imaginations of

---

[80] Adamson, *Pioneers of Modern Education*, pp. 112, 124, 129, 130, 139. Hartlib's contributions to practical learning are especially noteworthy. He was largely responsible for popularizing the utilitarian views of Comenius by translating from him *A Reformation of Schooles* (1642).

[81] Hartlib was born of a match between a Polish merchant and the daughter of an English merchant. When he came to England in 1628, he lived ostensibly as a merchant himself but actually conducted a general news agency and cultivated his hobbies. (See *Dictionary of National Biography*, sub Hartlib.) Dury gained business experience as minister to the English Company at Elbing, West Prussia, in 1628, and again as minister to the Merchant Adventurers of Rotterdam in 1642-43. Although Petty was later knighted by Charles II for his learning and became famous for his economic writings, he was the son of a Hampshire clothier and served his apprenticeship in trade. In 1646 he was practising his father's trade.

For detailed discussion of their educational theories, see Adamson, *Pioneers of Modern Education, passim.*

reformers and caused the Long Parliament to invite him to London to advise the government about educational matters.[82] It was natural, therefore, that Petty, having found suggestions in the works of both Comenius and Bacon, should set himself to recommend a similar method, which he believed would enormously improve the practical education of that part of society which would need vocational training. Not for nothing had Petty himself served an apprenticeship and later plied the trade of clothier just two years before he published *The Advice of W. P. To Mr. Samuel Hartlib For The Advancement of some particular Parts of Learning* (1648),[83] which advocates the establishment of a great technical college and the codification of all technical and useful knowledge into a vast "handbook" or encyclopedia to be the guide of youths, especially of apprentices. The author urges

That there be instituted *Ergastula Literaria*, Literary work-houses, where Children may be taught as well to doe something towards their living as to Read and Write. . . . That all Children of above seven yeares old may be presented to this kind of Education, none being to be excluded by reason of the poverty and unability of their Parents, for hereby it hath come to passe, that many are now holding the Plough, which might have beene made fit to steere the State. [Pp. 3-4.]

He recommends a sensible course of study adapted to the development of the child and adds a long list of manual-training projects suitable for children. For the advancement of all "Mechanicall Arts and Manufactures," Petty continues, "we wish that there were erected a Gymnasium Mechanicum or a Colledge of Trades-men."[84] This college would really be a research institute, as Petty outlines it, where "the Prime and most Ingenious Workman" in each trade would reside rent-free with brother master-craftsmen in other trades, in order to foster new inventions. Here would be the place for the compilation of the great encyclopedia of technical knowledge, where all useful information would be

---

[82] *Ibid.*, pp. 84-85.

[83] This treatise is reprinted in the *Harleian Miscellany* (1808-13), Vol. VI. My references are to the edition of 1648. Petty asserts his obligations to Bacon for suggestions of the plan for the codification of knowledge.

[84] P. 7.

classified with indices and tables. It would be, Petty asserts, a timesaver :

All Apprentices by this Book might learn the Theory of Their Trades before they are bound to a Master, and consequently may be exempted from the Taedium of a seven years bondage, and having spent but about three years with a Master, may spend the other foure in Travelling to learn breeding, and the perfection of their Trades. As it would be more profitable to Boyes, to spend ten or twelue years in the study of Things, and of this Book of Faculties, then in a rabble of words, so it would be more suitable to the naturall propensions we observe in them.   [Pp. 23-24.]

Petty, the son of a clothier and partly self-educated, was anxious to make learning easier and more intelligible to the youth of his own class.

Another mid-seventeenth-century treatise which summed up much previous thinking about practical education was published in 1649 by George Snell with the significant title, *The Right Teaching Of Useful Knowledg, to fit Scholars for som honest Profession*,[85] the author's purpose being to furnish a guide to utilitarian learning. Two dedications grace the work : one to "Mr. George Snel, Citizen and Gold-smith of Lombard street," a nephew and namesake of the author, and the other to "Mr. Durey and Mr. Hartlib," men known for endeavors to promote "more profitable learning, in English Schools." In the latter dedication, Snell hopes

that our english youths may no longer bee taught to bee emptie Nominalists and verbalists onely, and to have no knowledge of the necessarie things and matters, that should be taught in, and by their longsom and toilsom nouns and verbs ; but, by divine blessing, maie henceforth bee *realists* and *materialists;* to know the verie things and matters themselvs, and yet onely such matters as may best further a man for the sufficient doing of all duties and works perteining to his own profession & person ; . . .   [Sig. *6.]

Snell makes four divisions of learning. The first stage is for beginners who must be taught the fundamentals :

---

[85] *The Right Teaching Of Useful Knowledg, to fit Scholars for som honest Profession: Shewing so much skil as anie man needeth (that is not a Teacher) in all knowledges, in one schole, in a shorter time in a more plain waie, and for much less expens than ever hath been used, since of old the Artes were so taught in the Greek and Romane Empire* (1649).

The first of Learners, who without letters are to bee guided, by constant inurement in the waie of good manners, and of that happiness, of which in their low condition they may partake : for publick wisdom may prescribe some general rules, by which illiterate Parents and Masters may bee directed so to educate Children and Servants as they may becom most profitable for their Countrie, for their Educators, and for themselvs. [Sigs. A 2-A 2ᵛ.]

The second stage is for those who would be proficient so far as only the English tongue permits. The third stage is for those who would attain to some higher degree of learning than English alone permits. And the fourth stage is for those who would reach perfection.

Some of Snell's advice is specific ; some is merely general theory. He insists that English grammar and dictionaries must be studied to secure uniformity in the language. One should also learn to read shorthand, and the "rude and ragged writings of Laborers, Mariners, and vulgar Artificers."[86] All above artificers should have arithmetic. Good manners must be learned by all. Snell gives a list of titles and proper methods of address in all ranks of society ; there are sections on etiquette, on the preservation of the health of body and mind, on "The right use, and the deceitfulness of Rhetorick." All of this is for those in the first category, who are also advised to study logic, or the "well using of reason," and the most useful parts of English law. He advises against scaring children with tales of witchcraft, and provides a discussion of the proper choice of a profession or trade. The later chapters urge the usefulness of grammar, Latin, geometry, cosmography, geography, topography, limning, laws of moral virtue, natural philosophy, history, international and English law, civil government, a little theology "to strengthen Christian belief," "Instructions, how by prudence to maintein a Familie in an happie estate," and so on. The study of history should be confined to that of western Europe, in epitomes and tabulated forms "that may best agree with the dailie business of actual life."

The most important suggestion made by Snell is that of a "general college" to train teachers in "useful knowledge" and other colleges, in reality normal schools, where utilitarian knowl-

---

[86] Pp. 51-52.

edge, "accrewing for the benefit of the whole land," will be taught.[87] The rules prepared by Snell for this system so well illustrate the utilitarian point of view that they deserve quotation :

1. Care shall bee taken that no unprofitabel learning shall bee taught, to bee laid awaie so soon as the Scholar leaueth the School; for who looketh on School-books after hee hath left going to School? but in our intended Colleges onely shall bee taught such dictates and written lessons concerning most profitabel matters, of which the Scholar shall haue need and use so long as hee liveth.

2. By the varietie of knowledges here taught, the Scholars shall bee so throughly instructed in all necessarie learning, that when they put themselvs to any trade of living, they shall not finde want of any learning, they shall need to use.

3. In teaching of necessarie Arts, there shall bee no superfluous and over-teaching, which is a grievous losing of time, but everie knowledg shall bee taught so far onely as the learner shall have occasion to use it : and by this stinting and limiting of things to bee learned onely for need and use, a short time will serv to learn, as much as is needful of everie knowledg ; and so the Scholar may bee hasted from art to art, in such manner that within the time limited for his frequenting the School, all the arts afore-mentioned with eas may bee sufficiently learned, so far forth as the learner in his vocation shall have occasion to need and practise them. . . .

4. All Arts and Sciences shall bee taught in the english tongue, and every lesson shall be fairly written by the hand of the learner, . . .

5. All kindes of useful learning shall bee so taught, by demonstration and evidence of arguments and reason ; . . .

6. In the Colleges the learners shall not onely bee instructed in all things, which the wisdom of superiors shall foresee to bee profitabel for them ; but also their discretion shall bee informed how to use and practise all manners, and behaviors that may procure favor and acceptance in the hous where they live, and in all companies, and with all persons with whom they shall have occasions to convers.[88]

[Pp. 314-17.]

An attack on the futility of much of the university training was made in 1654 by John Webster in *Academiarum Examen, Or The*

---

[87] P. 313.

[88] A brief summary, but not a very complete account of Snell's ideas, is given by Foster Watson in "George Snell and Right Teaching," *Educational Review* (London), January, 1896, pp. 408-14.

Examination Of Academies.[89] Webster, who hints at his lowly origin[90] and apologizes for his lack of learning, condemns the traditional training in the universities, the "chains and fetters of cold and dead formality," the waste and uselessness of methods and subject matter. He uses Bacon in support of his arguments, which, although not always logical, are based on a common-sense observation of faults in the system of the day. He argues that the theological training of the universities unfits men for the ministry and is both useless and hurtful. He sees only futility in the study of languages in an effort to get back to the original meaning of the Gospels.[91]

---

[89] *Academiarum Examen, Or The Examination Of Academies. Wherein is discussed and examined the Matter, Method and Customes of Academick and Scholastick Learning, and the insufficiency thereof discovered and laid open; As also some Expedients proposed for the Reforming of Schools, and the perfecting and promoting of all kind of Science. Offered to the judgements of all those that have the proficiencie of Arts and Sciences, and the advancement of Learning* (1654). My references are to the copy in the Thomason Tracts in the British Museum.

Webster's attack on existing university education brought forth several replies. Seth Ward, who signed the initials "H.D." to his work, published in the same year *Vindiciae Academiarum Containing, Some briefe Animadversions upon Mr. Websters Book, Stiled, The Examination of Academies. Together with an Appendix Concerning what M. Hobbs, and M. Dell have published on this Argument* (1654). This treatise ridicules all of Webster's arguments and tries to make him out an ignoramus for his belief in astrology, which he had defended.

A kindred treatise is Thomas Hall's *Vindiciae Literarum, The Schools Guarded: Or The excellency and usefulnesse of Arts, Sciences, Languages, History, and all sorts of humane Learning, in subordination to Divinity, & Preparation for the Mynistry, by ten Arguments evinced, ten cavils raised against it by Familists, Anabaptists, Antinomians, Lutherans, Libertines, &c. are repelled and answered, and many cautions to prevent all mistakes are added* (1654).

[90] Epistle to the reader, sig. B iv: ". . . let not my education be blamed, but my negligence and stupidity, though I must confess I ow little to the advantages of those things called the goods of fortune, but most (next under the goodness of God) to industry: However, I am a free born *Englishman*, a Citizen of the world, and a seeker of knowledge, and I am willing to teach what I know, and learn what I know not, . . ."

[91] Pp. 6-9. Webster points out that languages change so much through the ages that it is impossible to ascertain the true language of God's dictation. Furthermore, scholars become so nearsighted through the study of languages alone that they lose sight of the true wisdom of God. "Lastly, while men trust to their skill in the understanding of the original tongues, they become utterly ignorant of the true original tongue, the language of heavenly *Canaan*, which no man can understand or speak, but he that is brought into that good Land that flowes with milk and honey, and there to be taught the language of the holy Ghost, for *he that is from heaven is heavenly, and speaketh heavenly things*, and all that are *from the earth, do but speak earthly things:* . . ." The mere knowledge of Greek, Hebrew, and oriental tongues is useless without divine inspiration. He would encourage language study and translations, but not as a means to the interpretation of God.

In the manner of Milton's Raphael rebuking Adam, he would condemn mere speculative study. The schools should emphasize those subjects which are of practical value to man. He describes the schools' division of subjects into

two sorts, *Speculative* and *Practick:* wherein their greatest crime lies in making some meerly Speculative, that are of no use or benefit to mankind unless they be reduced into practice, and then of all other most profitable, excellent, and usefull; and these are natural *Philosophy* and *Mathematicks*, both of which will clearly appear to be practical, and that in a few reasons.   [P. 18.]

Webster has no difficulty in justifying the study of natural philosophy or what to him is natural science. Mathematics he calls the peer of all knowledges because it has served the everyday needs of humanity. Furthermore, he insists upon emphasizing in the schools the practical application of the less obviously utilitarian studies, for, he asks, "what is *Grammar, Lodgick, Rhetorick, Poesie, Politicks, Ethicks, Oeconomicks*, nay *Metaphysicks*? if they serve to no other use than bare and fruitless speculation?"[92] He points out the folly of studying languages as mere exercises, and the need of training in the actual use of foreign tongues. He approves short-

---

[92] "Can the *Mathematicall* Sciences, the most noble, useful, and of the greatest certitude of all the rest, serve for no more profitable end, than speculatively and abstractively to be considered of? How could the life of man be happily led, nay how could men in a manner consist without it? Truly I may justly say of it as *Cicero* of *Philosophy*, it hath taught men to build houses, to live in Cities and walled Towns; it hath taught men to measure and divide the Earth; more facilely to negotiate and trade one with another : From whence was found out and ordered the art of Navigation, the art of War, Engins, Fortifications, all mechanick operations, were not all these and innumerable others the progeny of this never-sufficiently praised Science? O sublime, transcendent, beautifull and most noble Mistress! who would not court such a *Celestial Pallas*? who would not be inamoured upon thy Seraphick pulchritude? surely thy divine and *Harmoniacal* musick were powerfull enough to draw all after thee, if men were not more insensible than stones or trees. Is the admirable knowledge that *Arethmetick* afords worthy of nothing but a supine and silent speculation? Let the Merchant, *Astronomer*, Mariner, Mechanick and all speak whether its greatest glory stand not principally in the practick part? what shall I say of *Geometry, Astronomy, Opticks, Geography*, and all those other contained under them, as they are reconed up by that myrror of manifold learning Dr. *John Dee* in his Preface before *Euclide*? it were but to hold a candle to give the Sun light, to deny that they are practical. Nay are not all the rest also practical? what is *Grammar, Lodgic, Rhetorick, Poesie, Politicks, Ethicks, Oeconomicks*, nay *Metaphysicks*? if they serve to no other use than bare and fruitless speculation?"—Pp. 18-20.

cut methods of all sorts and commends the simplification of grammar teaching.[93] He wishes that someone would devise a universal language.

The study of pure logic is a waste of time, Webster thinks, because it is too speculative.[94] He condemns the schools for teaching the outworn Ptolemaic system of astronomy.[95] He would retain the good in Aristotle and throw aside the rubbish of fact and method, which has now been superseded.[96] He defends the teaching of modern history and economics and recommends the works of Bodin and Machiavelli.[97] Here again he would cast away Artistotelian tares, retaining only the good that is left.

Finally, Webster rather grudgingly admits that cultural subjects that serve for adornment have a place in human learning and must be reckoned with:

Lastly, for *Rhetorick*, or *Oratory*, *Poesie*, and the like, which serve for adornation, and are as it were the outward dress, and attire of more solid sciences; first they might tollerably pass, if there were not too much affectation towards them, and too much pretious time spent about them, while more excellent and necessary learning lies neglected and passed by: . . . [Pp. 88-89.]

Webster, then, typifies the practical man's rebellion against the affectations of Renaissance learning and the clinging vestiges of

---

An interesting earlier commentary on the growth of the materialistic outlook upon education is contained in a passage in Nicholas Breton's *A Poste With A Packet of Mad Letters* (ed. of 1633, pp. 66-68) in which an older man counsels a young friend, about to enter the university, to study arithmetic, which will provide a sure road to wealth as a merchant; and wealth, he emphasizes, ought to be his chief ambition: ". . . for howsoeuer honour may be sought or bought by them that haue enough, seeke thou wealth, and that will bring thee what the world can giue thee: for if thou fall into want, and impairing or spending thy stocke, be forced to take some meane course for thy maintenance, I wil tel thee what thou shalt find true: the honest will onely pittie thee, and say thou maiest keepe a Schoole, is it an honest trade, when a Churle will grutch at his groat for a shillings worth of labour in beating quicke sense into a dul wit: . . . beleeue me, if thou haue al the Sciences, be furnished with many languages, and art acquainted with honourable courses, and a heart as honest as can liue, yet if thou lack wealth to grace al the rest thou shalt haue a Foole come ouer thee, and a knaue abuse thee, . . ."

[93] Pp. 21-22. Webster argues for the direct method of language instruction and commends Joseph Webbe for his methods. Cf. Webbe's *A Petition To The High Court of Parliament, In the behalfe of auncient and authentique Authors* (1623).

[94] P. 40.   [95] Pp. 42-50.   [96] P. 103.   [97] P. 88.

scholasticism. In his resentment against the fantastic and the useless, he went to the other extreme and fashioned a criterion of pure utility which was to become in later bourgeois societies more and more the measure of the value of education. Even though most of Webster's middle-class contemporaries would not have shared all of his beliefs concerning the shortcomings of the universities, clearly the feeling was growing that the universities did not contribute enough to the practical instruction of their students. A few learned men had long complained about the sterility of the university discipline, but it was not until the middle of the seventeenth century that middle-class criticism gathered sufficient head to indicate that it was a significant portent of future changes. Even so, it must be remembered that the average citizen was still too unfamiliar with the curriculum of the universities to have any very definite opinions about it. He doubtless went his way believing, as he had always believed, that the universities were sufficiently justified because they provided the learning that would make a man a wise minister or, with good luck, a gentleman.

Before ending this discussion, one other manifestation of middle-class concern over learning, somewhat analogous to the interest in founding schools, deserves notice here : that is, the beginning of an effort on the part of citizens in the seventeenth century[98] to establish public libraries. Private book-collecting having already become firmly established among middle-class readers,[99] the creation of public libraries soon followed. Although England had no mer-

---

[98] One of the earliest instances of a merchant's interest in the establishment of libraries was the reputed foundation of the library of Grey Friars, later Christ's Hospital, by Dick Whittington in 1429. *See* Pearce, *op. cit.*, pp. 5-6.

[99] Since the days of Captain Cox (the Coventry mason whose library was described by Robert Laneham)—and even before—plain people had been collecting books, which were cheap enough throughout the sixteenth and seventeenth centuries for a person of very moderate circumstances to accumulate a few volumes, and in some cases sizable libraries. The most assiduous citizen-collector of books in the seventeenth century was Richard Smith, an undersheriff of London from 1644 to 1653, who resigned his office that he might have more time to make daily rounds of the booksellers' stalls. His collection is said to have been started by Humphrey Dyson, a notary who helped Edmund Howes with his continuation of Stow's *Survey of London. See* W. Y. Fletcher, *English Book Collectors* (London, 1902), p. 93. Another citizen of the mid-seventeenth century who showed zeal in book-collecting was Nehemiah Wallington, a turner of Eastcheap, who took pride in his "studdy" lined with books. Although he

chant-prince collectors who could equal the Fuggers of Germany, it had a few citizens who realized the service performed by libraries and sought to make books more easily available to the public. Under the mayoralty of Sir John Pettus, the city of Norwich founded a library in 1608 as a popular undertaking on the part of the citizens.[100] A public library was founded in Bristol in 1614 by Robert Redwood, "an eminent citizen," with the aid of Dr. Toby Matthew, himself the son of a Bristol mercer. This institution was designed "for the furtherance of Learninge," by making available books "of sound divinity and other learning, for the use of the Aldermen and shopkeepers."[101] A town library was founded in Leicester in 1632 under the direction of the Bishop of Lincoln, who "incited the Town Councillors to the effort." "There was," says the annalist,[102] "a general and voluntary collection throughout the Corporation . . . and likewise amongst the Ministers and Clergy in every Deanery in the county." One wealthy schoolmaster gave books "amounting to above six hundred, . . . being worthy books both divine and moral, and also many ancient and modern Chronicles and Historians, books of Philosophy and Poetry, Dictionaries, and divers other Tractates and Treatises."

The most important of the libraries founded in this period by a citizen was the reference library at Manchester, established by Humphrey Chetham (b. 1580; d. 1653), a linen draper who became a wealthy money-lender and merchant-trader. Besides founding a school and home for forty poor boys, he left at his death ample funds to provide both building and books

For or towards a Library within the town of Manchester for the use of scholars, and others well affected . . . the same books there to remain as a Public Library for ever; and my mind and will is, that care be taken that none of the said books be taken out of the said Library at any time . . . and that the said books be fixed or chained,

---

avidly bought news-books, he kept in prominent view such works as Richard Sibbes' *The Bruised Reed*, Thomas Beard's *Theatre of God's Judgments*, and the Geneva Bible. "Good books" were gifts which he liked to bestow on friends.—R. Webb (ed.), *Historical Notices of Events Occurring Chiefly in the Reign of Charles I. By Nehemiah Wallington*, 2 vols. (London, 1869), I, xxv.

[100] Edward Edwards, *Memoirs of Libraries*, 2 vols. (London, 1859), I, 737.

[101] *Ibid.*, pp. 740-42.

[102] *Ibid.*, pp. 747 ff.

as well as may be, within the said Library, for the better preservation thereof. [After enumerating various provisions] . . . Also, I do hereby give and bequeath the sum of £200 to be bestowed by my executors in godly English books, such as Calvin's, Preston's, and Perkins' works, comments or annotations upon the Bible, or some other parts thereof, or . . . other books . . . proper for the edification of the common people, to be chained upon desks, or to be fixed to the pillars, or in other convenient places, in the parish churches of Manchester and Bolton . . . [103]

The books, not all of which were purchased until 1663, were chiefly works of theology and history. Libraries, like schools, reflected the desire of citizens to foster "good learning."

The faith in learning—whether attained by the private reading of good books or acquired through the formal instruction of the schools—never waned in middle-class consciousness throughout the sixteenth and seventeenth centuries, for it was firmly believed that education was an instrument of salvation (religious, economic, and social) which would teach the way of life leading to business prosperity, social advancement, and an eventual seat at the right hand of God with Abraham and Isaac. Although an important part of the agitation for more utilitarian education came from reformers expressing the middle-class point of view, it must not be believed that this criticism indicates a repudiation of the older educational system. While there was a certain amount of discontent with the secondary schools and, to a smaller degree, with the universities, the public, generally, believed that the established learning, subject to a few changes, was sound and useful. Even though classical culture came more and more under suspicion as Puritanism increased in strength, until Ovid, Plautus, and Terence[104] became for a few honest citizens bogies as great as Darwin is in certain quarters today, a bit of pruning here and there to shear away such godless dross was sufficient to purify the grammar

---

[103] *Ibid.*, p. 635.

[104] Comenius, who exercised a great influence on education in the mid-seventeenth century, opposed the teaching of classical authors in the grammar schools and suggested that Christian authors in Latin be substituted.—*See* Foster Watson, *The English Grammar Schools to 1660: Their Curriculum and Practice* (Cambridge, 1908), p. 535.

schools and leave them high in the citizens' favor. Believing, as
he might, in universal depravity, the Puritan nevertheless looked
to the schools for help in alleviating the sinful condition of man
and in raising him to a position of dignity before men and God.
Since godliness and piety no longer have any importance in
modern education, it is difficult for the twentieth-century observer
to realize how extremely fundamental, and, if applicability to the
problems of life is the basis of determining what is practical, how
very "practical" was the moral instruction offered in the petty and
grammar schools. That worthy schoolmaster Charles Hoole, who
described in 1660 the successful practices which he had employed
a quarter of a century earlier,[105] nourished his petty-school pupils
on a diet of "orthodoxall catechisms and other books that may
instruct them in the duties of a Christian, such as the *Practice of
Piety*, the *Practice of Quietness*, the *Whole Duty of Man;* and ever
afterward in other delightful books of English History, as *The
History of Queen Elizabeth*, or poetry, as *Herbert's Poems, Quarles'
Emblems; . . .*" [106] Later, in the grammar school, the pupil continued his lessons in good morality with such aphoristic wisdom
as was to be extracted from Cicero, Seneca, Plutarch, Demosthenes, Aesop, Erasmus, Corderius, and a host of other moral
teachers, both ancient and modern. Even though a few hard-
thinking critics might believe that too many boys wasted their
time with such classical discipline, the average middle-class parent
did not think to question the practical quality of instruction that
obviously sought to inculcate so much good morality. To be sure,
he sometimes suggested that Christian authors were better than
pagan Greeks and Romans, and he would have liked to see more
utilitarian courses substituted for a few of the classic authors, but
in general he believed that even the boy who left the grammar
school early to begin an apprenticeship would receive valuable
training which would help him to become a godly and successful
man. This emphasis upon moral teaching, there can be no doubt,
maintained the classical grammar school in popular favor with a

---

[105] *A New Discovery Of the old Art of Teaching Schoole* (1660), edited by E. T. Cam-
pagnac (Liverpool, 1913).

[106] *See* Adamson, *Pioneers of Modern Education*, pp. 162-63 *et seq.*, and Watson, *The
Old Grammar Schools*, pp. 101 ff.

group who would be expected to demand utilitarian courses, and who, in fact, were moving toward more practical instruction. The argument that there was no other body of organized knowledge to take the place of the classical discipline is not sufficient to explain the long popularity of the traditional instruction. The grammar schools had come to symbolize both learning and morality, and so long as they retained this symbolism, the middle class supported them. Indeed, so great was the faith in their usefulness that the American colonists, despite the hardships of settling a new country, expended both treasure and energy in the establishment of the traditional discipline as the basis of English education in the New World.[107]

More important than the schools which citizens founded in the sixteenth and seventeenth centuries, more important than the theories of education which they supported, was the assurance, established in the creed of the middle class, that education would bring all good things in its train. Having crystallized into a faith in Tudor and Stuart commercial society, this doctrine became one of the most firmly fixed of later middle-class beliefs. Modern bourgeois civilizations have poured their money into schools, believing that here at last a miracle would be wrought, and every sow's ear, through the magic incantation of the teacher, would be made into a silk purse. Education, nebulous of definition and intangible as a wraith, has been followed like a will-o'-the-wisp through the fens and marshes of modern commercial civilization. It has become the Holy Grail of whatever knight-errantry business has bred, though Galahads yet are lacking. The beginning of this quest is clearly discernible in the middle-class attitude toward learning developed in the expanding commercial world of sixteenth- and seventeenth-century London.

---

[107] Watson, *op. cit.*, pp. 124-26.

IV

POPULAR LITERARY TASTE

THE most obvious result of the spread of education among the middle classes was the growth of the reading public. From the mid-sixteenth century onward, the number of average citizens who were buying and reading books was steadily increasing, and even before this time, a large portion of the output of the printing presses had been designed for ordinary readers. In the century that followed the accession of Elizabeth, the habit of reading became so widespread that by the outbreak of the Puritan revolution, the printing press was perhaps the most powerful single medium of influencing public opinion. Behind this extension in the scope of popular literacy lay something more than the mere increase in the ability to read and write. There had come an unconscious development in the public taste, an increase in the appetite for printed works, a fixed habit of book-buying among citizens whose fathers, if they read at all, had been content with an almanac and the Bible.

The urban development of the sixteenth century, which was responsible for so many changes in English life, contributed largely to the multiplication of the reading public, for the patrons of the booksellers were not isolated villagers and countrymen, who probably got along with as few books as their ancestors, but the citizens of London and the commercial towns that had business intercourse with the metropolis. While, for the most part, the country squire remained sodden, with no more intellectual interest than Justice Shallow, his town-bred contemporaries were waking up. With the improvement in communication as a result of commercial development, the exchange of ideas was made easier; and with the intellectual stimulation that followed, there came a new curiosity, a new desire to know more, a new zest for the delights that reading offered. London, of course, was the center from which the ideas of the awakened commercial classes emanated, to leaven, in a lesser degree, the citizens of other thriving communities. Conditions in London were unusually favorable for the growth of the reading public. At the heart of the business and political life of England, at the nerve center of commerce and trade, where every day brought news of explorations and adventures in foreign lands exciting enough to stir the most leaden spirit, not even the dullest apprentice could fail to feel something of the excitement around him, some mental stimulation, however faint. And with booksellers flaunting, under his very eyes, wares that often bore the most alluring titles, neither the tradesman nor his apprentice could resist the temptation to stop and read, and perchance to buy.

Not least important in the development of the reading public was the influence of the printers and booksellers of London, for the appetites of the populace grew by what they fed on, and the booksellers were shrewd enough to realize the value of encouraging readers. In the open stalls of Paul's Walk, any loiterer with time to spend was free to snatch the sense of a book or pamphlet without laying out a coin; and if his fancy led him to make a purchase, pamphlets could be bought for as little as a penny. The multiplication of printers and booksellers in sixteenth-century London (which increased that trade to the proportion of an important industry numbering ninety-seven stationers with the privilege of printing and selling books, when the Stationers' Company was incorporated in 1557) further extended their influence upon the widening circle of readers. Competition led to cheaper books and more diligent efforts to vend literary wares. By the end of the sixteenth century, booksellers were sending their products to every provincial fair, and the tradesman in the small town could see and buy, if he wished, a few of the books available to his London brother. As the market for books widened, the activities of the booksellers increased, to stimulate again the public demand. One has only to scan the titles in the *Short Title Catalogue* to gain some idea of the extent and variety of works produced for the literate public in England between the introduction of printing and 1640. This huge outpouring of books could not have been printed if there had not been an enormous demand from the generality of citizens. The publishers of Elizabethan England could no more live by the custom of learned and aristocratic readers alone than can modern followers of their trade.

The nature of the books printed for bourgeois consumption will be the theme of more detailed consideration in succeeding chapters of the present study, but some general survey of the background of middle-class literary taste is appropriate here, even at the risk of some repetition.

A numerous reading public is no guarantee, of course, of the quality of its taste. No Addison had yet arisen to prescribe proper standards for middle-class readers, who enjoyed the freedom in Elizabethan England of a catholic curiosity and an uncritical judgment. The bourgeois reader liked to be amused, but more important than the desire for amusement was the demand for information of every conceivable sort. Printers therefore hastened to supply publications as infinitely various as the life of the times. Trifling and serious works mingled on the booksellers' shelves. Jest books jostled collections of prayers, and encyclopedias of all useful knowledge found themselves in company with frivolous chapbooks describing the adventures of some absurd and mythical hero. Catholicity is the quality of middle-class taste that is most noteworthy.

But if the average literate citizen of Tudor and Stuart England read more widely than well, he at least managed to extract some virtue from the most unlikely places. He soon learned, as later chapters will make clear, to find a justifiable reason even for the trivial broadside that amused him. Although the deepening shades of Puritanism increased bourgeois interest in godly literature, and the gradual accentuation of utilitarianism sent the tradesman scurrying for "useful" books, the middle-class reader never lost his taste for diverse reading. Fashion never dictated to him set types and forms of literature, but he continued to seek out whatever he felt was of interest or profit.

While much of our knowledge of middle-class taste must be drawn from inference, some specific evidence remains. For example, Robert Laneham, gossipy mercer of London, writing to his friend Humphrey Martin, also a mercer, about the princely pleas-

ures of Kenilworth in July, 1575, comments on the library of a
prosperous mason of Coventry, one Captain Cox, a diligent collector of books which doubtless represented the taste of readers of
his social class. Captain Cox, Laneham assures us, "great ouer-
sight hath . . . in matters of storie" :

For az for King Arthurz book, Huon of Burdeaus, The foour suns of
Aymon, Beuys of Hampton, The squyre of lo degree, The knight of
courtesy, and the Lady Faguell, Frederik of Gene, Syr Eglamoour, Sir
Tryamoour, Sir Lamwell, Syr Isenbras, Syr Gawyn, Olyuer of the
Castl, Lucres and Eurialus, Virgils life, The castl of Ladiez. The
wido Edyth, The King & the Tanner. Frier Rous, Howleglas, Gargantua, Robinhood, Adambel, Clim of the clough & William of
cloudesley, The Churl & the Burd, The seauen wise Masters, The
wife lapt in a Morels skin. The sak full of nuez. The seargeaunt that
became a Fryar, Skogan, Collyn cloout. The Fryar & the boy, Elynor
Rumming, and the Nutbrooun maid, with many moe then I rehearz
heere : I beleeue hee haue them all at hiz fingers endz.

Then in Philosophy both morall & naturall, I think he be az
naturally ouerseen : beside poetrie and Astronomie, and oother hid
sciencez, as I may gesse by the omberty of hiz books : whearof part az
I remember, the Sheperdz kalender. The Ship of Foolz, Danielz
dreamz, the booke of Fortune, Stans puer ad mensam, the hy wey to the
Spitlhouse, Iulian of Brainfords testament, the castle of Loue, the
booget of Demaunds, the hundred Mery talez, the book of Riddels,
the Seauen sororz of wemen, the prooud wiues Pater noster, the
Chapman of a peniwoorth of Wit : Beside hiz auncient playz, Yooth &
charitee, Hikskorner, Nugize, Impacient pouerty, and heerwith
doctor Boords breuiary of health. What shoold I rehearz heer, what
a bunch of ballets & songs all auncient : Az Broom broom on hil.
So wo iz me begon, troly lo. Ouer a whinny Meg. Hey ding a ding.
Bony lass vpon a green. My bony on gaue me a bek. By a bank az I
lay : and a hundred more, he hath fair wrapt vp in Parchment and
bound with a whipcord.

And az for Allmanaks of antiquitee, (a point for Ephemerides) I
weene hee can sheaw from Iasper Laet of Antwarp vnto Nostradam of
Frauns, and thens vnto oour John Securiz of Salsbury. To stay ye no
longer heerin I dare say hee hath az fair a library for theez sciencez,
& az many goodly monuments both in proze & poetry & at after-
noonz can talk az much without book, az ony Inholder betwixt

Brainford and Bagshot, what degree soeuer he be.[1]

The diversity of subject matter in Captain Cox's library is characteristic of middle-class taste. Here are found types which continued in favor with the commonalty for years to come. Indeed, some of the Coventry mason's books were continually being reprinted throughout the seventeenth century. If his taste runs somewhat to romance, especially those stories dealing with legendary British history, Captain Cox need make no apology, for though ridicule of this type of fiction had already set in, it was still enjoying considerable favor, even with aristocratic readers, and was to continue in favor with the multitude for a century to come. But romances supplied only a portion of the mason's reading, which included popular tales, jest books, dream books, plays, books of riddles, ballads, treatises on health, almanacs, and domestic literature. It is remarkable that Captain Cox had little pious and moralistic literature. If he had lived a quarter or a half century later, even though he had not been a Puritan, his library would have had many theological, moral, and utilitarian items, with which the 1570's were somewhat less oppressed; for the tendency in bourgeois reading and book-collecting developed in the direction of the useful, either for temporal or spiritual benefit.[2]

---

[1] Robert Laneham, *A Letter* [1575], pp. 34-36. *See* F. J. Furnivall (ed.), *Robert Laneham's Letter*, New Shakespeare Society, Ser. 6, No. XIV (1890), pp. xii ff., which gives a long analysis of this book list, with descriptions of the items and brief extracts from some of them.

[2] One might compare the interest of William Gregory, Lord Mayor of London, 1451-52, as given by James Gairdner in *The Historical Collections of a Citizen of London in the Fifteenth Century*, Camden Society, N.S., XVII (1876). This is a reprint of a manuscript book containing (pp. i-ii):

"1. An English version of the poem called 'The Seven Sages of Rome' . . .

2. A short poem on the words: 'Memento, homo, quod, cinis es et in cinerem reverteris.' . . .

3. Notes of the 'properties' of a young gentleman, the conditions of a good greyhound, a vocabulary of the terms of venery, &c. . . .

4. A poem on courtesy, beginning—
　　　　Litylle chyldrynne here may ye lere
　　　　Moche curtesy that ys wretyn here.

5. A few scraps, among which are rules how to interpret the weather at Christmas, &c., as presaging future events. . . .

6. A classification of beasts of venery and the chace &c.; also of the different kinds of hawks; . . .

This increasing preoccupation with didacticism a little over seventy-five years later led William London, the bookseller, in *A Catalogue Of The most vendible Books in England* (1657) to regret that many people grow up in ignorance when they might learn something useful through their reading. Instead,

too many idly sit down in the Chaire of Ignorance, travelling by the fire side, with the *Wandering Knight Sir John Mandevil*, or it may be *Bevis of Southampton;* whilest the Laws of Nations, admirable foundations of Common-wealths, pass undiscovered or dived into.   [Sig. A 4ᵛ.]

William London harps on this theme in advertising further his useful books :

For *Romances*, *Playes* and *Poems*, I do indeed take less paines to promote their study though I hinder not their sale; their names are not so wiredrawn as others are; They are least usefull of any. The two first may properly be said to be *Incentiva vitiorum* to some; heare a Learned Author speak to the first; *Romances are the trash of writings, and they could never have the Credit so much as to allure my youth to delight in them.*
[Sigs. C 2-C 2ᵛ]

He continues his argument against romances and even expresses suspicion of poetry, the latter being "of late too much corrupted in the praise of Cupid and Venus."

Later in the seventeenth century Francis Kirkman in *The Unlucky Citizen* (1673), a story purporting to be the autobiography of the son of a London merchant, describes his first book purchases and his reading :

. . . Once I happened upon a Six Pence, and having lately read that famous Book, of the *Fryar and the Boy*, and being hugely pleased with that, as also the excellent History of the *Seven wise Masters of Room*, and having heard great Commendation of *Fortunatus*, I laid out all my mony for that, and thought I had a great bargain . . . now having read this Book, and being desirous of reading more of that nature; one

---

7. 'A nobylle tretys of medysyns for mannys body' . . .
8. 'Sapiencia phisicorum,' a poem on the preservation of health. . . .
9. 'For bloode latynge,' another poem, . . .
10. The assize of bread and ale, as in Statutes of the Realm, i. 199 . . .
11. The names of the churches in the City of London. . . .
12. A poem on 'The Siege of Rouen,' . . .
13. Lydgate's verses on the Kings of England. . . .
14. A Chronicle of London. . . ."

of my School-fellows lent me *Doctor Faustus*, which also pleased me, especially when he travelled in the Air, saw all the World, and did what he listed. . . . The next Book I met with was *Fryar Bacon*, whose pleasant Stories much delighted me: But when I came to Knight Errantry, and reading *Montelion Knight of the Oracle*, and *Ornatus* and *Artesia*, and the Famous *Parismus;* I was contented beyond measure, and (believing all I read to be true) wished my self Squire to one of these Knights: I proceeded on to *Palmerin of England*, and *Amadis de Gaul;* and borrowing one Book of one person, when I had read it my self, I lent it to another, who lent me one of their Books; and thus robbing Peter to pay Paul, borrowing and lending from one to another, I in time had read most of these Histories. All the time I had from School, as Thursdays in the afternoon, and Saturdays, I spent in reading these Books; so that I being wholy affected to them, and reading how that *Amadis* and other Knights not knowing their Parents, did in time prove to be Sons of Kings and great Personages; I had such a fond and idle Opinion, that I might in time prove to be some great Person, or at leastwise be Squire to some Knight: . . . [He scorns trade but at length decides to become a bookseller] because, by that means I might read all sorts of history Books, and thereby please myself with reading, but I was mistaken therein, for . . . I, since I dealt in Bookselling, have read fewer Books than formerly: but my Father would not allow of this Trade, because he who had never made use of any Book, but the *Bible* and *Practice of Piety*, and knew no more but some School Books, did suppose it to be an unprofitable Trade, and profit it was he aimed at. [Pp. 10-13.]

From the days of Captain Cox to the time of Francis Kirkman's boyhood in the mid-seventeenth century, middle-class taste was undergoing considerable development, but it is significant that there is a certain stability of interest. It may be useful to quote two advertisements of books designed to appeal to middle-class readers at the end of the seventeenth century. The first is from a leaf in the back of *The Renowned History of the Seven Champions of Christendom* (n.d.),[3] headed "Books Printed for and Sold by B. Deacon, at the Angel in Gilt-spur street, without Newgate."[4] The books listed

---

[3] Bodleian Douce R. 528.

[4] H. R. Plomer, *A Dictionary of Printers and Booksellers* . . . *1668-1725* (Oxford, 1922), p. 102, says that B. Deacon was a bookseller in Giltspur Street, 1699-1704—a partner of J. Deacon. They dealt in all sorts of cheap, popular literature.

are for the most part old favorites of the multitude, dating from early in the century or before :

The Arraignment of Lewd, Idle, Froward, and unconstant Women ; or, The Vanity of them : (Chuse you whether.) With a Commendation of the Wise, Vertuous, and Honest Women. To which is added, a Second Part, Containing merry Dialogues, witty Poems, and jovial Songs. Price Bound 1s.

The most famous History of Amadis of Greece, sirnamed the Knight of the Burning Sword, Price 1s. 4d.

Arcandam, that famous and expert Astrologian, to find the Fatal Destiny, Constellation, Complection, and Natural Inclination of every Man and Child by his Birth. Price 6d.

The Art of Legerdemain, with new Additions. Price 6d.

Sports and Pastimes for City and Country. Price 6d.

The most pleasant History of Tom-a-Lincoln, that ever-renouned Soldier, the Red Rose Knight. Price 6d.

Markham's Faithful Farrier, wherein the depth of his skill is laid open in all those principal and approved Secrets of Horsemanship, in 8vo. Price 4d.

Scogin's Jests : Full of witty Mirth, and pleasant Shifts. Price 4d.

A speedy Post, with a Pacquet of Letters and Complements : Useful for England, Scotland, and Ireland. Price 4d.

The Golden Garland of Princely Delight. Wherein is contained the History of many of the Kings, Queens, Princes, Lords, Ladies, Knights, and Gentlewomen of this Kingdom. Price 4d.

The Honour of the Cloathworking Trade : Or, The Pleasant and Famous History of Thomas of Reading. Price 3d.

The Merchant-Taylors Renown : Or, The famous and delightful History of Sir John Hawkwood, Knight. Price 3d.

The most Famous History of the Learned Fryer Bacon. Price 3d.

The Famous, Pleasant, and Delightful History of Ornatus and Artesia. Price 3d.

The History of the Valiant London 'Prentice. Price 3d.

The Noble Birth and Gallant Achievements of that Remarkable Outlaw, Robin Hood : Together with a True Account of the many Merry and Extravagant Exploits he play'd ; in Twelve several Stories. Price 3d.

The History of the Life and Death of that most Noble Knight, Sir Bevis of Southampton. Price 3d.

The Second Part of Mother Bunch of the West.

The History of Tom-Tipler, the Merry Tinker of Banbury.
The Birth, Life, and Death of John Frank.
These Three last are but a Penny a piece.

A similar list of late sixteenth- and seventeenth-century books appears at the end of *The Shooe-makers Glory: Or, The Princely History Of The Gentle Craft* (n.d.)[5] as "A Catalogue of several Pleasant and Delightful Books, which are to be sold by the Booksellers of Pye-corner and London-Bridge":

The famous and pleasant History of *Parismus*, the Valiant and Renouned Prince of *Bohemia:* In III. Parts. I. Containing his Triumphant Battles fought against the *Persians*, his Love to the Beautiful *Laurania*, the great Dangers he passed in the *Island of Rocks;* and his strange Adventures in the *Desolate Island.* II. Containing the Adventurous Travels, and Noble Chivalry of *Parismenos*, the *Knight of Fame*, with his Love to the Fair Princess *Angelica*, the Lady of the *Golden Tower.* III. Containing the Admirable Adventures and truly Heroick Achievements of *Parismenides*, Knight of the *Golden Star;* with his Love to the Fair *Astrea*, Princess of *Austracia*, and other Adventures. Price bd. 1s.

The Comical and Tragical History of *Fortunatus:* Wherein is contain'd his Birth, Travels, Adventures, and last Will and Testament to his two Sons, to whom he bequeathed his Purse and Wishing-cap; as also their Lives and Deaths. Illustrated with divers Pictures. In Octavo. Price bd. 1s.

The most Pleasing and Delightful History of *Reynard* the Fox, and *Reynardine* his Son. In two Parts. With the Morals to each chapter, explaining what appears Doubtful, or allegoricall. And every Chapter illustrated with a curious Device, or Picture, representing to the Eye, all the material Passages. Done in the most Refined English. Price bd. 1s.

The Compleat Book of Knowledge: treating of the Wisdom of the Ancients; and shewing the various and wonderful Operations of the Signs and Planets, and other celestial constellations, on the Bodies of Men, Women, and Children; and the mighty Influences they have upon those that are born under them. *To which is added*, The Country Man's Kalendar; containing his daily Practice, and the perpetual Prognostications for Weather; together with a Catalogue of all the

---

[5] Printed by and for W. O. "and are to be sold by C. Bates, in Pye-corner."—Bodleian Douce R. 528. Bates (Plomer, *op. cit.*, p. 26) was a dealer in popular literature, 1709-14.

Market-touns, Fairs and Roads in *England* and *Wales*. Compiled by *Erra Pater*, a Jew, Doctor in Astronomy and Physick, born in Bethany, in Judea; made English by W. *Lilly*, Student in Physick and Astrology.

The Garland of Delight: containing Thirty excellent Songs, being Chronicles and Histories of Kings, Queens, Princes, Lords, Knights, Gentlemen and Ladies of this Kingdom: together with several Love-sonnets, *Written by* Thomas Delone, Gent Octavo.

The Crown Garland of Golden Roses, gathered out of *England's* Royal Garden; being full of many pleasant and delightful Songs and Sonnets. Divided into two Parts. Octavo.

Robin Hood's Garland: Being a compleat History of all his merry Exploits and valiant Fights which He, *Little* John, and Will. *Scadlock*, fought on divers Occasions. Octavo.

The High Dutch and German Fortune-teller: wherein all those Questions relating to the several States, Conditions and Occasions of Humane Life, are fully Resolved and answered, according to the Rules of Art, used by the Ancient and Famous *Egyptian Magi*, or Wise Men and Philosophers. To which is added, The Art of Palmistry; as it was practised by the Ancient Egyptians (from whom the Art of Palmistry was Originally derived) shewing a Person's Good or Bad Fortune, by the Lines and Marks that are found in the Hand and Wrist. The whole being more Correct than anything of this Nature hitherto published. Quarto. Price 2d.

For a century after Captain Cox made his collection we see that the old types of romances, realistic tales, books of wonders, almanacs, literature concerned with domestic problems, historical tales either in verse or prose, and jest books remained staple items in the popular literary fare, and that many sixteenth-century books continued to be reproduced with astonishing frequency. This does not mean that public taste underwent no change, but it does indicate that the late sixteenth century developed a rich body of material which appealed so strongly to the average reader that it persisted in popularity until Defoe and his successors produced new works to succeed the old.

The unity of aristocratic tone in Elizabethan literature has been greatly emphasized by literary historians. "One can hardly exaggerate the aristocratic character of Elizabethan literature,"[6] one

---

[6] Vida D. Scudder, *Social Ideals in English Letters* (Boston and New York, 1923), p. 83. Miss Scudder mentions Heywood and Dekker in passing but finds little significance

writer asserts. So complete has been the preoccupation of students with the aristocratic tradition that they have almost forgotten the existence of any other point of view. If one means by "literature" the works that have stood the test of time and are still regarded as worth reading for their own sakes, then it is true that most literature was aristocratic; but if one considers the books that delighted the mass of Elizabethans, much will be found which does not show the touch of gentleman or scholar.

The extent of the invasion of the precincts of literature by the unlearned may be inferred from the documents in the battle waged by formal critics to preserve the world of letters from contamination by the multitude. After the manner of academic critics in whatever age, they set themselves up as the keepers of the true literary heritage and fought earnestly to protect their birthright from the rascal many, who went about the practical business of turning out works to delight the average man, unmindful of critical contempt. Poetry in particular was the branch of literature regarded by professors of letters as unfit for profane hands, because poetry was an esoteric learning, the peculiar province of a small number of the elect, the learned, and the highborn; and any unlearned meddler in the sacred art was guilty of impiousness. Not only was the welfare of poetry threatened by unlearned practicers, but "a further source of evil was found in an undiscriminating multitude of readers whose uncultured taste fostered low ideals and inferior work."[7] If the defense of poetry by aristocratic authors of treatises on the subject had been successful, it would have remained the exclusive privilege of a selected few initiates. But the vehemence of the recurring onslaughts upon the profaners of

---

in them. "Even the drama, popular in origin and appeal, shows few popular sympathies; one may search it almost in vain for democratic sentiments or social inspiration. The mob doth dearly love a king and on the Elizabethan stage, high-born lords and ladies were the only people in whose fate a serious interest could be taken."—P. 82. Speaking of the seventeenth century, she says: "It witnessed the rise of the middle class, and it conquered political freedom. . . . But in spite of its grim republican passion, the contribution of Puritanism to social literature is curiously slight."—P. 86. The middle class is always conservative, and one's failure to find much experimental social and political theory in the literature is no proof that its conservatism is purely aristocratic. Aside from the implications drawn from the foregoing statements, the factual assumptions are subject to question.

[7] G. A. Thompson, *Elizabethan Criticism of Poetry* (Menasha, Wis., 1914), p. 35.

poetry is an indication that the middle class was paying no attention to Brahman dictation. The critics, as usual, lagged behind the actuality of their world. While ballads and pamphlets poured from the press, stimulating a popular appetite for more, Webbe, Puttenham, E. K., and others railed at the rabble rout. William Webbe, in *A Discourse of English Poetrie* (1586), is especially violent against common writers who served the needs of citizens:

If I let passe the vncountable rabble of ryming Ballet makers and compylers of sencelesse sonets, who be most busy to stuffe euery stall full of grosse deuises and vnlearned Pamphlets, I trust I shall with the best sort be held excused. For though many such can frame an Alehouse song of fiue or sixe score verses, hobbling vppon some tune of a Northern Iygge, or Robyn hoode, or La lubber etc., and perhappes obserue iust number of sillables, eyght in one line, sixe in an other, and there withall an A to make a iercke in the ende: yet if these might be accounted Poets (as it is sayde some of them make meanes to be promoted to the Lawrell) surely we shall shortly haue whole swarmes of Poets: and euery one that can frame a Booke in Ryme, though for want of matter it be but in commendation of Copper noses or Bottle Ale, wyll catch at the Garlande due to Poets; whose pottical, poeticall (I should say), heades I would wyshe at their worshipfull comencements might in steede of Lawrell be gorgiously garnished with fayre greene Barley, in token of their good affection to our Englishe Malt.[8]

George Puttenham in *The Arte of English Poesie* (1589) declares that poets should rise above the common taste of tavern minstrels reciting such stories as Bevis of Southampton, Guy of Warwick, and their kind, "made purposely for the recreation of the common people."[9] The practice of poetry is the prerogative of the gentle and not of the base. He denies the "inferiour sort" even the privilege of being the subject matter of grave poetry. One of the few critics heretical enough to express an interest in the multitude was Samuel Daniel, who set forth his liberal views in *A Defence of Ryme* [1603].[10]

Thomas Nashe perhaps best represents the point of view of the academic professional man of letters towards the bourgeoisie.

---

[8] G. Gregory Smith (ed.), *Elizabethan Critical Essays*, 2 vols. (Oxford, 1904), I, 246.
[9] Thompson, *op. cit.*, p. 136.
[10] *Ibid.*, p. 23. For further objections to rabble poets, see Thompson, *passim*.

Described by the late Sir Walter Raleigh as probably the best product of the Italian Renaissance, he

loved poetry and hated the Puritans—with the hatred, not of a religious partisan, but of a scholar and a wit. He is always ready for a bout with these enemies of polite learning, and from his earliest work to his latest heaps contempt equally on them and on all "poor Latinless authors," and "lay chronigraphers, that write of nothing but of Mayors and Sheriffs, and the dear year, and the great frost."[11]

Nashe pays his respects to middle-class writers and their themes in *Pierce Penilesse* (1592):

. . . every grosse braind Idiot is suffered to come into print, who if hee set foorth a Pamphlet of the praise of Pudding-pricks, or write a Treatise of *Tom Thumme*, or the exployts of Vntrusse; it is bought vp thicke and threefold, when better things lie dead.[12]

In *Strange News* (1592) he refers to Gabriel Harvey's attacks on the balladist William Elderton and his kind of "drunken rimesters" and makes a sarcastic appeal to bourgeois writers to come to Elderton's rescue:

Hough *Thomas Delone, Phillip Stubs, Robert Armin,* &c. Your father *Elderton* is abus'd. Reuenge, reuenge on course paper and want of matter, that hath most sacriligiously contaminated the diuine spirit & quintessence of a penny quart.[13]

Further, in *The Anatomie of Absurditie* (1589), he sneers at the middle-class taste for poetry memorializing prudence and bourgeois glory:

It were to be wished, that the acts of the ventrous, and the praise of the vertuous were, by publique Edict, prohibited by such mens merry mouthes to be so odiouslie extolde, as rather breedes detestation then admiration, lothing then lyking. What politique Counsailour or valiant Souldier will ioy or glorie of this, in that some stitcher, Weauer, spendthrift, or Fidler, hath shuffled or slubberd vp a few ragged Rimes, in the memoriall of the ones prudence, or the others prowesse? It

---

[11] *The English Novel* (London, 1894), p. 83.
[12] Edited by G. B. Harrison (London, 1924), pp. 7-8.
[13] R. B. McKerrow (ed.), *The Works of Thomas Nashe*, 5 vols. (London, 1904-10), I, 280.

makes the learned sort to be silent, whē as they see vnlearned sots so insolent.[14]

In *Nashes Lenten Stuffe* (1599), a medley in praise of Yarmouth and the red herring, the author writes a good-natured burlesque of popular pamphlets, with a comical dedication to Humphrey King, a third-rate author of *An Halfe-penny-worth of Wit in a Penny-worth of Paper. Or the Hermites Tale*,[15] which Nashe describes as "the next stile to The strife of Loue in a Dreame, or the Lamentable burning of Teuerton."[16]

Although most of the writers ridiculed by such critics as Nashe were too busy trying to earn a living by their pens to pay much attention to jibes at their expense, a few retorted. For example, Barnabe Rich, satirized by Nashe as the favorite author of the barber of Trinity College, Cambridge,[17] makes a defense, in the *Allarme To England* (1578), of the right of the unlearned to literary expression :

But such is the delicacie of our readers at this time, that there are none may be alowed of to write, but such as haue bene trained at schoole with Pallas, or at the least haue bene fostered vp with the Muses, and for my parte (without vaunt be it spoken) I haue bene a trauayler, I haue sayled in Grauesende Barge as farre as Billings gate, I haue trauayled from Buckelers bery to Basingstocke, I haue gone from S. Pankeridge church to Kentish towne by lande, where I was combred with many hedges, ditches, and other slippery bankes, but yet I could neuer come to those learned bankes of Helicon, neither was I euer able to scale Parnassus hyl, although I haue trauailed ouer Gaddes hyll in Kente, and that sundrie tymes and often.

No marueill then good reader, although I want such sugered sape, wherewith to sauce my sense, wherby it might seeme delightfull vnto thee : such curious Coxcombes therefore, which can not daunce but after Apollos pype, I wish them to cease any further to reade what I haue written : but thou which canst endure to reade in homely style of matters, more behooueful and necessarie, then eyther curiouse or fyled, . . .   [Sig. *3ᵛ.]

---

[14] *Ibid.*, p. 24.

[15] *Ibid.*, IV, 374. (The third impression of King's treatise is dated 1613.)

[16] *Ibid.*, III, 149.

[17] *Ibid.*, p. 16 (in *Haue with you to Saffron-walden*).

Although an occasional writer defended the literature favored by the common people, the ridicule that formal critics lavished upon popular writers increased rather than diminished in the seventeenth century, as the differentiation in literary taste as well as in the social structure became more clearly marked. But in spite of the commentary of aristocratic cynics and university Brahmans, the energy of the people's writers never flagged. While critics scoffed, authors who understood the tastes of the multitude busily turned out journalistic pamphlets and ballads, "improving" literature of many kinds, and an infinite variety of works to delight the average man. Adverse criticism had little, if any, effect upon either the quantity or the quality of literary productions designed for the middle class.

Some of the allusions to popular literature, however, furnish interesting commentaries on the taste of the people and the quantity of material written for their consumption. W. Parkes in a preface to *The Curtaine-Drawer Of the World* (1612) regrets the lost Golden Age before the days of unlearned authors:

Then were there not halfe so many puling Ballet-mongers, nor a quarter of so many fashions, nor halfe a quarter of so many Taylors, Poets and Taylors as they here stand within the length of a paire of sheares together, so in their Arte & vse in the world, they differ not much. The Poet stands all vpon invention : so doth the Taylor. . . .

Then was not I cloyed with so many Idle Pamplets, not Pamphlet stitchers. If a search had been made neuer so curiously betwixt Temple-barre and Pauls, was not aboue two to be found, now drawne to a large multiplication. [Sig. B 3.]

Henry Parrot, in *The Mastive, Or Young-Whelpe of the Olde-Dogge* (1615), expresses his contempt for common readers, at the same time enumerating certain types of works which he despises:

Ile not enioyne thee, but request in loue,
Thou so much deigne my Booke to dignifie ;
As first it bee not with your Ballads mixt,
Next, not at Play-houses, mongst Pippins solde:
Then that on Posts, by the 'Eares it stand not fixt,
For euery dull-Mechanicke to beholde.
Last, that it come not brought in Pedlers packs,
To common Fayres, of Countrey, Towne, or Cittie :

> Solde at a Booth mongst Pinnes and Almanacks ;
> . . . . [Sig. A 4ᵛ.]

The reading of the lower classes, Parrot mentions in a description of visitors to a bookstall :

> Next after him, your Countrey-Farmer viewes it,
> It may be good (saith hee) for those can vse it.
> Shewe mee King *Arthur, Beuis,* or Syr *Guye,*
> Those are the Bookes he onely loues to buye.
> Well, that he likes and walkes. Then comes a Diuell,
> With sober countenance, and Garments ciuill.
> A *Puritane,* or pure one, choose you whether,
> (For both as one makes selfe-same sense together.)
> Hee lookes on some, and finding this the next.
> With very sight thereof his minde is vext.
> Fye ont't (saith he) that any man should buye,
> Such Bookes prophane of fained Poetrie,
> That teacheth vice, worse then your Playes on Stages,
> And is a shame to olde and future Ages.
> To louing Brother-hoods Communitie,
> That are defiled by such impuritie.
> Away retires my fained *Publican,*
> And after him next comes my Seruing-man.
> Who calls for new Bookes, heres one sayes the Boy,
> He reads, and tells him, tut, this is a toy,
> And nere will please our Maides that take delight,
> In bookes of Ladies or some valiant Knight.
> Those wittie workes buyes hee, and thence he passes,
> . . . . [Sig. I 1.]

Henry Fitzgeffrey, in his *Satyres: And Satyricall Epigrams* (1617), comments caustically on the popular journalism of the day, the pamphlets, tracts, ballads, stories, and nondescript reading matter of the less learned portion of the population :

> Let Natures causes (which are too profound
> For euery blockish sottish *Pate* to sound.)
> Produce some *monster:* some rare *spectacle:*
> Some seauen yeares *Wonder:* Ages *miracle:*
> Bee it a worke of nere so slight a waight,
> It is recorded vp in *Metre* straight,

And counted purchase of no small renowne,
To heare to *Praise* sung in a Market-toune.
    How many *Volumes* lye neglected thrust
In euery Bench-hole? euery heape of dust?
Which from some *Gowries* practise, *Powder* plot,
Or *Tiburne Lectur's*, all their substance got:
Yet tosse our Time-stalles youll admire the rout
Of carelesse fearelesse *Pamphlets* flye about.
    Bookes, *made of* Ballades: Workes: *of* Playes,
Sights, *to be* Read: *of my* Lo: Maiors *day's:*
Post's *lately set forth:* Bearing (*their Backe at*)
Letters, *of all sorts: An intollerable Packet.*
Villains discouery, by *Lanthorn and Candle-light:*
(*Strange if the author should not see it to hādle right*)
A Quest of Inquirie: (Iacke a Douer's)
The Iests of Scoggin: *and diuers others*
(*which no man Better the* Stationer knowes)
Wonderfull Writers; Poets *in* Prose.
What poste pin'd *Poets* that on each base *Theame*,
With Inuocations vexe *Apollo's* name.
    Springes for Woodcockes: Doctor Merriman:
Rub and a good Cast: Taylor *the Ferriman.*
Fennor, *with his* Vnisounding E'are word;
The vnreasonable Epigramatist of Hereford:
Rowland *with his* Knaues a *murniuall;*
Non worth the calling for, a fire burne em all:
And number numberlesse that march (vntolde)
Mongst *Almanacks* and *Pippins*, to be solde.   [Sigs. A 7ᵛ-A 8ᵛ.]

Utter scorn of the unlearned reader is Fitzgeffrey's attitude:

Let not each *Pesant*, each *Mecannick Asse*,
That neer knew further then his *Horn-booke* crosse.
Each rauin-*Rusticke:* each illiterate *Gull:*
Buy of my *Poesie*, by pocket full.
Bookes like *Made-Dishes* may for *Daintyes* goe,
Yet will not euery *pallate* taste 'em so:
. . . . [Sig. G 4ᵛ.]

With the exception of one or two of Fitzgeffrey's personal animosities like John Davies of Hereford, most of the writers here alluded to were favorites of the multitude. Such things as Breton's letter

book, Dekker's rogue pamphlets, John Taylor's and Samuel Rowlands' miscellaneous hack-work, the lord mayor's pageants, the
wonder books, last confessions, collections of anecdotes, and almanacs constituted staple items of middle-class literary consumption.

Popular journalism is roundly condemned, along with many
other types of literature, in A. H.'s addition to John Davies' *A
Scourge for Paper-Persecutors* (1625), entitled "A Continued Inquisition against Paper-Persecutors." A. H. sneers at popularizers who
rhyme the Bible—a jibe at the type of thumb Bible written by
John Taylor. Country people read old ballads of Chevy Chase,
new accounts of hangings at Tyburn, and descriptions of monstrosities. Every post is stuck with bills of books to appeal to the
crowd :

> To runne through all the Pamphlets and the Toyes
> Which I haue seene in hands of Victoring Boyes,
> To raile at all the merrie *Wherrie-Bookes*,
> Which I haue found in Kitchen-cobweb-nookes :
> To reckon vp the verie Titles, which
> Doe please new Prentices, the Maids, and rich
> Wealth witti'd Loobies [*sic*], would require a Masse
> And Volume, bigger than would load an Asse :
> . . . .   [P. 3.]

He urges inferior poets to give over their heavy rhymes, which

> Would make one quite abiure all Poetrie,
> And studie *Stow* and *Hollinshed*, and make
> Tractates of Trauells, or an Almanake :
> . . . .   [P. 6.]

Particularly obnoxious to A. H. are the compilers of lying news
pamphlets, especially purveyors of foreign news. This type of
journalism had grown in popular favor in the 1620's because of
the interest in the Spanish marriage, the troubles in the Palatinate,
and the possibilities of foreign complications of vital importance
to English business and religious interests. A sneer at Nathaniel
Butter's news-books is contained in a punning allusion :

> . . . . But to behold the wals
> Butter'd with weekely Newes compos'd in Pauls,
> By some *Decaied Captaine*, or those *Rooks*,

Whose hungry braines compile prodigious *Books*,
Of *Bethlem Gabors* preparations, and
How termes betwixt him and th'*Emperor* stand :
Of *Denmarke*, *Swede*, *Poland*, and of this and that,
Their Wars, Iars, Stirs, and I wote not what :
The *Duke of Brunswicke*, *Mansfield*, and *Prince Maurice*,
Their Expeditions, and what else but true is,
Yea of the *Belgique state*, yet scarcely know,
Whether *Brabant* be in *Christendome* or no :
To see such *Batter* euerie weeke besmeare
Each publike post, and Church dore, and to heare
These *shamefull lies*, would make a man in spight
Of Nature, turne *Satyrist*, and write
Reuenging lines, against these shamelesse men,
Who thus torment both *Paper*, *Presse*, and *Pen*.   [Pp. 6-7.]

The popular ballad and the pamphlet of miscellaneous lore are represented as the work of the inferior poet who appeals to the lower classes, in John Earle's character of "A Pot-Poet" in his *Micro-cosmographie* (1628) :

The Presse is his Mint, and stamps him now and then a sixe pence or two in reward of the baser coyne his Pamphlet. His Workes would scarse sell for three halfe-pence, though they are giuen oft for three Shillings, but for the prety Title that allures the Country Gentleman : and for which the Printer maintaines him in Ale a fortnight. His Verses are like his clothes, miserable Cento's and patches, yet their pace not altogether so hobbling as an Almanacks. The death of a great man, or the fiering of a house furnish him with an Argument, and the nine Muses are out strait in mourning gownes, and *Melpomine* cryes Fire, Fire. He is a man now much imploy'd in commendations of our Nauy, and a bitter inueigher against the Spaniard. His frequent'st Workes goe out in single sheets, and are chanted from market to market, to a vile tune, and a worse throat, whilst the poore Country wench melts like her butter to heare them. And these are the Stories of some men of Tyburne, or a strange Monster out of Germany : or sitting in a Baudy-house hee writes Gods Iudgements. . . . [Sig. F 1v-F 3.]

The multiplicity of poets and the lack of learning among them aroused the indignation of Henry Reynolds, who in *Mythomystes Wherein A Short Survay Is Taken Of The Nature And Value Of True Poesy* [1632] likewise set forth the doctrine that poetry should convey esoteric wisdom and should not be the prerogative of the many. He is particularly bitter against popular poets, even though they make a pretense that they offer good morality :

But our Rimes (say they) are full of Morall doctrine. be it so. But why not deliurered then in plaine prose, and as openly to euery mans vnder-standing, as it deserues to be taught, and commonly knowne by euery one.   [P. 45.]

The aristocratic critic naturally chose for his attacks the weakest spots in middle-class literary taste. Yet despite the truth of aristocratic taunts that the populace consumed vast amounts of trivialities provided by ballad writers and journalistic pamphleteers, the bourgeoisie was developing a definite criterion of judgment, and that criterion was one of utility. The first demand made of a book was that it serve some useful end. As a later discussion of fiction will show, the romances were brought up to date, often expurgated, and set forth as inspirational treatises. What Spenser accomplished in the romance tradition for courtly readers, Richard Johnson did for the plain citizen. The general feeling that books had to be justified in the eyes of their public led to countless sanctimonious dedications and prefaces in which authors claimed much of virtue for their works. Pamphlets describing murders and other crimes were recommended as warning pieces and were so interpreted by their readers. Almost invariably a claim to didacticism was made by those books that sought the favor of the substantial middle class. Trivial from a literary point of view as was much of this reading matter, it laid claim to being definitely useful. Although the modern reader hardly classifies historical reading as utilitarian, the Elizabethan believed history to be a sovereign teacher of practical lessons and good conduct. Since morals and religion, always the concern of the merchant class,[18] were regarded

[18] An example is the pious undertaking of Alderman Rowland Heylin, London ironmonger (resigned as alderman, 1632), about whom Anthony Munday writes as follows in his 1633 edition of John Stow's *Survey of London:* "Alderman Heylin charitably and nobly at his own cost, at the beginning of King Charles reign, caused the Welsh Bible to be printed in a more portable bulk, being previously only printed in a large volume for the use of churches. He also caused the book, called the *Practice of Piety,* to be printed in Welsh, for the use of the Welsh people, and a Welsh or British Dictionary to be made and published for the help of those that were minded to understand that ancient language."—Quoted by J. J. Baddeley, *The Aldermen of Cripplegate Ward* (London, 1900), p. 61.

as one and the same thing, pious works needed no further justification of purposefulness. Yet abundant as were "good books,"
they were not numerous enough to satisfy some middle-class
writers who found the reading of less edifying works alarming.
Philip Stubbes, for example, in *The Anatomie of Abuses* (1583), after
recommending the utility of the lessons to be gleaned from the
Bible and Foxe's *Acts and Monuments*, mourns over the multiplicity
of iniquitous works, for

. . . bookes and pamphlettes of scurrilitie and baudrie, are better
estemed, and more vendible, then the godliest and sagest bokes that
bee : But if it be a godlie treatise, reprouing vice, and teaching vertue,
a waie with it, for no manne (almost) though thei make a flourishe of
vertue, and godlinesse, will buie it, . . .   [Sigs. R 3-R 3ᵛ.]

Notwithstanding Stubbes's pessimistic view, from the Puritan
standpoint, of the state of literary taste, the fact is that the middle
class were consuming sermons and devotional books in what
seem today unaccountable numbers, largely because these works
were regarded as improving to both mind and soul.[19]

Although Stubbes found abominable any book that was not
pious, other writers were preparing the average reader to utilize
for good a variety of profane works. The method was to extract
a lesson even from literature which on the surface seemed barren
of utility. George Whetstone in the preface to *The Rocke of Regard*
(1576) suggests the proper procedure :

I giue thee to witt, that there is nothing written so clearkely (Diuine
causes excepted) but there may bee some follie wrested out of the same :
and nothing againe so fonde, but it conteyneth matter of moralitie.
Vppon which warrant, Poets of worthie memorie, as *Virgil*, *Ouid*,
Horace, *Mātuan* and others, by your leaue, sometimes sauced their
grauest discourses with wanton deuises.   [Sig. ¶ 3ᵛ.]

Like Jaques, who could suck melancholy from any theme as a
weasel sucks eggs, so the middle-class reader sought to wring a
good lesson out of the most unpromising books. As Henry Peacham comments in *The Compleat Gentleman*,

I imagine not that hereby I would binde you from reading all other

---

[19] *See* Chap. VIII, *infra*.

bookes, since there is no booke so bad, euen Sir *Beuis* himselfe, *Owle-glasse*, or *Nashes* herring, but some commoditie may be gotten by it.[20]

W. B.'s handbook on conversation, *A Helpe To Discourse* (1619), purely a middle-class treatise, has a concluding question as to the "perfect vse of Bookes," with the answer that it is

To increase knowledge, confirme judgement, compare the times past with the present, and draw vse out of both for the future; to bring forth the dead speaking and conferring their knowledge to the liuing . . . What continuall Physicke hath the World receiued to purge out the dulnesse of naturall capacitie, and the very Image of death as the Poet stiles it? . . .[21]

The desire for a literature complying with the notion that books should improve the mental and spiritual furniture of the reader colored the taste and appreciations of the middle class. Recreation and entertainment were not sufficient to justify reading. But since humankind, even in periods of Puritan influence, cannot completely resist amusement, utilitarian qualities and virtues were attributed to much Elizabethan literature that might otherwise have been damned as idle and frivolous. An age that could justify contemporary jest books as aids to health by reason of their allevia-

---

[20] Quoted by McKerrow, *Works of Thomas Nashe*, V, 154.

[21] Ed. of 1627, pp. 191-92. Cf. Sir William Cornwallis' *Essayes* (1600), "Of the obseruation & vse of things." Sir William with aristocratic disdain speaks contemptuously of popular treatises but believes nevertheless that they may be useful : "All kinde of bookes are profitable, except printed Bawdery; they abuse youth : but Pamphlets, and lying Stories, and News, and two penny Poets I would knowe them, but beware of beeing familiar with them : my custome is to read these, and presently to make vse of thẽ, for they lie in my priuy, and when I come thither . . . I read them, halfe a side at once is my ordinary . . . I see in them the difference of wits, and dispositions, the alterations of Arguments pleasing the world, and the change of stiles : . . .

"I haue not beene ashamed to aduenture mine eares with a ballad-singer, and they haue come home loaden to my liking, doubly satisfied, with profit & with recreatiõ. The profit, to see earthlings satisfied with such course stuffe, to heare vice rebuked, and to see the power of Vertue that pierceth the head of such a base Historian, and vile Auditory."—Sigs. I 7-I 7v.

"If out of these blotters of paper many things may be extracted not vnworthy of note, what may we expect from *Homer*, *Virgil*, and such Poets? If in *Arthur of Britaine*, *Huon of Burdeaux*, and such supposed chiualrie, a man may better himselfe, shall hee not become excellent with conuersing with *Tacitus*, *Plutarch*, *Salust*, and fellowes of that ranke?"—Sig. I 8v.

tion of melancholy could easily find sermons in stones, and good in everything. This very capacity for discovering a justification for many different types of literature explains the infinite variety of printed works which the average reader found acceptable. If at times the robust appetites of citizens led them to devour trivial books and ballads more lewd than preachers and moralists would approve, usually the literary fare, entertaining or dull as the case might be, held out the promise of some form of improvement. Undeterred by the scoffing of satirical critics, writers who knew the demands of the people, abetted by thrifty printers, produced multitudinous works to amuse or edify the plain man, whose taste was varied enough to enjoy everything from treatises on the duty of man to ballads on the frailties of woman. In addition to the satisfaction over reading to some good purpose, the citizen found a far greater amount of entertainment and recreation in books than we may have supposed, for it is difficult for the scholar to project himself into the spirit of an age that could delight in the printed sermons of William Perkins or the romances translated by Anthony Munday and Margaret Tyler. Undiscriminating but vigorous, the taste of the middle-class reader led him to dip into many books and to enjoy what to us seems savorless and dull. The Elizabethan citizen read widely and, to his own way of thinking, profitably.

In even a brief survey of the background of bourgeois literary taste, the importance of a new class of readers, composed of women from the middle ranks of society, deserves attention,[22] because the influence of feminine opinion, an influence which has grown continually more powerful in English and American literature, began to be felt in the sixteenth century.

Undoubtedly we have been prone to underestimate the literacy of the Renaissance populace, whether we spoke of men or of women. Mr. J. W. Adamson has recently advanced the belief that reading in the vernacular in the sixteenth century was "an art widely disseminated among the humblest social ranks irrespec-

---

[22] *See* Louis B. Wright, "The Reading of Renaissance English Women," *Studies in Philology*, XXVIII (1931), 671-88, the relevant portions of which essay are reprinted here.

tive of sex."[23] Many girls, he points out, learned to read from private teachers. Although girls, except perhaps in isolated cases, did not attend the grammar schools, both sexes seem to have attended the petty schools, where they learned to read English. Richard Mulcaster, defending the theory of education for women in his *Positions* (1581), implies that it was customary to teach girls English, as well as other tongues, for, he says, "We see yong maidens be taught to read and write, and can do both passing well; we know that they learne the best, and finest of our learned languages, to the admiration of all men"; and he adds, "I dare be bould therefore to admit yong maidens to learne, seeing my countrie gives me leaue, and her *custome* standes for me."[24] Discussing what the girl should be taught, Mulcaster comments:

To learne to read is very common, where conuenientnes doth serue, and *writing* is not refused, where oportunitie will yeild it.

Reading if for nothing else it were, as for many thinges else it is, is verie needefull for religion, to read that which they must know, and ought to performe, if they haue not whom to heare, in that matter which they read. . . . Here I may not omit many and great content-mentes, many and sound comfortes, many manifoulde delites, which those wymen that haue skill and time to reade, without hindering their houswifery, do continually receiue by reading of some comfortable and wise discourses, penned either in forme of historie, or for direction to liue by.[25]

---

[23] "The Extent of Literacy in England in the Fifteenth and Sixteenth Centuries: Notes and Conjectures," *The Library*, 4th Ser., X (1929-30), 163-93.

[24] R. H. Quick (ed.), *Positions of Richard Mulcaster* (London, 1888), Chap. XXXVIII, pp. 167 ff.

[25] *Ibid.*, pp. 176-77. Several writers preceding Mulcaster had written on the education of women. *See* Foster Watson, *Vives and the Renascence Education of Women* (London, 1912). Under the learned Katherine of Aragon, her preceptor, Ludowick Vives, and such men as Sir Thomas More, Sir Thomas Elyot, and Richard Hyrde, set forth ideas favoring the education of women in the learned languages. Watson (p. 159) calls Hyrde's preface to Margaret Roper's translation of Erasmus' treatise, *Precatio dominica in septem portiones distributa* (tr. 1524), the "first Renascence document in English on the education of women."

One should compare Mulcaster's theories with those of Comenius as laid down in his *Great Didactic* (1628-32). Comenius is insistent on the education of girls and boys alike. *See* J. W. Adamson, *Pioneers of Modern Education, 1600-1700* (Cambridge, 1905), p. 60.

Sir Balthazar Gerbier advertised public lectures in London in 1650 on the languages, arts, and sciences, to which "not onely the Fathers of Families, but also the Mothers

Mulcaster's language indicates that women were, in general, sufficiently educated to read English works. This assumption is borne out by other allusions to women's reading. For example, in R. C.'s translation of Huarte's popular work on physiology and psychology, *Examen de Ingenios. The Examination of mens Wits* (1594), there is a marginal note opposite a passage concerning procreation, "This is no chapter for maids to read in sight of others."[26]

Improvement in the education of women is one of the concerns of Edward Hake in *A Touchestone for this time present . . . Wherevnto is annexed a perfect rule to be obserued of all Parents and Scholemaisters, in the trayning vp of their Schollers and Children in learning* (1574). After a dedication to his "knowne friende mayster Edward Godfrey Merchaunt," Hake laments the depravity of the age, and among other evils finds that girls are provided with improper reading matter, which helps to keep them from better learning: "Eyther shee is altogither kept from exercises of good learning, and knowledge of good letters, or else she is so nouseled in amorous bookes, vaine stories and fonde trifeling fancies, that shee smelleth of naughtinesse euen all hir lyfe after, . . ." [sig. C4]. Like Hake, Thomas Salter, in *A Mirrhor mete for all Mothers, Matrones, and Maidens, intituled the Mirrhor of Modestie* (1574),[27] condemns unwise fathers who

---

(mutually interested in the good educations of their Sonnes)" were invited.—*Ibid.*, pp. 186-87.

Perhaps the popularity of the French-language text prepared by Pierre Erondelle, entitled *The French Garden: for English Ladyes and Gentlewomen to walke in* (1605), was a result, not only of an intellectual interest among women, but of a desire for the social improvement which French gave. Samuel Daniel appended a prefatory verse declaring that

"Ladies haue long'd to match old *Holliband*,
That they with men might parle out their parte,"

and Erondelle himself wrote a preface flattering English women for their studiousness and quick wits.

It seems hardly necessary to point out that the dedication of a book to "ladies" or "gentlewomen" need not be taken as a proof of its aristocratic appeal. An author, if tactful, even in Elizabethan England, would thus attempt to ingratiate himself with his feminine readers, notwithstanding the fact that he expected his book to be read chiefly by the wives of London shopkeepers.

[26] P. 269.

[27] Reprinted in J. P. Collier (ed.), *Illustrations of Old English Literature*, 3 vols. (London, 1866), Vol. I.

doe give them [their daughters], so sone as they have any under-standyng in readyng, or spellyng, to cone and learne by hart bookes, ballades, songes, sonettes, and ditties of daliance, excityng their memories thereby, beyng then most apt to retayne for ever that whiche is taught theim, to the same maner . . . therefore I would wish our good matrone [who teaches young girls] to eschew suche use as a pestilent infection ; . . . But in steede of suche bookes and lacivious ballades, our wise matrone shall reade, or cause her maidens to reade, the examples and lives of godly and vertuous ladies, whose worthy fame and bright renowne yet liveth, and still will live for ever, whiche shee shall make choice of, out of the holy Scripture, and other histories, both auncient and of late dayes ; whiche bookes will not onely delight them, but as a spurre it will pricke and incite their hartes to follow vertue, and have vice in horror and disdaine. . . . for you shall never repeate the vertuous lives of any such ladies as *Claudia, Portia, Lucretia,* and such like were, but you shall kindle a desire in them to treade their steppes, and become in tyme like unto them. . . .[28]

Although Salter emphasizes that woman reads, and ought to be encouraged to read further, he strongly condemns allowing her to choose her own books. She should be advised to avoid moral philosophy and should have recommended to her such Christian poets as "Prudentio, Prospero, Juvenco, Nazianzeno," and their kind. On no account should she read Ovid, Catullus, the stories of Aeneas and Dido in Virgil, or of "filthie love" among the Greek poets. Proper reading matter may be found in ". . . the holie Scripture, or other good bookes, as the bookes of *Plutarche*, made of such renowmed and vertuous women as liued in tyme paste, and those of *Boccas* tendyng to the same sence, or some other nerer our tyme ; . . ."[29]

In the preceding passages quoted from Hake and Salter, the object of woman's training in good learning was a devout or useful application of her knowledge. With the growth of Puritanism, the impetus to the acquirement of the rudiments of education grew stronger in the lower classes, who regarded reading as the means to the study of the Bible and pious works—a ruling motive, incidentally, inspiring many of the pupils at the present time in American schools for illiterate adults. The mother was expected

---

[28] *Ibid.*, pp. 10-11.   [29] *Ibid.*, p. 21.

to read the Bible to her children and, in the absence of her husband, to conduct family worship, which the whole household, children, servants, and apprentices, were expected to attend. Hence it was a godly duty—indeed, a necessity—for mothers to know how to read. Without doubt the average middle-class woman could read and teach members of her household the rudiments of learning.[30] Unfortunately, our records of the learning of bourgeois women are scanty. We know that Elizabeth Lucar, the daughter of a tradesman and the wife of a merchant tailor,

> Latine and Spanish, and also Italian,
> She spake, writ, and read, with perfect utterance;
> And for the English, she the Garland wan,
> In Dame Prudence Schoole . . .[31]

Elizabeth Wallington, wife of John Wallington, a turner in Eastcheap, was a diligent reader of the Bible, Foxe's *Acts and Monuments*, and the English chronicles.[32]

---

[30] A passage in Thomas Deloney's *Thomas of Reading* [1598-99] seems to indicate that among the lower orders of servant maids reading was not common at the end of the sixteenth century. The maids who meet fair Margaret, daughter of the banished Earl of Shrewsbury, on her way to enter domestic service, are amazed that she can read and write. In reply to their inquiries as to what she can do, Margaret replies:

". . . I can read and write, and sowe, some skill I haue in my needle, and a little on my Lute: but this, I see will profit me nothing.

"Good Lord (quoth they) are you so bookish? wee did neuer heare of a Maide before that could reade and write. . . .

"I pray you (qd. another) seeing you are bookish, will you doe so much as to reade a loue-letter that is sent me, . . . "—F. O. Mann (ed.), *The Works of Thomas Deloney* (Oxford, 1912), p. 223. Not all maids were so ignorant, and in many households some, at least, were trained by their mistresses to read.

[31] From her epitaph.—Quoted from George Ballard, *Memoirs Of Several Ladies Of Great Britain, Who Have Been Celebrated For Their Writings Or Skill In The Learned Languages, Arts, And Sciences* (Oxford, 1752), p. 36.

[32] R. Webb (ed.), *Historical Notices of Events Occurring Chiefly in the Reign of Charles I. By Nehemiah Wallington*, 2 Vols. (London, 1869), I, xi.

Perhaps the literary habits of Lady Margaret Hoby, a pious Puritan woman of Yorkshire, who left behind a diary, were not unlike those of the more prosperous tradesmen's wives. Lady Hoby's maids and serving women were able to read to her when she was too busy to read herself. Most frequently read were her herbal, her book of physic, the *Acts and Monuments*, Perkins's sermons, or similar useful and godly works. *See* Dorothy M. Meads (ed.), *Diary of Lady Margaret Hoby* (Boston and New York, 1930), pp. 93, 94, 175, and *passim*.

A brief survey of the learned ladies of the Renaissance, whose accomplishments may give some inkling of the possible learning of their less aristocratic sisters, is contained

The amount of pious literature read by the Elizabethans is amazing, and we may be sure that the average middle-class woman consumed her share. Death, imminent and fearful, haunted woman's consciousness; if she survived the dangers of childbirth, she was beset by fears for the lives of her children, who remained during their infancy in the shadow of a mortality frightful in its toll. Small wonder it is that the Elizabethan woman kept by her side Michael Sparke's *Crums of Comfort*, or some similar work. Salvation and another world were often her only consolation. Some of the devotional books were addressed directly to women and were read by aristocrats and commoners alike. For example, Nicholas Breton, in dedicating "To the Ladies and Gentlewomen Reeders" his collection of prose prayers, *Auspicante Jehoua. Maries Exercise* (1597),[33] indicates that religious material is especially suitable for woman's reading. A book small enough to be carried conveniently in a pocket, that she might have its comfort always at hand, was the anonymous *A Iewel For Gentlewomen. Containing diuers godly Prayers, fit to comfort the woūded consciences of all penitent sinners* (1624). Such books, presumably, devout women read in their odd moments.[34] For more extended reading, there

---

in the first chapter of Myra Reynolds, *The Learned Lady in England, 1650-1760* (Boston and New York, 1920). *See also* Rachel Weigall, "An Elizabethan Gentlewoman," *Quarterly Review*, CCXV (1911), 119-38; Evelyn Fox, "The Diary of an Elizabethan Gentlewoman," *Transactions of the Royal Historical Society*, 3d Ser., II (1908), 153-74; G. C. Williamson, *Lady Anne Clifford* (London, 1922); and Ballard, *op. cit.* Dorothy Gardiner, *English Girlhood at School* (Oxford, 1929), gives a useful survey of the education of women.

William Harrison was impressed with the reading capacities of English gentlewomen. In his *Description of England* (1577), Pt. I, edited by F. J. Furnivall, New Shakespeare Society, Ser. 6, I (1877), pp. 271-72, he comments: "And to saie how many gentlewomen and ladies there are, that beside sound knowledge of the Greeke and Latine toongs, are thereto no lesse skilfull in the Spanish, Italian, and French, or in some one of them, it resteth not in me: sith I am persuaded, that as the noble men and gentlemen doo surmount in this behalfe, so these come verie little or nothing at all behind them for their parts: . . . [of the women of the court] some [occupy their time] in continuall reading either of the holie scriptures, or histories of our owne or forren nations about vs, (and diuerse in writing volumes of their owne, or translating of other mens into our English and Latine toong,) . . ."

[33] Reprinted by A. B. Grosart (ed.), *The Works in Verse and Prose of Nicholas Breton*, 2 vols. (Chertsey Worthies' Library, 1879), Vol. II.

[34] Practically all the devotional books, of course, gave space to crises peculiar to women's lives. Many prayers were designed especially for women. See a later little

were sermons like those of William Perkins and Richard Green-ham, the ever present *Book of Martyrs*, and writings of the early church fathers, like St. Augustine's *City of God*.[35]

Not only was woman concerned in her reading with proper and useful means of attaining the kingdom of God, but she kept on her table for ready reference books designed to help mortals here below. The first duty of the wife, from the duchess to the tailor's helpmeet, was housewifery, which included vastly more than keeping a house in order, for she was often doctor, surgeon, and apothecary. She consulted her almanac to learn about the times for letting blood. She read in the latest herbal about the medicinal use of countless plants. The popular books on medicine, abundantly printed in the sixteenth and seventeenth centuries, found women of all classes among their most conscientious readers.

Many books of pure utility were available to the Renaissance woman. Cookbooks, of course, were numerous, a fact which may throw some light on the literacy of the average housewife. The preface to *A Booke of Curious and strange Inuentions, called the first part of Needleworkes* (1596), giving illustrations of lace patterns, emphasizes the fact that even maids may use the book.[36]

Despite Puritan objections to idle reading—perhaps in part as a result of it—the Renaissance woman, like her modern sister, found in fiction the literature of escape which the strenuousness of her life demanded. John Lyly recognized the importance of the courtly feminine audience and frankly catered to it, while Robert Greene, who succeeded him, became, in Nashe's sarcastic com-

---

book, Robert Aylett's *Devotions, Viz., 1. A good Woman's Prayer. 2. The humble man's Prayer* (1655). In the good woman's prayer, the author weaves into verse-stanzas the good women of the Scriptures, whom the woman-reader prays to be like.

[35] Certainly women in the upper ranks of society read these books (as is evident from the diary entries of Lady Hoby and the records of the reading of Lady Anne Clifford), and there is no reason to believe that the same books did not also appeal to women in the lower ranks. *See* Reynolds, *op. cit.*, p. 32.

[36] It commends industry in such arts as a means of improving their social position :

> "This worke beseemth Queenes of great renowne,
> And Noble Ladies of a high degree :
> Yet not exempt for Maids of any Towne,
> For all may learne that thereto willing be :
> Come then sweet gyrles and hereby learne the way,
> With good report to liue another day.

ment in the *Anatomie of Absurditie*, "the Homer of women," both aristocratic and common. Since women in general have never subscribed to realism, romance in strange opera lands and love stories with happy endings found favor with the Elizabethans even as with feminine readers today. The chivalric romance, as one might expect, remained a popular literary form with women throughout the sixteenth and early seventeenth centuries.[37] Many allusions testify to the interest in romances of all types. The reading

---

> "For many maidens but of base degree,
> By their fine knowledge in this curious thing:
> With Noble Ladies oft companions be,
> Sometimes they teach the daughter of a King:
> Thus by their knowledge, fame, and good report,
> They are esteemed among the noblest sort.

> "Then prettie maidens view this prettie booke
> Marke well the works that you therein doe finde,
> Sitting at worke cast not aside your looke,
> They profit small that haue a gazing minde:
> Keepe cleane your Samples, sleepe not as you sit,
> For sluggishnes doth spoile the rarest wit."

[37] Vives, in *Instruction of a Christian Woman*, translated by Richard Hyrde and printed about 1540, after condemning filthy songs and Ovid's works, adds: "And this the laws ought to take heed of, and of those ungracious books, such as be in my country in Spain, the *Amadis*, Florisand, Tristan [of Lyons] and Celestina the bawd, mother of naughtiness; in France, Lancelot du Lac, Paris and Vienne, Ponthus and Sidonia, and Melusine, and here in Flanders; the histories of Flor[ice] and Blanchefleur, Leonella and Canamorus, Pyramis and Thisbe. In England, Parthenope, Genarides, Hippomadon, William and Melyour, Libius and Arthur, Guy, Bevis, and many other. And some translated out of Latin into vulgar speeches [i.e., languages], as the unsavoury conceits of Pogius and Aeneas Silvius, Euralus and Lucretia, the hundred fables of Boccaccio, which books but idle men wrote unlearned, and set all upon filth and viciousness, in whom I wonder what should delight men but that vice pleaseth them so much."—Watson, *op. cit.*, pp. 58-59. Later, in *The office and duetie of an husband*, translated by Thomas Paynell [1553?], Vives further condemns romances.— *Ibid.*, p. 196. Vives's criticism is not wholly destructive, for in place of idle love stories, he suggests in his *Plan of Studies for Girls* (1523): "Let her be given pleasure in stories which teach the art of life. Let these be such as she can tell to others—*e.g.*, the life of the boy Papirius Praetextatus in Aulus Gellius, of Joseph in the Holy Books, of Lucretia in Livy, of Griselda and others, as found in Valerius, Sabellicus, and other writers of the same kind—stories which tend to some commendation of virtue, and detestation of vice."—*Ibid.*, pp. 144-45. Among other authors recommended are Cicero, Seneca, Plutarch, some dialogues of Plato, the epistles of Jerome, some works of Ambrosius and Augustine, some of Erasmus, More's *Utopia*, histories of Florus, Justinus, and Valerius Maximus, the Christian poets, Prudentius, Sidonius, Paulinus, Aratus, Prosper, Juvencus, and others of like character.—*Ibid.*, p. 146.

of Greene's works and of chivalric romances extended even to chambermaids, if one can believe a description of "A Chambermaid" in Sir Thomas Overbury's *Characters* (1614) : "She reads Greenes works over and over, but is so carried away with the *Mirror of Knighthood*, she is many times resolv'd to runne out of her selfe, and become a lady errant."[38] Adventurous love stories are again described as the literary fare of maids, by Wye Saltonstall in *Picturae Loquentes. Or Pictures Drawne forth in Characters. With a Poeme of a Maid* (1631). Of "A Mayde" he says :

> Nor should they reade books which of some fond Loues,
> The various fortunes and aduentures show ;
> Nor such as natures secrets do discouer,
> Since still desire doth but from knowledge grow : . . .[39]

Again he comments, ". . . she reades now loues historyes as *Amadis de Gaule* and the *Arcadia*, & in them courts the shaddow of loue till she know the substance."[40] That the *Arcadia* had become the reading matter for middle-class women is further attested by Thomas Powell's *Tom of All Trades, Or The Plaine Path-way To Preferment* (1631) in a passage on the education of women :

In stead of Song and Musicke, let them learne Cookery and Laundrie. And in stead of reading Sir *Philip Sidneys Arcadia*, let them read the grounds of good huswifery. I like not a female Poetess at any hand. Let greater personages glory their skill in musicke, the posture of their bodies, their knowledge in languages, the greatnesse and freedome of their spirits, and their arts in arreigning of mens affections at their flattering faces : This is not the way to breed a private Gentlemans Daughter.[41]

The implication is that even women in the lower social orders were laying claims to more abstract culture and greater familiarity with idle romance than Powell approved.

Other allusions indicate that romances made the favorite reading of middle- and lower-class women in the early seventeenth

---

[38] Quoted by Henry Thomas, *Spanish and Portuguese Romances of Chivalry* (Cambridge, 1920), pp. 292-93.
[39] Sig. B 1v.
[40] Character 19, "A Maide," sig. E 6v.
[41] Reprinted by F. J. Furnivall, New Shakespeare Society, Ser. 6, No. II (1876), p. 173.

century. The goldsmith's daughter in *Eastward Hoe* (1605), the victim of Sir Petronel Flash's desertion, exclaims, "Would the Knight o' the *Sun*, or *Palmerin* of England, haue vsed their Ladies so?" Her maid adds her favorites: "Or sir *Lancelot?* Or sir *Tristram?*" (V, i).[42] The confidante in Massinger's *Guardian* declares to her mistress not only that she has read the romances but that she believes in them:

> Seek no more president:
> In all the books of *Amadis de Gaul,*
> The *Palmerins,* and that true Spanish story
> *The Mirror of Knighthood,* which I have read often,
> Read feelingly, nay more, I do believe in 't,
> My Lady has no parallel.   [I, ii.]

A chambermaid described by William Browne in "Fido, an Epistle to Fidelia" is a keen student of the romances. After hearing the mistress read "one epistle that some fool had writ,"

> Her chambermaid's great reading quickly strikes
> That good opinion dead, and swears that this
> Was stol'n from Palmerin or Amadis.

To woman's reading of voluptuous love stories was attributed much of her moral depravity, so lamented by Puritan writers. It may be inferred from the extant comment that women of all classes were equally guilty.

As bad as the love stories, or worse, were the amorous poems that women of every social station were accused of reading, to their detriment. Robert Anton in *The Philosophers Satyrs* (1616) complains that women not only read but also compose bawdy verse:

> And I much wonder that this *lustie lime,*
> That women can both *sing* and *sigh* in rime,
> *Weepe* and *dissemble* both in *baudie meetre,*
> Laugh in luxurious pamphlets, like a *creature*
> Whose very *breath,* some *Ouid* did create
> With *prouocations,* and a *longing fate*
> After some *stirring meates: wiues* couet *bookes,*

---

[42] This and the two succeeding quotations are cited by Henry Thomas, "The Palmerin Romances," *Transactions of the Bibliographical Society of London,* XIII (1913-15), 97-144.

Not penn'd by *Artists*, but the *fruits* of *Cookes*
Prescribing *lustie dishes*, to enflame
Their lustie fighting *broode* vnto their *game*
Confections with *infections* of their *kinde*,
Rot both their *body*, and corrupts the *minde*.   [P. 52.]

John Davies in *A Scourge for Paper-Persecutors*, referring to *Venus and Adonis*, maintains that

. . . . the coyest Dames
In private reade it for their Closset-games.[43]

Love poetry and amorous fiction, including *Venus and Adonis*, made up the library of the heroine of Thomas Cranley's *Amanda or the Reformed Whore* (1635):

And then a heape of bookes of thy devotion,
Lying upon a shelfe close underneath,
Which thou more think'st upon then on thy death:
They are not prayers of a grieved soule,
That with repentance doth his sinnes condole,
But amorous Pamphlets that best likes thine eyes,
And Songs of love, and Sonets exquisit:
Among these Venus and Adonis lies,
With Salmasis and her Hermaphrodite:
Pigmalion's there with his transform'd delight,
And many merry Comedies with this,
Where the Athenian Phryne acted is.[44]

Other women of Amanda's profession were readers of prose and verse, chiefly sentimental, we are told by other writers. Thomas Lodge describes a harlot who kept a pathetic ballad over her

---

[43] Quoted by J. P. Collier in *A Bibliographical and Critical Account of the Rarest Books in the English Language*, 4 vols. (New York, 1866), I, 229. Collier also notices the reference to *Venus and Adonis* cited here from Cranley's *Amanda*.

[44] Reprinted privately by Frederic Ouvry (London, 1869). A second edition of *Amanda* in 1639 bore the title, *The Converted Courtezan, Or The Reformed Whore. Being a true Relation of a Penitent Sinner, shadowed under the name of Amanda*. Cranley in an epistle to the reader states that he particularly hopes that his work will appeal to women readers. It is a sentimental story in verse and prose, describing the wickedness of a fair woman whom the author saw from his own prison window and rebuked in a series of verse letters until she repented her way of life. It is the forerunner of many stories like it in the later seventeenth and eighteenth centuries.

8

chimney piece ;[45] Humphrey Mills a little later tells of a harlot whose house was equipped "with [Martin] Parker's workes, and such like things" ;[46] an anonymous pamphlet near the middle of the seventeenth century, *The Yellow Book* (1656), describes Mrs. Wanton's chamber ". . . where there is nothing but four or five naked Pictures, a Song book, a Play book, a Lute, a History, two or three great Looking-glasses," and similar equipment.[47] Poetry for women seems to have become suspect, at least if they sought to write it, for Thomas Heywood in *A Curtaine Lecture* (1637) thinks "it is a question disputable" whether any virgin should "bee pleasant in lookes, free in language, wanton in carriage, to poetize, or the like," and he further enjoins maidens "to be wary in their words, and weighty in their writings, . . ."[48]

The foregoing allusions give some clue to the literary tastes of women at the end of the sixteenth and the beginning of the seventeenth century. Did professional writers realize the importance of the new reading public? The evidence is that they did. The feminine audience had reached such proportions by the last quarter of the sixteenth century that many authors were making a definite and frank appeal to women. Best known, perhaps, to modern readers are John Lyly's efforts to please the ladies of rank with courtly fiction. But Lyly's contemporaries were equally solicitous about having their books read by women,[49] whether fine

---

[45] Quoted from *Wits Miserie* (1596), by Hyder E. Rollins, in "The Black-Letter Broadside Ballad," *Publications of the Modern Language Association*, XXXIV (1919), 301, n. 30.

[46] Quoted from *Night's Search* (1646), in *ibid.*

[47] Thomason Tracts, Brit. Mus., E. 878. (1), pp. 7-8.

[48] Pp. 41-47.

[49] Cf. J. J. Jusserand, *The English Novel in the Time of Shakespeare* (London, 1899), p. 147.

Authors frequently made efforts to attract the attention of women by their dedications. For example, a certain R. B., who signed the dedication to George Pettie's *A Petite Pallace of Pettie his Pleasure* (edition of 1576), addressing himself "To the gentle Gentlewomen Readers," openly says of his audience that "by my will I would haue Gentlewomen." Barnabe Rich, anxious to win the favor of women, in *Riche his Farewell to Militarie profession* (1581) declares he wrote "for the onely delight of the courteous Gentlewoemen bothe of England and Irelande." He makes a further conscious bid for the patronage of women in *Don Simonides* (1581). William Warren in addressing *A pleasant new Fancie of a Fondlings deuice. Intitled and cald the Nurcerie of Names* (1581) "to the Gentlewomen of England" refers to himself as "youre poore Poet, and your olde friend."—Thomas Corser, *Collectanea Anglo-Poetica*, Pt. XI (1883), pp. 359-62.

ladies of the court or tradesmen's wives. Many books, particularly collections of stories and prose romances, though they bore flattering dedications to the "gentlewomen" of England, provided literature for women in less exalted positions. The attempts of Robert Greene to reach an audience of women in his numerous collections of love stories are obvious even to the casual turner of his pages. Such a title as *Penelopes Web: Wherein a Christall Myrror of faeminine perfection represents to the viewe of euery one those vertues and graces, which more curiously beautifies the mynd of women, then eyther sumptuous Apparell, or Iewels of inestimable valew* (1587) is typical of his efforts to ingratiate himself by flattery, a motive which dictated title-pages, dedications, and subject matter. Perhaps Nashe had Greene in mind when he wrote of the desire of some authors to lavish their praise upon women :

Many of them [writers] to be more amiable with their friends of the Feminine sexe, blot many sheetes of paper in the blazing of Womens slender praises, as though in that generation there raigned and alwaies remained such singuler simplicitie, that all posterities should be enioyned by duetie, to fill and furnish theyr Temples, nay Townes and streetes, with the shrines of the Saints.[50]

Writers, Nashe again comments, think "by compiling of Pamphlets in their Mistresse praises, to be called the restorers of womankind."[51]

The middle-class woman, it is clear, was a great reader of sentimental romances like those of Greene. Some of Greene's successors openly catered to her. Samuel Rowlands, author of miscellaneous works appealing to the London bourgeoisie, addressed a jolly transcript of London life, *'Tis Merrie when Gossips meete* (1602), "To all the pleasant conceited London Gentle-

---

[50] *Anatomie of Absurditie*, in McKerrow, *Works of Thomas Nashe*, I, 11.

[51] *Ibid.*, p. 19. A mournful commentary on the dead laureate of women is found in R. B.'s *Greenes Funeralls* (1594), edited by R. B. McKerrow (Stratford-upon-Avon, 1922), Sonnet III, sig. B 1 :

> "He is dead, that wrote of your delights :
> That wrote of Ladies, and of Parramours :
> Of budding beautie, and hir branched leaues,
> Of sweet content in royal Nuptialls.
> He he is dead, that kild you with disdaine :
> And often fed your friendly hopes againe."

women, that are friendes to mirth, and enemies to dull Melan-
choly." Later, in a prefatory address to *The Famous History of Guy
Earle of Warwick* (1609), he holds up Guy "To the Honourable
Ladies of England"[52] as a notable savior of women.

Rowlands had an established precedent for dedicating a chivalric romance to women. Although by the end of the sixteenth
century romances had come to be the literary fare of the lower
classes, they were not completely abandoned by any group and
remained popular with women of all classes. Indeed, a woman
who has been given too little credit in the annals of her sex, a
certain Margaret Tyler, came forward in 1578 as the translator of
The First Part of the Mirrour of Princely deedes and Knighthood. In a
long epistle to the reader she asserts the virtue-provoking qualities
of romances and the prerogative of women to read and to write
them. Furthermore, she defends herself against critics who carp
that she has not spent her time

penning matters of great waight & sadnesse in diuinitie, or other studies,
ye profession wherof more neerely beeseemeth my yeers, other some
discoursing of matters more easie and ordinary in common talke,
wherein a Gentlewoman may honestly imploy hir travaile. . . . But
my defence is by example of the best, amongst which, many haue
dedicated theyr labours, some stories, some of warre, some Physicke,
some Law, some as concerning gouernment, some diuine matters, vnto
diuerse Ladies and Gentlewomen. And if men may & doe beestow
such of theyr trauailes vpon Gentlewomen, then may wee women read
such of theyr woorkes as they dedicate vnto us, and if wee may read
them, why not farther wade in them to the search of a truth. . . . But
amongst all my ill willers, some I hope are not so strayght that they
would enforce mee necessarily either not to write or to write of diuinitie. . . . And thus much concerning this present storie, that it is
neither vnseemely for a woman to deale in, neyther greatly requiring
a lesse stayed age then mine is.[53]

Margaret Tyler's bold assertion of woman's equality in reading
and writing is a document in the history of woman's rights, as

---

[52] From what we know about Rowlands and his popularity, it is plain that he was
writing for the wives of tradesmen, who would be flattered, of course, by such courteous
forms of address. Other writers similarly flattered them.

[53] Title quoted from the edition of 1599. My quotations are also from this edition
(sigs. A 3ᵛ-A 4ᵛ), which has the same preface as the edition of 1578.

well as an interesting commentary on feminine taste.

The effort to appeal to women readers is obvious in the sequence of chivalric romances which followed Margaret Tyler's labors in translation. For example, in L. A.'s *The Seuenth Booke of the Myrrour of Knighthood* (1598) the translator calls attention to the fact that in many places he has addressed his speech "& directed the Historie as it were particulerly to one or more Ladies or Gentlewomen." *The Ninth part of the Mirrour of Knighthood* (1601) is much concerned, the title-page advertises, with "the high cheualrie of the gallant Ladyes." A little later William Webster declares in a preface "To The Faire Reader, Of The Fayrer Sex"[54] that his romance, *The Most Pleasant And Delightful Historie of Curran, a Prince of Danske, and the fayre Princesse Argentile* (1617), was written solely for women. John Kennedy even provides the 1631 edition of *The Historie of Calanthrop and Lucilla* (1626) with a title-page describing it as *The Ladies Delight, or, The English Gentlewomans History of Calanthrop and Lucilla*.

The controversial pamphlets of the first quarter of the seventeenth century, in which women were in turn satirized and defended, indicate that women in the middle ranks of society were reading both the satires and the encomia, and were turning a hand to defend themselves.[55] From Margaret Tyler's time onward, they were asserting their literacy in definite terms. After Robert Greene, writers who hoped to earn their livelihoods by their pens could no longer despise the feminine reader. Thomas Heywood, perhaps woman's staunchest literary advocate in the first half of the seventeenth century, was convinced of her capacity to read and appreciate, and he provided for her such useful works as his *Gunaikeion: or, Nine Bookes of Various History Concerninge Women* (1624) and *The Exemplary Lives and memorable Acts of nine the most worthy Women of the World* (1640). Here woman could find the biographies of virtuous and noble women, so insistently recommended more than a half century earlier by Thomas Salter. In the first of these works she might also find some equally interesting

---

[54] Cf. Robert Hayman's dedication of his translation of the first four books of Owen's *Epigrams*, appended to his own *Quodlibets* (1628), "To The Far Admired, Admirably Faire, vertuous and witty Beauties of England."

[55] *See* Chap. XIII, *infra*.

lives of the wicked. Writers no longer felt that woman's reading was limited to works of divinity and books of physic. The increase in the reading public in the later sixteenth and early seventeenth centuries was in part a result of the widening of woman's literary taste and the development of a desire for books among the women of the substantial middle class.

PART II

THE WHOLE DUTY OF THE CITIZEN

V

HANDBOOKS TO IMPROVEMENT [1]

THE discovery of some Northwest Passage to learning, some short route to the information and culture demanded by the "complete citizen," was sought during the sixteenth and seventeenth centuries with a zeal which equaled that of the traders and voyagers who strove to find quicker passages to the material wealth of the Orient. Prosperous merchants, thrifty tradesmen, all that increasing multitude of citizens who made up a commercial class ambitious for advancement, were eager for self-improvement. While the Renaissance courtier perhaps cultivated the arts and graces that made him the accomplished personality described by a Castiglione or a Peacham, his cousin, the tradesman, was pursuing an ideal of education that multiplied his accomplishments and increased his stock of useful and cultural information. For the Renaissance spirit was confined to no class, however different its manifestations might be in different groups. Since, however, the citizen had less time and means than the courtier for attaining his ends, he required speedy methods of instruction and usable compendiums of facts. The answer to his demands was the handbook, the printed guide, the Tudor and Stuart counterpart of the modern fifteen-easy-lessons which lead to bourgeois perfection. What the schools did not or could not accomplish, the citizen attempted to do for himself by private study of a convenient manual. The day of handbook-learning for the generality of men had arrived.

Not that the compendium was a new thing in the Renaissance, for the goal of much medieval effort had been the reduction of all knowledge to orderly encyclopedic form so that it might be

---

[1] This chapter includes material previously published in an essay, "Handbook Learning of the Renaissance Middle Class," *Studies in Philology*, XXVIII (1931), 58-86.

more easily mastered. But the invention of printing made easier the multiplication of encyclopedic works and increased the feasibility of publishing cheap manuals. Moreover, a relatively widespread literacy[2] gave such manuals a utility greater than they could have had in an earlier period. Some of the first books printed by Caxton and his contemporaries in England were encyclopedic collections of knowledge, published in the vernacular, that plain men might learn. As the eagerness for learning was stimulated, printers hastened to supply the means of satisfying it, until bookstalls were amply furnished with manuals which promised short and easy ways of acquiring all manner of information, from correct social forms to seamanship.

Nor was the handbook peculiarly the property of middle-class readers. Courtier and citizen alike thanked the gods of learning for the Elizabethan equivalent of the works that make up the modern five-foot shelf containing books of general information. The rediscovery of ancient learning, the opening up of new fields of knowledge, and the general ferment of the Renaissance had enormously expanded the interests of all classes. Furthermore, in Elizabethan society, which was still topsy-turvy as a result of commercial expansion and the breakdown of feudal institutions, a vast number of upstarts were seeking to better their social conditions by rising to the rank above them or by increasing the dignity of the rank in which they found themselves. Never before had there been such widespread zeal for knowledge, so great a return upon an investment in learning, such necessity for an acquaintance with a common stock of knowledge with which every intelligent man was expected to be reasonably familiar. "Slothful ignorance" came to be a term fit to damn one to the company of cowherds and plowmen. The effect was, not to make every man in the street a scholar, but to cause an unusual scrambling after scraps of learning and a determined effort to master those externals of behavior that indicated *savoir faire*—the goal of the ambitious, whatever his social position. In this scramble to learn, or to seem learned, the middle class found handbooks particularly helpful, though one should always bear in mind that many a gentleman also conned the same books.

---

[2] *See* Chap. III, *supra*, n. 2.

The courtesy book is, perhaps, the best-known type of Renaissance manual. It ranged in material from the little primer of behavior illustrated by Erasmus' *De Civilitate Morum Puerilium . . . A lytell booke of good maners for chyldren* (1532) to the philosophic treatise on education and culture exemplified in Castiglione's *The Courtyer,* translated by Sir Thomas Hoby in 1561. Various forms of both types remained popular[3] throughout the period and were not confined to the reading of any particular class, though books like *The Courtyer* and some of its imitations were of course predominantly concerned with the training of the gentleman. But since many middle-class persons were social climbers, the gentleman's manual of education was a volume desired above others. Moreover, as Sir Walter Raleigh long ago pointed out,[4] the term "courtier" must not be understood to denote merely an aristocratic sycophant of the sovereign, for its meaning was quite otherwise in an age that awarded tokens of honor to many low-born persons because of their services to the state. Indeed, a considerable number of business men, not least of whom was Sir Thomas Gresham, were, in the Renaissance sense, courtiers and trusted servants of the commonwealth, to whom the counsels of Castiglione were as appropriate as they were to the noble Sir Philip Sidney. Nor was Castiglione's work totally useless to lesser folk. When William Martyn, the recorder of Exeter,[5] compiled *Youths Instruction* (1612), a treatise of advice exhorting his own sons and the sons of other citizens to lead lives of piety, thrift, and diligence, he took occasion to recommend "the deliberate reading and meditating vpon that excellent and euer most praise-worthie worke of *Balthazar Castilion,* who by his choise precepts, hath cast young gentlemen into a fairer moulde then

---

[3] The book of manners had been in use long before the Elizabethan period and has remained popular to the present day. For early versions of the manners books, see F. J. Furnivall (ed.), *The Babees Book,* Early English Text Society, Orig. Ser., XXXII (London, 1868).

Gabriel Harvey ridiculed the taste for conduct books. *See* a note on Harvey's *Letter-Book* in G. Gregory Smith (ed.), *Elizabethan Critical Essays,* 2 vols. (Oxford, 1904), I, 376.

[4] Introduction to *The Book of the Courtier,* The Tudor Translations (London, 1900), p. lxii.

[5] He is said to have been a cousin of Richard Martyn, recorder of London.

their fathers did."[6] Martyn's own work represents an effort to adapt some of the moral lessons of Castiglione to the tastes of common citizens. While *The Courtyer* was not a popular book in the sense that every shopkeeper was familiar with it, undoubtedly its influence was wider than the audience to whom its title commended it, and it was a source of inspiration for other books which more directly influenced middle-class ideals.

Other Italian courtesy books, less philosophic and more utilitarian, made a conscious appeal to burgher taste. Most famous of these was Giovanni della Casa's *Il Galateo*, translated by Robert Peterson and published in 1576. Of this work one writer has said that it was "a frank handbook of manners, a manual for the schoolboy and the parvenu, and became popular in England under the titles of *Refined Courtier* and the like, given to it by later editors and adapters. . . . The Elizabethan scholar or merchant was interested, we can believe, in the argument for learning and for wealth as titles of *gentilezza*, when birth and skill in arms could not be pleaded."[7] *Il Galateo* was an intensely practical book providing directions for behavior under all circumstances. Its utility is attested by the fact that it was appended to Walter Darell's *A Short Discourse of the life of Seruingmen, plainly expressing the way that is best to be followed, and the meanes whereby they may lawfully challenge a name and title in that vocation and fellowship* (1578),[8] a manual which provided serving men, not only with advice on social procedure, but also with a rationale of conduct that would lead to a position of reputation and credit. *Il Galateo* was added to give further concrete suggestions about behavior. Nearly forty years later Thomas Gainsford still thought it the best instrument for inculcating good manners in citizens, for whom he prepared *The Rich Cabinet* (1616), a handy outline of miscellaneous information including "An Epitome Of Good Manners extracted out of the treatise of Mr. Iohn Della Casa called Galateo." Thus

---

[6] P. 109.

[7] W. H. Woodward, "English Universities, Schools, and Scholarship in the Sixteenth Century," *Cambridge History of English Literature*, III, 438.

[8] The only known copy is preserved in the Huntington Library. For a reprint and discussion of the little treatise, see Louis B. Wright, "A Conduct Book for Malvolio," *Studies in Philology*, XXXI (1934), 115-32.

was *Il Galateo* long regarded as a standard work on behavior, suitable for the guidance of plain men.

Another Italian treatise on conduct, not quite so specific in its advice as *Il Galateo* but more serviceable to commoners than *The Courtyer*, was Stephano Guazzo's *Civile Conversation*, the first three books of which were translated by George Pettie and published in 1581. A second edition, with the fourth book translated by Bartholomew Young, appeared in 1586. Guazzo himself planned his work as a "treatise that confined itself strictly to the great middle classes as distinguished from the patricians of a higher social order: and herein lies the reason of its popularity at the date of its publication."[9] No mere conversation manual, it taught precisely that philosophy of conduct which was most pleasing to grave burghers, and incidentally suggested many ways for improving one's bearing and behavior. No one could fail to see the value of the lessons in the first book describing "the fruites that may be reaped by conversation, and teaching how to know good companie from yll"; even more obvious were the benefits of the succeeding books, which promised to teach not only the manner of conversation but also many "particular points" to be observed by people of all classes.

Still plainer were the precepts laid down for common men by Giovanni Battista Gelli, a tailor of Florence, who wrote a conduct book, translated by W. Barker as *The Fearfull Fansies of the Florentine Couper* (1568), a second edition of which appeared in 1599. This tailor-author, described in the translator's preface as "chief of the vulgar vniversitie of Florence," imagines a certain cooper named Just discussing with his Soul the manifold problems affecting his temporal and spiritual welfare. When Just objects to the moralistic regimen prescribed by the Soul, his arguments are demolished by proofs of the profitableness of well-doing. If, instead of wasting precious time in idle and frivolous amusements, honest craftsmen like Just would devote themselves to self-improvement, they would win thereby much honor and profit. Other tradesfolk, the Soul points out, have distinguished themselves through the pursuit of learning. Just is reminded of the fame of a

---

[9] *The Civile Conversation of M. Steeven Guazzo.* . . . *With an Introduction by Sir Edward Sullivan, Bart.*, The Tudor Translations (London, 1925), I, xxviii.

humble apothecary of Florence who applied himself to learning
with such good results that he became ambassador to Naples.
What the apothecary did, other plain men might accomplish. To
help those who thus choose to instruct themselves, Gelli gives a
variety of useful and moral advice, including practical suggestions
about diet, exercise, and recreation.

Such, in brief, were some of the typical Italian courtesy books
which influenced the ideals of Elizabethan conduct among those
of high and low degree. The belief in the well-rounded personality and the capacity of the individual, whatever his status,
for infinite self-improvement penetrated to all classes, partly as
a result of the diffusion of Renaissance ideals through the instrumentality of the courtesy books, both foreign and native,
which included in the scope of their instruction far more than the
mere externals of etiquette. The best of them, indeed, were guides
to the whole wide field of self-education and, as such, found
readers in all classes. Even so obviously aristocratic a treatise as
Sir Thomas Elyot's *The boke named The gouernour* (1531), eight
times printed by 1580 (being superseded then only by more
recent works), by its high moral lessons must have attracted
readers not of the governing class, with whose upbringing the
book was concerned. Similarly, the royal but less aristocratic
treatise, *Basilikon Doron* (1599), written by King James for the
education of his son and often reprinted, undoubtedly influenced
many humble subjects who devoutly believed King James's opening verse, "God giues not Kings the stile of *Gods* in vaine." What
the great ones said, the lesser read and utilized as best they could.

This quality of moralization, so emphatic in many English
courtesy books, prevented their being exclusively aristocratic in
appeal, for the concern over moral virtues was by no means the
prerogative solely of the gentry; indeed, no social group showed
such zeal for moral literature as did the middle ranks of citizens.
In the seventeenth century, as the bourgeois and Puritan influences became more pronounced, the emphasis on moral virtues
grew stronger in the conduct books, and, by the same token, their
appeal to the middle class was increased. This development is
best exemplified in Richard Brathwaite's *The English Gentleman*
(1630) and *The English Gentlewoman* (1631), which present a

philosophy of conduct in striking contrast to Henry Peacham's *The Compleat Gentleman* (1622), a work which summed up the earlier Renaissance ideal of courtly training.[10] In Peacham the emphasis is placed upon the cultivation of the qualities that make the gentleman an accomplished, versatile personality as well as a capable servant of the state. In Brathwaite, the aim is to produce a godly man whose Christian character will be an example to others. Moreover, Brathwaite formulates the doctrine that the perfect gentleman should be intent upon doing good to his fellow man. In short, in the new conception it is better to *do* than to *be*. And the logical consequence is an emphasis upon the gospel of work, which is a cardinal point in all middle-class doctrine, as its opposite, idleness, is first of the bourgeois seven deadly sins. Though Brathwaite himself was a country gentleman, bourgeois ideals are strongly reflected in his treatises.[11] His gospel of work, for example, merely echoes Puritan ministers, who were preaching a doctrine pleasing to middle-class prejudices.[12] From the Scriptures and the classics Brathwaite quotes many passages "inveighing against Idleness" and insisting that it is better to wear out than to rust out in slothful ease.[13] No man, however high his position, is exempt from the necessity of laboring in a vocation. Indeed, "Men in great place (saith one) are thrice servants; servants of the Soveraigne, or State; servants of Fame; and servants of Businesse. So they have no freedome, neither in their persons, nor their actions, nor in their times."[14] Thus Brathwaite set forth not only the growing conviction that all men must work

---

[10] This distinction is pointed out by W. L. Ustick, "Changing Ideals of Aristocratic Character and Conduct in Seventeenth-Century England," *Modern Philology*, XXX (1932-33), 147-66. Cf. E. N. S. Thompson, "Books of Courtesy," in *Literary Bypaths of the Renaissance* (New Haven, 1924), p. 160.

[11] Ustick, *op. cit.*, pp. 156-58.

[12] Cf. *infra*, pp. 170-72, 175-85, where William Perkins's *A Treatise Of The Vocations* is mentioned.

[13] *The English Gentleman*, p. 108: "So as this *rust*, which indeed is *rest* from imployment, doth no lesse consume the *Light* or *Lampe* of our *Life*, than labour or exercise."

[14] *Ibid.*, p. 115. *See also* p. 124: "How necessary then is it for all estates to be carefull, lest they incurre a heavy and fearfull censure, to addresse themselves to especiall *Vocations*, beneficiall to the state, and pleasing to God, whose *glory* should be our *aime*, without any by-respect unto our selves? Wee shall see in most places both at home and abroad, how such trades or *Vocations* are most used, as may best suit with the nature and condition of the place."

but also the modern belief in the virtue of "service." *The English Gentleman*, for all its title, was as useful to merchants and shop-keepers as it was to the proudest squires. And it must have been widely read, for the first edition was soon exhausted and a second edition, "revised and enlarged," was published three years later. Again in 1641 it was republished, with its companion work, *The English Gentlewoman*, in a handsome folio volume. Brathwaite him-self had desired to make his work into a small and convenient manual suitable for the pocket, but the quantity of his material had prevented it.[15]

In the shifting social order of sixteenth- and seventeenth-century England, all things were possible, and the merchant, the tailor, or the shoemaker today might be the wealthy alderman tomorrow, who at length would acquire lands and titles of gentil-ity. Since the upward progress might be hastened by a knowledge of the technique and philosophy of social relations, the middle class set themselves to learn from all the sources available to them. The most obvious instruments of this education were of course the treatises on conduct, which abounded in an infinite variety throughout the period, as we have seen.[16] The great multiplica-tion of handbooks which sought to guide the uninitiated over the hazardous seas of social progress was largely stimulated by the demands of middle-class readers, whose desire for manuals teach-ing the proper way of life and the correct procedure therein was never satisfied. Since good manners soon came to be equated with good morals, which were the concern of shopkeepers no less than

---

[15] *Ibid.*, a note following the preface to the reader: "I had purposed that this Worke should have been digested into a *portible Volume*, to the end it might be more familiar with a *Gentlemans* pocket, not to picke it, but that he might picke some good from it: But since the *Volume* would not beare it, you must with patience beare with it, and with more trouble beare it: by enlarging your pocket to containe it.

"Now for the *Title*, I am not wholly ignorant, how a Subject intitled *The Complete Gentleman*, was heretofore published; which (I can assure you *Gentlemen*) consorts with this rather in *Title* than *Tenour*, *Name* than *Nature;* the proofe whereof I referre to the generous and judicious Reader."

[16] For a general discussion of courtesy books and the relation of their theories to Elizabethan life, see Ruth Kelso, *The Doctrine of the English Gentleman in the Sixteenth Century*, University of Illinois Studies in Language and Literature, XIV (Urbana, 1929). A more exhaustive treatment of courtesy books is to be found in a manuscript dissertation, in the Harvard College Library, by W. L. Ustick, "The English Gentle-man in the Sixteenth and Early Seventeenth Century" (1931).

of gentlemen, much of the moral and pietistic literature especially favored by the middle classes contained advice on the externals of behavior; in the same way, the books on domestic relations frequently provided sections dealing with general conduct.[17] Occasionally the same book combined all these useful elements, as in the case of William Vaughan's *The Golden-groue, moralized in three Bookes: A worke very necessary for all such, as would know how to gouerne themselues, their houses, or their countrey* (1600). As was suggested in an earlier chapter, one reason for the faith of the middle class in the grammar schools was the belief in their capacity to teach good manners, which of course meant good morals. Some of the books used in such formal instruction in manners were, for generations, popular guides to polite behavior. Of these school manuals, one of the most famous was Francis Seager's *The Schoole of Vertue, and booke of good Nourture for chyldren and youth to learne theyr dutie by* (1557), which was still being recommended by John Brinsley in 1612[18] and which was reprinted as late as 1626. Another manual, prepared for school children and apprentices and also approved by Brinsley, was William Fiston's *The Schoole of good manners* (licensed, 1595).[19] This book so successfully combined advice on morals and rules of behavior that Charles Hoole in 1660 was still advising its use in the schools. Little change, indeed, occurred, from decade to decade, in the subject matter and treatment of these books, which were studied both in the schools and in the homes. A popular book of the mid-seventeenth century, translated from a Jesuit treatise by Francis Hawkins as *Youths Behaviour, Or Decency In Conversation Amongst Men,*[20] repeated much of the counsel that had been part of the common stock of such works since the

---

[17] *See* Chaps. VII and VIII, *infra*, for discussions of these treatises.

[18] Foster Watson, *The English Grammar Schools to 1660: Their Curriculum and Practice* (Cambridge, 1908), p. 102.

[19] *The Schoole of good manners, Or A new Schoole of Vertue, teaching children and youth how to behaue themselues in all companies: Also the manner of seruing and taking vp a table. With diuers godly prayers for mornings and euenings. And certaine new Graces very necessary to be vsed both of young and old. Newly corrected and augmented by W. F.* (1629).

[20] The title, which appears in full as follows, is quoted from the edition of 1646: *Youths Behaviour, Or Decency in Conversation Amongst Men. Composed in French by grave persons for the Use and benefit of their Youth. Now newly turned into English By Francis Hawkins. The fourth Edition, with the Addition of twenty sixe new Precepts (which are marked thus*).* An earlier edition appeared in 1641.

9

broadside ballads as source of lessons on etiquette

time of Erasmus' *De Civilitate*. Used as both a school text and a private manual, it lived to influence George Washington's own rules of behavior![21] Its advice, like that constantly repeated in many of the more specific books on manners, is often painfully concrete. For example, "Cleanse not thy teeth with the Table-cloth, or Napkin, nor with thy finger, forke, or knife : much worse would it be to do so with thy nailes; but use thy picktooth."[22] The tradesman of Tudor and Stuart England did not lack for guidance, both general and detailed, which would help him to cultivate the behavior of a gentleman.

In addition to formal treatises on manners, there were other even cheaper sources of instructions for the citizen or apprentice who did not wish to lay out more than a penny on good conduct, for the broadside ballads did not neglect to give advice as to both the details of behavior and the general rules of life. Most of these ballads of good counsel mix admonitions to godliness with practical suggestions. The best example of this type is *A Table of Good Nurture. Wherin is contained a Schoolemaster's admonition to his Schollers to learne good manners; the Father to his Children to learne vertue; and the Houshoulder to his Servants to learne godlinesse.*[23] The first part of the ballad (which is in two parts) urges neatness in dress, diligence and earnestness in work or study, and general correctness of conduct. The second part reads like a paraphrase of Polonius' advice to Laertes. The young man is instructed to follow the example of some grave man, to avoid waste of money in riotous living, to preserve his credit, to beware of too much courtesy in a new acquaintance—the whole ballad being an exhortation to the prudential virtues. Similar to this broadside are the "A B C" ballads. *A right Godly and Christian A,B,C, Shewing the duty of every degree*[24] is a compilation of pious and useful precepts, the successive stanzas beginning with the consecutive letters of the alphabet. It stresses the profitableness of godliness :

---

[21] *See* Charles Moore (ed.), *George Washington's Rules of Civility and Decent Behaviour in Company and Conversation* (Boston, 1926), p. xiv.

[22] Edition of 1646, p. 49.

[23] Temp. Jac. I. (Printed in *Roxburghe Ballads*, II, 569 ff.)

[24] Temp. Jac. I. (*Ibid.*, III, 159 ff.)

Oppress no man by usury,
   refuse unlawfull gaine:
Give plenteously unto the poore—
   Christ will thee pay againe.

The Virgin's A.B.C; Or, An Alphabet of vertuous Admonitions for a chaste, modest, and well-governed Maid [1620-29][25] is another ballad of good conduct, urging modesty, constancy, loyalty, obedience, and similar virtues. Especially does it warn against extravagance, pride, and hasty marriages. Practical guidance is the aim of *An Hundred Godly Lessons, That a Mother on her Death-Bed gave to her Children, whereby they may know how to guide themselues towards God and Man, to the benefit of the Commonwealth, joy of their Parents, and good to themselves;*[26] the general theme is, "Do well and thou wilt be rewarded":

They that upon the Poor bestow
   unto the Lord doth lend;
And God unto such men again
   a thousand fold will send.

The profitableness of righteousness and the temporal advantages of correct relations with one's fellows echoed like a refrain in many of these ballads of good conduct.[27] The persistence of their popularity is attested by a quotation from "The Exchange in its

---

[25] *Ibid.*, II, 650 ff.

[26] Temp. Eliz. or early Jac. I. (*Ibid.*, I, 427 ff.)

[27] Professor Hyder E. Rollins, *Old English Ballads, 1553-1625* (Cambridge, 1920), pp. 226 ff., reprints from Add. MSS 15,225 an undated ballad, *Seek wisdom chiefly to obtain*. Of this ballad he says that it "is a sort of *Poor Richard's Almanac* that must have delighted the pious Catholic who composed the MS.: seek wisdom, it advises; waste not, shun borrowing, value true friends, avoid drink and dice, lose no time, envy not thy neighbor—good advice expressed in a pithy line or two, every item of which was both before and after the date of this MS. fully emphasized in separate ballads."

In connection with the ballads may be mentioned a broadside sheet of advice preserved by the Society of Antiquaries. It bears the title of *Table-Observations, or Rules for Conduct at Table, put in a tabular form, as,*

Tell			Long Tales
Take	*no*		Tobacco
Touch			State Matters

[temp. Jac. I]. *See* Robert Lemon, *Catalogue of a Collection of Printed Broadsides in the Possession of the Society of Antiquaries of London* (London, 1866), p. 71.

Humours" in *A Garland for the New Royal Exchange* (1669) : ". . . Here be your story-ballads, your love-ballads, and your ballads of good-life ; fit for your gallant, your nice maiden, your grave senior, and all sorts of men beside."[28] The popular interest in advice about manners and correct behavior is reflected in the burlesque of such counsel in Dekker's *The Guls Horne-Booke* (1609) and in R. F.'s translation of Dedekind's *Grobianus* (1605).

More specialized than the books on manners and the conduct of life were the manuals of conversation, which, though not scorned even by the upper classes, were a veritable godsend to the less cultured, who made haste to add such works to their equipment for self-improvement. "I had rather than forty shillings I had my Book of Songs and Sonnets here," exclaimed Master Slender, and presently demanded of his servant, "You have not the Book of Riddles about you, have you?"[29] As Slender proposed to show his wit by apt quotation from his anthologies, so others made use of literary allusions, polite phrases, and witty jests garnered from dictionaries of compliments, anthologies of similes, books of anecdotes, and guides to polite discourse. Edward Guilpin in *Skialethia* (1598), Satire V, says of a fop :

> Thys is the Dictionary of complements,
> The Barbers mouth of new-scrapt eloquence,
> *Synomicke Tully* for varietie,
> And Madame Conceits gorgeous gallerie.

John Taylor in *Divers Crab-tree Lectures* (1639) describes a maiden whose tradesman-lover woos her with cribbed compliments and an amorous tale :

. . . and what was it, but an old passage betweene *Venus* and *Adonis*, and that was all he did : onely hee presented me with a Coppy of Verses, and many Letters of Complements in writing, which I tooke on purpose to laugh at, and withall he intreated me to accept of them,

---

[28] Quoted by Hyder E. Rollins, "The Black-Letter Broadside Ballad," *Publications of the Modern Language Association*, XXXIV (1919), 308.

Related in tone to the broadside ballad of good counsel is a verse pamphlet by that inveterate balladist, Martin Parker, entitled *Harry White his humour* (1637). Such bourgeois virtues as sobriety, industry, and thrift are represented as bluff Harry's humors.

[29] *The Merry Wives of Windsor*, I, i, 205-9.

for they were of his owne invention. And when I had perused them, I remember'd that I had read them in Print, for hee stole them out of divers bookes of Complements on my knowledge, thinking thereby that I should account him witty, and the sooner to get my love.

[Pp. 202-3.]

Without doubt one reason for the popularity of Elizabethan verse anthologies was their utility in supplying quotable passages of the sort that persons desirous of making a good impression collected into commonplace books and kept against a time of need.

The desire to converse wittily and learnedly was confined to no rank or degree. The printer of T. T.'s *The Schoolemaster, or Teacher of Table Philosophie* (1576),[30] one of the best of the sixteenth-century manuals of conversation, specifically declares in "The Printers preamble to al estates" that the purpose of the treatise is to teach "Demeanour meet from hie vnto the low," from the Prince to "The marchant eke that makes the merie sale." Forthwith the little book provides ammunition which all estates might find effective in the rapid fire of talk at dinner. A general principle of conversation at table is enunciated as follows:

Wherfore, it is generally expedient, that all table talke be either concerning the nature & qualitie of the meates and drinkes wherof we feede, or of table questions wherwith we may be made merie and sturred vp to mirth at the boorde, or els touching them their condition, and manners with whom we meete at the table, or lastly of such meriments and honest deuises wherwith we may be refreshed and delighted at our meate. [Sig. A 4.]

This suggestion is not unlike that made nearly fifty years later by Peacham:

---

[30] This work has been attributed to Thomas Twyne. Its full title is *The Schoolemaster, or Teacher of Table Philosophie. A most pleasant and merie companion, wel worthy to be welcome (for a dayly Gheast) not onely to all mens boorde, to guyde them with moderate & holsome dyet: but also into euery mans companie at all tymes, to recreate their mindes, with honest mirth and delectable deuises: to sundrie pleasant purposes of pleasure and pastyme. Gatherered out of diuers, the best approued Auctours: and deuided into foure pithy and pleasant Treatises, as it may appeare by the contentes* (1576). Daniel Tuvil published in 1614 a learned little treatise designed to provide a sort of philosophic basis for social and business communications. He gave it the fanciful title of *The Dove And The Serpent. In which is conteined a large description of all such points and principles, as tend either to Conuersation, or Negotiation.* It was dedicated to Sir Henry Montague, recorder of London.

In your discourse be free and affable, giuing entertainment in a sweete and liberall manner, and with a cheerefull courtesie, seasoning your talke at the table among graue and serious discourses, with conceipts of wit and pleasant inuention, as ingenious Epigrammes, Emblemes, Anagrammes, merry tales, wittie questions and answers, Mistakings, . . .[31]

Since every ambitious citizen was eager to talk as much like a gentleman as he might, he welcomed such expedient handbooks as *The Schoolemaster*, from which he could draw the miscellaneous information helpful to his conversation. For example, *The Schoolemaster*, packed like a miniature encyclopedia with facts gathered chiefly from classical authors, provides in Book I a discussion of foods and drinks, with stray bits of curious information about them; in Book II a description of the manners and customs of various people; in Book III witty questions and answers; and in Book IV merry jests.

Handbooks of encyclopedic information, anthologies of verse, and other convenient compilations were the sources of the cultural tags with which all classes throughout the period were pleased to decorate their conversation.[32] The *genre* reached its culmination in *A Helpe To Discourse. Or A Misselany of Seriousnesse with Merriment* (licensed, 1618),[33] compiled by W. B. and E. P., a work designed particularly for the needs of busy people. The time-saving qualities of the manual—a significantly modern note—are stressed by

---

[31] *The Compleat Gentleman*, p. 196.

[32] An interesting example of a late-sixteenth-century treatise on speech and writing is to be found in a manuscript, compiled by John Hoskins, with the title, "Direccons For Speech and Style. . . . Conteyning all the figures of Rhetorick and the Art of the best English exemplyfyed either all out of Arcadia wch it censureth, or by Instances . . . The matter whereof may Benefitt Conversation. The Quotacons being taken out of *Sr. Phillip Sidneys Arcadia* . . ." The manuscript is preserved in the British Museum, MS. Harley 4604. The Modern Language Association of America has desposited a rotograph of the manuscript (No. 93) in the Library of Congress. Hoskins' work, which was never published, was apparently designed particularly to aid students of the Inns of Court.

[33] *A Helpe To Discourse. Or A Misselany of Seriousnesse with Merriment. Consisting of witty Philosophicall, Gramaticall, and Astronomicall Questions and Answers. As Also, Of Epigrams, Epitaphs, Riddles, and Jests. Together with The Countrey-mans Counsellour, next his yearely Oracle or Prognostication to consult with. Contayning diuers necessary Rules and Obseruations, of much vse and consequence beeing knowne. Now the sixt time published, and much inlarged by the former Authors*, W. B. and E. P. (1627). My quotations are from this edition.

W. Lorte in a prefatory poem which emphasizes its utility :

> Take this Discourse or wits Monopoly.
> And such sweet profit of it shall ensue,
> (As what indeed is euery good mans due)
> Honour and fellowship among the wise,
> From whence this benefit or good doth rise,
> As hearing, reading, or calme conference,
> Where man's most safest, shunnes the base expence
> Of hasting time; time's onely lent to man,
> His wayes t'examine, Arts wide depth to skan.
> Be then aduertis'd this *Helpe to Discourse*
> Bespeaks thy future good, 'twill gently force
> Knowledge into thee; and the generous wise
> Will know thee fit for all societies.
> If in thee, all or none of these finde roome,
> Others will speake, whil'st thou with shame sits dumbe.

Not even the most sanguine of present-day correspondence schools and handbook-makers dare promise more than knowledge forced gently in to make their students brilliant in all societies. A further prefatory note by Thomas Brewer assures the user of *A Helpe To Discourse* that he can here get wisdom "with ease and little cost." The work is a miscellany of quotations, questions and answers, riddles, epigrams, jests, and diverse curious lore. There is even "A briefe Epitome of Chronicle Discourse"—a summary of history from Edward III to James I. Included also is "The History of St. George, St. Christopher and the seven Sleepers." In short, this handbook represents an effort to supply a demand for an epitome of knowledge in easy and inexpensive form. It is not surprising that a book which contained the promise of so much help to middle-class users should have been instantly popular. First published apparently in 1619, by 1638 it had gone through at least thirteen editions. Closely imitative of *A Helpe To Discourse* was *A Helpe To Memorie and Discourse* (1621),[34] a compilation which

---

[34] *A Helpe To Memorie and Discourse. The two Syrens of the Eare, and ioynt Twins of Mans perfection, extracted from the sweating braines of Physitians, Philosophers, Orators and Poets. Distilled in their Assiduous, and witty Collections: And which for the method, manner, and Referent handlings may be fitly termed: a second Miscelany, or Helpe to Discourse. The second Impression, corrected and enlarged by the Author* (1621).

contains preliminary advice on the care of the health and the improvement of the memory by diet. Then follow questions and answers, verses, and other matter suitable for conversational use.

To remove the danger of betraying a country origin through incorrect speech, to improve the chances of success in love, and to increase one's power of persuasion in good causes are the self-advertised reasons why the public was urged to buy another of the conversation manuals, *Cupids Schoole: Wherein Yongmen and Maids may learne diuers sorts of new, witty, and Amorous Complements. Newly written, and neuer any written before in the same kinde* (1632).[35] The publishers of this handbook reveal an insight into popular psychology which modern advertising specialists might envy. The sex element is emphasized in the title and the preface, both of which suggest the utility of the treatise as a manual of love-making. Next is created a fear motive—the fear of betraying a social inferiority. And finally, for those upon whom the first two selling points might be lost, it is claimed that the book is an invaluable help for serious persons who wish to persuade others to lead virtuous lives. Since the times have changed, as one learns from a prefatory statement, no longer is blunt speech good form, but it is now necessary to use graceful language if one hopes to be received acceptably.[36] Despite what might be expected from the title, *Cupids Schoole* is no gallant's guide to amorous adventure. The wooing taught is for the honest purpose of respectable marriage. Obviously intended for actual imitation were such

---

[35] The only copy recorded in the *Short Title Catalogue* is preserved in the Huntington Library. "A Complement to the Reader" (sig. A 4) is signed "W. S." There is no other clue to the authorship. An exemplar of another edition, published in 1642, is also preserved in the Huntington Library.

[36] The preface, entitled "The Character and description of a Complement," is a discussion of the place of polite speech in one's social equipment: "In the old time their Garments were plaine, and so were their words and meaning. But afterward, some more witty than the rest (finding what power perswasion hath ouer the mind of man) inuented a new Art of words, called Complements: which is indeed nothing but an affable and courteous manner of speech, and yet is now grown so necessary, that nothing can be done without them. For men now a-dayes regard not vertuous qualities, but onely a pleasingnesse of nature and condition, so that hee that speakes best, speeds best, and shall be sure to be preferred before the plaine meaning man. So that the necessity of these times doe enforce vs to learne the Art of Complements, which I will proue vnto you by particulars; and first in loue, hee that thinkes to win affection by telling a Maid in plaine tearmes that he loues her, is much deceiued, for

straightforward, seriously composed utterances as those here set forth, for example, in "The Seruingman's wooing of *Susan* a Chamber-maid." Nor is love the main theme of the treatise. The innumerable contingencies of polite conduct are provided for. The reader is taught the proper way to bid a friend farewell, to invite a guest home, to excuse one's self with thanks, to ask lodging of a gentleman, to thank one for a courtesy, to excuse the absence of a friend, or to comply with any of the social amenities. Though it bears an alluring title, *Cupids Schoole* sought to teach the manners of a gentleman to those who might without it betray a lower breeding.

Even if the conversation manual often claimed to be a gentle-man's treatise, its appeal to the socially aspiring burgher was obvious. Such a book was *The Mirror Of Complements. Or: A*

---

when she heares you begin so plainely, shee will start backe from you, and thinke you to bee some ignorant *Corydon* that know not *Cupid's* Language; when on the contrary, hee that can deliuer his minde in amorous words, doth seeme to keepe the keyes of their Maydenheads, of which hee can take possession when he list, for their hearts are at his deuotion, while the other poore Louer that cannot expresse his mind in a Comple-ment, may pine away with sorrow vnregarded, for he that loues most is many times neglected, and he that loues least is oftentimes most respected. Therefore it behooues a Louer now a-dayes to vse some Complement and Insinuation to procure affectiõ for a man can preuaile in nothing without Complements; your friend will not thinke you his friend without you salute him with a Complement; you cannot inuite one home, nor entertaine him afterward without Complements; neither can you keepe company or bee sociable without the mutuall enterchanging of complements. To conclude therefore, a Complement is the language of Gallants, the Conqueror of Maiden-heads, the quintessence of wit, the refiner of speech, and necessary both in City and Country: For though the Country man be plaine, yet faire and courteous words will preuaile much with the goodnes of his nature; and this may be seene by the Fable of *Mercury* and *Iupiter*. . . . Besides, as Complements are necessary in wooing, so you cannot counsell your friend to refraine from any vitious course, vnlesse you vse the Insinuation of a Complement, for truth is so sharpe, that it is displeasing to all men, and seemes to grate their eares, if it be not sweetned by some pleasant dis-course, and therefore when you are to doe the tendrest office of a friend, which is to lay his shame and vice before him, there is nothing can giue a more ready entrance to your words, or make him more willingly endure the sharpnesse of good counsell, than to begin in a louing and complementall manner. Seeing therefore that a Com-plement is so gracefull to the speaker, so delightfull to the hearer, and so powerfull to winne affection, I hope Yongmen will imbrace and loue this Booke, which teacheth them how to obtaine their loue. And I hope yong Maids will lay it vnder their pillow, and read it when they goe to bed, since it will instruct them how to giue an answer to their amorous Suters. And so wishing to all Yongmen and Maids the accomplish-ment of their desires, I leaue these Complements to their perusall."

pleasant and profitable Academy, for all such as have occasion to frequent the Court, or to converse with persons of worth and quality (1635), which, without doubt, many a new-made knight from the City found a useful and convenient work, for its duodecimo size made it an easily carried pocket manual. It contains a variety of useful helps, ranging from formulas for offering one's service to the sovereign to the proper way "To salute a Gentlewoman with an intention of marriage and to offer her service." A preface to the reader stresses the value of eloquence. In addition to graceful conversation formulas the compiler also gives brief suggestions for letter writing, and includes simple examples of letters likely to be used in social correspondence.

One of the most popular conversational manuals of the mid-seventeenth century was compiled by a certain Philomosus as *The Academy Of Complements* (1640).[37] In spite of a high-flown title, which claimed that the book was designed for scholars and gentlewomen, the appeal was chiefly to the commonalty. The dedication to the ladies of England promises that it will be useful even to maids. Here all persons may find

the best expressions of choise complementall language, for though by nature and custom, you can deliver your minds in a smooth and graceful manner; yet from hence, without study, or praemeditation, you may command necessary Ceremonies. Besides, your Ladyshippe's Chambermaids and waiting-Gentlewomen are to be pitied; who having by their good cariage compassed Suters, are often constrained to blush, in ignorance, for want of Complements, wherewith to answer them.

To meet the Puritan objection that forthright plain speaking is more honest than the courtly practice, the author says in refutation of the statement that

doune right dealing is best, I answer thou mayest somtimes be too plain in the way of thy preferment; if thou namest the word dissimulation thou errest, the whole heaven: this work relishes in respect of the

---

[37] *The Academy Of Complements. Wherein Ladyes, Gentlewomen, Schollers, and Strangers may accomodate their Courtly Practice with most Curious Ceremonies, Complementall, Amorous, High expressions and formes of speaking, or writing. A work perused and most exactly perfected by the Author with Additions of witty Amorous Poems. And a Table expounding the hard English words* (1640).

subject more of curtesie, unlesse thou abuse it by craft, accept it then as every way beneficiall to thee . . .[38]

The book is filled with speech formulas, letter models, and occasional verses. A glossary defines the harder words.

The need of help in letter writing was even greater than the need for conversational guidance, because epistolary style followed Ciceronian models, and, since not every Elizabethan could command the style demanded by convention, letter manuals were among the favorite handbooks. William Fulwood, a merchant, produced one of the most popular letter books of the period, entitled *The Enimie of Idlenesse: Teaching the maner and stile how to endite, compose and write all sorts of Epistles and Letters* (1568).[39] In the dedication to the master, wardens, and Company of the Merchant Taylors, the author insists that he offers a useful work for general utility, especially for the unlearned,

> Wherat grosse heads may grope :
> And finde therein some nedefull thing.

In a later preface, "To the reasonable Reader" (edition of 1578), Fulwood adds :

The cunning clearke hath small neede of a teacher. It is the vnskilfull scholer that wanteth instructions. Mine onely intent therefore at this instant is to place doune such praecepts, and set foorth such instructions, as may (in mine opinion) best serue to edifie the ignorant : and those not vnprofitable, but very needfull. The matter that I meane to intreat of, I haue intituled, *The Enimie of Idlenesse*. It consisteth chiefly vppon sundrie necessarie instructions and examples, for the inditing and composing of Epistles & Letters, whiche title I haue thought conuenient to be added therevnto, for that not onely, when weightie busines and vrgent affaires require, it may stand thee in good steede : but also at idle times, when opportunitie permitteth, for the auoyding of idlenesse (the capitall enimie to all good exercise, & common consumer of youth,) this woorke teacheth thee in what sorte thou mayest (I say at such vacant times) take thy penne in hande and gratifie thy friend with some prettie or pleasant conceite.

---

[38] Preface to the reader.

[39] *The Enimie of Idlenesse: Teaching the maner and stile how to endite, compose and write all sorts of Epistles and Letters: as well by answer, as otherwise. Deuided into foure Bokes, no lesse plesaunt than profitable. Set forth in English by William Fulwood Marchant, &c.* (1568).

So useful was the work that it went through eight editions between 1568 and 1621. In Fulwood's compilation, the citizen could find specimens of letters for most situations likely to arise. By imitating their form and style any merchant might write as clerkly as a scholar.

Even more important, both to serious students of epistolary style and to practical persons looking for models to follow, was Angel Day's *The English Secretarie* (1586)[40] which by 1626 also enjoyed eight editions. Frankly for general utility, Day's work is both a treatise on letter writing and a compilation of model letters. The title-page boasts that never before has there been "layd forth a Path-waye, so apt, plaine and easie, to any learners capacity." In a long essay prefatory to sundry examples of letters on almost every conceivable theme, Day discusses such matters as the tone of the letter, the use of rhetorical ornaments, methods of argumentation, and in general the theory of epistolary composition. The examples are in the stilted rhetoric of most Elizabethan letters, which sought to teach Ciceronian elegance rather than simple clarity.

Less popular but inspired by the same motive of aiding the unlearned was Abraham Fleming's *A Panoplie of Epistles, Or a looking Glasse for the vnlearned* (1576).[41] This is a collection of a vast number of model letters on all subjects, chiefly from classical sources. The letters are preceded by "An Epitome Of Precepts whereby the ignoraunt may learne to indite, according to skill and order, reduced into a Dialogue betweene the Maister and Scholer." Moralistic "Arguments" and marginal glosses[42] add to the value of the letters, for not only could Fleming's tradesman

---

[40] *The English Secretarie. Wherein is contayned, A Perfect Method, for the inditing of all manner of Epistles and familiar Letters, together with their diuersities, enlarged by examples vnder their seuerall Tytles. In which is layd forth a Path-waye, so apt, plaine and easie, to any learners capacity, as the like wherof hath not at any time heretofore beene deliuered. Nowe first deuized, and newly published, by Angel Daye* (1586).

[41] *A Panoplie of Epistles, Or a looking Glasse for the vnlearned. Conteyning a perfecte plattforme of inditing letters of all sorts, to persons of al estates and degrees, as well our superiors, as also our equalls and inferiours: vsed of the best and eloquentest Rhetoricians that haue liued in all ages, and haue beene famous in that facultie. Gathered and translated out of Latine into English, by Abraham Flemming* (1576).

[42] A reference to the use of letter books may be indicated in an allusion by Gabriel Harvey to Nashe in *Pierce's Supererogation* (1593): "I haue seldome read a more garish,

learn to write, but in the process he might also acquire moral virtues.

Though the earlier manuals helped to crystallize letter writing into set formulas of rather stilted Ciceronian verbiage, gradually in the late sixteenth and early seventeenth centuries there begins to be noticeable in model letters, especially those intended for the use of plain folk, a new note of simplicity of expression. Humor creeps in and the language of daily conversation finds its way into the handbooks. Fine phrases, one must hasten to add, were by no means discarded, in theory or practice, but gradually the colloquial tone grew stronger, to achieve at length a more natural and warmer mode of writing than had earlier been the fashion. Nicholas Breton contributed to this advance in *A Poste with a madde Packet of Letters* (1602), a collection which was enormously popular.[43] More than mere pedestrian letters to be imitated by unimaginative folk, Breton's specimens took the form of familiar essays, often distinctly bourgeois in tone.[44] At times whimsical or gay, Breton remembers to teach such virtues as thrift, industry, and sobriety. Yet his letters not only were read as light essays but served as well for models of correspondence and helped to further the familiar style.

The homespun style, suggested by Breton, was imitated by Gervase Markham, industrious compiler of utilitarian treatises, in *Hobsons Horse-load of Letters.*[45] A happy medium between affected ornamentation and dull matter-of-factness is the avowed aim of the compiler, who boasts of the worthiness of a work free "from

and pibald stile in any scribling Inkhornist; or tasted a more vnsavory slaumpaump of wordes, and sentences in any sluttish Pamfletter; that denounceth not defiance against the rules of Oratory, and the directions of the English Secretary."—R. B. McKerrow (ed.). *The Works of Thomas Nashe,* 5 vols. (London, 1904-10), V, 94.

[43] With its subsequent enlargements, this collection went through at least eleven editions by 1637.

[44] Professor Thompson in his essay on "Familiar Letters," *op. cit.,* pp. 105-6, observes that Breton's letters have in them "the middle-class prejudices that color many of the late English courtesy books."

[45] *Hobsons Horse-load of Letters: Or, A President for Epistles. The First Part. Being a most exact Method for men, of what quality soeuer, how to indight, according to the forme of these times, whether it be for serious Negotiations, priuate businesses, amorous accomplishment, wanton merriment, or the defence of Honour and Reputation.* Title quoted from the edition of 1617. An exemplar of an edition of 1613 is preserved in the Bodleian Library. The second part was first printed in 1614.

the lisping affectation of ill embrodered speech, or from the rude plainnesse of too much dulnesse.''[46] Though Markham tries to give his work an aristocratic tone by inserting a large number of letters of state and challenges to combat, even going so far as to prescribe a "Challenge, which may bee sent from one King vnto another,"[47] the chief interest of the book is in its honest kersey phrases. Particularly in the second part Markham abandons knightly cartels and high-flown letters that kings might use and inserts plain speech for merchants, apprentices, schoolboys, women, and lovers. The letters, even those that are jocular, are full of common sense and are clearly and directly expressed. Once more Markham calls attention to his simplicity of style, neither too plain nor too fancy:

. . . here are no farre fetcht Phrases to pusle and amaze people, nor any so rude and barbarous to distate the nobler spirits, but an euen & common language spoken vsually, and vnderstood of euery body, which the noble Roman (the glory of this kind) directly chargeth that we follow the ancient customes and behauior, but the present words and phrases.   [Sigs. I 2-I 2ᵛ.]

In this statement Markham seeks to justify the simple style demanded by plain-thinking people and to reconcile it with the point of view of those who still insisted upon following the rhetorical models of Cicero and Quintilian as laid down in both Continental and English works on epistolary style.

Fascinating pictures of seventeenth-century life may be reconstructed from clues furnished by *Hobsons Horse-load of Letters.* A father's letters about his son's studies at the university, the son's replies, an inquiry from a master on vacation in the country to his steward in London, a chapman's complaint to a tradesman of London about a shipment of goods—[48] these are some of the useful matters about which the writers concern themselves. One

---

[46] Preface, "To The Reader : of what quality soeuer."   [47] Sig. C 3ᵛ.

[48] This letter is closely akin to modern adjustment letters in its emphasis on good will. The chapman writes tartly to complain that a shipment of goods which he had ordered had not been brought by the carrier. He wonders if the merchant doubts his credit. The latter replies in the smoothest of tones in order to placate his customer :

"Truly it much grieues me you were so disappointed, and the negligence of my man

letter so clearly sets forth bourgeois pride in the practical that it deserves quotation, for if this specimen did not furnish the precise model for many such statements, at least its ideas have become a commonplace of middle-class thinking. It is the reply of an apprentice to his brother at Eton, who had written reproaching him for besmirching himself with trade when he might be climbing "vp to the flowrie hill of Pernassus" instead of striving to see that he has a "body richly cloathed," while he lets "the mind his Master go stark naked."[49] The apprentice retorts sarcastically that he has work more useful than traveling "vp Pernassus to pick flowers." And he makes the business man's jibe at the poverty of scholars, a poverty which to him is always proof of the impractical folly of merely theoretical learning :

Surely Brother, your Schollers haue but a poore crop in it without their mind (which no body can be witnesse to) be so well trapped, I am sure their bodies are bare inough ; and their clothes none of the whollest. It may be the sweetnesse of the water at Helicon haue made them loue it euer since ; for few of them can attaine to beere : And truly I do thinke wee doe really and indeede, enioy those fine and flourishing gardens you speake off, and you Schollers in conceit and discriptions : how euer Brother, enioy your happinesse, which with many wishes of much increase I louingly wish vnto you ; and I must be contented with my lot, which I will fashion to as neere a degree to goodnesse and generosnesse (led by your example) as the weakenesse of my minde will giue me leaue, and cease not to loue him who doth

---

went not away vnpunished, by whose default the Carrier went without them. Beleeue me on my word, and I accompt my selfe happier in being Master of that then much riches, no feare of paiment nor the least doubt of your estate was any hindrance to it. I haue well knowne you by others, and haue had so much experience in you my selfe, that you shall sooner want occasions for wares, then I confidence to trust you : your neighbours speake much good of you, and all men giue you a faire report, which makes me happy both in your custome and friendship. If sinister occasions shall by any time happen (as while wee are here they are incident vnto vs) I shal rather pittie your fortunes, then call your faire dealing into question : and know, wee are all men accountable euery instant for all our possessions. The Carrier this weeke brings those Commodities, better and more vendable you neuer had of me, and I verily beleeue, the Gentlemen will thinke themselues well repayed for their stay, with the exceeding goodnesse and lastingnesse of the ware. For our reckonings, at more leisure I will peruse and send them, in whose place receiue my kindest Commendations and entreaty for my mans carelesnesse. Your friend to his power, L. W."—Sigs. N 2-N 2ᵛ.

[49] Sig. I 4ᵛ.

most heartily loue you, and pray, you liue long, to be a comfort and stay to our Family. Your truly louing Brother. S. H. [Sigs. K 1-K 1v.]

The popular interest in handbooks of letters was enormous, and once compilers had learned the trick of providing in the same form amusing essays and useful models, collections further multiplied. Shortly after the second edition of *Hobsons Horse-load of Letters*, there appeared *Conceyted Letters, Newly Layde Open: Or A Most Excellent Bundle Of New Wit, Wherin Is Knit Vp Together All the perfections of arte of Episteling, by which the most ignorant may with much modestie talke and argue with the best Learned. A Worke Varying From The nature of former Presidents* (1618).[50] The psychology employed in this appeal is precisely that of modern correspondence schools and the sundry books which promise to make the student fit for any social or professional occasion. Certainly no seventeenth-century tradesman would have found it easy to resist an equipment which would make him capable of writing to or arguing with the most learned. The preface seeks still further to remove any doubt about the usefulness of the work:

Three things (Iuditiall Reader) make Books, and the publication of Bookes aboue good; excellent, to wit, *Necessitie, Vtility & Implicity*, & where any one of these are figured, no doubt but the Image is most comely, then how much more where all are contained, not *Helens* thirty perfections can challenge more admiration, and though it may sauor of Ostentation, to say this Pamphlet hath all, yet it shall not be against truth to approue the subiect, more then a Master, yea euen the soueraigne of all: . . .

Nicholas Breton undoubtedly is responsible for the popularization, in the early seventeenth century, of the handbook of familiar letters, so numerous after the publication of his first collection. His very title was adapted by a certain I. W. who published *A Speedie Poste With certaine New Letters. Or, The first fruits of new Conceits, neuer yet disclosed. Now published for the helpe of such as are desirous to learne to write Letters* (1629).[51] Another popular letter

---

[50] Another edition was published in 1632. The *Short Title Catalogue* attributes the collection to Breton, though Markham seems to have had a hand in the compilation. The preface to the reader is signed "I. M."

[51] Noticed by Thompson, *op. cit.*, pp. 105 ff. I. W. boasts in the epistle to the reader that "the varietie of matters and their answers are more capable to content the learned,

book in the Breton vein was M. R.'s *A President For Young Pen-Men. Or The Letter-Writer. Containing Letters of sundry sortes, with their seuerall Answers. Full of Variety, Delight, and Pleasure, and most necessary for the instruction of those that can write, but haue not the Guift of enditing* (1615). In a brief preface to the reader, the compiler observes that

In these latter times euery Ballad-maker will be a Poet, as if euery Pedler would seeme a Merchaunt, and euery Pettifogger a Lawyer : so hee that can scarce endite a Letter, will take vpon him to be a Secretarie : For myselfe, I dare not be so sawcy, as to put such a Title to my Book ; onely this I haue heere written a few Letters, which, I hope, are so composed as will be presidents for yong pen men, and not displeasing to elder yeeres : . . .

A combination of letter book and guide to practical wisdom was provided by Thomas Gainsford in *The Secretaries Studie: Containing New familiar Epistles: Or Directions, for the formall, orderly, and iudicious inditing of Letters* (1616). Although Gainsford uses the epistolary form with the evident intention of furnishing models for letter writers, he turns the letters into essays containing much prudential counsel. Under such headings as "Household Letters" he gives advice on domestic affairs. Under "Chiding Letters" are epistolary essays of reproval for various sins repugnant to the tradesman : drunkenness, frivolity, gaming, dishonesty in a servant. A letter book by "S. S. Gent.," *The Secretaries Studie* (1652), is based on Gainsford's collection.[52] The manual of letter writing and of conversation long continued to be popular ; when William London published his *Catalogue Of The most vendible Books in*

---

then the ignorant, howsoeuer, vseful to both, and chiefly necessary to instruct the youth, in the true methode of inditing and composing Letters."

Presumably this is the same "I. W. Gent." who brought out in 1622 a handbook for merchants, entitled *The Merchants Hand-Maide; or a booke containing very necessarie and compendious tables for the speedie casting vp . . . of any commodities whatsoeuer.*

[52] There were numerous other letter books in this period, many of them translated from foreign languages and designed for aristocratic audiences. *See* Watson, *The English Grammar Schools to 1660*, pp. 418-19.

An effort to attract readers by emphasizing the love interest is discernible in *Cupids Messenger: Or, A trusty Friend stored with sundry sorts of serious, wittie, pleasant, amorous, and delightfull Letters. . . . Newly written* (1629). Possibly it is by the author of *Cupids Schoole.* Although it purports to be a book of love letters, it includes letters on other subjects. As in many similar collections, old letters often do duty with but slight alter-

England in 1657, handbooks including such "helps" occupied a prominent place in his list.[53]

In the Renaissance, learning was fashionable, and all ranks were pleased to lard their discourse, written or spoken, with its evidences. Hence makers of books arose to supply quantities of easy erudition. The demand for works which would furnish the maximum amount of learned allusion explains the large number of books containing wise saws, "similes," quotations from good literature, classical references, and historical anecdotes. Printers were quick to publish works which were merely glorified notebooks of miscellaneous lore, such as schoolmasters had long labored to persuade their charges to keep. Indeed, the keeping of commonplace books in which pupils should enter fine sentences

ation. Here, for example, may be found the complaint of a chapman in the country to a London tradesman which had been used in Markham's *Hobsons Horse-load of Letters.*

In 1640 John Massinger brought out *The Secretary in Fashion: Or, A Compendious and Refined way of Expression in all manner of Letters. Composed in French By P. Sr de la Serre, Historiographer of France. And Translated into English, by John Massinger, Gent.* In an epistle to the reader, Massinger hopes that if his book is not accepted, the reader may "be condemned to the Reading of the English Secretary, as long as thou livest." He criticizes Breton's letters as vulgar and is equally severe on those of Jean Louis Guez, Sieur de Balzac, which had appeared in several English translations.

[53] E. g., London lists such works as the following:

"*Art of Memory,* a cure for weak Memory, usefull to all persons, from the Crown to the Clown."—Sig. T 4.

"*The Achademy of Eloquence,* containing a compleat English Rhetorique exemplified, with common places and formes, digested into an easie and Methodicall way to speak and write fluently according to the mode of the present times; with Letters both Amorous and Moral, upon emergent occasions."—Sig. T 4.

"*The Achademy of Complements* wherein Ladies, Gentlewomen, Scholars, and Strangers, may accomodate their courtly practice with gentle Ceremonies; complementall, amorous high expressions, and forms of speaking and writing of Letters most in fashion, with excellent similitudes, comparisons, fancies, and devices; with a Table resolving the most delightfull fictions of Heathen Poets."—Sig. T 4ᵛ.

"*An English Dictionary,* or an Interpreter of hard english words, enabling as well Ladies and Gentlewomen, young Scholars, Merchants, and others to understand the most hard words, for the more speedy attaining an ellegancy in speaking and writing."—Sig. U 3.

"*The Theatre of Complements,* or art of eloquence, and most refined way of speaking."—Sig. Y 4ᵛ.

"*Wits interpreter.* The English Parnassus, or a guid to those admirable accomplishments that furnish our English Gentry, in the most acceptable qualifications of discourse, or writings: The mystery of eloquence Theatre of court-ship: Inditer of letters alamode."—Sig. Z 1.

and worthy facts was an important element in grammar-school education. From their notebooks, schoolboys could draw much of the learned verbiage which they wove into their orations and epistles. This training in collecting classical allusions, proverbial wisdom, and useful bits of information was retained in later life by many an Elizabethan who kept his notebook by him. In conversation, public speeches, letters, and published works, he delighted in using such accumulated learning. Polonius in his advice to Laertes might have been reading aphorisms from his notebook, or from some volume published to supply what his notebook lacked. Both the schoolboy and the adult were amply provided with epitomes of information, which included a deal of aphoristic lore.[54] From the learned scholar to the busiest of merchants, all classes used these epitomes and handbooks, which furnished at least the semblance of learning.[55]

The later years of the sixteenth century saw a multiplication of books of aphorisms, similes, and flowers of rhetoric and history— a type of epitomized learning which scholars and educationists for generations had urged upon all who sought the fountains of erudition.[56] Originating as academic and aristocratic works, such compilations gained favor during the latter half of the sixteenth

---

[54] *See* Watson, *op. cit.*, pp. 428 ff. Mr. Watson lists many of the epitomes used in the schools.

[55] F. L. Schoell, *Études sur l'Humanisme Continental en Angleterre à la fin de la Renaissance* (Paris, 1926), *passim*, has shown that the Elizabethans were greatly indebted to compilations for many allusions to and apparent familiarity with foreign literature. *See also* Mr. Schoell's "G. Chapman's 'Commonplace Book,'" *Modern Philology*, XVII (1919-20), 199-218. He shows that Chapman is much indebted to books of quotations, especially to such works as Erasmus' *Parabolae* and the *Adagia*. Erasmus had urged youths to collect similes, metaphors, and proverbs for use in poems and orations. McKerrow, *Works of Thomas Nashe*, V, 112-15, shows that much of Nashe's learned reference came from collections of similes and from his commonplace book. Nashe used such sources for his classical quotations as Erasmus' *Parabolae*, the *De Incertitudine et Vanitate Scientiarum*, and other collections which McKerrow does not identify. Many Latin quotations came from Lily's *Grammar*. Leonhard Culmann's *Sententiae Pueriles* and the *Pueriles Confabulatiunculae*, attributed to Evaldus Gallus, a Dutch schoolmaster, were available. Erasmus' *Colloquia Familiaria* was, of course, popular. Similes, or "similitudes," were recommended in such works as Wilson's *Art of Rhetoric* and Puttenham's *Art of Poesie*.

[56] Erasmus had lent his great authority, both by precept and practice, to the compilation of aphorisms. Sixteenth-century writers on rhetoric and education strongly recommended the reading and gathering of aphorisms, which were regarded as help-

century until, by the end of the century, they were widely popular, not only with cultured readers, but also with busy middle-class folk who prized them because of their concentrated wisdom, their good morality, and their general utility as instruments of instruction.

No citizen would have questioned the value of the Latin adages and apothegms of Erasmus in the grammar-school curriculum, and schoolboys who cut their intellectual teeth on such fare grew up into earnest citizens who set great store by similar learning translated and presented in more palatable form.[57] For instance, William Baldwin, proof reader, preacher, and poet, was sufficiently alert to the tastes of the public to prepare *A treatise of Morall Phylosophie, contaynyng the sayinges of the wyse* (1547), a work which a scholar has recently described as "one of the most popular books in England,"[58] and which the compiler recommended as useful "to helpe and encourage other, whom eyther ignoraunce or neglygence holdeth backe."[59] This book, containing proverbs, similes and adages (in part from Erasmus), precepts, and fragments of the lives and sayings of the classic philosophers, was soon augmented by Thomas Palfreyman and was so widely read during the next century that it went through at least eighteen editions before 1640. One reason for its popularity was its compact wisdom expressed in neat sententious statements. For the Elizabethans liked their learning spoken trippingly from the tongue. Hence proverbs were greatly esteemed and even Chaucer was so prized for his good "sentences" that one printer, for the greater convenience of the reader, marked his aphorisms in the margin of the text.[60] An age that would read Chaucer for his proverbs would naturally be eager for anthologies and compilations of

---

ful both to the style and matter of one's speech or writing. *See* M. P. Tilley, *Elizabethan Proverb Lore in Lyly's Euphues and in Pettie's Petite Pallace with Parallels from Shakespeare,* University of Michigan Publications in Language and Literature, II (1926), 14-27.

[57] For an indication of the way Erasmus furnished material for compilers of wisdom-literature in English, see C. R. Baskervill, "Taverner's *Garden of Wisdom* and the *Apophthegmata* of Erasmus," *Studies in Philology,* XXIX (1932), 149-59.

[58] D. T. Starnes, "Sir Thomas Elyot and the 'Sayings of the Philosophers,' " University of Texas Studies in English, XIII (1933), 17.

[59] Edition of 1547, sig. I 1.

[60] *See* Louis B. Wright, "William Painter and the Vogue of Chaucer as a Moral Teacher," *Modern Philology,* XXXI (1933-34), 165-74.

Precept
aphorisms

concise wisdom of this nature. Printers saw to it that there was no lack.

More strictly concerned with the taste of the middle class than were some of the other compilers, Robert Greene, with an eye to popular favor, produced *The Royal Exchange. Contayning sundry Aphorismes of Phylosophie, and golden principles of Morrall and naturall Quadruplicities* (1590).[61] This work, set forth with a flattering dedication to the lord mayor and the sheriffs of London, is a collection of wise observations heavily glossed with good morality. Greene departed from his original sufficiently to draw on Chaucer, whom he is always fond of quoting, in a passage characteristic of the book :

Olde men, (saith Sir Iefferie Chawcer,) are then in their right vaine, when they haue *In diebus illis* in theyr mouth : telling what passed long agoe, what warres they haue seene, what charitie, what cheapenes of victuals, alwaies blaming the time present, though neuer so fruitful. Foure thinges doo belong vnto olde men. 1. To speake profitablie. 2. To counsayle. 3. To set enemies at concorde. 4. And to instruct them which are ignoraunt. [Sig. I 2ᵛ.]

Precepts of this sort, Greene assured the lord mayor and citizens, would teach the London tradesman "the duety of a Christian, the offyce of a Ruler, the calling of a Cittizen."

The "quadruplicities" found in Greene's *Royal Exchange* are examples of a strange fad for numerically grouped aphorisms, which were popular for many years. Nicholas Breton was the author of a little pamphlet called *The Figure Of Foure, Or A Handfull of sweet Flowers: Gathered out of diuers good Grounds, and set together in this little Garden within The Figure of Foure.*[62] In groups of fours are gathered such pearls of wisdom as these :

Scoffe not a wise Speech in a meane man, scorne not Vertue in a poore habit, refuse not good wine in a wooddern cup, nor deny not to

---

[61] *The Royal Exchange. Contayning sundry Aphorismes of Phylosophie, and golden principles of Morrall and naturall Quadruplicities. Vnder pleasant and effectuall sentences, dyscouering such strange definitions, deuisions, and distinctions of vertue and vice, as may please the grauest Cittizens, or youngest Courtiers. Fyrst written in Italian, and dedicated to the Signorie of Venice, nowe translated into Englishe, and offered to the Cittie of London* (1590).

[62] Title quoted from the presumably unique copy in the Huntington Library, dated 1631. The title was entered in the *Stationers' Register* in 1597.

take currant money out of a course canuasse bag.   [Sig. B 2ᵛ.]

Loue not a Tale of Robin Hood and his bow, beat not thy braines about the reading of a Riddle, listen to no Ballads of the Fox and the Crow, nor giue credit to newes till they be halfe a yeare old. [Sig. B 3.]

Keepe thy pocket from the Cut-purse, thy stable from the Theefe, thy body from a Harlot, and thy hand from a Bond.   [Sig. B 3ᵛ.]

Such pamphlets, though extant specimens are very rare, seem to have enjoyed a considerable vogue. The Huntington Library has a small octavo volume in which eight pamphlets, including the foregoing example from Breton, are preserved.[63] All contain homely bits of proverbial advice or information, occasionally spiced with humor of a sort to appeal to bourgeois readers.

Of all the handbooks of wisdom, the one having the greatest popular acceptance was *Politeuphuia, Wits Common-Wealth* (1597), edited by a shrewd publisher, Nicholas Ling. By about 1630 a twelfth edition had appeared. In a preface to the reader, Ling announces that the purpose of the work is to aid discourse and to give the reader profound utterance, without, he implies, too much exertion. Here the man in the street could crib a wise-sounding speech and a multitude of learned allusions. In a dedication to "Maister I. B." (perhaps John Bodenham, a compiler of similar material), Ling describes his book as a "burden of wit," "compendiously drawne from infinite varietie, diuine, historicall, poeticall, politique, morrall, and humane."[64] The appetite of the masses for easy learning could find in such a work adequate appeasement. The book is divided into sections, such as "Of God,"

---

[63] Included in the group, in addition to the Breton item already cited, are the following :

   (1) *The Figure Of Foure . . . The second part* (1626).

   (2) *The Figure Of Foure: Being a New Booke, Containing many merry Conceits, which will yield both Pleasure and Profit to all that reads or heare it. The Last Part* (1653).

   (3) *The Figure of Three: Or, A Patterne of good Counsell. Gathered for the Delight of the well disposed* (1636).

   (4) Martin Parker, *The Figure Of Five* [date clipped].

   (5) Martin Parker, *The Figure Of Seven. Very Pleasant to Reade, Plaine to Vnderstand, And Profitable to Practise* (1647).

   (6) D. N., *The Figure Of Six. Containing these Six things; Wit, Mirth, Pleasure, pretty Observations, new Conceits, and merry Jests* (1652).

   (7) D. N., *The Figure Of Six* (1654).

[64] Quoted from the dedication of the edition of 1598.

popular aphoristic wisdom books

"Of Heauen," "Of Vertue," "Of Hell," "Of Schoole," and many others treating of abstract virtues and vices. After a definition of the topic-heading, appropriate aphorisms bearing on the subject follow. Perhaps it is significant that Bacon's first collection of *Essays* appeared in the same year as *Politeuphuia* and bore an outward similarity in subject, arrangement, and aphoristic treatment. Bacon's utilitarian point of view, his concise statements of patent truths, his abundance of illustration and learned allusion, so appealing to an age that delighted in having learning reduced to the space of a handbook, may account for the enormous popularity of his *Essays* during the next fifty years. Many a reader undoubtedly kept Bacon's *Essays* by him as a source for such allusions as he also drew from *Politeuphuia* and kindred works.

Francis Meres contributed to what seems to have been a definitely planned series of popular aphoristic wisdom books (of which *Politeuphuia* was the first), with his own *Palladis Tamia. Wits Treasury Being the Second part of Wits Common wealth* (1598), which was followed in the next year by Robert Allot's *Wits Theater of the little World* (1599).[65] *Palladis Tamia* contains hundreds of useful similes ; for example, under the section on "Idlenesse," one learns that "As rust doth putrifie iron : so idlenesse doth corrupt the wit and disposition of man," or that "Standing water is sooner frozen, then the running streame ; he that sitteth is more subiect to sleepe, then he that walketh : so the idle man is farre more subiect to be ouercome of vice, then he that is exercised."[66] When Meres is finally done with his theme, the reader has been given an infinite choice of similitudes explaining all the qualities of idleness. So it is with each topic. *Wits Theater*, on the other hand, approaches the subject historically. Whatever the theme, innumerable historical examples are cited. Under a section headed "Of Prodigality," for example, Cleopatra, Lucullus, and a host of others are called up to bear witness by example to the sin of prodigality. With such handbooks as Ling, Meres, and Allot furnished in their *Wits Commonwealth* series, everyone, from the child in school to the merchant in the Royal Exchange, could utter his sentences with gravity and learning. Provided with such books, one did not need

---

[65] Cf. Starnes, *op. cit.*, pp. 23-25.   [66] Fol. 303.

to labor through pagan writers in search of apt phrases. Speeches, like that heard by Jack Wilton at Wittenberg, composed by the emptying of notebooks and "all by patch & by peecemeale stolne out of *Tully*,"[67] might now be more easily put together with the help of handbooks. Dozens of works similar to those already described made such creation easy.[68] The air of learning blew alike

---

[67] McKerrow, *op. cit.*, II, 246.

[68] Typical examples of other collections of aphorisms and bits of concise learning, which seem to have made an appeal to middle-class readers, are the following :

H. C., *The Forrest Of Fancy. Wherein Is Conteined Very prety Apothegmes, and pleasaut histories, both in meeter and prose, Songes, Sonets, Epigrams and Epistles, of diuerse matter and in diuerse manner. With sundry other deuises, no lesse pithye then pleasaunt and profytable* (1579). The author in an epistle to the reader promises a diversity of material so that even "the common sorte whose learning nor capacity cannot attaine to the full perfection or perfecte vnderstanding of such deepe misteries" can find something of use. The work contains verses and epistles, tales and short anecdotes, usually of an admonishing sort, urging the reader to virtue and good conduct.

William Fiston, *The Welspring of Wittie Conceites: Containing, A Methode, aswell to speake, as to endight (aptly and eloquently of sundrie Matters: as (also) see [sic] great varietie of pithy Sentences, vertuous sayings, and right Morall Instructions: No lesse pleasaunt to be read, then profitable to be practised, either in familiar speech, or by writing, in Epistles and Letters. Out of Italian, by W. Phist. Student* (1584). An anthology of aphorisms, similar to the books of similes. The author hopes the work will be "to the helpe and profit of many English Readers : & not anything hurtful to the learned, in other languages." —Sig. A 3ᵛ.

S. R., *The Choise of Change: Containing the Triplicity of Diuinitie, Philosophie, and Poetrie. Short for memorie, Profitable for Knowledge, and Necessarie for Maners: Whereby the Learned may be confirmed, the Ignorant instructed, and all Men generally recreated. Newly set foorth by S. R. Gent. and Student in the Vniuersitie of Cambridge* (1585). A vast array of moralistic aphorisms arranged in triplets.

Leonard Wright, *A Display of dutie, dect with sage sayings, pythie to reade, delightfull to heare, and profitable to practice, By L. Wright. Good nurture leadeth the way vnto vertue, and discreet behauiour plaineth the path to felicitie* (1589). Pious advice on conduct and duty to the state, followed by "certaine prety notes, and pleasant conceits"—a collection of jocular aphorisms, whose avowed purpose is "to beat down vice, and further vnto vertue."

Robert Hichcock (trans.), *The Quintessence of Wit, being A corrant comfort of conceites, Maximes, and poleticke deuises, selected and gathered together by Francisco Sansouino* (1590).

Anthony Fletcher, *Certaine very proper, and most profitable Similes, wherein sundrie, and very many most foule vices . . . are displaied* (1595).

Robert Cawdrey, *A Treasurie Or Store-house of Similies* (1600).

W. S., *The Country-mans Commonwealth. Containing diuers golden Sentences, very usefull and profitable both to read and practise* [1633-40?]. This late manifestation of the "Commonwealth" series of wisdom books is preserved in the Huntington Library. It contains many of the familiar proverbs as old as John Heywood's compilation. Many especially stress the virtues of thrift and industry ; e.g., p. 17 :

through the cloister and the market place, but the learning of the average citizen came more often than not from epitomes and outlines.

The value of history as material for culture was a convention of Renaissance educational theory,[69] and a knowledge of historical facts was sufficient to mark a man as well-read and cultivated. Moreover, history was considered useful as a means of inducing general wisdom. Richard Brathwaite in *The English Gentleman* commends history to young men as valuable "not onely in respect of discourse, but in respect of discipline and civill society."[70] The middle class believed implicitly in this utility of history and sought easy means of acquiring historical information by the use of epitomes and handbooks of chronologies. Thomas Heywood, most typical of the exponents of middle-class ideals, realized this demand and made an effort to capitalize on the popularity of condensed biographies and histories.[71] George Snell in *The Right Teaching Of Useful Knowledg* (1649) advocated the use of historical epitomes and tabulated forms as the ideal system for the busy man whose method of learning must be agreeable with "the dailie business of actual life." From an early date handbook history had been popular with the learned and unlearned alike. Epitomes such as Nicholas Bownd's edition of John More's *A Table From The Beginning of the world to this day* (1593)[72] provided tabular chronologies designed for the easy

---

"He that hopes to thriue,
    must rise at fiue :
He that hath thriuen,
    may lie till seuen :
But he that will neuer thriue,
    may lie till eleuen."

Most of the seventeenth-century epigram writers followed the flippant cavalier tradition, but a few provided assortments of bourgeois maxims. Such a collection is Robert Chamberlain's *Nocturnall Lucubrations: Or Meditations Diuine and Morall. Whereunto are added Epigrams And Epitaphs* (1638), which contains a good deal of pragmatic advice of the Poor Richard sort.

[69] *See* Chap. IX, *infra.*

[70] Edition of 1641, p. 117.

[71] Cf. Louis B. Wright, "Heywood and the Popularizing of History," *Modern Language Notes*, XLIII (1928), 287-93.

[72] *A Table From The Beginning of the world to this day. Wherein is declared in what yeere of the World euery thing was done, both in the Scriptures mentioned, and also in prophane matters.*

reference of busy people. The digests of history were sometimes more elaborate, as in the case of J. Philippson's *The Key of Historie* (1627),[73] which put into compendious form the history of Babylon, Persia, Greece, and Rome, besides furnishing explanations of obscure terms and place names. This work was a textbook as well as a general compendium for reference. The translator states in his preface a desire to make his style simple and direct "to satisfie a meere English Reader." This epitome was long used; later editions appeared in 1631, 1635, and 1661. The popularity of historical summaries at the beginning of the seventeenth century is attested by William Fulbecke in *An Historicall Collection Of The Continuall Factions, Tumults, and Massacres of the Romans and Italians* (1601); the epistle to the reader declares that "histories are now in speciall request" and that they are "teachers of vertuous life, good conuersation, discreete behauiour, politicke gouernement, conuenient enterprises, aduised proceedings, warie defences, grounded experience, and refined wisedome."

An outline of history and geography, so compact yet inclusive that it might shame the industry of modern outline-makers, was the learned Peter Heylin's *Microcosmus, Or A Little Description Of The Great World. A Treatise Historicall, Geographicall, Politicall, Theologicall* (1621). Heylin, who knew that his audience wanted a certain amount of entertainment along with its information, provided sufficient picturesque detail and observation to hold the reader's interest.[74] Brevity and simplicity of style, such as would

---

Written by that worthy member of the Church of God, M. Iohn More Preacher at Norwich. Seene and allowed by publike authoritie (Cambridge, 1593). The work is dedicated to the Bishop of Norwich and the mayor and aldermen of that town.

[73] *The Key of Historie. Or, A most methodicall Abridgement of the foure chiefe Monarchies, Babylon, Persia, Greece, and Rome, Being a generall and compendious Chronicle from the Flood. Digested into three bookes. Whereunto is added a marginall Chronologie of euery Roman Emperors Raigne, and of all the most memorable persons and accidents. Together with briefe illustrations vpon the more obscure names, places, and Offices. With a directory table for the more profitable reading of History. Written by that excellent and most learned man Iohn Sleidan* (1627). Philippson wrote under the name of John Sleidan.

[74] *See* Heylin's statement in the preface: "I know men are diuersly humoured, either according to their constitution or profession: to please all were impossible, to endeauour a generall satisfaction not amisse. I haue therefore entermingled with Geographie and History (which are my chiefe scope) many conclusions of pollicie: the diuersities, and different tenents of religions: Here I play the Heralt in matters both of blazon and Genealogies, there the Statist in matters of revennew and gouernment;

enable the busy reader to find the kernel of truth without winnowing it from a mass of chaffy verbiage, were Heylin's aims, for the seventeenth-century citizen was beginning to ask for facts instead of verbal gymnastics. Heylin gives warning that his work is for earnest readers rather than those who delight in Lylian word-juggling :

If itching eares which commonly follow shallow iudgements expect contradictory epithites, fustian phrases or a stile which no common capacity can goe ouer, I professe no satisfaction for them. I had rather informe the minde then please the hearing, and could wish my booke were laid rather next my readers heart then hung like a Iewell in his eare. Againe the brevitie which I vse, and the subiect concerning which I write are not capable of strong lines, and elegant raptures.[75]

The average reader, anxious to learn in the shortest time about the Romans, the early Britons, or the new Americans could find in this outline the essential facts desired. Furthermore, if his curiosity was great, he could find here also a critical bibliography, which would guide him to further and more learned reading. Although it is doubtful whether Heylin, a Laudian partisan in controversy, had much interest in the intellectual welfare of tradesmen and plain citizens, yet he nevertheless compiled a book which all classes, especially those who had little time for learning, would find unusually helpful. And it is clear that the public took advantage of the merits of the *Microcosmus*, because an eighth edition was required in 1639.

Since self-education and home study made a strong appeal to the aspiring members of the middle class, handbooks were designed for those who wished to teach themselves. Robert Record, one of the most learned of sixteenth-century textbook makers, declares in the preface to the reader of *The Ground Of Arts: Teaching The*

---

in some places an Astronomer, in others a Chronographer. I haue enterlaced those more serious affaires with Poeticall fables, and other pleasant relations ; yet so that neither these will bee offensiue to graver men, nor the serious matters tedious to the younger sort : but both shall pleasantly lead along all readers, that they may steale to the end before they thinke they are at the beginning. Finally, if mixing pleasure with profit, I doe not fully hit the nayle on the head, yet I hope suiting my selfe to all humours, I shall at last please some."

[75] Preface.

Perfect worke and practise of Arithmeticke:[76]

I doubt not but some will like this my Booke aboue any other English Arithmeticke hitherto written, and namely such as shall lacke instructers, for whose sake I haue so plainly set forth the Examples, as no Booke that I haue seen hath done hitherto: which thing shall be great ease to the rude Readers.

Therefore (gentle Reader) though this Booke can be but small aid to the learned sort, yet vnto the simple ignorant (which needeth most help) it may be a good furtherance and meane vnto knowledge.

Peter Bales promised in his *Writing Schoolemaister* [1590?] that orthography could be learned "by the right vse of this Booke without a Schoolemaster." The table of contents of Thomas Blundeville's . . . *Exercises, containing eight Treatises . . . verie necessarie to be read and learned of all yoong Gentlemen that haue not bene exercised in such disciplines, and yet are desirous to haue knowledge as well in Cosmographie, Astronomie, and Geographie, as also in the Arte of Navigation* (1597),[77] likewise promises "First, a very easie Arithmeticke so plainely written as any man of a meane capacitie may easily learn the same without the helpe of any teacher." Statements like the foregoing indicate something more than the natural desire of authors, prompted by booksellers, to advertise their works, for throughout the sixteenth and seventeenth centuries many scholarly writers and teachers displayed a sincere feeling of obligation to make learning available to those whose equipment and opportunity for formal study had been limited.[78]

The modern correspondence school is forecast in an advertisement following the title-page of Thomas Clay's *Briefe, Easie, and necessarie Tables, for the Valuation of Leases, Annuities, and Purchases* (1622), in which he not only offers to teach mathematics, navigation, and such studies, but also assures the reader that "Such as are desirous to attaine to knowledge in any of these faculties by their owne study; haue Bookes ready written of any the said

---

[76] Edition of 1623. The first edition appeared in 1542. By 1640 fourteen editions had been printed.

[77] This is the second edition. The first edition appeared in 1594. A seventh edition had been published by 1636 and another issue came out in 1638. Blundeville dedicated his labors to the interest of "young Gentlemen and seamen."

[78] *See* Chap. X, *infra.*

Subiects, applied to the vse of the best Instruments now in request." The most elaborate, as well as the favorite, among the
textbooks designed for home study was Edmund (or Edward)[79]
Coote's *The English Schoole-Master* (1596). This is an important
treatise in the history of self-education. The British Museum has
an edition of 1636, "now the 25th. time imprinted." An edition
of 1684 bears the legend, "now the 42th time printed." The last
edition recorded in the British Museum Catalogue is that of 1692.
Yet in spite of the numerous printings, the British Museum possesses only seven of the editions, and the *Short Title Catalogue* lists
only seven extant editions before 1640. Obviously, since it was
designed to make learning easy for the tradesman class, the
treatise was literally worn out with use. It was a handbook of
reading, spelling, grammar, arithmetic, and related subjects, not
neglecting the catechism and pious instruction. Coote intended
his book to be useful to schoolmasters who had little preparation,
as well as to those who wanted to teach themselves, particularly
"for an Apprentice, or any other his priuate vse," as he is careful to emphasize on the title-page of the edition of 1636, which
also has a significant "Preface for direction to the Reader":

. . . I am now therefore to direct my speech to the vnskilfull, which
desire to make vse of it, for their owne priuate benefit; and to such
men and women of trade, as Taylors, Weavers, Shoppe-keepers, Seam-
sters, and such others, as haue vndertaken the charge of teaching
others; . . . If peradventure for 2 or 3 daies at the first it may seeme
somewhat hard or strange vnto thee, yet be not discouraged, neither
cast it from thee: so if thou take diligent paines in it but 4 daies thou
shalt haue many very profitable things that thou neuer knewest; yea
thou shalt know more of the English tongue, than any man of thy
calling (not being a Grammarian) in *England* knoweth: thou shalt
teach thy Schollers with better commendation and profit than any
other, not following this order, teacheth; and thou mayest sit on thy
shop boord, at thy loomes or at thy needle, and neuer hinder thy worke

---

[79] He is listed as Edmund Coote by Pollard and Redgrave in the *Short Title Catalogue*, but the British Museum Catalogue gives his name as Edward Coote, the same
as that given on the title-page of the twenty-fifth edition, the earliest edition in the
British Museum with a whole title-page. The *Dictionary of National Biography*, sub Coote,
says, "In all the known copies of the 'English School-master' the author is misnamed
Edward Coote."

many technical handbooks

to heare thy Schollers, after thou hast once made this little Booke familiar to thee. . . . If thou canst not find out the meaning and true vse of any rule or word, and hauing none present to helpe thee, make a marke thereat with thy pen or pin, vntill thou meetest with your Minister, or other learned Scholler, of whom thou mayest inquire; and doe not thinke it any discredit to declare thy want, being in a manner pertaining to Grammar, or other such things as those of thy condition are vsually vnacquainted with : rather assure thy selfe, that all wise men will commend thee that desirest knowledge, which many reject . . .   [Sig. A 3.]

The author continues his advice to "my teaching Tradesmen" and recommends his book as the most perfect on the market. Doubtless his claims were justified.

A consideration of purely technical handbooks is outside the scope of the present study, but it is sufficient to say that the professions and trades were well supplied. When John Dee came to praise the translation of Euclid made by the learned merchant, Henry Billingsley, he recommended the work on geometry as a handbook useful to artisans :

Besides this, how many a Common Artificer, is there, in these Realmes of England and Ireland, that dealeth with Numbers, Rule, & Cumpasse : Who, with their owne Skill and experience, already had, will be hable (by these good helpes and informations) to finde out, and deuise, new workes, straunge Engines, and Instrumentes : for sundry purposes in the Common Wealth? or for priuate pleasure? and for the better maintayning of their owne estate?[80]

Perhaps we must credit to Dee's enthusiasm the extraordinary intelligence of common craftsmen implied in the foregoing passage, but it is quite clear that plain citizens of commerce and trade were turning to practical use much erudite information made available to them in handbooks. An excellent illustration of this type of manual is provided by William Bourne's *A booke called the Treasure for traueilers* (1578), a treatise which further popularized and adapted to utilitarian needs principles of geometry revealed

---

[80] Dee's preface to *The Elements Of Geometrie of the most auncient Philosopher Euclide of Megara. Faithfully (now first) translated into the Englishe toung, by H. Billingsley, Citizen of London* (1570), sig. A 4.

in the translation of Euclid.[81] Here travelers could learn how to measure by geometry the heights of buildings and mountains, the extent of land and water, the weight of ships and other bodies. Here also was found much other practical information, including the essentials of navigation and a table of longitudes and latitudes. But of greater interest to us is the author's statement of his purpose and plan to make his work understandable to the unlettered reader. No scholar himself, Bourne describes his station, in the dedication of the book to Sir William Winter, master of the Queen's ordnance, as "a poore Gunner, seruing vnder your worthinesse." If one so simple as he presumes "to open any Science," it is only "to profyte the common wealth," the author further declares in the preface to the reader. Learned men, he complains, find fault when others write books, but they do not sufficiently exert themselves to make useful knowledge available to the commonalty. The object of books, he says in a marginal note, should be to teach the unlearned. Therefore, he is determined to write for their capacity, and he warns the reader not to look for academic terminology, which should be reserved for subjects too abstruse for common understanding. His statement of utilitarian purpose so well expresses the point of view of other handbook-makers that it deserves quotation :

And furthermore, I doo not intende to make any booke to teach them that are cunning & learned : But the only cause of my writing of this booke is, to instruct or teach them that are simple and vnlearned : And therefore notwithstandyng, I shal the better lyke of it, if any learned man should write or set out any booke, as touching these causes, to re-fourme this. And my opinion is this, if that any Booke be set foorth vnto the common people in the world, that then it is to the ende, to teach the symplest sort of people that are not instructed in learned causes. But if that it be any high poynt in learned causes, then it is not for the common sort of people, but to be in learned mens Libraries, and ther-fore as it is not written by a learned man, so in lyke manner you must not looke for fyne or eloquent schole termes, but euen to take the substance of the matter rudely as it is, and more to regarde the neces-

---

[81] Bourne indicates that he used the translation. Preceding the first book of the treatise there is "A briefe note, taken out of M. Dees Mathematical Preface that goeth before Euclides Elementes nowe extant in our Inglish tongue."

sarinesse of the matter, whether it may doe any good to the commonwealth.   [Sig. * 4ᵛ.]

The opinion expressed by Bourne was shared by others, both
scholars and practical men, and, from this time on, technical
handbooks in many fields increased in numbers.

When even seamen were learning the groundwork of their
profession from handbooks, and were navigating by manuals,[82]
we may be sure that other crafts and trades were well supplied
with convenient helps. Merchants, for example, had many books
of computation, tables of interest, polyglot dictionaries, and manuals of similar utility.[83] But in addition to books of such specialized
use as these, there were other works attempting to epitomize all
the practical learning that the merchant's apprentice might need.
One of the best of these mercantile manuals of general information
was *The Marchants Avizo Verie Necessarie For their Sonnes and Seruants,
when they first send them beyond the Seas, as to Spayne and Portingale, or
other Countreyes. Made by their hartie wellwiller in Christ. I. B. Marchant*
(1591). The author, John Browne, a merchant engaged in the
Spanish trade,[84] explains in a dedication to the master and members of the Company of Merchants of Bristol that at first he had

---

[82] *See,* e.g., William Bourne, *A Regiment for the Sea: Conteyning most profitable Rules*
(1754); Captain John Smith, *An Accidence Or The Path-way to Experience, Necessary for
all Young Sea-men* (1626), and *A Sea Grammar* (1627).

[83] *See* I. W., *The Merchants Hand-Maide* (1622); Thomas Clay, *Briefe, Easie, and
necessarie Tables* (1622); William Webster, *Webster's Tables* (2d ed., 1629); [anon.],
The Treasurers Almanacke (1636); Richard Dafforne, *The Apprentices times entertainer
accomptantly, or a methodicall meanes to obtain the exquisite art of accountantship* (1640). (The
latter work is advertised among other technical handbooks in London's *Catalogue*,
sig. EE 1, from which the title is here quoted.) W. C. Hazlitt, *Schools, School-Books,
and Schoolmasters* (London, 1888), pp. 154 ff., mentions the popularity of polyglot
dictionaries.

[84] The dedication of the edition of 1591, preserved in the Huntington Library but
not listed in the *Short Title Catalogue*, is addressed "To the Worshipfull Master Thomas
Aldworth Marchant of the Citie of Bristowe: and to all the Worshipfull companie of
the Marchants of the saide Citie: your bounden in good will Iohn Browne, wisheth
vnto your Worships, felicitie in Heauen, and prosperitie in earth." The dedication
is signed "From my house in Bristow the 26. day of October. 1589. Your Worships
bounden in good will. J. B."

The *Avizo* was licensed in 1589. The *Short Title Catalogue* lists editions in 1607,
1616, and 1640. Doubtless there were others besides these and the hitherto unre-
corded edition represented by the exemplar in the Huntington Library, for the work
was long used by merchants and their apprentices.

made the book only for the private instruction "of me and mine" but had been persuaded to publish it for the good of his brother merchants, whom he wishes thereby to relieve of much worry :

But my chiefe purpose herein is, onely to worke a generall ease to all Marchants : whereby they may the lesse trouble themselues, either with writing, inuention, or thought of these matters. And likewise that it might be some stay to young and weake wits : yeelding them thereby the more freedome of minde toward their other businesse.

He has taken care to order it so that the book may be seen and allowed in other countries, but he adds a marginal suggestion that "If this booke may not bee thought tollerable beyond the Seas : then will it be yet a good exercise and but little labour, for euerie Prentise to copie it all out in writing : and so carie it with him for his instruction." Browne takes occasion here to urge "young nouices" in their correspondence to follow the author's example and "to vse greater breuitie in their writings then commonly they are wont." The text provides practical advice on a variety of subjects, including the means to post mail ahead of one's rivals, the discretion demanded of a foreigner, the technique of bargaining, the necessity of courtesy and forbearance, the value of thrift and sobriety. Even a prayer, discreetly short, "because of Merchants lets and hindrances in long prayer," is furnished. Next follow a series of model letters, tables of weights and measures, specimen accounts and business papers, facts about Portuguese, Spanish, and French wares, and finally, a set of maxims, prudential and moral, together with a sorrowful fable relating the unhappy end of a young lion that failed to take his aged parent's advice. These maxims epitomize the bourgeois philosophy that virtue pays in things of this world. Indeed, the very first one commands the youth who would be successful to "seeke the kingdome of God and the righteousnesse thereof : and then all things shall bee giuen thee that thou hast neede of." Then come other precepts which mix piety with shrewd observations of things as they are :

Applie thy selfe vnto labour while thou art young, least in thine old age thy bodie become full of diseases, and thy end be in reproach and pouertie.

The Godly and diligent man shal haue prosperitie in all his wayes :

11

but he that followeth pleasure and voluptuousnesse, shall haue much sorrow before he die. . . .

Couet not ouermuch familiaritie amongst men : for it maketh thee spend much losse of time.

Let not thy expences bee equall with thy gaines : for either sicknesse, naughty debtors, let of trade, or misfortune by the sea or land, may soone ouerthrow the.

Linke not in amitie with too many mē that are aboue thy calling : for it will much increase thy trouble and charge. . . .

If either of good wil or necessity thou must do a thing, see thou do it gladly & cheerefully : for so shall thy gift be well accepted, and thy labour cost neuer a whit the more. . . .

If thou wilt prosper well pray : if thou wilt haue blessings, restore what thou hast euill gotten : if thou wilt haue ioy of thy labours, be single in thy tongue and eye, vse no lying, nor deceipt. . . .

[Sigs. I 3-K 1v.]

With such good advice, the business man was prepared to prosper in both this world and the next.

If no succeeding handbook managed to crowd so much useful and moral information into as brief a compass as John Browne's *Avizo*, later compilations brought together material of similar utility. The most imposing work on commerce, in the first half of the seventeenth century, came from the pen of Lewes Roberts, merchant and captain of one of the trained bands of London, who published *The Merchants Mappe Of Commerce* (1638)[85] and, as further proof of his skill as a maker of compilations, two years afterward brought out *Warre Fare Epitomized, In A Century Of Military Observations* (1640). *The Merchants Mappe Of Commerce* is a

---

[85] The full title indicates the nature of the book : *The Merchants Mappe Of Commerce: Wherein, The Vniversall Manner and Matter of Trade, is compendiously handled. The Standerd and currant Coines of sundry Princes, observed. The Reall and Imaginary Coines of Accompts and Exchanges, expressed. The Naturall and Artificiall Commodities of all Countries for transportation declared. The Weights and Measures of all eminent Cities and Townes of Traffique, collected and reduced one into another; and all to the Meridian of Commerce practised in the famous Citie of London. By Lewes Roberts, Merchant. Necessary for all such as shall be imployed in the publique Affaires of Princes in forreigne Parts; for all Gentlemen and others that travell abroad for delight or pleasure, and for all Merchants or their Factors that exercise the Art of Merchandizing in any part of the habitable World* (1638). It is dedicated to Sir Morris Abbot, alderman of London and governor of the East India Company, and to Henry Garraway, alderman and governor of the Levant Company. It has a second dedication to members of the Harvey family, who were wealthy merchants.

compact folio crammed with facts which today would be classified as commercial geography. It also includes much information like that in the *Avizo*, but its emphasis is upon the sort of geographical information that would be of most service to traders. Izaak Walton thought so highly of the work that he wrote a prefatory poem commending it as a manual to success:

> If thou would'st be a *Merchant*, buy this Booke:
> For 'tis a prize worth gold; and doe not looke
> Daily for such disbursements; no, 'tis rare,
> And should be cast up with thy richest ware.

The inclusive manuals like Browne's *Avizo* and Roberts' *Merchants Mappe* supplemented the facts to be found in the rudimentary guidebooks which supplied travelers with concise knowledge about foreign countries, including useful phrases from foreign languages, explanations about monetary systems, distances between cities, and other necessary information. Books of this sort were common throughout the period. One of the best examples of the type, an ancestor of Baedeker's guides, was translated from the German by Richard Rowlands with a title that is sufficiently descriptive of the contents: *The Post of the World. Wherein is contayned the antiquities and originall of the most famous Cities in Europe. With their trade and traficke. With their wayes and distance of myles, from country to country. With the true and perfect knowledge of their Coynes, the places of their Mynts: with al their Martes and Fayres: And the Raignes of all the Kinges of England. A booke right necessary and profitable, for all sortes of persons, the like before this tyme not Imprinted* (1576). Fittingly enough, it is dedicated to the merchant prince Sir Thomas Gresham. Further illustrations of the practical guides for travelers in foreign countries are Robert Dallington's *The Method of Trauell* (1598), Thomas Palmer's *Essay of the Meanes how to make our Trauailes into Forraine Countries the more profitable and honourable* (1606), James Wadsworth's translation from the Italian, *The European Mercury. Describing the Highways and Stages from place to place, through the most remarkable parts of Christendome. With a Catalogue of the principall Fairs, Marts, and Markets for all Gentlemen, who delight in seeing forraign Countries; and instructing Merchants where to meet with their conveniences for trade* (1641), and James Howell's *Instructions For Forreine Trauell* (1642).

The Englishmen who believed in seeing England first had available handbooks of the type represented by John Norden's cosmographies, such for example as *Speculum Britanniae. The first parte An historicall, & chorographicall discription of Middlesex. Wherin are also alphabeticallie sett downe the names of the cyties, townes, parishes hamlets, howses of name &c. Wth direction spedelie to finde anie place desired in the mappe & the distance betweene place and place Without compasses* (1593). This work is typical of other guidebooks by Norden. John Taylor provided a still more local and specialized handbook in *The carriers cosmographie: or a briefe relation of the innes, ordinaries, hosteries, and other lodgings in and neere London, where the carriers, wagons, foote-posts, and higglers doe vsually come* (1637).[86]

The strangest of the manuals of travel was the handiwork of a tradesman whose advice to travelers was cast in the form of a pious poem, which he described as *The Tryall Of Trauell, 1. The Wonders of Trauell, 2. The Worthes of Trauell, 3. The Way to Trauell. In three bookes Epitomizd. By Baptist Goodall Merchant* (1630). Although Goodall does not give detailed information of any great value, he makes up for this lack by an enormous number of moral and practical suggestions of a general nature, documented with Latin tags from the Scriptures. When finally he has finished with such matters as an enumeration of famous travelers of antiquity, chief of whom were Noah and Jonah, he turns to a discussion of the proper conduct for success in travel and assures the reader that

> Prudence of morall virtues for her grace
> Merits her ranke in trauailes primest place.   [Sig. H 3.]

But being a thrifty merchant himself, Goodall emphasizes a practical morality which brings its own reward:

> Feare God aboue first honour then the King
> Preserue thy credit, and thy fellowes state
> Whose chance in trauaile is to bee thy mate
> Do as thou woulst be done by, Christ commands

---

[86] A list of English guidebooks has been compiled by Sir Herbert George Fordham, *The Road-Books and Itineraries of Great Britain, 1570 to 1850* (Cambridge, 1924).

> Let none here neyther enter a mistake
> Frugality next trauails worth I make.
> A sauing habit of both time, and state,
> Making a man thrifty and considerate.
> A worth if ere in any course required
> In this its ten times more to bee desired.
> Preuents a famine oft of store at sea,
> Yets mercifull when others wantings plea.
> Attends at pinch, and in extreames befriends,
> When lauish prodigallity still spendes.
>
> [Sigs. H 4ᵛ-I 1.]

Though Goodall, let us hope, was a better merchant than he proved a poet, the good morality of his versified handbook was sufficient to warrant a second edition of the poem in 1639.[87]

If prudential wisdom, which had as its objective the attainment of material success, could find its way even into manuals of travel, it is not surprising that some handbooks were devoted exclusively to counseling the way of life which leads to worldly prosperity. This sort of guide is best exemplified in William Scott's *An Essay Of Drapery: Or, The Compleate Citizen. Trading Iustly. Pleasingly. Profitably* (1635). This is an epitome of the bourgeois code of ethics, of a Poor Richard philosophy that honesty is the best policy for the tradesman who wishes to attain riches and honor. But Scott, who signs himself "Citizen" and boasts that he has managed business affairs successfully, would prescribe a "reasonable honesty," neither too rigid nor too lax: a tradesman's shop should be neither too light nor too dark.[88] In his dedication he adopts as a

---

[87] The prudential morality of Goodall's advice to travelers may be compared with that of Henry Peacham in *The Art Of Living in London, Or, A Caution how Gentlemen, Countrymen and Strangers, drawn by occasion of businesse, should dispose of themselves in the thriftiest way, not onely in the Citie, but in all other populous places. As Also, A direction to the poorer sort that come thither to seeke their Fortunes* (1642). Peacham preaches sobriety and industry, holding out as a reward that a worthy young man may rise thereby to the position of wealthy alderman.

[88] Although Scott condemns the usual forms of deceit, he maintains that a certain amount of dissimulation is sometimes necessary in the tradesman as "with one who hath married a wife, whom hee must use well, pretending affection to her, though hee cannot love her; and indeed Divines hold it in some cases lawfull, to pretend one thing and intend another; . . ."—P. 27. Although the citizen "must never turne his back to honesty; yet sometimes goe about and coast it, using an extraordinary skill, which may be better practis'd then exprest: . . ."—P. 137.

motto, "Wealth with peace of conscience bee multiplied unto you." Scott divides his treatise into two main divisions. The first is an essay that discusses the qualifications of a good draper and emphasizes the necessity of a utilitarian education.

In the second division, entitled "The Compleat Citizen," the author prescribes a system by which the tradesman "may carry himselfe, Justly, Pleasingly, and Profitably."[89] The citizen should be fair in his dealings with his fellows ; his prices should insure him a good profit but should not be extortionate ; he must avoid trusting others too far ; he must be pleasant, a good talker, thrifty and industrious, sober, modest, discreet of speech, and generous toward civic and philanthropic enterprises. Scott insists upon marital stability, for the home is the basis of society. A tradesman should honor his wife and treat her well, but he must not be ruled "with blinde affection." Care should be taken by the wealthy tradesman not to leave too much wealth to his sons, for money is the ruin of many youths. Finally, Scott pleads for coöperation and unity among business men, so that they may solve such problems as overcrowding in businesses where too many apprentices are being trained. In short, Scott presents in a brief handbook the creed of a seventeenth-century business man, stating a viewpoint that is modern in most of its prudential teachings. *An Essay Of Drapery* is the most significant of the success books that reflect the ideals of the commercial classes in this period.

Other works of the late sixteenth and seventeenth centuries, less manual-like in construction than the foregoing examples, served as handbooks to teach the same doctrines of success. For instance, a conduct book in fiction exhorting young tradesmen to high deeds by the example of famous apprentices who rose from low estates to positions of honor was produced by Richard Johnson under the title of *The nine Worthies of London Explayning the honourable exercise of Armes, the vertues of the valiant, and the memorable attempts of magnanimous minds. Pleasant For Gentlemen, not vnseemely for Magistrates, and most profitable for Prentices* (1592). Johnson, who describes himself as a former apprentice, dedicates this work to the lord mayor of London and addresses it particularly to apprentices. The nine

---

[89] P. 11.

Worthies were all valiant tradesmen whose bravery, thrift, and generosity are held up as examples to be followed. Closely related to the conduct book for apprentices is the same author's *Look on me London: I am an Honest English-man, ripping vp the Bowels of Mischiefe, lurking in thy Sub-vrbs and Precincts* (1613). In this reform pamphlet, Johnson warns young men against the follies of gambling, the loss of credit, and unthrifty living. The burden of his advice is more prudential than moral. A certain D. N., a former apprentice, writing from Rouen, presents a pamphlet of guidance entitled, *Londons Looking-Glasse, Or The Copy of a Letter, written by an English Trauayler, to the Apprentices of London* (1621). He appeals to London apprentices to mend their manners toward foreigners for the sake of business relations. In the course of his remarks, D. N. praises diligence, thrift, sobriety, and industrious exercises which result surely in business prosperity.

Since the attainment of worldly success was closely linked in middle-class thinking with the virtues which also lead to a comfortable assurance of heaven, guidebooks to celestial happiness, discussed in a later chapter, made an enormous appeal to lay readers, who found therein many lessons useful in the practical affairs of daily life. More numerous throughout the sixteenth and seventeenth centuries than any other type of manual, these works frequently urge the value of piety in the attainment of material prosperity as well as of spiritual salvation. Preachers did not overlook an opportunity to bring together religion and the conduct of everyday affairs. An indication of a desire to play upon the religious and business interests of tradesmen is evident in Immanuel Bourne's sermon, *The Godly Mans Guide: With A Direction For all; especially, Merchants and Tradesmen, Shewing how they may so buy, and sell, and get Gaine, that they may Gaine Heauen* (1620), William Loe's *The Merchants Manuell, Being A step to Stedfastnesse* (1628), and in others of like nature, both earlier and later. An elaborate handbook of practical piety for apprentices, stressing the necessity of observing social degree, the value of thrift, and the paying value of religion, was Abraham Jackson's *The Pious Prentice* (1640).[90]

---

[90] *The Pious Prentice, Or, The Prentices Piety. Wherein is declared, how they that intend to be Prentices, may 1. Rightly enter into that Calling. 2. Faithfully abide in it. 3. Discreetly ac-*

To point the way to success was one of the objects even of almanacs, the simplest form of handbook used by the populace. For in addition to the astronomical information obviously to be expected, the almanac frequently provided moral proverbs and facts believed to be of educational value. The supposedly utilitarian information also included such things as the elements of judicial astrology, prognostications of the weather and impending events, the dates of the fairs and law terms, and other facts of practical worth.[91] The most famous of the sixteenth-century almanacs of this type was *A Prognostication for euer, made by Erra Pater, a Iew, born in Iury, Doctour in Astronomie and Phisicke: very profitable to keepe the body in health: And also Ptolomeus saith the same.*[92] At least twelve editions appeared between 1536 and 1639. Erra Pater furnished, among other miscellaneous lore, a list of the kings of England, a deal of advice on thrift, and a rhyming table to show the cumulative value of saving a farthing a day. Almanacs with specialized handbook information are exemplified in Daniel Browne's *A Prognostication for this present yeare of our Redemption, 1627,* which announces that it is "Amplified with new additions very commodious and profitable; with new Tables and Rules thereto annexed, for all those that vse Purchasing or buying of Annuities, or borrowing; . . ." John Rudston in *A New Almanacke* (1627) promised "many necessary Rules, Tables and Directions not heretofore published." He gives lists of the kings and miscellaneous information. Such were the conventional contents of almanacs. A work like the popular *Kalendar of Shepherds,* early translated from the French, was popular with the lower middle class as well as with a rural audience. An edition of 1618, "Newly augmented and corrected," contains practical information, pious ballad material, a discourse on the seven deadly sins (with fearsome illustra-

---

complish it. *4. And how they may be satisfied in conscience in such doubts as may arise upon some particular occasions and occurrences proper to that Calling. By A. J.* (1640).

For further discussion of the handbooks of piety, *see* Chap. VIII, *infra.*

[91] Almanacs were extraordinarily numerous. *See* Eustace F. Bosanquet, *English Printed Almanacks and Prognostications, a Bibliographical History to the Year 1600* (London, 1917), and "English Seventeenth-Century Almanacks," *The Library,* 4th Ser., X (1929-30), 361-97. *See also* Carroll Camden, Jr., "Elizabethan Almanacs and Prognostications," *ibid.,* XII (1931-32), 83-108, 194-207.

[92] Title quoted from the edition of 1607(?) in the British Museum.

tions), diagrams for phlebotomy, health hints, and wise proverbs. Useful information in tabloid form was provided by John Tapp in *The Seamans Kalender, . . . Together with many most needfull and necessary matters, to the behoofe and furtherance principally of Mariners and Seamen: but generally profitable to all Trauailers, or such as delight in the Mathematicall studies* (1602). The popularity of almanacs, described by Nashe in his ridicule of John Harvey, led to many burlesque mock-almanacs.[93]

The handbook, ranging in its infinite variety from the treatise on a gentleman's training to the lowly almanac, was firmly established in Elizabethan England as a powerful instrument of popular education. Although the schools exerted a tremendous influence upon the intellectual development of the middle class, the handbooks proved a worthy supplement and no doubt actually contributed more than did the schools to the guidance and information of the populace because they were the means of self-instruction used by purposeful citizens who could retain them for constant reference. Believing implicitly in the value of the information to be obtained therefrom, citizens applied themselves earnestly to the study of handbooks from which they might derive, not merely utilitarian facts, but also instruction in good manners, profitable learning, and true religion, which the middle class regarded as the essential elements leading to a successful life. Nor was the hope of social and material success the only reason for bourgeois application to short-cut methods of self-education, for some of the Renaissance zeal to learn and to know had stirred even tradesmen to seek out epitomes that would supply them with facts from all fields of knowledge. Thanks in part to convenient handbooks, information, of a sort, became common property. No longer was learning a monopoly of clerk and aristocrat.

[93] Cf. Nashe's ridicule of Harvey in *Haue with you to Saffron-walden* (McKerrow, *Works of Thomas Nashe*, III, 72.) He says of the popularity and utility of almanacs: ". . . not the poorest walking-mate, or thred-bare cut-purse . . . can well be without them, be it but to know the Faires & Markets . . ." Among the mock-almanacs, see Dekker's *Ravens Almanacke* (1609).

VI

LESSONS IN DILIGENCE AND THRIFT

THE obligation of every good citizen to have a trade or profession and to labor in it, the virtue of diligence and persistence, the moral value and the dignity of labor—ideas fundamental in modern society—were a part of the gospel proclaimed by preachers of the Reformation, who saw in ascetic retirement from the world of activity only a relic of popish superstition.[1] In the rapidly developing commercial life of sixteenth-century England, the doctrine that man was called of God to labor in a particular calling and that he served God best by diligent application to his mundane duty found great favor with both clergy and laity, who accepted with thanksgiving a dogma that solved so many social problems. Although the lessons implicit in the doctrine were taught from many a pulpit throughout the sixteenth century, it was left to William Perkins, the learned theologian of Cambridge, to distill the essence of the gospel of work into an essay entitled *A Treatise Of The Vocations, Or, Callings of men, with the sorts and kindes of them, and the right vse thereof,*[2] which first appeared in the 1603 edition of his collected works. The influence of this treatise, the forerunner of many later works which discussed the same social ideas,[3] is incalculable, for not only was the author's personal influence great, but his writings were among the most popular of contemporary works of divinity. In such

---

[1] Max Weber, *The Protestant Ethic and the Spirit of Capitalism*, translated by Talcott Parsons (New York, 1930), pp. 79 ff.; R. H. Tawney, *Religion and the Rise of Capitalism* (London, 1929), pp. 240 ff.

[2] Title and quotations are from the edition of 1605 of Perkins's collected works in the Huntington Library.

[3] E.g., Richard Steele's *The Tradesman's Calling, being a Discourse concerning the Nature, Necessity, Choice, etc., of a Calling in General* (1684), and Richard Baxter's *A Christian Directory* (1673). Cf. Tawney, *op. cit.*, pp. 228 ff.

esteem were they held that they made up a part of the equipment which the early colonists to Virginia and New England deemed necessary to their success.[4] Perhaps Perkins's essay on vocations might be called the corner stone of that American faith in the virtues of industry and thrift which found supreme expression in Benjamin Franklin. Since the treatise epitomizes the whole bourgeois gospel of work and sums up practically all that other sixteenth- and seventeenth-century writers had to say on the subject, an analysis of it and its background will indicate the quality of this middle-class concept, which was fundamental in the education of the complete citizen.

That "the fulfillment of worldly duties is under all circumstances the only way to live acceptably to God"[5] was an idea developed by Martin Luther and amplified by the later Calvinists, who discovered in the "conscientious discharge of the duties of business . . . the loftiest of religious and moral virtues."[6] In England preachers of the early sixteenth century talked much about man's obligation to his calling, which was twofold—spiritual and temporal. In his spiritual call, man had received from God an invitation to salvation, and in his temporal call, an opportunity to serve God by demonstrating his capacity to labor for the good of the community.[7] Since God had established society in ranks and degrees according to the capacities and fitness of each person, it was a religious obligation for the individual man to labor contentedly

---

[4] Thomas G. Wright, *Literary Culture in Early New England, 1620-1730* (New Haven, 1920), pp. 37, 39, 139, and P. A. Bruce, *Institutional History of Virginia in the Seventeenth Century,* 2 Vols. (New York, 1910), I, 365.

[5] Weber, *op. cit.*, p. 81.

[6] Tawney, *op. cit.*, p. 241.

[7] Luther had maintained that every legitimate calling has the same value in the eyes of God and that labor in that calling is "the outward expression of brotherly love."—Weber, *op. cit.*, p. 81. A good example of the transmission of these ideas to England is found in William Tyndale's *The Parable of the Wicked Mammon* (1527), written at Worms under the influence of Luther. In comparing the service of a kitchen-page and an apostle, Tyndale shows that they are of equal importance in the sight of God. "Now thou that ministerest in the kitchen, and art but a kitchen-page, receivest all things of the hand of God; knowest that God hath put thee in that office; submittest thyself to his will; and servest thy master not as a man, but as Christ himself, with a pure heart, according as Paul teacheth us; puttest thy trust in God, and with him seekest thy reward. . . . Now if thou compare deed to deed, there is difference betwixt washing of dishes, and preaching of the word of God; but as touching

in the trade or profession to which he had been called; if God willed that he should occupy a higher place in society, he would call him to that office. Yet the doctrine of contentment in one's vocation was not that of mere resignation to fate: man should strive his utmost in order that he might capably fulfill the particular duty to which God might decide in his wisdom to call him. For it often happened that God was so impressed with the industry and virtue of an individual that he called him to better things and permitted him to change his vocation.

The surest method of pleasing God and succeeding to earthly happiness and heavenly bliss is to labor honestly in the vocation in which one finds himself, agreed the preachers. Hugh Latimer gave the best expression, before Perkins, of this belief in man's obligation to his occupation. Although St. Paul had warned in I Corinthians 7:20, "Let every man abide in the same calling wherein he was called," Latimer and his contemporaries did not interpret the passage as forbidding any progress. As it was the duty of certain of the apostles to leave their original trade of fishing, to answer a special call from God, so it is the duty of any man to heed a clear mandate to enter another vocation; but, Latimer declares, let him be certain about the validity of the call;[8] it is well not to be too hasty or too importunate in beseeching God to change our callings. That the essential matter is faithfulness

---

to please God, none at all: . . . Let every man therefore wait on the office wherein Christ hath put him, and therein serve his brethren. If he be of low degree, let him patiently therein abide, till God promote him, and exalt him higher. . . . Let every man, of whatsoever craft or occupation he be of, whether brewer, baker, tailor, victualler, merchant, or husbandman, refer his craft and occupation unto the common wealth, and serve his brethren as he would do Christ himself."—*Doctrinal Treatises and Introductions to Different Portions of the Holy Scriptures* by William Tyndale, Parker Society (Cambridge, 1848), pp. 101-2.

[8] Describing the call of Peter, James, Andrew, and John to the apostleship, Latimer says: ". . . they had a calling, they ran not before they were called: . . . and no doubt there be some that think in their hearts, 'What, shall I tarry till God call me? Then peradventure I shall never be called, and so I shall never get any thing.' But these be unfaithful men: they consider not that God seeth us every where: . . ." —"The Sermon Preached Upon Saint Andrew's Day, 1552," *Sermons and Remains of Hugh Latimer*, Parker Society (Cambridge, 1845), p. 29. Cf. *ibid.*, p. 34: "Well, Andrew, Peter, James, and John were not ambitious, they tarried their calling: so I would wish that every man would follow their ensamples, and tarry for their vocation, and not thrust themselves in till they be called of God."

to the appointed task is the message which Latimer and other preachers of the sixteenth century are eternally emphasizing. To the Reformation preacher, diligence in one's daily duty was a service to God more acceptable than monastic holiness. Latimer draws such a lesson from the fact that the shepherds to whom the angels revealed the birth of Christ returned to their daily labors:

They were not made religious men, nor monks; but returned again to their business and to their occupation. Where we learn every man to follow his occupation and vocation, and not to leave the same, except God call him from it to another: for God would have every man to live in that order that he hath ordained for him. And no doubt, the man that plieth his occupation truly, without any fraud or deceit, the same is acceptable to God, and he shall have everlasting life.[9]

And the preacher drives home his lesson with the story of a message from heaven to St. Anthony, telling him that he was less perfect than an industrious cobbler of Alexandria, who served God merely by spending the whole day in honestly earning his living without fraud or guile. "In this story [Latimer concludes], you see how God loveth those that follow their vocation and live uprightly, without any falsehood in their dealing. This Anthony was a great holy man; yet this cobbler was as much esteemed before God as he."

With a firm conviction that God was served by honest labor rather than by withdrawal from the world, as the monk in a previous age had sought holiness, the sixteenth-century preacher found it easy to take one further step in the sanctification of work. If ordinary labor in one's vocation was good, unusual diligence ought to be better. And so it was. The gospel of work emphasized industry and persistence. If we work uprightly in our callings, Latimer assures us, God will not let us lack in any necessary thing.

But we must labour and travail; as long as we be in this world we must be occupied. For St. Paul saith, . . . "Whosoever will not labour, let him not eat." Likewise David saith, . . . "Thou shal eat the labours of thy hand, and it shall go well with thee." For he that will labour, and is content to travail for his living, God will prosper him;

---

[9] "A Sermon Made on Christmas-Day, by Master Hugh Latimer, at Bexterly, 25 December 1552," *ibid.*, p. 94.

he shall not lack. Let every man therefore labour in his calling; for so did our Saviour himself, . . . [10]

Since diligence is enjoined, the problem of whether it is right to accumulate riches by our industry becomes pertinent. Although the clergy with one voice condemn covetousness, they by no means damn wealth. Even Latimer, who more than any other was an apostle to the poor, answers the question of the righteousness of riches :

And here, peradventure, you will say, that it is not lawful for a christian man to have riches nor to have honours, neither to bear high dignities. But I answer, We are not bounden by the commandment of God to cast away our substance and riches that God sendeth us, neither to refuse such honours as we shall be lawfully called unto. But we may not do, as many do, that greedily and covetously seek for it day and night : for some there are that have no rest, but still study and muse how thay may get riches and honours. We must not do so ; neither may seek for it after that sort. But if God call thee to honours, if our vocation requireth us so to do, then follow thy vocation with all humbleness and gentleness. Seek not for it; for it is the greatest madness that may be, to seek for honours or riches. If God sendeth them, refuse them not; as the scripture teacheth us, saying, . . . "If riches come unto you, set not your hearts upon them ; neither put your trust in them."[11]

From Latimer's day, throughout the rest of the sixteenth century, the ministry was concerned with the doctrine of voca-

[10] "The Third Sermon upon the Lord's Prayer" (1552), *Sermons of Hugh Latimer*, Parker Society (Cambridge, 1844), p. 359. *See also* a passage in "A Sermon Preached by Master Hugh Latimer, the First Sunday after the Epiphany, Anno 1552," *Sermons and Remains of Hugh Latimer*, pp. 154-55 : "But for all this, we may not tempt God ; we must labour and do our business, every one in his vocation and order wherein God hath called him. Labour thou, and God will bless thee, and increase thy labours ; so that thou shalt have no lack of necessary things, so long as thou walkest uprightly in thy vocation ; like as he provided for Mary and her child. But yet thou must labour and do thy business, as it is written : . . . 'Be content to work for thy living, and it shall go well with thee, and thou shalt have enough, for I will make thee a living :' . . ." Further along in the same sermon (pp. 158-59) Latimer comments on the example of labor which Christ has set : "This is a wonderful thing, that the Saviour of the world, and the King above all kings, was not ashamed to labour ; yea, and to use so simple an occupation. Here he did sanctify all manner of occupations, . . ."

[11] "A Sermon Preached by Master Hugh Latimer, on the Sunday Called Sexagesima, Being the 21st Day of February, Anno 1552," *ibid.*, p. 214.

tions, with increasing emphasis on the temporal side of man's calling.[12] The culmination of these doctrines came in the treatise on vocations by William Perkins, a worthy successor to Latimer in his social interest. Learned theologian though he was, Perkins, like Latimer, was concerned with the practical application of theology to life. As Fuller expressed it, he "first humbled the towering speculations of philosophers into practice and morality."[13] Perhaps the influence of his tutor, Laurence Chaderton, helped to turn his thoughts to social problems, for Chaderton gave his own sermons a practical turn.[14] At any rate, Perkins's productions show an intense interest in the social problems of his day; whether the subject was witchcraft or the relations of the ranks of the social classes, he wrote with such vigor and clarity that his published sermons remain important documents in the social history of the late sixteenth century.[15] Without the pedantry that obscures so much Elizabethan ecclesiastical writing, Perkins's works have both the dignity of learning and the simplicity necessary to their understanding by plain men. As his first biographer expressed it, "His Sermons were not so plain, but the piously learned did admire them; nor so learned, but the plain did understand them."[16] In none of his writings is there a better example of the adaptation of his theological learning to the problems of the day than in the essay on vocations, apparently a treat-

---

[12] The activities of the Elizabethan preachers are treated at greater length in Chap. VIII, *infra.*

[13] *Dictionary of National Biography*, sub Perkins.

[14] *See* Chaderton's *A Fruitfull Sermon* (1584). I have used the edition of 1618 in the Huntington Library. Chaderton stresses the necessity of dutiful application to one's vocation until God calls one to another (pp. 12-13). Most of the evils of unrest in the commonwealth, Chaderton discovers in the failure of citizens to follow properly the callings to which God had appointed them (p. 14).

[15] Perkins died in 1602 but the popularity of his works was undiminished for the next generation.

[16] Samuel Clark, *The Marrow of Ecclesiastical Historie* (1650), p. 415. Apparently his spoken utterances were extraordinarily effective, for Clark comments: "In his Sermons hee used to pronounce the word *Damn* with such an Emphasis, as left a dolefull Echo in his auditors ears a good while after: and when hee was Catechist in Christ's College, in expounding the Commandements, hee applied them so home to the conscience as was able to make his hearers hearts fall down, and their hairs almost to stand upright: . . . ."

ise worked over from a sermon.[17]

The text from which Perkins preaches his gospel of vocations is the favorite passage from St. Paul's first epistle to the Corinthians commanding everyone to abide in the vocation to which God has ordained him. In addition to the general calling which God has given all men to receive salvation (the author explains in the beginning), there is a "Personal calling [which] is the execution of some particular office, arising of that distinction which God makes betweene man and man in euery societie."[18] Since men are ranked by degrees in society, it follows that there is a distinction in the gifts with which they are endowed and hence a diversity in trades and professions. It is the duty of all men to labor in their personal callings faithfully, without resentment, regardless of how lowly their positions may be.

After this general statement of the organization of society, the author launches into a discussion of personal callings, asserting that the first condition of Christian society is that "Euery person of euery degree, state, sexe, or condition without exception must haue some personal and particular calling to walke in."[19] Even while Adam dwelt in innocence, he had a garden to dress, and at his fall God decreed, "In the sweat of thy browes shalt thou eate thy bread."

In the choice of occupations, Perkins lays down three rules:

I. Rule. That we are to choose honest and lawfull callings to walke in. . . . Heere we are warned by the holy Ghost, to make choice of such callings as be honest. . . . For better direction in the choice of an honest calling, this generall ground must be obserued : Euery calling that serueth to vphold & maintaine three seuerall estates and societies,

---

[17] A dedication to Master Robert Tailor, teller in the Queen's Exchequer, signed by T. P. [Thomas Pierson] and dated "Cambridge Febr. 16. 1602," condemns monks for their retirement from the world of activity and from "any calling or condition of life, wherein they might gaine glorie vnto God, or good vnto mē." Equally reprehensible are those men who are called to some certain vocation and yet fail to perform properly their duties. Pierson presents Perkins's treatise, "wherein are handled at large, out of the word of God, the differences and right vse of al callings whatsoeuer," as a "remedie for these and sundry more corruptions."

The treatise in the edition of 1605 occupies thirty-six folio pages, with the type set in double columns.

[18] Perkins's *Works* (ed. of 1605), p. 909.   [19] *Ibid.*

namely, the estate of the Church, or the estate of the Commonwealth, or the estate of the family, is grounded vpon the moral law ; and therfore lawfull, and consequently may be had, vsed, and inioyed with good conscience. . . .

II. Rule. Euery man must choose a fit calling to walke in ; that is, euery calling must be fitted to the man, & euery man be fitted to his calling. This rule is as necessary as the former : for when men are out of their proper callings in anie societie, it is as much, as if a ioynt were out of the place in the bodie. . . . [The author here advises men to choose callings for which their talents and tastes are best fitted. Parents likewise should select proper callings to fit the capacities of their children.]

III. Rule. He that is fit for sundry callings, must make choice of the best. Thus much S. Paul teacheth plainely in the next verse of this chapter : *Art thou* (saith he) *called, being a seruant? care not for it; but if thou maiest be free, chose it rather* [marginal note : "I Cor. 7.21."]. Where he giues this counsell, that a bondman hauing libertie in his choise, must accept of it, rather then continue a bond-man still.

[Pp. 913-15.]

According to these rules, which Perkins bases on scriptural authority, man has wide latitude in the choice of a vocation, but it is made a religious obligation to choose that which best fits his capacities and best serves family, church, and commonwealth —the holy trinity of middle-class solidarity. By the third rule, ambition is not discouraged, for it is a duty to better one's condition if God provides the means. This question is discussed further :

. . . it may be demanded, whether a man being to enter into a calling, may lawfully offer himselfe and make meanes to enter into it or no? *Ans.* This question S. Paul answereth, when he saith, *He that desireth the office of a Bishop, desireth a worthie worke* [marginal note : "I. Tim. 3.1"] : here he giueth vs to vnderstand how it is not vnlawfull to desire an office. It is true indeed, there be vnlawfull desires of places & callings, namely, when they are sought vpon a vaine and greedie minde, for pleasure, or for lucres sake ; yet when they are desired or sought for, vpon conscience to discharge a dutie vnto God and man, there is no offence. Now if the desire of an office be lawfull, then to shew the same desire by honest and lawfull meanes, is not vnlawfull. Therefore men may vse honest & lawfull means to enter into callings meet for them, if so be they bring sufficient gifts for the discharge thereof, and withall

12

submit themselues to examination, and election according to lawfull order.[20]   [P. 918.]

Lest men in their zeal overstep this privilege of ambitions, the preacher warns that the common good must determine the choice and practice of vocations. Since the question of whether two vocations may be practised is important in this connection, Perkins next discusses that problem and concludes that under certain conditions it is lawful, and under certain others it is unlawful, to practise more than one vocation :

An entrance may be made into two callings in three cases : first, when god hath combined two callings togither by his owne appointment. . . . Secondly, two callings may be combined, when the entring into them at once is not against the word, and for the common good. . . . Thirdly, two callings may be endured, when being ioyned, they hinder not each other, nor the common good. . . . Now I come to the second parte of my distinction, to shew that men may not enter into two distinct callings at once : and that in three cases. First, if God haue disioyned these callings by his word & commaundement. Secondly, if the practise of the one hinder the practise of the other. Thirdly, if the combining of them together, hinder the common good.   [P. 919.]

Under proper conditions it is not unlawful to practise two trades at the same time :

Furthermore it may heere be demaunded whether it be lawfull to enter into two trades at once, or no? *Answer:* It is not vnlawefull, if so be they hinder not each other, nor the combining of them hinder the common good of men, and the partie intend not filthy lucre, but the common benefit. Neuerthelesse it is inconuenient in a peopled commonwealth, for then one man shall hardely liue by an other : yet if one be not sufficient to maintaine the charge of a family, a second calling may be added vppon the former conditions. Again it may be demanded whether one may haue two farmes at once or no? *Answ.* Some haue thought it not conuenient; but the trueth is, it may as well be demaunded whether it bee lawfull to haue two coates at once or no : for in a common wealth all must not be equall : but some aboue, some vnder others in regard of wealth. And therfore such as haue sundry

---

[20] A warning against too much ambition is later given in a passage discussing the hindrances to persistence in one's calling.—*Ibid.*, p. 931. *See* discussion, *infra*.

farmes, whether it be by inheritance, or by honest purchase, may lawfully inioy them. [Pp. 919-20.]

Always Perkins insists that the calling followed must be proper
to the estate of honest Christians, that it must be profitable to the
commonweal, and that it must be necessary. Hence such parasites
as astrologers and alchemists are sinners, as are artisans and tradesmen who earn their livelihood in the manufacture and distribution
of useless commodities.[21] The Christian practiser of a vocation
must be governed by faith and love which so guide him that his
work will serve the best interests of church and commonwealth.[22]
Furthermore, these virtues will prevent the abuse of one's callings
through greed and self-seeking. Although Perkins is not one to
condemn the acquisition of wealth if it is put to right uses, he
agrees with the scriptural assertion that covetousness is the root
of all evil and reminds his readers that they will need nothing in
death except a coffin and a winding sheet. Therefore he implores
mankind to keep their desires in compass and to labor for "contentation," the state of obedience to the scriptural injunction to
"be content with that which you haue."[23] Moderation is desirable
above all things.

Now for the better restrayning of our affections from the world, two
things must be done: first of all, we must in this life resolue our selues
to seeke for no more, but things that be necessarie and sufficient for
vs and ours. For to seeke for aboūdance is not laweful, neither dooth
it stand with good conscience, which I prooue on this manner. We
may seeke for that which we may pray for: but we haue no warrant
to pray for aboundance: for things necessarie & sufficient, we haue
warrant to pray; . . . [Pp. 925-26.]

Abuse of one's calling, whether by greed or by some form of unjust
or fraudulent dealing with one's fellow men, is a grave sin. And
here Perkins enumerates various abusers of honest vocations:
unjust magistrates, grasping lawyers, quack doctors, dishonest
shopkeepers, rent-rackers, corn hoarders, printers and sellers of
wicked and heretical books.[24] Having been called to some honest

---

[21] *Ibid.*, pp. 920-21.   [22] *Ibid.*, pp. 930-31.   [23] *Ibid.*, p. 925. Cf. p. 910.
[24] Perhaps a commentary on the laxity of the censorship is the following statement
about printers and booksellers: "In the calling of the Printer, which should serue for

vocation, man must continue to practise virtue in his trade. "It is not sufficient for a man to doe the proper workes of his calling, but hee must do them in a good and godly manner."[25] Nor must man be satisfied merely with honest diligence, but he must have complete sanctification in Christian faith, without which "we can looke for no successe or righteous mans priuiledge, *Whatsoeuer he doth it shall prosper.*"[26] For success in this world and reward in the next, man is enjoined throughout the treatise to unite Christian doctrine with the practice of his trade, whatever it is. For example :

Euery man must ioyne the practise of his personal calling, with the practise of the generall calling of Christianitie, before described. More plainely. Euery particular calling must be practised in, and with the generall calling of a Christian. . . . And that wee may the better ioyne both our callings together, we must consider the maine end of our liues, and that is, to serue God in seruing of men in the workes of our callings. . . . The true end of our liues is, to doe seruice to God, in seruing of man : and for a recompence of this seruice, God sends his blessings on mens trauailes, . . . Secondly, by this we learne, how men of meane place & calling, may comfort themselues. Let them consider, that in seruing of men, by performance of poore and base duties, they serue God : and therefore that their seruice is not base in his sight : and though their reward from men be little, yet the reward at Gods hand, shal not be wanting. For seeing they serue God in seruing of men, they may iustly looke for reward from both. And thus may we reape maruelous contentation in any kind of calling, though it be but to sweep the house, or keep sheepe, if we can thus in practise, vnite our callings.   [Pp. 911-12.]

While God promises earthly as well as heavenly rewards to the faithful, the necessity of positive action on the part of the individual who hopes for earthly success is strongly emphasized by

---

the speciall good of the Church and common wealth, there is exceeding iniustice done to both, by the publishing of libels, and hereticall bookes, whereby errours are spread abroad, as also by publishing vnchast, immodest, and vnprofitable writings. And in the calling of the Booke-seller there is like iniustice, in that they sell all bookes, good and badde, of truth and falshood, and that hand ouer head, without any regard, to euery one that commeth. For at this day, in England, a papist may furnish himselfe almost with all kind of bookes of his owne heresie, and that in the shoppes of Protestants. A thing to be thought vpon, and that which greatly hinders the good of this our Church."—P. 929.

[25] *Ibid.*, p. 922.   [26] *Ibid.*, p. 923.

Perkins and other ministers of his day. That idleness is sin, diligence a necessity, efficiency a duty, and persistence a heavenly
virtue were then unquestioned axioms, and they have come to be
cardinal points in the modern creed of success. Especially had
idleness been reprehended by Calvin, Zwingli, and other reformers, for in mendicancy they saw a relic of superstitious popery,
which had encouraged begging friars.[27] Like Calvin before him,
Perkins preached a doctrine of diligence, which was opposed to all
forms of idleness. For success man must abide in the vocation to
which he has been called, lest like Samson, who went out of his
calling, he encounter misfortune; for constant labor in a specified vocation is a certain means of avoiding idleness. Furthermore
it must be remembered

That, *Euery man must doe the duties of his calling with dilligence:* and therefore Salomon saieth, *Whatsoeuer is in thine hand to doe, doe with all thy
power.* . . . Of this diligence there be two reasons : first of all, the ende
why God bestowes his giftes vppon vs, is, that they might be employed
in his seruice, and to his glorie, and that in this life. Therefore Paul
saieth, *Redeeme the time:* and Christ, *Walke while yee haue light:* And
againe, *I must doe his worke while it is day:* For wee see trades men and
Trauellers rise earely to their busines, lest night ouertake them. Secondly, to them which imploy their gifts, more is giuen, and from them
which imploy them not, is taken that which they haue : and labour in
a calling is as precious as golde or siluer. . . . Occupation is as good
as land, because land may be lost, but skill and labour in good occupation is profitable to the end, because it will helpe at a neede when land
and all things faile. And on the other side, wee must take heede of
two damnable sinnes that are contrarie to this diligence. The first
is idlenesse, whereby the duties of our callings, and the occasions of
glorifying God, are neglected, or omitted. The second is Slouthfulnesse,
whereby they are performed slackely and carelesly. God in the Parable
of the husbandman, calls them that are idle into his vineyard, saying,
Why stand ye idle all the day? Matth. 20. And the seruant that had
receiued but one talent, is called an euill seruant, because he was
slouthfull in the vse of it. . . . St. Paul giueth this rule to the Thessa-
lonians. *He that will not labour, must not eate* [marginal note: "2. Thes.
3.6"] : . . . And by this he sheweth, that slouth and negligence in the
duties of our callings, are a disorder against that comely order which

---

[27] Tawney, *op. cit.*, pp. 114 ff.

God hath set in the societies of mankinde, both in Church and Com-mon-wealth. And indeede, Idlenesse and slouth are the causes of manie damnable sinnes. The idle body and the idle braine is the shoppe of the diuell. The sea, if it mooued not, could not but putrifie: and the bodie, if it be not stirred and mooued, breedeth diseases. Now the idle & slouthful person is a sea of corruption; and when he is most idle, Sathan is least idle; for then he is most busie to draw him to manifolde sinnes.   [Pp. 905-6.]

Thus diligence and the avoidance of idleness by application to the appointed task were made moral issues upon which the very soul's salvation depended. Thus the Puritan felt that the slightest deviation from duty to his vocation involved not only business failure but the danger of hell-fire in the world to come. Not only was it a utilitarian necessity to labor ceaselessly and dutifully in one's calling, but it became a moral and a religious obligation.

It was a logical corollary that social evils caused by idleness were sinful and should be banished from the Christian state. Hence, in a plan for poor relief devised by Zwingli for Zurich in 1525, beggary was strictly forbidden,[28] and in England throughout the last half of the sixteenth century preachers and laymen alike advised relief for the poor in the form of work. No longer was it a virtue to distribute largess indiscriminately. Indeed, the indis-criminate giver was an enemy of society, for he encouraged lazi-ness and removed the incentive to self-help. Perkins clearly sums up the attitude of the Protestant clergy toward mendicancy:

. . . it is a foule disorder in any Cōmonwealth, that there should be suffered rogues, beggars, vagabonds; for such kind of persons com-monly are of no ciuil societie or corporation, nor of any particular Church: and are as rotten legges, and armes, that droppe from the bodie. Againe, to wander vp and downe from yeare to yeare to this ende, to seeke and procure bodily maintenance, is no calling, but the life of a beast: and consequently a condition or state of life flatte against the rule; That euery one must haue a particular calling. And therefore the statute made the last Parliament [marginal note: "Anno. 39"] for the restraining of beggars and rogues is an excellent statute, and beeing in substance the very lawe of God, is neuer to be repealed. Againe, hereby is ouerthrowne the condition of Monkes & Friers:

---

[28] *Ibid.*, p. 114.

who challenge to themselues that they liue in a state of perfection, because they liue apart from the societies of men in fasting and praier : but contrariwise, this Monkish kinde of liuing is damnable ; . . . Thirdly we learne by this, that miserable and damnable is the state of those that being enriched with great liuings and reuenewes, doe spende their daies in eating and drinking, in sports and pastimes, not imploying themselues in seruice for Church or Commonwealth. It may be happily thought, that such gentlemen haue happie liues ; but it is farre otherwise : considering euery one, rich, or poore, man, or woman, is bound to haue a personall calling, in which they must performe some duties for the common good, according to the measure of the gifts that God hath bestowed on them. Fourthly, hereby also it is required that such as we commonly call seruing-men should haue, beside the office of waiting, some other particular calling, vnlesse they tend on men of great place and state : for onely to waite, and giue attendance, is not a sufficient calling, as common experience telleth : for waiting-seruants, by reason they spend the most of their time in eating and drinking, sleeping, and gaming after dinner and supper, doe prooue the most vnprofitable members both in Church and Commonwealth. For when either their good masters die, or they be turned out of their office for some misdemeanour, they are fit for no calling beeing vnable to labour ; and thus they giue themselues either to begge or steale. The waiting man of Cornelius the Centurian, was also by calling a souldier [marginal note : "Act. 10.7."] : and it were to be wished now a daies, that gentlemen would make choise of such seruants, that might not onely tend on their persons, but also tend vpon some other conuenient office. It is good for euery man to haue two strings to his bow. [P. 910.]

Having banished idleness as a sin before God and set forth the doctrine of necessary diligence, the preacher is concerned to urge the good of persistence and perseverance in the calling. Perkins lays down a rule that

Euery man must iudge that particular calling, in which God hath placed him, to be the best of all callings for him : . . . The practise of this dutie is the stay and foundation of the good estate both of Church and common wealth : for it maketh euery man to keepe his owne standing, and to imploy himselfe painfully within his calling : but when we begin to mislike the wise disposition of God, and to thinke other mens callings better for vs then our owne, then followes confusion and disorder in euery societie.   [P. 910.]

In following his calling, man must be careful to practise that constancy which is "nothing else, but a perseuerance in good duties," and to avoid "three lets of Constancie : Ambition, Enuy, Impatience."[29] Of these hindrances to perseverance in the following of a vocation, Perkins warns against that type of ambition which makes a man "malecontent with his particular calling." Adam and Absalom were brought low by their discontent with the lot to which they had been called. Just as too much ambition can cause ruin, so envy, which prevents mutual coöperation for the common good, and impatience, which causes discontent "arising from the continuall troubles that are incident to all callings," are both injurious to that state of diligence which brings success in plying the trade or occupation in which man finds himself.

Like Latimer, Perkins holds that the injunction to persevere in a vocation does not prevent a lawful change of occupations, but that hasty changes are evil both for the individual and the commonwealth. Yet Perkins has too much common sense to take literally the apostle's words about abiding in the calling to which man has been called :

A change of a calling, is a lawful going from one change to another. It is not the Apostles meaning to barre men to diuert from this or that calling, but he giues them an *item* to keepe them from chaunging vpon euery light conceit, and euery sodaine occasion. And that changes may lawfully be made, it appeareth thus. Amos by calling was first a heird man, but after a prophet. The Disciples were first fishermen, and after Apostles. Our Sauiour Christ himselfe was by calling a Carpenter, in his first and priuate liue, till he was thirtie yeares old : yet after his baptisme, he shewed himselfe to be the Messiah, & Sauiour of the world. Neuertheles, a chãge may not be made, but vpon vrgent and weightie causes, and they are two especially ; *Priuate necessitie* and the *common good*. *Priuate necessitie*, is when men cannot maintaine themselues and theirs by the callings in which they are ; for then they may betake themselues to other callings. Thus a Merchantman may become an husbandman, and an husbandman, a Merchant. . . . The second cause of making change lawfull, is *the publike good*. Thus may a priuate man become a magistrate. And it must be remembered, that so oft as we change, it must be to better and more excellent callings, in

---

[29] Perkins, *op. cit.*, p. 931.

which we may glorifie God more, and bring greater benefit to the church & Common-wealth.   [Pp. 934-35.]

With great good sense, he even advises such vacations and changes as will make the laborer more efficient,[30] for the individual and the state will profit thereby.

The necessity of shaping the vocations of men to serve the best interests of church and commonwealth finds constant iteration in Perkins, who identifies the highest good of the individual with the common good. The logical consequence of such an economic creed would be to create a society composed of individuals who make work the handmaid of morality and religion, and who find in the earnest pursuit of honest vocations the greatest service that can be rendered to church and state. Such, indeed, was the ideal that the Protestant clergy tried to inculcate in the English public, and so well did they succeed that by the beginning of the seventeenth century there were few to gainsay their teachings. Although this earnest devotion to one's trade or profession is often described as a Puritan quality, it was not peculiar to the Puritans. As we have already noticed, Martin Luther expressed this ideal, which was developed in England by the preachers of the Reformation and amplified by later clergymen. It is true, however, that the preachers who had come under the influence of Calvinistic teachings were more vigorous than others in the application of religious texts to the problems of daily life, and the gospel of work as outlined by Perkins, himself a mild Puritan, became a fundamental dogma in the religion of the Puritan middle class of the seventeenth century. This gospel of work, founded on Scripture and corroborated by the common sense and desires of the burgher society that was becoming so powerful in seventeenth-century England, was reinforced by the necessities of frontier conditions in the early American colonies, where idleness was a positive and very real sin against society. Not until the development of machinery so ingenious that human labor has become almost futile has man thought to question the value of ceaseless industry.

A logical consequence of the glorification of the gospel of work was an intense emphasis upon thrift, a virtue which predicated

---

[30] *Ibid.*, pp. 933-34.

diligent industry and carried connotations of self-denial, sobriety, and frugality. If there was a single maxim above others which the Elizabethan youth of the commercial classes heard constantly dinned into his ears, it was one which exhorted him to ways of thriftiness. Since God had enjoined man to labor and had shown him ways of increasing his earnings by conscientious application to duty, the neglect of divinely appointed opportunities was simply flying in the face of Providence and would assuredly entail misfortune. Because the ways of good morality brought prosperity, the puritanical citizen was more than ever convinced of the goodness of the code to which he subscribed, and he could see only the machinations of Satan in the sneers of scoffing critics who found in the tradesman's ethics merely self-interest and sordid hypocrisy. Having been taught by his practical good sense that the prudential virtues necessary to the exercise of thrift were commercially valuable as well as ethically desirable, the Elizabethan citizen believed in them with the sincerity of fervent conviction. If he talked overmuch about virtue, a volubility often ridiculed on the stage, it was not to offer a sop to his conscience for his shady dealings—as dramatists like Jonson and Middleton would have us think—but rather to deliver a message that he believed divinely inspired by a God who was pleased with sacrifices on the altar of business. The thrift-worshiping citizen of Elizabethan England was the ancestor of the correct Whig of the eighteenth century.

To encourage their countrymen to follow the path of prudential morality and acquire the virtues of thrift, preachers and poets, novelists and essayists, ceaselessly strove to warn erring youth of the dangers of prodigality and to picture the rewards of circumspect living. The tone of this literature of thrift is much the same, whether it comes from the mid-sixteenth or the mid-seventeenth century, but it increases in quantity, if it does not alter in its essential quality, as the seventeenth century moves toward the Puritan outburst.

The implications of the doctrine of thrift are obvious in Perkins's essay on vocations, but in addition to such specialized treatises, there was a diverse literature that taught the same lessons. First in point of circulation and popular consumption were the broadside ballads. For example, William Fulwood, the merchant, wrote

A New Ballad against vnthrifts [1562],[31] which inveighs against drunkards, "raging louts with feble braines," "rufling roisters," "liuely lads," "lasie loiterers," and "doting dolts," and finally traces the course of unthrifts to Newgate and Tyburn, with this proper moralization in conclusion :

> Wherfore al ye that vse this trade
> leaue of betimes yf ye be wise :
> Lest that perchaunce this way ye wade,
> ful sore against your owne deuise.
> For heer ye see the end of suche :
> as litle haue and wil spend muche.

The thrift ballads and broadsides greatly increased in the seventeenth century, as the merchant class became more imbued with the doctrine. A single-sheet broadside in the British Museum,[32] bearing the title *The Good Hows-holder* (1607), has a woodcut of a patriarchal merchant delivering his views on good management :

> The good Hows-holder, that his Howse may hold,
> First builds it on the Rock, not on the Sand,
> Then, with a warie head and charie hand
> Prouides (in tyme) for Hunger and for Cold :
> Not daintie Fare and Furniture of Gold,
> But handsom-holsome (as with Health dooth stand).
> Not for the Rich that can as much command
> But the poor Stranger, th' Orfan & the Old.

Many of the ballads which recounted the judgments of God on evildoers chose as their subjects unthrifty sinners, as does *A new Ballad, intituled, A Warning to Youth, shewing the lewd life of a Marchant's Sonne of London, and the miserie that at the last he sustained by his riotousnesse*.[33] This youth squandered his fortune, seduced a maid after making her drunk, and came to a miserable end—all of which inspired the ballad writer to emphasize the waste of

---

[31] Brit. Mus. Huth. 50 (59).

[32] Brit. Mus. 4474. aa. 90. (1).

[33] Temp. Eliz. or early Jac. I? (Printed in *Roxburghe Ballads*, III, 36 ff.) Cf. *A Warning to all Lewd Livers. By the Example of a disobedient Child, who rioutously wasted and consumed his Father's and Mother's goods, and also his own, among strumpets and other lewd Livers, and after died most miserably on a Dung-hill*, attributed to Martin Parker [temp. Car. I?]. (*Roxburghe Ballads*, III, 23 ff.)

wealth. The anonymous ballad of good counsel entitled *A Table of good Nurture*[34] is a compilation of maxims, with particular advice to be prudent, industrious, sober, temperate, and to protect carefully one's credit. Advice against marital infidelity and libertinism, purely for financial reasons, is contained in the ballad *I tell you, John Jarret, you'l breake: Or, John Jarrets wiues counsell to her husband, to haue care to his estate in this hard time, lest he turne Bankerout* (1630).[35]

The first stanza ends,

> If your time you wast away at Alehouse boords,
> I tell you, Iohn Iarret, you'l breake,

and the lessons become increasingly strong as his sins become worse. A parallel piece of advice is contained in *Charles Rickets his recantation. Warning all good Fellowes to striue, To learne with him the way to thriue* (1633).[36] Rickets claims to be an Oxfordshire trader who has given over thriftless ways and unprofitable sins to settle down to an industrious life:

> I will follow my Vocation
>   with industry and regard,
> And maintaine my reputation,
>   in this world thats growne so hard.
> Markets are naught,
> Ware is not bought,
> As twas since I the Trade did know,
>   tis time therefore
>   now to giue ore
> Such spending, and no more doe so.[37]

---

[34] Temp. Jac. I. (*Roxburghe Ballads*, II, 569 ff.)

[35] Hyder E. Rollins (ed.), *A Pepysian Garland* (Cambridge, 1922), pp. 337 ff.

[36] *Ibid.*, pp. 420 ff.

[37] Cf. Richard Climsell's *John Hadland's advice; Or, a warning for all young men that have meanes, advising them to forsake lewd company, Cards, Dice, and Queanes.* (*Roxburghe Ballads*, III, 267 ff.)

Charles Mackay (ed.), *A Collection of Songs and Ballads Relative to the London Prentices and Trades*, Percy Society, I (1841), 52 ff., reprints *A Ballad* from *Wit and Drollery* (1656), which gives an apprentice's warning to his fellows to be honest and thrifty and to avoid evil. The ballad seems to date from an earlier period. The unfortunate apprentice advises:

> "Farewell, dear fellow prentices all,
> And be you warned by my fall:

Martin Parker, one of the most prolific ballad writers of the seventeenth century, is fond of preaching a philosophy of industry and thrift. A typical example is *The honest plaine dealing Porter: Who once was a rich man, but now tis his lot, To proue that need will make the old wife trot* [1630?].[38] The porter, though fallen on evil days, is sturdily independent and urges that all landless youths learn a trade and occupy their time wisely:

> Let him who hath no house nor land,
>   some honest calling take in hand,
> Whereby a liuing may be got,
>   *For need will make the old wife trot.*
> If thou hast learning, strength, or wit,
>   to vse it lawfully tis fit,
> To sharke and shift from place to place,
>   doth thee and all thy kin disgrace.
> Tis base to beg, tis worse to steale,
>   then if thou honestly doe deale,
> Be not ashamed of thy lot,
>   *For need will make the old wife trot.*

The pamphlet literature of the latter part of the sixteenth and first half of the seventeenth century is also rich in advice urging thrift and industry. The warning-history technique, popularized

---

> Shun usurer's bonds, and dice and drabs,
> Avoid them as you would French scabs;
> Seek not to goe beyond your tether,
> And cut your thongs unto your lether,
> So shall you thrive by little and little,
> Scape Tyborne, Counters, and the Spittle."

[38] Rollins, *A Pepysian Garland*, pp. 365 ff. Of this ballad, Professor Rollins says: "A didactic ballad of a type characteristic of Martin Parker. There is a sturdy independence, a pride in honest labour, in almost everything he wrote. That pride may also explain his deep veneration for the nobility and the throne."

Similar to Parker's ballad advice is the insistence on thrift in his little verse pamphlet entitled *Harry White his humour* (1637): "Item He esteems it a point of no good husbandry for any man to loyter and bee drinking all the working dayes, and to follow his labour on Sundayes, or holy-dayes: neither doth he commend the custome of those Journey men or labourers, who hauing receiued their wages on Saturday night, doe spend all (or the most part of it) on Sunday: and the next weeke following are forced to make more fasting-daies than the Church commands."—Sig. B 2. It is Harry White's humor to dislike the sins of gaming, borrowing, excess, and double-dealing.

in the *Mirror for Magistrates*, is utilized in John Carr's *The Ruinous fal of Prodigalitie: with the notable examples of the best aprooued aucthours which hath bin written of the same* (1573). Gathering instances from Greek, Roman, and English history, Carr shows that prodigality and wastefulness bring disaster: ". . . I doo write this to the intente that they should not spend that whiche they haue, in superfluitie, as in gaminge, in gay apparell, in keppynge of such companie as are edicted vnto riotousnesse."[39] This is the burden of much comment from bourgeois writers. Philip Stubbes, George Whetstone, and Thomas Churchyard are always ready to point out the unthriftiness of vice.[40] It becomes an important part of the propaganda of writers like Thomas Deloney and Thomas Heywood. The emphasis on thrift runs through much of Deloney's prose fiction and many similar lessons are inserted in Heywood's plays.[41] For example, Deloney, in *The Gentle Craft* [1597-98?], delights to praise the conduct of Richard Casteler, who finds that thrift procures for him the love of the maidens of Westminster:

The louely Maidens of the Citty of *Westminster*, noting what a good husband *Richard Casteler* was and seeing how diligently hee followed his businesse, iudged in the end he would proue a rich man: for which cause many bore vnto him very good affection, and few there was that wished not themselues to be his wife. . . . [They] would say thus one to another: Now verily, there goes a proper ciuill young man, wise & thrifty: yea such a one as in time will proue wondrous wealthy, and without all doubt, will come to great credit and preferment.[42]

The Gentle Craft also recounts the story of the industrious Harry Neuell, whose thrift is responsible for his marriage to the widow of his master.[43] In *Thomas of Reading* [1598-99?] Deloney relates

---

[39] Sig. B 2v.

[40] Cf. Stubbes's *The Anatomie of Abuses* (1583), Churchyard's *Challenge* (1593) and his *Mirror and Manners of Men* (1594), and Whetstone's *The Rocke of Regard* (1576) and *The Enemie to Vnthryftinesse* [1586].

[41] Heywood's plays are filled with advice to sobriety and thrift. Cf. the "much ale, little thrift" expression of the clown in *The Rape of Lucrece* (Pearson's reprint of Heywood's *Plays*, V, 183); Old Forrest's disgust at drinking parties in *Fortune by Land and Sea* (I, i); Thersites' temperance lecture in *The Iron Age*, Pt. I (I, i); Robin's lament over his master's riotous and wasteful life in *The English Traveller* (I, ii); etc.

[42] F. O. Mann (ed.), *The Works of Thomas Deloney* (Oxford, 1912), p. 141.

[43] *Ibid.*, pp. 193 ff.

the misfortunes of Thomas Dove, whose poverty and distress result from his extravagance and prodigality.[44]

The works of Samuel Rowlands are filled with lessons of thrift and industry. In *Looke to it: For, Ile Stabbe ye* (1604)[45] he satirizes in a series of characters various types that are distasteful to the middle class. Death threatens to stab spendthrifts, prodigals, idle housewives, miserly misanthropes, and kindred offenders. Similarly, in his *Knave* pamphlets Rowlands again ridicules the types repugnant to the citizenry.[46] *The Knaue of Harts* (1612) includes as the objects of its satire "A proud Knaue, a shifting Knaue, a dissembling Knaue, an hypocriticall Knaue, a drunken Knaue, a swearing Knaue, a theeuing Knaue, a slothful Knaue, a busie Knaue, a Prophane Knaue, a prodigal Knaue," and other knaves equally reprehensible. Throughout these satires the prudential virtues of thrift and sobriety are upheld, and their opposite sins are condemned. In *The Night-Raven* (1620) the author reads a lesson "To all slothfull Seruants" who are responsible because of their carelessness for many disastrous fires and similar calamities.[47] Rowlands reproves all sorts of prodigality, especially the extravagance of merchants' wives, in *Heavens Glory* (1628):

Euery man is an eye-witnesse of this vanity, the more is the pittie that it should be so common: your Lady, the Merchants wife, the tradesmans wife, nay, all of all sorts are a degree aboue their estate. Your Gallant is no man, vnlesse his haire be of the womans fashion, dangling and wauing ouer his shoulders; your women no body, except (contrary to the modesty of her sexe) shee be halfe (at least) of the mans fashion: she jets, she cuts, she rides, shee sweares, she games, shee smoakes, shee drinkes, and what not that is euill . . . *O tempora! O mores.*[48]

The popular domestic treatises on the care and management of the home usually taught the necessity of economy and thrifty living. For instance, Robert Cleaver's *A Godlie Forme Of Householde Government: For The Ordering Of Private Families* (1600) con-

---

[44] *Ibid.*, pp. 267 ff.
[45] *The Complete Works of Samuel Rowlands*, 3 vols., Hunterian Club (Glasgow, 1872-80), I, 35-42.
[46] Edited by E. F. Rimbault as *The Four Knaves*, Percy Society (1843).
[47] *Works*, II, 14. [48] *Ibid.*, III, 98-99.

tains several long discourses, which he supports from Scripture,[49] on the need for diligence and thrift. Insisting upon the necessity of labor for all men, he condemns sloth, gluttony, prodigality, the keeping of evil company, idle pastimes, and kindred iniquities, as enemies of prosperity. Frugality is enjoined as a good rule of the household, and sobriety, of course, is regarded as essential to success.

Many evils of the times were attributed to sins of prodigality and failure to remember lessons of thrift. Richard Johnson's *Look on me London: I am an Honest English-man, ripping vp the Bowels of Mischiefe, lurking in thy Sub-vrbs and Precincts* (1613)[50] is avowedly a utilitarian treatise of advice intended for young men coming to London, with particular warnings against gambling, frequenting bawdyhouses, and borrowing money from usurers. The advice is always prudential rather than moral. Johnson's dedication to the lord mayor, Sir Thomas Middleton, stresses the fact that "it concerneth the prosperity of our children and kinsmen," while a further dedication to the young men of London urges them to lead virtuous and thrifty lives and to preserve their credit. The climax of the arguments against sin is always the financial ruin which ensues. Writers labored unceasingly to impress upon the apprentice the necessity of avoiding all offenses leading to prodigality. Anthony Nixon produced a dull satire in prose entitled *A Straunge Foot-Post, With A Packet full of strange Petitions* (1613), ridiculing the groups objectionable to Puritan business men : harlots, bawds, spendthrifts, and ne'er-do-wells. In a concluding poem he addresses apprentices directly and holds out to them the reward of wealth and civic dignity if they eschew vice and live thriftily :

> Liue carefully young Prentise, be no waster
> Of others goods, abandon filthy whores,
> And dissolute assemblies : Please thy Maister
> And all the night keepe close within his dores,

---

[49] Pp. 61 ff. Scripture is easily found to prove "That euery one should haue some honest and good calling, and should walke diligently in it : that it may bring in honest gaine, whereby necessaries for the families may be prepared." Cf. Chap. VII, *infra*.

[50] Reprinted by J. P. Collier (ed.), *Illustrations of Early English Popular Literature*, 4 vols. (London, 1864), Vol. II.

Roue not about the suburbes and the streetes
When he doth thinke you wrapt betweene your sheets.

Too many take such courses vile and base
To their owne miseries and maisters fall
But if thou doe thy duty in thy place
And prouidently keepe within thy stall,
When they ride bound, or lurke in some by-lane
Thou maist ride with thy foot-cloth, and gold chaine. [Sig. G 4ᵛ.]

The arguments against drunkenness, advanced in several treatises of this period, emphasize the calamities that overtake sots because of their unthriftiness. William Hornby's *The Scourge of Drunkenness* (1618)[51] is a confessional piece of verse in which the author describes the evils of dissolute company and the waste of one's substance in alehouses. He also relates the bad ends of drunkards and reproves ale-drinking parsons, lawyers, and constables. The anonymous *A Looking-Glasse for Drunkards* (1627) likewise recounts the terrible mishaps that befall drunkards and stresses the poverty that unthrifty habits bring to the drunkard and his family. Richard Rawlidge in *A Monster Late Found Out And Discovered, Or the Scourging of Tiplers* (1628) announces that though he is a simple "Mechanicall man," he is earnest and honest in his efforts to expose the evils of tippling and the large number of alehouses, which he appeals to the authorities to limit. Considering both the moral and economic problems involved, he attributes to drinking much poverty and distress. At the end of his treatise Rawlidge appends a list of judgments of God against drunkards.[52] Thomas Heywood contributed a humorous treatise, in *Philocothonista, Or, The Drunkard, Opened, Dissected, and Anatomized* (1635). Even here, however, amidst droll tales of the behavior of sots, he is careful to point out the wastefulness of the vice. R. Junius [Richard Young], in *The Drunkards Character, Or, A True Drunkard with such sinnes as raigne in him* (1638), traces to drunkenness much unthrifty idleness with its resultant poverty.[53] This treatise is a

---

[51] Edited by J. O. Halliwell-Phillipps (London, 1859).

[52] Rawlidge pays a tribute to George Whetstone's *A Mirror for Magistrates of Cities* (1584), which had treated, *inter alia*, the same theme. He recommends Whetstone's treatise to the general reader.—Sig. A 3ᵛ.

[53] *See* pp. 62 ff., 72 ff., 267 ff.

13   .

vast onslaught against the evil, but its purpose is rather to deter than to reclaim. The disastrous effects of drunkenness became a conventional theme with the later character writers. For instance, Thomas Jordan, in *Pictures of Passions, Fancies, & Affections* (1641), rounds off a character of a drunkard with these lines:

> To conclude all, Drink is the souls disquiet,
> The wrack of Reputation, Road to Riot;
> The Port to pains Eternal, the decay
> Of Life, Goods, Honour; Hels broad beaten way.[54]

Many pamphleteers throughout the first half of the seventeenth century and after, aside from the conventional reformers ubiquitous in every age, were urging upon youth a stricter observance of codes of conduct, by pointing out the business advantages of an improved standard of behavior. A certain D. N., in *Londons Looking Glasse. Or The Copy of a Letter, written by an English Trauayler, to the Apprentices of London* (1621), ostensibly writes an appeal for greater consideration of foreigners at the hands of Londoners, but he adroitly inserts propaganda for "industrious exercises" to tame the outrageous rudeness of apprentices, whom he plies with lessons of abstinence from drink and other wasteful vices.

The exaltation of thrift reached the dignity of an imposing poem, partly in Spenserian stanzas, in Robert Aylett's *Thrifts Equipage: Viz Fiue Diuine and Morall Meditations Of 1. Frugalitie. 2. Prouidence. 3. Diligence. 4. Labour and Care. 5. Death* (1622). Displaying a middle-class interest in philanthropy, Aylett is careful to show that true frugality is the golden mean between avarice and prodigality. Thrift is a master quality:

> We *Temp'rance, Abstinence,* and *Modesty,*
> With *Continence,* in this word THRIFT contain;
> And yet exclude not Liberality.   [P. 2.]

He includes the usual illustration of the grasshopper and the ant to show the value of providence, and then proves from history that many persons in antiquity, some of them patriarchs of Israel, by thrift rose from poverty to wealth:

---

[54] Cf. Richard Watts, *Bacchus Banner Displaied* (1641).

See how great Princes, and the sonnes of Kings
Are not ashamed of *Frugality*.

. . . .

Paul had a trade, although a Pharisie;
And though he to th' Apostleship attaine,
Yet workes he in his Trade and Mysterie,
His liuing with his labour here to gaine,
Nor will he charge the Church, though bound, him to
     maintaine. [P. 8.]

Like Poor Richard, he insists on early rising in the interest of wealth of body and purse:

Thus *early rising* as the Prouerbe sayes,
Brings *Thrift* in body, in *estate*, and *mind*. [P. 12.]

Thus throughout the poem he stresses the value of all the virtues that make for success. Man must be equipped with an abundance of prudential wisdom, but Aylett, Milton-wise, rebukes him for being curious about hidden or speculative things.

The middle-class conception of thrift is evident even in such a courtier as Francis Lenton, whose description of the follies of youth, *The Young Gallants Whirligigg: Or Youths Reakes* (1629), points the usual contrast[55] in emphasizing the lesson of the poem, that prodigality brings misery and thrift happiness. Later, in his *Characterismi* (1631), amidst many satirical characters Lenton praises thrift and generosity in the character of "A good Husband":

Hee drinkes onely for thirst, and eats only for hunger, knowing superfluity to be the heyre of prodigality, and liberality the daughter of good husbandry, and medium betwixt two extremes. He is the sole happinesse of a good wife, and the torment of a Waster. His children neuer liue to curse him, nor his seruants to accuse him for their want of wages. He seriously viewes the folly of Profusenesse, and is inwardly sorry to see the fall of any. He is not so niggardly as to grutch himselfe or his friend a good meale, but tasts freely (though temperately) of that God hath lent him, and thinkes himselfe no loser by lending a little to the needy. His moderate diet giues him longer dayes, and his

---

[55] Pp. 16-18. Lenton points out that God dislikes prodigals and often sends his judgments upon them. Cf. p. 9.

care in his calling frees him frõ idlenesse (the bait of his greatest enemy) for in doing nothing men learne to do ill.[56]

The handbooks of success[57] obviously stressed the prudential virtues as strongly as the modern business world emphasizes the assets of character and reputation. In *Tom of All Trades. Or The Plaine Path-Way To Preferment* (1631),[58] Thomas Powell has a passage of mocking satire on the conditions of the day, which includes common-sense advice to be thrifty. He recommends that apprentices be diligent in learning some essential trade.[59] But a far more serious and imposing guide to success—commending especially thrift, honesty, stability of the home, courtesy, and philanthrophy —is William Scott's *An Essay Of Drapery: Or, The Compleate Citizen. Trading Iustly. Pleasingly. Profitably* (1635).[60] Scott, himself a citizen of London, announces to the reader that he proposes to imitate Socrates, who "turned all his acquir'd knowledge into morality." After describing a purely prudential system of ethics for the "complete citizen," Scott insists that diligence and thrift are essential to any success. Of the habit of saving, he declares: "I would have him think it more honourable to stoope to petty savings, then to base gettings; let him imitate the thriftie King of *France*, who thought it no discredit to tye a knot in a broken poynt, and reweare it."[61] After inveighing against the unthrifty sins of drunkenness, gluttony, the haunting of taverns, and foolish extravagances, Scott urges that the home be made a school of thrift where the husband and father may lay down a code that will lead to temporal success.

---

[56] Sigs. G 6v-G 7v.

[57] *See* Chap. V, *supra.*

[58] *Tom of All Trades. Or The Plaine Path-Way To Preferment. Being A Discovery of a passage to Promotion in all Professions, Trades, Arts, and Mysteries. Found out by an old Travailer in the sea of Experience, amongst the inchanted Islands of ill Fortune. Now published for Common good* (1631). Reprinted by F. J. Furnivall, New Shakespeare Society (1876).

[59] Edition of 1631, pp. 33-34. Powell stresses particularly skilled manufacturing trades: "Besides, it is no matter of difficultie, burthen, or disgrace, for a Shopkeeper, yea, a Merchant, or a Gentleman, to have the skill of some one of these Manufactures, besides his Revenew, or profession, to accompany him, what fortune soever may carry him into Countries unknowne. To my knowledge, a great *Earle* lately of this Land, did thinke it no scorne to indeavour the attaining of the Craft, and trade of a Farrior, wherein he grew excellent."

[60] Discussed further, pp. 165-66, *supra.*   [61] P. 122.

The ascendency of the Puritans and the increasing consciousness of the middle class, in the mid-seventeenth century, of the temporal necessity of prudential virtue perhaps account for the multiplicity of pamphlets on domestic themes, including advice for the guidance of youth. One of these pamphlets is Richard Watts's *The Young Mans Looking Glass. Or, A summary Discourse between the Ant and the Grashopper. No lesse pleasant than necessary to bee followed. Whereto is annexed a Poeme, intituled, Bacchus Banner displayd, Or The seuerall humours of the drunken crue* (1641). Watts announces that he is a shoemaker, in an epigram advising other tradesmen to read his book of verse, which sets forth the now classic tale of the grasshopper and the ant as an exhortation to providence and thrift. In conclusion the author lets the foolish grasshopper warn young men :

> And you, O young men of these present dayes,
> Walke wary, wise, and circumspect alwayes :
> Lothing the ground-work of all mis'ry, sloth,
> That doth consume a man, even as a moth
> That frets a garment ; and be sure to fly
> Envie, with Ambition (falling) high,
> Pride, and security see you suppresse ;
> With gluttony, and beastly drunkennesse ;
> Riot, and luxury, abandon quite ;
> In wrath, and avarice, do not delight.
>
> .   .   .   .
>
> Striue to become as truly provident.
> Be humble, chaste, and temperate, for this
> Is the roade way to gaine eternall blisse.
>
> .   .   .   .
>
> I was addicted to mine own conceit,
> Pleasure, lewd company, (the Divels bait)
> To women, and to musick lend mine eare,
> To costly viands, pallet pleasing cheare.
> Now wanting bread to feed my hunger, I,
> Prest hard with famine, ready am to dy :
> I had my full fill'd bowles of dainty wine,
> Now, wanting some warme liquor, here I pine.[62]

[62] Pp. 19-20. Bourgeois propaganda is evident in such an execution pamphlet as *The Apprentices Warning-piece. Being A Confession of Peter Moore Servant to Mr. Bidgood,*

Henry Peacham, with a schoolmaster's delight in didacticism, produced a popular treatise, which went through several editions,[63] entitled *The Worth Of A Penny: Or A Caution to keep Money. With the Causes of the scarcity and misery of the want hereof in these hard and mercilesse Times. As also, How to save it in our Diet, Apparell, Recreations, &c. And also, What honest Courses men in want may take to live* (1647). This is a semi-ironical discussion of the times, lamenting the current distress and urging thrift, sobriety, and industry as a means of alleviation. Peacham relates an anecdote to show that many Englishmen would prefer to suffer even hanging rather than to demean themselves with work, and quotes finally "that homely (but true) distich of old Tussers":

> Thinke no labour slauerie,
> That bringes in pennie sauerlie.[64]

The municipal glory that may come from a life of industrious sobriety is the tempting bait held out to the apprentice in *The Wandering Jew telling Fortunes to Englishmen* (1649),[65] in the Jew's prophecy that any apprentice by a thrifty life might eventually be lord mayor, sheriff, alderman, or the recipient of some similar dignity. With a warning against riotousness, he insists that it is the apprentice's place "to follow Industry, not bravery."[66] After the apprentice earns his freedom

---

Apothecary in Exeter, executed there the last Assizes, for poysoning his said Master. Wherein is observed such lamentable expressions proceeding from him, as may produce a trembling to all who reade or heare thereof, and be a warning to such leud servants who walk the same steps, lest they receive the same punishment (1641). The luckless youth advises others to "let your study be, first, to please your heavenly Master, and then your Masters upon earth."

See also *The Birth, Life, Death, Wil, And Epitaph, Of Iack Puffe Gentleman* (1642), a five-page satire of a cavalier debtor who will not pay his debts to a citizen, skips off to France, has to return, dies in the Counter, and has a bad epitaph.

[63] The British Museum Catalogue lists eight editions between 1647 and 1704.

[64] P. 35. Thomas Tusser, author of *A hundreth good pointes of husbandrie* (1557), amplified to *Fiue hundreth pointes of good husbandry*, appended to later editions a poem entitled "The Ladder to Thrift," a modernized version of which is reprinted by Dorothy Hartley (ed.), *Thomas Tusser* (London, 1931), pp. 159-60. Tusser gives a sequence of axioms for the guidance of the husbandman who would live thriftily.

[65] Reprinted by J. O. Halliwell-Phillipps in *Books of Characters* (London, 1857).

[66] Pp. 35 ff.

by good husbandry, you may arrive at riches, and riches in the end bring you to honor : if you disdaine not to weare a Prentices Cap, you may live to see the Cap of Maintenance, worne before you as the Cities Praetor. Put on those clothes of a servant cheerfully, which your Master shall bestow upon you, and this City which is now your Nurse, shall at length, be your Mother, and put you into Robes of Scarlet.

Even more specific advice as to industry and thrift is given the serving man :

Would you rise higher then you are? drinking stiffly, or domineering proudly cannot do't. Are you in a good Service? keepe it ; least when you would such another, you goe without it : would you thrive? catch Time by the shoulder, for if you let him passe by, hee comes no more at your call : for Time, though hee bee an old man, is an excellent footman ; . . . If you gather no eares of Corn in the Summer of your youth, in the Winter of Age, you shall eat no bread ; but either leape at a crust, and begge or starve : . . . Are you in a good place? strive to deserve it : what you get keep ; what you spend make use of : Are you trusted? deceive not such a Master : By this small harvest, you may gather golden sheaffes enough to fill your little Barne.[67]

When the conception of "the moral duty of untiring activity"[68] was fused with a belief in the godliness of thrift, the foundation was laid for the apotheosis of business efficiency. This faith in business, taking shape in the early sixteenth century, crystallized into a bourgeois dogma in the seventeenth, and has been practically unquestioned by the middle class ever since. That God is always on the side of the diligent and thrifty was the belief carefully fostered by propagandists who reflected the opinions of the middle class. William Holbrooke, for instance, in *A Sermon Preached before the Antient Company of Blacksmiths in S. Marie Magdalens Church in London* (1612) was at pains to emphasize that God on the last day would show no mercy to parasitic loafers and wasters but would reward those who had lived industrious and thrifty lives. Sub-

---

[67] This advice to the serving man is paraphrased from *The Man in the Moone telling Strange Fortunes* (1609) by W. M., also reprinted by Halliwell-Phillipps, *op. cit. The Wandering Jew* gives a much more favorable picture of the serving man, but the advice on thrift and sobriety is practically the same.

[68] Tawney, *op. cit.*, p. 248.

scribing without question to these beliefs, the "complete citizen" trained himself to practise industry and thrift, and became a voluble advocate of these virtues. The philosophy of Poor Richard, in which Franklin expressed the code of a great bourgeois society rising in America, was anticipated by the middle-class writers and reformers of sixteenth- and seventeenth-century England, whose maxims of success were so piously cultivated by a mercantile society that they grew into a religion as firmly fixed in the national consciousness as any of the theological tenets of Puritanism. Indeed, the faith in the gospel of work and thrift became so ingrained that until recently it was far less subject to skepticism than the purely theological beliefs upon which the Puritans based their hope of heaven.

VII

INSTRUCTION IN DOMESTIC RELATIONS

THE thrifty citizen, bent upon making his life a success according to mercantile ideals, might encompass all the knowledge of the schools and digest every epitome of erudite information and still fail in his essential knowledge if he neglected what in every bourgeois society is the *sine qua non* of collective and individual welfare : the understanding of the domestic relations that lead to the stability of the home. But one need have no fear that the Elizabethan tradesman was lax in his duty of self-instruction in so fundamental a subject, for, like all true believers in the divine right of property, he was aware of the positive service rendered by so important a functional unit as the home to the organization of that society which made his goods safe and gave his accumulated possessions continuity. Hence, he was seriously concerned to maintain a code fostering ideals useful in the efficient conduct of the household, so that the home might make the greatest possible contribution to the happiness of its component parts, without friction and waste, either material or emotional. In this middle-class code of domestic relations, the husband was recognized as the primary earner of wealth, while upon the wife devolved the duty of the thrifty utilization of the income for the comfort of her household. Therefore the wife became, acknowledged or unacknowledged, the factor determining the success of the individual home. If the wife were a railing shrew, a slattern, an extravagant, gossipy, or faithless creature, the domestic efficiency and happiness so earnestly desired by every worthy husband would be jeopardized. Since humankind, especially womankind—for so it was then believed—has ever been prone to error, assistance was needed in the encouragement of the conventional ideals and in the enforcement of the bourgeois code of conduct.

Hence, the handbook, the printed guide, which sought to give advice upon all the intricate questions of domestic relationships, became a prized work in the utilitarian libraries of the Elizabethan middle class. Nor has the popularity of the type vanished, for nearly every newspaper still prints columns of common-sense, if often platitudinous, advice to husbands, wives, and lovers.

The beginnings of advice of this sort probably go back to the origin of commercial society. In England evidences of a bourgeois spirit in the counsel upon domestic problems is discernible in some of the early treatises on the subject. Although the little books on manners, translated into English in the Middle Ages from foreign originals, contained some suggestions about domestic problems, and the fourteenth-century treatise attributed to Wiclif, *Of Weddid Men and Wifis and of Here Children also*,[1] dealt with the duties of husbands and wives, the first important stimulus to the spread of the typically middle-class sort of treatise came with the advent of printing in the Renaissance. It is not without significance that one of Caxton's early publications, *The Book of Good Maners* (1487), a translation from Jacques Le Grand, contained a section on "thestate of the comynalte and of the people," in which material common to later domestic treatises appeared.[2] But ease in the multiplication of books was not the chief reason why such works increased so rapidly in popularity with the less learned type of reader. Actually, as the social consciousness of the average burgher awoke with a fresh zest for improvement, the book of domestic advice became a work regarded as necessary in the household of every honest and thoughtful citizen.

Political and social changes conspired to focus the attention of the English citizen of the Renaissance upon the relations of the sexes. While it is true that the medieval woman of the mercantile and craftsman class had borne her share of responsibility and enjoyed considerable freedom, the break with medieval conventions in the late fifteenth and early sixteenth centuries had greatly

---

[1] Chilton Latham Powell, *English Domestic Relations, 1487-1653* (New York, 1917), p. 101. Mr. Powell's discussion, to which I am indebted for a number of facts and suggestions, provides a useful survey of the major works of the period. Certain phases of the problem have been very briefly discussed in the introductory portion of Joachim Heinrich, *Die Frauenfrage bei Steele und Addison*, in *Palaestra*, CLXVIII (1930), 1-50.

[2] Powell, *op. cit.*, pp. 102-3.

increased woman's liberties. Likewise, commercial expansion and more widely distributed wealth, which so rapidly multiplied the middle class, had augmented the responsibilities and obligations of women. Furthermore, the divorce proceedings of Henry VIII against Queen Katherine, an event which must have set wagging the tongues of clerics and tradesmen alike, fixed attention upon a pertinent domestic problem. Out of the effort to clarify and codify marriage relations, an effort which was stimulated to a considerable degree by the popular interest in the discord in the royal household, a whole literature developed. Yet there were still other influences at work. After the break with the Church of Rome, with its conservative attitude toward all sex relations, new opinions regarding woman, marriage, and the home gained favor. For one thing, the reformed doctrine tended to give greater dignity to the married woman. No longer, as in the medieval church, was virginity held to be the highest good, but a chastity of marriage was glorified by the Protestants. As Puritanism further modified church beliefs, the insistence upon the sterling virtues of the home became louder. If the Puritan possessed some of the asceticism of his medieval forbears, he regarded marriage as a God-given expedient for evading the damning sin of sexual indulgence. Thus he began to concentrate his interest upon preserving the purity of the married state rather than the physiological purity of the individual. From the first half of the sixteenth century onward, English writers on domestic themes busied themselves in the propagation of their notions about the best methods for maintaining the proper harmony between husband and wife in the government of the home. It is worth noting that most of these treatises were patently written from the middle-class point of view and express the ideals of the rising mercantile classes.[3]

---

[3] Powell, *ibid.*, p. 129, remarks that the domestic conduct book was not influenced by the Italian types of courtesy book: "One would expect that the two types of Italian book illustrated by the *Principe* and the *Cortegiano* would have exerted a strong influence in our field; but, although both of these works were translated and imitated in the period, they do not seem to have affected the domestic book as a whole in the slightest, and although they were popular among aristocratic circles, it is doubtful if they were read by our authors." The Elizabethan writers of domestic treatises seem to have drawn chiefly upon their common sense and their Bibles in an effort to justify their points of view.

In social theory and in legal practice, woman throughout the Renaissance was subservient to man. If Eve in acknowledging Adam as her "guide and head" seems too foolishly humble to an age long since accustomed to female dominance, nevertheless she was following the conventionally prescribed formula for wives, as Milton might have learned from dozens of writers of the early seventeenth century. Nor was the author of *Paradise Lost* creating an ideally meek wife to compensate for his own marital misadventures, as the unwitting might assume. Eve was the embodiment of what the handbooks said a wife should be. Yet despite the theoretical subordination of women, in actuality women of the commercial classes in the later sixteenth and early seventeenth centuries had a remarkable amount of independence.[4] Women were admitted to some guilds on an equal footing with men; they occupied an important place in the retail trade as shop managers and assistants; they often proved invaluable allies of their husbands in the conduct of many small businesses; and after the death of their husbands they not infrequently carried on alone the family calling. For example, the records of the Stationers' Company reveal successful women printers and booksellers, most of whom had inherited their husbands' trades. To mold the sort of wife who would have just the proper amount of obedience and humility and yet would possess the spirit and capacity to be a real helpmeet of her husband was the aim of many a book on domestic relations which provided advice on every subject from dressing the hair to educating children.

The domestic works most popular with the rank and file of English citizens ranged from ballads of good counsel to solemn admonitory sermons, all of which managed to provide sufficient prudential advice to convince the middle-class reader of their obvious utility. Having drawn deeply upon the reservoirs of the general wisdom literature, the domestic treatises emphasized those elements which were most applicable to the problems of man's routine relation with his fellows in daily life. An early illustration of this type of book was Richard Whitford's *A werke for housholders*

---

[4] *See* Alice Clark, *Working Life of Women in the Seventeenth Century* (London, 1919), pp. 29-30, 93, 150, 161, 194-95, 197.

(1530),[5] which, like many of its successors, combines abstract wisdom and practical suggestions, with an emphatic insistence upon the value of industry as a preventive of sin. Long before Benjamin Franklin, Whitford urged "some certeyn occupacyon that may be profytable, and euer to auoyde ydlenes ye mother and nurse of all synne & euyll." After a commentary on the Ten Commandments, in which he warns against unthrifty pastimes, Whitford appends a seven-page translation from Bernard Sylvester giving maxims useful in the conduct of the household. The work enjoyed such popularity that it was published in at least seven editions.

Another early book of practical utility, which offered the additional appeal of a sound classical origin, was Gentian Hervet's translation from Xenophon, entitled *Xenophons Treatise Of Housholde* (1532). In a preface crediting Geoffrey Pole with inspiring the work, Hervet asserts that "for the welthe of this realme" he deems it "very profitable to be red." Apparently his contemporaries shared this opinion, for the little dialogue, which discusses chiefly woman's household duties, went through at least six editions by 1573.

Practical and utilitarian advice which would aid him in the conduct of his domestic establishment was the concern of the serious-minded citizen of the sixteenth century. Merely a pleasant discussion of household duties, such as the dialogue from Xenophon provided, was not sufficient. What was needed, especially in the early years of the century, was some work that would stabilize popular ideas about marriage, the relations of the sexes, and the government of the home. This need was not long unsatisfied, for Miles Coverdale hastened to translate from Heinrich Bullinger *The Christen state of Matrimonye* (1541), which summed up so well the essential facts demanded of a treatise on domestic relations that its successors could do little more than amplify elements found in the earlier work. Its influence is attested by the fact that it went through nine printings by 1575. The scope of the treatise is indicated by the description on the title-page, which promises a book

---

[5] For further details about Whitford and his successors, *see* Powell, *op. cit.*, pp. 108 ff. *See also* the Bibliography given in the same work, pp. 245-56.

wherin housbandes & wyfes maye lerne to kepe house together wyth loue. The originall of holy wedlok : whā, where how, & of whom it was instituted & ordeyned : what it is : how it ought to proceade : what be the occasiōs, frute and commodities thereof. Cōtrary wyse : how shamefull and horrible a thinge whordome and aduoutry is : How one ought to chose hym a mete & conuenient spouse to keepe and increace the mutuall loue, trouth and dewtye of wedloke : and how maried folkes shulde bring vp theyr chyldren in the feare of God. . . .

This treatise opposes divorce, insists upon the recognition of the husband as head and governor of the house, and enumerates the proper duties of both him and his wife. It advises parents to take care not to force their children into unsuitable marriages. As in many of the later treatises, man is warned that he is head "euen as Christ is the heade of the congregation," but not as a tyrannical overlord. In tones almost modern the book insists upon forbearance and mutual sympathy as the basis for successful marriage. If it devotes much space to what we may call the theory of marriage, with lengthy discussions of the dignity of the institution and its ceremonials, it nevertheless furnishes ample information about strictly concrete problems such as housekeeping, proper dress, the direction of servants, and the education of children. In short, the Bullinger-Coverdale treatise epitomizes the theoretical and practical subject matter that remained the theme of similar works for the next century. Such works as this and its successors were the sort which the plain citizen[6] found most useful in time of domestic need.

---

[6] Books on domestic relations, of course, were of interest to all classes, though the type here discussed was designed to reach and teach the average man. In courtly circles, the interest was just as keen. Works of the instructor to Katherine of Aragon, Joannes Ludovicus Vives, who was regarded as an authority on domestic affairs, were translated and widely read. For example, Richard Hyrde's translation, *A very frutefull and pleasant boke called the instructiō of a Christen womā* [1529?], had eight editions by 1592. This work is more concerned with the duties of woman than with general domestic problems. Another work of Vives, translated by Thomas Paynell, *The office and duetie of an husband* [1553?], was less popular.

Erasmus shared with Vives a reputation for wisdom in domestic affairs because of the comments in his various works, even though his longest contribution to the subject, *Matrimonii Christiani Institutio*, was not well known in England.—Powell, *op. cit.*, p. 112. Richard Taverner translated from Erasmus *A ryght frutefull Epystle . . . in laude and prayse of matrymony* [1530?]. This was followed by a translation by N. L'

Like ecclesiastics in all ages, the Protestant clergy of the sixteenth and seventeenth centuries had a firm conviction of their
divine inspiration to advise the lay brethren on every problem
of human economy, and they were convinced of their duty, not
only to set forth rules of conduct for husbands and wives and to
establish the ethical bases of their relationships, but also to give
directions for the everyday guidance of the household. Since many
of the treatises prepared by the ministers asserted the dignity of
matrimony in a way unknown in previous works, and since they
were often savored with common sense and provided just the
proper ecclesiastical approval for what the average man was
willing to believe, they won much popular approval. Coverdale's
translation from Bullinger, which established the *genre* and was
typical in its treatment, soon had a worthy successor in the work
of Thomas Becon, industrious preacher of God's word and publisher of advice, who was already famous as the author of that
much-read book of devotions, *The sycke mans salue* [1561]. Becon,
who had already shown an interest in Coverdale's translation by
writing a preface for it, presently brought out a tractate of his own,
The Boke of Matrimony.[7] Although there is no evidence that this
treatise enjoyed the vogue of Becon's popular devotional work, it
was focussed, like most of his works, for the average citizen, even
though the author does at times rebuke the aristocracy for setting
bad examples in morals to lesser men. A rigid observance of certain

---

entitled *Modest means to marriage pleasantly set foorth* (1568).

The reputed wisdom of Vives and Erasmus in such affairs helped to give point to
an early attempt to popularize the domestic treatise, in semi-fictional form, by Edmund Tilney, Master of the Queen's Revels, in *A brief and pleasant discourse of duties in
Mariage called the Flower of Friendshippe* (1568), three times printed by 1577. The exposition is cast in a framework with a speaker telling of discussions at a certain lady's
house at which were also "Loudouic Viues, and an olde Gentleman called M. Erasmus." In the manner of "Boccacce" they engage in a discussion at dinner, followed
on the next day with pronouncements by Master Pedro, who holds forth on married
men, marriage customs, duties in marriage, chastity, faithfulness, and allied subjects.
The following day's conversation, which deals with the duties of a wife, stresses skill
in housewifery and obedience to husbandly authority. Putting their trust in God, man
by gentleness, and woman by obedience and industry, may attain to happiness.

[7] Powell, *op. cit.*, p. 114, points out that printers capitalized upon Becon's popularity
by attributing to him versions of *The Christen state of Matrimonye* bearing the title of
The Golden Book of Matrimony. Becon's *The Boke of Matrimony* formed a part of his
collected works, published 1560-64.

prudential virtues is stressed, as the author insists that thrift and industry are necessary to the well managed home, that wives must lead modest lives, free from extravagance, and that parents must provide their children with training for some gainful occupation. But such useful advice was not Becon's sole concern, for he presents the most idealistic picture, up to his time, of marriage as a way of life in which men and women live together in a high, holy, and blessed state of mutual understanding and comradeship. This industrious divine also provided further directions to lead men into the paths of domestic bliss, in his *Catechism*, which, like *The Boke of Matrimony*, was published in his collected works. It furnishes fifty-eight pages of practical advice on household management.

Becon's successors in the ministry, who were prolific in the multiplication of treatises on domestic relations, reiterated many ideas found in their predecessors, though they occasionally emphasized particular phases of the subject that happened to be engaging public attention at the moment. For example, the prosperous Elizabethan tradesman, eager to establish his family and secure the most profitable marriage alliances possible for his children, found ready support for his authority over his children in such a pamphlet as John Stockwood's *A Bartholomew Fairing for Parentes . . . Shewing that children are not to marie, without the consent of their parentes, in whose power and choise it lieth to provide wiues and husbandes for their sonnes and daughters* (1589). After analyzing the situation, Stockwood finds that the plague is a judgment sent by God on account of the prevalent disobedience of children! This point of view is upheld stoutly by Henry Smith, a brother preacher (as prolific as Becon), who published an expanded sermon on the subject, *A Preparatiue To Marriage. . . . Whereunto is annexed a Treatise of the Lords Supper: and another of Vsurie* (1591), which went through three editions in the year of its publication. Although children are enjoined to obey their parents strictly in the choice of mates, the pamphlet shows an advance over some contemporary treatises in its command to husbands not to strike their wives. A marginal note opposite this passage observes: "Husbands must holde their handes and wiues their tungs."[8] Smith would permit divorce only because of adultery. Husbands and wives are urged

8 P. 58.

to study one another's natures so that they may live together in harmony.

Not all the preachers of the time were convinced, however, that parents should have an unlimited right to dictate the mates of their children. While the proper adjustment of parental authority remained a burning issue in bourgeois society for years to come, the trend in the later sixteenth century was toward greater freedom of choice in marriage. The theme of the miseries of enforced marriage, utilized in sermon, story, poem, and play, indicates a popular sympathy with this problem, which was debated at great length in the more specialized treatises. Charles Gibbon, author of obscure pious works, made an appeal to well-to-do citizens in *A Work worth the Reading. Wherein is contayned, fiue profitable and pithy Questions, very expedient, as well for Parents to perceiue howe to bestowe their Children in marriage, and to dispose their goods at their death: as for all other Persons to receiue great profit by the rest of the matters herein expressed* (1591). As usual, whatever the issue, the author turns to Scripture to prove his point, and Scripture proves, in Gibbon's dialogue, that parents should not force their children unwillingly into marriage, particularly since most of the domestic evils of the day originate in forced marriages. His lamentation is loud that the age is given over to greedy seeking after marriages for money, a subject which becomes one of the commonest themes of satire.

An effort to popularize the topics treated so solemnly by the ecclesiastics is evident in an anonymous journalistic pamphlet, *Tell-Trothes New-yeares Gift* (1593),[9] giving a discussion of middle-class family life and its problems. While the aristocratic sonneteer of the 1590's was cudgeling his brains for conceits to describe the pangs of love and jealousy, his tailor and his grocer, facing the same devastating emotions, were pondering the proper rationale of conduct. Wearied with heavier treatises, the tradesman could find edification as well as amusement in *Tell-Trothes New-yeares Gift*. Robin Goodfellow, just back from hell, relates to Tell-Troth the devil's boast that jealousy is one of the chief means of bringing

---

[9] Reprinted by F. J. Furnivall, New Shakespeare Society, Ser. 6, II (1876), along with *The Passionate Morrice* (1593) by A., apparently a sequel to *Tell-Trothes*. Furnivall remarks (p. viii) that the pamphlet "has great interest, so far as the family life of the middle classes is concerned."

14

people to his domain. There follows an account of the causes of jealousy and of unhappy marital relations, first of which is marriage for money.

The first cause (quoth he) is a constrained loue, when as parentes do by compulsion coople two bodies, neither respectinge the ioyning of their hartes, nor hauinge any care of the continuance of their wellfare, but more regardinge the linkinge of wealth and money together, then of loue with honesty: will force affection without liking, and cause loue with Ielosie. For either they marry their children in their infancy, when they are not able to know what loue is, or else matche them with inequallity, ioyning burning sommer with kea-cold winter, their daughters of twentye yeares olde or vnder, to rich cormorants of threescore or vpwards.   [P. 5.]

Lack of mutual discipline in domestic obligations, causeless discontent, men's follies and suspicions, ill counsel of busybodies and gossips, credence in reports of scandalmongers—all these, we learn, are fruitful causes of domestic disasters. In addition men are admonished against hard usage of their wives,

when as a man will brutishly vse his wife by strokes, and currishly barre her of matrimoniall kindnesse. The man that will lifte vp his hand against his wife, is like the horse that doth fling out his heeles to strike his keeper; the one hauing a knauishe, and the other a iadish tricke.   [P. 14.]

As husbands must be kind and considerate, so wives must be modest and faithful. Robin Goodfellow, evidently a man of sound experience, sets forth, in the second part of the work, the virtue of persuasion over force in managing women. Love, he has discovered, accomplishes more than wrath. On the whole, the little book is a common-sense appeal for justice and forbearance in domestic relations. Lest the reader grow weary, appropriate anecdotes are provided to illustrate the good lessons deduced.

An allegorical fiction to preserve the reader from tediousness during his instruction in similar social problems is the device of *The Passionate Morrice* (1593), the epistle to which is signed "A.," who purports to be the author of *Tell-Trothes New-yeares Gift*. A certain inquisitive soul named Honesty, finding "a troupe of lovers" at a house in Hogsdon, inspects the various couples and describes the follies of foolish and ill-considered love. Although he "honors the consent of Parents" in marriage, Honesty "abhorres such loue as is built on their liking." Shifts in the social ranks through improper marriages between persons of different classes, he deplores:

For men wil sooner match their daughters with my yong maister, a rich Coblers Sonne, though they be their heires, then with a Gentleman of a good house, being a yonger Brother. Heerby comes the decay of ancient gentilitie, and this the making of vpstart houses; . . . But fie of couetousnes, that is the roote of all mischiefe; for men that haue enough to make their Daughters Gentlewomen, by matching them with houses of no small antiquitie, will, with the desire they haue therevnto, wooe men of great liuing with large offers, to match their sons and heires with them; . . .   [Pp. 98-99.]

Furthermore, women of the middle class who marry into proud old families are warned that their lot will be unhappy. After such advice, Honesty ends the treatise with an extravagent description of virtuous love and loyal women, to whom he attributes most of the good that comes to man.

Although an occasional piece of lighter literature, as illustrated by the foregoing examples, found favor with middle-class seekers after domestic guidance, the works prepared by clergymen continued to express the voice of authority in such affairs. As if to sum up all that had preceded it during the century, the longest and most complete of the treatises on domestic relations to make a popular appeal, up to its time, was brought out by Robert Cleaver in 1598 under the pious title of *A Godlie Forme Of Householde Government*. The statement of purpose on the title-page indicates its scope :[10]

For The Ordering Of Private Families, according to the direction of Gods word. Whereunto is adioyned in a more particular manner, The seuerall duties of the Husband towards his Wife : and the Wifes dutie towards her Husband. The Parents dutie towards their Children : and the Childrens towards their Parents. The Masters dutie towards his Seruants : and also the Seruants dutie towards their Masters. Gathered by R. C.

---

[10] Edition of 1600.

Although he makes no claim to originality, Cleaver contrived to select such material from other writers on the subject that he produced a compendium of sentiments best approved by the average readers of his time. So popular was the work that it had two editions in 1598 and reached a total of seven editions by 1624.

Like all of his Puritan contemporaries, Cleaver demanded, as an essential to felicity, that the home have a Christian foundation. But after piously admonishing the head of the family to conduct the household regularly in worship and to see that all observed the Sabbath, the author turns to the more practical details of attaining to domestic success and provides directions in matters as useful as the care of the health, the inculcation of thrift, and the practice of economy. Though it was an axiom of the Puritan middle class that all men should have a vocation and labor in it, Cleaver proves at great length from Scripture and common sense "*That euery one should haue some honest and good calling, and should walke diligently in it:* that it may bring in honest gaine, whereby necessaries for the families may be prepared."[11] Sloth, gluttony, prodigality, the keeping of idle company, and trifling pastimes are condemned as the enemies of diligence and thrift. Frugality is an essential rule for the good governor of a family: "Cut thy coate according to thy cloath, and eat within thy teder." Wives, particularly urged to frugality—for "A good saver is as good as a good getter"[12]—must see that within the house there is no waste. Husbands are told to live discreetly with their wives, to "bee not bitter, fierce, and cruel," but to love, cherish, and nourish their mates. Husbands must neither flatter nor reprove their wives in public, and must bear with their infirmities. Wives must be obedient and serviceable, and "stand in a reuerend aw" of their husbands. Always they should be neat and as comely as possible. Both parents should unite to see that the children are brought up in godliness, thrift, and industry. A vast deal of detailed advice is provided, that the family may compass all these ends. A final section advises servants how to conduct themselves toward their masters.

Since one of the preoccupations of the middle classes—as of

---

[11] P. 62.   [12] Pp. 76-90.

the aristocracy, for that matter—was the proper choice in marriage to insure a stable and prosperous home and, if possible, to improve the economic position of the family,[13] Cleaver's book made a strong appeal on that score, for he provides "Sixe rules to be obserued in the choise of a good wife, or a good husband."[14] Though he includes husbands, he gives his attention chiefly to the choice of wives. The six rules insist that the prospective wife should have a good report among her acquaintances; that she should have a good countenance, neither given to angry glances, vain immodesty, nor proud looks; that she should be of modest talk, "for she

---

[13] The interest in the theme is illustrated by the catchy title of a play attributed to Thomas Heywood, *How a Man May Choose a Good Wife from a Bad* (acted *c.* 1602). A treatise which emphasizes the marriage problem is *The Court Of good Counsell. Wherein Is Set downe the true rules, how a man should choose a good Wife from a bad, and a woman a good Husband from a bad. Wherein Is Also Expressed, the great care that Parents should haue, for the bestowing of their Children in Mariage: And likewise how Children ought to behaue themselues towardes their Parents: And how Maisters ought to gouerne their Seruants, and how Seruants ought to be obedient towards their Maisters* (1607). Although it advertises prominently on the title-page the choice-of-mates topic, this work is a book of general guidance for the middle-class home.

Advice on the proper conduct to insure a profitable marriage is found in much of the domestic literature of the time. Perhaps nowhere is there a better expression of the Pamela sort of morality and procedure than in Thomas Heywood's *A Curtaine Lecture* (1637), in which Chapter III has the significant heading: "Encouragements to young Virgins and Damosells to behave themselves well in their single estate, that they may become eminent Wives & Matrons, by the example of others, drawne from divers selected Histories." Throughout, Heywood holds up the profitableness of virtue. For example (pp. 48-49), he comments: "To encourage all maides how to behave themselves, that they may be the better married . . . I hold it not impertinent to the present tractate in hand, to shew you an history or two (and those not common) how some Virgins, but of meane condition and quality, have, by their vertues meerely, and generous behaviour, attained to great preferment and honour . . ." Stories follow of how poor girls made wealthy matches by a parade of their virtue. Finally, Heywood concludes (p. 69): "And these out of infinite I have collected onely to shew unto you that Virgins, howsoever obscurely descended, who from their Ancestours could neither boast of wealth or Gentrie, yet by their vertues, beauty, and generous behaviour, have not only attained unto matches of most especiall remarke, but some also to dignities imperiall."

Intermarriage between tradesmen and gentry was common, and Heywood's advice was just the sort to appeal to the daughters of London citizens. Thomas Gainsford in *The Rich Cabinet* (1616) remarks on the social shifts (sigs. E 3-E 3ᵛ): ". . . Citizens in times past did not marry beyond their degrees, nor would a Gentleman make affinitie with a Burgesse: but wealth hath taught vs now another lesson; and the Gentleman is glad to make his younger sonne a tradesman, and match his best daughter with a rich Citizen for estate and liuing."   [14] Pp. 103 ff.

which is full of talke, is not likely to prooue a quiet wife"; that
she should wear modest apparel, "beseeming her estate and condition : to wit, honest and sober raiment"; that she should keep
good company; and finally, that she should have a useful education. The last two rules apply equally to both men and women.
Man is advised to choose a wife rather for virtue than for wealth
and to seek "no match in marriage above thy degree." To
strengthen man-made rules and to insure that no mistakes may
occur in so important a matter, the author offers one further
suggestion, that "A good wife is aboue all things to be craued of
God by prayer."[15] With these provisions, the most inexperienced
apprentice was equipped to seek a proper mate.

Cleaver's *A Godlie Forme Of Householde Government*, designed as a
practical guide for the average man in all matters domestic, makes
no great advance in ideas over similar works preceding it, but
it is more inclusive and explicit. Although Cleaver, like all of the
ecclesiastical writers, based his authority on Holy Writ, he was
not narrowly bound by texts and he anticipates, in his breadth of
interpretation, later writers who followed him in the seventeenth
century. Similar in point of view was William Perkins, whose
*Christian Oeconomie: or, a short survey of the right manner of ordering a
familie according to the Scriptures* was translated from the Latin
original by Thomas Pickering in 1609—a work which one critic
has described as "the best planned, best balanced, most practical,
and most informing of the whole series."[16] Though he was a
learned preacher and scholar, Perkins interested himself in the
welfare of the common man in this, as in other treatises, and
maintained a balance which enabled him to reconcile biblical
injunctions with everyday realities.

The zeal of seventeenth-century preachers to provide good
advice on domestic relations never waned, even if few of them
made any significant progress in ideology over their predecessors.
Indeed, the habit of giving domestic directions was so great that

---

[15] P. 152.

[16] Powell, *op. cit.*, p. 131. The Latin version of the work was written in 1590. Although some of Perkins's sermons had a tremendous vogue with the populace, this
treatise does not seem to have excited so much interest as some of its contemporaries
which did not come up to it in scholarship and organization of material.

many purely moralistic works are full of advice[17] to husbands and wives—advice which is often of a practical nature—and many books of devotions frequently include wise counsel on family affairs in addition to appropriate prayers for all domestic crises. But despite the ubiquitous nature of such counsel, the demand increased for books devoted exclusively to family affairs, and authors and printers labored to provide the works that found a growing sale with the multiplication of households which regarded them as things necessary. Before the echoes had ceased to ring from many a wedding sermon that repeated the ancient precepts of the handbooks, the preacher was hurrying it to the printing house, whence it appeared in due course as one more direction to married folk. The ministers of the seventeenth century were agreed that domestic felicity in the world below was a sight pleasing in the eyes of God and that such felicity would go far toward insuring celestial bliss. To that end, a certain pious person, who signed himself Sk. B., produced a pamphlet typical of its kind, entitled *Counsel To The Husband: To The Wife Instruction. A Short And Pithy Treatise Of Seuerall and ioynt duties, belonging vnto man and wife, . . . for their more perfect happinesse in this present life, and their eternal glorie in the life to come* (1608). But glory in the next world depends upon the skill with which husbands and wives unite to induce godliness in themselves, their children, and their servants. In order that the wiles of the devil may not disturb the happy home, the wife is instructed to obey her husband without question, but he is warned that his mate is a subordinate officer, not a slave. Then, if the "filthie sin of iealousie," the equally reprehensible iniquity of meddling in their neighbors' affairs, and other commonplace evils are avoided, the author hopes that such

---

[17] For example, included in the anonymous *The Anathomie of Sinne Briefely discouering the braunches thereof, with a short method how to detect and avoid it* (1603), sigs. D 5-D 6ᵛ, are two long passages on "The dutie of a Husband" and "The duty of a wife." Significantly enough, only nine duties are listed for the husband, whereas fourteen are provided for the wife. William Vaughan in *The Golden-groue, moralized in three Bookes* (1600) discusses the duties of husbands and wives. In Bk. II, Chap. VIII, sigs. O 5ᵛ-O 6 (ed. of 1608), he comments: "Let wiues bee subiect to their husbands . . . she must not be too sumptuous and superfluous in her attire, as, decked with frizled haire, embrodery, precious stones, gaudy raiments, and gold put about, for they are the forerunners of adultery."

godly husbands and wives may at length enter the kingdom of heaven.

With less theological ado but with the same pious hope of improving domestic relations, which impressed him as bad, Robert Snawsell set out to translate "a Dialogue betweene two women . . . by the reuerend learned man Erasmus," but because he found that women might "attaine to all that which hee counselleth there, and yet be damned," he contented himself with an adaptation of the Erasmian idea in *A Looking Glasse For Married Folkes. Wherein they may plainly see their deformities; and also how to behaue themselues one to another, and both of them towards God. Set forth Dialogue-wise for the more tastable and plainnesse sake* (1610). It was plain enough to make a popular appeal and to warrant another edition in 1631. In his preface Snawsell laments that husbands and wives have lived "wickedly and discontently together, to the dishonor of God, the offence and euill example of others, the losse of their credits, the wasting of their goods, the corrupting of their children and seruants ; and finally to the consuming of their owne bodies ; yea many to the destroying of their soules for euermore." In the dialogue between four women and one man, mutual forbearance is especially counseled. Abigail and Eulalie present the conventional good qualities of loyalty, obedience, and skilful housewifery, while Xantippe and Margerie serve as foils for the lessons that the other two teach. Ben-Ezer, husband of Xantippe, receives from Abigail a lesson in proper love and honor to a wife. In the end, he and Xantippe are reconciled, and with prayer set forth to live amicably together, each respecting the other's rights and privileges as emphasized by Abigail, who insists that a man has no right to criticize his wife in anger or ever to beat her ; in view of such patience, the wife should attempt always to please her husband.

In still more popular vein was Alexander Niccholes's *A Discourse of Marriage and Wiving, and of the greatest Mystery therein contained: How to choose a good Wife from a bad An Argument of the dearest Use, but the deepest Cunning, that Man may erre in; . . . Pertinent to both Sexes, and Conditions, as well those already gone before, as shortly to enter this honest Society* (1615).[18] Another edition of this common-sense and rather cleverly written treatise appeared in 1620. Niccholes is not excessively puritanical, but he stresses the value of chastity and a single standard of morality for both sexes. He inveighs against the "fashion much in use in these times to choose wives as chapmen sell their wares" and maintains, in his chapter on the way to select a wife, that marriage is an adventure in which companionship is an essential. After the usual virtue of modesty, Niccholes places education, "according as thine estate and condition shall best instruct thee, the education and quality of her thou hast so elected, her personage not being unrespected."[19] Parity in years and congeniality come next in the requirements of a good wife. Finally, Niccholes advises merchants, mariners, and "termers" to choose a wife "of some phlegmatic humour, that, like a rich creditor, with her large stock of virtue, without breaking out, can forbear thee, upon occasion, a month or two, a year or two, a term or voyage."[20] Certain cankers and blights of marital bliss, such as pride, ambition, and social climbing, should be firmly curbed, and excesses in dress and behavior, particularly painted faces, curled hair, and bared breasts, fashionable in the city and the court, should be avoided. After condemning widows for unseemly lust and advising husbands to set an example of faithfulness to their wives, Niccholes concludes with "Certain Precepts to be observed either in Wiving or Marriage," the first of which is "Woo not by ambassador."

As an epilogue to his *Asylum Veneris, Or A Sanctuary for Ladies* (1616), Daniel Tuvil added a brief treatise on domestic relations.[21]

---

[18] Reprinted in *Harleian Miscellany* (1808-13), Vol. II. My quotations are from this reprint. [19] *Ibid.*, p. 162. [20] *Ibid.*, p. 165.

[21] Pp. 137 ff. John Davies of Hereford in the same year published *A Select Second Husband for Sir Thomas Overburie's Wife, Now A Matchlesse Widow* (1616), which sought to give in verse a statement of the proper relations of man and wife. Unlike Tuvil, he stands out for the recognition of the husband as absolute head. The wife must be intelligent, but like Milton's Eve she must take her light from her husband:

> "His *Minde* with witty *Flashes* (fir'd aboue)
> Doth *lighten* oft, to giue his wife some *light*
> To mend her misse; . . ."—Sig. B 8v.

Arguing woman's equality with man in spirit and intellect, a view more advanced than most of his contemporaries fully accepted, Tuvil asserts that man's assumption of superiority comes merely from self-conceit, which "hath like a canker eaten into the hearts of Men." The logic of this belief determines the code of behavior prescribed by the author, a code based on mutual forbearance, which insures that "All Cynicall rigour therefore and austerity must bee quite diuorced from the nuptiall yoke." In such a household private admonitions will take the place of churlish prohibitions, which are merely invitations to their violation. Like Niccholes, Tuvil maintains that if husbands want virtuous wives they must first set an example of marital fidelity. This emphasis upon a single standard of sexual morality is evidence of an increasing influence of Puritan ideals and a growing insistence upon the necessity of maintaining carefully the integrity of the home.

But preachers and serious moralists, diligent though they were throughout this period, had no monopoly of domestic counsel. Among the numerous literary forms in which such treatises appeared was occasionally one in verse, such, for example, as Samuel Rowlands' *The Bride* (1617),[22] a poem on the virtues of marriage and the proper conduct of a wife to insure domestic bliss. Ringing praise of the married state is put into the mouth of the bride, who convinces her attending maidens that all girls should have, as their single ambition, marriage and the establishment of a home. She finally concludes with a speech on the "eight duties" which "doe concerne a wife."[23] Since she is yet only a bride, evidently she had been well brought up on some of the helpful handbooks. First the wife must

> . . . haue domestique cares,
> Of priuate businesse for the house within,
> Leauing her husband vnto his affaires.

The husband should be kind and considerate, but he must remain a firm governor who disciplines himself, and hence should also discipline his wife who is a part of him, made for his pleasure and honor. Yet "Blowes are brutish" unless the wife turns upon him "in *furious moode*"; in that case, the husband is admonished to beat her "for her good."—Sig. D 3.

[22] Edited by A. C. Potter (Boston, 1905).   [23] Sigs. D 4 ff.

Wives should not meddle in matters

> Beyond their element, when they should looke
> To what is done in Kitchin by the Cooke
> Or vnto childrens vertuous education
> Or to their maides that they good huswiues be.

The wife's second duty is to entertain her husband's friends and shun evil society. The third is to avoid extravagance,

> For many ydle huswiues (London knowes)
> Haue by their pride bin husbands ouerthrowes.

The fourth is to love her own house best

> And be no gadding gossippe vp and downe
> To heare and carry tales amongst the rest
> That are the newes reporters of the towne :
>
> .   .   .   .
>
> At publike playes she neuer will be knowne,
> And to be tauerne guest she euer hates . . .

Her fifth duty is obedience to her husband : "Women must neuer think their judgments best." The sixth is to pacify her husband's ire, and the seventh gives a similar injunction to observe his disposition and "thereunto conforme her selfe for euer" with meek submission. Lastly, she must remember all the other seven duties and have a chief regard for her husband's honor. And the poem closes with a benediction that "God send good husbands to you every one." As poetry, Rowlands' work is not distinguished ; but as an example of what a popular versifier thought worth his efforts, it indicates the contemporary interest in domestic guidance that was manifested by the middle-class group to whom Rowlands appealed in this and similar poems.[24] The lessons of *The Bride* were essentially the same as those which were often heard

---

[24] Somewhat akin to *The Bride* in theme, but aimed, perhaps, at more sophisticated readers, was *A Happy Husband Or, Directions for a Maide to Choose her Mate As also A Wives Behaviour towards her Husband after Marriage. By Patrick Hannay, Gent. To which is adioyned the Good Wife; together with an Exquisite discourse of Epitaphs, including the choysest thereof, Ancient & Moderne. By R. B. Gent.* (1618) (reprinted in *The Poetical Works of Patrick Hannay*, Hunterian Club [Glasgow, 1875]). Prefatory poems link Hannay's *Husband* with Sir Thomas Overbury's *Wife.* Such subjects were unusually popular at this period with all classes.

from the pulpit or gleaned from some preacher's tract.

The attainment of happiness in the married state was the object of the practical advice given by William Whately, known for his strong lungs and lusty sermons as "the Roaring Boy of Banbury," in a sermon expanded into a treatise bearing the title of *A Bride-Bush: Or, A Direction For Married Persons. Plainely Describing The Duties Common to both, and peculiar to each of them. By Performing Of Which, marriage shall prooue a great helpe to such, as now for want of performing them, doe find it a little hell* (1619).[25] The son of a former mayor of Banbury, Whately understood the problems of middle-class life, and his exposition is a good example of the way in which a few of the clergy were facing the practical aspects of domestic economy. A new spirit of realism is evident in the Banbury preacher's common-sense approach to the facts of human relationships. Failure in marriage, he maintains, is usually the result of a lack of sympathy, understanding, or applied intelligence in the contracting parties. Recognizing, as did few of his brethren of the cloth, that marriage had a fundamental sexual basis, Whately faced the problem squarely and stressed the necessity of a rational life. While he insisted upon temperance and moderation, with a consideration of the mutual desires of husband and wife, he made clear that sexual incapacity or refusal was a sufficient ground for divorce.[26] Throughout his work, this foresighted preacher pleads for reciprocal consideration and argues that marriage is a partnership, though the husband's authority as head of the household must be conceded by the wife. Intolerable as it is for a husband to beat his wife, Whately admits that such punishment may occasionally be necessary:

But if she will raile vpon him with most reprochfull termes, if shee will affront him with bold and impudent resistances, if she will tell him to his teeth, that she cares not for him, and that she will doe as she lusts for all him; if she will flie in his face with violence, and begin to strike him, or breake into such vnwomanly words or behauiour; then let him beare a while, and admonish and exhort, and pray; but if still she persist against reproofes and perswasion, if her father be liuing, let him be intreated to fight; if she haue none, or he cannot, or will

---

[25] The sermon, bearing essentially the same title, appeared in 1618. Another edition of the expanded treatise was published in 1624.   [26] Pp. 25 ff.

not, I thinke the husband shal not offend, in vsing a foole according to her folly, a child in vnderstanding; like a child in yeeres, and a woman of base and seruile condition in base and seruile manner.[27] [Pp. 107-8.]

Although the lay readers of Whately's treatise must have found his observations essentially sound, ecclesiastical opinion regarded his attitude toward divorce as such a scandal that the Court of High Commission ordered him to retract his statements. The re-cantation was the occasion for the publication of another little book, *A Care-cloth: Or A Treatise Of The Cumbers And Troubles Of Marriage* (1624). Even though the author bows to learned author-ity, the tone of his denial indicates that he, in common with many others of his time, was seeking for what he himself calls a "right vnderstanding" in such matters.[28] The text of the new work gives further sensible advice on the choice of mates and warns against overhasty marriages. The vigorous, if noisy, preacher of Banbury represents an opinion which was more and more inclined to analyze domestic situations from the point of view of the practical problems of the urban middle class.

More popular and more exhaustive than Whately's works was the encyclopedic production of the Reverend William Gouge, dedicated to his "beloued Parishioners, Inhabitants of the Precinct

---

[27] Opinion as to the merits of wife beating differed, but sentiment against physical punishment gained strength. William Heale in *An Apologie For Women* (1609) opposes the advocates of wife beating and insists upon woman's right of protection from bully-ing conjugal authority.—P. 66. The anonymous *Anatomy of a Woman's Tongue* (1638), reprinted in *Harleian Miscellany* (1808), II, 183 ff., provides a large amount of rhymed advice on the management of a wife, including this warning:

> "Some men will beat their wives, but that's the way
> To make them obstinate and go astray."

[28] In the Preface to *A Care-cloth*, Whately repudiates his earlier views: "Vnderstand, good Reader, that in a former Treatise about the duties of the married, intitled, A Bridebush, I did occasionally deliuer two positions: One this; The sinne of adulterie dissolueth the bond, and annihilateth the couenant of Matrimonie. Another this; The sinne of wilfull desertion doth likewise dissolue the bond of Matrimony. Giue me leaue now to aduertise thee of such reasons, as haue been obiected vnto me against these two positions. [He presents scriptural reasons against his former position and adds:] Sweyed by these arguments (to which, I confesse, that I cannot make a satis-fying answere) I depart from these opinions, wishing that I had not written them, and that no man, by what I haue written, would imbolden himselfe, in such cases, to take at least a doubtfull, and an hazzardfull liberty. So praying God to giue vs a right vnderstanding in all things, I bid thee farewell."

of Black-Fryers London" and entitled *Of Domesticall Duties* (1622).
A handsome folio edition was brought out in 1626, followed by a
third edition in quarto in 1634. Besides these, *Of Domesticall Duties*
also appeared as a part of Gouge's *Workes* (1627), which went
through three issues. Gouge made no advance in domestic thinking over his brother minister of Banbury, but the opinions of a
well known minister of London carried greater weight with the
citizens. Furthermore, Gouge was all-inclusive and had a ready
formula for any situation. He tells us in a preface that the domes-
tical duties were "first vttered out of the Pulpit"—a statement
which reveals much about the utilitarian quality of his preaching.
Like his predecessors, Gouge emphasizes that, although the wife
must acknowledge the husband as titular head, in reality the
family is a joint stock company and "he ought to make her a
ioynt Gouernour of the Family with himselfe."[29] To render his
treatise more easily used and to show that he sought just relations
between husband and wife, Gouge also drew up a table. Opposite
the "Particular duties of wiues" he set the "Particular duties of
Husbands," with page references to discussions in the text. Like
Whately, who had maintained that a husband should never play
the buffoon before his wife, Gouge was opposed to too much
familiarity of speech between husbands and wives:

Remember the feareful issue that had like to haue fallen out by reason
of such compellations giuen by *Sarah* and *Rebekah* to their husbands.
Not vnlike to those are such as these, *Sweet, Sweeting, Heart, Sweet-heart,
Loue, Ioy, Deare,* &c. and such as these, *Ducke, Chicke, Pigsnie,* &c. husbands Christian names, as *Iohn, Thomas, William, Henry,* &c. which if
they be contracted (as many vse to contract them thus, *Iacke, Tom,
Will, Hall*) they are much more vnseemely: seruants are vsually so
called. But what may we say of those titles giuen to an husband by
his wife, not seldome in passion, but vsually in ordinary speech, which
are not fit to be giuen to the basest men that be, as *Grub, Rogue,* and the
like, which I am euen ashamed to name, . . .
                                    [Edition of 1626, pp. 166-67.]

Of all the titles for a wife to use in addressing her husband, Gouge
thinks "Husband" is most meet. Despite such Puritan coloring,

---

[29] Sig. A 4. A table of contents in Gouge's work is given by Powell, *op. cit.*, pp. 234-37.

Gouge's work provides the union of pious and practical advice which was pleasing to the middle-class readers composing the author's flock. Clearly his work also reflects the ideas of urban mercantile society as to what should be the proper relationships in the family organization. By his time certain fundamental moral questions had been thoroughly established in the ideals if not in the practice of citizens. For example, Gouge emphasizes the devastation to organized society caused by all sexual laxity and declares that although a wife's infidelity may cause greater disaster to the family the same sin in the husband is no less iniquitous. Writers like Gouge welded the authority of religion to the persuasiveness of expediency and convinced middle-class readers of the good sense of the standards of conduct which they set forth.

Although the *genre* of domestic conduct books in the first half of the seventeenth century may culminate in Gouge,[30] other writers shared his audience if they did not rival his success in making an inexhaustible but useful compendium of counsel. The title of *Carters Christian Commonwealth; Or Domesticall Dutyes Deciphered* (1627) by Thomas Carter reads as if it had been suggested by Gouge's work, but one edition sufficed for its pious deciphering. Somewhat more popular, though even more pious if anything, was Matthew Griffith's *Bethel: Or, A Forme For Families* (1633), a substantial quarto of 528 pages, which appeared in four separate issues. Griffith announces on his title-page that the handbook will be useful to "all sorts, of both Sexes" to attain to the end described later in the preface as that which should be sought by every Christian—namely, to be "both a good *servant* to *God*, and a good *Subject* to the *King*," and he adds, "my scope in this *Manuall*, is to teach both." Perhaps Griffith realized that the handbooks of domestic guidance were growing too voluminous for ready use, because he makes this comment upon his own method of compilation : "Some few things are here *enlarged;* but the most I have purposely *contracted*, intending only a *Vade-mecum*. The *lighter* passages I use as *sauce*, to give the more *grave* a *better rellish;* that so I may both *please* and *profit*."[31] But if his contemporaries could savor the sauce, it has dried up for the modern reader who seeks

---

[30] *See* Powell, *op. cit.*, p. 137.
[31] Preface "To The Christian Reader."

it beneath a heavy crust of scriptural quotation. Griffith, like Gouge, drew upon most of his predecessors for material with which to instruct the family in all phases of its activities; but he added nothing new to the accumulated lore. Nor were these the only writers who served a public eager for help with problems eternally pertinent; but other works of the period only repeat what had already been said.[32] Sufficient illustrations have been given to show the vogue and influence of these manuals.

So keen was the interest in domestic relations that we find its evidences in many types of popular literature. The increasing demand for plays dramatizing domestic problems from everyday life, especially after the beginning of the seventeenth century, is partly a result of the more general realization of the significance and complexity of such ordinary human relations in a rapidly developing urban society. If many a play by Heywood, Dekker, Middleton, and others gave a living demonstration of the problems dealt with abstractly in the treatises, it is nevertheless true that the abstract discussions sharpened the perceptions and increased the concern of the public for problem plays. How important were the handbooks on family affairs in fertilizing the ground for the domestic novel, soon to develop to full strength, no one can say, but undoubtedly they had a significance that has not been realized. Throughout the late sixteenth and early seventeenth centuries the journalistic literature found material in the comedy and tragedy of domestic relations for innumerable broadsides and pamphlets. Frequently the ballads became the vehicle of domestic advice, both serious and jocular. Martin Parker, for example, near the middle of the seventeenth century found this subject worth his while in such ballads as *The Marryed Man's Lesson; Or, A disswasion from Jealousie*;[33] another directed to women, *Keep a good tongue in*

---

[32] Powell, *op. cit.*, pp. 136-37, 243-52.

The more generalized conduct books, of course, contained material similar to that in the manuals of domestic guidance. For example, Richard Brathwaite's *The English Gentlewoman* (1631), which made an effort to adapt itself to the use of all classes, necessarily devoted much space to family matters. A certain N. N. translated from the French a conduct book for the particular benefit of women, *The Compleat Woman. Written in French by Monsieur Du-Boscq* (1639), which essays to be a guide in matters concerning woman's social and intellectual training.

[33] *Roxburghe Ballads*, III, 231 ff.

your head;[34] another on hasty marriage, *The Married-womans Case. Or, Good Counsell to Mayds, to be carefull of hastie Marriage*;[35] and many others of like nature.

Crude as were the ballads of good counsel, they sometimes anticipated themes of domestic conduct which Addison and Steele later treated more urbanely in their journalistic essays. The literature of domestic relations was for the middle class of the sixteenth and seventeenth centuries intensely vital, whether it appeared in the form of direct advice, as in the handbooks, or in oblique suggestions, as in the drama and other literary forms.

The social significance of the literature of domestic relations, particularly of the manuals, in the formation of middle-class ideals was incalculable. Since this literature, to a large extent, was written by preachers, it was intensely moralistic, but it described a morality that was practically possible, not merely theoretically desirable. These preacher-writers, who gave expres-

---

[34] *Ibid.*, pp. 237 ff. This ballad was answered by Parker himself in *Hold your hands, honest men*, a warning to men not to strike their wives.

[35] Hyder E. Rollins (ed.), *A Pepysian Garland* (Cambridge, 1922), p. xxi. Parker, like many of his ballad-writing contemporaries, was fond of the domestic-advice ballad. *See* the satirical, half-in-earnest ballad beginning,

> "A Prouerbe old, yet nere forgot,
> Tis good to strike while the Irons hott.

> Or

> Counsell to all Young men that are poore,
> To Marry with Widowes now while there is store." —*Ibid.*, pp. 229 ff.

On a similar theme was Parker's

> "The wiuing age.

> Or

> A great Complaint of the Maidens of London,
> Who now for lacke of good Husbands are vndone,
> For now many Widowes though neuer so old,
> Are caught vp by young men for lucre of gold."   —*Ibid.*, pp. 234 ff.

John Cart replied to *The Wiuing age* in

> "The cunning Age.

> Or

> A re-married Woman repenting her Marriage,
> Rehearsing her Husbands dishonest carriage.
> Being a pleasant Dialogue between a re-married
> Woman, a Widdow, and a young Wife."   —*Ibid.*, pp. 239 ff.

Scores of ballads on such themes found ready buyers in seventeenth-century London.

15

sion to a theory of conduct appealing especially to the middle class because of its expediency and its prudential qualities, were extremely influential in crystallizing theories into a code, because they based their work not merely upon biblical revelation but upon the practices of the times. Particularly did the clergy of Puritan sympathies—men like Whately, Perkins, and Gouge— preach a doctrine in which morality and utility were united. Such a combination made a rational approach to the solution of vexing problems, an approach which recommended itself because of its good sense. When the average citizen was facing many new social problems as well as many old problems grown more acute on account of changing conditions, he welcomed the efforts of writers who sought to help him by clarifying and codifying those complexities of domestic relations which are eternally in the forefront of social agitation. The extent of the influence exerted by the handbooks can only be guessed at, but from the persistence of the printers in publishing them and from the number of editions which some of them attained, it is reasonable to suppose that few households among the substantial middle class were without benefit of printed guidance in the management of their affairs, guidance which in many cases was prepared specifically for the burgher household.

The literary historian who likes to trace an evolutionary development in literature will find the manuals of domestic guidance peculiarly disappointing, for there is a strange sameness in point of view and treatment in the books read by the burgher of 1558 and by his grandson in 1640. For one thing, the genesis of all these handbooks was the unchanging Bible, and even if the reinterpretations of the old injunctions sought to reconcile the Scriptures with approved contemporary conventions in morality, these conventions remained essentially static. Except for differences of opinion regarding divorce and occasional differences about the subordination of woman, there is far more agreement than divergence in the treatises throughout the period. But this does not mean that there was no social development. While the fundamental moral conventions showed little change, there was considerable shifting of emphasis, which in itself pointed toward significant changes. For example, it cannot be doubted that a gradual improvement in the position of woman is discernible in the works treating of marriage and the home, an improvement which they no doubt helped to foster, for the manuals continually insist that woman must be treated as the lieutenant of her husband, sharing his confidence and trust, and not as his chattel and slave. Though the husband remained the commander, with powers of discipline if necessary, the increased emphasis upon woman's spiritual and material rights paved the way that led toward theoretical equality—a position which a few writers in the early seventeenth century were already beginning to maintain. If in general, however, the guides to domestic felicity reiterated for decade after decade the same counsel, it merely indicates the fundamental quality of much of the advice, which remains to this day valid in bourgeois society. The books on domestic relations were important factors in establishing burgher ideals and educating the citizen in his social obligations.

VIII

GUIDES TO GODLINESS

NO phase of Elizabethan literary interest seems stranger today than the inordinate appetite of that age for "good books." The zest for collections of pious aphorisms, books of prayers and religious guidance, printed sermons, adaptations of the Psalms, and moralized allegories was limited only by the ability of the printers to pour out such works. Nor was the zeal for godly reading confined merely to a few Puritan fanatics; in every rank of society from the dissolute courtier to the ribald apprentice, pious books found their place. Whatever the personal conduct of the individual might be, he recognized that books teaching good morality were second only to the keys of salvation—that salvation toward which the whole creation moved, even fat John Falstaff and the unregenerate Robert Greene (or so they both hoped, in periods of sober remorse). An Elizabethan who would not buy one of the countless pathways to piety offered by the booksellers of St. Paul's was indeed but little better than one of the wicked.

The intricacies of theology never bothered the average reader, for, except in its broadest outlines, even in that period of intense religious controversy the divines held a monopoly of theological learning. The average citizen was governed by his prejudices—he knew whether or not he hated the papists, or whether in his heart he accepted the Book of Common Prayer and the bishops, but for erudite details the ministers could do the wrangling. It is true that he looked on with considerable interest when theological problems were in dispute, and occasionally bought controversial treatises, but for general usefulness he preferred a book of sermons teaching good morality and Christian doctrine, or one of the handbooks giving advice on everything from the proper prayer at childbirth to the means to die well. Just as the average citizen, regardless of his manner of applying the lessons in godliness, attended regularly at the preaching of sermons and noted carefully the main points of the discourse, so he bought the printed works and read with sincere interest expositions that he earnestly believed were helpful. The buying and reading of pious books was more than a gesture, more than a Puritan obligation; it was a symbol of an age of faith, a faith still almost as profound as that of the Middle Ages despite the dissensions of Protestants and Catholics or the faint murmurs of such freethinkers as Giordano Bruno and Christopher Marlowe.

The imminence of eternity oppressed the Renaissance. The hope of immortality was still the refuge of a world where human life hung by the frailest of threads. The specter of the plague, dread weapon of an avenging Jehovah, ever stood in the mind's eye. The judgments of God upon blasphemers, profane swearers, Sabbath breakers, and unbelievers were known to every citizen. The havoc of the plague, which laid waste London with inexorable regularity, which multiplied graves in Paul's Churchyard until a minister at Paul's Cross complained of the stench, which made every heart chill at the sight of a cross-marked door and its "God Have Mercy Upon Us"—all this was only the condign punishment sent upon a city which had forgotten God. As every preacher and pamphleteer knew and declared, the plague would cease when London repented. Needless to say, London sought helps to repentance and salvation, and found them in the bookstalls.

Tradesmen were naturally concerned with the problem of piety, since commerce and religion found themselves mutually useful. By the proper consideration for conduct, disaster might be avoided, for God would not turn his face from the righteous, and he was known to prosper the devout. A profitable venture to the Indies, a successful return from one's speculations, even, indeed, a gainful meeting with a golden galleon of Spain, were the handiwork of the Disposer of all things. Success was the meed of those who loved the Lord and turned from their sins. This the Elizabethan citizen believed as implicitly as did Abraham and Jacob. Hence the East India Company included among the supplies necessary to be sent out to their factors Foxe's *Acts and Monuments*, a book "of that worthy son of Christ, Mr. William Perkins," books of Psalms, Bibles, and service books.[1] Furthermore, preachers were regularly employed as chaplains and sent out to the Indies. The London Company, seeing its efforts at colonization in Virginia thwarted by the epidemics which swept the infant settlements, urged a rigid care for God's ordinances, that his heavy hand might be lifted.[2] The echoes of piety were heard even in the tavern, for, however ill his life, the Elizabethan liked to see the outward signs of virtue. Sir William Cornwallis, in his *Essayes* (1600), writing under the influence of the skeptical Montaigne, describes an alehouse in a mean town where he had been driven by nightfall :

The first note here is to see how honestly euery place speakes, and how ill euery man liues : not a Poste, nor a painted cloth in the house, but cryes out, *Feare God*, and yet the Parson of the Towne scarce keepes this Instruction. It is a straunge thing how men bely themselues : euery one speakes well, and meanes naughtily.[3]

But there was virtue in the precept which God in his infinite wisdom would appreciate.

Unthrifty idleness is always the Great Devil of those ranks of

---

[1] Arnold Wright, *Early English Adventurers in the East* (London, 1917), pp. 70-71.

[2] T. J. Wertenbaker, *The First Americans, 1607-1690* (New York, 1927), p. 179. *See also* Edward Eggleston, *The Transit of Civilization from England to America in the Seventeenth Century* (New York, 1901), pp. 149-50. Pirates prayed before battle, and profanity was forbidden to the early colonists on undertaking an Indian expedition. Eggleston further comments : "The Virginia Company thought the Indian massacre of 1622 due to the 'sins of drunkenness and excess of apparell' in the colony. The Massachusetts Company in London wrote to Endecott, in charge of their pioneer settlement, to 'make good laws for the punishing of swearers' and other offenders 'if you ever expect a comfort or blessing of God upon our plantation.' The first church was organized in Massachusetts during an epidemic, 'to pacify the Lord's wrath.' "

E. P. Cheyney, *A History of England from the Defeat of the Armada to the Death of Elizabeth* 2 Vols. (London, 1926), II, 57-58, cites the rules for the fleet that captured Cadiz in 1596. These regulations, drawn up by an old sea captain, John Young, provided for common prayer twice a day and stipulated "that no man, soldier or mariner do dispute of matters of religion, unless it be to be relieved of some doubts." In such a case he should seek out one of the clergymen with the fleet, "for it is not fit that unlearned men should argue of such mystical matters." "This was no meaningless requirement," Professor Cheyney observes, "since Essex took with him four chaplains, the lord admiral three, and Ralegh, Howard, and the Earl of Sussex, a volunteer, each one."

[3] Essay 22, sig. M 6.

society intent upon commercial success. The fear of idleness was one of the obsessions of the Puritans; idle reading, therefore, early became identified with the very essence of unthriftiness. Books described as lewd, but usually harmless except for their dearth of direct moral instruction, were regarded as instruments of seduction to be kept from the eyes of the young and the inexperienced. When even the formal critics emphasized that the function of poetry was to teach and delight—and by teaching they meant ethical instruction—professional moralists might be expected to forget delight in the preoccupation with edification.

Preachers and moralists were profuse in their condemnation of the unprofitable reading poured out by the printers. At least one, however, among many profane printers, was piously anxious to set forth good books untainted with frivolousness, if we may believe Thomas Rogers's tribute to Henry Denham in the "second Epistle" prefacing *Of the Imitation of Christ* [1580] :

And this whatsoeuer I haue done, was taken in hand at the motion of the Printer hereof; whose zeale to set forth good bookes for the aduancement of virtue, and care to publish them as they ought to be, would some printers folowe, neither would the sale of good workes be mard manie-times for lack of wel handling; nor vaine and vile bookes to the dishonor of God, the infamie of this land, to the confirming of the wicked in naughtines, and alienating of the wel disposed from virtue, I saie, to the discredite of the Gospel, and abuse of printing would not dailie be so broacht as they are.

Perhaps Denham was not altogether unmindful of the increasing taste for pious works. Edward Dering, a popular preacher of the 1570's and 1580's, after commenting on the taste of the past generation for romances and for such trifles as Howleglasse, Esop, Robin Hood, Adam Bell, Friar Rush, and the Fools of Gotham, complains :

. . . but as though the wickedness of our fathers were not yet full, we will make up their measure . . . To this purpose we have printed us many bawdy songs . . . our sonnets, our palaces of pleasure, our unchaste fables, and such like sorceries, more than man can reckon. Yea, some have been so impudent as new-born Moabites, which wallow in their own vomit, and have not been ashamed to entitle their books the

Court of Venus, and the Castle of Love, and many such other as shameless as these.[4]

William Perkins, probably the most popular preacher of the late sixteenth century with the commonalty, is fearful of ungodly idleness. Conversation must be about serious matters, even at table, he declares in *A Direction For The Government Of The Tongue according to Gods Word*, which appeared in 1593 and had eight editions by 1634. Laughter he permits but advises that it be as sparing as one's speech, which ought not be superfluous, for "Hee that speaketh many wordes, either speaketh false things, or superfluous, or both: . . ."[5] Finally, the same standard should be applied to writing and reading:

All this which is set down concerning speech, must as well be practised in writing, as in speaking. Wherby are condemned ballads, books of love, all idle discourses and histories, being nothing else but enticements and baites unto manifolde sinnes: fitter for *Sodome* and *Gomorrha*, then for Gods Church.   [Pp. 91-92.]

Henry Holland, editor of *The Workes Of The Reverend . . . M. Richard Greenham* (1599), smells popery in idle reading:

The diuell in elder ages in the blinde Papacie, fed blinde soules with fables, and idle Friers inuentions: now mens wits be refined, they can no more feede on such drie stubble. He feedes daintie eares with choise of words, and vncleane hearts with the vnchast and wanton loue-songs of Italian Poetry. Such food breeds many vncleane beasts in citie and countrie. Such men cannot loue the truth and holines, because they are repleate with error and vncleanenes. M. Ascham, a man greatly to be commended for his learning and good affection to pietie, of this matter writes on this manner. These inchanters of Circes (saith he) brought out of Italie, marre mens manners in England; much by example of life, but more by precepts of fond bookes, translated out of Italian into English. Againe, tenne Sermons at Pauls Crosse doe not so much good for mouing men to true doctrine, as one of those bookes doth harme with enticing to ill liuing. I say further, these bookes tend not so much to corrupt honest liuing, as they doe to subuert true re-

---

[4] Quoted by J. O. W. Haweis, *Sketches of the Reformation and Elizabethan Age Taken from the Contemporary Pulpit* (London, 1844), p. 148, from the preface to Dering's *Necessary Catechism*, the earliest edition of which appeared in 1572.

[5] Quoted from the edition of 1632, p. 88.

ligion : More Papists be made by your merry bookes of Italie, then by your earnest bookes of Louaine. This complaint ought wise men to consider well of, for that the world was neuer more full of Italian conceits, nor men more in danger for the long contempt of Gods trueth to be Italianated.   [Sigs. A 4-A 4ᵛ.]

The populace should be weaned from its taste for frivolous reading, believed Arthur Dent, compiler of the extraordinarily popular manual *The Plaine Mans Path-way to Heauen* (1601). In a discussion of books between Asunetus, an ignorant man, and Antilegon, a caviler, the latter tries to cheer his ignorant acquaintance, who has been thinking of damnation :

> *Antil.* Tush, tush : now I see you are in a melancholy humor. If you will go home with me, I can giue you a speedy remedy : for I haue many pleasant and merry bookes, which if you should heare them read, would soone remedie you of this melancholy passion. I haue the Court of *Venus*, the Palace of Pleasure, *Beuis of Southampton, Ellen of Rummin:* The merrie iest of the Frier and the Boy : The pleasant stori of *Clem* of the *Clough, Adam Bell,* and *William* of Cloudesly ; The odde tale of *William, Richard,* and *Humphrey:* The pretty conceit of *Iohn Splinters* last Will and Testament : which all are excellent and singular bookes against heart-qualmes, and to remoue such dumpishnesse as I see you are now faln into.
>
> *Asune.* Your vaine and friuolous bookes of tales, iests, & lies would more increase my grief, & strike ye print of sorrow deeper into my hart.[6]

Ever fearful of misspending his time, the Puritan could see no virtue in books that did not tend toward some good or useful purpose. The multiplicity of useless books was a frequent complaint. An adapter of a dialogue of Erasmus, one F. S., in *The Picture Of A Wanton: her leawdnesse discouered* (1615), thinks that useless and idle works should be burnt, leaving only such as are conducive to honest conduct :

> . . . I know that the multitude of Bookes in this age, are many : but good Bookes, which tende either to the instruction of Vertue, or to the destruction of Vice, are to be regarded, and diligently read : But filthy and vnchast Pamphlets, (whereof the World is too full) are fitter to be

---

[6] Edition of 1622, p. 371.

burned as corrupters of Youth: And who soeuer doth so misspende his time, and abuse his Witte, and peruert the good guiftes and graces of God, shall receiue condigne punishment, and his owne Bookes shall be produced as witnesses against him.   [Sig. A 3.]

The folly of idle reading and the iniquity of frivolous writing are nowhere better expressed than in Owen Feltham's *Resolues Diuine, Morall, Political* [1623]. Even beauty of style is not sufficient justification either for the reading or the writing of useless works. Feltham's own dignified statement of the sinfulness of idle books and the necessity of a union between the Graces and the Muses deserves attention:

Idle bookes are nothing else, but corrupted tales in Inke and Paper: or indeed Vice sent abroad with a Licence: which makes him that reades them, conscious of a double iniurie: they being in effect, like that bestiall sinne of brutish Adulterie. For if one reades, two are catched: hee that angles in these waters, is sure to strike the *Torpedo*, that in stead of beeing his food, confounds him. Besides the time il spent in them, a two-fold reason shall make me refraine: both in regard of my loue to my owne soule, & pitie vnto his that made them. For if I be corrupted by them, the Comprisor of them is mediately a cause of my ill: and at the day of Reckoning (though now dead) must giue an accoūt for't, because I am corrupted by his bad example which hee leaues behinde him; . . . A lame hand is better then a lewde pen: while I liue, I sinne too much; let me not continue longer in wickednesse, then life. If I write ought, it shall be both on a good subiect, and from a deliberated pen: for a foolish sentence drop't vpon paper, sets folly on a Hill, and is a monument, to make infamie eternall. . . .   [Pp. 1-4.]

Some men read Authors as our Gentlemen vse flowers, onely for delight and smell; to please their fancy, and refine their tongue. Others like the Bee, extract the hony, the wholesome precepts, and this alone they beare away, leauing the rest, as little worth, of small value. In reading I will care for both; though for the last, most: the one serues to instruct the mind; the other fits her to tell what she hath learned: pitty it is, they should be deuided: he that hath worth in him, and cannot expresse it, is a chest keeping a rich Iewell, and the key lost. Concealing goodnesse, is vice; vertue is better by being cōmunicated. A good stile, with wholesome matter, is a faire woman with a vertuous soule, which attracts the eyes of all; . . . Quaint phrases on a good

subiect, are baits to make an ill man vertuous : how many vile men
seeking these, haue found themselues Conuertites? I may refine my
speech without harme : but I will endeuour more to reforme my life.
'Tis a good grace both of Oratory, or the Pen, to speake, or write
proper : but that is the best work, where the Graces, and the Muses
meet.   [Pp. 81-85.]

Some limitation upon the distribution of idle and frivolous books
was requested in the famous Root and Branch Petition presented
by Londoners to the Parliament of 1640. A major evil, as the
petitioners saw it, was

The swarming of lascivious, idle and unprofitable Books and Pamphlets, Play-books and Ballads ; as namely, *Ovid's Fits of Love, The Parliament of Women,* which came out at the Dissolving of the last Parliament ; *Barns's Poems, Parker's Ballads,* in disgrace of religion, to the
encrease of all Vice, and withdrawing of the People from Reading,
Studying and Hearing the Word of God, and other good Books.[7]

The allusions to the unprofitable reading of profane literature
might be multiplied endlessly. What the preachers declared, the
rank and file of the laity doubtless agreed to in theory, though
they godlessly purchased lewd ballads and dangerous love lays.
But Elizabethan preachers were too clever to be content merely
with destructive criticism. Of their labors toward the positive
influencing of Elizabethan thought and taste in reading there is
abundant proof. Scores of industrious preachers busied themselves
with the production of handbooks of religious guidance, helps
to the reading and interpretation of the Bible, and sermons, which
lay in the bookstalls thicker than the leaves in Vallombrosa. One
writer, satirically comparing a politician to a bookshop, comments
on the quantity of pious works : "He is therefore much like a
bookesellers shoppe on Bartholomew day at London : the stalls of
which are so adornd with bibles and prayer-bookes, that almost
nothing is left within, but heathen knowledge."[8]

---

[7] Quoted from John Rushworth, *Historical Collections* (1692), Pt. III, Vol. I, p. 99.
The same petition deplored that the authorities had previously been guilty of "hindering of Godly Books to be Printed" and of favoring by means of the censorship works
which were anathema to the petitioners.

[8] J. Stephens, *Essayes and Characters* (1615), Character XII ; reprinted by J. O.
Halliwell-Phillipps, *Books of Characters* (London, 1857).

The Bible naturally was the foundation of all religious reading. The abundance and cheapness of printed Bibles placed them within reach of every Elizabethan citizen. Although some high churchmen, notably Archbishop Whitgift, looked upon the reading and exposition of the Bible in the home, particularly when outsiders were present, with outspoken distrust,[9] the average preacher urged the constant reading of the Scriptures, and the average citizen at least provided himself with the necessary means. All manner of Bibles found their way into English households : Bibles printed in Cambridge, London, Amsterdam, Geneva, even some from Douai and Rouen. Whatever Bible best suited the citizen's creed, he sought out and purchased. Perhaps more Bibles were bought than read. Early in Elizabeth's reign, Nicholas Robinson, a preacher, complained that ". . . for fashion's sake merchantmen have Bibles, which they never peruse ; for fashion's sake some women buy Scripture books, that they may be thought to be well disposed."[10] But certainly there was widespread reading among the laity. The popularity of various "helps" cannot be explained purely by ecclesiastical demand. Indeed, some of the concordances and commentaries were avowedly prepared for the unlearned reader. The obligation of the ministry to make scriptural interpretation available to the average man is strongly expressed by John Udall in the preface to *A Commentarie Vpon The Lamentations of Ieremy* (1593), a work which had five editions by 1637 :

. . . For, whilest some giue themselues, vpon the least occasion, to enter into a common place of Diuinitie, and to handle it most largely (which is the right way in Catechising and laying the foundations of Religion) and others labour to shewe themselues learned in the tongues, and humaine Artes, or of great reading in diuine and heathen writers, we see that the people is brought either into such amazednesse, as they thinke that any thing may be made of the Scriptures, or to such an vnsetlednesse in iudgement, as they rather hunt after varietie of teachers for their straunge manner of preaching, then for sound instruction for their owne edification.

---

[9] Henry Gee and William John Hardy (eds.), *Documents Illustrative of English Church History* (London, 1896), p. 481.

[10] Haweis, *op. cit.*, pp. 161-62.

Udall's own work is a line-by-line exposition of the meaning of Jeremiah's lamentation, with the present application to be made.

Thomas Wilson's *A Christian Dictionarie* (1612), which had four editions by 1627(?), sought to explain the difficult terms that would puzzle the reader. A certain H. S. prepared *A Divine Dictionarie; Or, The Bible abreviated* (1615), a summary by chapter and book, so that the reader might ascertain the chief contents of any book and thereby more easily find the material he sought. The best expression of the desire to help the average man in his biblical study was given by Clement Cotton, himself a member of the London Company of Drapers. In the preface to *The Christians Concordance: Containing The Most materiall words in the New Testament* (1622), he comments:

Deare Christian Reader, who, it may be, art such a one as my selfe, simple and illiterate, & yet endeuourest to know Christ, and him crucified for eternal life: . . . The learned, I doubt not, are euery way so furnished alreadie in this kinde, with all sufficient helps in other languages, that in respect of them, this is but as a candle lighted vp to the Sunne.

The need and desire of the middle-class reader for such a help as Cotton's *A Complete Concordance To The Bible Of The Last Translation* (1631) is again expressed in the preface addressed to the Christian reader:

For whom is this worke? Schollars can haue recourse to *Concordances* in Hebrew, Greek, and Latin. And the illiterate as little need this work, as they can make use of it. To this objection the diligent Composer hereof might answer as Lucilius in Tulli, that *he wrote not his bookes for the most learned, or for the most unlearned*, but for the middle sort.

Obviously, the "middle sort" not only read, but they also looked up biblical allusions often enough to need concordances.

To the Bible, English citizens looked for guidance and help even in the practical undertakings of life. In the Bible was revealed all the advice which the Creator had to offer man. Proof of the certainty of the promises of God was found in the fulfilment of the prophecies. In the British Museum there is a thin quarto entitled *The Mariage Of The Old And New Testament* (1620), with the following brief dedication:

To The Two Noble Examples of Friendship and Brotherhood, Mr.
Richard Fishborne, Mr. Iohn Browne. This Sacred Worke is conse-
crated, as a Testimonie of his Loue and Seruice, to Worth and Vertue.
By Tho : Middleton, Chronologer for the Honourable Citie of London.

Without more ado the book falls to its task, a harmony of the
prophecies of the Old with the fulfilments in the New Testament,
arranged in parallel columns. That the cynical Middleton should
have undertaken such a commission argues that the two dedicatees,
or perhaps the aldermen officially, had commanded their chronologer to compile a work of usefulness for London. A knowledge
of the Bible was an essential in the education of every citizen.

The eagerness of the public for an easy access to biblical knowledge accounts for the four editions which favored Henoch Clapham's *A Briefe Of The Bible, Drawne First into English Poësy, and
then illustrated by apte Annotations* (1596). The versified Scripture-
history is followed by a vast array of explanation, doctrinal exposition, and questions and answers on the Bible. Later editions,
dedicated to Prince Henry, are amplified with prayers and further
biblical synopses.[11] Popularization of the Bible reached its utmost
extreme in John Taylor's *Verbum Sempiternae*[12] [*sic*] (1614), a tiny
"thumb Bible" giving a rhyming paraphrase of the Old Testament
and Apocrypha. Bound with it was *Salvator Mundi*, a rhymed
paraphrase of the New Testament. The latter has a brief preface
stressing the inexpensiveness of the book :

> Heere, Reader, maist thou read (for little cost)
> How thou wast ransom'd, when thou quite wast lost.
> Mans gracelesnes, and Gods exceeding Grace
> Thou heere maist read, and see, in little space.

---

[11] Similar in appeal was Henry Lok's *Ecclesiastes, Otherwise Called The Preacher. Containing Salomons Sermons or Commentaries (as it may probably be collected) vpon the 49. Psalme
of Dauid his father. Compendiously abridged, and also paraphrastically dilated in English poesie,
according to the analogie of Scripture, and consent of the most approued writer thereof.* . . . .
Whereunto are annexed sundrie Sonets of Christian Passions heretofore printed (1597).

[12] The work was reissued in 1616 with the title corrected to *Verbum Sempiternum*.
My quotation is from the 1616 issue. Taylor's thumb Bible has had a long biblio-
graphical history, having been constantly reprinted throughout the seventeenth and
eighteenth centuries, in both England and America. It was also translated into French.
For a history of this book see Wilbur Macy Stone, *The Thumb Bible of John Taylor*
(Brookline, Mass., 1928). Mr. Stone asserts (p. 12) that Taylor's work was suggested

To the end that all good citizens might know the Bible and its doctrines, preachers, abetted by thrifty printers, produced scores of treatises which expounded the Scriptures. The necessity for popular instruction had long been recognized ; even in the Middle Ages little handbooks of religious instruction called primers had helped to familiarize the laity with the doctrines and service of the church. After the break with Rome, Henry VIII placed in the hands of the unlettered laity a primer that taught the essentials of religion without reference to the older unreformed faith.[13] Further instruction was also provided in the short catechism inserted in the Order of Confirmation in the prayer books of Edward VI and Elizabeth ; and at the request of the Puritan element in the church, this instruction was amplified by an additional explanation of the sacraments. The catechism early became an instrument of instruction in the schools and in private households. Edward VI issued an official catechism ; and unauthorized catechisms by Erasmus, Calvin, Bullinger, and others[14] were also widely used. The most influential Elizabethan catechism, however, was that prepared by Alexander Nowell and printed in an authorized edition in 1570. An abbreviated version was published for less advanced students.[15] This catechism, which went through numerous editions, was a part of the routine instruction in the schools,[16] and was used extensively in private religious instruction.

Do what the church could, however, it was unable to discourage the circulation of unauthorized manuals of religion. Calvin's *Catechism* continued to be printed, and many others, influenced by his work, found their way into English households. The authorities apparently made no serious effort to curb the printing of Puritan manuals so long as they did not meddle too obviously with controversial questions of doctrine and church government. At any rate, doctrinal and devotional works by preachers of marked

---

by John Weever's *An Agnus Dei* (1601), a rhymed version of the Bible. Weever's book had at least three editions before 1640.

[13] Norman Wood, *The Reformation and English Education* (London, 1931), pp. 154-55, 257-58, 261. *See also* Francis Proctor and Walter Howard Frere, *A New History of the Book of Common Prayer* (London, 1914), p. 599.

[14] *Ibid.*, p. 601, n. 4.

[15] *Ibid.*, p. 602, n. 4.

[16] Wood, *op. cit.*, pp. 133, 149, 174.

Puritan tendencies were published in increasing quantities throughout the reigns of Elizabeth and the first two Stuarts. A ponderous monument of Protestant faith, albeit the faith of Calvin in its less controversial form, was translated from Zacharias Ursinus by Henry Parry as *The Summe Of Christian Religion: . . . Wherein are debated and resolued the Questions of whatsoeuer points of moment, which haue beene or are controuersed in Diuinitie* (1587). The translator corrects whatever seems to him unpalatable to English religious tastes at the moment. So well did he succeed in putting forth a manual which summed up Christian doctrine, that the work had eight editions by 1630, besides two editions in Latin. An antidote to the more extreme doctrines of the Puritans, as well as a statement demolishing popery, was Bishop John Jewel's *Apologia Ecclesiae Anglicanae* (1562), translated by Lady Bacon, and published in numerous editions in both its Latin and English versions.

Works dealing with the theological approach to religion were not, however, the sort that profoundly influenced the citizenry. The literate populace was more interested in the substance of Christianity and its practical applications than in arguments over subtle points of doctrine. Devotional works for the layman, which sprang up rapidly in the beginning of Elizabeth's reign and continued to multiply during the next two reigns, furnished spiritual guidance for practical citizens. The influence of these books, written for the most part by moderate Puritans, is incalculable. They prepared the minds of the public for independence in religious worship. Through prayer and meditation, models for which they could find in a score of books, the draper, the butcher, and their apprentices soon learned to approach God without ecclesiastical assistance. Unaware of what they were doing, the authors of popular devotions were undermining the future authority of the church. The London citizen who had learned to hold worship in his own household, whose prayer was as sonorous and as eloquent as the curate's, who had studied God's promises and had learned that faith combined with prudent morality might bring him riches in this world and certainly a haven of bliss in the next, gradually came to depend upon his own dealings with the Master. Lacking the services of the chaplain usually attached to aristocratic households, the heads of middle-class families assumed the duty of teaching religion to their children and apprentices. As one Jacobean preacher later expressed it,

. . . let him instruct them in the principles of Religion; teaching them some good Catechisme, according to their capacitie; at least labouring to drive into their heads, the maine points of Christian Doctrine; and that in such familiar sort of questioning with them, that they may make him perceive they know what they speake.[17]

Religious instruction was no longer left to a teacher in holy orders, and the hierarchy of the Established Church found itself more and more in conflict with the citizenry, whose reverence for bishops was giving way. No longer was a bishop nearer the throne of God than a baker; no longer was it necessary for the parson to serve as spokesman for his parishioners at the Court of Heaven. Thanks to countless manuals, the private citizen had become articulate in the presence of the Deity.

A further social influence was exercised by the religious handbooks, which taught or implied man's obligation to man. Peace, charity, generosity, harmony in the household, city, or state, reverence for constituted authority, the recognition of the necessity of social degree in the commonwealth—these were positive contributions pleasing to magistrates. Much is to be learned of human nature and Elizabethan life from the books of prayers, meditations, and instructions which illuminated religion for the common man. Of all the works that poured from the press in the sixteenth and seventeenth centuries, these had the widest circulation and remained popular longest.[18] In quantity and numerousness of editions, only a few often-reprinted textbooks can compare with some of the books of devotions, like, for example, the famous *Practise of Pietie*.

The interest in private devotional works was already widespread

---

[17] William Whately, *The New Birth: Or, A Treatise of Regeneration* (1618). My quotation is from the edition of 1635, pp. 178-79.

[18] A valuable contribution to our understanding of the devotional literature of the early seventeenth century has been made by Miss Helen C. White, *English Devotional Literature [Prose], 1600-1640*, University of Wisconsin Studies in Language and Literature (Madison, 1931). I wish to acknowledge many helpful suggestions from Miss White.

early in the reign of Elizabeth. Thomas Becon, a noted preacher with keen social interests,[19] prepared several treatises of prayer and contemplation, which he gave such metaphorical names as *The Pomāder of Prayer* (1558)[20] and *The Sicke Mans Salue, Wherein all faithful christians may learne both howe to behaue themselues patientlye and thankfullye in the time of sicknesse, and also virtuouslie to dispose of their temporall goods, and finally to prepare themselues gladly and godly to die*, first printed in 1561.[21] The latter work was enormously popular. By 1632 it had gone through at least seventeen editions; but preserved exemplars are extremely rare today. Although it is concerned with the themes of holy living and holy dying—themes often treated by later writers—the treatise gives much practical advice. The sick man is told how to make a will, how to exhort his wife and household to lives of virtue. He is urged to be generous, to provide properly for his children and servants, to forgive his debtors, to assist the poor, and

to remember the poore schollers of the Vniversities of Oxford & Cambridge. For if they be not maintained, all learning and vertue will decay, and a very barbaritie shall burst in among vs, and at the last bring this our realme into destruction.   [Pp. 97-98.]

Many poor scholars now have to leave the universities and become serving men, one of the speakers in the dialogue maintains—a condition that will continue unless benefactors are generous. How influential were such persuasions to philanthropy, there is no way of knowing; but it is worth noting that bequests to charity and education became a convention in middle-class wills, even in seventeenth-century America.

The models for many of the early Protestant devotional books may be found in works known to the pious long before the Reformation. St. Augustine's *Prayers* and Thomas à Kempis's *Imitation of Christ* contain most of the elements developed in later manuals. Both works were themselves extremely popular throughout the Renaissance, though, obviously, alterations were necessary to

---

[19] *See* Chap. VII, *supra*, where Becon's work on marriage and household government is mentioned.

[20] Five editions of this book of prayers are recorded by 1578.

[21] Title and quotations from the edition of 1604.

make them suitable for Protestant use. To Thomas Rogers, Protestants were indebted for the expurgation of Catholic doctrine and symbolism from both authors. By way of the French, Rogers translated *Of the Imitation of Christ* [1580], thus providing a version which had at least fourteen editions by 1640. His defense of his liberties with the text reveals a method of "improving" Catholic works which was to become conventional with later translators and editors. He trusts that no one will mislike his corrections,[22] since the changes have been made in the interest of good doctrine. He has omitted some popish words and phrases and has purged the text of some corruptions (also popish). He marvels why previous translators have not so corrected the author. Not even a note will he give to betray to the simple reader, for whom his work is prepared, the places where superstition occurred:

It maie be obiected that I might haue giuen some note by the waie, and so let them passe; as doth *Erasmus* in his translations. Surelie *Erasmus* might better do so in Latine, than I maie in English. For asmuch as most are learned, & haue iudgement which read his; and I do that which I do for the simpler sorte.

Such purging of superstitious books should be greatly pleasing to God, Rogers believes. To the end that other good works might be cleansed of Catholic error, he translated *A right Christian Treatise, entituled S. Augustines Praiers: . . . purged from diuers superstitious points* (1581), which also included *St. Augustines Manuel.* Expressing a hope that the word "manual" will be interpreted literally, Rogers describes the method of reading undoubtedly followed by some of the devout:

I do cal this booke, as also the author doth, a Manuel, because my wish is, that Christians would vse, and haue it in their hands, not onlie when they are at home in their chambers, and studies priuatelie, but also when they are abroad in the fields, gardens, and else-where idlelie: and that not to dandle, and to handle onlie, but diligentlie, and zealouslie, as the part of Christians is, to reade the same for their spiritual exercise.   [Sig. a 2v.]

Various other versions of the works of St. Augustine and Thomas

---

[22] Second epistle of the translator.

à Kempis were available and served to popularize this type of prayer and meditation.

The practice of drawing on Catholic works to furnish good doctrine for Protestants reached the level of comedy in the notorious thefts of the traveling preacher, Edmund Bunny, from the Jesuit, Robert Parsons. In 1584 appeared a treatise bearing the title, *A Booke of Christian exercise, appertaining to Resolution, that is shewing how that we should resolv our selvs to becom Christians in deed: by R. P. Perused, and accompanied now with a Treatise tending to Pacification: by Edmund Bunny.*[23] Finding a well written treatise persuading mankind to leave his vanities, serve God, and spend much time in meditating upon the goodness of God and the mercies of Christ, as well as upon the rewards[24] and punishments likely to be received, Bunny was not deterred because it was clearly the work of a Catholic propagandist. His zeal, indeed, was even stirred to turn the weapon against the papist author; hence he deleted all elements of Catholicism and presented to a piety-reading nation a treatise so popular that it was to be constantly reprinted for generations. When Parsons indignantly protested, in a new edition of his work with the changed title of *A Christian Directorie,* Bunny replied with *A briefe Answer vnto those idle and friuolous quarrels of R. P. against the late edition of the Resolution* and continued to reprint the first treatise. With self-righteousness, in the dedication of the *Christian exercise* to the Archbishop of York he had expressed his desire to correct a work which was already being widely read:

. . . I perceived, that the booke insuing was willingly read by divers, for the persuasion that it hath to godlines of life, which notwithstanding in manie points was corruptly set down : I thought good in the end, to get the same published againe in some better manner, than now it is come foorth among them ; that so the good, that the reading therof might otherwise do, might carrie no hurt or danger withal, so far as might be prevented.

---

[23] Title quoted from edition of 1585. For a discussion of Bunny and Parsons, see White, *op. cit.,* pp. 143-49.

[24] Opposite a section on God's rewards is a pertinent marginal note, "God the best pay-master."—P. 129.

He had the precedent of "Maister Rogers" "in that little booke of *Kempicius,* that is called *The Imitation of Christ,* leaving out the corruption of it, and taking onlie that which was sound."[25] Aside from any interest which may have attached to the treatise because of the notoriety of Parsons and the clever trick played upon him by Bunny, as a religious manual the book struck the note that appealed to the popular audience. Despite its strange origin, it steered clear of controversial matters and directed men to think upon the fundamentals of Christian belief, urging always the temporal as well as the spiritual advantages of the virtuous over the wicked life.

Most of the widely read devotional books combined meditations and prayers with much prudential wisdom. Edward Dering, author of popular catechisms, sermons, and prayers, boiled down his wisdom into a one-page epitome, opposite the title-page of *Godly priuate prayers for housholders to meditate vpon, and to say in their families* (1576), and labeled it "Maister D. his councell, to all that are his : as also a briefe lesson for all estates." Urging man not to speak all he knows, or to believe all he hears, Dering suggests that he think of his death, and practise abstinence, which is good for the health and wealth of the soul, mind, and body. Particularly should man flee idleness, fear God, and combine good morality with worldly prudence, as the following passage advises :

Keepe counsell. Use not manye wordes. Tell the truth. Be slow to speake. Brydle thine anger. Appease debate. Hinder no mans good name. Take heede of drinke. Remember thy ende. Be mercifull. Trie before thou trust. Repose no confidence in a reconciled aduersarie. Sorowe not for that which can not be got agayne. Reioyce not in thy

---

[25] Sig. A 2. The necessity of drawing upon Catholic works for such treatises is mentioned a little later by T. Pickering, in his edition of William Perkins's *The Whole Treatise Of The Cases Of Conscience,* first printed in 1606. In the dedication to the second and third books, Pickering complains : ". . . in this flourishing estate both of our Church and Commonwealth, none haue employed their indeauours in the vnfolding and displaying of this Subiect : yea, whereas they of the Popish church haue bene so plentifull, or rather lauish in their Summes, Manuels, Aphorismes, Instructions, Determinations, &c. for direction of their Confessours in Case-points : that our Protestant Divines for the most part haue bene so sparing and silent in speaking or writing of this argument." He is glad that Providence has raised up a help in Master Perkins. (Quotation from the edition of 1608.)

neyghbours crosse. Striue not with thy ouer match. Reueale not thy secretes to thy wife, nor to thy children : for women, and children, say all they know. Three things vndid the Romanes reigne : priuie grudge, yong heades, and priuate gayne. Beare with others, as thou would haue others beare with thee. Be not to rashe, hasty, bolde, nor wyse in thine owne conceyte.[26]

Surely the teachings of Machiavelli and the Man of Galilee must have been combined to produce this prayer book, which was reprinted six times by 1615. Its expansions of the Lord's Prayer and the simple, direct prayers for all occasions, must have been useful in many a tradesman's household worship.

The belief in the efficacy of aphoristic wisdom, in the utility of the pat phrase—a convention of Renaissance educational theory—found its way into the training of the common people partly through the devotional books. One of the best illustrations of the guide to piety, divided into pithy numbered statements for memorizing and easy reference, is Abraham Fleming's *The Diamond of Deuotion, Cut and squared into six seuerall points: Namelie, 1. The Footpath to Felicitie. 2. A Guide to Godlines. 3. The Schoole of Skill. 4. A Swarme of Bees. 5. A Plant of Pleasure. 6. A Groue of Graces. Full of manie fruitfull lessons, auaileable to the leading of a godlie and reformed life* (1581). In the section on the "Schoole of Skill," the material is "Digested into three sententious sequences of the A, B, C. Wherein the weake haue their full measure of pure milke, and the strong their iust weight of sound meate." Under the D's, for example, one finds such suggestions for the improvement of one's reputation as, "Drawe towards the wise to learne wisedome, so shalt thou be had in reputation."[27] The first section, concerning the "Footepath to Felicitie," is more expositional than the rest, but even it is devoted to the terse statement of pious and practical maxims.

What the average man wanted when he approached God is clearly set forth in the religious writings of John Norden, whom we may now safely identify with the author of numerous works

---

[26] In the Huntington Library copy, opposite the words "Reueale not thy secretes to thy wife" (which have been scratched through with a pen) some seventeenth-century woman, it seems, has written with indignation, "[Y]f thy wife be a foolish woman or a whorish woman."   [27] P. 193.

on surveying and topography. Norden understood the religious
point of view of his contemporaries and prepared for them *A
Pensiue Mans Practise. Very profitable for all persons: wherin are contained very deuout and necessary prayers for sundry godly purposes, with
requisite perswasions before euery Prayer. Newly corrected and amended
by the Author after aboue forty Impressions* (1627), the first edition
of which appeared in 1584. The forty impressions here claimed
did not end the popularity of this work, for at least two other
editions appeared between 1627 and 1640. Preceding each prayer
is "The Motiue," a short explanatory passage and meditation.
The prayers themselves are so simple and direct that "to the
faithfull, exercising them, they will be profitable, of whatsoeuer
estate, degree, calling, or ministery they be of."[28] By profit,
Norden means something more than bliss in a future life, for he
has included such necessary petitions as "A short Prayer for a
competent liuing"[29] and "The prayer for a prosperous iourney."[30]
The general belief in the profitableness of godliness in the affairs
of this world was a little later to provoke Henry Smith to preach
against mercenary praying, but it remained imbedded in the
faith of man.

The concern for the unlearned, obvious in Norden's work, is
one of the noteworthy characteristics of the industrious and influential William Perkins, whose sermons, as we shall see, were widely
read and approved in all classes of society. Though he was an
erudite teacher of theology at Cambridge, Perkins labored earnestly to provide religious guidance for the ignorant, perhaps with
less emphasis on the utilitarian quality of prayer than Norden
expressed. A volume of instruction in the fundamentals of religion,
entitled *The Foundation of Christian Religion: Gathered into sixe Prin-*

---

[28] Preface. Norden's concern for the simple man is expressed quite clearly in the
dedication of *A Pensive soules delight* (1603), his versified history of the plots against
Queen Elizabeth. The subject is "worthie of a more serious labour. But because many
worthie workes are extāt of their discouery, some too great of price for poore men, and
some too learned for the simple. And such serious Treatises oftē neglected, because
they delight not all humours, I thought it not vnfit to put the inferiour multitude in
minde, in this kinde of writing, what causes they haue to sighe and to sing, to grieue
and reioyce : . . ." Norden's title, *A poore mans rest: now the eight time augmented*
(1620), is further indication of the audience to whom his work was directed.

[29] P. 120.   [30] P. 212.

ciples. And it is to be learned of ignorant people, that they may be fit to heare Sermons with profit, and to receiue the Lordes Supper with comfort (1590),[31] had a widespread use over a long period, going through fourteen editions by 1638, not including the reprints in Perkins's collected works. Preceding the text is a two-page epitome of certain vulgar errors, addressed "To all ignorant people that desire to be instructed." In numerical order, he lists the popular fallacies which he wishes to correct; for example:

13 That it is the safest, to doe in Religion as most doe.

14 That merrie ballads and bookes, as *Scoggin, Beuis of Southampton, &c.* are good to driue away time, and to remoue hart quames.

. . . .

19 That it was a good world when the olde Religion was, because all things were cheape.

20 That drinking and bezeling in the alehouse or tauerne is good fellowship, & shewes a good kinde nature, & maintaines neighbourhood.[32]   [Sig. A 2.]

Thus it appears that the fundamentals of religion, as interpreted by Perkins, have to do not only with heaven but with common matters of economics and everyday life. This work, in substance, is a catechism-like question-and-answer book to prepare the laity for worship.[33]

The end of the sixteenth century saw a great multiplication of devotional books, many of which concerned themselves with the

---

[31] Title quoted from the edition of 1595.

[32] Perkins's interest in the ignorant is further indicated in *An Exposition of the Lords Prayer: In the way of Catechising seruing for ignorant people. Hereunto are adioined the Praiers of Paule, taken out of his Epistles* (1595), bound with the edition of *The Foundation* cited here.

[33] Another of the much-read catechisms for popular study was *The Way To True Happiness: Leading to the Gate of Knowledge. Or, An entrance to Faith: without which it is vnpossible to please God. By Questions and Answers, opening briefly the meaning of euery seuerall Booke and Chapter of the Bible, from the beginning of Genesis, to the end of the Revelation.* The first edition with this title appeared in 1610; the foregoing title is quoted from the edition of 1632. The work had ten editions in this form by 1640. Before 1610 it had appeared in several editions as *The doctrine of the Bible.* Equally popular was Stephen Egerton's *A briefe methode of Catechizing,* the earliest preserved edition of which, listed in the *Short Title Catalogue,* is the sixteenth, in 1610; the last recorded is the thirty-ninth, in 1631.

problem of how to die well.[34] Perhaps the raging of the plague made this a timely theme; perhaps the general disillusionment and uncertainty that crept into the national consciousness in the last years of Elizabeth may be reflected in the somber tones of the books of meditations, which often savor of stoicism despite the effort to set forth the glowing hope of Christian optimism. Again it was William Perkins who produced a book in the language best understood by the simple, *A salve for a sicke man, or, A treatise containing the nature, differences, and kindes of death; as also the right manner of dying well. And It may serue for spirituall instruction to 1. Mariners when they goe to sea. 2. Souldiers when they goe to battell. 3. Women when they trauell of child* (1595). To the distressed and to those for whom death seems imminent, Perkins holds out the rewards to be expected in a better world; death is merely the door which leads to a fuller life. Anticipating the queries which might arise in the mind of the reader, Perkins gives many hypothetical questions and objections, with the proper answers. The preserved exemplars of this pamphlet, which had six editions by 1632, are frequently ragged and soiled with use. The Huntington Library copy is thumb-marked, as if some grimy-handed mariner had often conned it. In an age when buccaneers fell to their prayers before overhauling a Spanish carvel, the sailor with his book of meditations might exist in the flesh rather than in the bizarre dream of a zealot of the Bible Society.

More widely read even than Perkins's treatise was a work published in 1600 by Christopher Sutton, *Disce Mori. Learne to Die.*[35] This was followed in 1602 by *Disce Vivere. Learne to Live.*

---

[34] The art of holy living and holy dying, which was to reach its finest literary expression in the seventeenth century in Jeremy Taylor's *Holy Living* (1650) and *Holy Dying* (1651), was no new theme, of course. The craft of dying well had been a popular subject in the Middle Ages. Attributed to Richard Rolle was a treatise on the subject, *The boke of the craft of dying* (cf. C. Horstmann, *Richard Rolle of Hampole and His Followers* [London, 1895-96], II, 406 ff.). One of the most popular of medieval works was *De Arte Moriendi*. (Cf. Frances M. M. Comper [ed.], *The Book of the Craft of Dying and Other Early English Tracts concerning Death* [London, 1917], p. ix.) A translation of one of the versions of this work was published by Caxton. The theme of the coming of death had also been made familiar to the populace by the Dance of Death literature and the morality plays.

[35] *Disce Mori. Learne to Die. A Religious discourse, moouing euery Christian man to enter into a serious remembrance of his ende. Wherin also is contained the meane and manner of disposing*

Both treatises were later published together. *Disce Mori* is a dignified discussion of the approach of death, calling upon man to
live so that he may meet his end with decorum. The evanescence
of this life and the ephemeral quality of things of the earth, which,
like dross, should be put aside, are emphasized throughout. Sutton's style is learned, though frequently eloquent, as when he
speaks of the futility of earthly vanity. Life is only an interlude.
The dead have finished their parts; we wait to recite our epilogue.
Death comes, like a sergeant in an action of debt, at the suit of
nature to attach and arrest us all. The world is a weak world and
all its people

. . . shall one day find, that death will haue to do with them, when
hee shall strip them into a shrowding sheete, binde them hand and
foote, and make their last bed to be the hard and stony graue.

[Pp. 19-20.]

But Sutton is not merely interested in painting a vivid picture of
the worthlessness of earthly ambition; practical in his outlook,
he is imbued with the new humanitarianism born of the modern
spirit which has nurtured the idea of progress. He includes, therefore, a chapter on "How the sicke shoulde dispose of worldly
goods and possessions." It is a blessed thing to give, says Sutton,
but our giving must be tempered with reason. Hence the dying
philanthropist ought to be governed by advisers possessed of
learning and discretion, who will know how to bestow his goods
where they will be of greatest use to society:

In which giuing, the maintenaunce of Churches, Colledges, Schooles,
Hospitalles, and such like godly vses, should where abilitie is answerable, be chiefly remembred; for by these deeds of mercie we doe not
onely ourselues acknowledge Gods goodnesse, but make many others,
when we are long since dead & gone, blesse him in the participation
of the same. . . . To giue vnto the poore in time of sicknesse tis good:
but more acceptable were it to do it dayly, and in time of best health.
This giuing is the shippe that will neuer strike against the rocke, but

himselfe to God, before, and at the time of his departure. In the whole, somewhat happily may be
obserued, necessary to be thought vpon, while we are aliue, and when we are dying, to aduise our
selues and others. Title quoted from edition of 1601. Nine editions appeared by 1620.
Disce Vivere had six editions by 1620. In 1629 both were published together, followed
by another edition in 1634. Several reprints appeared in the nineteenth century.

bring our marchandise home in safetie. This giuing is the most gainfull interest, when the mercifull shall receiue a thousande for one, and find in another world the rewarde of lending vnto God, that is to say, of giuing vnto the poore.   [Pp. 174-75.]

Sutton is socially minded throughout his treatise. He objects to extravagance, especially in dress, but his objection is not Puritan fanaticism—and the Puritan objection to ostentation has frequently been misunderstood—for Sutton is troubled over economic waste :

The pride of the world in attire, the needlesse superfluitie in dyet hath eaten vp hospitalitie and mercie towardes many hungrie soules : and causeth that wee haue little to leaue at our departures for the good of others : neuer more at the table, but neuer lesse at the doore : neuer more sumptuous in clothing our selues, neuer lesse respectiue of others.
                                                   [Pp. 176-77.]

The open house maintained in the establishments of the wealthy, and the free-handed dispensation of food to the poor, were giving way in the face of rising prices and the retrenchments necessary to keep pace with the changing standards of living and the increasing desire for new luxuries. Hospitality, the decay of which is regretted by Sutton, connoted much more than the modern word. It meant not only charity but employment for countless retainers. Hence its decay became the theme of moralists and economists. Sutton further shows his social interest by counseling a mode of life that will make for harmony in society. Men should live in peace, ply their callings, and not meddle with the affairs of their neighbors; especially should they avoid the unchristian practice of going to law "for some vile vnconscionable gaine."[36] Strangely enough, *Disce Vivere* is more mystical and less concerned with practical matters than the treatise on dying well. The author gives an exposition of the life of Christ and suggests that man improve his condition by contemplation and imitation of his Savior.

Printers were diligent, at the turn of the century, to supply the demand for books of prayer and instruction in the pious life, and

---

[36] P. 397. In this connection it may be worth noting that lawyers were long looked upon with hostility in Puritan New England.

authors were careful to prepare their works so that they might be understood by the less erudite. Josias Nichols simplified his book so thoroughly that he was constrained to give it the self-advertising title of *An Order of Houshold Instruction: By which euery master of a Familie, may easily and in short space, make his whole houshold to vnderstand the principall and chiefe points of Christian religion: without the knowledge whereof, no man can be saued* (1596). This was a manual of interpretation to guide the head of the house in explaining the Bible to his children and apprentices. Thomas Tymme produced a small handbook of prayers for the lower classes, entitled *The Poore Mans Pater noster, with a preparatiue to praier: Wherto are annexed diuers godly Psalmes and Meditations* (1598).[37] More widely read was a later work by Tymme, *A Silver Watch-Bell. The Sound whereof is able (by the Grace of God) to winne the most profane worldling, and carelesse liuer . . . to become a true Christian indeed* (1605).[38] The author is convinced that his treatise contains

matter of greater consequence, then *Plato* his Commonwealth or *Aristotles Summum Bonum,* or *Tullius Oratour,* or *Moores Vtopia;* for that it comprehendeth not onely an *Idaea* of good life, but also a plat-forme of good workes, which leadeth the way to true sempiternall felicitie.[39]

Evidently the public agreed, for there appeared in 1640 an eighteenth impression of this little book, which warned against the vanities of the world and the horrors of hell and provided the reader with a guide to the attainment of heaven. Francis Meres in *Granados Devotion* (1598) and *The Sinners Guyde* (1598), and Thomas Lodge in *The Flowers of Lodowicke of Granado* (1601), pillaged from Catholic Spain material for the benefit of Protestant readers. John Brinsley compiled *The True Watch, And Rule Of Life* (1606), which had at least eleven editions by 1637. Thomas Sorocold, rector of St. Mildred's in the Poultry, was the author of *Supplications of Saints. A Booke of Praiers and Prayses* (licensed, 1608),[40] a work so long popular that at least forty-five editions were pub-

---

[37] This is the earliest preserved edition; the title-page declares that it is "newly imprinted the second time." It was recorded in the *Stationers' Register* on July 5, 1591.
[38] Title quoted from "The tenth Impression" (1614).
[39] *Ibid.,* dedication to Sir Edward Coke.
[40] Title quoted from the eleventh edition, 1623. The earliest extant edition recorded is that of 1612.

lished before 1754. Thomas Hearne remembered a pious woman who yearly gave large numbers of Sorocold's book of prayers to the poor.[41] Even Thomas Dekker turned his hand to piety in *Foure Birds Of Noahs Arke* (1609) and produced a collection of prayers in which he achieved some of his finest prose.[42] Mindful of the needs of the "yong & the meanest people," Dekker includes prayers for the schoolboy, the apprentice, the serving man, the maid, the tradesman, the mariner, and other simple folk; nor is he forgetful even of the galley slave and "men that worke in dangerous works, as Coale-pits."

Of all the treatises of devotion, however, which appeared in the last years of Elizabeth's reign, the most influential was *The Plaine Mans Path-way to Heauen. Wherein euery man may clearly see, whether he shall be saued or damned. Set forth Dialogue wise, for the better vnderstanding of the simple. By Arthur Dent, Preacher of the word of God at South-Shoebery in Essex* (1601). Both the ignorant and the learned can find something of use in his treatise, Dent asserts in the dedication:

As concerning the manner, heere is no great matter of learning, wit, art, eloquence, or ingenious inuention: (for I haue heerein, specially respected the ignorant, and vulgar sort, whose edification I doo chiefly aime at) yet somewhat there is which may concerne the learned, and giue them some contentment.

A moderate Puritan in his religious convictions, Dent, like the majority of his kind, wished to steer clear of controversy in dealing with the multitude; and the multitude, caring more for salvation than for argument, responded for the next generation by buying his book. Satan and sin are the objects of his attack, he declares in the preface. Man's misery in nature and his means of recovery, the iniquity and common corruptions of the world, the differences between reprobates and the children of God, the signs of damnation and salvation—these are Dent's themes. Especially does he inveigh against unthrifty sins, of which woman's extravagance in dress is prominent. Of the signs of damnation there are nine: Pride, Whoredom, Covetousness, Contempt of the Gospel, Swear-

---

[41] *Dictionary of National Biography*, sub Sorocold.

[42] *See* the introduction, F. P. Wilson (ed.), *Foure Birds Of Noahs Arke by Thomas Dekker* (Oxford, 1924).

ing, Lying, Drunkenness, Idleness, and Oppression. Thus had Calvinism improved upon the Seven Deadly Sins. A "Five and twentieth" edition in 1640 and a translation into Welsh proved how keen was Britain's interest in whether it were damned.[43]

Hard on Dent's heels came Robert Hill, himself a London preacher and a member of the Vintners' Company, with another directory to the proper life, similarly called *The Pathway to Prayer, And Pietie: Containing, 1 An exposition of the Lords Prayer. 2 A preparation to the Lords Supper. 3 A direction to a Christian life. 4 An Instruction to a Christian death. With Divers Prayers, and thanksgiuings, fit for this Treatise* (1610).[44] Like Dent's treatise it is in dialogue; questions and answers regarding the practical problems of ethics affecting London citizens are exchanged between Euchedidascalus, a teacher of prayer, and Phieluches, a lover of prayer.

No pious work of the period so well represents the commercial point of view or so completely indicates the fusion between religion and materialism which has always been a characteristic of bourgeois civilizations. In the first section, which provides an exposition of the Lord's Prayer, the whole economy of man in relation to God is explained. The discussion of the problem of whether God should be petitioned for wealth is particularly significant. Although it is "very inconuenient, if not vtterly vnlawfull"[45] to pray for riches, man may pray for the prosperity of himself and others. For his daily bread, of course, he is commanded to pray; this injunction is interpreted largely to mean not only actual bread but

figuratiuely all things, which are, or may be for the good of my bodie, and this naturall life : as strength by nourishment, health by Physicke, warmth by apparel, sufficiencie by labour, and the blessing of God in the vse of al these & such like.   [Pp. 30-31.]

---

[43] A suggestion of imitation of Dent's title, to catch the eye, was William Webster's *The Plaine Mans Pilgrimage. Or Journey Towards Heaven. Wherein if hee walke carefully he may attaine to euerlasting life* (1613), a sermon-like treatise exhorting men to virtue and piety.

[44] Title from the Huntington Library exemplar, which is described on the title-page as "The fourth Edition." According to the *Short Title Catalogue*, an earlier edition, with a different title, appeared in 1606. An eighth edition was published in 1629.

[45] P. 35.

The repetition of this prayer is useful to impress upon the petitioner the divine origin of property,

To teach me that all riches, whether of inheritance, or by gift, paines, trades, office, seruice, witte, mariage, or any other meanes are the gift of God, who only giueth man power to get riches. [P. 31.]

Since property comes from God, the recipient is advised to remember God's creatures, his own poor brethren, and be liberal in his charity.

While it is improper to appear greedy in petitions to the Dispenser of all good things, man should be diligent and thrifty. The implication is that God helps those who help themselves:

I must pray neither for riches, nor pouertie, but go on in my calling, with faithfull diligence: and waiting for a blessing from the Lord, be thankfull for whatsoeuer he shall send. [P. 36.]

By the examples of Joseph and even the apostles, who practised "frugalitie and thriftinesse," we are taught to save something for the morrow. Though Christ did command us not to lay up treasures on earth, he meant in such a manner "so as to neglect to lay vp treasure in heauen."[46] A final list of the things to pray for is a summary of the bourgeois conception of a well ordered commonwealth:

1 I pray here for al means by which I and others may haue our daily bread; as seasonable weather for ye fruits of the earth, sympathie of all creatures, that the heauens may beare the earth, the earth the corne, and it vs. For godly Magistrates, for the maintenance of peace, and procuring of plentie: For valiāt souldiers to defend our land: for painful husbandmen, & trades-men in al callings: for prudent huswiues, faithfull seruants, and that euē our beasts may be strong to labor.

2 I pray for peace in all kingdoms, plentie in our borders, and that the staffe of bread be not taken from vs.

3 I pray for humilitie in acknowledging Gods good gifts, and blessings to me: contentednes in our estates, diligence in our callings, faithfulnes in our dealings, prouidence to get, frugalitie to lay vp, liberalitie to giue out, magnificence in doing great works, thankfulnes

---

[46] P. 37.

for our goods, ioy at the good of others, and that God would giue vs all that which is fit for vs.   [Pp. 40-41.]

A list of things to be prayed against comes next. They are chiefly the opposites of the foregoing desires: unseasonable weather, disease among animals, ungodly laws, wars and disturbances of the peace, discontent and want, pride in abundance, parsimony in hoarding, prodigality in spending, and unmercifulness toward the poor.

No heresy can be more unchristian in bourgeois eyes than the doctrine of community of goods, which violates all that is holiest in the structure of society. It is not surprising, therefore, to find Hill directing an attack on Anabaptists, declaring once more the familiar creed that we must labor diligently to be true followers of Christ, that we must recognize that God meant his people to be ranked by degree. Hill tabulates a little creed of things good to remember:

1 That I must labour to bee in Christ.
2 That I may so get riches, that I may say they are mine.
3 That I may labour to maintaine my estate.
4 That communitie of goods is an Anabaptisticall fancie.
5 That God wold not haue al alike rich.
6 That I must impart my goods to the poore.   [Pp. 39-40.]

Almost as wicked as communism—indeed, its handmaiden—is idleness. If prosperous citizens of the early seventeenth century, instead of the church Fathers, had formulated the Seven Deadly Sins, Pride would have had to give up its place in the van to Idleness, for in bourgeois eyes, to do nothing is grievously to sin. Moreover, it is a worse sin if one's neighbor does nothing. Therefore Robert Hill set himself to cope with this Dragon of Error. His method, again, is to draw up a tabulation of things to remember:

I must meditate, 1 That God commandeth all men to labour.
2 That Euah fell in Paradise by idlenesse.
3 That it was one of ye sins of Sodom.
4 That it is a cushion for Satan to sleepe on.
5 That labour puts Satans assaults away.
6 That idlenesse consumeth the bodie.

7 That a slothfull hand maketh poore, as a diligent hand maketh rich.

8 Without diligence we cannot prouide for a familie, or the time to come.

9 All creatures, euen to the pismire, are diligent.

10 God our Father is euer working.

11 By it we may be able to do good to others.

12 All good men haue laboured in a calling. And why haue people hands, and wits, but to vse them : and the more both are vsed, the better they are.   [Pp. 82-83.]

Falstaff's jest about laboring in his calling is a satirical thrust at a fundamental bourgeois axiom. The doctrine of contentment with one's lot, also insisted upon by Hill, is in no way contradictory to the injunction to be diligent; if man labors and is content, God will take care of the rest. Prosperity is the reward of faith and industry.

All of this practical guidance to bourgeois piety is not yet enough. Under a separate title-page, Hill gives *A Direction To Live Well*—a collection of suggestions on everyday matters. Even the choice of clothes in some mystical way is bound up with godliness. Clothes must be neat and suitable for one's occupation, neither too gay nor too somber but such as indicate sobriety of mind. No one must dress above his degree, for to do so is to "giue testimonie of idlenes."[47] Moderation in diet is enjoined. Recreations are permitted, if they are not offensive to any man and provided the participant returns immediately afterward to his calling.[48] There are rules on the observance of the Sabbath, a catechism on the obligations which husbands and wives owe to each other, and, finally, a section on the relations of masters and servants. Masters are told to have a care for their servants' health, to see that they observe the Sabbath, to correct their faults, to avoid familiarity with them, to teach them a trade or occupation, and to help them when they set up for themselves. Servants are warned to be diligent, honest, careful to become masters of their trades, circumspect for their master's good, silent and discreet, willing and cheerful, respectful of their betters, peaceful to their fellows, to set a good example to the children of the family, and to

---

[47] Pp. 165-66.   [48] P. 167.

remember that a thriving master was never a slothful and wicked apprentice. More specific and detailed advice is given to serving men and maids, the essence of which is that diligence and honesty are pleasing in the sight of God and man. After this come rules and duties of good magistrates and good subjects. Obedience and reverence for authority, even to the point of concealing the faults of a ruler, are emphasized. Lastly, Hill appends, with a separate title-page, *A Direction To Die Well*, urging, like Sutton in his *Disce Mori*, a life so lived that death may be met with dignity and without fear. Weary with well-doing in the following of Hill's prescription for the good life, the citizen doubtless found in death a deserved rest.

Hill's *Pathway to Prayer, And Pietie*, more clearly than any other document, sets forth the tradesman's ideal of life and his conception of God as the master business man. In Hill's philosophy, which is the philosophy of the bourgeoisie, industry, honesty, and obedience to the laws of God and man lead to success in this life and at length to a seat with Abraham and Jacob.

Urged though they were by countless treatises and sermons, apprentices were not so zealous in the cause of righteousness as the moralists desired. To make the attainment of virtue easier for them, a certain B. P. wrote *The Prentises Practise In Godlinesse, and his true Freedome. Diuided into ten Chapters* (1608), dedicated to the "Religiously disposed and vertuous yong men, the Apprentices of the City of London." The author, who refers to himself as a "new conuerted Prentise," finds a cause for the discouragement met with by the children of light in

the bookes that are written, not of vertue and verity, but of vilenes and vanity, which many offer now a daies, as so many Sacrifices to the diuell (by the which as with so many cups of poison, he infecteth the hearts of millions of people).   [Preface.]

His own contribution promises to serve as an antidote to such lewd books. Among the means to further the journey toward salvation, B. P. urges pious reading when one might otherwise be indulging in the heinous sin of unthrifty idleness:

Another meanes to set vs forward in the way of repentance, is the reading of good bookes, & mutuall conference, and exhortation one of another. These doe both after one sort bob vs continually on the elbowe, and euen importune vs to well doing, and would worke some good effect if we were not negligent & carelesse in the vsing of them. But so it is, how much time do we spend idlely doing nothing, or vn-thriftily in doing naught, neuer taking a good booke in our hands all the weeke long, though we haue choice of manie, and our trades will beare it; or if wee begin, it growes irksom straight before wee haue turned one leafe ouer; or if we haue the patience to goe thorow to the end (slightly enough;) wee cast it in a corner to be moulded and moath-eaten, and are as much the better as he that hath lookt in a glasse is, after his backe is turned : because wee do not stirre vp and whet our remembrance by a second more aduised reading, esteeming our olde bookes as olde friends, which must euer now and then be visited, that acquaintance may be renewed and not lost. [Pp. 35-36.]

Rebukes for Sabbath breaking, idleness, riotous behavior, and disobedience, mingled with exhortations to religious devotion, make up the contents. Despite the flattering dedication to them, apprentices neglected the book, and it died in its first edition. They and their masters bought such works as those by Dent and Hill, which offered a fuller and more acceptable view of salvation.

Very soon appeared two other handbooks, which were to rival all the previous works in popularity. The first was Samuel Hieron's *A Helpe Vnto Devotion. Containing certaine Moulds or Formes of Prayer, fitted to seuerall occasions, and penned for the furtherance of those, who haue more desire then skill, to poure out their Soules by Petition vnto God.*[49] The other was Lewis Bayly's *The Practise of Pietie,*[50] for generations the common man's guide to godliness—a book imported in large quantities into early America.[51]

---

[49] The first preserved edition of *A Helpe Vnto Devotion*, described as the fourth, dates from 1612. It was licensed in 1608. A twentieth edition was published in 1636. My citations are from the reprint included in *The Sermons of Master Samuel Hieron* (1620).

[50] The first preserved edition, called the third, dates from 1613. The work was licensed in 1612. At least forty-three editions were printed by 1640 and it continued in popularity until the nineteenth century. *See* J. E. Bailey, "Bishop Lewis Bayly and his 'Practice of Piety,'" *Manchester Quarterly*, No. VII (1883), 201-19.

[51] Edward Eggleston, *The Transit of Civilization*, pp. 168-71. Eggleston declares that "Colonists frequently carried it to Virginia and elsewhere, sometimes in company with the Bible, the prayer book, and Barrough's Method of Phisicke, . . ." It is frequently met with among the heirlooms of New Englanders and it was translated by Eliot for the Indians. Reading of the *Practise of Pietie* was believed to be good to ward off witches.

Hieron's *A Helpe Vnto Devotion*, written by a preacher who had
been a favorite with Londoners,[52] gives evidence of the attitude
of the citizenry toward formal prayers. Although many Puritans
objected to the Prayer Book of the bishops and to any form of
private worship dictated by ecclesiastical authority, the rank and
file welcomed such "helps" as that which Hieron provided. The
author tactfully suggests the good sense of a middle course in
regard to printed prayers:

I am not ignorant (good Reader) that set forms of Prayer are very dis-
tastfull vnto many: they are aiudged to be a kind of confining & limiting of Gods Spirit. And some which do allow them a lawful vse in the
Congregation, doe yet not so well approue them for priuate purposes.
For mine owne part, as I fauour neither their fondnesse, who scarce
account it praying, vnlesse it be by a Booke; nor their carelesnesse,
who labour not to attaine to an ability of commending their personall
occasions (euen in words of their owne conceiuing) vnto God: so I
could neuer see good reason, why platformes of direction for those,
who are yet but beginners in this spiritual exercise of Prayer, should
be thought any way inconuenient or needlesse amongst Christians.

Impressed with the ignorance and the unskilfulness of many who
wished to pray, Hieron deemed it well to give them aid:

Hereupon I thought with my selfe, that as familiar Catechismes and
plaine Treatises haue their vse, being ioyned to the publike Ministry,
to bring those . . . which haue as yet but stammering and lisping
tongues, vntill they shall bee able, hauing tongues as fined siluer,
plainly and distinctly to speake the language of Canaan. For this
cause I gaue my Booke no greater title then A Helpe vnto Deuotion,
because I would not be mistaken, or thought to intend any thing
else, . . .   [Preface.]

The prayers are simple and direct, designed for all crises in the
lives of ordinary folk. There are supplications to be said in time
of tempest, dearth, plague, or war, prayers for the sea traveler,
the soldier, and even one for a malefactor condemned to die. In
"A Morning Prayer for a priuate Person," once more appears the
familiar doctrine of industry:

---

[52] *Dictionary of National Biography, sub* Hieron,

Idlenesse and godlinesse cannot agree : & it is thy will, that in the sweat of my face I should eate my bread : preserue me from all fraudulent, guilefull, oppressing, greedy courses.   [P. 695.]

Like many of the earlier devotional books, *The Practise of Pietie* combined meditations and prayers. Furthermore, it summarized in simple language the non-controversial elements of the Protestants' conception of Christian practice. The reader learns at once the nature and attributes of God ; he sees contrasted the miseries of the natural or unregenerate man and the happiness that comes from regeneration ; and after the enumeration of seven hindrances to piety, he is exhorted to lead the godly life. Then follows a direction for proper conduct to insure the attainment of heaven. In order that the advantages of godliness might be impressed upon the reader, Bayly cited notable examples of God's judgment against sinners. A repetition of fires at Tiverton, for instance, served as an illustration of the result of profane Sabbath breaking. So influential was Bayly's work that collectors of funds for the stricken town complained after a third burning that "the *Practice of Piety* had done them much wrong."[53] Prayers, long and short, for all occasions are provided, as well as consolations for the dying and those about to die. The book, furthermore, was conveniently small, so that it could be easily carried in one's pocket. In short, it combined all the qualities useful to a traveler along the somewhat thorny seventeenth-century way of life. Puritan and Anglican alike read it. Men singled it out in their wills for special mention along with the Bible. Bunyan's wife brought as her marriage portion Dent's *Plaine Mans Path-Way to Heauen* and Bayly's *Practise of Pietie*—books which had been reverently bequeathed to her by her father. The justice of the peace kept it on his table along with his handbook on the duties of magistrates. Finally, it became, in the fashionable Restoration drama, a byword for the old-fashioned religion of the much-lampooned London citizen.[54] Its influence in the direction of independent religious thinking is incalculable.

The technique of self-analysis, the instrument for determining one's place in the eyes of God, set forth in the treatises of Dent and Bayly, came to occupy a large place in books of religious

---

[53] J. E. Bailey, *op. cit.*, p. 208.   [54] *Ibid.*, pp. 203-4.

instruction. Such works, again, helped unconsciously to make the priest less important as an intermediary between God and man. With a book to tell him of doctrine and the means of knowing his state of salvation, with a manual of biblical interpretation and a handbook of meditations and prayers, any apprentice or trades-man could deal with God for his soul.

A combination of good instruction was prepared by Nicholas Byfield, a Middlesex preacher, as *The Marrow Of The Oracles Of God. Or Divers Treatises, containing Directiõs about six of the waightiest things can concerne a Christian in this life* (1620),[55] a work which had eleven editions by 1640. The firm faith of the moralist in the virtue of prescriptive wisdom is clearly illustrated in Byfield, who shared the belief of so many preachers, that one of man's greatest needs was a set of godly rules which "reduced to a method" all morality and ethics for the aid of sinners. The lay public, more-over, had an equal faith in the efficacy of catalogued knowledge. Knowing the taste of his audience for neat moral prescriptions, Byfield provided a sequence of aphoristic statements to cover all religious experiences and needs. With this hoard of pious lore,

---

[55] In reality a group of several smaller treatises with separate title-pages, its scope is sufficiently indicated by the descriptive titles of the sections:

"The Beginning Of The Doctrine Of Christ. Or, A Catalogue of Sinnes: Shewing how a Christian may finde out the euils he must take notice of in his Repentance. With Rules, that shew a course, how any Christian may be deliuered from the guilt and power of all his sinnes.

"The Spirituall Touchstone: Or, The Signes Of A Godly Man: Drawne in so plaine and profitable a manner, as all sorts of Christians may trie themselues thereby. Together with directions, how the weake Christian, by the vse of these Signes may establish his assurance.

"The Signes Of The Wicked Man. Together with Directions that shew how the seuerall Gifts and Graces of Gods Spirit may be attained. Needfull for such as want those Graces, and for such as desire to increase in them.

"The Promises: Or, A Treatise shewing how a godly Christian may support his heart with comfort, Against all the distresses which by reason of any afflictions or temptations can befall him in this life. Containing all the most comfortable places through the whole Bible, orderly digested.

"The Rules Of A Holy Life. Or, A Treatise containing the holy order of our liues, prescribed in the Scripture, concerning our cariage, Towards God, Towards men, Towards our selues. With generall Rules of Preparation, that concerne either the helpes or the manner of a holy conuersation.

"The Cure Of The Feare Of Death. Shewing the course Christians may take to be deliuered from those Feares about Death, which are found in the hearts of the most. A Treatise of singular vse for all sorts."

the literate citizen had only himself to blame if he went astray. Without the need of further ecclesiastical interpretation, he was now able to say for himself what was necessary for his own salvation. Furthermore, he had ample advice to enable him to live in harmony with his fellow men and to succeed in his mundane affairs, for Byfield offers such pertinent counsel as "Take heede of idlenesse, and prouide to walke faithfully & diligently in some honest calling of life."[56]

The demand for religious works increased as the seventeenth century wore on. As men grew more apt in studying their own religious conditions, they became more eager for adequate prayers. No work speaks more eloquently of the use to which devotional books were put than Michael Sparke's *The Crums of Comfort with godly Prayers. Corrected and amended. 7. Edition* (1628). This is the earliest edition of which there is record of a preserved copy. Only three exemplars before 1640 are listed in the *Short Title Catalogue*: two copies of the seventh edition and one of the tenth (1629). Yet Sparke could boast in 1652, in the preface to *Crums Of Comfort*, that

Although there have been fourty Impressions of the first Part of the Crumms of Comfort Printed, which amount unto about 60000 and these being sold, to satisfie the desire of such Christians, as long for such spirituall food, I have penned this second Part, to chear thy sin-full sinking soul.[57]

Allowing even for exaggeration, the distribution of Sparke's book must have been extensive. That only three copies of the earlier editions are preserved, argues that they were read out of existence. Sparke was a printer rather than a preacher, and his choice of the material for his book is an indication of a business man's judgment of what would sell. The actual labor of compilation, he claims, was performed by "some godly Ministers of mine acquaintance." In substance, the "booke of Crummes," as Sparke calls it, consists

---

[56] P. 269.

[57] *Crums Of Comfort. The Second Part To Grones Of The Spirit in Prayers, Meditations Consolations and Preparation for Death With his and Times last Legacy A Coffin and Winding Sheete.* In this preface Sparke attacks the Laudian conception of episcopacy, as well as such unruly folk as "Ranters, Quakers, Shakers, Seekers, &c. with their Raptures, Visions, and Revelations [who] will be the only Saints."

of prayers, meditations, and apt scriptural passages. The whole is pitched to the level of middle-class needs.

Books to direct the lives and souls of commoners increased in number in the reign of Charles I. The Anglican church might move toward formalism, but thousands of its citizen-members, particularly those of Puritan leanings, took their spiritual guidance from preachers who did not subscribe to Laud's doctrines and who wrote books to justify the simpler ways of God to men. The older devotional works continued to be reprinted, and new compilers, eager to instruct the multitude, arose to supply the increasing demand. John Davenport, who edited Henry Scudder's *The Christians Daily Walke in holy Securitie and Peace*,[58] enumerates great writers on religion before him—Rogers, Egerton, Bishop Hall, and others—but he believes that there can never be too many good works, especially those which have their matter "digested in such a Method, with such brevity and perspicuity, as was necessarie to make the Booke a vade mecum, easily portable, and profitable to the poore, and illiterate."[59] *The Christians Daily Walke*, a conduct book for the godly, had seven editions before 1640 and was reprinted at least twice in the nineteenth century.[60] Like the more secular courtesy books, it deals with the rationale of behavior—not the behavior of any man, but the behavior of a Christian. To that end it gives instruction in such matters as

How a man should behave himselfe in all Company.   [P. 213.]
How a man should make good use of himselfe by all Company.
    [P. 218.]
Meanes of good speech, and carriage in all Company.   [P. 225.]
Rules wherby a man may wel order himselfe in evill Company.
    [P. 228.]
How to demeane a mans selfe in good Company.   [P. 231.]
Rules for Eating and drinking.   [P. 64.]
A Table of Duties commanded & of Vices forbidden in the Moral Law.   [P. 90.]

---

[58] The first edition was published in 1628. My citations are from the edition of 1635, described as the sixth.

[59] Preface signed by Davenport.

[60] The British Museum Catalogue lists a fifteenth edition in 1813 and another edition in 1826.

How to reade mens writings profitably.[61]   [P. 194.]

These themes are typical of the subject matter of the work, which, besides such practical considerations, goes into much detail regarding purely religious matters: the avoidance of temptation, the prevention of sin against the Holy Ghost, the removal of fears by trusting in the Lord, the value of fasting, resignation in bearing one's crosses, and similar themes which harassed the souls of the faithful. Man is exhorted to pray much, to live in harmony with his neighbors, to be charitable, and to model his life after that of Christ. The influence of courtesy books in the sixteenth and seventeenth centuries was enormous. It is small wonder, then, that writers like Scudder should have produced pious courtesy books founded on the ample material so suitable to the purpose in the New Testament.

The inculcation of virtue in young men, particularly apprentices, was one of the great concerns of sixteenth- and seventeenth-century moralists. Treatises were often directed particularly to them. Such was the aim of William Loe in *The Merchants Manuell, Being A step to Stedfastnesse, tending to settle the Soules of all sober minded Christian Catholiques, as they haue beene taught, and learned the Lord Iesus the Sauiour in the Holy Catholike Church* (1628). Needless to point out, Loe is speaking of the Anglican and not the Roman church. He was a favorite preacher of London tradesmen,[62] having

---

[61] The advice on reading (pp. 194-95) will give some idea of the tone of the whole:

"1. In reading mens writings, reade the *best*, or at least those by which you can *profit* most.

"2. Read a good booke thorowly, and with due consideration.

"3. Reject not hastily any thing you reade, because of the meane opinion you have of the author. Beleeve not every thing you reade, because of the great opinion you have of him that wrote it. But (in all bookes of faith and manners) *try all things by the Scriptures*. Receive nothing upon the bare testimony or judgement of any man, any further then hee can confirme it by the *Canon of the word*, or by undoubted experience, alwayes provided that what you call reason and experience, be according unto, not against the Word. If the meanest speake according to it, then receive and regard it: but if the most judicious in your esteeme, yea, *if he were an Angell of God* should speake or write otherwise, refuse, and reject it. Thus much for private reading. Onely take this *Caution*. You must not think it to be sufficient that you reade the Scriptures and other good Bookes at home in *private*, when you shall by so doing neglect the hearing of the *Word* read, and preached in *publike*."

[62] *Dictionary of National Biography*, *sub* Loe. Perhaps one reason for Loe's popularity was his humor. One of Loe's colleagues, a minister named Adam, was in the habit of

been for a time chaplain to the English merchants in Hamburg, and it is to the fellowship of the Merchants Adventurers[63] that he dedicates his handbook:

That I call this collection the Merchants Manuell, it is for that I principally desire it should be fostered, fauored, and followed in the practise thereof, by the younglings of your society: as for others, whose yeares require stronger meate, it may bee to them onely as a remembrancer is to a great Person of State.

An exposition of the Ten Commandments and the Lord's Prayer and certain religious exhortations make up the contents of the manual.

More complete was the direction to proper Christian behavior laid down for apprentices by Abraham Jackson in *The Pious Prentice, Or, The Prentices Piety. Wherein is declared, how they that intend to be Prentices, may 1. Rightly enter into that Calling. 2. Faithfully abide in it. 3. Discreetly accomplish it. 4. And how they may be satisfied in conscience in such doubts as may arise upon some particular occasions and occurrences proper to that Calling* (1640). As in most of the popular treatises on religion, *The Pious Prentice* identifies godliness with the support of the established social order, for in the ethics of the tradesman, nothing was so vile as rebelliousness and a froward

---

failing to appear for his services. It is related that on one occasion, when Adam was scheduled to preach at the same church in the evening, Loe chose for the morning text, "Adam, where art thou?" Adam, not to be outdone, preached in the evening from the text, "Lo, here am I."

[63] In other works Loe showed his interest in the Merchants Adventurers. He published in Hamburg, in 1620, *Songs of Sion*, a collection of religious verses in monosyllables. Each division of the book is dedicated to an English merchant in Hamburg. These verses were reprinted by A. B. Grosart (ed.), *Miscellanies of the Fuller Worthies' Library* (1870), Vol. I.

The English merchants abroad were strong Protestant protagonists, especially favoring the tenets of Calvin. The Puritan leader at Cambridge, Thomas Cartwright, was for a time a factor for English merchants at Middelburg. *See* A. F. Scott Pearson, *Thomas Cartwright and Elizabethan Puritanism, 1535-1603* (Cambridge, 1925), pp. 169-71. The merchants, be it noted, claimed that Puritan factors were more honest than those who felt it a pious act to trick a Protestant tradesman. The thrifty merchants of the Scottish Staple, having suffered from defalcations of Catholic factors, declared, in June, 1582, that only Protestants should be factors for them (*ibid.*, pp. 169-70). Pearson further comments upon the English merchants: "Through their association with the exponents of the reform movement on the Continent many of them became the staunchest protagonists of Protestantism, and it was a notorious fact that wealthy merchants were among the most generous supporters of Puritanism."

spirit, or the iniquitous yearning for change. The ancient doctrine of degree—the constant theme of preachers—is clearly set forth :

Let every man abide in the same calling, wherein he was called. Art thou called being a servant? care not for it, but if thou mayest bee made free, use it rather. For he that is called being a servant is the Lords free man : likewise hee that is called being free, is Christs servant. [P. 9.]

. . . .

To this end consider, that the calling you are placed in, was appointed unto you by Gods particular providence, as knowing better what was fit for you then you your selfe. To be discontented therefore with your calling, is to repine at Gods Providence, which is a cursed effect, proceeding either,

     1. From envie : or,
     2. From ambition : or,
     3. From impatience. [P. 54.]

To the young man who has his success at heart, Jackson recommends that "Upon week daies, when you have any leasure from your particular imployments, you spend it in reading of Gods Booke, and the bookes of Holy men, tending to piety and devotion"[64]—an injunction not without practical value in an age that extracted a philosophy of success from the Bible. Temperance in all things, especially in drinking and in other unthrifty sins, is an essential to the success that Jackson holds out as the reward of virtuous apprentices, who are warned to observe particularly "1. Sobriety 2. Chastity 3. Contentment."[65] Persistence, of course, is another virtue to be regarded by the ambitious youth, who is advised to "take heed of abandoning your calling upon every idle fancy, or fond conceit, or sudden occasion, or humorous dislike, or malecontented sullennesse."[66] Submission to discipline is likewise necessary in the training of the apprentice, and here Jackson charges every servant always to obey his master without question except in direct violation of the laws of God. Where there is uncertainty in the servant's mind, "If the thing commanded be of an indifferent or doubtful nature, it is better to doubt and obey, than doubt and disobey."[67] In short, Jackson

---

[64] P. 39.   [65] P. 43.   [66] P. 116.
[67] P. 113. The problem of obedience to wicked commands was a troublesome one. In 1611 Nicholas Byfield advised John Brerewood, a Chester youth who had become

wrote a treatise bringing religion to bear on the practical relation of the apprentice to his environment. It is a guidebook to
temporal success. It holds out prosperity as the reward for adherence to the code laid down. It argues cogently for the ideals
of capitalistic civilization.

Not all the manuals of piety and devotional works are so pre-
occupied with social instruction as *The Pious Prentice*; but through
the scores of religious treatises and handbooks which the Elizabethan middle class accepted as second only to the Bible, there
runs much the same theme. Religion is not merely an emotion
for the inner sanctuary; it is rather the mainspring of human
conduct which brings success or failure according to our obedience
to its mandates. Religion is soon shaped to fit the peculiar wishes
of a rising capitalistic nation. Protestantism, particularly its Calvinistic branches, develops into a faith supporting property and
the prudential virtues. Christ and the New Testament become
the bulwarks of trade and commerce.[68] All of these tendencies are
discernible in the manuals of prayer, the volumes of meditations,
and the pious conduct books which furnished so much of the
reading matter of sixteenth- and seventeenth-century citizens.

What was the attitude of the minister in the pulpit, we may well
ask after observing the trend of the manuals prepared by him.

---

an apprentice in London, that he did right to refuse to run errands for his master on
the Sabbath. The boy's uncle, John Brerewood, professor of astronomy at Gresham
College, declared that the fourth commandment was binding only on the master, and
therefore the master's commands should be obeyed. A correspondence with Byfield
on the subject was published at Oxford in 1630 as *A Learned Treatise of the Sabaoth*.
See *Dictionary of National Biography*, *sub* Nicholas Byfield.

[68] The complex relations of business and religion are treated by R. H. Tawney,
Religion and the Rise of Capitalism (London, 1929). Cf. Professor Tawney's critique (pp.
319-21) of Max Weber's *Die protestantische Ethik und der Geist des Kapitalismus*, in which
Tawney warns against the oversimplification of English Calvinism in Weber's thesis
that Calvinism contributed largely to the development of modern capitalism: "Both
the 'capitalist spirit' and 'Protestant ethics,' therefore, were a good deal more complex than Weber seems to imply. What is true and valuable in his essay is his insistence
that the commercial classes in seventeenth-century England were the standard-bearers
of a particular conception of social expediency, which was markedly different from
that of the more conservative elements in society—the peasants, the craftsmen, the
many landed gentry—and that that conception found expression in religion, in politics, and, not least, in social and economic conduct and policy."

A detailed treatment of sixteenth- and seventeenth-century preaching is beyond the scope of the present study ; but sermons, which had been conspicuous in the entertainment and instruction of plain people since the Middle Ages,[69] played such an important part in the development of middle-class ideas that they cannot be overlooked in a consideration either of literary taste or of political and economic influence, for sermons, both spoken and printed, provided the intellectual food of large masses of the people. An examination of the sermons popular enough to be often reprinted shows that their content was much the same as that of the manuals. Indeed, the pulpit was as much a place of instruction as of exhortation, and many of the sermons when published took the form of treatises.

The Tudor and Stuart pulpit surpassed any other medium of expression in its possibilities for molding public opinion. It was a medium for the dissemination of government proclamations and official announcements. Government authorities early realized its capacity for propaganda and sought to utilize its influence. William Cecil, Lord Burleigh, was assiduous in his efforts to make the pulpit express views pleasing to the government. As early as the reign of Edward VI we find Cecil preparing notes to be given to Gardiner to preach from at Paul's Cross.[70] Throughout Burleigh's long official life he was constantly on the side of moderation, constantly scheming to keep the English pulpit from going to extremes, constantly pursuing a policy of reconciliation between factions.[71] Walsingham likewise, though a Puritan in his personal

---

[69] The medieval background of Elizabethan sermon literature is discussed by G. R. Owst in *Preaching in Medieval England* (Cambridge, 1926), and in the same author's *Literature and Pulpit in Medieval England* (Cambridge, 1933). For later sermons, see W. Fraser Mitchell, *English Pulpit Oratory from Andrewes to Tillotson* (Society for Promoting Christian Knowledge, London, 1932), and Caroline Francis Richardson, *English Preachers and Preaching, 1640-1670* (New York, 1928).

[70] Haweis, *op. cit.*, pp. 42-43 : "In 1548, Gardiner was summoned before the council, and forbidden to leave town until he preached at the Cross, in defence of Edward's reforms, from notes brought to him by that steady votary of expediency, Cecil. He was desired to write this discourse, and submit it for inspection previous to delivering it. This indecent demand he would not comply with, but expressed his readiness to speak on most of the subjects indicated." *See also* W. H. Frere, *The English Church in the Reigns of Elizabeth and James I* (London, 1911), p. 3.

[71] Martin A. S. Hume, *The Great Lord Burghley* (London, 1898), pp. 459-60.

leanings, strove for a church free from dissension. Through their counsels there developed an ecclesiastical policy, encouraged by Elizabeth, that fostered a church so broad that moderate elements in all parties could be satisfied.[72] To this end, early in Elizabeth's reign the pulpit itself was enlisted, and, as in the reign of Edward VI, an official book of homilies was decreed by the new Queen, as *Certayne Sermons appoynted by the Queenes Maiestie, to be declared and read, by all Parsons, Vicars, and Curates, euery Sunday and Holyday, in theyr Churches: and by her Graces aduise perused and ouerseene, for the better vnderstanding of the simple people.*[73] An official statement prefaces the work, in which Her Majesty wills ministers

to read and declare to their parishioners plainly and distinctly one of the said Homilies, in such order as thei stand in the booke, except there be a sermon, according as it is inioyned in the booke of her highnes Iniunctions, and then for that cause only, and for none other, the reading of the saide Homilie to be deferred vnto the next sunday or holiday folowing. And when the foresaid booke of Homilies is read ouer, her Maiesties pleasure is, that the same be repeated & read againe, in such sort as was before prescribed.

Ministers are also commanded to expound the Ten Commandments, the Articles of Faith, and the Lord's Prayer, to the end that all men may learn to pray. The homilies are prescribed "to auoyd the manyfolde enormities which heretofore by false doctrine haue crepte into the Churche of God." Furthermore, plain orthodox sermons are necessary, since many of the clergy "haue not the gift of preaching sufficiently to instructe the people whiche is committed vnto them, wherof great inconueniences might arise, and ignorance still be mainteyned, if some honest remedy be not speedily founde and prouided." The homilies officially decreed are models of simplicity and directness. Carefully avoiding matters of dispute, they preach a doctrine useful to the state. The

---

[72] Conyers Read, *Mr. Secretary Walsingham and the Policy of Queen Elizabeth*, 3 vols. (Oxford, 1925), II, 271. Of Elizabeth's policy Mr. Read says: "She sought primarily to keep England at peace without and within and to make her people prosperous and happy. To obtain this she was quite willing to juggle more or less with creeds and dogmas. . . . She insisted upon uniformity, but she tried to make her Church broad enough to satisfy the moderate elements in all parties."

[73] The book of homilies seems to have been first reprinted under Elizabeth in 1559. My citations are from the edition of 1569.

first book has for its themes the necessity of reading the Scriptures, the misery and salvation of man, faith, good works, love and charity, swearing and perjury, the fear of death, whoredom and adultery, strife and contention, and an exhortation to obedience. *The second Tome of Homilees*, as revised in 1571,[74] contains much the same material, with certain expansions to take care of timely needs. A sermon in three parts on the dangers of idolatry provides a place for the condemnation of popish superstition. The volume closes with a sermon in six parts condemning disobedience and wilful rebellion, particularly significant after the recent troubles in the North.

The arguments against rebellion are precisely those to make an appeal to the self-interest of the substantial commoners. The sermon writer pictures the punishment sent by God upon rebels, from Lucifer down to the latest traitor fresh in the memory of the populace. He describes the suffering and waste through civil strife. To unthrifty sins and the desire of the indolent to take the goods of the industrious, he ascribes the beginnings of rebellion :

As for enuie, wrath, murther, and desyre of blood, and couetousnes of other mens goodes, landes and lyuynges, they are the inseparable accidentes of all rebelles, and peculier properties that do vsually stirre vp wycked men vnto rebellion. Nowe suche as by riotousnesse, gluttonye, drunkennesse, excesse of apparell, and vnthriftie games, haue wasted their owne goodes vnthriftily, the same are moste apte vnto and most desyrous of rebellion, whereby they trust to come by other mens goodes, vnlawfully and vyolentlye. And where other gluttons and drunkardes take to muche of suche meates and drynkes as are serued to tables, rebelles waste and consume in short space al corne in barnes, feeldes, or elswher, whole garners, whole storehouses, whole cellers, deuour whole flockes of sheepe, whole droues of oxen and kyne. And as rebels that are maryed, leauyng their owne wyues at home, do moste vngratiously : so much more do vnmaryed men worse then any stallandes or horsses, beyng now by rebellion set at libertie from correction of lawes whiche brydled them before, whiche abuse by force

---

[74] *The second Tome of Homilees, of such matters as were promised, and intituled in the former part of Homilees. Set out by the aucthoritie of the Queenes Maiestie: And to be read in euery parishe Church agreeably. 1571.* The volume closes with "A thankesgeuing for the suppression of the last rebellion."

other mens wyues, and daughters, and rauishe virgins, and maydens, moste shamefully, abhominably, and damnably.   [P. 577.]

Shrewdly the sermon continues to play on the prejudices of the bourgeoisie, stressing their losses through disorder, the disruption of their homes, and the deflowering of their women. Finally, it warns men not to be misled by the catchwords of rebels, though their banners do bear "the image of the plough paynted therein, with GOD SPEEDE THE PLOUGH, wrytten vnder in great letters," for "none hynder the plough more then rebels, who will neither go to the plough them selues, nor suffer other that would go vnto it."[75] The necessity of the strict observance of degree is proved by Holy Writ and is evident throughout the natural world. As children recognize the authority of their parents, so subjects should regard their rulers.

The homilies stress the value of following the prudential virtues and avoiding the unthrifty vices. Drunkenness and gluttony, excessive apparel, and idleness are the subjects of separate sermons. Again it is self-interest that the sermon writer emphasizes. Good English woolens, the dress of their fathers, made from the fabric which created English commerce, ought to suffice for the dress of Englishmen. He deplores the lust after finery which takes money from the country and brings simpler styles into disrepute. In the old days when men wore simpler clothes, they were hardier and could stand more cold. Now fine clothes have brought with them ills of the flesh as well as the purse.[76] Diligence in our vocations is enjoined, for God has commanded us to live by the sweat of our brows; it is a part of the condemnation brought by the sin of Adam. If we refuse to labor honestly, if we lurk slothfully, if we give ourselves over to "wylful wandering, & wastefull spending, neuer setling our selues to honest labour, but liuing like drone bees by the labours of other men," we violate the express ordinances of God and will be damned accordingly. Workers are cautioned that God's eye is ever upon them and that in times of sickness he will remember to cherish those who labored diligently in their vocations.[77]

---

[75] Pp. 591-92 (misnumbered 590, 593).   [76] Pp. 213 ff.

[77] Pp. 496 ff. Another reward of industry vouchsafed to the laborer is his greater chance for salvation, for the diligent are freer from temptation: "And to conclude

The profitableness of philanthropy is the message of the three parts of the homily on almsdeeds. With an increasing problem in the care of the poor, the government was eager to stimulate charity. The sermon is careful to point out that salvation is not assured merely from good works, but that God will not cause to suffer those who remember him by succoring the poor. God makes the goods of the generous to multiply; therefore we should be charitable that we may

be made partakers, and feele the fruites and rewardes that folowe such godly lyuyng, so shall we knowe by proofe what profite and commoditie doth come of geuyng of almes, and succouring of the poore.[78]

[P. 331.]

All the problems of life, including the important considerations of matrimony, are treated in the official homilies in such a simple, direct style that any man however unlearned—or sleepy—might understand. The lessons which a paternalistic government believed best for the commonwealth are stressed in such a manner as to make an appeal to the common sense of the intelligent citizenry. Theology is subordinated to good sense, and, when necessary, doctrine is made to convey such promises as will encourage a commercial society to live for the greatest prosperity of the state. The influence of these homilies, repeatedly read in every pulpit, and without doubt read in private by the populace, must have been enormous in crystallizing the bourgeois philosophy which they express. The influence of their crisp, forcible style on the development of English prose must also have been considerable. The two books of homilies were regarded as the essence of Christian doctrine. In 1622 King James, in a direction to preachers

---

the labouryng man and his familie whyles they are busilie occupied in their labour, be free from many temptations and occasions of sinne, which they that liue in idlenesse, are subiect vnto. And here ought Artificers and Labouring men, who be at wages for their worke and labour, to consyder theyr conscience to God, and theyr duetie to their neighbour, least they abuse their tyme in idlenesse, so defraudyng them whiche be at charge both with great wages, and deare commons."—P. 505.

[78] One further statement emphasizes the profitableness of generosity: "So mightily doth God worke to preserue & mainteine those whom he loueth, so carefull is he also to feede them who in anye state or vocation do vnfaignedly serue him. And shal we nowe thinke that he wylbe vnmyndfull of vs, yf we be obedient to his worde, & accordyng to his wyl haue pitie vpon the poore?"—P. 338.

18

which he is said to have drawn up himself, again called attention
to the value of the homilies. He warned that no preacher under a
bishop or a dean of a cathedral or collegiate church should expound any Scripture or preach any sermon not comprehended
or warranted by inference in the Articles of Religion and the
two books of homilies, which he urged the clergy to read over
carefully.[79]

By providing official sermons, by rigidly licensing ministers, and
by supervising the choice of preachers for such important occasions as the sermon at Paul's Cross,[80] Elizabeth and her successors
sought to control the pulpit and direct its influence into the
channels most serviceable to the state. Complete success was not
to be hoped for,[81] but it is significant that the clergy were usually
on the side of civil authority. Especially in the published sermons,
where the censor, of course, had a better opportunity than in the
spoken utterance, the sermons prevailingly stress such fundamental matters as Christian faith and the good life, obedience to
authority, and the prudential virtues. Sermons displeasing to
civil and ecclesiastical authorities were preached and published,

---

[79] Gee and Hardy, *op. cit.*, pp. 516 ff., "Directions Concerning Preachers." James
also warned against controversial sermons, references to the jurisdiction or prerogative of the sovereign, or other state matters, and invectives against other sects. The
"Directions Concerning Preachers" is an interesting document in the history of the
government's efforts to control pulpit utterance.

[80] Haweis, *op. cit.*, pp. 51-52. There seems to have been much confusion in the early
years of Elizabeth in the matter of authority over the preachers at Paul's Cross. At
various times the Bishop of London, the Archbishop of Canterbury, the Lord Mayor,
or even the Earl of Leicester or some other noble felt privileged to appoint a preacher
for the sermon. From the later years of Elizabeth onward, civil and ecclesiastical authorities seem to have kept a stricter eye on Paul's Cross. The Queen several times
vetoed appointments of preachers. Sermons unfavorable to the authorities naturally
became less frequent than in earlier times.

One of the best examples of sermons preached at Paul's Cross at the express command of the authorities was that delivered by William Barlow after the execution of
the Earl of Essex, whom Barlow had accompanied to the scaffold as one of his three
spiritual advisers. The sermon was printed as *A Sermon preached at Paules Crosse, on the
first Sunday in Lent; Martii 1. 1600. With a short discourse of the late Earle of Essex his confession, and penitence, before and at the time of his death* (1601). It is significant that Barlow
felt called upon to defend himself against the charge that his sermon was a timeserving
piece preached merely to please the authorities.

[81] Haweis, *op. cit.*, p. 98. The sensational preacher managed to make himself heard
and to draw crowds, much to the disgust of Bishop Whitgift, who, in *A Godly sermon
preached at Greenwich* (1574), condemned sensation-mongering itinerant preachers: "If

it is true, and bitter attacks, such as those in the Martin Marprelate controversy,[82] were launched against the Anglican church; but, by and large, the majority of Elizabethan and Jacobean sermons were fairly orthodox. The Elizabethan policy was sufficiently

---

a man in some congregations commend the magistrates, if he move unto peace, if he confirm the rites and orders by public authority established . . . he shall scarcely be heard with patience—nay he shall be sent away with all kinds of opprobries. But if he nip at superiors and reprove those that be in authority, if he shall inveigh against laws and orders established, and talk of matters that lead to contention rather than edification (though it be done never so untruly, never so unlearnedly, as commonly it is), they flock to him like bees, they esteem him as a god, they extol him up to heaven." Whitgift here gives an interesting implication of what the lesson from the pulpit ought to be, by contrast with the sensation-monger's practice.

Another example is cited by Haweis (pp. 99-100) from L. Barker's *Sermons begun at Paul's Cross, and continued before an honourable audience* [*c.* 1600?] : The public disdains grave and godly divines, "but if you can tell them of a trim young man that will not quote the fathers, (and good reason, for his horse never eat a bottle of hay in either of the universities), that never yet took orders, but had his calling approved by the plain lay elders, (for he was too irregular to be ordered by a bishop), . . . that will not stick to revile them that were in authority, that his sectaries may cry he is perse-cuted when he is justly silenced. If ye can give them intelligence of such a man, oh, for God's sake, where teacheth he? To him they will run for haste without their din-ners, sit waiting by his church till the door be open ; if the place be full, climb up at the windows, pull down the glass to hear him, and fill the church-yard full, send him home everything, one man plate, another hangings, this gentlewoman napery, that good wife money ; let him want nothing so long as he is new, though within two years after they leave him on a lee land and never heed him." It may be worth noting that the writer assumes that as a matter of course the sensational preacher will be silenced.

[82] J. R. Tanner, *Tudor Constitutional Documents* (Cambridge, 1922), pp. 194-95 : "The Marprelate libels against the bishops attracted much public attention, but some writers have taken them too seriously. The charges made were so impossible and the expres-sions used were so violent that they must be regarded as having a humorous intention, and they were so accepted at the time except by the government and by those whom they attacked. But underlying their satire there was always bitter indignation, and often effective argument."

Cf. also G. P. Gooch, *English Democratic Ideas in the Seventeenth Century* (2d ed., Cam-bridge, 1927), p. 35. Though Cartwright was opposed to the combination of civil and ecclesiastical authority, "There was, however, no desire to meddle with the office of magistrate, nor, indeed, with anything but the admonition and excommunication of the obstinate. Some justices were desirous to have a quarrel with the Precisians, as they were called, for their conscience ; but the author wished the government might find better subjects. An organization supplemental to that already in operation was outlined in the following year ; but so little danger was seen in the movement that Travers was assisted by Burleigh in his candidature for the Mastership of the Temple. Cartwright himself strongly expressed his disapproval of the Marprelate Tracts, and, when Barrow blamed him for not leaving the Church, replied that separation was unjustifiable."

liberal to make it possible for Puritans like William Perkins to preach and publish without seriously disturbing ecclesiastical harmony. Although Presbyterianism increased in intensity under James to reach its climax in the reign of Charles, civil and ecclesiastical authorities maintained a reasonably tractable pulpit until the Puritan outbreak. Indeed, the popular preachers who swayed public opinion in their spoken and printed sermons throughout the reigns of Elizabeth and James and the earlier years of Charles were not eager to meddle in affairs of state. Though, for the most part, of Puritan leanings, the preachers who were the favorites of the multitude steered a middle course. Learned men like Richard Greenham, William Perkins, Henry Smith, Richard Sibbes, and Samuel Ward represented the mind of the intelligent middle class who suspected episcopacy of a Roman taint but preferred to give attention in spiritual matters to more fundamental concerns. If Charles could have had the advice of the expedient Burleigh instead of that of Laud, he might have kept the citizenry loyal to himself and his church. The preachers influential with the masses would have been on his side. And the influence of the preachers in the sixteenth and seventeenth centuries was a force to be reckoned with.

Probably the political power of the clergy is less important than their subtler influence in the molding of social and cultural ideals. We have seen how the authorized homilies not only expressed the opinions which the state desired the public to accept as its own, but actually did reflect conceptions which a property-loving society found useful to receive as fundamental beliefs. Scores of sermons, in addition to the homilies, similarly reflect the interests of the middle class.

Before noticing some of these sermons, we might well consider the attitude of the public toward sermons, both spoken and written. The modern finds it hard to appreciate the place sermons occupied in the life of the average citizen of the sixteenth and seventeenth centuries. Sermons furnished entertainment and intellectual exercise. Everybody went perforce to hear the preacher and most listened attentively.[83] From the devotional books, it is

---

[83] F. E. Hutchinson, "The English Pulpit from Fisher to Donne," *Cambridge History of English Literature*, IV, 257 ff.

clear that the master of the household often felt it his duty to catechize his children and servants about the preacher's utterances. Note-taking at the service was usual. Not merely was it the whim of the devout to put down in commonplace books the sayings of the minister, but ordinary laymen preserved ecclesiastical wisdom. John Manningham, for example, was not peculiarly pious; yet in his diary for 1602-3 he preserves scores of sermon extracts, epitomes, and allusions to services which he attended.[84] The zeal of the note-taking laity and the greed of printers led to the publication of corrupt versions of sermons, to the embarrassment of the authors. For example, the reason for publication given by John Dod and Robert Cleaver in the dedication to *A Plaine And familiar Exposition of the Ten Commaundements*[85] is the corruption of the unauthorized printed versions,

. . . since some of the ordinarie hearers had published their notes (as themselues could gather them in the time of the Sermon) without our knowledge or consent, and many faults were escaped in writing and printing, which by due care and foresight might haue beene prevented.

The vogue for copying down and printing sermons is attested by Ambrose Wood, editor of Samuel Ward's *A Coale From The Altar To Kindle The Holy fire of Zeale*,[86] who affirmed in a preface addressed to the author that he copied the sermon "partly from your mouth, and partly from your Notes." Scornful disgust at the pride of listeners in their notes is expressed by A. B., editor of John Stoughton's *XIII Sermons, Preached In The Church of Aldermanbury, London* (1640). He is convinced that his labors will be exposed to many censures, for "some there are, whom no Sermon pleaseth, longer than it is in hearing, or otherwise than it is extant in their own broken notes."[87] A little later Sir Ralph Verney com-

---

[84] John Bruce (ed.), *Diary of John Manningham*, Camden Society, XCIX (1868), *passim*.

[85] The first edition was in 1603. The title and citation here given are taken from the edition of 1606.

[86] First edition, 1615. My quotation is from the reprint in *A Collection Of Such Sermons and Treatises as haue beene written and published By Mr. Samuel Ward, Preacher of Ipswich* (1627).

[87] Preface. In one of his sermons, *The forme of wholsome Words, or an Introduction to the body of Divinity* (p. 33), Stoughton recommends that men preserve sermons : "Have a *copie* of them about thee *written;* and if possibly *printed*, . . ."

plained that women learned shorthand in order to take down sermons, pride in which "hath made multitudes of woemen most unfortunate."[88]

Ecclesiastical authorities were sometimes as eager as the populace to see pleasing sermons in print. Thomas Playfere, for example, in the dedication, to Sir George Carey, of *The Path-Way To Perfection. A Sermon preached at Saint Maries Spittle in London on wednesday in Easter-weeke. 1593*,[89] asserts that the Bishop of London, as well as divers others, had importuned him for a copy to print. Only because of the corruptions in an unauthorized version of another of his sermons which he was obliged to print from a true copy, was Playfere persuaded to see *The Path-Way To Perfection* through the press. Doubtless many sermons were perpetuated in print through the desire of the authorities to insure a wider dissemination of the ideas therein.

Political histories, as well as histories of the religious sects in the age of Elizabeth and the first two Stuarts, emphasize the theological controversies which raged about every conceivable question, from Sabbath observance to the dress of the clergy. Bitter though these disputes were, and important as the results proved, the rank and file of the citizenry showed far more interest in pragmatic religion and Christianity applicable to daily life than in such questions, for example, as whether the clergy should wear vestments or not. As the Puritan Revolution approached, one must

---

[88] Margaret M. Verney, *Memoirs of the Verney Family during the Commonwealth, 1650 to 1660*, 4 vols. (London, 1894), III, 72. Sir Ralph Verney wrote in a letter in 1650: "Let not your girle learne Latin, nor Short hand; the difficulty of the first may keepe her from that Vice, for soe I must esteeme it in a woeman; but the easinesse of the other may bee a prejudice to her; for the pride of taking Sermon noates, hath made multitudes of woemen most unfortunate."

[89] First edition, 1596. My citation is taken from the edition of 1616. Playfere says: "Sir, as soone as I had preached this Sermon, it pleased the Lord Bishoppe of *London* last deceased, both by his Letter, and by word of mouth, to request a Copie of it for the Presse. The like did diuers others also. But in truth I had then no Coppy of it. Or if I had beene possessed of any, yet I was resolute to yeeld to no such motion. Which some (I know not who) vnderstanding, that being by so many, and so many times importuned, to print this, or some other Sermon, I alwayes vtterly refused so to do, haue presumed to print the *Meane in Mourning*, altogether without true iudgement, or calling me to counsell therein. . . . Therefore after I was, not onely perswaded by the aduice of all my friends, but euen enforced by the necessitie of the thing it selfe, to print that Sermon as it was preached: I thought good likewise to let this goe with it."

add, there was a rush to take sides, and every man's partisan-
ship developed bile ; but, during most of the preceding period,
London citizens found moderate Calvinism best suited to their
inclinations. They hated papists, suspected High Church tendencies, watched such a cat-and-dog fight as the Marprelate
controversy with considerable glee, and looked to the milder
Puritans within the Church of England for spiritual leadership.
It is significant that the sermons which enjoyed the greatest
popularity in print are not those which open questions of dissension, but those which show the way to earthly harmony and
eventual salvation.

The universal fondness for homilies that expounded the means
of proper living may be seen in the themes of the "occasional"
sermons, especially those preached at weddings, funerals, meetings
of the city companies, at Paul's Cross, and at fairs. These for the
most part extol virtue and rebuke vice ; they give good counsel on
sundry subjects ; and they urge the necessity of repentance as they
hold up the horrors of hell and the rewards of heaven. Simple,
direct expositions appealed to the people. Hugh Latimer's homely
sermons, for instance, were reprinted until 1635. In the same year
*A Godly Sermon no les fruitfull thē famous, made in the yeare of our Lord
God M.CCC.lxxxviii. and found out beyng hyd in a wall,*[90] a plain-
spoken little treatise on sin, had a fifteenth edition. Even the
sermons preached before the sovereign sometimes became popular
favorites. Such a one was *A Sermon Preached Before The Queenes
Maiestie, the. 25. day of February, by Maister Edward Dering, in Anno.
1569,* which had twelve printings before the accession of James.
Perhaps the attack on the corruption of the clergy, no less than
the description of the goodness of God in giving England so able
a ruler, accounts for its popularity.

Though the fashion of learned display in pulpit oratory was
the curse of many sermons, especially after pedantic King James
had expressed a preference for that type, the preachers who had
the good sense to be plain were favored by the citizens. Arthur
Dent, in the preface to *A Sermon Of Repentaunce* (1583), disclaims
any desire for vainglory, because, as he says, "I seeke especially

---

[90] Title from edition of 1575. It is attributed to R. Wimbledon, the printed version
being tentatively dated 1550.

the saluation of the simple and ignorant: and therefore stoope downe to their reach and capacitie." He reached the level of the multitude so successfully that this sermon, stressing the calamities to befall the unregenerate, had twenty-one editions by 1638.[91] Conscious of his obligation to lead into spiritual light, rather than to confuse the common man, even when dealing with such abstruse points as free will and predestination, Dent tries to simplify his words and to emphasize only matters which he considers of fundamental importance.[92]

An absence of theological bickering, in place of which one finds subject matter dealing with the substance of religion, is noticeable in most of the sermons popular enough to go through several editions. Richard Greenham, the learned Cambridge preacher, though cited for nonconformity by the Bishop of Ely, remained loyal to the church and preached against schism.[93] After he came to London, about 1588-89, he was a favorite preacher with the citizens, and his *Workes*, published in 1599 and four times thereafter, supplied both spiritual guidance and practical advice. Individual sermons took shape as treatises in the printed versions— a frequent transformation in the period.[94] The problems discussed range from Christian faith and Sabbath observance to the relations of betrothed persons before marriage and the proper educa-

---

[91] The same goal is indicated in the title of John Hawkins's *A Salade For The Simple. Gathered out of the fourth verse of the first chapter of the Prouerbes of Salomon* (1595), a sermon stressing the homely virtues of diligence, industry, and obedience.

[92] *See* Dent's *The opening of Heauen gates, Or, The Ready Way to euerlasting life. Deliuered in a most familiar Dialogue, betweene Reason and Religion, touching Predestination, Gods word and Mans Free-will, to the vnderstanding of the weakest Capacitie, and confirming of the more strong. The fifth edition* (1624). The first edition was published in 1610. This work, left in manuscript by the author, is described by the writer of the preface as being so clear "that the meaner capacity may be instructed, and the skilfuller more confirmed." Even here Dent avoids a tone of controversy.

[93] *Dictionary of National Biography*, *sub* Greenham.

[94] Many sermons were edited as expositional treatises or guides to devotion. John Dod and Robert Cleaver were the joint authors of numerous popular "expositions" of the Scriptures. Perhaps the best-known was *A Plaine And familiar Exposition of the Ten Commaundements, with a methodicall short Catechisme, containing brieflie all the principall grounds of Christian Religion. Newly corrected by the Author* (1606) [first edition, 1603]. By 1635 nineteen editions had been printed. This treatise had been first delivered from the pulpit in a sequence of sermons.

John Preston's sermons were widely read in the treatise form which his editors, Richard Sibbes and John Davenport, gave them. *The Saints Daily Exercise. A Treatise*

tion of children.[95] Through the power of his personality and, after his death, through his printed sermons, Greenham did much to mold the religious opinions of commoners.[96]

One of the great preachers popular with the commonalty, one who came under Greenham's influence at Cambridge, was William Perkins, whose printed works became the religious authority for middle-class readers. It takes nearly three pages in the *Short Title Catalogue* merely to list the labors of this industrious minister, and in all these works—which include prayers, commentaries, and sermons, as well as treatises on conduct, economics, witchcraft, and a dozen other subjects—he pitches his style to the level of the average reader. He has no interest in the frills of learning evident in the court preachers, even in the sermons of so worthy a minister as Lancelot Andrewes. Perkins simplified the language of theology and made his sermons, as Thomas Fuller says, "not so plain but that the piously learned did admire them, nor so learned but that the plain did understand them."[97] Though he was ready to defend a fellow Cambridge man against the attacks of Bishop Whitgift, Perkins, like Greenham, opposed fanatical Puritanism. Especially was he fond of preaching simple truths,

---

Vnfolding the whole dutie of Prayer. Delivered in fiue Sermons vpon 1 Thess. 5, 17, which first appeared in 1629, had at least ten editions and two additional issues by 1636. Like the devotional books, the treatise is a revelation of the art of prayer.

William Whately's *The New Birth: Or, A Treatise Of Regeneration. Delivered in certaine Sermons* (1618), which had six editions by 1635, was a handbook on the means of salvation and the way to be certain of it.

[95] One sermon, *A Treatise Of A Contract Before Mariage*, insists that the marital relation must not be consummated until after the actual marriage ceremony. Another sermon, *Of The Good Education Of Children*, emphasizes the necessity of pious training in the home. Greenham is a strict moralist and a Sabbatarian. In *A Treatise Of The Sabbath* he declares that even in vocations which must continue their duties on the Sabbath, time should be given to worship. He urges a more strict attention to this by sailors and suggests that the merchant fleets take care to provide the ships with chaplains.—Pp. 362-63. Greenham's opinions on Sabbath observance exerted wide influence, much more than the formal statements on the subject by his stepson, Nicholas Bownd, in the latter's *The Doctrine of the Sabbath* (1595), though Bownd is frequently given credit for first codifying the Puritan notions of strict Sabbath observance. *See* Edward Eggleston, *The Beginners of a Nation* (London, 1897), pp. 129-30.

[96] Like John Wesley in a later generation, Greenham was accustomed to preach at dawn at Dry Drayton, Cambridgeshire, for the benefit of laborers on their way to work.

[97] *Dictionary of National Biography*, *sub* Perkins.

such as the need of Christian faith. Sermons on this topic were collected into a volume published by his executors under the title of *A Cloud Of Faithfull Witnesses, Leading To The Heavenly Canaan* (1608),[98] a favorite book with the merchant class, for it shows by the countless examples of the Old Testament how success will come through faith in the Lord. One John Hill, a London trader, on setting out for New England in 1636, was presented by his brother with a copy of this useful work to hearten him for his dangerous ventures. John read the book and prospered.[99]

A group of lectures and sermons delivered by Perkins in Cambridge were assimilated from his notes into an exceedingly popular treatise on practical Christian ethics by T. Pickering and "published for the common-good" as *The Whole Treatise Of The Cases Of Conscience* (1606).[100] Here the reader can find the answer to almost any question of right and wrong which might arise in his daily life. No better illustration of the bourgeois attitude toward the prudential virtues can be found than in Perkins's treatment of temperance,[101] which, incidentally, further disproves the hoary myth of Puritan asceticism. Under temperance Perkins discusses the pursuit of wealth, which, he finds, must be determined by the condition and degree of the individual. No wrong can come from laboring to acquire all that is necessary. Evil comes in the accumulation of what he calls "abundance," interpreted to mean a greater surplus than can be utilized.[102] The same principle controls man's eating, drinking, and recreations. Food and drink are to

---

[98] At the executors' directions, the work was edited by William Crashaw and Thomas Pierson, "Who heard him preach it, and wrote it from his Mouth," says the title-page. I have used the edition of 1622.

[99] The copy of the edition of 1622 in the Huntington Library has an inscription in the back of the book, in a contemporary hand, reading : "John: Hill His Booke giuen vnto him by his Brother Edward Vallentine Hill at his Departure out off old England into new England : in anno domm 1636." John had added, in his own hand, "Finis : per me Iohannem Hill." The Hill family became prominent in early New England. This book was evidently highly valued, for the same copy bears an inscription in front : "Boston N. E. Nov. 16, 1725. For Mrs. Jane Colman. The Gift of the Honorable Judge Sewall."

[100] My quotations are from the edition of 1608. Eight editions are recorded by 1636.

[101] In the last book of the treatise, entitled *The Second And Third Bookes Of The Cases Of Conscience, Concerning Man Standing In Relation to God and Man.*

[102] *Ibid.*, pp. 53 ff.

be enjoyed, but we must remember moderation and conduct ourselves for the glory of God.[103] Wholesome recreations, chiefly sports which will improve the body and stimulate the brain, are recommended :

Games of wit, or industrie are such, as are ordered by the skil and industry of man. Of this sort are Shooting in the long bow, Shooting in the caleeuer, Running, Wrastling, Fensing, Musicke, the games of Chests, and draughts, the Philosophers game, and such like. These, and all of this kind, wherein the industry of the mind and body hath the chiefest stroke, are very commendable, and not to be disliked.
[Pp. 121-22.]

Gaming, of course, Perkins will not condone, for this is a hazard that leads to waste and prodigality ; but games which mix hazard and wit and have in them no direct harm, as certain games with cards, he neither commends nor condemns.[104] Even in the matter of almsgiving, Perkins counsels moderation, for he realizes that indiscriminate charity is an evil. Sturdy beggars who will not work are not to be relieved. Philanthropy is desirable, but it must be intelligent.[105] This treatise by one of the favorite preachers of the day, constantly reprinted for three decades, must have had important results in giving form to the ethical opinions of plain people.

The Works[106] of Perkins, sometimes called *A golden Chaine: Or The Description Of Theologie*, from the title of the first treatise, were frequently reprinted with various additions of sermons and treatises. Not only does the author reveal the hidden mysteries of theology, even to predestination, but he provides a hoard of miscellaneous wisdom. Here is to be found *A Treatise Of The Vocations, Or, Callings of men,* which boils down the whole bourgeois creed of diligence, industry, and the necessity of social degree,[107] always emphasizing the doctrine that our labors must be for the good of "Church and Commonwealth"—a formula repeated like a constant refrain in Perkins's works.[108] Here also may be found

---

[103] *Ibid.*, pp. 69 ff.   [104] *Ibid.*, p. 123.   [105] *Ibid.*, pp. 130 ff.

[106] First edition in 1600. I have used the edition of 1605 in the Huntington Library.

[107] See Chapter VI, *supra,* for more extensive discussion of this treatise.

[108] The same refrain—with a somewhat different connotation, incidentally—is to be found in Laud's works. *See* Tawney, *op. cit.*, p. 171.

one of his vivid occasional sermons, *A Faithfull And Plaine Exposition vpon the two first verses of the second Chapter of Zephaniah,* delivered at Stourbridge Fair in the fields.[109] If the reader expects to find Perkins taking advantage of such an opportunity to preach of sensational matters, he will be disappointed. The common sins of England are his theme as he exhorts the crowds at the fair to root out their own ignorance of God's word, to give up their blasphemies and lies, their chicanery and sharp practice. He warns that God watches their sins and will winnow them with "the fearfull fan of his iudgement."[110] As they may better their estates through buying and selling at the fair, so they should help their souls by taking home some grain of the gospel, some good word in their hearts. To the great towns of London, York, Bristol, Manchester, Hull, Colchester, and others, the preacher urges the visiting crowds to carry back the lessons of salvation, the warning that a judge sits in waiting. Eloquent and forceful, Perkins at times has the simple vividness of Bunyan. Good lessons, practical in their application, sensible in their logic, such as appeal to the common sense of ordinary citizens[111]—these are the matters commonly found in his works.

A preacher whose sermons were more widely read even than those of Perkins was Henry Smith (called for his eloquence

---

[109] The sermon is edited by William Crashaw, with a dedication to Sir William Gee, dated August 7, 1605. Crashaw implores, in a preface to the reader, that persons having copies of the sermons of Perkins do not publish them in corrupt versions, but wait until his own true copies can be printed. He places a curse on all who rush into print with the sermons and thus defraud Perkins's children of their right. He speaks of his proposed edition "to be published, with the allowance of our Church, and for the benefit of his children." Crashaw also appends a list of Perkins's works in his hands.

[110] P. 21.

[111] Frequent advice is directed from the pulpit to tradesmen. Immanuel Bourne was the author of *The Godly Mans Guide: With A Direction For all; especially, Merchants and Tradesmen, Shewing how they may so buy, and sell, and get Gaine, that they may Gaine Heauen. . . . Preached in a Sermon at Paules Crosse, the 22. of August, 1619. Being the Sunday before Saint Bartholomew Day. By Immanuel Bourne Master of Artes and Preacher of Gods Word at Saint Christophers neere the Exchange* (1620). This pastor of tradesmen warns them against the sins peculiar to their occupations : greed, covetousness, deceit, and fraud. He appeals to them to use their talents for the glory of God and not labor merely for earthly gain. Buying and selling is a commendable occupation, albeit fraught with dangers. Though pointing out certain failings of tradesmen, Bourne is too much one of them not to vaunt his pride in the nobility of trade : "And hence it comes to passe that as Mer-

"silver tongued Smith"), a Cambridge man and a student under Greenham. Like his master and Perkins, Smith was tinged with Puritanism, but, though suspended from preaching for a time in 1588 by the Bishop of London, he defended the Established Church. Through his stepmother, who was a sister of Lord Burleigh, Smith gained the support of the lord treasurer, and repaid favors from him by preaching to the populace a doctrine of contentment. Appointed lecturer at St. Clement Danes in the Strand in 1587, Smith had an opportunity of reaching London's multitudes, who came in vast throngs to hear him and diligently wrote down in their notebooks the sermons which printers reproduced by the score for the next fifty years. Smith's bibliography is a bewildering confusion occupying three pages in the *Short Title Catalogue*. Publishers, eager for such popular works, printed from whatever copy they could lay their hands on; hence many sermons exist in several forms.[112] One of the most widely distributed of Smith's sermons, and doubtless one of the most pleasing to his step-uncle, Lord Burleigh, was *The Benefit of Contentation*, apparently first printed in 1590, in which year it had three editions; it was constantly reprinted for the next half century.[113] Rebuking

---

chandise hath beene auncient, euen in the dayes of *Noah* (as *Iosephus* affirmes) so it hath beene glorious in former Ages; By this we haue gotten acquaintance with forreigne Nations, and the Kingdome of *Christ* hath beene enlarged; By this we haue leagues of amitie, contracted with people of diuers Languages: By this we haue gotten knowledge and experience in seuerall Sciences. Yea, some Merchants haue been builders of great and famous Cities (as *Plutarke* in *Solon* reporteth). And not to trauell like a Merchant beyond the Sea, if we make a search neerer home, how many religious Merchants and Tradesmen, haue been Benefactors to the Vniuersities, for the maintenance of learning and Pietie. Yea, this Citie can witnesse their workes of charitie to the poore; and this Place is not silent of that good, it hath and doth dayly receiue from them." —Pp. 26-27.

   Sermons at fairs, and just before fairs, were often directed to the trading classes. See *The Marchant. A Sermon Preached At Paules Crosse on Sunday the 24. of August, being the day before Bartholomew faire. 1607. By Daniell Price Master of Arts, of Exeter Colledge in Oxford* (1608), a conventional sermon dedicated "To The Honorable Companie of Merchants of the Cittie of London."

   I have not had an opportunity to see Thomas Wilson's *A sermon in Canterbury to the corporation of black-smiths* (1610), preserved in Lincoln Cathedral Library.

[112] *Short Title Catalogue*, p. 529: "Smith's sermons having been largely taken down by his hearers in charactery, several publishers issued similar collections of them. The separate sermons in these have often different imprints."

[113] My quotations are taken from the version appearing in *Three Sermons made by*

Londoners for their greed, Smith preaches powerfully against discontent, which leads men into ungodly schemes for personal aggrandizement. Though he does not minimize the necessity of industry and thrift, he stresses the wickedness of unrest over failure to accumulate as much material wealth as one's neighbor. One should work hard, trust the Lord, and be satisfied with what he sends, for, as the apostle Paul taught us,

a man should be contented, not with 1000. pounds, nor 100. pounds, nor 20. pounds, but with that he hath : and there is great reason, why hee should so : because no man knoweth what is fit for him, so well as his caruer. [Sig. B 3.]

Zealously Smith attacks the excessive materialism of his day, the covetousness which he describes as "the Londoners sinne,"[114] the lust for wealth that produces cutthroat competition, the greedy inhumanity that would make slaves of apprentices. He even insists that a more spiritual reason for godliness than the hope of temporal gain must be found. While commending philanthropy, he warns that no deathbed gift will wipe out the stain of ill-gotten gains, "for a man may be hanged for stealing the money which he giues to the poore."[115] Smith realized the dangers of a materialism that was already menacing the welfare of the state and the happiness of individuals, as England was periodically swept by waves of speculation. Smith's attack is not on money or capitalistic industry, but only on excesses which the citizens themselves readily acknowledged.[116]

Maister Henry Smith (1599), where *The Benefit of Contentation* is the first sermon. This collection alone had thirteen editions by 1637.

[114] Sig. A 2. For the evolution of the ecclesiastical attitude toward usury and covetousness, see Tawney, *op. cit., passim.*

[115] Sig. C 2.

[116] Sermons on contentment were frequent with the ministers who were in close contact with the people, especially as the rumblings of dissensions grew more distinct. Richard Sibbes, son of a wheelwright, but a learned Cambridge preacher, included *The Art of Contentment* as the first sermon in his collection entitled, *The Saints Cordials. As They Were Delivered In Sundry Sermons upon speciall Occasions, in the Citie of London, and else-where. Published for the Churches good* (1629). Although there is no immediate social application, man is advised to be content with his lot and not be rebellious under misfortune. Sibbes's sermons were popular. He was deprived of his lectureship at Holy Trinity, Cambridge, but by the influence of Sir Henry Yelverton was chosen preacher at Gray's Inn, and in 1626 returned to Cambridge as master of St. Cath-

Many of the same eloquent preacher's sermons were almost as popular as *The Benefit of Contentation*. Eleven separate editions, not including the reprints in collections, are recorded of *Gods Arrowe Against Atheists* (1593), which sums up the evidence for Christian belief and condemns unbelievers. Extravagance, pride, usury, and drunkenness were themes of other much-read productions. Prevailingly, Smith sticks to condemnations of sin or exhortations to the leading of a good life and meddles little with theological controversy.

Many spoken and printed sermons in the first four decades of the seventeenth century emphasize the necessity of respect for authority—a theme which had been greatly stressed in the early years of Elizabeth. Conservatives in the general public and in the ministry perceived a gathering current of unrest and feared it. Although as early as Thomas Cartwright and Walter Travers[117] the foundation for rebellion against the ecclesiastical hierarchy had been laid, these staunch Puritans made far less impression on the popular imagination than their place in the history of Nonconformity would lead one to believe. Their presbyterian doctrines, with the logical but generally unrealized consequence of resistance to civil authority, spread with relative slowness among the bourgeois laity, who preferred less schismatic teachings.[118] Indeed, the public favor showered on conservative preachers is

---

arine's Hall. Sibbes showed himself anxious to keep the favor of the authorities and in 1633 received the perpetual curacy of Holy Trinity, Cambridge. See *Dictionary of National Biography*. Some of his printed sermons went through five or six editions.

[117] Tanner, *Tudor Constitutional Documents*, pp. 166 ff.

[118] It should be remembered that the Puritan leaders themselves did not foresee the logical implications of their opposition to the Established Church. Democracy in the sense of political leveling was not dreamed of by the moderate Puritans. Only extreme left-wing sectarists, condemned by the majority of Anglicans and Puritans alike, had a good word to say for the political theories of such radicals as the Anabaptists. The necessity of social degree and obedience to civil magistrates are constant themes of preachers representing the popular opinion until the approach of the Rebellion. For the Puritan attitude see A. F. Scott Pearson, *Church and State: Political Aspects of Sixteenth Century Puritanism* (Cambridge, 1928), especially pp. 50-51, for the point of view of Cartwright and Travers. Sixteenth-century Puritans developed the two-kingdom theory of politics, in which they separated religious from civil matters in so far as the exigencies of the state as then constituted permitted. Mr. Pearson shows (pp. 130-31) that Cartwright thought his platform harmless and attempted to steer clear of the political tendencies that reached their culminating expression in the seventeenth century with a momentum unrealized by the Puritans themselves.

frequently overlooked in our preoccupation with the stormier apostles of the Puritan Revolution. Since freedom from civil strife and national security were prized by the commercial classes, ministers who reflected their opinions constantly stressed these benefits. Even preachers who were against episcopal church-government vigorously denounced trouble-makers in the state. London citizens, later to oppose their sovereign, listened respectfully to John White, chaplain in ordinary to King James, when he took it upon himself to preach and print the doctrine of divine right, recognition of the royal prerogative, content with one's lot, and even the justice of taxes—themes which were treated in sermons at Paul's Cross and the Spital and reprinted at least four times as *Two Sermons: The Former Delivered At Pauls Crosse The Foure And twentieth of March, 1615. being the anniuersarie commemoration of the Kings most happy succession in the Crowne of England. The Latter At The Spittle On Monday in Easter weeke, 1613.*[119] White shows that obedience to royal authority is simply the culmination of the logic of the social system that is built on the notion of degree. Libeling magistrates and persons in authority smacks of the revolutionary methods of Wat Tyler's kind. The satires of poets and dramatists are dangerous as tending to bring authority into contempt.[120] To the social ambition of the apprentice, to his desire to become a respected alderman, White appeals in his rebuke of their impudence to their

---

[119] My quotations are from the reprint in *The Workes* of John White (1624). The first edition of the two sermons was in 1615. Ministers became too meddlesome in the matter of the authority of kings, it appears from King James's "Directions Concerning Preachers" (1622), which provided that "no preacher of what title or denomination soever, shall presume from henceforth in any auditory within this kingdom to declare, limit, or bound out, by way of positive doctrine, in any lecture or sermon, the power, prerogative, jurisdiction, authority, or duty of sovereign princes, or otherwise meddle with these matters of state and the references betwixt princes and the people, than as they are instructed and presidented in the homily of obedience, and in the rest of the homilies and Articles of Religion, set forth (as before is mentioned) by public authority; but rather confine themselves wholly to those two heads of faith and good life, which are all the subject of ancient sermons and homilies."—Gee and Hardy, *op. cit.*, p. 517.

[120] In the Paul's Cross sermon, p. 8: "And not onely the King himselfe is of God, but all the eminency and distinction of authority that is vnder him, his Nobles, his Councellors, his Iudges, his Magistrates, his Officers, his Courts are all of God; to maintaine his State and royalty, and to manage the affaires of the Common wealth, which one man cannot doe: and it is but a sauage and popular humour to backbite or

masters and to the magistrates.[121] To the citizens' anxiety to maintain a stable government where property will be safe, he appeals
in his condemnation of their resentment against tax-paying,[122] for
he shows that Constantinople fell through the churlishness of
the people in refusing to support the Greek Empire. Extravagance, waste, and prodigality brought by too much wealth
and too little knowledge of how properly to spend it, are ruining
the commonwealth :

---

despise this *eminency* in whomsoeuer. Those rhymes, *When Adam delued and Eue span, &c.*
were liker to be made in Wat Tylers campe than any where else ; and the practise of Li-
belling against Magistrates and great persons, at this day, that neither the liuing can
walke, nor the dead sleepe, cannot be iustified. If any thing be amisse, there is cause
rather of sorrow than laughter, and it is fitter to pray, than to lay our heads together
at a scurrilous Pasquill : which tending to nothing but the bringing of authority into
contempt and disgrace, the end may bee the ouerthrow of all at the last, when nothing
is more dangerous in a State, than for Statesmen to lose their reputation : and the
Stage and Poet, with iests and Satyrs to deride sinne, which by the Bishops and Pas-
tors of the Church is grauely and seuerely to be reproued. It is true indeed that among
the Greekes, *in veteri Comoedia* the persons of men were taxed : but they were Barbarians,
whom Christians must not imitate ; and the Magistrates thereby were disgraced, and
the rude people armed against them to the ruine of the best men, as we haue examples
in *Socrates* and others, and therefore the best States put them all downe."
[121] In the Spital sermon, p. 24 : ". . . Thus it fares at this day among vs ; seruants
despise their masters, the people reuerence not the Magistrate, the graue Magistrates
of this very Citie receiue not the pledges of respect. . . . Now young men, Prentices,
seruants, the common sort, are so farre from hiding themselues, or rising vp, that I
haue often seene the Magistrate faced, and almost brow-beaten, as he hath gone by :
but that due obseruance and honour, that, by baring the head, bowing the knee,
shewing awfull respect, they should yeeld to so publike Magistrates in so honourable
a Citie, I haue seldome seene. The reason is, that Presumption and arrogancy followes
youth and basenesse, as well as wealth. A paltry cottage will send out as much smoke
as a great house. A rotten log that is all sap, will yeeld as much saw-dust, as sound
timber. The best motiue I can propound to all young people and seruants, is this ;
so to carry themselues toward their masters, as they would their owne seruants another day should carry themselues toward them : and so to honour their Magistrate,
as themselues would looke to bee honoured, when by their well-doing, God should
hereafter aduance them to the like place."
[122] *Ibid.*, p. 32 : "And whereas subsidies, and loanes of mony, and other taxations
when need is, are part of those duties whereby the goods and wealth of the subiect is
communicated to the State ; let me say something of that too. It is a thing that we should
readily yeeld to. A good King is no burden to his State, if it be considered that whatsoeuer the stomacke receiues from the mouth, is for the benefit of the whole body.
The Magistrate *is eies to the blinde, feet to the lame, father to the poore*, watchman to the
common wealth, *Iob.* 29.15. whiles priuate men sit in rest, without care or feare of the
enemy ; which hee cannot be, without these things."

19

When God bestowed this abundance of wealth vpon the land, he neuer intended that it should be so abused, in prodigality and excesse : Drinking, and dicing, and gaming, and apparell, consume the most part of many a mans estate ; to say nothing of whoredome, *and suits at Law*, and other actions of prodigality. Many hundreds sell their land, which God gaue them to enioy, and destroy their estates, to maintaine these things : this is it that makes our gallants trudge so fast betweene the Broker and the Vsurer. The excesse of apparell is such, both in men and women, from the Lady to the milkmaid, that it should seeme they imagine, God gaue them their riches for nothing but to decke themselues. The walls of old *Babylon* might haue beene kept in repaire with as little cost as our women are ; and a Ladies head is sometime as rich as her husbands rent day. There is as much, possible, to be said of men. I haue little hope to controll it.   [P. 29.]

Like Henry Smith, White sees the dangers of material excesses. Not love of asceticism, so often charged against the preachers of the day, especially the Puritans, but prudential realization of the dangers to organized society explains the anxiety of such moralists as these. White believes that the open wickedness of the times tends "to the dissolution of all humane societie." The very bases of civilization are threatened in the disrespect to law and order, in greedy self-seeking without a care for the good of the commonwealth :

Three things maintaine societie, Religion, Iustice, and Order. Religion is pitifully violated by Atheisme, Blasphemy, Heresie, horrible Profanenesse. The Stages now in this City, woe is mee that I should liue to see it, tosse the Scripture phrase as commonly, as they doe their Tobacco in their bawdy houses. Iustice is destroied by oppression, rapine, bribery, extortion, partialitie. . . . Gouernment and order is profaned by contention, by contemning the Magistrate, by whoredome, incest, Sodomy, pride, drunkennesse. . . . The great Nobleman, that thinkes God hath made him greater than others, for no purpose but that he might be bolder to sinne, than others : the wealthy Gentlemen that turne townes into sheepe-walkes ; sell Benefices for ready money ; contriue hospitality into the narrow roome of a poore lodging taken vp in the Citie ; that subuert the strength of the land by vnreasonable renting the tenants : the Iudge that takes bribes, that iudges for fauour, that vpon the bench makes lawes, and iustice, and religion, stoope to his lust ; the Lawyer that pleads against the right, leads Iurie into periury: spends Sabbath after Sabbath among clients, openly defying God to his face thereby, and protesting that he loues his fee better than Gods ordinance: the sharking Officer that receiues bribes, and spares neither the King nor the subiect, but sucks from them both what he can; and the Clergie man too that failes, either in life or teaching, or labours not effectually to feed the flocke whereof the holy Ghost hath made him Ouerseer: for all that are such as these, and all whatsoeuer that lay the foundation of sinne, must needs build vpon condemnation.

[Pp. 35-36.]

Though the citizens of London who gathered to hear White's sermons and later bought his books might receive with reservations his support of cheerful taxation and the divine right of kings, in general they applauded the social doctrine laid down. Obedience to the law, respect for authority, adherence to religion, and avoidance of unthrifty sins—these are fundamental in bourgeois philosophy.

Sermon literature, as is evident from the few examples that we have been able to consider here, was diverse in its subject matter and complex in its appeal to the plain citizen. The entire explanation of the tradesman's interest is not to be found in his simple piety. Nor is it enough to say with a vague gesture that the age was Puritanic, and hence given to pious pursuits. The sermons that influenced the multitude, that were listened to and read by the populace, might be from the pen of a Puritan or the King's chaplain. They were popular because they reflected the fears, the hopes, and the ideals of the middle class. They rebuked sin—and the anatomy of sin has ever fascinated the populace— they told of "faith and good life" (to use King James's phrase), and they exhorted the multitude to adhere to the virtues that upheld the commercial society so rapidly determining English thought and policy. Englishmen liked to hear of salvation and security in this world and the next. For the most part, the sermons that won the greatest favor were conservative and "safe." Only on this basis can one explain the vogue of the dull sermons by John Stoughton, preacher of Aldermanbury.[123] Even in the heat

---

[123] Various collections of Stoughton's sermons were published. Typical examples may be found in *XV. Choice Sermons, Preached Vpon Selected Occasions* (1640) and *XIII Sermons, Preached In The Church of Aldermanbury, London* (1640). The latter is dedicated

of ecclesiastical disputes, the sermons which were still most highly esteemed were not denunciations of episcopacy, but lessons in the good life. Samuel Ward, staunch Puritan of Ipswich, published much-sought-after sermons on such safe themes as Christ crucified, faith, death, drunkenness. In the often printed *A Coale From The Altar To Kindle The Holy fire of Zeale*,[124] Ward opposes turbulent zeal and bitter zeal, insisting only upon zeal for Christian right-eousness. Likewise, *Balme from Gilead To Recouer Conscience. In a Sermon Preached at Pauls-Crosse, Octo. 20. 1616*[125] dwells on the healing quality of Christ's mercies. *Woe To Drunkards* tells of the fearful judgments of God upon many common sots, alewives, serving men, a miller, a butcher, and others, "such as might make their hearts to bleede and relent."[126] Robert Harris, like Ward a Puritan in his beliefs, steered away from controversy and preached so well of sin and salvation that his printed works were eagerly sought by middle-class readers, who found therein much discussion of God's goodness and mercy, of David's comfort at Ziklag, of Judas's misery, or of the drunkard's cup[127]—all sermons useful to any citizen.

Not until the bitter years of the 1640's did the average citizen begin to prefer controversial works to those of good morality and Christian practice. Though the violent William Prynne published a score of pamphlets before 1640, there is little evidence that the public at large paid much attention to them. Ecclesiastics read them, and ecclesiastics replied, but the interest of shopkeepers was awakened only when the author lost his ears over *Histrio-Mastix*, and when not only Prynne, but his dissenting brethren,

---

to a group of city officials and merchants. The sermons are conventional and unin-spiring helps to heaven.

[124] First edition, 1614. A fifth edition was published in 1627, in addition to the re-prints in collections.

[125] First edition, 1616. Six separate editions by 1628.

[126] First edition, 1622. Three separate editions by 1627. My quotation is taken from the version in *A Collection Of Such Sermons and Treatises as haue beene written and published By Mr. Samuel Ward, Preacher of Ipswich* (1627), p. 19.

[127] These phrases were subjects of sermons which had several editions each. *The Drunkards Cup* (1619) paints a vivid picture of drunkenness at fair-time, when taverns, streets, and lanes are filled with brutish sots. He emphasizes the waste to the common-wealth and the danger to the individual, of excessive drinking. Citations are from *The Workes of Robert Harris* (1635).

Burton and Bastwick, through persecution had become heroes to an increasing number of sympathizers. Samuel Smith—destined to be famous among the Presbyterian preachers of the Commonwealth—attained his popularity before the Civil War, not by controversy, but by such sermons as his discussion of sin, original and otherwise, in *Davids Repentance: Or, A Plaine and Familiar Exposition of the 51. Psalme first Preached, and now Published for the benefit of Gods Church*, of which a fourteenth edition was published in 1640.[128]

The zeal for works of piety and godliness, so clearly shown in the widespread distribution of all varieties of devotional books and collections of sermons, manifested itself in every form of literature. Even on the stage, especially in the theaters frequented by the less aristocratic audiences, biblical plays still enjoyed a considerable vogue.[129] Many of the writers who were regarded as most profane turned a hand to pious and didactic works. For instance, Robert Greene, periodically remorseful, made a tremendous appeal to bourgeois readers with his repentance pamphlets. Londoners likewise attended, if they did not always applaud, his and Thomas Lodge's moral play, *A Looking Glasse for London And England* (1594), because it rebuked their sins. Thomas Nashe in *Christs Teares Over Ierusalem* (1593), Thomas Deloney in *Canaans Calamitie Ierusalems Misery, Or The dolefull destruction of faire Ierusalem by Tytus* (licensed, 1598),[130] Thomas Dekker in his *Foure Birdes of Noahs Arke* (1609), Samuel Rowlands in *The Betraying Of Christ. Iudas in despaire. The seuen Words of our Sauior on the Crosse. With Other Poems on the Passion* (1598) and other equally religious works, Thomas Middleton in *The Wisdom of Solomon Paraphrased* (1596), Henry Lok in *Sundry Christian Passions Contained in two hundred Sonnets* (1593), and the ballad writers in scores of pious broadsides[131]—these all catered to a taste for religious literature, which surely cannot be

---

[128] The second edition, 1614, is the earliest extant version. It was entered in the *Stationers' Register* on July 9, 1613.

[129] *See* Louis B. Wright, "The Scriptures and the Elizabethan Stage," *Modern Philology*, XXVI (1928), 47-56.

[130] This is also attributed to Dekker.

[131] In the ballads may be found all types of pious exercises. In W. Elderton's *A Ballad intituled, Prepare ye to the plowe* [1570] is an exhortation of obedience to God and the Queen, which urges the profitableness of goodness. If men would not break God's law,

explained in the one word "Puritan." Anglican, Puritan, and Catholic alike believed in the efficacy of good lessons, which they looked for in the things they read. Hence, collections of aphorisms, pious poems, biographies of virtuous persons,[132] religious allegories,[133] philosophic treatises,[134] treatments of death,[135]

"Then would the honour duly hit,
To parents, lord, or king;
Then would ther be doubt a whit
To haue store of euerything."—*A Collection of 79 Black-Letter Ballads and Broadsides* (London, 1870), p. 177.

This is typical of a point of view frequently found in the ballads. Of the pious ballads Professor Hyder E. Rollins, *Old English Ballads, 1553-1625* (Cambridge, 1920), remarks (p. xxv): "Religious verse enjoyed great vogue in Elizabeth's day. Ninety metrical versions of the Psalms, with music, are said to have been printed during the period 1560-1600. Poets like Googe, Turbervile, Whetstone, Edwards, and Churchyard contributed their full quota; professional ballad-mongers, either from expediency or taste, followed their example; so that there was an enormous production of 'pious chansons'. Of this flood of verse, the ballads of piety here reprinted are thoroughly representative. Most of them are sickled o'er with didacticism. . . . all are an effective answer to those critics (and their name is legion) who persist in describing non-traditional ballads as 'lewd and scurrilous journalism'. Fearful warnings of the imminence of Death and the Judgment Day abound . . . as do invectives against pride . . . and the sins of society. . . . Several are melancholy lamentations by sinners, whose penitence demanded a poetical outlet . . . ; others are mosaics of general advice on holy living and holy dying . . . There are, also, didactic ballads on Tobias . . . and Job."

[132] For example, Philip Stubbes's eulogistic biography of his wife, *A Christal Glasse for Christian Women*, had sixteen editions between 1591 and 1640. The popularity of Foxe's *Acts and Monuments* in part may be accounted for by the same desire to read the lives of good men. *See* Donald A. Stauffer, *English Biography before 1700* (Cambridge, Mass., 1930), p. 142: "The growth of the mercantile classes in independence and power brings a new class within the range of biography, and the lives of the London and provincial burghers and squires are interesting for their pious and conscious pride." He mentions in this connection Anthony Nixon's *Londons Dove: Or A Memoriall of the life and death of Maister Robert Doue, Citizen and Marchant-Taylor of London* (1612), the chief purpose of which was to elaborate on the charity of a pious business man.

[133] The religious allegory of Richard Bernard, *The Isle of Man: Or, The Legall Proceeding in Man-shire against Sinne* (1626), had eleven editions by 1640. The title quoted here is from the edition of 1627. For further details about Bernard's work, see Chap. XI, *infra*. Another example of pious allegory is Anthony Nixon's *The Christian Navy. Wherein is playnely described the perfit course to sayle to the Hauen of eternall happinesse* (1602), a long poem describing the best course to avoid the rocks and whirlpools in the sea of life.

[134] It should be remembered that Richard Hooker's *Of The Lawes of Ecclesiasticall Politie* was a popular book. Apparently it was read by many besides the learned, for the *Short Title Catalogue* distinguishes eleven editions and two issues between 1594 and 1640.

[135] Plague literature was extremely popular, as is evident from the frequency of the

and all manner of other virtue-provoking books found eager
readers. Even jest books turned pious. John Singer's *Quips Vpon
Questions, Or, A Clownes conceite on occasion offered, bewraying a moral-
lized metamorphoses of changes vpon interrogatories* (1600) gives that
clown's rhymed replies to questions at the Curtain theater in a
series of moralistic, philosophic quips. The culmination of the
taste for piety in all forms of literature may be found in George
Wither's "A rocking hymn,"[136] a lullaby that is made to teach
the infant in the cradle the process of salvation. Wither explains
in a prefatory note :

Nurses usually sing their children asleep, and through want of pertinent
matter, they oft make use of unprofitable, if not worse, songs. This was
therefore prepared that it might help acquaint them, and their nurse-
children, with the loving care and kindness of their heavenly Father.

Usefulness is always the criterion of value in bourgeois civilizations. Pious literature achieved utility in Tudor and Stuart England by teaching prudential morality, by spreading the beliefs
peculiarly favored by a mercantile society, and by holding up the
hope and method of attaining a greater reward in the world to
come. Not even the infant's lullaby was spared in the dissemination of this message, because the steps of progress leading to success began at the cradle and continued to the grave. The secrets
of successful living and dying were revealed by innumerable "good
books" read by the multitude. The Puritan has been called a
man of one book. But surely no man ever had more books to
teach the same thing than did the Elizabethan citizen, representing that group who won the loose appellation of "Puritan." With
the aid of his books, the citizen became independent of the priest ;
he acquired the habit of self-improvement ; and he developed self-
confidence. Through the help of God and prudence he achieved
success in this world and the assurance of celestial reward in the
next. In no literature are the ambitions and hopes of the middle

---

theme in such writers as Dekker and Samuel Rowlands. Sermon writers, likewise,
were fond of using it. *See* William Ward's *Gods Arrowes, Or, Two Sermons, concerning the
visitation of God by the Pestilence* (1607).

[136] Reprinted by J. W. Hebel and Hoyt H. Hudson (eds.), *Poetry of the English
Renaissance, 1509-1660* (New York, 1929), pp. 596 ff., from Wither's *Halleluiah, or
Britain's Second Remembrancer* (1641).

class better reflected than in the pious books that were read for pleasure and instruction. Here may be found the expression of the intellectual compromise which the English middle class made in accepting that portion of Calvinism suited to their desires. Throwing aside the economic collectivism laid down at Geneva and later attempted in the theocracy of New England, the English business mind evolved a spirit of individualism,[137] which still found in the strict tenets of Calvin the code essential to the development of personal integrity, reputation, and character that leads to credit and the virtues on which modern business flourishes. To this end tended the vast literature of godliness so eagerly consumed in Tudor and Stuart England.

[137] *See* Tawney, *op. cit.*, p. 234.

IX

THE UTILITY OF HISTORY[1]

THE Elizabethan citizen shared the belief of his learned and courtly contemporaries that the reading of history was an exercise second only to a study of Holy Writ in its power to induce good morality and shape the individual into a worthy member of society. This view, classical in its origin, ever since the sixteenth century has exerted a powerful influence to place historical reading high in the favor of the middle class. Poetry on imaginative themes has been received often with unconcealed suspicion; prose fiction has had to fight a long hour by Shrewsbury clock to justify its existence; the drama still savors of idle and frivolous amusement; but history is joyfully hailed as an open-sesame to learning and culture, a help in time of conversational need, a teacher of virtue and patriotism, and a stimulus to material and professional success. Renaissance criticism was unanimous in acclaiming the inherent virtues of history, for whatever else the critic might destroy, he preserved a shrine for Clio. History needed no apology, and even the sternest Puritan or the busiest tradesman might enjoy reading the annals of the past without prick of conscience, because he was certain that the chronicled examples of virtue and vice alike would be useful in teaching good lessons. "The reading likewise of histories," commented Henry Billingsley, a learned merchant and translator of Euclid, "conduceth not a litle, to the adorning of the soule & minde of man, a studie of all men cōmended : by it are seene and knowen the artes and doinges of infinite wise men gone before vs. In histories are contained infinite examples of heroicall vertues

---

[1] An earlier draft of this chapter appeared as an essay, "The Elizabethan Middle-Class Taste for History," *The Journal of Modern History*, III (1931), 175-97.

to be of vs followed, and horrible examples of vices to be of vs eschewed."[2]

Since practically all Renaissance writers on education advocated the study of history for the sake of the lessons useful in the service of the state, the subject early became an established part of the gentleman's training ;[3] and what was useful in aristocratic education was soon recommended as a means of inculcating good qualities in the sons of shopkeepers. Historical works, indeed, were supposed to be inspirational treatises, which would furnish moral, political, and even financial guidance, as well as encouragement, to Englishmen in their struggle for success. So great was the presumed value of these works that scholars felt a missionary urge to make them available to the commonalty, and no one disputed the good which they brought to the individual and to the state. Thomas Blundeville, a country gentleman with a zeal to popularize knowledge, published *The true order and Methode of wryting*

---

[2] "The Translator to the Reader" prefatory to *The Elements Of Geometrie* (1570).

[3] W. H. Woodward, *Studies in Education during the Age of the Renaissance, 1400-1600* (Cambridge, 1906), p. 313. *See also* D. T. Starnes, "Purpose in the Writing of History," *Modern Philology*, XX (1922-23), 281-300. Professor Starnes discusses the learned and aristocratic traditional belief in the power of history to promote virtue. Of the Elizabethan historians he observes that "in the sixteenth century, the moral purpose in writing was probably emphasized because of the Puritan attacks on poetry and the stage."—Pp. 293-94.

An example of the persistence of the Renaissance notion of the virtue-provoking quality of history is found in a recommendation from Oliver Cromwell to his son Richard that the latter read Raleigh's *History of the World*. In a letter dated April 2, 1650, Cromwell says : "Take heed of an unactive vain spirit. Recreate yourself with Sir Walter Ralegh's History : it's a body of History, and will add much more to your understanding than fragments of story."—S. C. Lomas (ed.), *Letters and Speeches of Oliver Cromwell*, 3 vols. (London, 1904), II, 54. Raleigh himself in the preface to his *History* had several times emphasized the general usefulness of historical learning.

The preface of nearly every work of history contained some allusion to the use and profit of such learning. E.g., Thomas Cooper's edition of Lanquet's chronicle, *An Epitome of Cronicles* [1549], sets forth the value of history as a guide for governors of commonwealths and stresses its utility to the average person because it shows the goodness of God to the virtuous and his just vengeance on the wicked. John Daus in *A Famouse Cronicle of oure time, called Sleidanes Commentaries* (1560) maintains that historians deserve better of the commonwealth than any other writers because of the usefulness of their work to the common country.—Sig. A 2.

For a discussion of the place of history in the schools, see Foster Watson, *The Beginnings of the Teaching of Modern Subjects in England* (London, 1909), pp. 45 ff.

and reading Hystories (1574)[4] in order to emphasize the didactic possibilities of history. "All those persons whose lyues haue beene such as are to bee followed for their excellencie in vertue, or else to be fledde for their excellencie in vice, are meete to be chronicled,"[5] the treatise suggests, for, as it says later, "nothing is more meete to drawe vs from vice, and dishonest dealing, than the examples of euill successes, which God hath giuen to the wicked, as punishments for theyr euill deserts."[6] Blundeville sincerely believed that writers of history should be urged to present their material so emphasized as to exert the maximum moral influence upon the reader, a theory of historical composition which moved Richard Brathwaite forty years later to declare that "A good Historian will alwaies expresse the actions of good men with an Emphasis, to sollicite the Reader to the affecting the like meanes, whereby hee may attaine the like end."[7] To writers of this type, Brathwaite assigns the highest place in the literary realm : "To be short, my opinion positiuely is this : That Historian which can ioyne profite with a modest delight together in one body or frame of one vnited discourse, grounding his story vpon an essentiall truth, deserues the first and principall place."[8] The views of Blundeville and Brathwaite represent an opinion held by most scholars and almost all laymen in the sixteenth and the first half of the seventeenth century.

The belief in the civilizing influence of history was so great that Barnabe Rich in his *Allarme to England* (1578) declared that one reason for the sad state of the Irish was the dearth of historical reading matter in Ireland. The Irish, he thinks, are little better than savages because they are

---

[4] *The true order and Methode of wryting and reading Hystories, according to the precepts of Francisco Patricio and Accontio Tridentino, two Italian writers, no lesse plainly than briefly, set forth in our vulgar speach, to the great profite and commoditye of all those that delight in Hystories* (1574).

[5] Sig. C 2.   [6] Sig. H 2.

[7] *The Schollers Medley, Or, An Intermixt Discourse Vpon Historicall And Poeticall Relations* (1614), p. 6. Brathwaite gives more extensive expression of his views on history and scholarship in the expansion of *The Schollers Medley* which he later published as *A Survey Of History* (1638).

[8] *The Schollers Medley*, p. 68.

. . . Baereued of one of the greatest benefites, that giueth light & vnderstanding, which is by reading of histories : considering there is nothing whiche may be either pleasant, profitable, or necessarie for man, but is written in Bookes, wherein are reported the manners, conditions, gouernments, counsels, and affaires of euerie countrie : the gestes, actes, behauiour, and manner of liuing of euerie people : the fourmes of sundrie Common wealthes, with their augmentations, and decayes, and the occasions thereof : the preceptes, exhortations, counsels, and good persuasions comprehended in quicke sentences : to conclude, in Bookes and Histories are actually expressed, the beautie of vertue, and the loathsomenesse of vice. . . . Which knowledge and light commeth chiefely vnto vs by reading of histories.   [Sig. D 3ᵛ.]

If history could have tamed the Irish, its effect upon ordinary Englishmen must have been infinitely greater. At any rate, the belief in its power was unquestioned. Every man who aspired to gentlemanly cultivation was urged by Brathwaite in *The English Gentleman* (1630), a work much read by ambitious burghers, to adopt history as his principal literary diet.[9] When citizens at the end of the sixteenth century were eagerly buying anthologies and the highly prized epitomes of information, the compiler of *Wits Theater of the Little World* (1599), a volume of biographical and historical gleanings, assured the reader that his time would not be wasted in the perusal of the book because the "profit that ariseth by reading these epitomized histories is, to aemulate that which thou likest in others, and to make right vse of theyr examples."[10] No man was so simple that he could not turn to account the lessons to be picked out of histories, according to Henry Wright, a London citizen, who published *The First Part Of The Disquisition Of Truth, Concerning Political Affaires* (1616), a curious little compilation of political philosophy expressed in a series of rhetorical questions. After praising London for its loyalty and the virtue of its citizens, Wright discusses studies which produce these good qualities, and suggests in one passage that history is the most effective way to the attainment of a worthy character :

Is it because that by reading of Histories, a man shall truely find *Vertue*, to haue her due praise, and honour giuen her, as contrariwise to *Vice*, her due shame and reproofe? Or may this bee the reason, for

---

[9] *See* Chap. V, *supra*, p. 153.   [10] Epistle to the reader.

that History is auaileable to instruct any priuate man (of what degree soeuer) how to frame his life, and carry himselfe with commendation in the eye of the world, when, as in a glasse, he shall see how to beautifie & compose it, according to the patterne of other mens vertues?
[Pp. 71-72.]

The faith in the didactic value of history was not confined, of course, to any social group in Tudor and Stuart England, because the belief was almost universal that a knowledge of the past furnished a valuable guide to the present. But middle-class readers especially came to regard history as the perfect literature, for it was safe, entertaining, instructive, and useful; and not even the grimmest Puritan, who might condemn most other forms of literature, could gainsay its value.[11] Moreover, a knowledge of the national history was an evidence of patriotism, just as an interest in the antiquities of London was a mark of the citizen's civic pride. Therefore historical works of manifold types found their way into the libraries of plain men, who added to their resources of learning by committing to memory the chronology of the kings of Israel or of England, storing away anecdotes garnered from classical historians, and reading diligently in the native annals.

First in popularity with the citizens were the chronicles of England, particularly those chronicles which emphasized the glory of London and her people, for London citizens had a pride in their own importance not unjustified by the facts of history. From early times Londoners had kept, or had caused to be kept, chronicles of the city recording the succession of mayors with lists of other municipal officers and the principal events in each mayoralty.[12] Chronicles of this sort occupied the leisure of many citizens in the fifteenth and early sixteenth centuries. For instance, William Gregory, skinner, and lord mayor in 1451-52, seems to

---

[11] Many worthless chapbooks, therefore, tried to bolster their reputations by calling themselves "histories." The term "history" was, of course, loosely used by Renaissance writers and sometimes included works of fiction. There was, however, a gradual narrowing of the sense to the modern meaning. Brathwaite, for example, in *The Schollers Medley* draws a distinction and uses the expression "feigned history," as some others had done, to describe imaginative work.

[12] *See* C. L. Kingsford (ed.), *Chronicles of London* (Oxford, 1905), Introduction, pp. v ff.; *idem, English Historical Literature in the Fifteenth Century* (Oxford, 1913), pp. 70 ff.

have been responsible for at least a portion of the chronicle that now goes under his name ;[13] Robert Fabyan, a draper, and city sheriff in 1493, was the compiler of *Fabyan's Chronicle*, first printed in 1516 and at least three times reprinted by 1559 ;[14] Richard Arnold, London citizen and haberdasher in the Flanders trade, compiled a popular hodgepodge of information about London, printed at Antwerp in 1503(?) and republished in Southwark in 1521.[15] His chronicle includes such diverse but useful matter as

the Names of ye Baylifs, Custōs, Mairs, and Sherefs, of the Cite of Londō, from the Tyme of King Richard the First; and also th' Artycles of the Chartur and Libarties of the same Cyte; and of the Chartur and Liberties off England, wyth odur dyuers mat's good and necessary for euery Citizē to vndirstond and knowe.

The "good and necessary" information provides, among other things, a recipe to take spots out of clothes. Arnold's chronicle represents the kind of commonplace book kept by citizens,[16] who believed that the compiling of annals was not only a useful enterprise but also an object of civic piety which enabled them to keep fresh in memory the glorious deeds that had made great their capital and their country.

Throughout the sixteenth century printers were busy republishing the older chronicles or bringing out new ones to satisfy the craving of a populace eager to read of England's past glories, which were believed to forecast greater things to come. Scholars and plain citizens alike composed "the noteworthy group of sixteenth-century historians, who wrote for London publishers and had at their command a wide class of interested readers."[17] The public of common men was being stirred by a national patriotism which, before the century was out, would flame through the country until even the most lethargic peasant discerned England's

---

[13] Edited by James Gairdner as *The Historical Collections of a Citizen of London in the Fifteenth Century*, Camden Society, N. S., XVII (1876).

[14] Edited by Sir Henry Ellis as *The New Chronicles of England and France by Robert Fabyan, 1516* (London, 1811).

[15] Edited by Francis Douce as *The Customs of London* (London, 1811).

[16] *See* C. L. Kingsford (ed.), *Two London Chronicles*, Camden Miscellany, 3d Ser., XVIII (1910), x.

[17] Kingsford, *English Historical Literature*, p. 261.

glorious destiny. It is no wonder that chroniclers and historians, pricked by the spur of patriotic duty, encouraged by rulers pleased at their flattery, and urged on by profit-scenting printers, set themselves with a right good will to turn out histories designed for the understanding of plain men. From the days of Henry VIII to the Puritan Revolution, histories which aimed to show the greatness of England came from the press in an unbroken stream. John Rastell, the lawyer-printer, was the author of one of the earliest of the histories planned to suit the tastes of commoners. He gave it the punning title of *The Pastyme of People. The Cronycles of dyuers realmys, and most specyally of the realme of Englond* (1529)[18] and sought to make it more enticing by printing full-page wood-cuts of the English sovereigns from William the Conqueror to Richard III, with whom he discreetly stopped. Not so timid was Edward Hall, barrister of Gray's Inn, who sought to glorify the house of Tudor in *The Union of the Two Noble and Illustrious Families York and Lancaster* (1542), which met with so much popular favor that it went through five editions in the next ten years. But for those who found the larger folios of Rastell and Hall too expensive or cumbersome, there were cheap little octavo volumes, which placed within reach of the lightest purse the skeleton at least of English history. Although Caxton and his immediate successors had published English chronicles, their works were not so widely distributed as the somewhat later epitomes that attracted great numbers of readers about the middle of the sixteenth century and continued in use for many years. The trifling little summary, *A breuiat cronicle contaynynge all the kings from brute to this daye* [1551], must have served as a handbook for many persons who could afford no better work, for in the next ten years it was frequently reprinted, exemplars from nine editions remaining extant. Another well liked and better abridgment of the chronicles was that be-gun by Thomas Lanquet and finished by Thomas Cooper in 1549 as *An Epitome of Cronicles*. Like other contemporary chronicles, it begins with the creation and briefly traces ancient history, which leads up to a more extensive treatment of England. Prefacing the work was a short essay, "Of the vse and profite of histories, and

---

[18] Edited by T. F. Dibdin (London, 1811).

with what iudgement they ought to be redde," which emphasizes the usual moral reasons and points out the value of witnessing the manifestations of the prophecies of God in historic events. So evident was the utility of the work for unlearned readers that Robert Crowley, the social reformer, published an unauthorized edition in 1559, causing Cooper to write a bitter prefatory note to his own edition of 1560, condemning "certaine persons, [who] for lukers sake contrarie to honestie, had caused my chronicle to be prynted without my knowlage." Still another edition was published in 1565. Though Cooper had maintained that his work was useful for the instruction of magistrates and rulers, the populace found it equally acceptable for their own instruction.

It is significant of the middle-class interest in chronicle-history that the two most important and prolific chronicle writers of the last half of the sixteenth century were both tradesmen who retained their connections with trade as long as they lived. Richard Grafton, printer and prosperous member of the great Grocers' Company, and John Stow, more learned if less prosperous member of the Merchant Taylors' Company, throughout their industrious lives were rivals in the craft of setting forth the glory of England. Each abused the other for inaccuracy, but both were imbued with the same zeal to make available to the commonalty a record of England's fame.[19]

Of the two, Grafton was the better business man and made history pay him a profit—something Stow, who apparently remained a practising tailor through most of his life, never managed to do. Grafton began his publishing career with the pious and not unprofitable venture of distributing the translation of the Scriptures printed in Antwerp, known as "Matthews' Bible," which he and another grocer, Edward Whitchurch, managed to have licensed in 1537. Displaying a canniness characteristic of him, Grafton sought a license under the privy seal to prevent other dealers from underselling him.[20] Having made money, first on the distribution and then on the printing of Bibles, Grafton next turned his attention to publishing historical works. His first un-

---

[19] *See* C. L. Kingsford (ed.), *A Survey of London by John Stow*, 2 vols. (Oxford, 1908), I, ix-x.

[20] *Dictionary of National Biography, sub* Grafton.

dertaking was an edition of *The chronicle of Ihon Hardyng* (1543), a second edition being published in the same year. To Hardyng's verse history, the printer himself compiled a prose continuation from Edward IV to Henry VIII, translated in part from Polydore Vergil, the source of a great deal of later history. The public having shown its approval of his labors in history, Grafton was now encouraged to publish a new edition of Edward Hall's chronicle, with a later history of his own composition, bringing the narrative down to the death of Henry VIII. Again the venture was so successful that the work went into a second printing before the new year and was twice again reprinted by 1552. The experience as a historian, derived from continuing other men's work, was not lost upon the printer-grocer, who compiled *An abridgement of the Chronicles of England*,[21] published by Tottell in 1562 after Grafton himself seems to have retired from the printing business. How many busy tradesmen gained a knowledge of history from this convenient little quarto, prepared by their fellow citizen, no one can tell, but five editions were required before 1572, when Stow's abridgment definitely superseded its rival.

Grafton sincerely believed that he was doing the country a service in furnishing a better epitome of history than it had previously had. In a dedication to Lord Robert Dudley he declares that he was persuaded to make the compilation because he saw "vsed and occupied in euery common persons hande a certeyne booke bearyng lyke tytle, wherein was conteyned lytle truthe and lesse good order." Perhaps Grafton was criticizing *A breuiat cronicle*, a new edition of which had appeared in 1561, for Stow's work was not licensed until three years later. If Grafton hoped to make a useful compendium that every common person could use, he succeeded admirably, for his style is simple, and if he has no new information, he furnishes forth the old in language easily understandable by the shopkeepers in Cheapside. In a further effort to provide the commonalty with an even simpler text, Grafton brought out in 1565 a tiny sextodecimo handbook entitled *A Manuell of the Chronicles of England. From the creacion of the worlde, to this yere of our Lorde 1565*, which he prayed the Com-

---

[21] Title quoted from the edition of 1563.

20

pany of Stationers to declare the only authorized epitome, to the end "that the Quenes Maiesties subiects, which couet suche litle colleciõs, for the helpyng of their memory maie not be abused, as heretofore thei haue been." The making of a volume "more portatiue & also to be sold at a meane & small price," has been his aim, he assures the reader, whom he expected to allure by the cheapness and convenience of a book that could be tucked into a pocket. As in the *Abridgement*, he includes an almanac and a rule to tell the beginning of the law terms. Furthermore, to remove the danger that the unlearned reader might find anything confusing, he employs Arabic numerals instead of Roman figures, "for the helpe of suche as are not acquainted with the vse of Figures." Having reduced history to its simplest form, Grafton was proud of his handiwork and not disposed to permit others to share his glory. The possibility of a recent compilation of Stow's encroaching upon his chronicle-domain disturbed him to the point of declaring, in the preface of the *Manuell*, that his rival had "coũterfeated my volume and order of the Abridgemente of the Chronicles, and hath made my trauaile to passe vnder his name also"—an attack that he continued in later prefaces. As a matter of fact, Grafton himself had borrowed from his rival's book in the effort to meet Stow's competition.

But Grafton was not content to let his fame rest upon abridgments, useful as these were, and he brought his historical studies to fruition in 1568 with the publication of *A Chronicle at large and meere History of the affayres of Englande and Kinges of the same*,[22] a ponderous folio running to nearly fourteen hundred pages, grandly dedicated to Sir William Cecil, and summing up all that Grafton thought worth recording from the creation to the year 1568, though he had the prudence to devote only a little more than two colorless pages to the doings of Queen Elizabeth. Aware that his was the most stupendous history up to its time, Grafton proudly calls Cecil's attention to its worth, as "neyther altogether needelesse nor vnprofitable":

For among so many writers, there hath yet none to my knowledge, published any full, playne and meere Englishe historie. For some of

---

[22] Title quoted from the edition of 1569.

them of purpose meaning to write short notes in maner of Annales, commonly called Abridgementes, rather touch the tymes when things were done, then declare the maner of the doyings, leauing thereby some necessitie of larger explication, and referring the desirous Reader to a further serch and study. Other haue dealt but with the reignes of a few kings, & yet therof haue made long bookes, with many tedious digressions, obscure descriptions & friuolous dilations : which forme of writing if it should not be reformed, coulde not in the whole be folowed without pestering the Reader with importable Volumes.

Other shortcomings of historians, such as intermingling the affairs of foreign countries and distorting the facts of English history (a fault attributed to alien historians), are not to be found in his work, the author insists. Lest the reader be not convinced of the value of the work and the qualifications of its author, a fellow Londoner, Thomas Norton, wrote a prefatory epistle affirming the profit to the kingdom of the history and asserting the worth of the author, one who had "not spent one quarter of hys lyfe to his owne ease or commoditie, but as a good Citezen for the benefite of the Citie of London, as a good Englisheman for the profite of the Realme of Englande, and as a good Christian for the further-aunce of true religion" had labored in good causes, which ought to move others "to be suche Citezens as he hath beene." Grafton had proved himself a public-spirited and generous citizen, by giving time and money to charities, by making the English Bible available to the commonalty, and now, "beside a number of good bookes by him published," by giving to the nation the great chronicle which crowned his labors! Surely, Norton thinks, citizens should be proud of their learned and magnanimous brother-in-trade. Although the huge chronicle, in spite of its costliness, attracted sufficient attention to make a second edition necessary in the year following its publication, it was to be superseded before many years by other and better books, for despite his patriotism and good intentions, Grafton had succeeded merely in bringing together in chronological order a vast deal of traditional lore, which, even for his time, represented uncritical credulity. Nevertheless, Grafton's historical works were widely read until late in the sixteenth century and were extremely important in the dissemination of historical knowledge.

It was Grafton's misfortune to be a competitor in the trade of historiography with John Stow, who possessed a better critical sense and keener antiquarian instincts. Stow's devotion to historical research, unlike Grafton's publishing enterprises, brought him little financial reward but it gave him a reputation for learning among the antiquarians of his day. Born of a London family who for generations had plied the trade of tailor in the parish of St. Michael, Cornhill, Stow inherited a love of the city and a pride in its citizens which added zeal to his painstaking investigations into the ancient glory of London and the kingdom. To the shame of these same citizens, their chronicler was allowed to die in poverty, with a pittance of charity from his own trade guild and letters patent from the state to "collect voluntary contributions and kind gratuities."[23] But if the citizens failed to see the basins which the old man placed in the streets for the collection of alms in his last days, they had for years bought works of his compilation, which gave them the best and briefest accounts of the history eagerly desired by all men. It was a vagary of Elizabethan publishing that an author whose works were widely read received only a trivial remuneration.

Although Stow had been busy with antiquarian research for a number of years and had in 1561 published an edition of Chaucer, his first contribution to popular history came in 1565 with the appearance of *A Summarie of Englyshe Chronicles,* a fat little octavo that traced the history of England from the arrival of Brute at Totness in Devonshire in 1108 B.C. to the year of publication, with rather more Elizabethan history than Grafton had elected to give. Acknowledging his debt to previous chroniclers, Stow modestly asserts in his preface that he has corrected them in accordance with facts discovered "partly by paynfull searche, and partly by diligent experiēce." He hopes that "though it be written homely, yet it is not (as I trust) writē vntruly." From the first, the *Summary* was enormously popular; simple, readable, and carrying an air of truth, it emphasized facts from the history of London and hence made a particular appeal to the citizens of the metropolis. Continually reprinted and brought down to date until well into the

---

[23] *Dictionary of National Biography,* sub Stow.

seventeenth century, fourteen editions before 1618 are extant, the continuations after Stow's death in 1605 being the labor of Edmund Howes; perhaps other editions were read out of existence. Although Stow had prided himself on the smallness of the original octavo volume, some of the succeeding editions further improved upon this format by appearing as sextodecimos. Certainly so much history had never before been packed into so convenient a pocket manual.

Stow sincerely believed that the lessons of history were of paramount value to the commonwealth, and in an epistle prefixed to the 1570 edition of the *Summary* he calls attention to the good to be derived from the study of such history:

Amongeste other Bookes, which are in this our learned age published in gret nombers, there are fewe, eyther for the honestie of the matters, or commoditie whiche they bringe to the common wealth, or for the plesauntnes of the studie and reading, to be preferred before the Chronicles and Histories: what exāples of men deseruinge immortalitye, of exploits worthy great renowne, of vertuous liuing of the posteritie to be embraced, of wise handeling of waighty affayres, diligently to be marked, and aptly to be applyed: what incouragement of nobilitie to noble feates, what discouragement of vnnatural subiectes from wicked treasons, pernitious rebellions and dānable Doctrines: to cōclude, what perswasiōs to honesty, godlines, & vertue of all sort, what disswasions from the contrarie is not plentifully in them to be found? So that it is as hard a matter for the Readers of Chronicles, in my fansie, to passe withoute some colors of wisdome, inuitaments to vertue, and lothinge of naughtie factes, as it is for a welfauored man to walke vp and downe in the hotte parching sonne, and not be therwith sonneburned.

But Stow was too good an antiquarian to permit instruction in morality to be his sole aim. Actually, as he goes on to say in the same preface, he had sought to discover the true facts of history, and to remedy "the confuse[d] order of oure late englishe Chronicles, and the ignoraunt handelinge of auncient affaires" even to the extent of contradicting statements made in the earlier editions of his own *Summary*. And he concludes his preface with a jibe at Grafton, who, Stow hints ironically, had plagiarized the errors which he corrects in this edition.

Stow's next historical work was a more extensive chronicle—but one still brief and cheap enough to find favor with the populace—which he published in 1580 as *Chronicles of England from Brute vnto this present yeare 1580*, a quarto volume, better known as *The Annales Of England*, the title employed in the edition of 1592. From a statement in the dedication of the latter edition to the Archbishop of Canterbury, it is clear that Stow would have preferred to publish the results of more original research, "had not the Printer, for some priuate respects, beene more desirous to publish Annales at this present." The "priuate respects" moving the printer were the demands of the public for general histories of England in portable volumes. The Armada victory had fanned national patriotism to such a fever heat that even stage players could draw crowds better with a history play than with any other theme. Small wonder it is that printers thought it a good time to bring out new editions of popular histories. Stow had managed to pack more interesting detail into a briefer compass than any preceding historian; hence his *Annals* for more than fifty years enjoyed a vogue as great as his *Summary*: eight editions before 1631 remain to testify to the long life of the work.

Stow's career as an antiquarian was crowned with a work that peculiarly expresses the spirit of the honest tradesman, proud of his native city, and all succeeding historians have cause to thank the industry that produced *A Survay Of London* (1598), a work which contained, as the title-page said, "the Originall, Antiquity, Increase, Moderne estate, and description of that Citie," as well as "an Apologie (or defence) against the opinion of some men, concerning that Citie, the greatnesse thereof." In a dignified dedication addressed to the lord mayor and the commonalty of London, Stow declares that the writing of this history has been a pious duty:

It is a duty, that I willingly ow to my natiue mother & Countrie. And an office that of right I holde my selfe bound in loue to bestow vpon the politicke body and members of the same: what *London* hath beene of auncient time, men may here see, as what it is now euery man doth behold: I know that the argument, being of the chiefe and principall Citie of the land, required the penne of some excellent Artisen, but fearing that none woulde attempt, and finish it, as few haue assayed any, I chose rather (amongst other my Laboures) to handle it after my plaine manner, then to leaue it vnperformed.

The *Survey* is far more than a chronicle of mayors and aldermen, of great frosts and prodigious happenings; it is the record of the growth of a city made great by the industry, thrift, and daring of a body of citizens whom one of their wisest members chose to exalt in a history that has preserved their fame to posterity. Needless to say, a work so compendiously describing the splendors of the metropolis and the virtues of its citizens was soon exhausted and new editions were demanded. Stow himself prepared a second edition in 1603; Anthony Munday, the draper, produced a third edition with continuations in 1618; and, aided by Humphrey Dyson, still another edition, in folio, in 1633. Stow's *Survey* has been the basis of all later histories of London. If the author, who described the infinite philanthropies of generous citizens, ever reflected bitterly on his own lot as he waited in his latter days for passers-by to toss alms into his basin, there is no record of it; Henry Holland described him as a merry old man. He believed to the last in the grandeur of his city and the goodness of its people.

If the citizenry generally were negligent of their chronicler, at least one tradesman was moved to remind his brethren that Stow had performed yeoman service in their honor and should be rewarded. Preserved among the Stow papers in the British Museum[24] is a poem by William Vallans, salter, dated 1583 and addressed to Stow, who, the author asserts, deserves more profits than he has received for praising citizens. Even though citizens have an obligation to speak in commendation of themselves, Stow's work is so noteworthy in this respect that it should be given tangible recognition, Vallans maintains:

> Let citizens themselues declare
> What dedes theyre mayors haue done,
> What benefactors they haue had,
> What honor they haue wonn.
> And though your selfe a Cytezen
> Regard there lastying fame
> Yet reason is they should reward
> Or recompense the same.

---

[24] MSS Harley 367; quoted by Kingsford, *Survey*, I, lxxxviii.

The publicity value of city history of the right sort was early recognized by the municipal authorities of London, who established the office of city chronologer. An effort seems to have been made to procure the best talent available, but the city was not always successful in getting adequate returns from the office-holders. Thomas Middleton, Ben Jonson, and Francis Quarles were among the holders of this office. The duties were chiefly "to collect and set down all memorable acts of this City and occurrences thereof,"[25] but Ben Jonson seems to have neglected all of them, for we find the city fathers refusing in 1631 to pay him "until he shall have presented unto this Court some fruits of his labours."[26]

The interest of the citizenry in their magistrates led the printer William Jaggard to publish in 1601 a cheap little volume entitled *A view Of all The Right Honourable the Lord Mayors of this Honorable Citty of London,*[27] which purports to give the portraits of all the mayors from the accession of the Queen to the date of printing. Unfortunately Jaggard had less than a dozen crude woodcuts of magisterial citizens, but he repeated them at intervals through the book to serve as the likenesses of all forty-five mayors whose administrations were briefly described. In a dedication to the mayor then in office, Sir William Ryder, Jaggard declares that he, "a poore Citizen," had been moved to publish the work because of "the examples of good iustice done by your predecessors," "the christian and charitable patterns left for after ages, by their examples," their liberality and godly provisions for charity, and the great mercy of God in blessing the country with so worthy a queen under whom these mayors had been able to flourish. Bad as were the pictures and the printing in this little book, it must have furnished pleasing municipal publicity.

The glorification of the middle class in some of the chronicles aroused the sarcasm of writers like Nashe, who usually catered to the aristocratic point of view. In *Pierce Penilesse* (1592) Nashe speaks scornfully of bourgeois chronicle writers and maintains that only poets can confer immortality:

---

[25] W. H. and H. C. Overall, *Analytical Index to the Series of Records Known as the Remembrancia* (London, 1878), p. 305.   [26] *Ibid.*

[27] The presumably unique copy is preserved in the Huntington Library.

Gentles, it is not your lay Chronigraphers, that write of nothing but of Mayors and Sheriefs and the deare yeere, and the great Frost, that can endowe your names with neuer dated glory : . . . it is better for a Nobleman or Gentleman, to haue his honours story related, and his deedes emblazond by a Poet, than a Citizen.[28]

Again in *Summers Last Will and Testament* he has Winter list among the idle rogues of the realm historiographers whom he charges with honoring tinkers, cobblers, and such like in the hope of earning from them a paltry reward.[29] In similar fashion, John Davies in *A Scourge for Paper-Persecutors* (1625) gives a satirical characterization of chroniclers like Stow :

> But that which most my soule excruciates,
> Some *Chroniclers* that write of Kingdomes States,
> Doe so absurdly sableize my White
> With *Maskes* and *Enterludes* by day and night;
> Balld *Maygames*, *Beare-baytings*, and poore *Orations*
> Made to some *Prince* by some poore *Corporations*
> And if a *Brick-bat* from a *Chimney* falls
> When puffing *Boreas* nere so little bralls :
> Or else a Knaue be hangd by iustice doome
> For cutting of a Purse in selfe-same roome :
> Or wanton Rig, or letcher dissolute
> Do stand at Pauls-Crosse in a Sheeten Sute;
> All these, and thousand such like toyes as these
> They clap in *Chronicles* like *Butterflees*,
> Of which there is no vse; but spotteth me
> With Medley of their Motly Liuery.
> And so confound graue Matters of estate
> With plaies of *Poppets*, and I wot not what :
> Which makes the Volume of her Greatnesse bost
> To put the Buyer to a needlesse Cost.   [Pp. 11-12.]

Edmund Bolton makes a disparaging comment on chronicles in his *Hypercritica* [1618], describing them as "vast vulgar Tomes procured for the most part by the husbandry of Printers, and not by appointment of the Prince or Authority of the Common-

---

[28] G. B. Harrison (ed.), *Pierce Penilesse* (London, 1924), pp. 59-60.
[29] R. B. McKerrow (ed.), *The Works of Thomas Nashe*, 5 vols. (London, 1904-10), III, 276.

weal."[30] But the taunts of scoffing critics had no influence upon the taste of the multitude, who had learned in the last quarter of the sixteenth century to relish chronicle-history with a zest accorded few other forms of writing.

The summary chronicles of Grafton and his predecessors stimulated the public appetite, which a little later was further supplied with the often printed works of Stow; but these cheap histories were not the exclusive source of the historical information possessed by the middle class, who would as willingly spend money for histories as for Bibles. The belief in the financial profits to be derived from historical works was responsible for the publication, by a sort of syndicate,[31] of *Holinshed's Chronicle* (1577), an enormous work which appeared first in two great folio volumes. The compiler, Raphael Holinshed, had been employed by Reginald Wolfe, the printer, to help in the production of a universal history, but when Wolfe died in 1573 before the completion of the task, the printers who carried on the publication decided to limit the work to a history of England, Scotland, and Ireland. Even so, the history ran to nearly three thousand pages; yet despite the costli-

---

[30] Joel E. Spingarn, *Critical Essays of the Seventeenth Century*, 3 vols. (Oxford, 1908-9), I, 97-98.

Although the public might continue to call for the old-fashioned chronicle type of history, some of the historians sought to eliminate the human-interest material in the belief that it was trivial. John Trussell, for example, in the preface to *A Continuation Of The Collection Of The History of England, Beginning Where Samuel Daniell Esquire ended* (1636) announces that he has "pared off these superfluous exuberances, . . . 1. Matters of Ceremony, as Coronations, Christenings, Marriages, Funeralls, solemne Feasts, and such like. 2. Matters of Triumph, as Tiltings, Maskings, Barriers, Pageants, Gallefoists, and the like. 3. Matters of Noveltie, as great inundations, sudden rising and falling of prizes of Corne, strange Monsters, Iustice done on petty offenders, and such like executions, with which the *Cacoethes* of the Writers of those times have mingled matters of state."

A reaction against this "pared" style is hinted at by Sir Richard Baker in the epistle to the reader of his *Chronicle Of The Kings Of England* (1643). He maintains that he has compiled his work in chronicle style rather than attempt to give a summary of state matters in the reigns treated. Others have done "excellently in the way of History" but not "so well in the way of Chronicle": "For whilst they insist wholly upon matters of State, they wholly omit meaner Accidents, which yet are Materials as proper for a Chronicle, as the other."

[31] *Dictionary of National Biography*, *sub* Holinshed. The two volumes of the work now called *Holinshed's Chronicle* had different title-pages when published in 1577: *The Firste volume of the Chronicles of England, Scotlande, and Ireland* . . . and *The Laste volume of the Chronicles of England, Scotlande, and Irelande, with their descriptions*. . . .

ness of the work, it must have become the prized possession of many a well-to-do citizen, for it was regarded as the most authoritative history of its time. The sale of the first edition was encouraging enough to induce the printers to bring out a still more extensive edition, in three volumes, in 1587. This great chronicle, which provided much of the history utilized by Shakespeare and his contemporary dramatists, was the coöperative enterprise of London citizens, having been inspired and partly compiled by a printer, edited and completed by a humble though able scholar hired for the task, and put through the press by a group of businesslike publishers. Its style, like the promoters of the undertaking, was plain. Holinshed in the preface to the first edition comments :

My speech is playne, without any Rhetoricall shewe of Eloquence, hauing rather a regarde to simple truth, than to decking wordes. I wishe I had bene furnished with so perfect instructions, and so many good gifts, that I might haue pleased all kindes of men, but that same being so rare a thing in any one of the best, I beseech thee (gentle Reader) not to looke for it in me the meanest.

But at times Holinshed achieved prose that the greatest poet believed good enough to use as he found it.

The widespread and increasing interest in the antiquities of Britain is further indicated by the popular reception accorded one of the most learned works of the age, William Camden's *Britannia* (1586), a combination of cosmography and history giving a county-by-county description of England, Scotland, and Ireland. Although the work was in Latin, the interest in it was so great that the Latin version was seven times reprinted by 1607. Three years later, Philemon Holland, assisted by the author, translated it into English and expanded the original octavo into a folio volume bearing the title *Britain, Or A Chorographicall Description Of The Most flourishing Kingdomes, England, Scotland, and Ireland, and the Ilands adioyning, out the depth of Antiquitie* (1610), which was again reprinted in 1625. John Bill, the King's printer, published in 1626 *The abridgment of Camden's Britañia,* and two other epitomes were published in Holland. Noblemen, gentlemen, and citizens, proud of their municipalities, anxiously read Camden's *Britannia* to see what he had said about their families, their landed possessions, or their towns. And not all of them were pleased, for Camden was a historian rather than the publicist of lords or cities. "Some will blame me for that I have omitted this and that towne and Castle," he comments, "as though I purposed to mention any but such as were most notorious, and mentioned by ancient authours. Neither verily were it worth the labour once to name them, when as beside the naked name there is nothing memorable."[32] But if a few of the gentry thought themselves scantily honored, and if a few citizens were displeased that their towns were not properly advertised, there was nevertheless so much interesting information about the past and present of Britain that the book enjoyed a long life and became the basis of similar works that followed its lead.

Camden himself is one of the great personalities of the age. Born in London, the son of Sampson Camden, a skilled craftsman of Lichfield, who had removed to London and become a member of the Guild of Painter-Stainers, William Camden never lost interest in the trade life of the metropolis, even though he became Clarenceux King-of-Arms and could have been knighted had he not refused the honor. Wise enough to despise "newly blossomed" gentility, the man who knew more about the antecedents of the British nobility and gentry than any other living person preferred the company of scholars, whatever their rank, and chose at his death to record his connection with trade by bequeathing to the Company of Cordwainers and the Guild of Painter-Stainers each a piece of plate inscribed, "Guil. Camdenus filis Sampsonis pictoris Londinensis."[33]

Camden's other historical works were almost as popular as the *Britannia*. The only book in English which Camden prepared for

---

[32] "The Author To The Reader," Holland's translation of 1610. In another passage preceding the one cited above, Camden observes a trifle ironically: "There are some peradventure which apprehend it disdainfully and offensiuely that I have not remembred this or that family, when as it was not my purpose to mention any but such as were more notable, nor all them truly (for their names would fill whole volumes) but such as hapned in my way according to the methode I proposed to my selfe; And with Gods grace I may have a more convenient occasion to deserve well of the Nobility and Gentry. But happily they will be most offended heerin who have least deserved of their country, or overvallew themselves most, or whose Gentry may be but newly blossomed."

[33] *Dictionary of National Biography, sub* Camden.

the press was a collection of precisely the sort of antiquarian lore that would appeal to the history-hungry public. This he brought out in 1605 as *Remaines Of A Greater Worke, Concerning Britaine, the inhabitants thereof, their Languages, Names, Surnames, Empreses, Wise speeches, Poesies, and Epitaphes*. The author himself described it in the dedication to Sir Robert Cotton as "only the rude rubble and out-cast rubbish (as you know) of a greater and more serious worke." But the multitude delighted in what Camden called his rubbish, and found much amusement as well as wisdom in the book, for in addition to historical facts, it supplied the material for useful moralizations. For example, what grave merchant would have failed to use this anecdote to point a moral for his son :

A lusty gallant that had wasted much of his patrimony, seeing master *Dutton* a gentleman in a gowne, not of the newest cut, tolde him that hee had thought it had beene his great grandfathers gowne, *It is so* (saide maister *Dutton*) *and I have also my great grandfathers lands, and so have not you.*   [P. 234.]

A work known to have been written by the great Master Camden, which combined fascinating tidbits of history, scraps of miscellaneous information, and witty anecdotes, was certain to attract many readers; in fact, it was so well received that a fifth impression was required in 1636.

Camden's history of Queen Elizabeth, published in Latin in 1615 as *Annales Rerum Anglicarum, Et Hibernicarum, Regnante Elizabetha, Ad Annum Salutis M.D. LXXXIX*, was not intended to tickle the ears of the multitude, but it too had a rather wide circulation. It was reprinted at Leyden, and a French version was published in London. Abraham Darcie translated the first three books from the French into English in 1625, and Thomas Browne translated Book 4 in 1629. In 1630 Robert Norton, the engineer and gunner, published a complete translation, which had a third edition in 1635.

The works of William Camden were not written for any class, but it is proof of the active historical interest of an extensive reading public embracing large numbers of the middle class, that works as learned as Camden's should have been so widely distributed.

Only the willingness on the part of ordinary citizens to pay for expensive histories accounts for the popularity of another important work produced by a London tradesman, John Speed—like Stow, a tailor who became a learned antiquary. Speed published in 1611 what must have been one of the most expensive books printed in his time, a combination of cosmography and history which appeared as an enormous folio in two parts, bearing the title of *The Theatre Of The Empire Of Great Britaine*, the historical portion having a separate title-page describing it as *The History Of Great Britaine*[34] from the Roman conquest to King James. Resplendent with maps and numerous engravings, the work was handsomely printed and proved a volume worthy to lie conspicuously in the parlors of the well-to-do, beside the new translation of the Bible which was published in the same year. Never before had two such splendid books, representing the ideal reading of the citizen, enticed the purse of every man able to buy them. Not every shopkeeper, of course, could afford Speed's magnificent cosmography and history, but the popularity of the work was remarkable. A Latin version of the *Theatre* was published in 1616, and new editions in English appeared in 1627 and 1631. The *Short Title Catalogue* also records separate printings of the *History* in 1611, 1614, 1623, 1627, and 1632. Clearly many a plain man who could ill afford the expense must have bought the books, to warrant so many printings. A learned and scholarly description of the geography and history of England—owing much to Camden, it is true—Speed's contribution to popular learning deserves to rank with the great works of the age. Though bred a tailor, John Speed, "His Maiesties Most lowly and most loyall Subiect and Seruant," as he describes himself in dedicating his book to King James, managed to become a historian capable of digesting more documents and facts than anyone hitherto in a history better planned and more discriminating than any previously published—a work respected by scholars and laymen alike. The air of Elizabethan tailor shops must have borne some strange elixir, to produce two

---

[34] The full title explains the contents of this portion of the work: *The History Of Great Britaine Under the Conquests of ye Romans, Saxons, Danes and Normans. Their Originals, Manners, Warres, Coines & Seales: with ye Successions, Lives, actes & Issues of the English Monarchs from Iulius Caesar, to our most gracious Soueraigne King James* (1611).

antiquarians of the ability and zeal of Stow and Speed. Like his predecessor, Speed was inspired by loyalty to his country, as he piously and humbly explains in the preface of the 1611 edition of the *Theatre*:

But how the Lord then composed my mind for the worke, or rather how his owne great power would be seene in my weakenes, is now in some measure made manifest by raising the frame thereof to this height; which here from the Presse sheweth his aspect vnto the world. But with what content to thy eye (gentle Reader) I stand in suspence, so many Maister-builders hauing in this subiect gone before me, and I the least, not worthy to hew (much lesse to lay) the least stone in so beautifull a Building; neither can I for my heedlesse presumption alledge any excuse, vnlesse it be this, that the zeale of my countries glory so transported my senses, as I knew not what I vndertooke, . . .

The accentuated interest in the history of Britain indicated by the popularity of the works discussed in the preceding pages is further manifested by the infinite variety of popular histories that appeared from the last quarter of the sixteenth century onward. While the annals of England naturally aroused the greatest interest of Englishmen, the histories of other nations, especially the history of the ancient world, soon came to occupy an important place in the reading of the public. After the late sixteenth century, the variety of histories was as wide as the known world.

A certain means of attracting popular attention to a work dealing with English history was to discuss the national ancestry, for speculation about the origins of the English was no mere academic question. That problem, for example, was the excuse for a curious work by Richard Harvey, the almanac maker, who published in 1593 *Philadelphus, or a Defence of Brutes and the Brutan History*, described by one scholar as "partly an attack upon Buchanan for his skepticism as regards the legend of Brutus, and partly a sort of summary of early English history (or what the writer supposed to be history) arranged in more or less tabular form."[35] A little nearer in time and interest than the mythical Brutus, was the slightly less mythical King Arthur, who was the subject of much speculation, both learned and popular. To prove to unscholarly

---

[35] McKerrow, *Works of Thomas Nashe*, V, 72.

readers the historical truth of Arthur's existence, Richard Robin-son, citizen of London, translated from Leland *The Assertion of K. Arthure* (1582). Years later an unknown editor of Malory published, as true history, that author's work, purged of oaths and popish superstition in such a way that it might be pleasing to Puritan readers.[36] Thomas Heywood, a patriotic popularizer of history,[37] paid tribute to both Brutus and King Arthur. After the experiment of making a translation of Sallust's *Catiline* (1608), Heywood turned his efforts to historical matters more appealing to his countrymen, by publishing *Troia Britanica: Or, Great Britaines Troy* (1609), which repeats the legends of the founding of London and mingles with them stories of modern heroes from Henry V to Francis Drake. In addition to biographical works like the *Gunaikeion* (1624), Heywood late in his life completed a sort of outline of history, called *The Life of Merlin* (1641), which an-nounced itself as "a small Manuell" for those who wished to be informed "in the knowledge of our English Annals"—for the *Life of Merlin* is more than the title indicates : it is a compendium of British history which uses the prophecies of Merlin as a basis for a journalistic presentation of the facts. Heywood was honestly trying to put within reach of the commonalty historical reading matter of a quality better than the hack work of some of the penny scribblers. But since he was living by his pen, he would not have elected to write this type of literature had not public interest been sufficient to create a constant market for popularized history.

For making a short history that would be available to the un-learned, Thomas Twyne received the praise of the authors of the poems prefatory to *The Breuiary of Britayne* (1573), Twyne's translation of Humphrey Lloyd's history in Latin. Nearly thirty years later, John Clapham in the preface to his own epitome of early British history, *The Historie of England. The first Booke. Declaring the estate of the Ile of Britannie vnder the Roman Empire* (1602),

---

[36] *The Most Ancient And Famous History Of The Renowned Prince Arthur King of Britaine . . . Newly refined, and published for the delight and profit of the Reader* (1634). Cf. Chap. XI, *infra*, p. 394.

[37] For further details of Heywood's historical activities, see Louis B. Wright, "Hey-wood and the Popularizing of History," *Modern Language Notes*, XLIII (1928), 287-93.

expressed his commendation of books brief and readable enough to gain a popular audience :

I Haue oft times wished, that (among so many large Volumes, and Abridgements of our English Chronicles, as are now extant) wee might haue one continued History collected out of approued Writers, and digested in such maner, as the Reader might neither be tired with the length of fabulous, and extrauagant discourses : nor left vnsatisfied in any materiall pointes, or circumstances worth his knowledge.

He then recommends the use of imaginary conversations "as things both allowable and commendable" to enliven the narrative. William Martyn, the recorder of Exeter, published in a reasonably brief folio *The Historie, And Lives, Of Twentie Kings Of England* (1615), a work praised because, as a relative of the author said in a prefatory poem, the reader could "gaine, With little reading, profit mixt with pleasure." Martyn himself was convinced that it was a disgrace that young gentlemen should travel abroad without knowing something of their own history, but, recognizing that memories are short and books too frequently long, he offers his work, which does not extend history "into a needelesse and vnprofitable length." In addition to the young gentleman-travelers whom Martyn wished to inform, others must have found the history useful, for it was twice reprinted. After the compendious labors of such historians as Grafton, Holinshed, Camden, and Speed, no historian could hope to achieve more complete and exhaustive works. The tendency, therefore, among most of the historians of the early seventeenth century was to write brief and, if possible, readable histories. If the popular historians did not all achieve the goal set for himself by courtly Samuel Daniel, who declared in the preface to his frequently printed work, *The Collection of the Historie of England* [1618], that he "had rather be Master of a small peece handsomely contriued, then of vaste roomes ill proportioned and vnfurnished," there was nevertheless an effort to boil down histories into more readable form than that of some of the earlier works.

As the historical horizons widened in the late sixteenth century, readers sought a knowledge of the past of lands other than their own. General histories, some of which were designed to lead up to a history of England, therefore became popular, and foreign histories, translated from most of the languages of Europe, found their way into the hands of English readers.[38] Translators like Arthur Golding, Edward Grimeston, and Philemon Holland were indefatigable in their labors to turn into English the stores of historical knowledge locked from all but scholars in the classical and modern European languages. Grimeston has over a dozen works to his credit; Holland was almost as diligent, and in his translations of Livy, Pliny, Suetonius, Xenophon, and others, he is always mindful of the understanding of the ordinary reader. Thomas North translated Plutarch for the "common sorte." The complaint was even made that England was better supplied with foreign histories than with her own, though this criticism seems unjustified in view of the vast amount of historical publication in England. John Clapham, in the preface in which he had urged briefer and better histories, makes this comment apropos of the learned Camden :

And were the Historical part as exactly set forth in English as his Description in Latin : I suppose that few Natiõs might then match vs for an History, whereas now, (in that one poynt) we come short of all others, that are not meerely barbarous. For like vnnaturall children, altogether carelesse of those dueties we owe to that place, where we first receiued our being, we spend our time eyther in catching flies with Domitian, or else in decking forraine stories with our best English furniture : suffering our Owne, in the meane time, to sit in ragges, to the blemish of our Countrey, . . .[39]

When William London published his *Catalogue Of The Most Vendible Books in England* (Newcastle, 1657) it took twenty-seven pages to list the works of "History with other Pieces of Human Learning Intermixed." Many of these items were translations of foreign histories.

The increasing general interest in classical history was the reason given for the publication of a work by an Oxford scholar, William Fulbecke, who sought to supply a condensed Roman

---

[38] *See* Chap. X, *infra*.
[39] *The Historie of England* (1602), sig. B 3.

history in *An Historicall Collection Of The Continuall Factions, Tumults, and Massacres of the Romans and Italians during the space of one hundred and twentie yeares next before the peaceable Empire of Augustus Caesar* (1601). The fashion of reading history receives Fulbecke's hearty approval, for he discerns much good to the public therefrom :

. . . considering likewise that histories are now in speciall request and accompt, whereat I greatly reioyce, acknowledging them to be the teachers of vertuous life, good conuersation, discreete behauiour, politike gouernement, conuenient enterprises, aduised proceedings, warie defences, grounded experience, and refined wisdome.[40]

Learned men and hack writers alike were kept busy supplying history to the multitude, with the result that pedantically academic works jostled chronicles in doggerel on the booksellers' shelves. An example of learned dullness attempting to impress the popular mind is furnished by Lodowick Lloyd, who published, among other historical gallimaufries, a sort of epitome of ancient histories, which he entitled *The Consent Of Time, Disciphering the errors of the Grecians in their Olympiads, the vncertaine computation of the Romanes in their Penteterydes and building of Rome. . . . Wherein is also set downe the beginning, continuance, successsion, and ouerthrowes of kings, kingdomes, States, and gouernments* (1590). Considerable rivalry developed among even the learned suppliers of historical lore. For example, Edmund Bolton takes occasion to berate the makers of epitomes, which he describes as "but Anatomies" ; yet that very phrase is taken from the dedication of Bolton's translation of an epitome, *The Roman Histories of Lucius Iulius Florus* (1618), which the translator recommends as a "perfect body" of history.

Among the hacks, Thomas Churchyard and Anthony Munday were typical of the popular writers who turned historian. After an unconscionably long life, in which he had written many nondescript historical pieces, Churchyard in his old age called to his aid Richard Robinson and translated from Emanuel van Meteren

---

[40] Preface. To make the acquisition of a knowledge of classical history easy for schoolboys, Thomas Godwin prepared a textbook which he published as *Romanae Historae Anthologia. An English Exposition Of The Romane Antiquities, Wherein many Romane and English offices are paralleld and divers obscure phrases explained. By Thomas Godwyn Master of Arts: For the vse of Abingdon Schoole* (Oxford, 1614). Nine editions by 1638 are recorded.

A True Discourse Historicall, Of The Succeeding Governours In The Netherlands, And The Ciuill warres there begun in the yeere 1565. with the memorable seruices of our Honourable English Generals, Captaines and Souldiers, especially vnder Sir Iohn Norice Knight, there performed from the yeere 1577. vntill the yeere 1589. and afterwards in Portugale, France, Britaine and Ireland, vntill the yeere 1598 (1602). The emphasis on the gallantry of the English in the Dutch wars for independence was sufficient to arouse the patriotism of English citizens, whose interest in the Low Countries was already keen because of the trade relations between the two nations. To assure the reader of the value of the work, the translators point out on the title-page that it is "meete for euery good subiect to reade, for defence of Prince and Countrey."

Although Anthony Munday himself was a draper, he did not lose an opportunity to flatter outrageously the Guild of Merchant Taylors and the Goldsmiths' Company, and to seek the favor of citizens generally in the dedications to his outline of universal history, *A Briefe Chronicle, of the Successe of Times, from the Creation of the World, to this instant* (1611). In the first dedication to the lord mayor and city officials, Munday traces the origin and honor of aldermen from the time of the Saxon kings, when one of royal blood was alderman of all England—from which it "appeareth, that the Title of Alderman, in those ancient, reuerend, and respectiue times, was an addition of honor and high repute" (a condition that has, of course, continued). The Merchant Taylors are equally glorious in their origins and later history, having had seven kings and innumerable noblemen as brethren of their body; and the Goldsmiths, not to be outshone, can even find records of their illustrious distinction in the Holy Scriptures, not to mention the luster shed by the eminence of later worthy members of their craft in London. For all of these tributes, prefacing his chronicle-history of the world, which never misses an opportunity to record the splendor of citizens, Munday was rewarded by gifts from both guilds, and shortly was busy about a pageant for the Goldsmiths.[41] If Munday could find in universal history a subject with which to exalt citizens, we may

---

[41] Celeste Turner, *Anthony Mundy, An Elizabethan Man of Letters,* University of California Publications in English, II (1928), 157-58.

be certain that he made the most of his opportunity when he came to prepare his continuation of Stow.

Yet, strangely enough, the draper's work was not the universal history that had the greatest vogue with citizen-readers of the seventeenth century; instead, *The History Of The World* (1614) by the courtly Sir Walter Raleigh attracted readers in every walk of life and became the favorite historical work of the Puritans. Between 1614 and 1687, ten editions were published, and the work was once reprinted in the eighteenth and twice in the nineteenth century.[42] The emphasis upon the high moral purpose of history, stressed by Raleigh in his preface, was sufficient to account for the favor that Puritan readers bestowed upon the work, for they agreed with the author that "wee may gather out of History a policy no lesse wise than eternall; by the comparison and application of other mens forepassed miseries, with our owne like errours and ill deseruings." Moreover, as Sir Charles Firth points out in discussing the reasons for Puritan interest in the history, Raleigh's "theological conception of History agreed with theirs: it was a belief in which the events of the Civil War confirmed them; they saw in their initial defeats and their final triumph the working of the same power."[43] If the poorer citizens could not afford the expensive folio volume in which the history was published, they at length were able to buy a little epitome of the prized book, for Alexander Ross, with a Scot's consideration of cost, abridged the work and published *The Marrow Of Historie* (1650). In the preface he recommends epitomes in general and his own in particular:

This Epitome hath this three fold advantage; it is more portable, more legible, and more vendible, then the great Book: this may bee a pocket companion, and it is soon read over; for everie one will not take pains to read great volumes, and manie cannot for want of leasure. There is also divers that have three or four shillings to bestow on this, which have not twentie or thirtie to impend upon the great Book.

The universal histories usually devoted sufficient space to biblical history to satisfy the average layman's interest in the background of his religion, but specialized histories of the Jews gained a

---

[42] Sir Charles H. Firth, "Sir Walter Raleigh's History of the World," *Proceedings of the British Academy*, VIII (1919), 13.   [43] *Ibid.*, p. 15.

wide circulation. For example, the medieval history of the chosen
people, *Sefer Yosippon* by Joseph Ben Gorion, translated into English by Peter Morwyng in 1558 as *A Compendious and most mar-
ueilous History of the latter tymes of the Jewes commune weale*, had at
least ten editions by 1615. This book was the basis of Nashe's
Christs Teares Over Ierusalem (1593), in which he pointed a moral
for London.[44] Josephus's Jewish history was also extremely popular. Translated in 1602 by Thomas Lodge, five editions and three
reissues appeared before 1640. A mere tabulation such as John
Speed's *The Genealogies Recorded In Sacred Scriptures, According to
euery Family and Tribe* (1611) went through innumerable editions,
thirty-five before 1640 being listed in the British Museum Catalogue.[45] Speed made his book more attractive by adding "A
Description of Canaan and the bordering Countries" with a map
of the Holy Land.

In the zeal for history, not even learned poets scorned to belabor
their Muses to turn historical facts into verses plain enough to
enlighten the ignorant and teach them their patriotic duty, if we
may judge from the example of John Sharrock, who made a verse
translation from Christopher Ocland, avowedly for the unlearned,
with the flag-waving title of *The Valiant Actes And victorious Battailes
Of The English nation* (1585).[46] Prefatory verses point out that the
translation is not for scholars but for the unlettered :

> And such as could not *Romaine* letters scanne,
> Their Grandsiers acts ; and courage haut might see,
> Whereby high laude, and endlesse fame they wanne,
> And they incenst of corage like to bee,
> For Prince and Countrie, dire daungers none to flee.

[44] McKerrow, *Works of Thomas Nashe*, IV, 212-13. A desire to furnish a cheap
and portable book was the intention of both translator and printer ; the epistle to
the reader in the edition of 1561 announces : ". . . it was thought most conuenient not to burthen the desirous hereof with the prouyding of so chargeable a volume,
as is ye greate Hystory of Flauius Iosephus, . . . but that we shuld plenteously content mens desires, and satisfie our prefixed end abundauntly, with a farre more briefe,
much lesse costlye, and as sufficient a commentarye for our purpose, nothyng inferiour
to the other in veritie : . . ."

[45] In 1611 Speed was granted a patent for ten years to print and insert these genealogies into the King James Bible. *See* the *Short Title Catalogue*, note *sub* Speed.

[46] The full title gives a more complete description of the work : *The Valiant Actes And
victorious Battailes Of The English nation: from the yeere of our Lord, one thousand, three hun-*

Let learned Clearkes the Authours poeme vewe,
This worke is wrought for the vnlearned crue.

Poetical histories of many kinds rivaled plain prose works in their effort to instruct the multitude.

The cheapest form of poetical history was of course the broadside ballad which epitomized the reigns of the kings into a single sheet, a good example of the type being *The Cronycle of all the Kynges: that haue Reygned in Englande: Sythe the Conquest of Wyllyam Conqueroure* [1590?],[47] a single sheet preserved among the Britwell ballads. This broadside, decorated with a woodcut of William the Conqueror and symbols of the Seven Virtues, reduces history to a few crude stanzas of verse, but it doubtless was a help to patriotic apprentices struggling to remember the names of the kings. Broadsides that made history the theme of their rhymes had long been popular and continued to provide entertainment and information for generations to come. R. M.'s *A New Ballade* [*c.* 1559],[48] which furnished citizens with information about the predecessors of the new queen down to the reign of her sister Mary, was a type that long flourished. Patriotism, of course, inspired many of these poets of the people, as a sort of versified general history by Thomas Churchyard indicates. In order to prove the happy state of England in comparison with other nations Churchyard published *The Miserie Of Flaunders, Calamitie of Fraunce, Misfortune of Portugall, Vnquietnes of Ireland, Troubles of Scotlande: And the blessed State of Englande* (1579). Smugly the author proves from history that England is the best and greatest of the nations of the earth.[49]

---

dred twentie and seuen: being the first yeare of the raigne of the most mightie Prince Edward the third, to the yeere 1558. Also, *Of The Peaceable And quiet state of England, vnder the blessed gouernement of the most excellent and vertuous Princesse Elizabeth: A compendious declaration written by C. O. And newly translated out of Latine verse into English meeter. By I. S.* (1585).

[47] The presumably unique copy is now in the Huntington Library.

[48] Preserved by the Society of Antiquaries and listed by Robert Lemon, *A Catalogue of a Collection of Printed Broadsides in the Possession of the Society of Antiquaries of London* (London, 1866), p. 17.

Andrew Clark (ed.), *The Shirburn Ballads, 1585-1616* (Oxford, 1907), Introduction, pp. 7-8, calls attention to the historical settings of some of the ballads. *See* Nos. xlvi, li, and lxxvi.

[49] For a bibliography of Churchyard's historical and pseudo-historical contributions, see George Chalmers (ed.), *Churchyard's Chips Concerning Scotland* (London, 1818).

With patriotism running high and the appetite for historical reading unsated, it was natural that a writer who so completely represented the taste of the tradesman-public as Thomas Deloney should have turned out ballad history. Deloney's first contribution was *The Garland of Good Will* (licensed, 1593), an assortment of verse tales from the chronicles, which proved so successful that the author followed them later with *Strange Histories, Or Kings, Princes, Dukes, Earles, Lords, Ladies, Knights, and Gentlemen. With the great trouble and miseries of the Dutches of Suffolke. Verie pleasant either to bee read or sunge, and a most excellent warning for all estates* (1602), a collection of ballad versions of chronicle material, several times reprinted. Properly enough, from the citizen's point of view, Deloney ends with the history of Sir William Walworth, the valiant fishmonger who slew Wat Tyler. As a warning to rebels, he pointedly describes the discomfiture of Jack Straw and his followers. Although Will Kemp could make in his *Nine Days' Wonder* a sarcastic reference to "the great ballet-maker T. D. alias Tho. Deloney, Chronicler of the memorable liues of the 6 yeomen of the west, Jack of Newbury, and such like honest men, omitted by Stow, Holinshed, Grafton, Hal, froysart, and the rest of those well-deseruing writers,"[50] Deloney was careful enough to stick to well known chronicle figures for the subject of his history ballads.

Another notable contributor to ballad history was Richard Johnson, the citizen-romancer, who imitated Deloney by publishing in 1612 *A Crowne Garland of Golden Roses: Gathered out of Englands Royal Garden*,[51] several times reprinted with additions. Most of the selections are ballad narratives based on ancient or recent British history. Johnson had already proved himself intent upon the exaltation of the citizen-hero in a semi-historical poem, *The nine Worthies of London Explayning the honourable exercise of Armes, the vertues of the valiant, and the memorable attempts of magnanimous minds. Pleasant For Gentlemen, not vnseemely for Magistrates, and most profitable for Prentices* (1592), which the author intended to be an inspiration to apprentices; it was history, to be sure, but, more than that, it was a conduct book which would lead future trades-

---

[50] Quoted by Alexis Lange (ed.), *The Gentlecraft*, in *Palaestra*, XVIII (1903), xv.
[51] Title quoted from the edition of 1631.

men to deeds of patriotism and virtue. In a dedication to Sir William Webbe, lord mayor, he calls himself only a "poore apprentice"; and in a preface "To the Gentlemen Readers, as well Prentices as others," he emphasizes the downright simplicity of his style:[52] "his simple truth shewes he is without deceyt, and his plaine speech proues, he flatters not. He can not boast of Art, nor claime the priuiledge of scholasticall cunning." In plan, the author has Fame conduct Clio to the Elysian Fields, where they find the Worthies sleeping. As Fame awakens each in turn, Clio writes down what the hero relates—in none too perfect verse. Fame in conclusion urges Clio to publish afar the report of the noble citizens, who may be an example to others,

because I would haue malicious mindes that enuye at the deserts of noble Citizens, by proofe of these mens worthienesse to repent their contempt, and amend their captious dispositions, seeing that from the beginning of the world, and in all places of the world, Citizens haue flourished and beene famous. [Sigs. F 4-F 4ᵛ.]

The nine Worthies selected by Fame are Sir William Walworth, fishmonger; Sir Henry Pitchard, vintner; Sir William Sevenoaks, grocer; Sir Thomas White, merchant tailor; Sir John Bonham,

---

[52] A plea for simplicity and directness of expression in writing history had been made earlier by Ulpian Fulwell in the preface to *The Flower Of Fame. Containing the bright Renowne, & moste fortunate raigne of King Henry the viii* (1575), a popular history in verse and prose. Fulwell's criticism of prose style makes the passage worth quoting: ". . . I confesse I haue not the gifte of flowing eloquence, neyther can I enterlace my phrase with Italian termes, nor powder my style with frenche Englishe or Inkhorne Rhethoricke, neyther cowche my matter vnder a cloake of curious inuentions, to feede the daintie eares of delicate yonkers. And as I cannot: So if I could, I woulde not. For I see that manye men are so affected with these premisses, that manye good matters are obscured, the Aucthours encombred, the woorkes but meanely commended, and the Reader deceaued. For while he coueteth to come to the purpose, he is lead amasked in the wylde Desert of circumstance and digression, seeking farre and finding little, feeding his humor on pleasant woordes of slender wayght, guyded (or rather giddyed) with plaucible eloquence. I do not herein condempne, neither discomende the noble Science of Rhethorike, nor the eloquent Rhethoritian, but rather wishe that excellent skill to be employed onlye on such matters as may both commende the speaker, and the thing spoken, or the writer and the thing written: hauing alwayes the cheefe respect to tyme & place. For as it would sounde very absurde to the eares of the skilfull Musitian to heare a gallyard, or any other daunce playde on the solemne Organs: So no lesse contrarie is it to daunce after an Hymn or other cunning voluntarie."—Sigs. B 2ᵛ-B 3.

mercer; Sir Christopher Croker, vintner; Sir John Hawkwood, merchant tailor; Sir Hugh Caverly, silk weaver; and Sir Henry Malevert, grocer. Praising each for his valor, generosity, and loyalty, Johnson is careful to show that any London apprentice by observing the same virtues might rise to equally high success.

Other histories in verse, written to the capacity of the simplest reader, appeared in the early seventeenth century. Such a work was *The Poores Lamentation for the Death of our late dread Soueraigne, the high and mightie Princesse Elizabeth* (1603), an anonymous doggerel history of the late queen. Not long afterward John Taylor, the catchpenny sculler, produced a rhyming history, with pictures of the sovereigns, under the modest title of *A Briefe Remembrance Of All The English Monarchs, From the Normans Conquest vntill this present* (1618), which Taylor continued and slightly amplified in later editions. Almost as brief and bare as broadside chronicles, these small octavo volumes, which sold for a penny, helped to give a modicum of instruction to unlearned readers. Taylor's picture-history may have been suggested by Thomas Tymme's cheap little illustrated history, which he called *A Booke, Containing The True Portraiture Of The Countenances and attires of the kings of England, from William Conqueror, vnto our Soueraigne Lady Queene Elizabeth now raigning: Together With A Briefe report of some of the principall acts of the same Kings, especially such as haue bene least mentioned in our late writers. Diligently collected by T. T.* (1597). An alleged portrait of each ruler is given, with a small amount of unimportant commentary.

But ballads were not the only verse history that the public read, and, as was true of the prose histories, many learned poems, long since neglected, gained an audience among all classes of readers. The public had been prepared for poetical history by the popularity of *A Myrroure For Magistrates* (1559), which was constantly read for three-quarters of a century. Originally, of course, written for the courtly circle, it soon had readers among all literate classes because the rapidly increasing interest of the public in its own history, and in the personalities who made it, invested the *Mirror* with a peculiar fascination, since it provided a vast amount of picturesque detail about the lives of noble Englishmen, glossed with appropriate moral lessons. Furthermore, the *Mirror* in turn exerted an enormous influence upon the development of the taste for historical poetry and became the source for a great deal of the dramatic and non-dramatic literature that followed it.[53] Many dramatists, hard pressed for new plays based on English history, found ample material in the old *Mirror*, which remained for years a productive mine of theatrical plots. In fact, it is probable that the education in legendary history furnished by the *Mirror* made possible the success of many plays, the subject matter of which would have been unfamiliar if it had not been for the earlier verse histories.

The growth by accretion of the *Mirror for Magistrates* over a period of fifty years, until the relatively small number of stories in the 1559 edition had been augmented to nearly a hundred in the edition of 1610, is sufficient proof of the enduring popularity of the work. Although aristocratic critics in the latter days sometimes scoffed at the old tales, the reading populace continued to enjoy the tragic stories in the *Mirror*, assured of reward in so doing. As late as 1620 a reissue of the *Mirror* was demanded. In the more recent versions, as the effort to cater to popular taste becomes more apparent, there is greater emphasis on entertaining details in some of the revisions; for instance, the amplifications in "The Tragedy of Bladud" in the edition of 1587 provide a striking illustration of this tendency. In the 1610 edition the attempt to profit from a popular interest in the late queen by including Richard Niccols's poem, "Englands Eliza," is obvious. Declaring that he had first intended to publish his poem as a separate work, Niccols asserts that he has been "since perswaded by the Printer to publish it with this worke : it being, though no fall, yet a worthie Mirrour answerable to that of the Empresse Helena in the first part of this volume." The canny printer, bent upon pleasing the public, also inserted pictures of the subjects of Niccols's additional tragedies, which ranged from King Arthur to Richard III, with a tearful account of the two little princes murdered by Richard's command. But however much the later tragedies might have been altered to attract public interest, the tone of didacticism was never lost, a fact which doubtless further

---

[53] *See* J. H. Roberts, "Samuel Daniels' Relation to the Histories and Historical Poetry of the Sixteenth Century," *Abstracts of Theses* (Chicago, 1923-24), pp. 402-3.

explains the long appeal that the *Mirror* had for middle-class, as well as for aristocratic, readers.

Later poets of the learned or courtly group, who looked to the Muse of History to inspire their verses, frequently found an audience among citizens and courtiers alike. If the concealed history of Spenser's patriotic epic proved too recondite for the man in the street, it is nevertheless true that the same man often read some of Spenser's learned contemporaries in poetry. For example, William Warner's *Albions England* (1586) met with such favor that it had at least six distinct editions before 1612. Warner provided in verse an outline of British history sufficiently in-inclusive to please all tastes.[54] After amplifying the work in the versions that followed the first, Warner finally in 1602 appended to his poem a prose epitome, because he had observed that even skillful readers sometimes had trouble staying in the channel of chronicle-history, and the "lesse literate" were much handicapped. "To helpe therefore these latters," he declares, "I haue, as yee shall now heare, opened to them so short and facile a Passage, that whosoeuer, in one or two howers, may cut thorough, vnin-terrupted, the whole Legend of the maine."[55] Then in forty-seven pages he boils down the entire history of England from Brute to Queen Elizabeth.

Another example of a learned poet who produced what be-came almost a best-seller was Michael Drayton, whose *Englands Heroicall Epistles* was printed in 1597 and frequently thereafter.[56] The author had hit upon a rich vein, often worked by later histo-rians, in which the pure metal of history was mingled with a pleas-ing alloy of romantic love story. Beginning with the life of Fair Rosamond and ending with Lady Jane Grey, Drayton was certain

---

[54] The complete title is sufficiently descriptive: *Albions England. Or Historicall Map of the same Island: prosecuted from the liues, Actes, and Labors of Saturne, Iupiter, Hercules, and Aeneas: Originalles of the Brutons, and English-men, and Occasion of the Brutons their first aryuall in Albion. Continuing the same Historie vnto the Tribute to the Romaines, Entrie of the Saxones, Inuasion by the Danes, and Conquest by the Normanes. With Historicall Intermixtures, Inuention, and Varietie: proffitably, briefly, and pleasantly, performed in Verse and Prose by William Warner* (1586).

[55] Edition of 1602, preface to the epitome, p. 350.

[56] Six distinct editions are extant for the period from 1598 to 1630. The first four editions followed in yearly succession.

of a success that made edition after edition of the poem necessary. The same writer's *Poly-Olbion* [1612], which sought to give, in verse, descriptions similar to those found in Camden's *Britannia*, was not quite so popular, though it illustrates what a poet in the seventeenth century thought was a proper subject for his muse.

A form of history that delighted the Elizabethans—as the vogue of the *Mirror for Magistrates* and its successors makes clear—was the relation of biographical details from the lives of historical figures, both good and bad, with proper moralizations. Innumerable were the works describing in whole or in part the lives of persons who had been famous for their virtues or notorious for their iniquities. As in many of the formal histories, these works set out consciously to inculcate good morality, with an insistence upon order, peace, sobriety, and loyalty to the commonwealth as cardinal principles of their doctrine. Most famous of the prose collections of biography was John Foxe's *Actes and Monuments* (1563), which for generations was a sort of second Bible in Puritan households; the great three-volume folio edition of 1632 announced that it had been seven times previously printed, and other editions followed. A pious and patriotic desire to educate the public in Protestant church history prompted Foxe to make the compilation, despite the fact that he believed the world to be "pestred . . . with a superfluous plenty" of books, "especially touchinge writing of historyes." Nevertheless, he was driven forward by a faith in the "cōmon vtilitie, which euery man plentifully may receiue by this our history," for he was certain that a knowledge of the sufferers for religion would be of greater value to the commonwealth than the history of "600. Alexāders, Hectors, Scipioes, and warring Iulies."[57]

Even though Foxe planned his work to reach the multitude, it proved too expensive and bulky for every citizen to buy and read; but that fault was soon remedied by epitomes which summarized the most noteworthy of the biographies. The first of the epitomes was the work of the physician Dr. Timothy Bright, who took time from his practice to edit *An Abridgement Of The Booke Of Acts And Monumentes Of The Church: . . . for such as either thorough want*

---

[57] Edition of 1563; prefatory note, "A declaration concerning the vtilitie and profite of this history."

of leysure, or abilitie, haue not the vse of so necessary an history (1589).
In a dedication to Walsingham, Bright points out that "a booke
that concerneth so manie, who by reason of the charge of price,
and largeness of volume, cannot either for want or busines, enioy
the full ·benefite of the same" deserves printing in a form that
would make it available to all. His example in epitomizing the
martyrology was later followed by the Reverend Thomas Mason,
who gave his summary the fanciful title of *Christs Victorie Over
Sathans Tyrannie* (1615), which the author "abstracted out of the
Book of Martyrs, and diuers other Bookes." Dedicating it to
church and state in an epistle to the Archbishop of Canterbury
and Lord Chief Justice Edward Coke, Mason repeats Bright's
complaint about the size and price of the unabridged work which,
for the good of the realm, he has "pared" and "made it tractable
for all sorts of people; they may buy it with little charge, and
peruse it with small paines; and I dare promise them that they
shall reape as much profit by reading this abridgement, as by
reading of the Book at large." An even briefer and more portable
volume was compiled by Clement Cotton as *The Mirrour Of
Martyrs* (1613), which offered in a small space the notable sayings
of the martyrs with a concise description of their sufferings and
fortitude. Foxe's *Book of Martyrs*, as the work was popularly called,
exercised a remarkable influence on the English populace, and
to it, as much as to any single cause, must be credited the middle-
class devotion to Protestantism.

Other works contemporary with the *Book of Martyrs* utilized
biographical material as an instrument in teaching good citizen-
ship and loyalty to the state. George Whetstone, for example,
used biographical history to further such a cause in *A Mirour For
Magestrates Of Cyties* (1584), which had as an appendix "A Touchstone for the Time: Containyng many perillous Mischiefes, bred
in the Bowels of the Citie of London." Citing from Roman history
examples of iniquitous citizens, Whetstone points a moral by
showing how their wickedness was put down. The dedication to
the lord mayor, recorder, and aldermen of London expresses
Whetstone's pride in his own city, which he hopes to benefit by
his biographical warnings. A more imposing work, dedicated to
the Queen herself but intended to instruct the general public, was

the same author's *The English Myrror. A Regard Wherein al estates may behold the Conquests of Enuy: Containing ruine of common weales, murther of Princes, cause of heresies, and in all ages, spoile of deuine and humane blessings, vnto which is adioyned, Enuy conquered by vertues. . . . A worke safely, and necessarie to be read of euerie good subiect* (1586). History, ancient and modern, is ransacked for examples of the dangers of envy, a term made to include most political crimes, as Whetstone piles up illustrations of the inevitable end of treason and the success that follows rulers who crush out rebellions and establish peace. In one of the couplet mottoes with which the book concludes, Whetstone suggests to the citizens the profitableness of honesty:

> In euery trade an honest gaine well gotten
>   good men hight
> And God will surely blesse the hand, that wayes
>   and measures right.[58]   [P. 248.]

The lives of traitors came to be a popular type of deterrent history. Thomas Lodge used the name of a traitor as a catchpenny title to a collection of stories of pirates and other malefactors which he published as *The Life and Death of William Longbeard, the most famous and witty English Traitor, borne in the Citty of London. Accompanied with manye other most pleasant and prettie histories* (1593).

---

[58] Closely allied to the historical treatise was Whetstone's pamphlet dealing with contemporary events, *The Censure of a loyall Subiect: Vpon Certaine noted Speach & behauiours of those fourteen notable Traitors, at the place of their executions, the xx. and xxi. of September, last past. As also, of the Scottish Queen, now (thankes be to God) cut off by iustice, as the principal Roote of al their treasons. On Wednesday the 8. of Februarie 1586. Wherein is handled matter of necessarie instruction and comfort for al duetiful Subiectes: especially the multitude of ignoraunt people.*

> *Feare God: be true to thy*
> *Prince: and obey the Lawes* (1587).

There is a great deal of "warning literature," somewhat similar to this, which is outside the scope of the present study.

Whetstone cites a number of warning examples from history in *A Remembraunce of the woorthie and well imployed life, of the right honorable Sir Nicholas Bacon* [1579?].

Similar in spirit to Whetstone's works were some of the kindred historical efforts of Thomas Churchyard, who developed a taste for "tragedy" when contributing to the *Mirror for Magistrates.* His *A generall rehearsall of warres* [1579] relates "fiue hundred seuerall seruices of land and sea: as sieges, battailles, skirmishes, and encounters." A dedication states the desire to encourage virtue. The verse "histories" at the end include such things as "A Pirates Tragedie" showing the bad end of pirates.

Thomas Gainsford, a writer of popular treatises, finding in Perkin Warbeck an example to deter traitors, published *The True and Wonderfull History of Perkin Warbeck, Proclaiming himselfe Richard the fourth* (1618), which draws the usual moral and warns the commonalty against "such facinorous attempts, breaking out to finde fault with men in authority, and audacious inuections against the gouernment."[59] Gainsford followed *Perkin Warbeck* with *The True Exemplary, And Remarkable History of the Earle of Tirone: . . . Not from the report of others or collection of Authors, but by him who was an eye witnesse of his fearefull wretchednes, and finall extirpation* (1619). The author professes in the dedication a desire to write a book which will be an example to traitors. In an introduction he reviews civil wars of the past, both English and foreign, and shows how foolish it is to rebel against constituted authority, all of which doubtless met the hearty approval of the censor.[60] A little later we find Henry Peacham attempting to instruct the multitude with *The Duty Of All True Subiects To Their King: As also to their Natiue Country, in time of extremity and danger. With some memorable examples of the miserable ends of perfidious Traitors* (1638). He urges peace among all estates and cites the bad ends of traitors, drawn chiefly from Roman history. On the verge of the troublous times of the Puritan rebellion an anonymous citizen, loyal to the king, published *The iust reward of Rebels, Or The Life and Death of Iack Straw, and Wat Tyler* (1642), in which once more the valorous deed of Sir William Walworth is held up as the proper example of citizen conduct.

The value of historical and biographical material, presented in such a way that it would serve as a warning to those who might contemplate crimes against the state, needed no argument before Elizabethan readers, who accepted this type of instruction as a patriotic and not uninteresting duty. Gabriel Harvey, in a letter to Arthur Capel, gives the weight of his opinion to the encouragement of such works against sedition:

---

[59] Sig. M 2.

[60] Gainsford's further contributions to historical literature are illustrated by *The Vision And Discourse Of Henry the seuenth* (1610), a warning recommending unity in the state, and the *Historie of Trebizond* (1616).

M. Capel, I dout not I, but you have ere this sufficiently perusid or
rather thurroughly red over thos tragical pamflets of the Quen of
Scots, as you did not long ago that pretti elegant treatis of M. Cheke
against sedition : and verry lately good part of the Mirrur for Magistrates, thre books iwis in mi judgment wurth the reading over and over,
both for the stile and the matter.[61]

The vast influence of historical reading upon the rank and file
of Tudor and Stuart society cannot be measured, but clearly it
was a potent factor in the intellectual progress of the citizenry.
In history they sought and found moral and political lessons ;
they learned to value the past glory of the nation and to prize its
future ; they learned of the valor of citizens and the accomplishments that plain men had wrought ; they learned a loyalty to the
state, which made Englishmen love their country with a patriotism equaled only in Holland ; and they learned lessons of state-
craft, which helped make it possible for commoners to shoulder
greater responsibilities of government. Perhaps the Elizabethan
evaluation of history as the greatest of secular studies is no exaggeration of its importance. History did much for the Elizabethan
citizen and deserves the panegyric of one who knew as well as
any the feelings of the plain man of his age :

. . . O Histories! you soueraigne balmes to the bodyes of the dead,
that preserue them more fresh then if they were aliue, keep ye fames
of Princes from perishing, when marble monuments cannot saue their
bones from being rotten, you faithfull entelligensers betweene Kingdomes and Kingdomes, your truest councellors to Kings, euen in their
greatest dangers! Hast thou an ambition to be equall to Princes! read
such bookes as are the Chronicles of Ages, gone before thee : there
maiest thou finde lines drawne (if vertue be thy guide) to make thee
paralell with the greatest Monarch : wouldest thou be aboue him,
there is ye scale of him ascending[.] Huntst thou after glory? marke
in those pathes how others haue run, and follow thou in the same
course. Art thou sicke in minde? (and so to be diseased, is to be sicke
euen to ye death) there shalt thou finde physicke to cure thee. Art

---

[61] E. J. L. Scott (ed.), *Letter Book of Gabriel Harvey, A.D. 1573-1580*, Camden Society,
N. S., XXXIII (1884), 167.

thou sad? where is sweeter musicke even in reading? Art thou poore? open those closets, and invaluable treasures are powred into thy hands.[62]

---

[62] Thomas Dekker, *Worke For Armorours* (1609), sigs. B 2ᵛ-B 3. The history of London and Westminster furnished Dekker with part of the material for his amorphous pamphlet, *The Dead Terme. Or, Westminsters Complaint for long Vacations and short Termes. Written in manner of a Dialogue betweene the two Cityes London and Westminster* (1608). The two debate their merits by relating their respective histories. This device is in reality a pretext for a popularized history of London and its environs. Dekker also improved the occasion by condemning London's current vices.

X

THE PATHWAY TO FOREIGN LEARNING
AND LANGUAGES[1]

THE intellectual background of the Elizabethan was as varied as the universe which the Renaissance had opened before him, because the materials that went into the creation of his mental outlook were as diverse as the literatures of the world, ancient and modern. To serve him, translators, from the time of the earliest printers in England until the end of our period, were diligent in their labors to place before him the stores of learning that, without translation, would have remained hidden from the majority of readers. Moreover, the increased communication with foreign countries during the later sixteenth century and after, so stimulated the desire for a knowledge of the languages encountered abroad that the study of modern tongues became widespread, both as a discipline in the education of gentlemen's sons and as a part of the useful training of merchants' apprentices. Thus, through the medium of innumerable translations and by actual contact with foreign countries, those Renaissance ideas which were at first so slow in reaching England, at last became widely disseminated. But it was mainly through translations, of course, that a knowledge of the culture and learning of other nations reached the great body of intelligent citizens. Even though the study of modern languages increased remarkably from the late sixteenth century on, and though Latin remained the backbone of grammar-school education, the majority paid only lip service to Latin and knew no modern language other than their own.

---

[1] Material in this chapter first appeared in two essays: "Translations for the Elizabethan Middle Class," *The Library*, 4th Ser., XIII (1932-33), 312-31; and "Language Helps for the Elizabethan Tradesman," *Journal of English and Germanic Philology*, XXX (1931), 335-47.

Realizing this, patriotic scholars exerted themselves to translate a multitudinous literature that was believed profitable to the commonwealth.

An insistence upon the desirability of the vernacular was one result of the spirit of nationalism, which gathered intensity throughout the Tudor period; but in addition to the patriotic impetus to translation, there was a utilitarian motive of gain—a motive which sent printers searching for an infinite variety of works, with the result that all European literature, ancient and modern, was pillaged for books worth decking in an English dress. Industrious translators drew upon Dutch, Italian, French, Spanish, and Latin works for treatises on navigation, warfare, trade, geography, pharmacy, medicine, architecture, painting, horse breeding, and many other useful subjects. Nor was humanistic literature slighted by translators who supplied England with an ample store of histories, books promoting good morality, and learned works in general. The tradition of translating for the benefit of the commonwealth had started with the first English printers, for so destitute was England of original works worth publishing that for many years after the beginning of printing, Caxton and his immediate successors were forced to feed their presses with translations of foreign books; it is significant that many of these versions were frankly utilitarian and were published in cheap little editions within the reach of any citizen able to read them. As one scholar has expressed it, "Elizabethan translation began in patriotism no less than in commercialism and literary taste, and its aim was to present Englishmen with foreign literature in the most attractive or useful guise."[2] Having learned the value of translation in the early days of printing, scholars and publishers for the next century and a half combined their efforts to supply England with foreign learning.

Translation came to be regarded by Elizabethan men of letters as a legitimate literary art in itself, but it was the translators'

---

[2] O. L. Hatcher, "Aims and Methods of Elizabethan Translators," *Englische Studien*, XLIV (1912), 174-92. *See also* C. H. Conley, *The First English Translators of the Classics* (New Haven, 1927), pp. 35, 60, 70 ff., 103 ff.; Flora Ross Amos, *Early Theories of Translation* (New York, 1920), pp. 88-89, 91; F. O. Matthiessen, *Translation, An Elizabethan Art* (Cambridge, Mass., 1931), pp. 177, 179, 190.

sense of obligation to the good of the commonweal that was responsible for a great deal of their efforts. The first English renderings of the Bible, for example, were inspired by a desire to place the Scriptures in the hands of unlatined readers who could not read the Vulgate; and zealous merchants, eager to benefit their countrymen, enabled William Tyndale to make his version and send it into England. Translators were convinced that they owed a service particularly to the alert and vigorous middle ranks of citizens who could profit by their labors—a fact which John Dolman clearly states in his translation from Cicero, *Those fyue Questions, which Marke Tullye Cicero, disputed in his Manor of Tusculanum* (1561):

Besydes the raskall multitude, and the learned sages, there is a meane sort of men : which although they be not learned, yet, by the quicknes of their wits, can conceiue al such poyntes of arte, as nature could give. To those, I saye, there is nothing in this book to darke.[3]

The sense of obligation to this mean or average sort of reader prompted many a zealous translator to use his learning for the profit of a reading public that was demanding in English what it did not have the knowledge, the time, or the inclination to read in the original.

But despite the obvious benefits to the state of adequate translations, there were some academic objectors who did not approve of the practice. As late as 1627 Dr. George Hakewill in *A Apologie Of The Power And Providence Of God* criticized Hakluyt for compiling his works in English : "It were to be wished as well for the honour of the English name, as well as the benefit that might thereby redound to other nations, that Hakluyt's *Collections and Relations* had been written in Latin."[4] Sir Thomas Hoby in the famous dedication of Castiglione's *The Courtyer* (1561) to Lord Henry Hastings declares that ". . . our learned menne for the moste part holde opinion, to have the sciences in the mother

---

[3] Conley, *op. cit.*, p. 84.

[4] Quoted by Foster Watson, *Richard Hakluyt* (London, 1924), p. 61. The charge was made by pedants that learning was corrupted by translation. Conley, *op. cit.*, pp. 86 ff., overemphasizes the opposition to translation, in his treatment of the "Zoili," whom he identifies as "anti-humanists" and calls (p. 93) an "unwashed company"—hardly an accurate conclusion from the evidence.

tunge, hurteth memorie and hindreth lerning . . ."[5] But academic objections proved futile in the face of popular demand, and scholarly translators themselves set out manfully to justify their labors. It was to answer "our learned menne" that Hoby penned the great passage prefacing his own translation. The "unlatined," he suggests, are in need of aid which the more learned should lay before them. After commenting on the selfishness of scholars who acquire knowledge "to no other ende, but to profite themselues," he launches a defense of popular learning through the vernacular:

. . . where the Sciences are most tourned into the vulgar tunge, there are best learned men, and comparing it wyth the contrarie, they shall also finde the effectes contrarie. [He cites in proof the case of the great advance in knowledge in Italy "where the most translation of authors is"] . . . not onely of their profounde knowledge and noble wit, but also that knowledge may be obtained in studying onely a mannes owne native tunge. So that to be skilfull and exercised in authours translated, is no lesse to be called learning, then in the very same in the Latin or Greeke tunge. Therefore the translation of Latin or Greeke authours, doeth not onely not hinder learning, but it furthereth it, yea it is learning it self, and a great staye to youth, and the noble ende to the whiche they oughte to applie their wittes, that with diligence and studye have attained a perfect understanding, to open a gap for others to folow their steppes, and a vertuous exercise for the unlatined to come by learning, and to fill their minde with the morall vertues, and their body with civyll condicions, that they may bothe talke freely in all company, live uprightly though there were no lawes, and be in a readinesse against all kinde of worldlye chaunces that happen, whiche is the profite that commeth of Philosophy. And he said wel that was asked the question, How much the learned differed from the unlearned. 'So much' (quoth he) 'as the wel broken and ready horses, from the unbroken.' Wherfore I wote not how our learned men in this case can avoide the saying of Isocrates, to one that amonge soundrye learned discourses at Table spake never a woorde : 'Yf thou bee unlearned, thou dooest wiselye : but yf thou bee learned, unwyselye,' as who should saye, learnyng is yll bestowed where others bee not profited by it. . . .[6]

---

[5] Conley (op. cit., p. 103) quotes Hoby but fails to emphasize the correct inference of academic opposition to translation.

[6] The Tudor Translations (London, 1900), pp. 8-9.

Although the dignity and sincerity of Hoby's defense of translation mark it out in English letters, it had been preceded by other assertions of the value of translations and the obligation of the learned to the common people. Thomas Wilson, for instance, in both theory and practice, sought to impress his age with the capacity of the commonalty for learning. In the dedication to the King of *The rule of Reason, conteinyng the Arte of Logique, set forth in Englishe* (1551), Wilson asserts that he hopes by using plain English to make logic as familiar as other sciences to his countrymen :

For, considering the forwardenesse of this age, wherein the very multitude are prompte & ripe in al Sciences that haue by any mans diligence bene sett forth vnto them : weighyng also that capacitie of my country men the Englishnaciō is so pregnaunt and quicke to achiue any kynde, or Arte, of knowledge, whereunto wit maie attain, that they are not inferiour to any other : And farther pōdering that diuerse learned mē of other coūtreis haue heretofore for the furtheraunce of knowlege, not suffred any of the Sciences liberal to be hidden in the Greke, or Latine tongue, but haue with most earnest trauaile made euery of them familiar to their vulgare people : I thought that Logique among all other beyng an Arte as apte for the English wittes, & as profitable for there knowlege as any the other Sciences are, myght with as good grace be sette forth in Thenglishe, as the other Artes, heretofore haue bene.[7]

---

[7] Richard Sherry, citizen of London, made an interesting defense of English in *A treatise of Schemes & Tropes very profytable for the better vnderstanding of good authors, gathered out of the best Grammarians & Orators by Rychard Sherry Londoner* (1550). This is a treatise designed for the common understanding. The dedication to Master Thomas Brooke refutes charges that English is barbarous, by citing Gower, Chaucer, Lydgate, Sir Thomas Elyot, and Sir Thomas Wyatt. Sherry then announces that he has set forth his rules "in so playne an order, that redelye may be founde the figure, and the vse whereunto it serueth. Thoughe vnto greate wittes occupyed wyth weightye matters, they do not greatelye pertayne, yet to such as perchaūce shal not haue perfect instructoures, they may be commodious to helpe them selues for ye better vnderstandynge of such good authors as they reade." Cf. also *The Artes Of Logike And Rethorike, plainelie set foorth in the Englishe tounge, easie to be learned and practised: togeather with examples for the practise of the same, for Methode in the gouernment of the familie, prescribed in the word of God* (1584), attributed to Dudley Fenner. The preface maintains the necessity of making these arts "common" to all by the use of plain English. John Rastell's earlier plea for plain English for the common understanding, in the Messenger's speech prefatory to the *Nature of the Four Elements* [c. 1517-18], is well known. Since he is making a conscious effort to popularize learning, his words are significant :

It is doubtful whether the "vulgare people" made much use of Wilson's learned work on logic but it is significant that a scholar of his standing was striving to benefit them. The same patriotic zeal inspired him to make a translation of *The three Orations of Demosthenes* (1570),[8] a work which he declared should be read of "yong and olde, of learned and vnlearned," by all who love their country.[9] In the dedication to Burleigh he quotes Sir John Cheke to prove the utility of Demosthenes to the citizenry:

Moreouer he was moued greatly to like Demosthenes aboue all others, for that he sawe him so familiarly applying himselfe to the sense and vnderstanding of the common people, that he sticked not to say, that none euer was more fitte to make an English man tell his tale praise worthily in any open hearing, either in Parlament or in Pulpit, or otherwise, than this onely Orator was.

With the spirit of Hoby, Wilson asserts the duty of the learned to provide for the understanding of the many:

But such as are grieued with translated bokes, are lyke to them that eating fine Manchet, are angry with others that feede on Cheate breade. And yet God knoweth men would as gladly eat Manchet as they, if they had it. But all can not weare Veluet or feede with the best, and therefore such are contented for necessities sake to weare our Countrie cloth, and to take themselues to harde fare, that can haue no better. . . . And may not I or any other sette downe those reasons by penne, in our English language, the which are vttered daily in our common

---

"For dyuers pregnaunt wyttes be in this lande
　As well of noble men as of meane estate
　Whiche nothynge but englyshe can understande
　Than yf connynge laten bokys were translate
　Into englyshe wel correct and approbate
　All subtell sciens in englyshe myght be lernyd."—Julius Fischer (ed.), *Das "Interlude of the Four Elements,"* in *Marburger Studien zur englischen Philologie,* Hft. 5 (1903), p. 41.

[8] In view of the tradition that Wilson translated Demosthenes to incite England to resist Spain (*see* Conley, *op. cit.,* p. 52) the full title may be significant: *The three Orations of Demosthenes chiefe Orator among the Grecians, in fauour of the Olynthians, a people in Thracia, now called Romania: with those his fower Orations titled expressely & by name against Philip of Macedonie: most nedefull to be redde in these daungerous dayes, of all them that loue their Countries libertie, and desire to take warning for their better auayle, by example of others. Englished out of the Greeke by Thomas Wylson Doctor of the ciuill lawes* (1570).

[9] Preface to the reader.

speach, by men of vnderstanding? Now wicked is that minde the
whiche doth enuie welfare or wisedome to an other bodie, bicause the
same man can not be so welthie, or as wise as the best. And therefore
in my simple reason, there is no harme done I say to anye body by
this my English translation, except perhaps it be to my selfe. . . . 🔲🔲

In Wilson the patriotic element is uppermost, but he is thinking
of the state in terms, not of the courtier, but of the strong middle
class.

John Dolman's desire to translate for the mean sort of men
has been mentioned. His chief fear was the objection of scholars
that he was "prophaning of the secretes of Philosophy, whiche
are esteemed onelye of the learned, and neglected of the multitude.
And therefore, vnmeete, to be made commen for euerye man."[10]
These fears beset other translators. Even such a veteran as Arthur
Golding writes a defensive preface to *Thabridgment of the Histories of
Trogus Pompeius, Collected and wrytten in the Laten tonge, by the famous
Historiographer Iustine* (1564). He hopes to escape critics who will
accuse him of having "taken in hand a vaine and friuolous trauell,
namely to put forth that thyng in rude Englisshe whiche is written
in good & pure Latin." He cites, in defense, the examples of others
and craves favor for the work "in his playne and homely English
cote." Elsewhere, in the dedication to the Earl of Oxford of *The
Psalmes of David and others* (1571), Golding announces his desire
to serve the commonalty:

I haue sincerely performed the dutie of a faithfull Interpreter, rather
indeuering too lay foorth things plainlye (yea and sometimes also
homely and grossely) too the vnderstanding of many, than too indyte
things curyously too the pleasing of a fewe. For in this and such other
workes, the rude and ignorant haue more interest, than the learned
and skilful.

That the failure of learned men to translate useful works would
be nothing short of a national misfortune is the contention of Nicholas Haward in his dedication to Master Henry Compton of *A
briefe Chronicle, Where in are described shortlye the Originall, and the suc-
cessiue estate of the Romaine weale publique . . . Collected and gathered*

---

[10] Preface to *Those fyue Questions, which Marke Tullye Cicero, disputed in his Manor of
Tusculanum* (1561).

first by Eutropius, and Englyshed by Nicolas Haward, studiente of Thauies In (1564). History, he maintains, is particularly instructive to the unlearned laity. Scholars have been wise in making translations heretofore, and should continue their labors, for the knowledge of history

had to diuers euen to thys daye lien hidde, bene vnknown, and vnattained vnto, had not that theyr default in learning, bene aided by some others, able to further thē in this behalfe. Which imperfection of many diuers here to fore vnderstandyng, (to whome the talent of lernynge hath ben more aboūdantly graūted,) endeuoringe them selues, to remedy & supply yt want & defalt in others, haue to theyr great cōmendation and praise immortall, by their industry and paines taking in translating diuers Histories and Chronicles, (as in theyr myndes best seemed to them) out of sondry languages into this our mother tounge, made perfect and healed that maime, which otherwyse the want of knowledge of the same Historyes for want of learninge, had bred to dyuers of this our country.

In his preface to the reader Haward uses the fable of the dog in the manger to describe the opponents of translation. For a precedent he cites the examples of the Greeks and Romans, who drew their wisdom from all tongues.

Reform zeal and the desire to improve the reading of the common people stirred Edward Fenton to translate a marvelous hodgepodge of prodigies entitled *Certaine Secrete wonders of Nature . . . Gathered out of diuers learned authors as well Greeke as Latine, sacred as prophane* (1569). Unprofitable Arthurian stories are to be supplanted by this new compilation, for

We see in daily experience, with howe great earnestnesse and delight the vnlearned sorte runne ouer the fruitlesse Historie of king Arthur and his round table Knights, and what pleasure they take in the trifeling tales of Gawin and Gargantua : the which bisides that they passe all likelihood of truth, are vtterly without either graue precept or good example. Whereby I am in better hope that this booke containing suche varietie of matter bothe plesant to read and necessary to know, being sprinkled throughout with great wisdome and moralitie, shall be the rather embraced and allowed of all.[11]

---

[11] Dedication to Lord Lumley. The book contains such marvels as the story of King "Nabuchodonozer." A woodcut shows the king on all fours, grazing in the fields with

To translation are credited good morality and prosperity, by Henry Billingsley, a merchant of London, who discusses the value of moral philosophy, of history, and of mathematical arts, in the preface to his translation of Euclid, *The Elements Of Geometrie* (1570). Lamenting the lack of zeal to translate such works when "many good wittes both of gentlemen and of others of all degrees" are frustrated for lack of them, Billingsley hopes his own work may

excite and stirre vp others learned, to do the like, & to take paines in that behalfe. By meanes whereof, our Englishe tounge shall no lesse be enriched with good Authors, then are other straunge tounges : as the Dutch, French, Italian, and Spanishe : in which are red all good authors in a maner, found amongest the Grekes or Latines. Which is the chiefest cause, that amongest thē do florishe so many cunning and skilfull men, in the inuentions of straunge and wonderfull thinges, as in these our daies we see there do. Which fruite and gaine if I attaine vnto, it shall encourage me hereafter, in such like sort to translate, and set abroad some other good authors, both pertaining to religion (as partly I haue already done) and also pertaining to the Mathematicall Artes. . . .

Since history was regarded as the study, next to philosophy, most conducive to wisdom and good morality, translators felt an especial obligation to make historical works available to the generality of men. *The Foreste or Collection of Histories, no lesse profitable, then pleasant and necessarie, dooen out of Frenche into Englishe*, by Thomas Fortescue (1571), bears a preface in which Fortescue declares that "To profite neuerthelesse generally, was my desire, but chiefely the lesse learned, with this present Foreste. . . ." It is a miscellany ultimately from Pedro Mexia. Because a history of Britain from the time of Brute, written in Latin by a Welshman, Humphrey Lloyd, was not likely to stir the patriotism of the commoner, Thomas Twyne translated it as *The Breuiary of Britayne* (1573) with prefatory verses by his brother Lawrence praising the translator for his services to the unlettered :

> Loe now in English tongue by true
>   report, and cunnings skill,

---

the rabbits. Another of the illustrated tales of good morality is the story of the Archbishop of Mayence who was eaten by rats.

Twyne hath set forth th'unlearned sort,
   their pleasure to fulfill.

. . . .

But Brother, sure in my conceit
   thou thanks deseruest more,
Of *Britaynes,* and of British soyle,
   which makst them vnderstand.
A thinge more meete (me thinks) for them
   then for a forren land.
Wherin as thou by toyle, hast wonne
   the spurres, and prayses got:
So reape deserued thanks of those,
   for whom thou brakst the knot.

Service to the state through the education of the common people is one of the purposes of his translation of Plutarch, Thomas North declares in the dedication to the Queen of *The Lives Of The Noble Grecians And Romanes* (1579), Englished out of Amyot's French: ". . . yet I hope the common sorte of your subiects, shall not onely profit themselues hereby, but also be animated to the better seruice of your Maiestie."[12]

  The benefits to middle-class readers rendered by the translators of travel accounts were especially valuable, since the mercantile population, in common with other Elizabethans, read travel literature not only because it was intrinsically fascinating but also because it was exceedingly useful to a society that was pushing its trading ventures to the ends of the earth. As will be seen in a later discussion, Richard Hakluyt was prompted by patriotic and utilitarian purposefulness to translate many travel narratives and insert them in his *Principall Navigations* (1589) in order that unlearned readers might acquire profitable information. Before Hakluyt, Richard Willis had realized the need for making travel literature easily understood. In the preface to his expansion of Richard Eden's *The Decades of the newe worlde*, entitled *The History of Trauayle in the West and East Indies* (1577), Willis complains of Eden's excessive Latinity:

Many of his Englyshe woordes cannot be excused in my opinion for

---

[12] North later stresses the teaching value of his translation of fables, *The Morall Philosophie of Doni* (1601).

smellyng to much of the Latine, as *Dominators, Fol.* 5. *Ponderouse. Fol.* 23.
Ditionaries. Fol. 25. *Portentouse. Fol.* 28. *Antiques. Fol.* 31. *despicable. Fol.*
387. *Solicitate. Fol.* 76. *obsequiouse. Fol.* 90. *homicide. Fol.* 390. *imbibed.*
Fol. 395. *Destructive. Fol.* 276. *Prodigious. Fol.* 279. with other such lyke :
in the steede of Lords, weyghtie, subiectes, wonderfull, auncient, lowe,
carefull, duetifull, manslaughter, drunken, noysome, monstrous. &. the
which faultes he confesseth in other his owne verses, wrytyng thus
of hymselfe.

> *I haue not for euery worde asked counsayle*
> *of eloquent Eliot, or Sir Thomas Moore:*
> *Take it therefore as I haue intended,*
> *the faultes with fauour may soone be amended.*

The conception of the duty of the learned to serve the commonwealth by revealing hidden stores of knowledge to the popular
understanding gathered further strength as the middle class gained
in power in the early years of the seventeenth century. The self-
styled "Resolute" John Florio never spoke with more conviction
than in his declaration concerning the popular service of translation in the opening passages of the epistle "To the curteous
Reader" of *The Essayes Or Morall, Politike and Millitarie Discourses
of Lo: Michael de Montaigne* (1603). Translation, he maintains,
does not subvert learning but rather aids it, for did not the Greeks
translate their learning from the Egyptians? Are not the mathematical and all useful sciences indebted to translation? To answer
the Brahman criticism that translation made learning too common, Florio comments with asperity :

Yea but Learning cannot be too common, and the commoner the better. Why but who is not iealous, his Mistresse should be so prostitute?
Yea but this Mistresse is like ayre, fire, water, the more breathed the
clearer ; the more extended the warmer ; the more drawne the sweeter.
It were inhumanitie to coope her vp, and worthy forfeiture close to
conceale her. Why but Schollers should have some privilege of pre-
heminence. So have they: they onely are worthy Translators. Why
but the vulgar should not knowe all. No, they can not for all this ; nor
even Schollers for much more : I would, both could and knew much
more than either doth or can. Why but all would not be knowne of all.
No nor can : much more we know not than we know : all know something, none know all : would all know all? they must breake ere they
be so bigge. God only ; men farre from God. . . . Why, but it is not

wel Divinitie should be a childes or old wives, a coblers, or clothiers
tale or table-talke. There is vse and abuse: vse none too much: abuse
none too little. Why but let Learning be wrapt in a learned mantle.
Yea but to be vnwrapt by a learned nurse: yea, to be lapt vp againe.

Florio and his learned contemporaries practised the doctrine
of popularization which they so fervently preached. Thomas
Blundeville, an industrious translator of works on mathematics,
navigation, and even riding, is careful to declare in the preface to
The Theoriques of the seuen Planets (1602) that he has translated
"so plainely, and with such facilitie, as I hope that euery man of
a meane capacitie may vnderstand the same." William Fowldes,
translator of the pseudo-Homeric *Batrachomyomachia* as *The Strange,
Wonderfull, and bloudy Battell betweene Frogs and Mise* (1603), hopes
that his work will serve to spur "the riper wits of our time" further
to translate the works of Homer and other famous poets,[13] that
they "may not still lie hidden, as vnder a vaile or mysterie, from
the weake capacitie of meaner iudgements."[14] For the ease of the
unlearned, Fowldes inserts the translations of the allegorical names
in the text instead of in marginal notes so "that the inferiour
Readers should not bee wearied with looking in the margent."
Thus early do we have a scholar sacrificing his footnotes in the
interest of popularization.

Among all the early seventeenth-century translators, none took
his duty more seriously or felt his obligation to the unlearned more
keenly than Philemon Holland, described by Thomas Fuller as
the "Translator General" of his day. Coming from the middle
class himself, the Coventry doctor-schoolmaster showed in his
translations that he remembered the needs of his people. A simple
style, easy to be understood, is the aim expressed in the preface
to *The Romane Historie Written By T. Livius* (1600):

. . . I framed my pen, not to any affected phrase, but to a meane and
popular stile. Wherein, if I haue called again into vse some old words,
let it be attributed to the loue of my countrey language: if the sentence
be not so concise, couched and knit together, as the originall, loth I
was to be obscure and darke: . . .

---

[13] Preface to the reader.

[14] Noticed in Henrietta R. Palmer's *List of English Editions and Translations of Greek
and Latin Classics Printed before 1641*, Bibliographical Society (London, 1911), p. xxvi.

Yet despite this patriotic purpose, Holland was condemned by pedants, to whom he replies in the preface to *The Historie Of The World. Commonly called, The Naturall Historie of C. Plinius Secundus* (1601):

Why should any man therefore take offence hereat, and envie this good to his naturall countrey, which was first meant for the whole world? And yet some there be so grosse as to give out, That these and such like books ought not to bee published in the vulgar tongue. It is a shame (quoth one) that *Livie* speaketh English as hee doth : Latinists onely are to bee acquainted with him : As who would say, the souldiour were to have recourse unto the universitie for militarie skill and knowledge; or the schollar to put on arms and pitch a campe. What should *Plinie* (saith another) bee read in English, and the mysteries couched in his books divulged : as if the husbandman, the mason, carpenter, goldsmith, painter, lapidarie, and engraver, with other artificers, were bound to seeke unto great clearks or linguists for instructions in their severall arts. Certes, such *Momi* as these, besides their blind and erroneous opinion, thinke not so honourably of their native countrey and mother tongue as they ought : who if they were so well affected that way as they should be, would wish rather and endeavour by all means to triumph now over the Romans in subduing their literature under the dent of the English pen, in requitall of the conquest sometime over this Island, atchieved by the edge of their sword.

In Pliny, Holland asserts, he has an example of simple style adapted to the common understanding,

furnished with discourses of all matters, not appropriat to the learned only, but accomodat to the rude paisant of the countrey; fitted for the painefull artizan in town and citie; pertinent to the bodily health of man, woman, and child; and in one woord, suiting with all sorts of people living in a societie and commonweale.

Pleased that Plutarch and Tacitus have found translators, he hopes that other rich stores will be opened for the commonwealth of knowledge.

Continuing his labors for popular learning, Holland equipped his translation of *The Historie Of Twelve Caesars . . . By C. Suetonius Tranquillus* (1606) with notes to help "those among you, who are not so conversant in such concise writings." *The Roman*

Historie . . . written first in Latine by Ammianus Marcellinus (1609) he dedicated to the mayor and aldermen of Coventry out of gratitude for their encouragement of learning. In all his works Holland reveals an ideal of simplification for a group eager to learn but frustrated by the difficulties of a foreign tongue. Always he sacrifices brevity for full explanation, for he believes that the utmost enlightenment is his mission.[15]

A direct, simple style that all may understand becomes the ideal, in theory at any rate, of history translators. Edward Aston, dedicating to Sir Walter Aston, a Staffordshire knight, *The Manners, Lawes, And Customes Of All Nations* (1611), says he has translated it "for the benefit of such as are vnskilful in the Latin tongue." He has made his authors speak "in a phrase though not eloquent, yet I hope plaine and intelligible." W. Shute declares in the preface to his translation of *The Generall Historie Of The Magnificent State Of Venice . . . Collected by Thomas de Fougasses, Gentleman of Auignon* (1612) that

Touching my stile, I haue not made it so high, but that the lowest vnderstanding may get ouer, not affected any thing so much, as not to affect. For my chiefe ambition was, that my lines might rather be fit to crowne my Readers braine, than hang in his eare, and make him a Man, than a Parrot.

Because John Willis believed that a work of his own, which he describes as a "Tractate in Latine called Mnemonica," could not be understood by the unlearned, he translated the third book of the treatise as *The Art Of Memory* (1621), "plaine and easie for any mans vnderstanding."[16] Kingsmill Long felt that the English public was losing the profitable lessons implicit in *Argenis*, the Latin allegorical romance by their countryman, John Barclay.

---

[15] Equally industrious but less patently concerned over the high purpose of translation was Edward Grimeston, who Englished a large number of historical works, for the most part concerning modern European affairs. The popular appetite for such translations seems to have enabled Grimeston to eke out a livelihood while waiting for some remunerative preferment. *See* G. N. Clark, "Edward Grimeston, the Translator," *English Historical Review*, XLIII (1928), 585-98.

[16] Preface to the reader. The first two books he did not translate, since they were "for Schollers onely, that are skilfull in Logicke and Poetrie." Willis's *The Art Of Stenographie* (1602) had been written "to the capacitie of the meanest, and for the vse of all professions," as the title-page asserted.

Four years after the publication of the Latin version Long translated it as *Barclay His Argenis: Or, The Loves Of Poliarchus and Argenis* (1625). In a dedication to William Dunche of Avesbury, Long discusses the profitable nature of *Argenis* and mentions the continued hope that

our Nation might not be depriued of the vse of so excellent a Story: But finding none in so long time to haue done it; and knowing, while it spake not *English*, though it were a rich iewell to the learned Linguist, yet it was close lockt from all those, to whom Education had not giuen more Languages, than Nature Tongues: I haue aduentured to become the Key to this piece of hidden Treasure, and haue suffered my selfe to bee ouerruled by some of my worthy friends, . . .

Formal defenses of translation became less numerous as the seventeenth century wore on, because even the academic public was conceding that the commonalty could be improved by a judicious induction into the worth-while literature of divers languages rendered into English. And "improvement" was the goal of the first half of the seventeenth century. I have not attempted to cite all the passages that urge the usefulness of translation. Some of these are perfunctory; some are in the nature of advertisements of the works. Many translators, however, were so seriously impressed with their duty to the unlearned that they urged others to follow their examples. Assembled here are what seem the most significant of such statements of the obligation to translate.

The Elizabethan middle class were as aware of the value of translated learning as the scholars who felt the missionary urge to supply their needs. I have already mentioned the activities of such bourgeois scholars as Philemon Holland. Many other citizens turned their hands to foreign learning because they were impressed with its utility. The merchants who traded in the Low Countries, for example, envied the Dutch and sought by translating their treatises of trade and navigation to stir Englishmen to commercial emulation.[17] George Baker, a surgeon, who trans-

---

[17] G. P. Gooch, *English Democratic Ideas in the Seventeenth Century* (2d ed., Cambridge, 1927), p. 45.

For an example of the utilitarian treatise, see Edward Wright's *The Haven-Finding Art, Or The Way To Find any Hauen or place at sea, by the Latitude and variation. Lately published in the Dutch, French, and Latine tongues, by commandement of the right honourable*

lated from Conrad Gesner *The newe Iewell of Health* (1576), alludes in the preface to the eminence in science of the Italians and the French and the need for translation of their works into English :

And nowe in these our dayes, we see howe other Nations doe followe their examples. For what kinde of science or knowledge euer was inuented by man, which is not nowe in the Italian or French? And what more prerogatiue haue they than we English men (of the which many learned men haue made sufficiēt proofe within these few yeres, fully to furnish & satisfie our Nation with many goodly works.) For our English is as meete & necessary for vs, as is the Greeke for the Grecians, though in the translation we be constrayned to make two or three words sometyme for one. For if it were not permitted to translate but word for word, thē I say, away with all translations, ye which were great losse to the cõmon weale, considering that out of one language into another haue ben turned many most excellent works, the which the best learned haue both receyued & approued to the singular commoditie of all men.

John Frampton is typical of the intelligent English merchants who utilized the knowledge gained in foreign business, to benefit their country. After Frampton's retirement from the Spanish trade, he translated *Joyfull Newes Out Of The Newe Founde Worlde* (1577) from the Spanish of Nicolas Monardes.[18] This popular pharmacopoeia, describing the drugs found in America, was reprinted in 1580 and again in 1596. Not content with this labor, Frampton translated Marco Polo as *The most noble and famous trauels of Marcus Paulus* (1579). In the dedication to Edward Dyer, he regrets that some more learned man has not undertaken the work, but at the request of divers merchants, pilots, and mariners, he presents his plain translation that it "mighte giue greate lighte

---

Count Mauritz of Nassau, Lord high Admiral of the vnited Prouinces of the Low countries, . . . And now translated into English, for the common benefite of the Seamen of England (1599). The treatise is by Simon Stevin. In a dedication to the Lord Admiral Charles Howard, Wright says he has been led to make the translation, that English sailors might not fall behind those of other nations, especially the "Netherlanders."

See also Robert Peake's *The first Booke of Architecture, made by Sebastian Serly, entreating of Geometrie. Translated out of Italian into Dutch, and out of Dutch into English* (1611). In the preface the translator declares that he has Englished this work for the good of the artisans of England and the common profit which will ensue.

[18] Reprinted in The Tudor Translations with an introduction by Stephen Gaselee (2 vols., London, 1925).

to our Seamen, if euer this nation chaunced to find a passage out of the frozen Zone to the South Seas, and otherwise delight many home dwellers, furtherers of trauellers." Frampton also translated a work on China from Bernardino de Escalante, *A discourse of the navigation which the Portugales doe make to the Realmes and Provinces of the East partes of the worlde* (1579), and a treatise on navigation from Pedro de Medina, *The Arte of Navigation* (1581).

As one would expect, travel literature appealed strongly to the merchant-translators. To be plain and forthright was their intention, for this literature was not Englished merely for the entertainment it might afford but for the instruction it would provide English adventurers.[19] Thomas Nicholas, for example, in the dedication to Dr. Thomas Wilson of his *The strange and delectable History of the discouerie and Conquest of the Prouinces of Peru . . . by Augustine Sarate* (1581) insists upon the value of such a history, though he

cā not polish [it] as learned mē might require. Yet the troth and pith of the matter vttered in plaine sort shall suffice giuing licence, as much (as in me lieth) to whosoeuer that will take the paines, to write it ouer againe, to beautifie the same, as to him or them shall seeme conuenient: as often times, hath happened among the Greeke and Latine Historiographers and Translators.

In an earlier translation, *The Pleasant Historie of the Conquest of the Weast India, now called new Spayne* (1578), Nicholas concludes his dedication to Sir Francis Walsingham with an apology for the homespun style of the book,

The whiche I haue translated out of the Spanish tong, not decked with gallant couloures, nor yet fyled with pleasant phrase of Rhetorike, for these things are not for poore Marchant trauellers, but are reserued to learned Writers: yet I trust the Author will pardon mee, bycause I haue gone as neere the sens of this Historie, as my cunning woulde reach vnto.

Michael Lok, a member of a merchant family, in editing and translating *De Nouo Orbe, Or The Historie Of the west Indies* (1612) by Peter Martyr, part of which had been previously translated by

---

[19] For some examples of the interest of traders in translation, see J. G. Underhill, *Spanish Literature in the England of the Tudors* (New York, 1899), pp. 157 ff., 176, etc.

Richard Eden, declares that he is impelled by a desire to stir Englishmen

to performe the like in our *Virginea*, whiche beeing once throughly planted, and inhabited with our people, may returne as greate bene-fitte to our Nation in another kinde, as the Indies doe vnto the Span-yard : for although it yeeld not golde, yet, is it a fruitfull pleasant coun-trey, replenished with all good thinges, necessary for the life of man, if they be industrious, who inhabite it.[20]

Great as was the interest of the mercantile class in utilitarian learning, tradesmen-translators did not confine themselves to treatises of practical use. As early as 1550 Thomas Nicolls pro-duced *The hystory writtone by Thucidides the Athenyan of the Warre, whiche was betwene the Peloponesians and the Athenyans, translated oute of Frenche into the Englysh language by Thomas Nicolls Citizeine and Goldesmyth of London.* Like the good tradesman he was, Nicolls in his dedication to Sir John Cheke objects to writers of trivial histories who have "bestowed theyr laboure, more in adournynge, garnyshinge and fylyng of theyr woordes, then in serchynge and declaryng of the trouth." He himself has not troubled with frothy matters of style but has "trauayled for to translate playnelye & truly owte of the Frenche into the Inglyshe tonge, thys hystorye."

Richard Robinson was another citizen who turned out transla-tions designed to help and uplift the commonwealth. Typical of his selections was *A Moral Methode of ciuile Policie. Contayninge A learned fruictful discourse of the institution, state and gouernment of a common Weale. Abridged oute of the Cõmentaries of . . . Franciscus Patricius . . . Done out of Latine into Englishe, by Rycharde Robinson, Citizen of London* (1576). Robinson dedicated his work to Sir William Allen, London alderman. Prominent in the epitome of Booke I is the discussion of means "Of maintayning husbandry, trades of marchandize, and handicraftesmen." Mixing as it does the moral, philosophic, and practical, this work is the kind which appealed to a London citizen.

Other London tradesmen have translations to their credit. Perhaps none took his duty more seriously than Joshua Sylvester, the translator of Du Bartas. Although the necessity of engaging

---

[20] Preface to the reader.

in trade sometimes irked him, he was proud to sign himself "Marchant Adventurer."[21]

Throughout the Elizabethan period both scholars and learned citizens felt a patriotic impulse to aid the commonwealth by revealing to all classes the stores of wisdom locked in foreign tongues. National pride urged them on to see that England did not fall behind Holland, Italy, Spain, or France. It is not my intention to imply that tradesmen greedily snatched up all the translations which scholars solemnly asserted were for their benefit, but without doubt the enormous quantities of translated learning did materially affect the intellectual development of the middle class, as well as all Elizabethan society. One has only to consult such bibliographies as Miss Mary Augusta Scott's *Elizabethan Translations from the Italian* to see how vast was the debt to foreign literature. Like Kipling's Tommy, what the Elizabethan wanted he went and took. And to aid in the taking, patriotic men of letters demolished the walls around learning, smashed the idols of academic objection, and invited the lay brethren to choose what suited their use.

Although the wisdom of the world could be brought to unlettered Englishmen by means of translations, the necessities of foreign trade forced merchants to turn their attention to the learning of languages. Since Latin was almost universally studied in the schools, it was an important instrument of communication throughout Europe, and merchants frequently made use of it. Indeed, in the third decade of the seventeenth century a London merchant, Baptist Goodall, urging the study of languages upon travelers and merchants, declared that since a knowledge of all vernaculars was impossible of attainment, it would be well to learn Latin, Greek, Hebrew, and "High Dutch," for with these key languages business could be transacted in most countries visited by Englishmen.[22] If few or no tradesmen attained to such

---

[21] *See* his early use of this style of signing himself in *A Canticle of the Victorie obteined by the French King, Henrie the fourth. At Yvry* (1590).

[22] *The Tryall Of Travell* (1630), a travel book in verse, bearing a prefatory epistle "To all the sonnes of Noble trauaile whether Merchant, Martiall, or Maryne Negotiators." The passage on language follows:

philological erudition as Goodall suggests, many nevertheless acquired sufficient knowledge of both ancient and modern languages to serve their practical necessities. In addition to the study of languages as a discipline, there was a gradual increase in the emphasis upon the utility of the tongues themselves, and the movement for the simplification of language-teaching in the early seventeenth century was dictated partly by the need for practical instruction in a shorter time than had been previously required. Attempts were made to simplify and popularize Lily's Latin grammar;[23] and, not satisfied with improving Lily, Christopher Syms published in Dublin in 1634 an ambitious Latin handbook, which he recommended not only to "any boy howsoever dul" but also to intelligent men who wished to instruct themselves.[24] The year before Syms's effort to produce a self-instructor in Latin, John Anchoran brought out an expansion of Comenius' *Porta Linguarum* for the use of those who needed a quicker introduction to foreign tongues than the usual academic texts provided. This book, which he entitled *The Gate of Tongues Vnlocked And Opened*,

---

> "But let vs note language collatral mixt
> Vnder both Poles by prouidence is fixt
> And generall tongues for generalls lead way.
> Which generals each way specials ouer sway.
> Ould Roman Latin in the westerne lands
> Italian, Spanish, French, and vs commands,
> Ould Greeke the spacious Adriaticke climes
> Hebrue the East, honourd in first of times.
> High Dutch the danish pole, and Northerne tracke
> So hauing one we cannot wholly Lacke
> And by the generall language that way vsd
> Perticulars will more esily be infusd
> Since a propensitions causd in tongues confusion
> Many as members haue to one head allusion
> Then fit thy selfe such specialles to collect
> And lazinesse worths canker worke reiect."   —Sig. G 3ᵛ.

Goodall's advocacy of learning a few master languages faintly suggests the belief in the possibility of constructing a universal language. Although this notion was toyed with by Bacon and others in the first half of the seventeenth century, it did not gain much favor until later. *See* Otto Funke, *Zum Weltsprachenproblem in England im 17. Jahrhundert*, in *Anglistische Forschungen*, Hft. 69 (Heidelberg, 1929).

[23] Foster Watson, *The English Grammar Schools to 1660: Their Curriculum and Practice* (Cambridge, 1908), pp. 268 ff.

[24] *An Introduction to, or, the Art of Teaching the Latine Speach* (1634).

Or else, A Seminarie or seed-plot of all Tongues and Sciences (1633), promised "A short way of teaching and thorowly learning within a yeere and a halfe at the farthest, the Latin, English, French, and any other tongue, together with the ground and foundation of Arts and Sciences."[25] Published as an answer to the criticism being made by practical reformers, many of whom came from the middle class, that too much time was being wasted in the study of grammar without acquiring a usable knowledge of the language, this work admits the validity of the criticism and recommends itself as a solution of the difficulty.[26] Such works as these were useful not only to students in the schools but to persons who were pursuing their own studies at home.

Long before the period of educational reform in the seventeenth century, however, the necessity of mastering modern European languages had occupied the attention of English tradesmen. English was said to be a useless language beyond the Channel, and as sharp competition with Dutch, Spanish, Flemish, and Italian merchants forced the English trader to realize the handicap of his linguistic ignorance, he set himself resolutely to master the essentials of the languages that he encountered in foreign trade. Because of its widespread currency, French assumed the greatest importance in the minds of traders, and as Miss Kathleen Lambley has shown, many early French-English dialogues were prepared for the aid of merchants.[27] At first, English merchants made use of the polyglot conversation-books published in France and Flanders, the basis of many similar works being the poly-

---

[25] Quoted from the title-page.

[26] *See* the statement in the preface, signed "Iohn Anchoran I.A. Comenius" : "Lastly, if for the Tongues alone, so many yeares are to be spent by any one, when shall he arriue at realities? When shall his mind receiue the tincture of more solide Philosophy? When shall he overcome the difficulties of Theology? or finde out the secrets of Physick? or turne over the Voluminous writings of the Law? When shall he compasse the end of his studdies? and (which is the greatest) when will he be able to exercise the praxis of his, solicitously sought for, learning for the benefit of Church and Commonwealth? Surely (such is the brevity of life) that not at all, or very late ; and then he will perceive that ha's spent in onely preparing to live."

[27] *The Teaching and Cultivation of the French Language in England during Tudor and Stuart Times* (Manchester, 1920), Chap. VIII, "The Study of French among Merchants and Soldiers," pp. 239 ff. To this discussion I am indebted for the facts in the next few pages. Titles of books which I have been unable to see are also quoted from Miss Lambley's work.

glot vocabulary of Noel de Barlement (or Barliament) printed at Antwerp in 1511, and many times thereafter. A Louvain edition of 1556 contained Flemish, French, Latin, and Spanish, and in later polyglot vocabularies English was added. In 1557 Gabriel Meurier of Antwerp dedicated a French grammar to the English merchants. From Antwerp also came in 1563 *Familiare communications no leasse proppre then proffytable to the Inglishe nation desirous and nedinge the ffrench language*, dedicated to John Marsh, governor of the local English colony and intended for the use of "Marchands, Facteurs, Apprentifs, and others of the English nation." An edition nearly eighty years later, this time from Rouen, makes improvements for the benefit of tradesmen, as its title indicates: *A treatise for to learne to speake Frenshe and Englishe together with a form of making letters, indentures, and obligations, quittances, letters of exchange, verie necessarie for all Marchants that do occupy trade or marchandise* (1641).

While grammars and dialogues were being printed abroad solely for the use of English business men, the students and printers at home were combining to supply their needs. Alexander Barclay in 1521 described his French grammar as helpful to merchants. In 1557 Edward Sutton received license to print "a boke intituled Italian, Frynshe, Englesshe and Laten"; in 1568 a "boke intituled Frynsche, Englysshe and Duche" was licensed to John Alde.[28] These were doubtless vocabulary and phrase books similar to those employed by English merchants on the Continent.

The treatise on French by Claudius Hollyband was probably the most popular with all classes. Its title advertised the self-help nature of the work and indicated its utility to such groups as merchants and traders who needed to pick up a working knowledge of the language: *The French Schoolemaister, wherein is most plainlie shewed, the true and most perfect way of pronouncinge of the French tongue, without any helpe of Maister or Teacher: set foorthe for the furtherance of all those whiche doo studie priuately in their own study or houses* (1573). Not only did Hollyband prepare textbooks to be used by plain people, but he also kept a school where children of tradesmen, in large classes, were instructed in French. Another teacher of

---

[28] *Ibid.*, p. 241.

tradesmen was Adrian à Saravia of Southampton, from whom Joshua Sylvester learned his French. Two years after Hollyband's treatise, there appeared *A plaine patheway to the French Tongue, very profitable for Marchants and also all other which desire the same, aptly deuided into nineteen chapters* (1575). John Wodroeph, an English soldier in the Low Countries, got out a useful combination of French grammar, dictionary, and phrase book, which he called *The Spared Houres of a Souldier in his trauells. Or The True Marrowe of the French Tongue* (Dort, 1623). A second edition was printed in London in 1625. Wodroeph describes his phrases as "more profitable for the merchants than for the loathsome courtier who cannot digest such coarse meats."[29] James Howell felt it peculiarly appropriate in 1650 to dedicate his edition of Cotgrave's *Dictionarie* to the "merchant adventurers as well English as the worthy company of the Dutch here resident and others to whom the language is necessary for commerce and foren correspondence."[30]

The polyglot works had the value of being equally useful for both English and foreign tradesmen. Such a one was *The English French: Latine Dutch Scholemaster or an introduction to teach young Gentlemen and Merchants to trauell or trade. Being the only helpe to attaine to those languages* (1637). Michael Sparke, the printer, brought out another edition in 1639 as *New Dialogues or colloquies or a little Dictionary of eight languages. A Booke very necessary for all those that study these tongues either at home or abroad, now perfected and made fit for trauellers, young merchants and seamen, especially those that desire to attain to the use of the tongues.* A large space is devoted to terms for buying and selling.

At least one London merchant repaid in a practical way the debt English tradesmen owed Flemish and French compilers of language helps. He was George Mason, who brought out for the benefit of the French merchants in London his *Grammaire Angloise. Contenant reigles bien exactes & certaines de la Prononciation, Orthographe, & Construction de nostre langue; En faveur des estrangiers qui en sont desireux. Par George Mason Marchand de Londres. A Londres. Chez Nat. Butter. 1622.*[31] Another edition appeared in 1633.

---

[29] *Ibid.*, pp. 246 ff.   [30] *Ibid.*, p. 240.

[31] Edited with an introduction by R. Brotanek in *Neudrucke Frühneuenglischer Grammatiken*, Hft. I (Halle a. S., 1905).

The polyglot vocabularies frequently included both Spanish and Italian, along with Latin, French, English, and Dutch, so that traders found them of equal utility wherever their business carried them. Although Spanish did not attain to the importance of French, the trade with Spain fostered a new interest in the language in the late sixteenth century. The standard grammar and dictionary used by the merchants was Richard Percyvall's *Bibliotheca Hispanica. Containing a Grammar, with a Dictionarie in Spanish, English, and Latine, gathered out of diuers good authors, very profitable for the studious of the Spanish toong. By Richard Percyvall Gent. The Dictionaire being inlarged with the Latine, by the aduise and conference of Master Thomas Doyley Doctor in Physicke* (1591). In the previous year John Thorius had published *A Spanish Grammer*. W. Stepney, who seems to have conducted a school in London for instruction in Spanish, conceived the idea of making the study more attractive by devising a dialogue for each day in the week in *The Spanish Schoole-master. Containing Seven Dialogues, according to euery day in the weeke, and what is necessarie euerie day to be done. . . . Newly collected and set forth by W. Stepney, professor of the said tongue in the famous Citie of London* (1591). In the epistle to the reader, Stepney commends others for publishing a grammar and a dictionary of Spanish. He believes that to be the language which holds the greatest utility for Englishmen : "I doubt not but that in the future age the Spanish tongue will be as well esteemed as the French or the Italian tongues, and in my simple iudgement, it is farre more necessary for our countrey-men then the Italian tongue is." Spanish was more necessary at the moment because of the increasing trade contacts, despite the political unpleasantnesses between England and Spain.

John Minsheu's labors as lexicographer and grammarian were of great help to tradesmen. He was the compiler of *A Dictionarie in Spanish and English* (1599), *A Spanish Grammar* (1599),[32] and a *Vocabularium Hispanico-Latinum et Anglicum copiosissimum* (1617). His *Guide into Tongues* (1617), with its eleven languages, was published in part by merchants' subscriptions. Joshua Sylvester is listed

---

[32] In the *Dictionary of National Biography, sub* Minsheu, it is stated that the Spanish dictionary and grammar were founded on Richard Percyvall's earlier work.

among the subscribers as "Secretary to the English Company of Merchants at Middleburgh."[33]

The study of Italian seems to have been regarded at first as a gentleman's exercise. Indeed, the necessity of English merchants' knowing Italian was not so pressing in the sixteenth century as it later became, for the Italian trade was largely in the hands of the Italians themselves, who sent traders to England in large numbers. Their need for helps to the English language was recognized by John Florio, who provided useful dialogues for them in *Florio His first Fruites: which yeelde familiar speech, merie Prouerbes, wittie Sentences, and golden sayings. Also a perfect Induction to the Italian, and English tongues, as in the Table appeareth. The like heretofore, neuer by any man published* (1578). Florio has a dedicatory address "A tutti i Gentilhuomini, e Mercanti Italjani, che si dilettano de la lingua Inglese, ogni Felicitá, è Gratia da Dio." In this he emphasizes the utility of the book to all gentlemen who want to learn Italian and to all merchants who want to learn English. Since it is a long phrase book with Italian in one column and English in the other, followed by a vocabulary and a grammar, it was equally useful for the study of either language.

When the English companies' trade with the Levant sprang into importance in the seventeenth century, the necessity for a knowledge of Italian increased, because in many of the trading ports of the Near East, Italian was the European language most easily understood. Furthermore, English merchants extended their factories to Italian cities and began to exploit the trade once monopolized by the Italians. The progress of Italian study by the merchant class is summed up in *The Italian Tutor Or A New And Most Compleat Italian Grammer* (1640) by Giovanni Torriano, who describes himself as a professor of Italian in London. In the dedication of his grammar to "The Right Worshipfull And Now Most Flourishing Company Of Turkey Marchants," he discusses their diligence in the study of Italian:

Thrice worthy Sirs: Of all the famous Companies of this Citie, none

---

[33] A. B. Grosart (ed.), *The Complete Works of Joshuah Sylvester*, 2 vols., Chertsey Worthies' Library (Edinburgh, 1880), I, xx. Grosart's edition is a reprint of the folio of 1641.

affecting the Italian Tongue so much as yours, and withall I standing ingaged to none more then to yours, through many respects, I cold doe no lesse then present you with these my weake indeavours, as an acknowledgement of what I owe to your goodnesse. This is a booke which is intended for the good of all the English Nation, but especially you who are in a continuall commerce with most parts of *Italy*, as well as *Turkey*, where the *Italian Tongue* is all in all. Yet mistake me not, I intrude not so farre as to dedicate it so much to you who are seniors, whereby I should instruct you, who are all-knowing in the language already; but to the end that the hopefull youth which is dayly traind up under your care whether your sonnes or your servants might reape most benefit thereby, which doubtlesse will the sooner accrew unto them, if you shall vouchsafe to countenance it, and no further then it shall seeme to deserve. I shall stand to your censure: Meane time hoping that you will be as willing to accept of it, as I am ambitious to present you with it; I rest, wishing you all from above, all the increase of health, wealth, and happinesse whatsoever. Your observant servant to his power, Gio: Torriano.

Torriano calls attention to his own *New and easie directions for the Thuscan Italian Tongue*, published the previous year, and designed apparently for students from the middle class. He also issued in 1640 *A Display Of Monasyllable Particles Of The Italian Tongue By Way Of Alphabet. . . . Also, certaine Dialogues*. The dialogues were prepared with a view to teaching Italian idioms; one of the longest of them, "The Seventh Dialogue. Concerning buying and selling," is devoted to the mercantile vocabulary. An effort to appeal to bourgeois interest is evident in another seventeenth-century collection of Italian-English dialogues, *The Passenger: Of Benvenuto Italian, Professour of his Natiue Tongue, for these nine yeeres in London* (1612). Dialogue 5 relates a discussion between a citizen and a countryman as to which is the greater idol, the country gentleman's pursuit of pleasure or the citizen's struggle for gain. The citizen gets the better of the argument and drives it home with the patriotic declaration that "our traffic redounds to the augmentation of Common-wealths renowne, reputation, and strength: but yet your pleasures dissipate, and confound all: Moreouer, they begin in pleasure, and end in discontent: the entring into them is with laughter, but the comming out of them, is sorrowfull, with lamentation."   [P. 333.]

With the exception of the study of Hebrew for its biblical implications, the first and greatest impetus to the study of oriental tongues came from travelers and traders in the East. Richard Hakluyt was interested in these languages, and Samuel Purchas included in his collections of travels examples of Turkish, Chinese, Japanese, and other eastern tongues, which commercial explorers were trying to master. Sir George Buck in describing the educational opportunities of London in 1615 mentioned teachers of the less known European and oriental languages, from whom merchants and commercial agents could learn the languages that were becoming more necessary with every year's expansion of the great chartered companies in the eastern trade. If we may believe Buck's statement, almost any speech needed in trade could be learned in London: "And here bee they which can speake the Persian and the Morisco, and the Turkish, & the Muscovian Language, and also the Sclauonian tongue, which passeth through 17. Nations. And in briefe diuers other Languages fit for Embassadors and Orators, and Agents for Marchants, and for Trauaylors, and necessarie for all Commerce or Negotiation whatsoeuer."[34] The practical value of Arabic and the importance of that language for business was recognized by the learned minister, William Bedwell,[35] who prepared an Arabic lexicon (left in manuscript at his death) and in 1615 published *The Arabian Trudgman*, a dictionary of Arabic titles, place names, and miscellaneous terms. Since Aleppo and Smyrna were centers of trade for the Levant Company, English merchants made their residences there and set about learning the languages in use around them. At Aleppo, Edward Pococke, chaplain of the Levant Company from 1630 to 1636, learned Arabic so fluently that on his return to England, Archbishop Laud appointed him professor of Arabic at Oxford. Pococke also boasted a knowledge of "Hebrew, Samaritan, Syriac, and Ethiopic."[36]

Since merchants trading in the East Indies were greatly handi-

---

[34] *The Third Vniuersitie Of England* [printed in the 1615 edition of John Stow's *Annales*], p. 983.

[35] See *Dictionary of National Biography*, *sub* Bedwell.

[36] Foster Watson, *The Beginnings of the Teaching of Modern Subjects in England* (London, 1909), pp. xxxvii-xxxviii.

capped because of the difficulty of the languages and the lack of adequate aids for learning them, no small service was performed by an industrious English merchant, Augustine Spalding, who prepared a phrase book of Malay, translated from the work of Gothard Arthus, a Danish linguist, with the title: *Dialogues In The English And Malaiane Languages: Or, Certaine Common Formes Of Speech, First Written in Latin, Malaian, and Madagascar tongues, by the diligence and painfull endeuour of Master Gotardus Arthusius, a Dantisker, and now faithfully translated into the English tongue by Augustine Spalding Merchant, for their sakes, who happily shall hereafter vndertake a voyage to the East-Indies* (1614). The Malayan words and phrases, selected for their utility in commercial intercourse, are given their approximate sound in Roman letters, but there is no formal discussion of pronunciation or grammar. In a dedication to Sir Thomas Smith, "Gouernour of the East India, Muscouia, Northwest Passages, Sommer Ilands Companies, and Treasurer for the first Colonie in Virginia," Spalding describes the former's efforts in behalf of useful learning necessary to commerce, and attributes to him the fostering of the study of languages:

Honourable Sir, the world hath iust occasion to take knowledge of your continuall trauels, cares and endeuours for the good of those sundry Companies, whereof by publike assent you haue been chosen Gouernour. Your erecting of the Lecture of Nauigation at your own expences, for the better instruction of our Mariners in that most needfull art: your setting downe of better orders in dispatching forth of our East-Indian fleetes: your employment with extraordinarie entertainment of skilfull Mathematicians and Geographers in the South and North parts of the world: This your providence and liberalitie is like, in time to come, to worke many speciall good effects. Lastly, you haue caused these Dialogues of the languages of the Isle of Madagascar and of the Malaian tongues, presented vnto you by Master *Richard Hackluyt*, a singular furtherer of all new discoueries and honest trades, to be set forth in our English tongue: because of the speciall vse and benefit which your Factors and seruants, residing in all the Southeast Islands of the world, may reape thereby. And that nothing might be omitted on your behalfe, it hath pleased you further to aske mine opinion, and to enioyne me to take speciall care for the correction of such errors as were committed in the first edition, because of my eleuen or twelue yeeres employment in those Countries, as seruant and Factor for your Worship and the Companie : . . .

Not only in the study of foreign tongues but in the interest bestowed upon English as well, the Elizabethan showed a developing language consciousness evident even among the less erudite middle class. That the power of persuasion depended upon the speaker's linguistic agility was as well known to the Elizabethan salesman as it is to his modern counterpart ; hence many a tradesman who expected to spend all his days in Cheapside found it worth his while to cultivate the graces of conversation and to keep by him a glossary of hard words. Bourgeois fathers early saw the value of having their sons and apprentices taught good English and particularly the vocabulary of trade. One of the most interesting of the helps to vocabulary building, designed for the use of merchants' children and apprentices, was Thomas Newbery's *A booke in Englysh metre, of the great Marchaunt man called Diues Pragmaticus, very preaty for children to rede: whereby they may the better, and more readyer, rede and wryte wares and Implementes, in this world contayned* (1563).[37] After exalting the trade of merchandising, in the verse preface, the author proceeds in the poem proper to enumerate all the wares which a merchant may sell or require, from books to ships stores. Following an exhortation to virtue and thrift comes this conclusion :

> With this mery Iest, and poore simple Ryme :
> For Seruantes and Chyldren, to passe with the tyme,
> At conuenient leysure, no hurt it wyll be.
> Honest myrth in measure, is a pleasaunt thyng,
> To wryte and to rede well, be gyftes of learnyng :
> Remember this well, all you that be young,
> Exercise vertue, and rule well your toung.

Edmund Coote's *The English Schoole-Master* (1596) was a much more serious treatise, a general handbook for use at home, prepared especially for the tradesman, in which directions for language study occupied a prominent place. The long description

---

[37] No. 21 in Henry Huth's *Fugitive Poetical Tracts*, 1st Ser. (privately printed, 1875). This little work has also been reproduced as No. 2 of *The John Rylands Facsimiles* (Manchester, 1910).

on the title-page of the twenty-fifth edition (1636) advertises the utility of the work in the acquisition of a knowledge of the English language :

The English Schoole-Master : Teaching all his schollers, of what age soever, the most easie, short, and perfect order of distinct Reading, and true Writing our English-tongue, that hath ever yet beene knowne or Published by any. And further also, teacheth a direct Course, how any vnskilfull person may easily both vnderstand any hard English words, which they shall in the Scriptures, Sermons, or elsewhere heare or reade : and also bee made able to vse the same aptly themselues ; and generally, whatsoever is necessary to bee knoune for English speech : so that he which hath this booke onely, needeth to buy no other to make him fit, from his Letters vnto the Grammar-Schoole, for an Apprentise, or any other his priuate vse, so farre as concerneth English. And therefore is made not onely for children (though the first Booke be meere childish for them) but also for all other, especially that are ignorant in the Latine-tongue.

A further advertisement following the title-page emphasizes the efficiency of the treatise in the improvement of one's understanding of English :

I Professe to teach thee, that art vtterly ignorant to read perfectly, to write truely, and with iudgement to vnderstand the reason of our English-tongue with great expedition, ease, and pleasure.

I will teach thee that art vnperfect in either of them to perfect thy skill in few dayes with great ease.

I vndertake to teach all my Schollers, that they shall be trained vp for any Grammer-Schoole, that they shall neuer erre in writing the true Orthography of any word truely pronounced : which, what ease and benefit it will bring vnto Schoole-masters, they best know : and the same profit doe I offer to all other, both men and women : that now for want hereof, are ashamed to write to their best friends : for which I haue heard many Gentlemen offer much.

.   .   .   .

I hope by this plaine and short kind of teaching, to incourage many to read, that neuer otherwise would haue learned. And so more knowledge will be brought into this land, and more Bookes bought than otherwise would haue beene.

I shall ease the poorer sort, of much charge that they haue been at, in maintaining their children long at schoole, and in buying many Bookes.

Strangers that now blame our Tongue of difficultie, and vncertainty, shall by mee plainely see and vnderstand those things which they haue thought hard.

. . . .

I haue set doune a Table, containing and teaching the true writing and vnderstanding of any hard English word, borrowed from the Greeke, Latine, or French and how to know the one from the other with the interpretation thereof, by a plaine English word : whereby children shall be prepared for the vnderstanding of thousands of Latine words before they enter the Grammar Schoole, which also will bring much delight and iudgement to others. Therefore if thou vnderstandest not any word in this Booke not before expounded, seek the table.

If I be generally receiued, I shall cause one vniforme manner of teaching, a thing which as it hath brought much profit vnto the Latine tongue, so would it do to all other languages if the like were practised.

Coote provides directions to assist the "teaching Tradesman" who desires to instruct his own children and apprentices, or to learn himself. His treatment of grammar, spelling, and vocabulary, not to mention the other subjects touched, must have had an important influence upon the language of the middle class by helping to create in the popular consciousness the semblance of a standard of correctness, for the book went through forty-two printings by 1684. His appeal to the tradesman's pride and his insistence on the value of mastering the standard language have all the modernity of the present-day correspondence school.

The need for instructing less erudite readers was one of the preoccupations of the makers of English dictionaries in the early seventeenth century. Robert Cawdrey stresses the help that the unscholarly might find in *A Table Alphabeticall, or the English expositor* (1604), which the title-page of the 1617 edition further describes as

containing and teaching the true writing and vnderstanding of hard vsual English words, borrowed from the Hebrew, Greeke, Latine, or French, &c. With the Interpretation thereof by plaine English words, gathered for the benefit and helpe of all unskilfull persons. Whereby

24

they may the more easily and better vnderstand many hard English words, which they shall heare or read in Scriptures, Sermons, or else-where, and also be made able to vse the same aptly themselues.

Cawdrey insists upon plain speech that all may understand.

Among the classes to whom Henry Cockeram thought his *English Dictionarie* (1623) would be especially useful were mer-chants. The descriptive title, as given in the second edition of 1626, makes the purpose of the book clear:

The English Dictionarie: Or, An Interpreter Of Hard English Words: Enabling as well Ladies and Gentlewomen, young Schollers, Clarkes, Merchants; as also Strangers of any Nation, to the vnderstanding of the more difficult Authors already printed in our Language, and the more speedy attaining of an elegant perfection of the English tongue, both in reading, speaking, and writing.

In the preface Cockeran insists that by use of his dictionary "the capacity of the meanest may soone be inlightened."[38]

Joshua Sylvester, a merchant adventurer himself, with the in-terest of his social class at heart, took care that the reader of his translation of Du Bartas's *Divine Weeks* (edition of 1608) should not go astray for want of the meanings of words. He compiled a glossary, or, as he called it, "A Briefe Index, Explaining Most Of The hardest words scattered through this whole Worke, for ease of such as are least exercised in these kinde of readings."[39]

The didacticism of the middle class, who often mixed piety with useful learning, helps to account for the popularity of *A Christian Dictionarie, Opening the signification of the chiefe wordes dispersed generally through Holie Scriptures of the Old and New Testament, tending to increase Christian knowledge* (1612) by Thomas Wilson, minister of St. George's, Canterbury. In his preface to the reader Wilson explains the commonalty's need for a dictionary that would define

---

[38] A desire to help the less learned is expressed by Thomas Blount, compiler of the *Glossographia* (1656). In the preface to the second edition (1661) he says: "It is chiefly intended for the more-knowing Women, and the less-learned Men; or indeed for all such of the illiterate, who can but finde, in an Alphabet, the word they understand not; yet I think I may modestly say, the best of Schollars may in some part or other be obliged by it." *See* James A. H. Murray, *The Evolution of English Lexicography* (Oxford, 1900), pp. 30-31.

[39] Quoted from Grosart, *Complete Works of Joshuah Sylvester*, II, 69-81.

hard words and save the preacher the necessity of expounding every difficult phrase. This dictionary is an alphabetical arrangement of scriptural words which, the author felt, needed interpretation. Not merely were the definitions valuable for their biblical connotations, but many of the explanations were of such general utility that the book became a standard work of reference among pious readers, bent on mental and spiritual improvement.[40]

The interest of the Elizabethan citizen in his own language increased in the seventeenth century as his sophistication grew.[41] In addition to a realization of the commercial advantages of a fluent vocabulary, he acquired a further desire to conform to the manner of speech practised by those who had arrived socially. Since fine speech is often believed to be the mark of the fine gentleman, the aspiring tradesman was eager to improve his language. Hence one of the appeals made by Cockeram's *Dictionarie* was the help it gave in changing homely speech into elegant phrases.[42] Love of fine language, a prominent characteristic of Elizabethan aristocratic taste, was not confined to the upper levels of society.

If improvement of the native speech was an asset, the learning of foreign languages, as we have seen, was often a necessity. When

---

[40] The British Museum Catalogue lists an eighth edition in 1678.

[41] The steady stream of books on orthography and pronunciation, which appeared from the later years of the sixteenth century onward, is an indication of the general interest in language. *See* Henry B. Wheatley, "Notes on Some English Heterographers," *Transactions of the Philological Society* (1865), pp. 13-59; A. G. Kennedy, *A Bibliography of Writings on the English Language from the Beginning of Printing to the End of 1922* (Cambridge and New Haven, 1927), pp. 203-5, 267, and *passim;* M. Rösler and R. Brotanek (eds.), *Simon Daines' Orthoepia Anglicana (1640)*, in *Neudrucke Frühneuenglischer Grammatiken*, Bd. 3 (Halle a. S., 1908), Introduction; C. C. Fries (ed.), *A Special Help to Orthographie, by Richard Hodges* (1643), in *Michigan Facsimile Series*, No. 2 (Ann Arbor 1932) ; Watson, *The English Grammar Schools*, pp. 183-85.

[42] Cockeram explains in the preface that "The second Booke contains the vulgar words, which whensoeuer any desirous of a more curious explanation by a more refined and elegant speech shall looke into, he shall there receiue the exact and ample word to expresse the same : Wherein by the way, let me pray thee to obserue, that I haue also inserted (as occasion serued) euen the *mocke-words* which are ridiculously vsed in our Language, that those who desire a generality of knowledge, may not bee ignorant of the sense, euen of the *fustian termes*, vsed by too many who study rather to be heard speake, than to vnderstand themselues."

merchants, engaged in the trade with the Continent, the Levant, or the Indies felt the need of the foreign language involved, they set to work to learn it. To these hard-trading pioneers is due much of the credit for the stimulation of interest in modern-language study in the early seventeenth century.

PART III
THE CITIZEN'S LITERATE RECREATIONS

XI

STORIES FOR AMUSEMENT AND EDIFICATION

WEARY with didactic books intended to save his soul or to guide him along the paths of worldly success, even an Elizabethan tradesman, for all his preoccupation with self-improvement, at times yearned for stories that helped him to escape into the realms of gold, where knights jousted for the hands of ladies fair and adventures were more plentiful than cutpurses at a hanging. For despite the daring deeds of the Sidneys, the Drakes, and the Raleighs, the everyday life of the plain citizen often seemed savorless and dull, and he was glad to seek excitement in company with Amadis of Gaul, or Guy of Warwick, or some such hero of the romances that were to feed the imaginations of middle-class readers for generations to come. The sixteenth- or seventeenth-century ancestor of the shopkeeper who now indulges in vicarious adventures in the shadowland of the cinema sought his escape from the humdrum existence of buying and selling, in the copious literature of romance.

An important part of the output of the early printing presses in England consisted of romances.[1] Caxton translated and published a number of French prose romances in rather expensive format, since he was consciously appealing to aristocratic readers. His successor, Wynkyn de Worde, continued Caxton's labors in publishing prose romances, but he also printed a number of the

---

[1] Ronald S. Crane, *The Vogue of Medieval Chivalric Romance during the English Renaissance* (Menasha, Wisconsin, 1919), pp. 5 ff. I am indebted to Professor Crane's discussion for a number of facts cited here. No effort has been made in the present study to treat in detail all Elizabethan popular fiction, which has been discussed at considerable length in the histories of prose fiction. See especially J. J. Jusserand, *The English Novel in the Time of Shakespeare* (London, 1908); Lord Ernle, *The Light Reading of our Ancestors* (New York, 1927); and E. A. Baker, *The History of the English Novel*, 4 vols. (London, 1929), Vol. II.

older metrical romances, such as *Bevis of Hampton*, *Guy of Warwick*, *The Squire of Low Degree*, *Richard Coeur de Lion*, *Sir Eglamour*, and others of the type, which appeared in a cheaper dress than the longer and more expensive prose romances like *Paris and Vienne*, *The Four Sons of Aymon*, *Le Morte Darthur*, *Huon of Bordeaux*, and *Valentine and Orson*. With Wynkyn de Worde's cheaper publications there began an appeal to lower-class readers which was continued and emphasized by the printers flourishing about the middle of the sixteenth century. William Copland, John Kynge, Thomas Marsh, John Alde, and several others were active in publishing inexpensive versions of chivalric fiction in both prose and verse, but they were content, for the most part, merely to reproduce stories that had already appeared in print. Although lords and ladies and men of letters continued to read the romances to some extent throughout the sixteenth century, the appeal was made more and more to readers of the less favored classes, while academic critics and moralists began to level their darts against the iniquity of romance-reading. From the mid-sixteenth century onward, the old-fashioned tales of chivalry were gradually relegated to the more unsophisticated readers, and romances, which had begun as aristocratic works, appeared in cheap quartos and at last reached the nadir of their fame as penny-chapbooks to be hawked by peddlers at fairs. Published in such cheap editions that anyone could buy them, these knightly romances provided the populace with a literature of escape analogous to that now supplied by a deluge of short stories and novels.

But eager though he was for the excitement furnished by stories of adventure, the middle-class reader—and to a less extent, his aristocratic contemporary—had a holy fear of vain and idle works. Feeling the stab of his conscience whenever he succumbed to the allurements of mere amusement, he wanted to believe that there was mingled in his literary entertainment both profit and instruction. Fortunately, authors connived to assure him on innumerable title-pages and in countless prefaces that virtuous precepts were obtainable if he looked diligently and well. "As Bees out of the bitterest flowers, and sharpest thornes, doe gather the sweetest hony: so out of obscene and wicked fables some profit may be extracted," commented Francis Meres in a passage of advice on reading.[2] The moral justification of the story-teller's art, already established as a literary convention in the Middle Ages, when many a purveyor of broad tales managed to extract therefrom ingenious moral lessons, remained insistent under the influence of Puritanism in the sixteenth and seventeenth centuries, and, as a result, one finds an exaggeration of moral sentiments and professions of good purposes in Elizabethan fiction. But since human nature, even under Puritanism, remains unregenerate, some stories, frankly amusing and sometimes impiously coarse, got into print and doubtless were read with equal avidity by the apprentice and his master, each being careful to prevent the other from catching him wasting time with such lewd and idle toys. In general, however, authors, editors, translators, or printers attempted to give the stories they set forth a coat of moral varnish that would disguise gross faults. Not even the irregular behavior of the heroes of romance was beyond the pale of bourgeois respectability when the work had been properly glossed with assurances of its virtue-provoking qualities.

Not only did the appetite of the populace for romance-reading, briefly discussed in an earlier chapter,[3] feed upon traditional stories of chivalry that had circulated in England for generations, but it also demanded further satisfaction from translators, who ransacked Europe for new tales to delight their countrymen. The already copious literature of romance, as illustrated by the collections of Captain Cox, the Coventry mason, whose interest in "matters of storie" had excited the comment of Robert Laneham in 1575,[4] was augmented in the last quarter of the sixteenth century by importations from Spain and Portugal of the *Amadis of Gaul* and the *Palmerin* romances, which were destined to become the literary recreation of innumerable middle-class readers. Recounting the most extravagant deeds of knights in pursuit of love and adventure, these tales never attained to much popularity with cultured people,[5] but they increased the eagerness of tradesmen and other plain folk for histories of knight errantry in strange and

---

[2] *Palladis Tamia* (1598), fol. 267^v.

[3] Chap. IV, *supra*.   [4] Pp. 83-85, *supra*.

[5] Henry Thomas, *Spanish and Portuguese Romances of Chivalry* (Cambridge, 1920), pp. 262, 293.

wonderful opera lands. One of the appeals made by the romances was the vision of high life which they opened to the astonished eyes of simple folk, who learned from them precisely how noble heroes conducted themselves in all the crises of life. Like Ralph, the grocer's boy, in the *Knight of the Burning Pestle*, every apprentice was stirred by the daring deeds of Amadis of Gaul in overthrowing the Irish, or rescuing the Princess Oriana from the lustful Romans, or defeating the hundred knights who had attacked Lisuarte, King of England, or by some other of the thousand and one incredible performances of a hero who made the reader forget the dull business of traffic and trade. "What lack ye," cried the shopkeeper's apprentice in Cheapside, but his thoughts were far away with Amadis on the Firm Island jousting for the honor of his princess and declaiming : "O my deere lady Oriana, from you onely proceedeth all the strength and courage that euer I had : I beseech you now not to forget him, who so constantly requireth your aid and good assistance."[6]

The vogue of the Spanish-Portuguese romances began about 1578 with the publication of Margaret Tyler's translation from Ortuñez of the first part of *The Mirrour of Princely deedes and Knighthood*,[7] which "shewed the worthinesse of the Knight of the Sunne, and his brother Rosicleer, sonnes to the great Emperour Trebetio : with the strange loue of the beautifull and excellent Princesse Briana, and the valiant actes of other noble Princes and Knightes." Of the profit that readers might reap from a contemplation of the deeds chronicled by the Spanish author of this romance, the translator comments in the preface :

I doubt not gentle reader, but if it shal plese thee after serious matters to sport thy self with this Spaniard, yt thou shalt finde in him the iust reward of mallice & cowardise, with the good speed of honesty & courage, beeing able to furnish thee with sufficient store of forren example to both purposes. And as in such matters which haue bene rather deuised to beguile time, then to breede matter of sad learning, he hath euer borne away the price which could season such delights with some profitable reading, so shalt thou haue this straunger an honest man

---

[6] *The Second Booke Of Amadis de Gaule* (1595), sig. C 4ᵛ.

[7] For further comment on Margaret Tyler, see pp. 116-17, *supra*.

when neede serueth, & at other times, either a good companiō to driue
out a wery night, or a merry iest at thy boord.

Likewise, Thomas East, the printer of *The Third Part of the first
booke, Of The Mirrour of Knighthood* [1586?], assured the reader that
he had been moved to procure the translation by "sundry persons,
as also being willing of my selfe to further so worthie a worke,
adorned with all good examples of honour & magnanimitie, that
may serue to the exalting of vertue and weldoing, and to the
repressing of vice."[8] For nearly a quarter of a century, new portions of the *Mirror* were printed, until the saga of chivalry was
completed in 1601 with the publication of the ninth part.[9] From
the opening pages until the ultimate chapter, adventure is piled
upon adventure without stint, as princes, kings, and emperors
wander from Great Britain to Trebizond, and through all the
realms between, fighting battles, wooing princesses, and begetting
more and braver heroes. Very early in the story we see the
Emperor Trebatio pursuing the beauteous Princess Briana with
such success that presently "by the grace of the Almightie, were
begotten these two noble children, The Knight of the Sunne, and
Rosicleer. The beames of whose knightly deeds so shined through
the world, as that the worthy prowesse of their predecessors were
thereby eclipsed."[10] Certainly the deeds of the unborn princes
were to equal, if not indeed to eclipse, any romance-heroes that
the English populace had yet taken to its heart. And the transla-

---

[8] Dedicatory epistle. Even more vigorous was East's insistence upon the virtue-
provoking qualities of *The Second part of the first Booke of the Myrrour of Knighthood* (1599).
He makes this statement in the dedication :
"Considering also that as well the spirit of God hath by the hands of Moses, and of
many good men since, published, and that greatly commending them, the valiaunt
acts and puissant exploits of sundrie both good and mightie men at armes, as did
Homere, Titus Liuius, Salust, with many mo, the right martiall and euer memorable
acts of the Greekes, the Romans, &c. All which records of Chiualrie tending to animate others vnto imitating the like, and beeing as a spur to instigate and prick vs
forwards vnto prowesse, who else would bee idle and lie in obscuritie : I haue thought
it not fruitlesse to publish this *Mirrour of Knighthood* also, inuented and set forth rather
to encourage dastards and to teach the readie minded what excellencie is in puissant
and inuincible mindes, passing common iudgement, then to feede the reader with an
vntruth."

[9] The history of these romances in England is treated by Thomas, *op. cit.*, pp. 242-
301, to whose discussion I am indebted for some details.

[10] *The Mirrour of Princely deedes and Knighthood* [1578], sig. C 4.

tor redeems her promise that the acts of violence would not be permitted to offend the moral sense of worthy citizens, for we are assured that the Knight of the Sun and Rosicleer were somehow begotten in lawful wedlock, though, as is the way of romances, the details are a bit obscure. At any rate, the Princess Briana consoles herself in this manner over the violent love-making of her Emperor : "This was the Plaudite of his passion, and the beautiful princesse now became a wife somewhat against hir will, but when she sawe no remedy to that which was past, she comforted hir selfe in that he was hir lawfull husband, and therefore she pardoned him his boldnesse in troubling hir." Thus were romantic adventure and good morality wedded to produce a story that would entertain and edify citizens for generations.

It is indicatory of the sort of audience to whom the Peninsular romances were directed that the most active person in their translation was Anthony Munday, described by Professor Fitzmaurice-Kelly as "a dismal draper of misplaced literary ambitions," who, another literary historian asserts, "aided and abetted by various English publishers, started in this country a factory for the translation of chivalresque romances of foreign origin."[11] Munday began his labor of romance-translation probably with *Palmerin of England* about 1581, though the first extant version dates from 1596. The earliest surviving product of Munday's romance mill is a portion of *Palmerin de Oliva*, which he divided into parts, according to his own device, in order to turn out a book cheap and brief enough to appeal to all tastes and pocketbooks, as he himself explains, because

a Booke growing too bigge in quantitie, is Profitable neither to the minde nor the purse : for that men are now so wise and the world so hard, as they love not to buy pleasure at unreasonable price. And yet the first Part will entice them to haue the second, when (it may be alledged) the cost is as great, though it had come altogether : yet I am of the minde, that a man grutched not so much at a little money, payd at seuerall times, as hee doth at once, for this advantage he hath, in meane time he may imploy halfe his money on more needfull occasions, and raise some benefit toward buying the second part.[12]

---

[11] Thomas, *op. cit.*, p. 249.

[12] *Palmerin D'Oliva. The First Part* (edition of 1637), "To the Reader." This passage is also quoted in part by Thomas, *op. cit.*, p. 249.

Having made it possible for even the poorest apprentice to buy fiction on the installment plan, Munday now dared his middle-class readers to find fault with the substance of his tales. To do so would damn them as persons of low tastes:

Yet herein I am encouraged, that what hath past with so great apply-ance in divers Languages, can hardly merite to be despised in *England*, being matter altogether of delight, and no way offensive: For Noble and Gentle minds, are farre from iniuring the Historie, that hath so highly pleased the Emperours, Kings, and mighty Potentates, if then the Inferiour sort mislike, it is because they are not capable of so especiall deservings.

After thus advertising his wares as cheap, entertaining, profitable, and fashionable, the industrious draper continued his production of romances until he translated during the next two decades eight or nine parts of the *Palmerin* series narrating the adventures of the original Palmerin de Oliva and his knightly descendants to the third and the fourth generation.[13] The *History of Palmendos* and *Primaleon of Greece*, for example, relate the activities of the original Palmerin's sons, while *Palmerin of England*, though prob-ably translated first, describes the career of Palmerin's grandson. Although some of the action of the last mentioned romance takes place in England, it occurred in the dimly distant reign of Fred-erick, King of England, when Palmerin de Oliva was Emperor of Constantinople. Hence no one need expect to recognize the landscape, which is marvelously cluttered with enchanted castles, wizards, dragons, griffins, giants, and warlike gentry bearing strange titles, such as the Knight of Death, the Knight of the Savage Man, and other fear-provoking appellations. No ingredient of romance was too absurd to find its way into the *Palmerin* stories, which Peele must have had in mind in his delightful travesty of the genre in *The Old Wives' Tale*.

Not content with these contributions to the entertainment of

---

[13] The intricate questions of the relation of the various parts of these romances to each other, and of the order of their printing, are discussed by Gerald R. Hayes, "Anthony Munday's Romances of Chivalry," *The Library*, 4th Ser., VI (1925), 57-81, and the same author's "Anthony Munday's Romances of Chivalry: A Postscript," *ibid.*, VII (1926), 31-38. *See also* Celeste Turner, *Anthony Mundy, An Elizabethan Man of Letters*, University of California Publications in English, II (1928), 180-83.

his countrymen, Munday also translated about 1590 the first part of *Amadis of Gaul*, and in 1619 brought out a folio edition of the first four parts of that romance, "Discoursing The Adventures, Loues and Fortunes of many Princes, Knights and Ladies, as well of Great Brittaine, as of many other Kingdomes beside," as the title-page promised. Moreover, in addition to these Peninsular romances, which Munday translated by way of the French, he also rendered into English two other romances from the French, *Gerileon of England* (Part I, 1583; Part II, 1592) and *Palladine of England* (1589). And despite the absurdities of these romances, which outdid each other in fantastic adventures, many a reader reveled in them and took comfort from John Webster's assurance in a commendatory poem prefacing the third part of *Palmerin of England* (1602) : "Nor for the fiction is the worke lesse fine : Fables haue pith and morall discipline."

Romances, of which the examples just cited merely illustrate some of the most popular pieces appealing to middle-class taste, fell from the presses like leaves in autumn, throughout the sixteenth and seventeenth centuries, but the great period of productivity both for translation and original composition was the last quarter of the sixteenth century, when enough chivalric stories were produced to supply printers with subject matter for the next generation. The output was various and was not confined to works appealing merely to unsophisticated readers, for this was the period of Sidney's *Arcadia*, inspired by Greek romance as practised by Renaissance writers. Even though Sidney's *Arcadia* was designed for noble persons, there is every indication that they did not enjoy an exclusive monopoly of the story, which must have been bought by many a well-to-do tradesman, for it was frequently reprinted. A cheap edition was published in Edinburgh by R. Walgrave in 1599 in an effort to undersell the more expensive folio version published by Ponsonby in London. Imitations by later writers who were aiming at middle-class readers utilized the title of the *Arcadia* to attract attention. For example, Gervase Markham published in 1607 *The English Arcadia, Alluding his beginning from Sir Philip Sydneys ending*, which he described in the preface as a "morall historie" and again in the head-title over the first page of text as "the Morall English Arcadia." Though the *Arcadia* in its origins was completely aristocratic, like all popular stories it found its way at last into the consciousness of simpler folk.

This also was the history of John Lyly's twin didactic stories, founded ultimately on Greek romance,[14] *Euphues. The Anatomy Of Wyt* [1578] and *Euphues And His England* (1580), which were written to appeal to aristocratic readers, but which at length became the reading matter and the guide to conduct of aspiring upstarts, as a remark by Tysefew to Crispinella in Marston's *The Dutch Courtezan* (1605) suggests: "By the Lord, you are grown a proud, scurvy, apish, idle, disdainful, scoffing—God's foot! because you have read *Euphues and his England*, *Palmerin de Oliva*, and the *Legend of Lies*."[15] Expressing much good morality and copious advice in the manner of the conduct books, these two novels could not fail to attract the attention of burgher readers, as the multiplicity of editions and imitations indicates. Of the first novel, the *Short Title Catalogue* lists thirteen editions before 1640; of the second, twelve; and of both together, three editions and one issue. Besides the moralizing wisdom in Lyly, Englishmen (particularly Londoners) found much to tickle their vanity in *Euphues And His England*, which provides near the end "Euphues glass for Europe," where Europeans might see reflected the nobility of England and English institutions, the grandeur of London with its magnificent river spanned by a bridge lined with rich shops, and the splendor of its churches, hospitals, and Royal Exchange. The citizens, the court, the Queen, even Lord Burghley, are all painted in splendid colors to prove to others the greatness of the English. Here was a work which added truth to fiction so aptly that any citizen might approve.

Lyly's *Euphues* quickly impressed the popular as well as the aristocratic audience, and imitators began to make capital of his title. Munday was soon in the field with a Lylian novel, *Zelauto. The Fountaine of Fame. Erected in an Orcharde of Amorous Aduentures. Containing a Delicate Disputation, gallantly discoursed betweene two noble Gentlemen of Italye. Given for a friendly entertainment to*

---

[14] S. L. Wolff, *The Greek Romances in Elizabethan Prose Fiction* (New York, 1912), pp. 248 ff.

[15] Quoted by Thomas, *op. cit.*, p. 290.

Euphues at his late arrival into England (1580). Other imitations
followed Munday's.

The romancer, however, who knew best how to write for both
courtier and citizen was Robert Greene, whose prose fiction
enjoyed a continuous popularity from 1583, when he published
the first part of *Mamillia*, an opportune imitation of Lyly's *Euphues*,
until far into the seventeenth century.[16] Since it was "one of
Greene's most deep-rooted characteristics to write what he
thought he would have a market for,"[17] he naturally took advantage of the great demand for romantic stories in the last two
decades of the sixteenth century and produced a huge quantity
of fiction which, despite high-sounding dedications to ladies and
gentlemen, in reality found its greatest favor among the citizens
of London.[18] Although Greene did not confine himself to romance
and was capable of turning out a realistic fabliau, a large number
of his stories were strongly influenced by Greek romance and the
Italian *novelle*, many of which themselves are derivatives from
Greek sources. Greene's public had already learned to like this
type of romance in Thomas Underdowne's highly moralized
translation from Heliodorus of *An Aethiopian Historie* [1569?],
which was extremely popular,[19] and Greene himself may have
learned a lesson from Underdowne about loading an unmoral

---

[16] For a discussion of Greene's romances, see J. C. Jordan, *Robert Greene* (New York,
1915), pp. 34 ff., and Wolff, *op. cit.*, pp. 367 ff.

[17] Jordan, *op. cit.*, p. 19.

[18] Wolff, *op. cit.*, pp. 367-68.

[19] The translation went through five editions by 1617, and was only superseded by
William Lisle's verse translation in 1631. In editions after the first, Underdowne
claimed to have improved the translations so that the story surpassed the older romances because "the losenesse of these dayes rather requireth graue exhortations to
vertue, then wanton allurements to leudnesse, that it were meeter to publish notable
examples of godly christian life, then the most honest (as I take this to be) historie of
loue." But this romance is different from others, Underdowne continues in the preface,
for it shows evil punished and virtue rewarded : "If I shall compare it with other of like
argument, I thinke none commeth neere it. Mort Darthure, Arthur of little Britaine,
yea, and Amadis of Gaule, &c. accompt violente murder, or murder for no cause,
manhoode : and fornication and all vnlawfull luste, friendely loue. This booke pun-
isheth the faultes of euill doers, and rewardeth the well liuers. What a kingi? Hidas-
pes? What a patterne of a good prince? What a happy successe had he? Contrariewise,
what a leawde woman was Arsace? What a paterne of euill behauiour? What an euill
end had shee? Thus might I say of many other." Underdowne filled his margins with
notes which frequently pointed the moral or gave a bit of prudential wisdom. For

tale with sufficient moralization to make it palatable to the
puritanical middle class who consumed so many of his stories.
Although he later claimed to repent his idle "love pamphlets,"
the public was so well assured of the moral value of these works
that their consciences did not trouble them, and the more popular
of his pieces of prose fiction appeared in numerous editions. For
example, *Arbasto, The Anatomie of Fortune* (1584) had at least five
editions by 1626;[20] *Pandosto* (1588), eight editions by 1636; *Men-
aphon* (1589), four editions by 1616; and *Ciceronis Amor. Tullies Loue*
(1589), nine editions by 1639. Set in an idealized Arcadian world
and filled with sugary talk of love and sentimental morality,
these novels were even more in demand than the framed collections of stories that Greene was also publishing about the same
time.

Best known of the romances today is *Pandosto*, the unreal plot
of which is familiar in Shakespeare's *The Winter's Tale*. As in all
of Greene's work, we are assured that the story discloses the
triumph of the moral verities, for though "Truth may be concealed yet by Time in spight of fortune it is most manifestly
reuealed." Moreover, the tale is "Pleasant for age to auoyde
drowsie thoughtes, profitable for youth to eschue other wanton
pastimes, and bringing to both a desired content." With such
assurances, any citizen might comfortably follow the sentimental
fortunes of Dorastus, "in whome rested nothing but Kingly valor,"
and Fawnia, who possessed "such singular beautie and excellent
witte, that whoso sawe her, would haue thought shee had bene
some heauenly nymph, and not a mortal creature." The other
romances are identical in the quality of their appeal. The heroes
are brave and generous; the heroines are supernally beautiful,
virtuous, and wise; the villains are at heart good, capable of
eventual remorse and repentance.

Most popular of the romances was *Ciceronis Amor. Tullies Loue*
which closely follows the usual formula. Again the title-page

---

example, in the 1587 quarto : "The discomdities [*sic*] of a wandring life" (fol. 95ᵛ);
"Sorcerie is a thing against nature" (fol. 87ᵛ) ; "This beggery is no better described
by Heliodorus then counterfeted of some of our beggers" (fol. 85) ; "The giftes of the
Gods ought not to be refused" (fol. 68).

[20] These figures are based on the number of extant editions recorded in the *Short
Title Catalogue*.

provides a certification of the good morality of the novel, which tells the story "of Ciceroes youth, setting out in liuely portratures how young Gentlemen that ayme at honour should leuell the end of their affections, holding the loue of countrie and friends in more esteeme then those fading blossomes of beautie that onely feede the curious suruey of the eye." Moreover, the work is "profitable as conteining precepts worthie so famous an Orator." Cicero, noble-hearted but lowly-born friend of Lentulus, the patrician, is loved by the beauteous Terentia, to whom Lentulus himself is paying court. When Cicero pleads the cause of his friend, Terentia—like the Puritan maid, Priscilla—bids him speak for himself. Mindful of the honor between friends, Cicero will not betray Lentulus, but the latter finally realizes the hopelessness of his suit and relinquishes his claim. The course of love does not run smoothly in romance, however, and there is a certain Fabius, who desires Terentia so hotly that he raises a revolt in the city of Rome against Cicero and Lentulus. The quarrel is finally concluded by an oration in the Senate, in which Cicero begs to die for having caused so much strife. And the story concludes with an ending dear to the hearts of the people :

The common people at this began to murmour, pleased with the plausible Oration of *Tullie*, which one of the Senators seeing stoode vp and saide thus. *Terentia? Cicero* here hath shewed reasons why thou shouldst loue *Lentulus* and *Fabius*, but what reason canst thou infer to loue so meane a man as *Tullie? Terentia* blushing made this aunswere. Before so honorable an audience as these graue Senators and worthy Romayne Citizens, womens reasons would seeme no reasons, especially in loue, which is without reason, therefore I onely yeld this reason, I loue *Cicero*, not able to ratefie my affection with anie strong reason, because loue is not circumscript within reasons limits, but if it please the Senate to pacifie this mutinie, let *Terentia* leaue to liue, because she cannot leaue to loue and only to loue *Cicero*. At this she wept and stayned hir face with such a pleasing vermilion die, that the people shouted, none but *Cicero*. Whereupon before the Senate *Tully* and *Terentia* were betrothed, *Lentulus* and *Fabius* made friends, and the one named *Lentulus* as the *Annales* make mention maried to *Flauia*, and *Fabius* wedded to the worthy *Cornelia*.[21]

[21] A. B. Grosart (ed.), *The Life and Complete Works in Prose and Verse of Robert Greene*, 15 vols., Huth Library (1881-86), VII, 216.

But being an Elizabethan romance, this is not a simple tale of love. There is much moralizing about friendship and other abstract qualities, and furthermore, the story is not permitted to close without a pastoral note so common in the fiction of the day. Terentia, wandering with her companions in a meadow one day, encounters a shepherd, who protests that "now in yeaning time the wolues are verie busie," but is persuaded to neglect his sheep long enough to tell a tale of the love of Coridon and Phillis. Though Phillis was so beautiful that Roman senators had sought her hand, she loved her simple shepherd and married him amidst much piping and feasting "as soon as the sheepehards coulde come together."[22]

As a romancer, Greene invented nothing, but he made the didactic tale more readable than most of his contemporaries. Although his early stories out-Lyly Lyly in their euphuistic adornment, his later novels are more simply told and unite edification and a good story so painlessly that they were enormously popular. His amazing industry enabled him to produce a sufficient quantity of fiction to supply the average Elizabethan with a respectable library of novels and stories even if no one else had written in this vein. For middle-class readers Greene performed a worthy service by providing them with a quantity of reading matter which furnished amusement without smelling too strongly of damnation.

Several of Greene's contemporaries who tried their hands at romance-writing likewise met with popular success. One of the most widely read romances of this period was Thomas Lodge's *Rosalynde. Euphues golden legacie* (1590), which went through twelve editions by 1642 and furnished the plot for Shakespeare's *As You Like It*. Following the methods of Greene, Lodge wrote a sweetly sentimental romance set in the pastoral atmosphere of the Forest of Arden. And again like Greene, he emphasized the good lessons that the story might teach; and lest the instruction should be missed, he concluded his tale by warning "that such as neglect their fathers' precepts, incur much prejudice; that division in nature, as it is a blemish in nurture, so 'tis a breach of good fortunes; that virtue is not measured by birth but by action;

---

[22] *Ibid.*, pp. 177-84.

that younger brethren, though inferior in years, yet may be superior to honours ; that concord is the sweetest conclusion, and amity betwixt brothers more forceable than fortune."[23] Though Lodge attempted other romances, none was received with such favor as *Rosalynde*.

Henry Robarts, a middle-class writer who reflects the taste of the London citizens of his day,[24] wrote three romances that combined elements of the chivalric stories with the newer Arcadian tales. His first attempt at romance was *A Defiance to Fortune. Proclaimed by Andrugio, noble Duke of Saxony . . . Whereunto is adioyned the honorable Warres of Galastino, Duke of Millaine* (1590), which he followed with *Pheander, The Mayden Knight* (1595), a chivalric tale in the manner of the Peninsular romances, which was popular enough to be reprinted in 1617 and again in 1661. After these two efforts, Robarts tried to whip up interest by emphasizing patriotic elements in his next novel, *Honours Conquest. Wherin is conteined the famous Hystorie of Edward of Lancaster: . . . With the famous victories performed by the knight, of the vnconquered Castel, a gallant English Knight* (1598). The reader is entertained and edified with the deeds of the noble Edward in the Holy Land and sundry other countries, in the course of which he utters many brave and pious sentiments. At one moment we read of him "whose heart neuer was seene to faynt, arming himselfe to defende, casting his Sheelde on his arme, putting himselfe amongest the rowte of them, still crying *Lancaster*, God and Saint George for Englande, laying so about him . . . that euerie one that coulde make shift for one, was willing to giue him rowme, and to bee gone."[25] Presently, however, we see him taking another rôle : "In which extremitie, our braue English Caualere playing the part of a heauenly Phisitian, comforted his weake patient, in the promises of Christ Jesus, and his passion, earnestly perswading him, to remember his time euill spent in this worlde."[26] But the gentle strain soon gives way to an Englishman's righteous defiance as Edward exclaims, "But as I am a Knight, and a true English man, or euer haue hope to beholde my natiue Country, were they

[23] W. W. Greg (ed.), *Lodge's Rosalynde*, The Shakespeare Library (New York and London, 1907), p. 165.
[24] *See* pp. 415-17, *infra.*   [25] Sig. E 4.   [26] Sig. H 2v.

a thousand to my selfe alone, armed as I am, in the name of my God, and hope of my rightful cause, I would assaile them."[27] Thus Robarts created a hero certain to appeal to the patriotic tradesmen who read his works.

Another romancer who furnished fiction for the less sophisticated readers of the late sixteenth and seventeenth centuries was Emanuel Forde, whose novels of chivalric adventure were continually reprinted in cheap editions for the next hundred years. *The Most Pleasant Historie of Ornatus and Artesia*, which appeared first about 1595, had four editions before 1640 and many afterwards; *Parismus, The Renoumed Prince of Bohemia* (1598-99) had at least five editions before 1640; the earliest preserved edition of *The Famous Historie of Montelyon* is the quarto of 1633, though many editions after 1640 exist. One historian of the novel, commenting on Forde, declares that only Sidney ran so close in sustained popularity with generations of readers. The vogue of Forde and his acceptance by the reading herd he calls "a curious incident in the literary history of the English," which has little to do with English literature.[28] But if Forde's romances lacked the qualities that modern critics seek in good literature, they nevertheless pleased the London tradesman and his apprentice, who were enabled by them to escape from the realities of buying and selling, to go adventuring with Parismus and his colleagues.

Although the popular audience displayed a catholic taste for romances of all types, consuming with avidity the older romances of medieval chivalry, the newer Spanish romances, and the varied adaptations of Greek romance, national prejudices did, however, favor stories dealing with English heroes. Hence tales of Arthur and his knights, of Bevis of Hampton, of Guy of Warwick, and of other British worthies continued to edify and delight Englishmen throughout the sixteenth and seventeenth centuries. Undoubtedly the reputed Trojan origins of Britain did much to keep alive the interest in the Troy romance, first printed by Caxton in 1477 and regularly thereafter until the eighteenth century. Even though critics and moralists found much fault with these old tales, such fiction remained in high favor. The older stories were

---

[27] Sig. I 3.   [28] Baker, *op. cit.*, II, 124.

linked with the newest inventions of the romancers, in Francis Meres's condemnation in *Palladis Tamia:*

As the Lord *de la Nouue* in the sixe discourse of his politike and military discourses censureth of the bookes of *Amadis de Gaule,* which he saith are no lesse hurtfull to youth, then the workes of *Machiauell* to age: so these bookes are accordingly to be censured of, whose names follow ; *Beuis of Hampton, Guy of Warwicke, Arthur* of the round table, *Huon of Burdeaux, Oliuer* of the castle, the foure sonnes of *Aymon Gargantua, Gireleon,* the Honour of Chiualrie, *Primaleon of Greece, Palmerin de Oliua,* the 7. Champions, the Myrror of Knighthood, *Blancherdine, Meruin, Howleglasse,* the stories of *Palladyne,* and *Palmendos,* the blacke Knight, the Maiden Knight, the history of *Calestina,* the Castle of Fame, *Gallian* of France, *Ornatus* and *Artesia,* &c.   [Fols. 268-268v.]

Numerous allusions to the old romances, both before and after Meres's time, indicate that they long enjoyed the favor of the populace.

The legend of Guy of Warwick, which was solemnly related as true history by the chroniclers, excited interest in bourgeois readers because of the low origin and high achievements of a hero who not only could fight Saracens, giants, and dun cows, but also could gloriously defend his native land against the Danes.[29] Although the old metrical version of *Guy of Warwick,* like all the other metrical romances except *Bevis of Hampton,* passed out of existence about 1575,[30] new ballad histories of the valiant Guy began to appear in the last decade of the sixteenth century and continued to entertain unsophisticated readers for more than a century. Samuel Rowlands was patriotically stirred to revive the memory of "this dust consumed champion"—a labor which he accomplished in a poem of twelve short cantos, *The Famous History of Guy Earle of Warwick* (1609). Described as "Warwick's worthy Knight," a "Countrey-man of ours," Guy is treated as a figure of serious history. Though Rowlands could burlesque the romances of Arthur, Lancelot, and their kind in *The Melancholie Knight* (1615), he knew that his middle-class audience still liked the very thing at which he laughed. They approved his history of Guy

---

[29] R. S. Crane, "The Vogue of *Guy of Warwick* from the Close of the Middle Ages to the Romantic Revival," *Publications of the Modern Language Association,* XXX (1915), 125-94.   [30] *Ibid.,* pp. 141-42.

sufficiently to call for new editions in 1632 and 1635. Another poet of the people, Martin Parker, wrote a *Guy Earl of Warwick* (licensed 1640), but his production, mercifully, has been lost.[31] Bevis of Hampton, almost as great a champion as Guy, was known to Elizabethan readers in the frequently reprinted versions of the old metrical romance which continued in circulation throughout the seventeenth century. John Bunyan was one of the countless readers who were entertained and instructed by Bevis's heroic deeds.

A romance combining all the elements that appealed to bourgeois interest and patriotism was *The Most famous History of the Seauen Champions of Christendome* (1596) by Richard Johnson, the author of several other works intended to please citizens. A second part of the *Seven Champions*, "shewing the Princely prowesse of St. Georges three Sonnes, the liuely Sparke of Nobilitie," appeared in 1597, and the two parts went through six editions before 1640 and continued to be reprinted down to the middle of the eighteenth century. After wishing his readers "increase of vertuous knowledge," Johnson launches into a chronicle of the daring adventures of his Champions, emphasizing particularly the deeds of St. George, the English hero, and also the exploits of St. George's three brave sons. Since these lads were concerned with adventures in "the famous Cittie of London" and their entertainment there, tradesman interest was magnified, though Johnson omits "what sumptuous Pageants and delightfull Showes the Citizens prouided, and how the streets of London were beautefied with tapestry."[32] As Spenser was inspired to employ romance material in the *Faerie Queene* to encourage virtue in aristocratic breasts, so Johnson sought to stir the citizens with tales of heroism and magnificent deeds. The conduct-book ideal is even clearer in his chronicle of tradesmen heroes, the *Nine Worthies of London* (1592).[33] Keenly aware of the tastes of his unsophisticated romance-readers, Johnson never forgot their requirements, either

---

[31] Parker's interest in romantic legend is further indicated by his *A True Tale of Robbin Hood . . . Carefully collected out of the truest Writers of our English Chronicles* [temp. Car. I] and *The most admirable Historie of that most Renowned Christian Worthy Arthur King of the Britaines* (licensed, 1660).

[32] *The Second Part*, sig. A 2.   [33] *See* Chap. II, *supra*.

in his subject matter or his style. Even if aristocratic critics made sport of bourgeois taste, Johnson was undeterred and continued to write the romances that his public demanded, though he did break a lance on such critics, in the preface to the second part of the *Seven Champions:*

I have no eloquent phrases to inuite thy willingnes to read, onely a little barren inuention, whereof I haue no cause to boast, so excellently the wits of many in these daies in that kind exceed. Onely thy curtesie must be my Buckler, against the carping malice of mocking iesters, that being worst able to doe well, scoffe commonly at that they cannot mend, censuring all thinges, doing nothing, but (monkey like) make apish iests at any thinge they see in Print : and nothing pleaseth them, except it sauor of a scoffing or inuectiue spirite.

Johnson's next labor in romance was the *History of Tom a Lincoln* (licensed, 1599),[34] another tale likely to excite the interest of simple readers. Tom of Lincoln, bastard son of King Arthur and Angelina, daughter of the Earl of Lincoln, is brought up as a commoner by a countryman who later becomes a rich landowner. After a sort of Robin Hood career, Tom joins the Round Table and sets out on still other adventures, which include marriage with the daughter of Prester John, the fruit of this union being two brave sons, the Black Knight and the Fairy Knight, who prove even doughtier than their father. The author emphasizes the virtuous deeds and generosity of the sons, who, after many deeds of heroism, settled down and "liued a life zealous and most pleasing to God : erecting many Almeshouses for poore people, giving thereto great Wealth and treasure."[35] Surely such instructive examples were pleasing to respectable burghers, who must have felt a qualm earlier in the story over Tom's begetting. With one more romance, *The History of Tom Thumbe, the Little, for his small*

---

[34] The full title, quoted from "The Ninth Impression" (1655) in the British Museum, gives an indication of the nature of the story : *The Most Pleasant History of Tom A Lincoln That Euer Renowned Souldier The Red Rose Knight Who for his Valour and Chivalry, was Sirnamed The Boast of England. Shewing his Honourable Victories in Forrain Countries, with his strange Fortunes in the Fayrie-Land:* and how he married the Faire Anglitora, Daughter to Prester John, that renowned Monark of the World. Together with the Liues and Deaths of his two famous Sons, the Black Knight, and the Fairy Knight, with diuers other memorable accidents, full of delight.*   [35] Sig. L 3.

stature surnamed, King Arthurs Dwarfe (1621), Johnson closed his career as a maker of fiction for common folk.[36]

If there was any change in the attitude of middle-class readers toward the romances in the seventeenth century, it was to increase rather than diminish their appetites for this sort of fiction. Innumerable cheap chapbook versions were published and sold, not only to London shopkeepers and apprentices, but to countrymen who might buy them from peddlers or from hucksters at fair time.[37] A strong recommendation of the romances that had been in circulation for nearly a century was made by Francis Kirkman, the bookseller, in his preface to the third part of *The Honour of Chivalry* in 1673. Kirkman's enumeration is practically a roll call of the old romances, which, he maintains, are both entertaining and improving. "I my self have been so great a Lover of Books of this Nature," he declares, "that I have long since read them all; and therefore shall give thee some Account of my experience, that

---

[36] In the preface to this tale, Johnson gives a summary of some of the more plebeian of the native romances: "My merry Muse begets no Tales of Guy of Warwicke, nor of bould Sir Beuis of Hampton; nor will I trouble my penne with the pleasant glee of Robin Hood, little Iohn, the Fryer and his Marian; nor will I call to minde the lusty Pindar of Wakefield, nor those bold Yeomen of the North, Adam Bell, Clem of the Clough, nor William of Cloudesly, those ancient archers of all England, nor shall my story be made of the mad merry pranckes of Tom of Bethlem, Tom Lincolne, or Tom a Lin, the Diuels supposed Bastard, nor yet of Garagantua [*sic*] that monster of men, but of An Older Tom a Tom of More Antiquity, a Tom of a strange making, I meane Little Tom of Wales, no bigger then a Millers Thumbe, and therefore for his small stature, surnamed Tom Thumbe . . . The Ancient Tales of Tom Thumbe in the Olde Time, haue beene the only reuiuers of drouzy age at midnight; old and young haue with his Tales chim'd Mattens till the cocks crow in the morning; Batchelors and Maides with his Tales haue compassed the Christmas fire-blocke, till the Curfew-Bell rings candle out; the old Shepheard and the young Plow boy after their dayes labour, haue carold out a Tale of Tom Thumbe to make them merry with: and who but little Tom, hath made long nights seem short and heauy toyles easie? Therefore (gentle Reader) considering that old modest mirth is turned naked out of doors, while nimble wit in the great Hall sits upon a soft cushion giuing dry bobbes; for which cause I will, if I can, new cloath him in his former liuery, and bring him againe into the chimney Corner, where now you must imagine me to sit by a good fire, amongst a company of good fellowes ouer a well spic'd Wassel-bowle of Christmas Ale telling of these merry Tales which hereafter follow."—Quoted from Joseph Ritson, *Ancient Popular Poetry*, 2 vols. (Edinburgh, 1884), II, 26-28.

[37] For some indication of the multiplicity of the chapbook versions of the romances, see Arundell Esdaile, *A List of English Tales and Prose Romances Printed before 1740*, The Bibliographical Society (London, 1912), *passim*.

may be both Pleasant and Profitable to thee. As first, I tell thee
be thou of what Age, or Sex soever, it is convenient for thee to
read these sorts of Historyes, . . ."[38]

Seventeenth-century publishers were so eager to emphasize the
improving quality of their fiction that in 1634 an editor of Malory
published the *Morte d' Arthur* as *The Most Ancient And Famous History Of The Renowned Prince Arthur King of Britaine . . . Newly refined, and published for the delight and profit of the Reader*, a version designed to appeal to Puritan readers by expurgating all profane
swearing of Arthur's knights and omitting all popish utterances,
as the printer is careful to indicate in the preface:

In many places this Volume is corrected (not in language but in phrase)
for here and there, King Arthur or some of his Knights were declared
in their communications to sweare prophane, and vse superstitious
speeches, all (or the most part) of which is either amended or quite
left out, by the paines and industry of the Compositor and Corrector
at the Presse; so that as it is now it may passe for a famous piece of
Antiquity, reuiued almost from the gulph of oblivion, and renued for
the pleasure and profit of present and future times.

Nourishing a subconscious hope that romantic fiction would in
some way be profitable, the middle class read it eagerly.

Closely related to the chapbook romances were the wonder
stories, which also circulated throughout the late sixteenth and
seventeenth centuries in chapbook versions. The stories of Fortunatus, of Friar Bacon and Friar Bungay, of the life and death
of Dr. Faustus, of Friar Rush, and of other similar worthies who
meddled with magic, were frequently printed. Indeed, *The Historie of the damnable life, and deserued death of Doctor Iohn Faustus*, first
printed in England in 1592, became one of the most popular
books of the seventeenth century and was one of the favorite
pieces of fiction in Puritan New England.[39] Its relation to the
witch hysteria might be worth study.

Experience in following the devious adventures of romantic
heroes may have helped readers to keep track of the plots of cer-

---

[38] Quoted by Thomas, *op. cit.*, p. 258.
[39] Thomas G. Wright, *Literary Culture in Early New England, 1620-1730* (New Haven,
1920), pp. 224-37, where invoice records of importations of this book are given.

tain highly instructive allegorical works of fiction[40] which edified middle-class readers of Tudor and Stuart England and prepared the way for Bunyan's *Pilgrim's Progress*, a work that owed almost as much to chivalric romance as to Christian piety.

An early anticipation of Bunyan's allegorical method is found in a translation from the French of Jean de Cartigny made by William Goodyear, a merchant of Southampton, entitled *The Voyage of the Wandering Knight. Deuised by Iohn Carthenie, a Frenchman* (1581). The title-page of the edition of 1607[41] advertises its good points by adding that it is a work "Shewing al the course of mans life, how apt he is to follow vanitie, and how hard it is for him to attaine to Vertue." It is dedicated to Sir Francis Drake, who is praised for his modesty, so unlike most travelers, who boast outrageously about crossing "a Sea of sixe daies sayling." Evidently the book was popular. Later editions appeared about 1609(?) and 1626(?). The narrative, related in simple prose and in the first person, tells of the Wandering Knight's adventures in the world of Folly, where he sees the Palace of Worldly Felicity, with a stately tower for each of the Seven Deadly Sins.[42] At length the Wandering Knight is redeemed from sin and is led by Faith to the City of Heaven. William Goodyear, who was careful to sign himself "Merchant," must have been hailed as a benefactor by tradesmen in search of pious tales.

[40] It may be worth noting that Sir Thomas More's *Utopia*, an allegorical romance of a different type from the ones discussed here, was first translated in 1551 "by Raphe Robynson Citizein and Goldsmythe of London, at the procurement, and earnest request of George Tadlowe Citezein & Haberdassher of the same Citie." In a dedication to Sir William Cecil, Robinson calls attention to the virtues of the work, which is "fruteful & profitable," full of "good, & holsome lessons, which be there in great plēty, & aboūdaūce." Robinson maintains that he was only led to translate the work by the unceasing persuasion of Tadlowe, the haberdasher, and "diuers other" citizens. He describes Tadlowe as "an honest citizien of London, & in the same citie well accepted, & of good reputatiō." The *Utopia* seems to have been read by citizens for the next century, five editions being recorded before 1640.

[41] All my references are to the 1607 edition in the British Museum.

[42] A part of the table of contents will give some idea of the plan and scope of the allegory:

"The contents of the first part of this present Booke.

"The Wandring Knight declareth his intent and foolish enterprise wishing and supposing in this world to find true felicitie. Chap. 1.

"The wandring Knight declareth vnto Dame Folly his gouernesse what is his intent. Chap. 2.

Even a serving man felt the allegorical urge, and James Yates turned out *The Castell of Courtesie, Whereunto is adioyned The Holde of Humilitie: With the Chariot of Chastitie thereunto annexed. Also a Dialogue betweene Age and Youth, and other matters herein conteined. By Iames Yates Seruingman* (1582). Yates identifies himself with Youth lost in a thorny wood. To his rescue comes Ayde who conducts him to the Castell of Courtesie, over the gate of which, in Yates's execrable verse, is a warning that

> No hoggish hob, nor currish carle
> may once presume so bolde
> To enter here within this Gate,
> this Castle to beholde.   [Sig. B 3.]

Clemencie is captain of the castle. Youth interests himself in the customs of the place and finds that Force does not prevail there, but "Good will is to be wayed though welthe doth want." Adjoining the Castle of Courtesie is the Hold of Humilitie to which the froward and stubborn are not admitted. After a long dialogue of

---

"Folly and Euill will prouides the Knight of apparell, armour, and horses. Chap. 3.

"Folly apparelleth and armeth the wandring Knight. Chap. 4.

"Folly vpon the way sheweth the Knight many of her auncient proceedings, and how many great and notable personages she had gouerned. Chap. 5.

"The wandring Knight finding two wayes, and doubtfull whether of them to take, there chanced to come to him Vertue and Voluptuousnesse, either of them offering to conduct and guide the Knight on the way. Chap. 6.

"The wandring Knight by the counsaile of Folly, left Lady Vertue, and followed Voluptuousnesse, which lead him to the Pallace of worldly Felicitie. Chap. 7.

"How the wandring Knight was receiued and welcommed to the Pallace of worldly Felicitie. Chap. 8.

"Voluptuousnesse sheweth the wandring Knight some part of the Pallace, and after brought him to dinner. Chap. 9.

"Dinner being done, Voluptuousnesse sheweth the wandring Knight the rest of the Pallace of worldly Felicitie, with the superscription of the Towers thereof: and by the Author is declared the euill fruit of certaine notorious sinnes. Chap. 10.

"The scituation or standing of the Pallace of worldly Felicitie. Chap. 11.

"The author declareth how the wandring Knight, and such like voluptuous liuers in the world, transgresse the ten cōmandements of almightie God vnder written. Chap. 12.

"The Knight went for to recreate himselfe, and viewed the warrens and Forrests, which were about the Pallace of worldly felicitie: anone hee saw it sinke sodainlie into the earth, and perceiued himselfe in the mire to the saddle skirts. Chap. 13.

"The Author cryeth out bitterly against worldlings, and their felicitie."

The foregoing gives the contents of Part One of the three parts into which the narrative is divided.

pious utterances between Youth and Ayde, they at length encounter Dilligence, who stresses the value of industry; and so
they make their tedious way to the Chariot of Chastitie. Such
allegories, to be put finally into Bunyan's simple prose, must have
found great favor with the common people. Several of this general
type have come down to us. Another example is *Laugh and lie
downe: or The worldes Folly* (1605), by a certain C. T., a dull
allegory about the inhabitants of the Fort of Folly.[43]

But the most popular of the pious allegories appealing to the
middle class was Richard Bernard's *The Isle of Man: Or, The
Legall Proceeding in Man-shire against Sinne*.[44] Like Goodyear's translation from the French, this is a Bunyanesque allegory describing
the arrest, arraignment, and trial of Sin and his many confed-
erates. Godly Jealousy, aided by Love-Good and Hate-Ill, is set
to watch and arrest Sin in Soul's Town, which has four principal
thoroughfares, Sense Street, Thought Street, Word Street, and
Deed Street. The chief inn is the Heart. Mistress Heart and all
the maids, who are the eleven passions of the heart, are harlots.
Other adversaries of Virtue in the town are Sir Luke Warm, Sir
Plausible Civil, Machiavell, Sir Worldly Wise, and similar characters. Sin and his ribald associates are at last arrested at the inn
by Sheriff True Religion and lodged in the jail of Subjection,
whence they are brought to trial, along with the Seven Deadly
Sins, before Lord Chief Justice Jesus. The whole second half of
the book is taken up with the trial and conviction of the malefactors, who by this time include the Old Man, a personification
of Original Sin. Much space is given to the trial of Covetousness
and Idolatry, two "Capitall Theeues," identified with Catholicism. Many witnesses testify against them, including Poverty,
who blames Covetousness for the depopulation of villages, the

---

[43] Described by J. P. Collier, *A Bibliographical and Critical Account of the Rarest Books
in the English Language*, 4 vols. (London, 1865), I, 452-53.

[44] *The Isle of Man: Or, The Legall Proceeding in Man-shire against Sinne. Wherein, by way
of a continued Allegorie, the chiefe Malefactors disturbing both Church and Common-Wealth, are
detected and attached; with their Arraignment, and Iudiciall triall, according to the Lawes of
England. The spirituall vse thereof, with an Apologie for the manner of handling, most necessary
to be first read, for direction in the right vse of the Allegory thorowout, is added in the end* (4th
ed., 1627). Esdaile, *op. cit.*, pp. 21-22, lists an eleventh edition in 1640. The earliest
edition listed in the *Short Title Catalogue* is 1626. A sixteenth edition appeared in 1683.

ruin of the poor, and other crimes. The sinners are convicted and the allegory closes with an invective against the Catholics.

After an explanation of the meaning of the allegory, Bernard adds at the end of the book an interesting comment on the fictional method of teaching morality:

These things are the substance of all this booke couched within the allegoricall narration: which is no dreaming dotage, no fantasticke toy, no ridiculous conception, no old wiues tale told; some haue an humour to delight in finding of faults; . . . Some are so ridgedly graue that, forsooth, it is a misse to reade that, wherein they may haue occasion offered any way to laugh or smile: when they may remember that euen *Abraham*, the gray headed, old aged, and graue father once laughed; as they themselues will also, whosoeuer they be, when the humour takes them. . . .

If the manner laying those things downe in a continued allegorie, bee the offence to some, I doe suppose they know, that *Nathan* did teach a *Dauid* by an allegorie: *Esay* and *Ezechiel* taught the Iewes so too, and that our Sauiour spake many parables to his hearers. . . .

But the fault, if a fault, peraduenture, is not simply imputed for making an allegorie: but in following it so largely, and for inserting (as it were interlude wise) some things, for the weightinesse of the matter therein conteined, not seeming graue inough as the parables of Christ, & his Prophets were. . . .

I knew the natures of men in the world: I persuaded my self that the allegorie would draw many to read, which might be as a bate to catch them, perhaps, at vnawares and to mooue them to fall into a meditation at the length of the spirituall vse thereof: . . .

If two or three passages carrie not that grauitie in shew, as some, perhaps, could wish they did: Let these consider therin those places the enforced nature of the allegory. . . . Lastly, that euen those few passages are sharpe reproofes; . . .

There is a kinde of smiling and ioyfull laughter, for any thing I know, which may stand with sober grauitie, and with the best mans pietie, iustly occasioned from the right apprehension of things, else had not *Abraham* fallen into it, nor holy *Iob*, nor the righteous in seeing (which is strange) matter of feare.[45]

Here at last Richard Bernard provides a justification for laughter, at least for thoughtful laughter, which even the most dolorous

---

[45] At end of book; no signatures or pagination.

Puritan would find it hard to refute, for it is based on the authority of Christ and his prophets. It is significant that Bernard felt it necessary to justify even so pious a fiction as *The Isle of Man*.

The liking for allegorical fiction was so strong with the middle class that when the merchant Gerard de Malynes, an industrious if misguided economist, wished to discuss the evils of foreign exchange, he at first tried an allegorical tale which he entitled *Saint George For England, Allegorically described: By Gerard De Malynes Merchant* (1601). A careful epistle "To the louing Reader" promises to lay bare the "effects of the subtill and cruell dealings of a Dragon, of whose manner and behauiour diuerse haue written heretofore." Malynes explains the significance of this dragon and the other allegorical figures:

This dragon is called Foenus politicum, his two wings are Vsura palliata and Vsura explicata, and his taile inconstant Cambium. The virgin is the kings treasure: the champion Saint George is the kings authoritie, armed with right armor of a Christian: who with the sword of the spirit of Gods most holy word, explained and corrobarated with seuerall other lawes, signified by the Pybal horse whereon he was mounted: did destroy the cruell dragon, rescuing the kings daughter, and deliuering the commonwealth, as by the circumstances of the historie may appeare: the Allegorie whereof requireth a due consideration, which would dilate vnto another treatise. [Sig. A 8.]

The allegory, beginning with a short paraphrase of the opening of the prologue to the *Canterbury Tales*, is a tiresome description of the dragon's misdeeds in the island. The author, who had the dragon revealed in a vision, ends his narrative with the pious wish that he might have St. George, "that valiant champion prefigured vnto me as the dragon was, for then no doubt the deliuerance expected and long required would ensue."

The taste for allegorical fiction had been inherited, of course, from the Middle Ages, when moral allegories had been a common medium of instruction and entertainment. It is not surprising, therefore, that some of the older forms should have persisted. Relics of the beast fables still remained, and the old story of Reynard the Fox, one of Caxton's first publications, was reprinted many times later in highly moralized forms. The title-page of an edition published in 1550 by T. Gaultier urges the usefulness of the lessons therein, not only to lords and prelates, but also to "marchaūtes & other comen people." One version, licensed in 1586, is extant in an edition which announces itself as *The Most delectable History of Reynard the Fox. Newly Corrected. . . . Also Augmented and Inlarged with sundry excellent Moralls . . . Neuer before this time Imprinted* (1620). Perhaps the inherited taste for beast stories made it easy for the classical fables of Aesop to gain wide circulation in the sixteenth and seventeenth centuries, when Latin texts were used for instruction in the schools and translated versions were widely read among all classes. The popularity of Aesop led to the publication of other fables which also had a great vogue. Thomas North's translation of the *Fables of Bidpai* as *The Morall Philosophie of Doni* (1570) had a second edition in 1601. In the prologue to this edition the translator urges the reader to look for the esoteric meanings, the "high doctrine" and the lessons therein, "For alwayes the worke of these sage Fathers carieth two senses withall. The first, knowne and manifest. The second, hidden and secret."[46] Animal fables make up a large part of that miscellaneous collection of highly moralized tales known in the Middle Ages as the *Gesta Romanorum* and published by Richard Robinson, a worthy citizen of London, as *A Record of auncient Histories, intituled in Latin: Gesta Romanorum. Discoursing vpon sundry examples for the aduancement of vertue, and the abandoning of vice* (1595). So popular was the work that it was frequently reprinted in the seventeenth century, until by 1713 it had gone through nineteen editions.[47] Samuel Rowlands employed the fable technique in part of *Diogines Lanthorne* (1607), a series of satires on the prevailing vices and foibles of the day, partly in verse, partly in prose. Some of the "Morralls" in verse are satirical fables. For example, he uses the old ant-grasshopper story to teach providence and thrift.[48] The work enjoyed such favor that no less than ten editions appeared before 1659. Another moralized tale of the fable type, much liked by the general public, was *The Pleasant History of Cawwood the*

---

[46] Sig. B 3.

[47] Esdaile, *op. cit.*, pp. 60-61.

[48] *The Complete Works of Samuel Rowlands*, 3 vols., Hunterian Club (Glasgow, 1872-80), I, 29-30.

Rook . . . also fit Morrals and Expositions added to every Chapter
(1640), which went through at least five editions.

The satirical tale with an allegorical twist often had a definite
middle-class appeal. Henry Chettle's *Piers Plainnes seauen yeres
Prentiship* (1595), for instance, comes in this category. Piers serves
seven masters, the description of whose vices gives an opportunity
for driving home a lesson of prudential morality, as in the case
of Piers's second master, a spendthrift courtier who has been
ruined by usurers and brokers through his unthriftiness. William
Rowley produced a timely bit of satirical allegory in *A Search for
Money. Or The lamentable complaint for the losse of the wandring Knight,
Mounsieur l'Argent. Or Come along with me, I know thou louest Money.
Dedicated to all those that lack Money* (1609). Throughout the city,
and later throughout the world, among merchants, innkeepers,
and usurers goes the search, in a year of depression, for vanished
Money, who is finally discovered in Hell. John Taylor's *A Shilling,
Or, The Trauailes of Twelue-Pence* (1621) chronicles the adventures
of a wandering shilling. In a dedication Taylor declares that the
travels of Sir John Mandeville, of the great Elizabethan explorers,
even of Coryate himself and the daring heroes of the romances,
were as nothing to this perambulation. Martin Parker wrote in
verse a fictional satire of the selfishness of the rich—a type of
criticism which the well-to-do are always ready to receive and
apply to their neighbors—in *Robin Conscience, Or Conscionable Robin.
His Progresse thorow Court, City and Countrey: with his bad entertainment
at each severall place* (1635). Robin Conscience seeks an asylum
among all classes—tradesmen, farmers, and aristocrats—but none
will have him except the poorest of laboring people, with whom
he finally elects to live.

Allegorical and didactic stories in verse and in prose, both
godly and utilitarian, found a receptive audience in the middle
class. George Whetstone, firmly convinced of the function of
literature to preach, was the author of a highly moralized collection of stories in verse and prose, set in an allegorical frame,
bearing the fanciful title of *The Rocke of Regard* (1576).[49] Though

---

[49] *The Rocke of Regard, diuided into foure parts. The first, the Castle of delight: Wherin is
reported, the wretched end of wanton and disolute liuing. The second, the Garden of Vnthriftinesse:
Wherein are many sweete flowers, (or rather fancies) of honest loue. The thirde, the Arbour of*

Whetstone writes a long address "To all the young Gentlemen of England," he provides much instruction useful to less aristocratic readers. In a later work, *An Heptameron of Ciuill Discourses* (1582), ostensibly a collection of prose romances for ladies and gentlemen, he suggests on the title-page that therein "the Inferiour, may learne such Rules of Ciuil Gouernmēt, as wil rase out the Blemish of their basenesse."

In the didactic vein was William Averell's *A Dyall for dainty Darlings* (1584),[50] a series of moralized stories, dedicated to a merchant, William Wrathe, warden of the Company of the Mercers. Averell's epistle to the reader gives assurance that the stories are "as gainsome as pleasaunt." The last piece will indicate the nature of the work. It relates

The rare vertue of a Maiden, and singular discretion of a young man, the one in her good and godlie gouernment, the other in his wise and prudent choise of a Wife. An excellent example to all Maidens, how they should exercise their golden tyme : and a perfect platform to young men, not to runne rashlie to the bayte of theyr pleasures, least they be caught in the hooke of follie, to their owne harme and hinderaunce.

[Sig. E 1.]

A likely young man encounters the pious heroine as she kneels in prayer instead of wasting her time "in trimming her head, in glaring in the glasse, in fingering her Lute, in singing of Sonnets, in deuising of Letters, in daunsing with her Louers, . . ." Impressed with her virtue, the youth marries the girl. This treatise in story form is filled with the doctrine that goodness receives an earthly reward and that evil is always punished.[51]

Vertue: Wherein slaunder is highly punished, and vertuous Ladies and Gentlewomen, worthily commended. The fourth, the Ortchard of Repentance: Wherein are discoursed, the miseries that followe dicing, the mischiefes of quareling, the fall of prodigalitie: and the souden ouerthrowe of foure notable cousners, with diuers other morall, natural, & tragicall discourses: documents and admonitions : being all the inuention, collection and translation of George Whetstone Gent. (1576).

[50] A Dyall for dainty Darlings, rockt in the cradle of Securitie. A Glasse for all disobedient Sonnes to looke in. A Myrrour for vertuous Maydes. A Booke right excellent, garnished with many woorthy examples, and learned aucthorities, most needefull for this tyme present (1584).

[51] Averell stressed the virtue-provoking quality of his rhyming love story entitled An excellent Historie bothe pithy and pleasant, Discoursing On the life and death of Charles and Iulia, two Brittish, or rather Welshe louers. No lesse delightfull for varietie, then tragicall in their miserie, not hurtfull to youthe, nor vnprofitable to age, but commodious to bothe (1581). He admits that in regard to amorous affections, "I haue somewhat louer lyke depaynted,

The mine from which most Elizabethan short stories were dug was, of course, the collections of Italian *novelle* which contained stories more often amusing than instructive. When Boccaccio, Bandello, Cinthio, Straparola, and other Italian authors and compilers of *novelle* were pillaged by Elizabethan writers, their tales were frequently given a coating of moral varnish to make them more acceptable to the puritanical tastes of Englishmen, and even so, they were regarded with suspicion. While some middle-class readers no doubt bought William Painter's two-volume collection of tales, fancifully called *The Palace of Pleasure* (1566, 1567), and Geoffrey Fenton's *Certaine Tragicall Discourses* (1567), the collection of Italian *novelle* that made the most widespread popular appeal was George Pettie's *A Petite Pallace of Pettie his Pleasure* [1576] which went through five editions by 1613. With a knowledge of what an English public demanded, Pettie heavily moralized his stories to take away some of the taint of Italian iniquity which always clung to the fiction that was imported directly. Although much Italian fiction was circulating in England in one form or another, the Elizabethan public viewed it skeptically until it had been provided with proper tags certifying its virtues. When Boccaccio's *Decameron* was first translated in 1620, the dedication emphasized the usefulness of the work. Previously published fragments, stolen out of Boccaccio, the translator observes, have not been savored with "his singular morall applications"— an omission which has done the author a disservice,

For, as it was his full scope and ayme, by discouering all vices in their vgly deformities, to make their mortall enemies (the sacred Vertues) to shine the clearer, being set downe by them, and compared with them : so euery true and vpright iudgement, in obseruing the course of these well-carried Nouels, shall plainly perceiue, that there is no spare made of reproofe in any degree whatsoeuer, where sin is embraced, and grace neglected ; but the iust deseruing shame and punishment thereon inflicted, that others may be warned by their example. In imitation of witty Aesope ; who reciteth not a Fable, but graceth

not that I bringe Oyle to maintaine the light of Venus lampe, but with the saciety therof quight to extinguish her flame, that Loouers perusing the wanton contracts of these two Venus darlings, may by the fulsomeness of theyr straunge euents, be driuen into disliking of so vaine a pastime, or rather a madnesse, . . ."—Preface, sigs. A 3- A 3ᵛ. In patriotic British fashion the ancestry of the lovers is traced to Brutus.

it with a iudicious morall application; as many other worthy Writers haue done the like.

This reads as if the translator sincerely believed it, and undoubtedly many a reader was reassured. When the printer Jaggard brought out a new edition of the *Decameron* in 1625 he was careful to entitle it *The Modell Of Wit, Mirth, Eloquence, and Conuersation,* hinting thereby that readers would find profit and utility in the stories. Italian stories had to emphasize whatever virtuous qualities could be discovered in them.

Probably the best disguised of the Italian *novelle* were presented to unsuspecting readers in the numerous stories that Robert Greene inserted in his nicely moralized frameworks. None could surpass him in giving a virtuous twist to short stories, and he proved as proficient in adapting Italian *novelle* to the taste of Elizabethan readers as he was at domesticating Greek romance. From Boccaccio and from other Italian sources he borrowed plots which he utilized in the tales that composed his collections of framed stories such as *Planetomachia* (1585), *Penelopes Web* (1587), *Perimedes* (1588), *Farewell To Folly* (1591), and a half dozen others. Invariably there were such obvious professions of good purpose behind the stories that most readers were convinced that the tales were as desirable for instruction as for pastime. For example, in *Penelopes Web,* the first tale presents a lesson of wifely obedience; the second, the virtue of chastity; and the third, the good quality of silence in women. But despite the morals, Greene never forgot that he was telling a story, and his audience was accordingly entertained. When some of the "graver sort" began to complain about the love stories which he had published in such abundance, Greene declared that he too regretted them, and soon brought out a group of prodigal-son stories, equally entertaining, and, the author implied, more edifying than some of his previous "love pamphlets."[52] All sorts of material proved grist for Greene's mill, however, and he managed to insert some rather broad fabliaux into settings which conveyed moral lessons so proper that any citizen could be easy in his conscience while enjoying these stories. Amidst the repentant moralizations, for instance, in a *Groats-Worth*

---

[52] Jordan, *op. cit.,* pp. 55 ff.

of witte (1592), Roberto stops the picaresque account of his career to tell a tale of how a farmer was cozened of his bride and induced to marry another. Greene's readers, let us hope, enjoyed the stories for what they were—entertaining yarns—but they were grateful that the author provided so many good reasons to assure them that they were not wasting their time in frivolous and unprofitable amusement.

But even the puritanical middle class, for all of their lust after moral lessons, sometimes grew weary of elevating stories and demanded something hearty and mirthful. And when they thought of merry tales, their minds turned to old Geoffrey Chaucer, who enjoyed a strange dual reputation as a teacher of good morality[53] and as a teller of broad stories, the quality of which had given a peculiar connotation to the Elizabethan use of the term "Canterbury tales." Chaucer's fame was kept alive in the sixteenth and early seventeenth centuries by fairly frequent editions, three having been published in the reign of Elizabeth. It was with an edition of Chaucer's works that John Stow, the learned antiquarian and tailor, began his literary career in 1561, and he contributed information used by Thomas Speght in his text of 1598, which went into a second edition in 1602. Writers of tales for common folk, moreover, imitated Chaucer's method in the *Canterbury Tales*, capitalized upon his name, and in some instances borrowed from him. Thomas Churchyard, for instance, included "A Tael of a Freer and a shoemakers wyef" in *The First Part of Churchyardes Chippes* (1575), a story written in obvious imitation of Chaucer, though the verse is in jog-trot ballad meter. One of the most popular collections of fabliaux in the Chaucerian manner was *The Cobler of Caunterburie* (1590),[54] the 1630 edition of which appeared with slight alterations and a new title, *The Tincker Of Turvey*. As they make their way in a barge from Billingsgate to Gravesend, a tinker, a cobbler, a smith, a scholar, and a seaman tell unedifying but amusing tales on such themes as cozening wives and cuckolded husbands. The tinker, into whose mouth the epistle to the reader of the 1630 edition is put, announces that

---

[53] Louis B. Wright, "William Painter and the Vogue of Chaucer as a Moral Teacher," *Modern Philology*, XXXI (1933), 165-74.

[54] Six editions between 1590 and 1681 are recorded. *See* Esdaile, *op. cit.*, p. 37.

the stories follow the model suggested by "old Chaucer, (the first Father of Canterbury-Tales)." Preceding each tale is what the author describes as a "Neate Character" of the narrator. The stories were not intended for courtly readers, but instead, as the tinker explains, "A Farmer sitting in's Chayre, and turning a Crab in the fire, may here picke out a Tale, to set his Chops a grinning till his belly akes. Old wiues, that haue wedded them-selues to *Robin Hood*, *Clim* a the *Clough*, *Tom Thumb*, *Fryer* and the *Boy*, and worthy Sir *Isenbras*, may out of this Budget finde some-thing to maintaine a Gossipping." Like the farmer and the old wives, many a citizen and apprentice must have found entertain-ment in this little book, though some of the stricter sort doubtless objected to it. Robert Greene (if, indeed, he is the author) de-clared in *Greenes Vision* [1592] that he had been "burdened with the penning of the *Cobler of Canterbury*," at which he "waxed passing melancholy."[55] In a trance, the author is visited by Chau-cer and Gower, who discuss morality in literature, Chaucer maintaining that "Canterbury tales" are justified, and Gower insisting that they are not. When Chaucer tells a fabliau about how Tompkins, the wheelwright of Cambridge, was cozened by his wife, Gower objects that it is too full of scurrility, even though Chaucer insists that it is a good invective against jealousy.

Imitative of *The Cobler of Caunterburie* was *Westward for Smelts*, probably first published about 1603, though the earliest extant edition dates from 1620.[56] It too is given a vivid, realistic setting, in which five fishwives going by boat from Queenhithe to Kings-ton, tell the usual fabliaux. Chaucer also gave a suggestion to Thomas Brewer in *The Life and Death of the merry Deuill of Edmon-ton. With the pleasant prancks of Smug the Smith, Sir Iohn, and mine Host of the George, about the stealing of Venison* (1631), a chapbook collection of jests of the fabliau type, including a version of Chaucer's *Miller's Tale* of "How Smug was reuenged vpon a Barber, (his riuall) that made him kisse his tayle." Thus did Chaucer furnish amusement for readers whose taste was not too queasy.

If Chaucer connoted tales of scurrility to some, as Gower in *Greenes Vision* suggests, others managed to extract some morality

---

[55] Grosart, *op. cit.*, XII, 197.   [56] Esdaile, *op. cit.*, p. 137.

even from his fabliaux. One of the best expressions of the good things to be derived from reading Chaucer's *Canterbury Tales* is put into the mouth of the countryman in Thomas Nash's dialogue, *Quaternio Or A Fourefoll Way To A Happie Life* (1633). Although it is a merry Chaucer whom the countryman reads, he gleans from the stories much wisdom:

And when I am disposed to spend an houre merrily, I take along with me, either *Guzman* the *Spaniard*, or *Bocchas* the *Italian*, or old *Ieffrey Chawcer* the *English-man*, in whose Company I take much delight, being full of wit and merry Conceits, without offence. And one while I draw out of him his Summers-tale; by which I learne how an honest Farmer rewarded a cousening Fryar with a Legacie, and how he was *perplexed about the division of it*. Sometimes his Plow-mans tale, wherein I see the pride, covetousnesse, hypocrisie, and dissimulation of the Abbots and Priors, Monkes and Fryars of former ages. Sometimes his Marchants-tale, by which I learne what inconveniences doe ensue when crooked age and youth, *Ianuary* and *May*, are linked in marriage together. Sometimes his Manciples-tale, where I behold the punishment due to tale-tellers and newes-mōgers, pictured to the life in *Phoebus* his Crow. Sometimes his pardoners tale, wherein I see the fruits and effects of covetousnesse, drunkennesse, dice, swearing and ryot. And sometimes his Nunnes Priests tale, by which I am taught to beware of *flatters*, smooth-tongu'd dissemblers, frothy Complementers, windie bladders, that vent out nothing els but smooth dissimulations, and hypocriticall delusions, that with their capring wits can delude the vnderstanding with as much dexteritie, as the jugling Mountebanke or deluding Mimicke can the outward sences, that can put a good dye vpon any hue, make blacke seeme to be white, & white to be blacke, fowle to be faire, and faire to be fowle, . . .   [Pp. 26-27.]

Abbreviated versions of the kind of anecdote forming the basis of the stories in *The Cobler of Caunterburie* found their way into the jest books, which contained the epitomes of stories that had been in circulation since the Middle Ages. Jest books were exceedingly popular throughout the sixteenth and seventeenth centuries, and show little change in subject matter or treatment between John Rastell's edition of *A C. mery Talys* [1525?] and John Taylor's *Wit and Mirth* (1629).[57] Along with old jokes and quips were

---

[57] Examples of these collections of anecdotes are to be found in W. C. Hazlitt (ed.), *Shakespeare Jest-Books*, 3 vols. (London, 1864).

printed tales in brief, which frequently represented longer fabliaux boiled down to the compass of an anecdote. Typical of the
jest books designed for the reading of the citizenry was Richard
Johnson's *The Pleasant Conceites of Old Hobson the Merry Londoner*
(1607), which purports to relate true anecdotes concerning a bluff
haberdasher who lived in the early years of Queen Elizabeth's
reign, though actually many of the stories are borrowed from
earlier jest books. One example, "Of Master Hobson teaching his
man to use money," will serve as illustration for the whole *genre:*

Maister Hobson had a servant so covetous, and withall so simple wit-
ted, that all the money he could gather together he hid in the ground,
of the which Maister Hobson having some inteligence fell a coniuring
for it in this maner. With a good wand he so belabored my yong man,
that he presently revealed where it lay, the which summe of money
Maister Hobson tooke quite away, all saving a smale summe, the which
the poore fellow put to so good a use, in buying and selling, that in
short time he greatly increased it. When Maister Hobson understood
what he had done, and what good use he put his money too, [he] sayd :
sirra [since] you can tell how to use money, and learne to make profit
thereof, I will restore to thee all againe ; and so he did, which made
the fellow ever after a good husband.[58]

And any thrifty citizen could have seen the apt lesson and moral
application of this little tale.

Some of the jest books dealt with the picaresque adventures
of a rogue-like character who was able to get along by wittily
cozening his way through the world. Such books were the *Merrie
Tales Newly Imprinted & made by Master Skelton* [1567], *Scoggins
Jests* (licensed, 1566-67), the *Merrie Conceited Iests of George Peele*
(1607), and *Tarltons Jests* (licensed, 1609)—all collections which
enjoyed widespread popularity and were akin to the more expanded rogue stories that gained favor in the later sixteenth century. In order that men should have a legitimate and purposeful reason for indulging in the light reading that the jest books
offered, the author of *Scoggins Jests* wrote this reassuring prologue :

There is nothing beside the goodnesse of God, that preserves health
so much as honest mirth, especially mirth used at dinner and supper,

---

[58] *Ibid.*, III, 44-45.

and mirth toward bed, as it doth plainly appear in the Directions for health : Therefore considering this matter, that mirth is so necessary a thing for man, I published this Booke, named, *The Jests of Scogin*, to make men merry : for amongst divers other Books of grave matters that I have made, my delight hath been to recreate my mind in making something merrie. Wherefore I doe advertise every man in avoiding pensiveness, or too much study or melancholie, to be merrie with honesty in God, and for God, whom I humbly beseech to send us the mirth of Heaven. Amen.[59]

Besides the inspiration from the native jest books, rogue fiction received an additional stimulus from the translation by David Rouland of *The Pleasaunt Historie of Lazarillo de Tormes* (1586), a picaresque Spanish novel which was at once liked by all classes. Finding few other virtues to emphasize, the translator in a dedication to the merchant prince, Sir Thomas Gresham, points out a utilitarian reason for reading a book that gives "a true discription of the nature & disposition of sundrie Spaniards. So that by reading hereof, such as haue not trauailed Spaine, may as well discerne much of the maners & customs of that countrey, as those that haue there long since continued." Sir Thomas and his mercantile brethren must have found *Lazarillo*, as a travel book, more diverting than informative, but at least the translator made the reading of it easier for their consciences. Though disdainful of flattering the taste of commoners, Thomas Nashe in *The Vnfortunate Traveller* (1594) produced a novel so close to the type of *Lazarillo*, already a public favorite, that a second edition was called for in the year of its publication.

"Guzman the Spaniard," mentioned in the dialogue *Quaternio* as one of the favorite pieces of the countryman, was another example of popular rogue fiction imported from Spain. James Mabbe in 1622 translated from Mateo Aleman *The Rogue: Or The Life of Guzman de Alfarache*, which went through three editions by 1634 despite its two folio volumes. The third edition was enlarged by the inclusion of the Celestina story. The Spanish penchant for sermonizing, evident in both this work and *Lazarillo*, doubtless helped them to public favor in England. An effort to profit by the popularity of Mabbe's translation is apparent in W. M.'s transla-

---

[59] *Ibid.*, II, 46.

tion from Carlos Garcia of *The Sonne Of The Rogue. Or, The Politick Theefe* (1638), in which the translator assures the reader that he relates the sleights of thieves "to teach thee to eschew them," and he presents his book as "an instrument to avoide the snares which leud fellowes ordinarily lay for honest men."

Back of the foreign rogue stories and the native jest books lay a literature of confessions, crime exposures, and rogue biographies, which also furnished interesting reading for the populace.[60] Precisely as the purveyor of modern crime stories has sometimes sought to allay public distrust of his material by stressing the value of the exposures, so the Elizabethan author soothed Puritan fears with assurances that his tales would lay open cosenage and prevent crime. Illustrative stories illuminate the cony-catching pamphlets of Greene and the descriptions of the London underworld in Dekker, Rowlands, Middleton, and others.[61] Romantic biographies of figures from low life made the same appeal to Elizabethan tradesmen as the counterpart lives of gangsters and their friends make to the present-day populace. Sometimes, as in similar modern literature, the author whitewashes the subject of his biography, presenting a romantic picture of a person more sinned against than sinning. Sometimes he paints a black picture to deter others from following in the footsteps of sin. One of the best examples of the semi-fictional biographies was *The Life of Long Meg of Westminster: Containing the mad merry prankes shee played in her life time, not onely in performing sundry Quarrels with diuers Ruffians about London: But also how Valiantly she behaued her selfe in the Warres of Bolloigne,*[62] first printed in 1582. A remedy against melancholy is the claim which the author makes for his tale, for "amongst the three Doctors of health, Doctor Merryman is not the least, and that longer liues a man of pleasant disposition, than a sad Saturnist."[63] Meg, the heroine, a country girl from Lancashire,

---

[60] *See* the discussion of journalistic literature and rogue pamphlets in Chap. XII, *infra*.

[61] Detailed discussion of the relations of the rogue literature will be found in F. W. Chandler, *The Literature of Roguery* 2 vols. (London, 1907), I, *passim*, and Baker, *op. cit.*, II, 126 ff. *See also* Frank Aydelotte, *Elizabethan Rogues and Vagabonds*, Oxford Historical and Literary Studies, Vol. I (Oxford, 1913).

[62] Title quoted from edition of 1635. Esdaile, *op. cit.*, p. 101, lists four editions, though the *Short Title Catalogue* records only two.   [63] Preface.

s portrayed as a dashing and essentially good-hearted person, able to exchange blows or repartee with equal zest. Her sins are passed over and she shines as a model of generosity, as the author describes how she freely fed the needy at her tavern, being especially mindful of poor soldiers, so that "Shee was famoused amongst all estates, both rich and poore, but chiefly of them which wanted or were in distresse, for whatsoever shee got of the rich (as her gettings were great) shee bestowed it liberally on them that had need."[64] Having beaten a band of thieves, Meg exacted a promise that they would never again rob the poor or distressed, but she made an exception of "euery rich Farmer and country chuffe that hoord vp money, and lets the poore want"; these the thieves are permitted to "spare not, but let them feele your fingers."[65] King Henry VIII, impressed with Meg's valor as a soldier in the wars against the French at Bulloigne, gave her a pension of eight pence a day, and she even excited the admiration of the rival French leader, "the Dolphin," by sending him the head of one of his soldiers whom she had slain in single combat, so that he "sent her an hundred Crownes for her valour."[66] At length, married to an English soldier, Meg proved an example to wives by submitting to a beating from her husband to show that women should never resist their lords. Such are the virtues represented in this tale of an English heroine, a companion of Skelton, Will Summer, and Sir Thomas More, in the court and camp of Henry VIII. The verve, spirit, independence, generosity, and bravery displayed by Long Meg become the typical qualities of many a hero and heroine of popular fiction. To comply with public taste, Thomas Heywood created for the stage a typical dashing heroine of the people in *The Fair Maid of the West, or a Girl Worth Gold*, and Dekker and Middleton romanticized a more vicious type in *The Roaring Girl*.[67] The portrayal of the life of a wicked woman, to deter others from vice, is the asserted aim

---

[64] P. 10. [65] P. 19. [66] P. 22.

[67] Apparently the dramatists based their play on a contemporary novel which is now lost. A. H. Bullen (ed.), *The Works of Thomas Middleton* (London, 1885), IV, 5, calls attention to an entry in the *Stationers' Register* in August, 1610, of "A Booke called the Madde Prancks of Merry Mall of the Bankside, with her Walks in Mans Apparel and to what Purpose. Written by John Day." A version entitled *The Life and Death of Mrs. Mary Frith. Commonly called Mal Cutpurse* (1662) is quoted by Bullen.

of Nicholas Goodman in *Hollands Leaguer: Or, An Historical Discourse Of The Life and Actions of Dona Britanica Hollandia the Arch-Mistris of the wicked women of Eutopia. Wherein is detected the notorious Sinne of Panderisme, and the Execrable Life of the Luxurious Impudent* (1632). Presenting the biography of a high-spirited girl, seduced and turned bawd, the author assures the reader that everything is "to the reformation of vice, . . . and to the aduancement of vertue."[68] Despite this avowal, the story ends with the successful resistance by the bawd ("the most famous that euer the Sun did looke vpon, in her most damned profession")[69] of a mob's attack on her castle of vice. And Goodman concludes satirically that such persons must remain in "Eutopia" because the laws of England are so strict that they cannot flourish in the latter kingdom. All the interest that a criminal career excites finds a place in this tale, which escapes criticism by being an exposure of wickedness.

The bad end of a traitor is the justification of a romantic pseudo-biography by Thomas Lodge, *The Life and Death of William Longbeard, the most famous and witty English traitor, borne in the Citty of London. Accompanied with manye other most pleasant and prettie histories* (1593),[70] dedicated to Sir William Webbe, a London citizen active in municipal enterprises and philanthropy. After an adventurous career in London, where William Longbeard becomes the hero of cobblers, tradesmen, and apprentices, an influence with the king, and the opponent of arrogant nobles, he at last is convicted as a traitor for stirring up sedition and encouraging idleness on the part of the rabble. He makes a fitting end with prose and verse repentances. At the conclusion of the biography Lodge includes a collection of miscellaneous stories of pirates, of "many learned men, ancient and moderne, who violently and infortunatelie ended their daies,"[71] and of other sad matters. Such fictional biography, properly moralized, became a literary form increasingly favored by the populace in the seventeenth century, until this variety of story reached its culmination in Defoe's narratives. The biographies of characters from low life were peculiarly attractive to substantial citizens because they provided a glimpse

---

[68] Sig. A 3.   [69] Sig. G 3.

[70] Reprinted by J. P. Collier (ed.), *Illustrations of Old English Literature*, 3 vols. (London, 1866), Vol. II.   [71] Pp. 74 ff.

of a segment of life within their own world, peopled by types familiar to them, yet fascinating because it was forbidden.

If the Elizabethan middle class liked to read of rogues and rascals, they also took delight in tales of honest tradesman-life, where they could see their own virtues upheld and the vices that they disliked condemned. The greatest contributor to this type of fiction was Thomas Deloney, himself a skilled artisan (a weaver), who wrote always from the tradesman's point of view, whether his handiwork was a ballad or a novel.[72] His tales range from pure romance (but always romance in some way connected with trade) to the realistic portrayal of apprentices and their masters. His style is simple and homely, and he manages to catch the flavor, the spirit, and the zest of life about him. Yet withal, his stories are filled with a vast deal of prudential morality appealing to the love of the didactic in his readers, who could see the ideals of the middle class exalted in his tales. He also flatters the tradesman's vanity and chooses themes especially pleasing to him.

Since the tradesman liked to imagine himself appreciated by kings, queens, and nobles, Deloney makes this a frequent theme. In *The pleasant Historie of Iacke of Newberie* [1596-97], Jack, the "poor clothier" as he calls himself, raises a hundred men for war on Flodden Field, equips them at his own expense, and is praised by the queen. He entertains the king so lavishly that he is accused of extravagance, but Deloney hastens to point out that this was only to show the magnanimous minds of weavers. The king is pleased with Jack's manufactory:

. . . and his Maiesty perceiuing what a great number of people were by this one man set on worke, both admired and commended him, saying further, that no Trade in all the Land was so much to bee cherished and maintained as this, which (quoth hee) may be called, The life of the poore.[73]

Jack declines a knighthood, preferring to "liue a poore Clothier among my people." He is the soul of bourgeois honor and gen-

---

[72] Abel Chevalley, in *Thomas Deloney. Le roman des métiers au temps de Shakespeare* (Paris, 1926), has made a study of Deloney's contribution to the fiction which glorified London craftsmen. *See also* the introduction by F. O. Mann (ed.), *The Works of Thomas Deloney* (Oxford, 1912).

[73] *Ibid.*, p. 36.

erosity, albeit canny and shrewd. No man bests him in a bargain but no man can complain of his unfairness. Throughout *The Gentle Craft* [1597-98?] and *Thomas of Reading* [1598-99?] Deloney continues to glorify business. The dignity of trade and the nobility of tradesmen are his constant themes, always imbedded in stories that have an interest for their own sakes. Proof that Deloney knew his audience is found in the numerous editions of the tales. The earliest editions seem to have been literally read out of existence. Esdaile lists twenty-four of one or both parts of *The Gentle Craft* between 1598 and the middle of the eighteenth century, twelve editions of *Jack of Newbery* by 1684, and ten of *Thomas of Reading* by the end of the seventeenth century.[74]

Deloney had a tremendous influence in the development of the bourgeois taste for simply told prose tales, which, without too great a burden of morality, taught lessons of thrift, industry, sobriety, and the business ethics which lead to success rather than directly to heaven. With the numerous printings of his stories, the populace must have become as familiar with Jack of Newbery, Simon Eyre, Thomas of Reading, and his other heroes as the modern audience is with the faces of motion-picture favorites. The stimulation given by Deloney to the writing of prose tales of the less obviously didactic type was perhaps partly responsible for the increasing number of chapbooks in the first half of the seventeenth century.

Themes of domestic relations (which Deloney frequently employed in his tales), such as the management of the household, the proper conduct of husbands and wives, and the behavior of children and apprentices, grew in popularity in the late sixteenth and seventeenth centuries. An example of the domestic tale is John Dickenson's *Greene In Conceipt. New raised from his graue to write the Tragique Historie of faire Valeria of London. Wherein Is Truly Discouered the rare and lamentable issue of a Husbands dotage, a wiues leudnesse, & childrens disobedience* (1598), which describes the marriage of the beautiful but wanton Valeria to Giraldo, an old bachelor, son of a London merchant. Much of the first part of the tale is consumed with arguments against the marriage of January and May. Since Valeria, whose faithlessness grieves

---

[74] *Op. cit.*, pp. 38-41.

Giraldo to death, marries a prodigal wanton, who spends her money and leaves her to die in beggary, the author has no difficulty in drawing a fitting moral. To Dekker is attributed[75] *Penny-Wise, Pound Foolish* (1631), the subtitle of which significantly explains that it is "A Bristow Diamond, set in two Rings, and both Crack'd. Profitable for Married Men, pleasant for young men, and a rare example for all good Women." The story relates the reform of a profligate Bristol merchant through the devotion of a faithful wife, whose wisely invested penny supports them and at length restores them to prosperity. The patient-Griselda story appeared in practically every literary form from ballad to play. As might be expected, it is one of the stories that set out to teach proper loyalty in a wife. Chapbook versions of *Patient Griselda* were published in England in 1619 and 1630(?), purporting to be translations from the French, but having all the traits of vernacular composition. The title-pages emphasize the domestic appeal; for example, the 1619 edition is entitled *The Antient, True, and Admirable History of Patient Grisel, A Poore Mans Daughter in France: Shewing, How Maides, by her example, in their good behauiour may marrie rich Husbands; And Likewise, Wiues by their patience and obedience may gaine much Glorie.*

One imitator of Deloney deserves notice here as a further example of the novelist from the ranks of the middle class. He is Henry Robarts, seafarer and citizen of London, upon whom literary historians have heaped opprobrium for plagiarizing from Deloney's *Thomas of Reading* in his own *Haigh for Deuonshire. A pleasant Discourse of sixe gallant Marchants of Deuonshire* (1600).[76] A native of Devonshire himself, Robarts found in Deloney's novel a suggestion for his own, but he did little more than imitate the plan and take the idea of having six sons of Devon for his heroes. These merchants engage in many lusty adventures in France. Finally William, one of the six, having returned to England, marries and becomes such a generous master of his servants that he does not complain when his factor, James, loses a fortune in

---

[75] M. L. Hunt, *Thomas Dekker: A Study* (New York, 1911), p. 188.

[76] *See* Louis B. Wright, "Henry Robarts: Patriotic Propagandist and Novelist," *Studies in Philology,* XXIX (1932), 176-99, which gives a fuller account of Robarts's career as a novelist and propagandist. The Huntington Library, in addition to the quarto of 1600 of *Haigh for Deuonshire,* has another quarto, dated 1612.

gaming rather than submit to the taunt of a Spaniard. Here
Robarts observes that none might wrong the poorest servant in
his house, that he took such care of his men that they had their
diet at his table and could drink "Claret Wine, and Sacke with
Sugar in Stone Pottes"[77] without fear of his disapproval. Much of
the story is concerned with the adventures of the factor in Spain;
irrelevant episodes in the narrative also relate the fitting out
by the merchants of twelve ships against the French and the
king's march on Exeter to besiege the Cornish rebels. Robarts
is intent, not only upon telling a tale that will interest his readers,
but also upon representing the type of tradesman-hero so dear
to Deloney, Dekker, Thomas Heywood, and others of their kind.
These merchants of Devonshire, who might equally well be London tradesmen, display the qualities of shrewdness, independence,
patriotism, generosity, and forthrightness which must have been
admired as much in life as on the stage and in fiction. In a preface
to the reader, Robarts prepares for the impression which he wants
his six merchants to make:

Amongst many famous Marchants inhabiting the Western confines of
this fertile Ile, there was dwelling neer, and in the renowned City of
Exeter, Totnes, Plymouth, Barnestable, and Tyuerton, many of great
substance, as wealthy for vertue, as rich in coyne and credit: such
they were as for pelfe passed not, niggardnesse came not neere their
Mansions: their gates to the stranger alwayes opened, and their liberall hands releeued the poore. . . . These men whom God blessed
with wealth, had thankfull mindes to the giuer, acknowledging his
goodnesse, whose stewards they were: Noblemen for their bountie,
myrth, and fellowship, loued them: and Gentlemen of their Country,
desired their familiar company: their neighbours well esteemed them,
holding their friendship in great regard: and the poore duly prayed
for them, whom they dayly comforted. . . . wrong they offered no
man, nor could they brooke iniuries: in good causes as readie to fight
as to feast: with vsury they dealt not: aduantages of bonds they sought
not: Couetousnesse they abhorred: their honest Trade they liued by,
gaining wealth with conscience, and worship by desert: . . .

Surely in this story of tradesmen, the middle class found itself
sufficiently glorified. This novel marked the culmination of

---

[77] Sig. I 3.

Robarts's efforts in fiction, which began with romances of knightly adventure but which ended, significantly enough, with a tale of the adventurous and patriotic careers of plain citizens.

As the preceding pages have attempted to show, the Elizabethan middle class had an eager craving for stories, a craving which was satisfied by a voluminous literature of fiction that ranged from chivalric romance to realistic tales of London life. Although little of this fiction possesses sufficient literary merit to make it readable today, the quality of its appeal was not very different from that made by the literature which the average citizen still reads. If the Elizabethan lacked detective stories, he nevertheless was abundantly provided with tales of rogues and cony-catchers. If the tradesman of 1600 did not have magazines filled with narratives describing the climb of business men to success, he at least had Deloney's and Robarts's tales of prosperous craftsmen and merchants. If there were no novels by George Barr McCutcheon detailing adventures in mythical Balkan kingdoms, there were innumerable romances, scarcely more absurd, that offered the tired business man of the sixteenth and seventeenth centuries the same avenue of escape from reality. Entertaining stories, then as now, were abundant, and those which received the greatest acclaim were filled with a multitude of incidents, for the Elizabethan relished action. One quality more obvious in Elizabethan fiction than in modern novels and short stories was the didactic element which occupied such a conspicuous place in the literature appealing to the bourgeoisie intent upon improvement. Some of the most popular fiction professed to improve the mind, help the purse, and save the soul. As a last excuse, mirthful tales were sometimes necessary "to purge melancholy from the minde, & grosse humours from the body."[78] Surely even the grimmest Puritan could laugh in defense of his health. Given proper justification for the reading of stories, the Elizabethan middle-class reader consumed fiction as voraciously and as uncritically as his modern descendant.

---

[78] Quoted from the title-page of Nicholas Breton's *Wonders Worth The Hearing* (1602), a collection of a few brief satirical tales.

27

XII

EPHEMERAL READING

THE deepest contempt, as we have seen, was expressed by contemporary aristocratic critics for the popular appetite which demanded for its satisfaction journalistic pamphlets and ballads. Yet of all the literary relics of unsophisticated Elizabethan public taste, modern scholars have given most attention to the broadside ballad.[1] Since Sir Charles Firth's series of papers on ballads as historical evidence, read before the Royal Historical Society, students have turned to these ephemeral pieces with renewed zeal. With minute care Professor Rollins has edited many of the surviving ballads and has prepared an index of the ballad entries in the *Stationers' Register*, which gives a remarkable measure of the people's interest in the varied themes that found

---

[1] Of particular value are the following works:

Hyder E. Rollins: "The Black-Letter Broadside Ballad," *Publications of the Modern Language Association*, XXXIV (1919), 258-339; *An Analytical Index to the Ballad-Entries (1557-1709) in the Registers of the Company of Stationers of London* (Chapel Hill, N. C., 1924); *Old English Ballads, 1553-1625* (Cambridge, 1920); *A Pepysian Garland* (Cambridge, 1922); *The Pack of Autolycus* (Cambridge, Mass., 1927); *The Pepys Ballads* (Cambridge, Mass., 1929), Vols. I-II; "William Elderton: Elizabethan Actor and Ballad Writer," *Studies in Philology*, XVII (1920), 199-245; "Martin Parker," *Modern Philology*, XVI (1918-19), 449-74.

Sir Charles H. Firth: "The Ballad History of the Reigns of Henry VII and Henry VIII," *Transactions of the Royal Historical Society*, 3d Ser., II (1908), 21-50; "The Ballad History of the Reigns of the Later Tudors," *ibid.*, III (1909), 51-124; "The Ballad History of the Reign of James I," *ibid.*, V (1911), 21-61; "The Reign of Charles I," *ibid.*, VI (1912), 19-64; "Ballads and Broadsides," *Shakespeare's England* (Oxford, 1916), II, 511-38; *An American Garland* (Oxford, 1915).

The texts of many ballads have been made accessible in the publications of the Ballad Society. A dissertation published by Matthias A. Shaaber, *Some Forerunners of the Newspaper in England, 1476-1622* (Philadelphia, 1929), treats the ballads and pamphlets in relation to journalistic development. Further bibliography on ballad and pamphlet material will be found in this dissertation and in the introductions to Rollins's *Analytical Index* and his editions of ballads.

their way into broadside verse. As the public today consumes
newspapers that bountifully supply what the newspaper profession technically describes as "features" and "human interest," so
the Elizabethan man in the street bought and read broadsides
and pamphlets that related sensational events, strange wonders,
the untimely ends of criminals, and the frailties of humankind.
But these were not the only themes. Ballads of commentary on
current happenings were frequent, sometimes to the misfortune
of a writer who meddled too far in political matters. Ballads of
good counsel supplied the place of the "advice" columns in the
modern newspaper. Pious ballads of warning were numerous.
The art of propaganda, so highly developed in modern life, was
not overlooked in sixteenth- and seventeenth-century England,
where ballads, a ready means of reaching the multitude, were
employed in times of national emergency to stir up patriotism.
Verse histories and narrative ballads recounting the deeds of
notorious villains, national heroes, pious maidens, resourceful
apprentices, or their opposites, found ready buyers. Love was the
subject of much broadside verse. And, to the grief of respectable
citizens of Puritanic leanings, ballads of ribaldry caused many an
ungodly snicker. In the broadsides, infinitely varied in theme,
conventionalized in form, the life of the citizenry is reflected with
a naïveté and a frankness not found in more literary productions.
From the middle of the sixteenth until the end of the seventeenth
century and even later, these trifling verses poured from the press
to edify or amuse the populace, with little change in either form
or type of subject matter.

The vogue of the broadside ballad, dreadful as its verses usually
are, can be easily accounted for ; indeed, it is no stranger than the
current appetite for drivel in prose, which occupies such an
enormous bulk in modern newspapers. Like the newspaper today,
the broadside was so cheap that any apprentice could soon accumulate a collection, which had for the Elizabethan somewhat
more permanency than present-day papers hold for their readers.
This form of reading matter had the saving grace of brevity—
surely a virtue in an age overmuch given to windy utterance and
interminable sentences. Even an "idle" ballad could not consume
much time, and an apprentice might soon learn by heart a

ballad of good advice or ribald merriment. The diction was the language of ordinary citizens, simple enough to be understood by anyone who could spell out the words. The tunes caught the ear of an age that loved songs, even bad ones. The craving for the subject matter of the ballads was stimulated by contemporary events, for the Renaissance had created in man a new interest in the world about him. Yet the medieval survival of a belief in the hand of God in each event of man's life, gave the warnings discovered in every eclipse, storm, accidental death, and other untoward happening a peculiar fascination when set forth in a fearsomely illustrated broadside. Explorations had aroused such curiosity about the distant and the strange that the exhibitions of monsters, particularly from afar, drew throngs, and descriptions of such things naturally found eager readers. The morbid curiosity about physical deformity—confined to no age—made descriptive ballads of two-headed calves and malformed children a regular item in the stock of the ballad vendors. Last confessions and the behavior of criminals on the gallows differed from modern accounts only in the rhymes. When half the town could crowd to see an execution, a ballad which purported to describe the victim's own reactions to his evil life had for the spectators a personal interest. Particularly when all these themes were properly moralized to take away the taint of frivolous waste of time, the appeal was irresistible.

The broadside ballad was a form that unlearned men could soon acquire the trick of writing, and through it common folk found a means of self-expression. Certain citizen-writers like Thomas Deloney, William Elderton, Martin Parker, and Lawrence Price show the effort of poets of the people to supply what their public wanted and to express the ideas and ideals of that public. In the same writer frequently are to be found contradictory sentiments, all set forth in the effort to catch some phase of current favor. Martin Parker, for example, could one day write a ballad in praise of women and, on the next, pen a satire of their frailties. Ballad writers answered each other, or whipped up interest in their own productions by writing replies to themselves. Always these professional writers, these "pot-poets," as more courtly authors scornfully called them, wrote to the level of the man in the street and produced a diverse literature having in it many elements that appeared in more serious literary forms. Many a play dealing with the complexities of human emotions had a humble counterpart in some ballad of love and misadventure. Narratives hidden in solid books of history, much admired by earnest citizens, were more accessible, and more easily read, in such informal ballad versions as those found in Deloney's *Strange Histories* (1602). Even precisians, who at times roundly condemned ballads for their lewdness, could find a broadside paraphrase from the Scriptures to suit their piety. Practically all types of reading matter favored by the public, from travel narratives to the jest books, were drawn upon by the ballad writers to furnish forth a versified broadside which could be sold for a penny. Though many a ballad was doubtless thrown aside by its reader as trash, the thrifty middle class found in the penny sheets much of consuming interest and supposed value.

The history of Elizabethan patriotism as it affected the literate populace could almost be written from broadside ballads. One evidence is the interest in the heroes of the past, who lived anew in execrable verse. Poetical histories of Robin Hood were reprinted throughout the sixteenth and seventeenth centuries. The feats of archery and the bluff courage of this hero of the people were equaled by the deeds of Adam Bell and William of Cloudesley, likewise the subjects of broadside poetry. Thomas Deloney, who about 1593 brought together a collection of ballads under the title of *The Garland of good Will*, included "The Noble Acts of Arthur of the round Table" to show the bravery of such English knights as Arthur and Lancelot. The ballad of Arthur is preserved in several variant forms.[2] Other ballads describing British heroes are included in the same collection and in Deloney's *Strange Histories*. King Arthur was not the only hero worthy of a citizen's reading, declares a ballad in the Pepys collection, entitled *Saint Georges commendation to all Souldiers* (1612),[3] which enumerates the favorite heroes of romance, stressing particularly Saint George, Bevis of Hampton, Guy of Warwick, Richard Coeur de Lion, and Henry V, all of whom had separate ballad existences. These and

---

[2] F. O. Mann (ed.), *The Works of Thomas Deloney* (Oxford, 1912), p. 570.

[3] Rollins, *Pepys Ballads*, I, 39 ff.

other worthies are the subject of another Pepys ballad, *A brave warlike Song* [c. 1626], which recounts the valor of Guy, Bevis, King Richard, and King Edward I, along with such citizens of renown as Sir William Walworth, lord mayor of London, and Richard Pike of Tavistock, who had distinguished himself in single combat against the Spaniards and had become the subject of a play, *Dick of Devonshire*. A stanza near the end enumerates others of recent memory whose daring appealed to citizen-interest because they had helped to enrich England!

> *Cumberland and Essex,*
> *Norris* and braue *Drake,*
> I'th raigne of Queene *Elizabeth*
> did many battels make.
> Aduentrous *Martin Frobisher,*
> with *Hawkins* and some more,
> From sea did bring great riches
> vnto our English shore.[4]

Ballad writer and popular historian occasionally were combined in the same person, as in the case of Richard Johnson, who glorified the citizen-hero in prose and verse.[5] The populace adored equally the hearty, bluff kings, who represented the qualities of strength, courage, and generosity, always admired by the common man, and the resolute heroes from their own ranks, who possessed the daring and prowess that every shopkeeper envied.

Patriotism, which never burned brighter in England than during the threat of the Spanish Armada, is reflected in scores of ballads, which not only describe the villainy of the Spaniards but also encourage native sons to do battle against a foe reputed to have loaded a ship with strange whips and instruments of torture to persuade the English to return to the popish fold. At least twenty-four ballads on the Armada are recorded.[6] Deloney, and many another balladist now unknown, set forth encouragements to Englishmen and exhausted their vocabularies of phrases incandescent with hatred of foreign foes. For years after the Armada

---

[4] *Ibid.,* II, 62.
[5] *See* Chap. IX, *supra.*
[6] Firth, in *Roy. Hist. Soc. Trans.,* III, 101 ff.

the demand continued for ballads descriptive of English valor against the Spaniards. The glory of the Queen; the nobility of the struggle against Spain on the sea, in France, and in the Netherlands; the riches of captured prizes—these are all themes of ballads that entertained tradesmen in London's streets. Numerous titles of other anti-Spanish ballads now lost are recorded in the *Stationers' Register*.[7]

The religious prejudices of the multitude found expression in broadside verse. The Pope and all his works were damned in dreadful rhymes, as any reader yet may see in such a ballad as the earliest preserved from Martin Parker's pen, *A Scourge for the Pope, Satyrically scourging the itching sides of his obstinate Brood in England* (1624), and in many others like it, both before and after.[8] Some of the early Catholic ballads had been equally violent. Bitter antagonisms against the Catholic church united with ebullient patriotism in an outpouring of balladry after every conspiracy and plot laid at Catholic doors. The rebellion in the North in 1569, Pius V's Bull of Excommunication and the execution of John Felton for nailing a copy to the Bishop of London's door, the execution of Thomas Howard, Earl of Norfolk, in 1572, the Babington Conspiracy, the Gunpowder Plot, and a dozen similar provocations begot for the populace an enormous amount of verse which condemned the Pope as the father of lies and the encourager of traitors, and lauded the faithfulness of true-born Englishmen. Largely because of its Protestant leanings, London was so deeply concerned with the fortunes of Elizabeth, daughter of King James, and her husband, Frederick of Bohemia, expelled in 1619 by the Catholic Tilly, that street singers attempted to stir up the citizens to armed intervention.[9] The ballad of *Gallants, to Bohemia*, a few years later, likewise exhorted Englishmen to defend Protestant Germany for the good of the church and the enrichment of their purses.[10] Many ballads on Gustavus Adolphus expressed London sympathies in the Thirty Years' War. Though

[7] *Ibid.*, pp. 106-7.
[8] This ballad is reprinted in Rollins, *Old English Ballads*, pp. 189 ff., and in *Pepys Ballads*, I, 219 ff.
[9] *Ibid.*, p. 214.
[10] Firth, in *Roy. Hist. Soc. Trans.*, V, 49.

the censorship made hazardous any comment on the unpopular Spanish marriage, with which diplomatic gesture King James sought to end the foreign troubles, manuscript ballads and some printed evidences reveal that the public was expressing itself in the usual verse.[11] In all national crises, patriotism and prejudice found the ballad a useful instrument for reaching the citizenry and voicing the feelings of the multitude.

In the ballads, protests of the common people against social wrongs and conditions distasteful to them found expression. From the time of Henry VIII onward, there was an abundance of verse complaint against taxes, monopolies, inclosing, rent-racking, the competition of foreign artisans, the oppression of the wealthy, and similar evils.[12] London citizens particularly resented evils that touched their pocketbooks. God's judgment was certain to fall on exorbitant money-lenders and profiteers in necessities. Especially did Londoners condemn farmers who hoarded corn to run up the price. Deloney was the author of a ballad, now lost, which complained of the dearth of corn in the year 1596 and brought in the Queen, "speaking with her People Dialogue wise in very fond and undecent sort"—a feat which sent the bailiffs in search of the author, "one noted with the like Spirit, in printing a Book for the Silk Weavers."[13] Whenever scarcity threatened, writers furbished up their ballads on the disasters befalling ingrossers. A remarkable punishment is described in *A Looking glasse for Corne-hoorders, By the example of Iohn Russell a Farmer dwelling at St Peters Chassant in Buckingham shire, whose Horses sunke into the ground the 4 of March 1631.*[14] This farmer, who had exacted a ruinous price from a poor man, thus becomes a warning to others :

> Let them take heed how they
>   doe oppresse, doe oppresse
> The poore that God obey,
>   and are beloued.
> God will not let these long
>   alone, that doe his wrong,

[11] *Ibid.*, p. 50.
[12] *Ibid.*, II, 35 ; III, 54 ; V, 35, 44 ; VI, 30, 31.
[13] Quotation cited, from Stow's *Survey of London*, by Mann, *op. cit.*, p. ix.
[14] Rollins, *Pepysian Garland*, pp. 370 ff.

> Though ne'r so rich and strong
> that are oppressors. •

Throughout the period, the rise in the price of foodstuffs was popularly attributed to the greed of farmers, who were blamed for inclosing common lands and ingrossing corn. As the modern paper magnifies news which carries its propaganda, so the ballad writer unearthed events which drove home his lesson of protest, as in *News from Antwerp, or a Glass for greedy Farmers* and *God's Judgment showed upon a covetous Encloser of common pasture in Germany, who was strangely trodden to death by his own Cattle*, entered in the *Stationers' Register* respectively September 3 and 4, 1607, at the time of the agrarian troubles in the Midlands.[15]

Of all the persons hated by the populace, the monopolist who lived by his indirect tax on every citizen's purchase received the bitterest measure of venom. Particularly after the accession of James, the critics of patentees became more outspoken. In *The French Whipper* [c. 1620],[16] "Vntrussing seuerally the noted abuse, In all sorts of people, which is most in vse," public opinion finds a voice against these and other evils :

> The briske Sickafanticall Courtier,
> that by begging Monopolies rise :
> Yet are not so deepe in my fauour,
> as the Plough-man that many despise :
> He's the cheifest prop of a Nation,
> though his hauiour & rayment be plain
> He begges of the King no pension,
> nor liues he on other mens paine.

Many other ballads are equally plain in their sentiments, sometimes exulting in the misfortunes of the monopolists, as in *The deserued downfall of a corrupted conscience* (1621)[17] describing the degradation of Sir Francis Michell, who, along with Sir Giles Mompesson, was one of the commissioners for enforcing monopolies.

The wickedness of London, real and imagined, was a theme dear

---

[15] Firth, in *Roy. Hist. Soc. Trans.*, V, 35. For another interesting, though a trifle later, example of the ballads against ingrossers of corn, see Rollins, *The Pack of Autolycus*, pp. 31 ff., where he reprints *A Warning-peice for Ingroosers of Corne* (1643).

[16] Rollins, *Pepys Ballads*, I, 142 ff.

[17] *Idem, Pepysian Garland*, pp. 144 ff.

to the heart of the ballad writers, who found therein material
for doleful predictions of disasters to befall the city. When it is
remembered that Jeremiahs in every pulpit were preaching the
same doctrine and that the belief in the visible judgments of God
on evildoers was almost universal, the interest in such metrical
gloom is understandable. The sack of Antwerp in 1576 stimulated
versifiers to warn London that it must make moral and military
preparations if it would avoid a like fate.[18] A morbid pleasure in
the contemplation of sin, especially in anatomizing those iniquities peculiarly distasteful to the bourgeois soul, is evident in
many moral ballads which treat of unthrifty vices. Such, for
example, is *A most excellent Godly new Ballad* (1624),[19] the subtitle
of which describes it as

[Shew]ing the manifold abuses of this wicked world, the intolerable
pride of people, the wantonnesse [of] women, the dissimulation of
flatterers, the subtilty of deceiuers, the beastlines of drunkards, the
filthinesse of Whoredome, the vnthriftines of Gamesters, the cruelty of
Landlords, with a number of other inconueniences.

Extravagance, idleness, disobedience of children, profiteering in
rents, and general moral license, we learn, are corrupting the land.
Verse commentary on the sins of tradesfolk provided a topic for
a group of ballads represented by Lawrence Price's *The Honest
Age, Or There is honesty in all Trades* (1632), which was answered in
the same year by Martin Parker with *Knauery in all Trades, Or,
Here's an age would make a man mad*.[20] Somewhat ironically, Price
calls the roll of the trades and finds each now reformed from its
proverbial sins. The miller no longer takes deep toll; the chandler
heaps his measure of coals; not even the tailor tricks a customer
out of an extra length of cloth. Now shoemakers, weavers, glovers,
painters, pewterers, and their kind bring credit to England
throughout all Europe by their industry and honesty. Such praise,
even though satirical, was too much for Parker, who saw an
opportunity of attracting attention to an answering broadside
asserting the knavery of tailors, tapsters, victualers, and cooks, as
well as of rich men, lawyers, and tradesmen:

---

[18] Firth, in *Roy. Hist. Soc. Trans.*, III, 97.
[19] Rollins, *The Pack of Autolycus*, pp. 3 ff.
[20] Both ballads are reprinted in Rollins, *Pepysian Garland*, pp. 406 ff.

One tradesman deceaueth another,
    and sellers will conycatch buyers,
For gaine one wil cheat his own brother,
    the world's full of swearers and lyars :
Men now make no conscience of oathes,
    and this I may boldly say,
Some Rorers doe were gallant clothes,
    for which they did neuer pay :
The rich shall a Saint be made,
    though his life be neuer so bad,
All honesty is decay'd,
    here's an age would make a man mad.[21]

The middle-class public, always interested in itself, read condemnations of its own shortcomings almost as eagerly as it consumed praise—a quality which accounts for much of the popular interest in satire.

Ridicule of the vices that lead to bankruptcy became conventional in ballad literature, especially as the middle class grew increasingly articulate in the seventeenth century. London poets were fond of picturing the disasters befalling the spendthrift, the prodigal, or the countryman who is caught in the toils of the city's dissipations. Such a ballad is *A merry Progresse to London to see Fashions, by a young Country Gallant, that had more Money then Witte* [*c.* 1620].[22] Wine, women, and tobacco proved this youth's undoing—a trio of hazards suggestive of another ballad, [*Dice, Wine, and Women*] *Or The vnfortunate Gallant gull'd at London* [*c.* 1625].[23] The Cornish gallant, who has sown his wild oats in the city, returns finally to his native heath with a warning to others :

Now to my countrey doe I hie :
    London and fashions I defie :
Farewell damd dice, & strong waters cleere :
    Farewell all punkes and double beere :
I am for *Cornwall* freely bound :
    For *London* doth my state confound :
    There by these three I was made poore:
    The Dice, Strong waters, and a whore.[24]

---

[21] *Ibid.*, p. 412.
[22] Rollins, *Pepys Ballads*, I, 148 ff. For further discussion of the literature of thrift, *see* Chap. VI, *supra.*   [23] Rollins, *Pepys Ballads*, I, 237 ff.   [24] *Ibid.*, p. 241.

Not the moral sin of her husband's keeping a half dozen mistresses, but the strain on his purse, disturbed the wife in *I tell you, John Jarret, you'l breake: Or, John Jarrets wiues counsell to her husband, to haue care to his estate in this hard time, lest he turne Bankerout* (1630).[25] Among many other ballads driving home the morality of expedience, rapidly becoming a rationale for the conduct of tradesmen, one other may be mentioned : *Charles Rickets his recantation. Warning all good Fellowes to striue, To learne with him the way to thriue* (1633).[26] This trader, known in all the market towns as a roarer, a drinker, and a spender, easy with his money, now reforms in the interest of good business :

> I will follow my Vocation
> with industry and regard,
> And maintaine my reputation,
> in this world thats growne so hard.
> Markets are naught,
> Ware is not bought,
> As twas since I the Trade did know,
> tis time therefore
> now to giue ore
> Such spending, and no more doe so.[27]

Throughout the sixteenth and seventeenth centuries, moral and religious ballads were innumerable.[28] For every lewd ballad, condemned by preachers and reformers, there were many moral broadsides to counteract its influence. The tone of these didactic ballads reflects bourgeois morality, with its emphasis on prudence for business reasons. Early in the sixteenth century the custom developed of moralizing even traditional ballads like *The Nut-Brown Maid*, a habit which the professional ballad-mongers continued to practise with such creations as *Row Well, ye Mariners Moralized.*[29] Didacticism in the seventeenth century, however,

---

[25] Rollins, *Pepysian Garland*, pp. 337 ff.

[26] *Ibid.*, pp. 420 ff.

[27] *Ibid.*, p. 423.

[28] Religious and moral ballads make up a large part of Professor Rollins's *Old English Ballads*, a volume which he describes as typical of Elizabethan and Jacobean balladry. Didactic pieces form a large proportion of the great Roxburghe and Pepys collections.

[29] Rollins, "The Black-Letter Broadside Ballad," *op. cit.*, p. 288.

leaned toward practical advice, especially of the sort that was serviceable to youth. The wiles of women, the disasters of drunkenness, and the bankruptcy in prodigality were the favorite themes.[30] The inordinate love of aphoristic wisdom sometimes manifested itself in balladry, as in *Good Admonition Or To al sorts of people this counsell I sing, That in each ones affaire, to take heed's a faire thing* (1633),[31] a versified collection of proverbs on good conduct. Frequently the ballad writer delighted his audience with the gloomy pleasure of reading dolorous verses on God's judgments, the day of doom, and the need of repentance during the plague's visitation.[32] When contemporary events were not impressive enough, Scripture history provided texts for good lessons.[33] The man in the street was willing to pay his penny for descriptions of his sins, and the ballad writer saw to it that he had the opportunity.

The ephemeral journalism of the ballad-monger also catered to the love of self-praise which the growth of class pride was stimulating in the citizen. Craftsmen and tradesfolk found in the ballads a means of vaunting their own professions. Thomas Brewer, author of a prose jest book, *The Merry Devil of Edmonton*, set forth *A newe Ballad, composed in commendation of the Societie, or Companie of the Porters* (1605),[34] which recounts the organization of the Company of Porters to improve the standards of the trade. Brewer, describing the first meeting of "a thousand fourtie one" porters, stresses the dignity of labor by mentioning God's own approval :

> To haue seene them so, you'd wonder,
> so many should maintaine
> themselues, by such a labour,
> but that, thats got with paine,
> God doth increase and blesse :
> for God himselfe hath sed,
> with paine and wearinesse,
> we all should get our bread.[35]

A quarter of a century later, Martin Parker, in *The honest plaine*

---

[30] Typical examples of this type of ballad are easily accessible in the excellent reprints by Professor Rollins. See *Pepys Ballads*, I, 122, 128, 262 ; II, 139 ; *Pepysian Garland*, pp. 189, 361, 376.

[31] Rollins, *Pepys Ballads*, II, 239 ff.

[32] Cf. Rollins, *Pepysian Garland*, pp. 176, 185.

[33] *Ibid.*, pp. 66, 350.   [34] *Ibid.*, pp. 11 ff.   [35] *Ibid.*, p. 16.

dealing Porter [1630?],[36] put into the mouth of a once-wealthy
citizen praise of the trade which now maintains him honestly. A
certain Thomas Neale, possibly a weaver himself like Deloney,
recited the honorable condition of the craft in *A Wench for a
Weauer* [1630?].[37] So moving is the persuasion of the craftsman-
hero of this ballad that he convinces a hesitating girl that a weaver
is a worthy match. Weavers, it is true, have fallen on uneasy days,
but once a weaver was king and the time was when Jack of Newbery kept two hundred and fifty looms.

> None like them then had prayse,
> they gained much treasure.
> Weauing did so excell,
> none like them did so well :
> Of all the trades they bare the bell,
> speake well of weauers.[38]

Shoemakers, for some reason unexplained, have been romantically
treated by writers from the Renaissance to modern times. Praise
of the gentle craft is conventional, and Lawrence Price only echoes
contemporary fashion in a song descriptive of the honest merriment of cobblers in *Round boyes indeed. Or The Shoomakers Holy-day*
(1637). No base companions are to be found when shoemakers
celebrate :

> But with those men of good report,
> that lead their liues in honest sort,
> A Iugg or two will make vs sport,
> *we haue money to serue our need.*[39]

Other trades likewise had their laureates, who praised them for
their industry and honesty.

City poets, though they might satirize particular weaknesses,
never wearied of praising London and its people above other
cities and towns. Richard Climsell, in *The praise of London* (1632),[40]
pictures the metropolis as the "flower of earthly ioyes," which
attracts all people to it :

---

[36] *Ibid.*, p. 365.
[37] Rollins, *Pepys Ballads*, II, 162 ff.
[38] *Ibid.*, p. 167.
[39] Rollins, *Pepysian Garland*, p. 446.   [40] *Idem, Pepys Ballads*, II, 219 ff.

> The Weauer, the Baker, the Brewer, the Miller,
>   the Glouer, the Tanner, the Butcher, the Barber
> The Ioiner, the Cooper, the Sawyer, the Turner,
>   the Tapster, the Hostler, the Clothier, the Taylor
> And many more Trades that here I might name,
>   that heare of braue *Londons* renowned high fame
> All these prepare both day and nights,
>   *To come to the City for their delights.*[41]

The commercial interests of London found a means of influencing the public in the ballad, which served the same end as newspaper propaganda at the present time. Since the prospects of rich gains from speculation in foreign ventures had penetrated the consciousness of most apprentices and small tradesmen, every particle of news about the New World, or about trade with the East, found eager readers among prospective investors, great and small. Ballads and pamphlets supplied the place of modern prospectuses and editorials. The best-known of the ballad-advertisements still extant is *Londons Lotterie: With an incouragement to the furtherance thereof, for the good of Virginia, and the benefite of this our natiue Countrie; wishing good fortune to all that venture in the same* (1612),[42] which persuades maids, widows, wives, farmers, craftsmen, merchants, and gentlemen, all to take a chance in the lottery which may make them rich and which also will provide a means to bring great riches to England from the new settlement in Virginia :

> Let no man thinke that he shall loose,
>   though he no Prize poscesse :
> His substaunce to *Virginia* goes,
>   which God, no doubt will blesse :
> And in short time send from that land,
>   much rich commoditie ;
> So shall we thinke all well bestowd,
>   vpon this Lotterie.[43]

---

[41] *Ibid.*, p. 221. For further material on the citizen's pride in London, *see* Chap. II, *supra.*

[42] Rollins, *Pepys Ballads*, I, 24 ff. *See also* Firth, in *Roy. Hist. Soc. Trans.*, V, 27, 57 ff. Both Firth and Rollins call attention to a broadside advertising the second lottery in 1615, entitled *A Declaration for the certaine time of Drawing the Great standing Lottery for Virginia; fixing the same to take place on the 26th of June next*, as well as a lost pamphlet advertising the first lottery.   [43] Rollins, *Pepys Ballads*, I, 29.

Long before this advertisement, ballads had described the undertakings in the New World. In 1563 appeared *A Commendation of the adventurous Viage of the wurthy captain, M. Thomas Stutely esquyer and others towards the land called Terra Florida*, which praised Thomas Stukeley, an adventurer who had found financial support in the City for a colonization effort. Stukeley turned pirate, and the failure of the venture prompted another ballad in 1564 describing the fiasco.[44] Trade propaganda usually attempted to minimize disasters. This purpose is evident in *Newes from Virginia of the happy arrival of that famous and worthy knight, Sir Thomas Gates, and well reputed and valiante captaine Newport, in England* (1610).[45] Though the company was wrecked in the Bermudas, they finally reached the distressed colony, which was soon succored by Lord Delaware, who is described in the ballad as encouraging the Merchants Adventurers to continue their support:

> Be not dismayed at all,
> For scandall cannot doe us wrong;
> God will not let us fall.
> Let England know our willingnesse,
> For that our worke is good;
> Wee hope to plant a nation,
> Were none before hath stood.

When trade rivalry with the Dutch in the East Indies very nearly precipitated a conflict between England and Holland in 1624, after the massacre of an English trading settlement in the island of Amboyna in February, 1623, the East India Company appears to have encouraged publicity about the disaster. Immediately after the news reached England, a pamphlet on the subject was published, and this was followed by a ballad, *Newes out of East India: Of the cruell and bloody vsage of our English Merchants and others at Amboyna, by the Netherlandish Gouernour and Councell there* (1624).[46] A little later a play on Amboyna was suppressed by the Privy Council for reasons of state. The ballad gives an account of the frightful tortures endured by the victims and ends with a list of

---

[44] Both ballads are described by Firth, in *Roy. Hist. Soc. Trans.*, III, 73-75.

[45] *Ibid.*, V, 26-27. The quotation cited here is taken by Firth from Alexander Brown, *The Genesis of the United States*, 2 vols. (London, 1890), I, 420.

[46] Rollins, *Pepysian Garland*, pp. 200 ff.

the names of those executed or pardoned. A concluding statement informs the reader that "You may read more of this bloody Tragedy in a booke printed by authority. 1624."[47]

As exploration and commerce brought large numbers of Englishmen in contact with foreign countries, the interest in news of the outside world increased. In periods of conflict with foreign powers, or during impending international crises, pamphlets and ballads giving accounts of events abroad multiplied enormously. Foreign pamphlets were translated and often versified by balladists.[48] The strange and the unusual in reports of travelers; the wars in the Netherlands, France, or Germany; sea fights against pirates or Spaniards; remarkable sights and happenings in foreign parts—all these went into the journalistic grist of the pamphleteers and ballad writers, to the delight of a news-hungry public.

To the modern antiquarian, interested in curious relics of Elizabethan literary taste, the ballads and pamphlets dealing with crime and monstrosities are the most familiar. Murders, fires, last confessions of condemned criminals, the deeds of witches, terrible storms, floods, God's fearful warnings in a fall of meteors, the casting up of monstrous fishes, the birth of deformed children or pigs—all these things were the materials of the sensation-mongers who fed an appetite increasing in voracity throughout the seventeenth century. A cursory glance at the Roxburghe and Pepys collections reveals the abundance of this type of literary fare among the ballads, which frequently had counterparts in hastily written pamphlets. Sometimes, particularly in the case of the murder ballads and pamphlets, the material found its way to the stage— a procedure familiar today when we frequently see crimes, made sensational by newspapers, appearing presently on the stage and screen. A wife's murder of her husband, or vice versa, and crimes growing out of illicit love provided the ballad writer and the pamphleteer with news certain to find ready purchasers. And as Elizabethan journalists were singularly adept at extracting good lessons from untoward events, murders became the subject of a persistent literature which pretended to instruct while it titillated the scandal-loving tastes of citizens. An excellent example of the

---

[47] *Ibid.*, p. 206.
[48] Many examples are cited by Shaaber, *op. cit.*, especially pp. 168 ff.

type is *The wofull lamentacon of mrs. Anne Saunders, which she wrote with her own hand, being prisoner in newgate, Iustly condemned to death* (1573),[49] a ballad descriptive of the murder of George Saunders, a London merchant, by his wife's paramour, with her connivance. Long after the execution of the principals, this murder—the sensation of the moment—lived in popular memory in Arthur Golding's *Briefe discourse of the late murther of master George Saunders* (1573), Anthony Munday's *View of Sundry Examples Reporting Many Strange Murders* (1580), the anonymous *Sundry Strange and Inhuman Murders Lately Committed* (1591), Stow's *Annals* (1592), and in the stage play *A Warning for Fair Women* (1599). The titles of the foregoing works indicate sufficiently their contents. In 1596 Thomas Lodge referred in *Wits Miserie* to one who would "reckon you vp the storie of Mistris Sanders, and weepe at it, and turne you to the Ballad ouer her chimney, and bid you looke there, there is a goodly sample."[50] This story of domestic tragedy, with its long literary history, is typical of such printed sensations, which were varied only by differences in the details of the crimes. With the regularity of the recurrence of murders, similar ballads and pamphlets appeared for the next century.[51]

As popular as the accounts of murders were the descriptions of miscellaneous sensations, like that provided by a certain T. F., who translated in 1616 a pamphlet entitled *Miraculous Newes, From the Cittie of Holdt, in the Lord-ship of Munster (in Germany) the twentieth of September last past. 1616. Where There Were Plainly beheld three dead bodyes rise out of their Graues, admonishing the people of Iudgements to come*—a subject also employed in a ballad.[52] The fame of the celebrated hog-faced gentlewoman, Mistress Tannakin Skinker, has been preserved to modern memory, when a thousand of her fairer sisters are as last year's snows, simply because of the tremendous journalistic reception accorded her when she appeared in London in 1639. Books, ballads, and woodcut portraits of the German woman with the swine's snout found fascinated buyers

---

[49] Rollins, *Old English Ballads*, pp. 340 ff.

[50] Rollins (*ibid.*, pp. 340-41) calls attention to this quotation and the pamphlets cited.

[51] For further details of the interest in murder stories and the literature concerned with the judgments of God, *see* pp. 459-63, *infra*.

[52] The pamphlet and ballad are referred to by Rollins, *Pepysian Garland*, p. 316.

in the English populace.[53] Neither in quality nor in subject matter was there much change in the type of such sensational material served up to the news-hungry citizen from the late sixteenth century for the next hundred years, although the demand for lurid journalism increased in the early years of the seventeenth century. The exhibitions by showmen, always sensitive to public taste, of deformed or strange creatures are further indications of the same appetite that devoured journalistic descriptions of the extraordinary.

One other type of ballad, popular with citizens, deserves mention—that describing the relations between the sexes. The middle class was peculiarly interested in domestic problems, a theme which occupied the attention of preachers, poets, and stage players.[54] The increasing freedom claimed by women, their extravagance and daring in dress, and the evils resulting from marriages for money were the constant themes of satirists and reformers, and the journalists hastened to make capital of these ever fresh subjects. Ballads—sometimes serious, sometimes mocking—describing the punishment of scolds, the chase after rich widows, the marriage of January and May, the ills and benefits of marriage, the means to attain happiness in the state of matrimony, were always a part of the street vendor's stock.[55]

The journalistic pamphlet literature, as the examples already incidentally noticed indicate, was similar to the broadside ballads in theme. News, propaganda, advice, descriptions of strange events, and the varied flotsam composing the stuff of human interest, were the subject matter of cheap little quartos, which littered the bookstalls. A glance at the titles listed and discussed in Dr. Shaaber's dissertation, *Some Forerunners of the Newspaper in England, 1476-1622*, will reveal the variety of human taste and journalistic purpose. As English insularity weakened through commercial enterprise, the eagerness of the populace for relations from the outside world grew keener. The late sixteenth and early seventeenth centuries saw the printing of countless pamphlets

---

[53] *See ibid.*, pp. 449 ff.

[54] *See* Chap. VII, *supra*.

[55] Good examples of these ballads may be found in Rollins, *Pepysian Garland*, pp. 72, 207, 229, 234, 239, 263, 356; Rollins, *Pepys Ballads*, I, 257; II, 16.

on travel, many of which were brought together in the ponderous compilations of Hakluyt and Purchas. News-books had been appearing with increasing frequency throughout the reign of Elizabeth, and from 1590 onward pamphlets of news grew in abundance.[56] The extended horizon resulting from the victory over Spain, the success of English buccaneers, and the activities of English traders abroad stimulated an interest in foreign news pamphlets called corantos, which were translated and reprinted in London. Enterprising printers in Holland in 1620-21 began publishing in English single-sheet corantos, which were the fore-runners of similar sheets published in London in 1621 by Nicholas Bourne or Nathaniel Butter. These, in turn, were followed by a series of quarto news-books, which appeared continuously until 1632, when they were suppressed until 1638.[57] A great outburst of journalism, exemplified in the numerous *Mercuries*, began with the increase of dissension in 1641. The translated news-books and the English corantos, which purported to give straightforward accounts of happenings in foreign countries, were the logical consequence of the developing interest among the commonalty in happenings abroad. The middle-class reader, though he might amuse himself with ballads and books describing monstrosities and strange creatures, also demanded something more in the way of news of the world as he came to realize the desirability of keeping informed about events that affected his trade and his purse. Dim and vague as was most of this news, it shows an alertness on the part of the average citizen toward world affairs. The news-books added one more item to the increasing variety of reading matter which attracted the eyes of busy tradesmen hurrying through St. Paul's.

The ephemeral journalism of Shakespeare's time was nearly as varied, and almost as abundant in proportion to the number of readers, as similar literature is today. The popular market for books and pamphlets of journalistic interest reached such proportions by the last decade of the sixteenth century that professional writers began to find it possible to eke out an existence by supplying whatever the public taste demanded. Greene, Deloney, Dekker,

---

[56] Shaaber, *op. cit.*, pp. 312-13, gives the titles of a dozen specimens of these news-books.   [57] *Ibid.*, p. 317.

Rowlands, Heywood, and others like them, turned their hands to anything that would bring in a penny. The result remains in nondescript pamphlets and verses, which have been left as monuments to the all-devouring habits of the reading public.

Since human nature finds an unholy fascination in the analysis of sin, the same interest that now induces the populace to listen to a reformed burglar preach at a revival service led the Elizabethans to buy pamphlets descriptive of misspent lives. Typical of the *genre* was a pamphlet recounting the life of Luke Hutton, a notable rogue, over whose name was published *The Blacke Dogge of Newgate: both pithie and profitable for all Readers* [1596?], later versions of which appeared in 1612 and 1638. With a dedication to the Lord Chief Justice of England and a pious epistle to the reader, Hutton describes his deeds in verse and prose, pretending also to reveal "the notable abuses daily committed by a great number of very bad fellows."[58] Hutton's criminal life, followed by a much advertised repentance, attracted so much attention that when he was hanged, the ballad of *Luke Huttons Lamentation* (1598), purporting to have been written by him the day before his execution, was hawked about the streets and long remained popular.[59] Scarcely a hanging passed without its crop of ballads and pamphlets relating the last words and warnings of a sorrowful victim on the scaffold. A good illustration of the execution pamphlet, with the conventional message from the criminal to deter others from following in the path of sin, was Gilbert Dugdale's *A True Discourse Of the practises of Elizabeth Caldwell, Ma: Ieffrey Bownd, Isabell Hall widdow, and George Fernely, on the parson of Ma: Thomas Caldwell, in the County of Chester, to haue murdered and poysoned him, with diuers others* (1604), the long subtitle of which emphasizes the life of Elizabeth Caldwell and implies the good lesson in the pamphlet:

Together with her manner of godly life during her imprisonment, her arrainement and execution, with Isabell Hall, widdow; As also a briefe relation of Ma. Ieffrey Bownd, who was the Assise before prest to death. Lastly, a most excellent exhortorie Letter, written by her

---

[58] Reprinted in a modernized version by A. V. Judges, *The Elizabethan Underworld* (London, 1930), pp. 265 ff.

[59] *Ibid.*, pp. 292 ff. Judges reprints a version dating from about 1660.

own selfe out of the prison to her husband, to cause him to fall into consideration of his sinnes, &c. Seruing likewise for the vse of euery good Christian. Beeing executed the 18. of Iune. 1603. Written by one then present as witnes, their owne Country-man, Gilbert Dugdale.

A similar pamphlet, with a lesson to apprentices neatly inserted, was *The Life and Death Of Griffin Flood Informer. Whose cunning courses, churlish manners, and troublesome Informations, molested a number of plaine dealing people in this City of London. Wherein is also declared the murther of Iohn Chipperford Vintner, for which fact the said Griffin Flood was pressed to death the 18. day of Ianuary last past* (1623). Flood's downfall began when he refused to live in harmony with his brother apprentices and, from quarrelsomeness, at length came to murder. This lesson of peaceful coöperation was clear to every young reader of Flood's fate.

The greatest professional success with the anatomy of misspent life was made, however, by Robert Greene, who discovered a rich vein of human interest in the revelation of his alleged iniquities described in a series of repentance pamphlets so filled with moralizations that no burgher could resist them. Being a clever journalist, Greene also inserted enough miscellaneous anecdotes and illustrative tales to keep the entertainment value of his pamphlets high. Although Greene's repentance pamphlets may possibly represent the catharsis of a sincerely remorseful soul, more likely they testify to the author's knowledge of popular psychology. Indications are clear that he shifted his point of view to attract a public turning from idle reading with a grim determination to find moral improvement and practical benefits in literary diversions : in *Greenes Mourning Garment* (1590), the author regrets that he had "ouer-weaned with them of *Niniue* in publishing sundry wanton Pamphlets, and setting forth Axiomes of amorous Philosophy," but having heard the cry of Jonas, "*Except thou repent*," he now writes in rebuke of wanton desires and "the fatall detriment that followes the contempt of graue and aduised counsaile."[60] The result is a prodigal-son story in pamphlet form. A sequence of repentance pamphlets follows : *Greenes*

---

[60] Dedication to George Clifford, Earl of Cumberland ; edition of 1616. In "The Conclusion" Greene further expresses his regret over his "many Pamphlets full of much loue and little Scholarisme."

Neuer too late (1590), *Greenes Farewell To Folly* (1591), *Greenes Groats-Worth of witte, bought with a million of Repentance* (1592), and *The Repentance of Robert Greene* (1592), all of which show the author's awareness of what would catch the eye of the casual buyer at the bookstalls. Some of these pamphlets were reprinted for the next generation. The *Groats-Worth of witte* had six editions by 1637, and *Neuer too late*, eight by 1631.

Revelations of life in the underworld were so alluring to Elizabethan readers that a whole literature of pamphlets descriptive of rogues and vagabonds[61] was produced by writers who set forth their exposures of the lives, habits, and language of rogues, as discoveries profitable to every citizen. The taste for books of roguery, discernible in the acceptance of such early works as *Cocke Lorelles Bote* [1510?] and Barclay's version of the *Shyp of Folys* (1509), received a stimulus from the publication of Robert Copland's *The hye way to the Spyttell hous* [1536?], describing the impostors and beggars who came to St. Bartholomew's Hospital. This book was followed later in the century by Gilbert Walker's(?) *A manifest detection of the most vyle and detestable vse of Diceplay* (1552), John Awdeley's galaxy of rogues, *The Fraternitye of Vacabondes* (1561), and Thomas Harman's even more inclusive description of the characters of low life, *A Caueat or Warening For Common Cursetors Vulgarely Called Vagabones* (1567). But again it was Greene who brought the rogue books or cony-catching pamphlets to journalistic perfection at the end of the sixteenth century by producing a brood of tracts which were eagerly bought for the next two decades.[62]

---

[61] The subject of Elizabethan rogues and the literature about them has been treated by F. W. Chandler, *The Literature of Roguery*, 2 vols. (London, 1907), Vol. I; Frank Aydelotte, *Elizabethan Rogues and Vagabonds*, Oxford Historical and Literary Studies, Vol. I (Oxford, 1913); and A. V. Judges, *op. cit.*, introduction and notes.

[62] Aydelotte, *op. cit.*, pp. 127-39. Greene and his contemporaries plagiarized from the earlier works on roguery and from each other until the later cony-catching pamphlets were a mosaic of much that had gone before. Mr. Aydelotte has shown (p. 127) that *A manifest detection* was the foundation for material in *Mihil Mumchance, His Discouerie of the Art of Cheating in False Dyceplay* (1597), Dekker's *The Belman Of London* (1608), and Samuel Rid's *The Art of Iugling* (1612). Greene borrowed from both *A manifest detection* and Harman's *Caueat*; Dekker and Rowlands borrowed from all three; and the process of stealing, one from another, increased in complexity as new authors arose to supply the demand for rogue literature.

Greene's first cony-catching pamphlet, *A Notable Discouery of Coosnage*[63] (1591), professed a deep moral purpose. Its subtitle was intended to recommend it to the average citizen, who might learn from it how to avoid the snares and pitfalls of card sharps and diceplayers, for it advertises the work as

Plainely laying open those pernitious sleights that hath brought many ignorant men to confusion. Written for the general benefit of all Gentlemen, Citizens, Aprentises, Countrey Farmers and yeomen, that may hap to fall into the company of such coosening companions. With a delightfull discourse of the coosnage of Colliers.

In a preface addressed to "Yong Gentlemen, Marchants, Apprentises, Farmers, and plain Countreymen" Greene further stresses the seriousness of his purpose : even at the risk of life and limb, he has undertaken this discovery based on his own experience. He has seen the havoc wrought by scheming gamblers and tricksters :

The poore Prentice, whose honest minde aymeth only at his Maisters profites, by these pestilent vipers of the commonwealth, is smoothly intised to the hazard of this game at Cardes, and robd of his Maisters money, which forceth him oft times eyther to run away, or banckrout all, to the ouerthrow of some honest and wealthy Cittizens. Seeing then such a daungerous enormity groweth by them, to the discredite of the estate of England, I would wishe the Iustices appoynted as seuere Censors of such fatall mischiefes, to shewe themselues patres patriae, by weeding out such worms as eat away the sappe of the Tree, . . .

Citizens and "poore ignoraunt countrey Farmers" who fall into the hands of rogues excite so much compassion in Greene that he pens the book to guide them in their dealings with London rascals. The success of the tract was immediate. Greene, the writer of tales, had not forgotten to supply illustrative stories—a feature which he elaborated in *The Second and last part of Conny-catching. With new additions containing many merry tales of all lawes worth the reading, because they are worthy to be remembred* (1592). The description of common thieves and rogues demands common language,

---

[63] Greene's rogue pamphlets have been reprinted by Professor G. B. Harrison in the Bodley Head Quartos (Oxford, 1923, 1924). My quotations are from these reprints.

the author maintains in answering those critics who had found the plain style of his previous tract faulty. Merchants, apprentices, and countrymen, however, evidently approved in sufficient numbers to warrant three other exposure pamphlets in quick succession.[64] To the previous types of low life, Greene added the alluring motif of woman's delinquency in *A Disputation, Betweene a Hee Conny-catcher, and a Shee Conny-catcher, whether a Theefe or a Whoore, is most hurtfull in Cousonage, to the Common-wealth. Discovering The Secret Villanies of alluring Strumpets. With the Conuersion of an English Courtizen, reformed this present yeare, 1592. Reade, laugh, and learne* (1592). The wickedness of women, the author warns, results in twin evils to those who patronize them : the consuming of wealth and the endangering of health. A tract like this, with the biography of a fallen woman, was irresistible. The most popular of all Greene's cony-catching pamphlets, it had five editions by 1637. A clever advertiser of his own works, Greene had promised a *Black Book* which would sum up his revelations about rogues and list them and their haunts. *The Blacke Bookes Messenger* (1592) took advantage in its title of the interest that had been aroused by his promised work. Here the author once more exploits the perennial interest of the public in the personalities of criminals as he lets a cutpurse narrate his jest-book deeds until he is finally hanged from a window in a French town. Greene finishes the story for him by painting a horrible picture of wolves scratching up and devouring his body, a notable example of the judgment of God upon evildoers. A preface to *The Blacke Bookes Messenger* reveals that the author was contemplating other criminal biographies, one of which he believed worthy to be put into the hands of children and servants for the good lessons therein.[65] Criminal

---

[64] *The Thirde and last Part of Conny-catching* (1592) ; *A Disputation, Betweene a Hee Conny-catcher, and a Shee Conny-catcher* (1592) ; and *The Blacke Bookes Messenger. Laying open the Life and Death of Ned Browne one of the most notable Cutpurses, Crosbiters, and Conny-catchers, that euer liued in England* (1592).

[65] Preface "To the Curteous Reader" : "I had thought to haue ioyned with this Treatise, a pithy discourse of the Repentance of a Conny-catcher lately executed out of Newgate, yet forasmuch as the Methode of the one is so far differing from the other, I altered my opinion, and the rather for that the one died resolute and desperate, the other penitent and passionate. For the Conny-catchers repentance which shall shortly be published, it containes a passion of great importance. First how he was giuen ouer from all grace and Godlines, and seemed to haue no sparke of the feare of God in him :

biography, especially if told in the first person with proper repentances, has remained popular even to the present day. A
little after Greene's time, John Clavell, a highwayman, repented
so well in verse that his *Recantation Of an ill led Life* (1628), giving
an account of his own career, with useful warnings against high-
way robbers, went through three editions. His rhymed apology
for his life won a pardon from the King and he claimed that his
Recantation was published by royal command.[66]

The world of knavery was now the theme of many hack writers
who followed in Greene's wake. Some clever journalist, writing
under the pseudonym of Cuthbert Conny-Catcher, answered
Greene with *The Defence Of Conny catching. Or A Confutation Of
Those two iniurious Pamphlets published by R. G. against the practitioners of many Nimble-witted and mysticall Sciences* (1592), in which,
maintaining that tricksters at cards were the least harmful of
rascals, he satirized other knaves in a series of brief tales. *The
Groundworke of Conny-catching* (1592), chiefly a plagiarism from
Harman's description of vagabonds, follows the current fashion.
Throughout the first half of the seventeenth century, imitations
of these rogue books remained popular and paved the way for
picaresque or realistic fiction.

Thomas Dekker, a prolific follower of Greene, found in the life
of London, especially in the low life, the subject matter for numerous pamphlets. With the same professions of moral purpose,
addressed to the same social classes, Dekker's pamphlets enjoyed
a circulation even wider than Greene's. *The Belman Of London*
(1608), a revelation of the vices of the city, borrowed in part from
preceding pamphlets, had a fifth impression in 1640. *The Belman*,
with *The Seven Deadly Sinnes of London* (1606), began a series continued in *Lanthorne and Candle-light* (1608), *O per se O* (1612), and
other pamphlets of similar character, which appeared regularly

---

yet neuerthelesse, through the woonderfull working of Gods spirite, euen in the dun-
geon at Newgate the night before he died, he so repented him from the bottome of
his hart, that it may well beseeme Parents to haue it for their Children, Masters for
their seruants, and to bee perused of euery honest person with great regard."

[66] Chandler, *op. cit.*, I, 114-15. For other works on criminal biography, *see* Chap.
XI, *supra*.

until 1640.[67] Buyers of cheap pamphlets from Dekker's pen had a choice of several vivid accounts of the knaveries of London. An arraignment of Dekker for his thefts from Harman occurs in *Martin Mark-all, Beadle of Bridewell* [1608?], a tract in which the author, perhaps Samuel Rid, gives an account of the Regiment of Rogues.[68]

The demand for literature exposing low life was responsible for other pamphlets after the school of Greene. Samuel Rowlands, if he was the author, followed the well beaten path of the exposure tracts in *Greenes Ghost Haunting Conie-catchers* (1602), a fabric of borrowings from previous works. One other pamphlet reflecting the taste of the populace for the lurid journalism of crime should be mentioned here. In 1595 William Barley printed a compilation of crimes, by a certain T. I., with the enticing title of *A World of wonders. A Masse of Murthers. A Covie of Cosonages. Containing many of the moste notablest Wonders, horrible Murthers and detestable Cosonages that haue beene within this Land.* With an air of pious sincerity, T. I. presents his exposure to "stirre and moue vs vp to prayer to God to amendment of our sinful liues, to the horror of such wicked actions and such like." The lesson will be plainer, the author believes, in the deeds of wicked Englishmen rather than crimes attributed to distant foreigners:

And for this cause I haue collected these examples, not from straunge languages or from forrain nations which might breed some ambiguitie or doubt as touching the trueth, but I haue taken them out of our owne natiue Cuntry (not without sorrow that such hainous sins & enormities should be so rife amongst vs) . . .   [Preface.]

The "Cosonages" reveal the tricks played on London tradesmen by sharp rascals. One ruse, similar to that described by Ben Jonson in *The Alchemist*, is the way in which Mistress Mascall, the tripe-wife, is persuaded to put her gold in the keeping of a wise woman who promises to call up the King of the Fairies. The cozener also deceived "a rich & greedy Churle in such sort that she sadled him and road vpon him as vpon an horse."[69] These

---

[67] Aydelotte, *op. cit.*, pp. 129 ff., gives a brief discussion of the relations of Dekker's pamphlets.

[68] *Ibid.*, pp. 133-35.   [69] Sig. C 4[v].

and other trickeries she is said to have confessed publicly "before the Honorable at the Sessions-house."

The "Wonders" are records of strange happenings, gathered from the chronicles of England, including such varied matters as the birth of monstrosities, the catching of great fish, the appearance of blazing stars, and the punishments visited upon enemies of the common good. Among the latter was a certain corn hoarder, no less a person than the Archbishop of York in the year 1234, who had a great stack of corn near the town of Ripon, but when workmen opened it,

there appeared in the sheaues the beds of wormes and of toades, and horrible serpents, yea and a voice was heard out of the mowe saying lay no handes one that corne for the Archbishop and all that he hath is the diuels. . . . Beholde this true example and repent thou couetous richman and doe good while time is offered thee, and God will blesse thee the better.   [Sig. D 3.]

Although the author omits "the cruell deuises of mother Bumby the witch of Rochester, the tirannie of the witches of Warboys, and many other," he does give an account of a piece of witchcraft, "the most straunge of all, committed in March 1592, near Harrow on the hill"—a situation which Thomas Heywood and Richard Brome used in *The Late Lancashire Witches* :[70]

One Master Edling hauing a barne at the townes end, his seruant Richard Bucte going thether with a mastiue dogge after him, suddainly espied an haire to start before him and set his dogge at her, but the mastiue refusing the chase ran round about the fellow whyning pittiefully, but the fellow left not till he saw the hare take in at one mother Atkins house, known to be a notorious witch.[71]

[Sigs. E 4-E 4ᵛ.]

After enumerating many woeful murders, the author concludes with an appropriate warning to masters to treat their apprentices fairly as a means of avoiding violence:

I might heer set before your eyes what mischeifes haue followed to masters by ouer hard vsages of their apprentices & seruants a matter

---

[70] II, 1.

[71] The riding of a man like a horse, mentioned earlier by T. I., is also used in the same play by Heywood and Brome, III, 1.

to be looked vnto for some are brought vp to idle to proudely, to wantonly with to much excesse both of meat and apparell which brings them to lewdnes, to dycing, to ryoting, to whoredome, to imbeasling of their masters goodes and such like, others on the contrary part want both apparell and sustenance & besides and most vnreasonable set to taskes to woorking vppon Sundayes and holydayes forbidden, beaten and corrected out of measure and most vnchristian like vsed, whereby they are forced for want of further remedie to runne away or to filch & steal to buye victualles or els to runne to a further mischeife amongst which I might remember the Pewterers seruant that sometime dwelt in Finchlane. Also George Collins sometimes Apprentice with Richard Haiton taylor in Fanchurch who being badly vsed his master sought to kill him which he perfourmed being vnable to doe such a fact, and was for the same executed, but because these and many others and yet fresher in memorie and writing then that they may be forgotten. It shall be needlesse to reporte vnto you the most hainous murther committed vppon the Chaundler neere broken Wharff in London the matter beeing so fresh in memorie, the malefactor still hanging as a notable example to our eyes, a greif to the godly a terrour to the wicked and reprobate : which God graunt for our Lord Iesus sake. Amen.

[Sig. F 4.]

Quotations have been given at some length from T. I.'s pamphlet, now one of the rarest of its kind, because it combines several types of subject matter which held for the London tradesman a consuming interest. Here he could read of cony-catching, of strange wonders, of murders, and of witchcraft—themes which supplied many another pamphleteer with matter for a book. T. I., perhaps a tradesman himself, knew intimately the tastes of his class and perceived accurately the demand for works useful to his readers, as his warning peroration shows.

The literature of low life, with its conventional preaching of reform, has remained for centuries a favorite item with the booksellers. Respectable tradesmen not only found entertainment in these revelations, but they also assured themselves that the information and warnings saved them from many a pitfall. Authors shrewdly encouraged this faith in the value of their works. We still see the same psychology at work, as motion-picture producers twist a moral into the shadiest film of the underworld and convince uncritical spectators that it serves a useful purpose.

Some of the early seventeenth-century tracts on prisons doubt-less helped to arouse some faint humanitarian impulses in an age callous to the treatment of criminals. They served, at any rate, as terrible warnings against the prodigal life, which led inexorably to prison horrors. William Fennor's *The Compters Common-wealth* (1617) pictured the evils of the debtors' prisons so well that new editions of his work, in slightly altered form, appeared in 1619 and again in 1629. Geffray Mynshul's *Essayes and Characters of a Prison and Prisoners* (1618) likewise was favored with three editions. In solemn aphoristic style, Mynshul describes the personalities and the conditions of prison life.[72] A pamphlet in verse, describing in mock-heroic vein the drunken brawls of prisoners in Wood Street Counter, was produced by Robert Speed as *The Counter Scuffle. Whereunto is added, the Counter-Ratt,*[73] first printed in 1623 (four editions appeared by 1639). The burlesque hero of the travesty is one Ellis, a goldsmith. The author describes the prisoners in the guise of rats.

Somewhat like the pamphlets of roguery were the tracts dealing with the plague—terrifying descriptions of an ever recurring horror which made every Londoner's blood run cold. The dance of death has from early times held for man a grisly fascination. For the Londoner of the sixteenth and seventeenth centuries, the plague meant a vision of frightened citizens fleeing from a stricken city; of carts, loaded with the dead, creaking to loathsome burials; of robbery and crime in a demoralized community; of haunting fear, always present, that the visitation would bring once more the tragic, red-painted invocations for the mercy of God. As pamphleteers and printers realized the value of works appealing to the morbid instinct that finds a fascination in horror, they supplied, with ghastly timeliness, fearful descriptions of the epidemics.

Dekker was one of the most vivid of the writers about the plague. Realistically he pictures the misery, suffering, and meannesses of London citizens, the mistreatment of the poor, and the selfish callousness which the constant devastation produced.[74] A grim and

---

[72] Chandler, *op. cit.*, I, 113.

[73] Title quoted from the edition of 1628.

[74] *See* F. P. Wilson (ed.), *Plague Pamphlets of Thomas Dekker* (Oxford, 1925). An ex-

ironical humor often illuminates Dekker's plague pamphlets, as in his description in *The Wonderfull yeare* (1603) of the merry tinker crying, "Haue ye any more Londoners to bury?"; or in the sort of jest found in *The Meeting of Gallants at an Ordinarie* (1604). Dekker lived to chronicle the two worst plagues of the first half of the century—those of 1603 and 1625—and produced the same type of pamphlet on both occasions. Sympathy with the distressed is mingled with a macabre spirit of jest as Dekker gives expression to a humor partly inspired, like that of the comic papers which flourished with the armies in the last great war, by an effort to alleviate rampant pessimism. In *A Rod for Run-awayes* (1625), relating the misadventures of Londoners who flee the city in time of plague, Dekker asks indulgence for his anecdotes :

. . . let mee a little quicken my owne and your spirits, with telling you, how the rurall *Coridons* doe now begin to vse our Run-awayes ; neyther doe I this out of an idle or vndecent merriment (for iests are no fruit for this season) but onely to lay open what foolery, infidelity, inhumanity, nay, villany, irreligion, and distrust in God (with a defiance to his power) dwell in the bosomes of these vnmannerly Oasts in these our owne Netherlandish Dorpes.[75]

Evidently, the numerousness of jesting or trivial pamphlets in time of plague did not meet with the approval of some of the stricter citizens, for the author of *Lachrymae Londinenses* (1626) warns his readers :

If you expect in these ensuing Lines any scarce credible or feigned matters of wonderment, made in some Tauerne or on some Ale-bench, to tickle your Eares and helpe you to sing Care-away, you will be deceiued : for there are enow, if not too many such like Spuriall Pamphlets, which the Presse hath of late already spewed out, (Broods of *Barbi-*

---

cellent study of plague conditions is the same author's *The Plague in Shakespeare's London* (Oxford, 1927).

[75] Wilson, *Plague Pamphlets*, p. 153. A reply to Dekker came in *The Run-awayes Answer, To a Booke called, A Rodde for Runne-awayes. In Which Are set downe a Defence for their Running, with some Reasons perswading some of them neuer to come backe* (1625). It is dedicated "To Our Much Respected And Very worthy Friend, Mr. H. Condell at his Countrey-house in Fullam" and signed, "Your most louing Freindes, B. V., S. O., T. O., A. L., V. S." The pamphlet is a defense of the practice of abandoning London. It describes some of the terrors of the plague and ends with an expression of longing to return to London.

can, *Smithfield*, and the *Bridge*, and *Trundled*, *trolled* and *marshalled* vp
and downe along the Streets ; and haply the Countries also :) and certes (excepting one ingenious and ingenuous Writer lately extant, and
published since this Tract was penned,) they are mad Mountebankes
that dare venture to vent their Quacksaluing Conceipts, to mooue
mirth, in time of a mightie Mortalitie.[76]

With every return of the plague or with each new plague scare,
the printers rushed off pamphlets dealing with the terror.[77] On
the bookstall shelves, collections of remedies and preventives for
the malady jostled prayers and calls to repentance. Dr. Thomas
Lodge turned from the writing of fiction and plays to pen *A
Treatise of the Plague* (1603), a professional work far above the
average book which sought the eye of frightened readers.

The recurrence of the plague made the theme of death unusually
prominent in popular thought and literature. Samuel Rowlands,
a diligent writer for the multitude, in *A Terrible Battell betweene
the two consumers of the whole World: Time, and Death* [1606?] presents
a dialogue in which Time and Death debate their respective
merits and places in society. The equality of all men before the
conqueror, Death—a conventional note in ballads and pamphlets
—is stressed :

> And wheresoeuer, or what ere he be,
> For countenance, for credit and condition,
> Dignity, calling, office, or degree,
> Pessant, or prince, patient, or els Phisition :
> Euen from the Crowne and scepter to the plow,
> I make all looke as I my selfe do now.[78]

Common poets and decorators of alehouse walls find in death a
subject for their labors, taunts Time :

> Thy picture stands vpon the Ale-house wall,
> Not in the credit of an ancient story,
> But when the old wiues guests begin to braule,
> She points, and bids them read *Memento mori*:

---

[76] Wilson, *Plague Pamphlets*, pp. 245-46.

[77] Many of these pamphlets are quoted by Wilson, *The Plague in Shakespeare's London*,
passim. Further evidence of the vogue of plague literature will be found in the doc-
umentation of the same work.

[78] *The Complete Works of Samuel Rowlands*, 3 vols., Hunterian Club (Glasgow, 1872-80),
I, 31.

Looke, looke (saies she) what fellow standeth there,
As women do, when crying Babes they feare.

No memory of worth to thee belongs,
To call thee famous is condemned error,
And though sometime th'art baletted in songs,
Thy names imploide vnto no vse but terror,
Thy companie both rich and poore defie,
Loathsome to eare, most vgly to the eie.[79]

Thomas Brewer, author of ballads and cheap pamphlets, turned his attention to London's sins, when the plague was once more threatening the city in 1636, with *Lord have Mercy upon Vs. The World, A Sea, A Pest-house. The one full of Stormes, and Dangers, the other full of Soares and Diseases* (1636).[80] Punishment is the companion of sin, declares the author, who compares the wicked world to the unstable sea and the noisome pesthouse. Another pamphlet, probably also by Brewer, *A Dialogue betwixt a Cittizen, and a poore Countrey-man and his Wife, in the Countrey, where the Cittizen remaineth now in this time of sicknesse* (1636),[81] recounts once again in verse the plight of the fleeing citizen. This time, however, a country family entertains the visitor hospitably, after having been assured that he is uninfected. Brewer evidently wanted to encourage a better reception for Londoners when they sought refuge from the disease. In a prose tract (which follows the foregoing dialogue), *London[s] Trumpet Sounding into the Countrey. When Death drives, the Grave thrives*, the author calls Londoners to repentance and reminds countrymen that God will deal with them according to their mercies :

To you I speake, your eies doe I wish to bee opened. To looke backe at your hard and unkinde dealings with Cittizens, in the two last great Sicknesses : Remember how your Infidelity then, hath beene punished since : And therefore welcome the Sonnes, and Daughters of London

---

[79] *Ibid.*, p. 36.

[80] Preserved in the Huntington Library. In the plague of 1625, T. B. (possibly Thomas Brewer) had published *The Weeping Lady: Or, London Like Ninivie In Sack-Cloth. Describing the Mappe of her owne miserie, in this time of Her heauy Visitation; with her hearty Prayers, Admonition, and Pious Meditations, as the occasions of them offer themselues in Her Passion. Written by T. B.* (1625).

[81] Preserved in the Huntington Library.

coming to you now, as if they were your owne.   [Sigs. C 1ᵛ-C 2.]

The pamphlet concludes with a verse dialogue between Life and Death, entitled *Have with you into the Countrey*. Preceding this dialogue is a woodcut of skeleton Death, standing with a spade in one hand and a trumpet in the other, blowing a blast to be heard in the country. At his feet are a coffin, a mattock, and fresh dirt from a new-made grave. Faith in Christ, Death confides to Life, would be a remedy against his darts, but Life groans that the flesh is frail. A prayer to Christ to spare "this sinfull English land, And give us grace to understand" ends the work. Here we see a London citizen, sometime laureate of the Society of the Porters, producing a pamphlet, in verse and prose, which is typical of scores that entertained, instructed, and terrified the populace.

Compilers of almanacs and prognostications—works conventionally associated with the taste of common folk—sometimes made use of a universal fear to advertise their pamphlets. A prognostication which promised a return of the plague was certain to attract readers. Dekker used such a title in his own burlesque prognostication, *The Ravens Almanacke Foretelling of a Plague, Famine, and Ciuill Warre* (1609). The popular vogue of almanacs, with their predictions and astrological lore, was sufficient to provoke a number of travesties from satirists, as well as serious attacks upon exponents of judicial astrology.[82]

From the flotsam of evanescent books and pamphlets issued by Elizabethan printers, there are left a few relics that give evidence of the desire of business men of that age to foster favorable public relations. Propagandic ballads and pamphlets dealing with colonization and speculation in trading ventures, we have already noticed. In a few pamphlets a sensitiveness to public criticism may be discerned. For example, the London grocers came forward

---

[82] *See* Carroll Camden, Jr., "Elizabethan Almanacs and Prognostications," *The Library*, 4th Ser., XII (1931-32), 83-108, 194-207, for a general discussion of the popularity and significance of almanacs.

Almost everybody probably kept an almanac, filled with miscellaneous information. John Greene, a young reader of Lincoln's Inn in 1635, found the blank pages of small almanacs a suitable place for keeping a diary, which he continued until 1657. *See* E. M. Symonds, "The Diary of John Greene, 1635-1657," *English Historical Review*, XLIII (1928), 386.

about 1592 with a tract zealously defending their honesty and up-rightness in the selling of spices, and proposing certain reforms in labeling to insure the buyer against adulterated products. The tract is entitled *A Profitable And necessarie Discourse, for the meeting with the bad Garbelling of Spices, vsed in these daies. And against the Combination of workemen of that office, contrarie vnto common good. Composed by diuers Grocers of London* [1592?].[83] A dedication to Sir William Webbe, lord mayor, mentions the abuses which had hitherto existed in the garbeling and certification of spices in the central warehouse set apart by law for such examination and labeling. A veiled threat of the power of public opinion is contained in this dedication, which suggests that the lord mayor take action :

. . . Or if that doo faile to follow the saieng of the Poet *Musaeus*, the which is thus set forth:
> *It is good sometime to sound in open street*
> *The wicked works which men do thinke to hide.*
meaning that by publishing of some smal pamphlet touching the same, suche good maye ensue, either the workemanne to grow better, or the buier to be more wiser, in the office of garbling (a matter right Honorable and worshipfull, full of rashnesse to breake open a discourse, whereinto a man may more easilie enter, then find the waie out againe.)

Quite in the spirit of modern business is the declaration that the authors had written to prevent misunderstanding and enmity between buyers and sellers :

Therfore to burie the hatred growne, both betweene the seller and the buier, we proposed a possible means to profit the marchant, satisfie al the retaylers, and to assure the buier and occupier of the goodnes of such spices without fraud.[84]

The grocers hoped through the exposure of current methods, and through the constructive suggestions offered, to make many reforms in the interest of the public. Surely here was a pamphlet which attracted much attention from the purchasers of spices, a commodity then regarded as essential in the diet and medication of every citizen.

The good opinion of the public, disregarded too often in earlier

---

[83] Preserved in the Huntington Library.
[84] Epistle "To the discreet and vertuous Readers."

times, was sought with increasing eagerness by seventeenth-century business men. The value of "educational compaigns," so potent in present-day commercial propaganda, soon dawned on company officials, and the use of the printing press was the logical outcome. John Wheeler, merchant of Great Yarmouth and secretary of the Merchants Adventurers, was one of the first to recognize fully the utility of pamphlets in fostering ideas favorable to his company. In 1601, when the Merchants Adventurers were facing a serious crisis and needed public favor, Wheeler published, first at Middelburg and later in London, *A Treatise Of Commerce, Wherin Are Shewed The Commodies [Commodities] Arising By A Wel Ordered, And Ruled Trade, Such as that of the Societie of Merchantes Adventurers is proved to bee, written principallie for the better information of those who doubt of the Necessarienes of the said Societie in the State of the Realme of Englande.*[85] The Merchants Adventurers were at the moment in disfavor with the people at home, who regarded them as greedy monopolists. At the same time, their monopoly of the white-cloth trade was being weakened abroad by interlopers, privileged by the Earl of Cumberland, who had an unlimited license for the exportation of white cloth for ten years, in violation, the Merchants Adventurers felt, of their rights. The Parliament of 1601 was to consider the question of monopolies. Wheeler wanted to be sure that his company was understood, and understood favorably, by the public. Before Parliament met, the pamphlet was printed in sufficient quantities to insure widespread circulation.[86] Its purposes, similar in aim to modern business publicity, are thus summarized by its recent editor :

(1) The *Treatise* must convince discontented members of the wisdom of remaining within the organization and obeying its rules. (2) It must convince the leaders of the cloth industry that they are benefited by the system of having their products marketed abroad through the chartered companies. (3) It must convince Parliament that the Merchants Adventurers should not be considered a harmful monopoly. (4) It must convince the Queen that failure to support the Company

---

[85] George Burton Hotchkiss (ed.), *A Treatise of Commerce, by John Wheeler* (New York, 1931). Professor Hotchkiss supplies an excellent introduction pointing out the significance of this treatise in the history of the Merchants Adventurers.

[86] Professor Hotchkiss (*ibid.*, p. 12) estimates that between 4,000 and 5,000 of the pamphlets were issued.

would endanger the Crown revenue and embarrass the kingdom finan-
cially. (5) It must convince friends of the Hanseatics that it is useless
to hope that they will be reinstated in England, and thus indirectly
influence Hamburg to invite the Adventurers back. (6) It must increase public respect for merchants in general and the Merchants
Adventurers in particular.[87]

When Wheeler has finished, the reader feels that the Merchants
Adventurers are great benefactors, unselfishly laboring for the
commonweal. Their private interest is the public interest. They
maintain peace with foreign countries, import foreign goods
cheaply, develop trade necessary to English prosperity, encourage
navigation, and bring honor and glory to the prince abroad. The
treatise apparently convinced enough contemporary readers to
effect its purposes for the next ten years.

The way opened by Wheeler for commercial propaganda was
quickly followed by others. Perhaps his own pamphlet had been
prompted by a prod from the same weapon. Thomas Milles, a
Kentish customs officer, wrote a pamphlet in 1601 called *The
Custumers Apology*, which he privately printed and circulated, and
later reprinted in several revised forms. Among other things, he
attacked the Merchants Adventurers for their monopolistic practices.[88] When Wheeler, in his *Treatise of Commerce*, took occasion to
reply to Milles, the latter retorted vigorously in *The Customers
Replie* (1604), once more condemning Wheeler's company.

Exposures of the machinations of big business soon had a place
in the popular literature of the time. An attack in 1615 on the
East India Company, entitled *The Trades Increase*, by a certain
Robert Kayll or Keale, who signed himself "I. R.," roused the
company to action and to a public reply. Innocently enough, the
author of *The Trades Increase* professes that his purpose is to encourage the fishing trade; but, under cover of this laudable intention, he assails the East India Company, accusing it of destroying
the power of the British navy by losing in distant voyages ships
needed at home, of running up the price of lumber by building
great vessels to be cast away, and of diminishing the number of
English sailors through sickness and drowning. While the East

---

[87] *Ibid.*, p. 65.   [88] *Ibid.*, pp. 60 ff., 81 ff.

India Company injures British commerce, he asserts, the Dutch fatten on the profits of the fishing trade. The pamphleteer suggests the abandoning of distant enterprises, which bring loss, and a concentration upon coastal fishing, in which he sees great profits. Though he was a Londoner who "was borne in the Citty, and liue amongst Sea-men,"[89] Kayll belonged to the minority opposed to the new imperialism. With a nose for journalism, he uses the name of one of the East India Company's ships, recently lost, as the title of his pamphlet, and appeals to the prejudices of the investors by comparing the company to "a bird that maketh her selfe gay with the feathers of all other fowles."[90] He is opposed to trade monopolies, and demands freedom of trade for all:

Now for a Corollary to all these imperfect lines, whereas in the superficiall suruey of want of shipping, we find most of our sea-trades either decaying, or at a stay; let me out of themselues, without offence, propound the consideration of one remedy thereto, euen by a *freedom of Traffique* for all his Maiesties subiects to all places; hereby his maiesties customes will increase, the nauy & sea-men will receiue nourishment out of more imployment, the whole incorporation of merchants reap comfort in that they may communicate with all aduentures, and the vniuersal body of the subiects of the land content, in that they may become merchants, being very ready in this aduentrous world to make new discoueries, whereas now otherwise merchandize sorting & setled in companies, confineth merchants into those limits that priuate orders tie them in, so that they may not helpe themselues through any discouragements in one trade, but by sute and submission of themselues to the other; . . .
                                                                    [P. 51.]

Corporate interests were enraged at the attack, and Dudley Digges, an officer of the East India Company, hastened to reply with *The Defence Of Trade. In a Letter To Sir Thomas Smith Knight, Gouernour of the East-India Companie, &c. From one of that Societie* (1615). The pamphlet, in the form of a letter, is a model for corporation defense, with all the arguments still used by business to justify its combinations and trusts. The convincing weapon of statistics is used to show that the yet unknown "I. R." had misrepresented the numbers of ships and seamen lost. Digges gains confidence by frankly admitting losses when they have occurred, such

---

[89] P. 56.   [90] P. 26.

as the "Trade's Increase," which was wrecked by misadventure while being overhauled, but he emphasizes the virtues of the company and the wealth which it has brought to England. If outsiders complain, the men who live on the company's pay roll are contented. Furthermore, the company does much philanthropic work in charity and support of preachers. Modern business has learned its lesson well from this seventeenth-century apostle of commerce, who thus extols the munificence of corporate blessings:

For my part, I that often visit *Philpot Lane*,* professe, I meet few sorrowfull *East India* Clients, but such as are refused to goe the Voyage. And though I would not wish the *East-India* Marchants to answere this imaginarie clamour with setting truly downe how many Hoggesheads of good Beefe and Porke, how many thousand weight of Biscuit they haue giuen to the poore, euen in the parishes and places which hee names; nor yet with telling what proportion weekely in pottage, beefe, and bread they send to the *Fleet, Ludgate, Newgate*, the two *Counters, Bedlem*, the *Marshalsea, Kings Bench, White Lion*, and *Counter* in *Southwarke*, besides good summes of money yearely to releeue poore painfull Preachers of the Gospell, whose meanes are small, and charges great. For which and other workes of charitie, God hath so wonderfully blest their labours. Yet if they should awhile forbeare their almes, and let the poore soules want it, because this man thus raild vpon them, think then what an armie of complaints and curses would fall on him and all his fained rabble, which he brought to fight like Satans seeming souldiers in the aire.   [Pp. 38-39.]
* Sir *Thomas Smiths* house, where the Companie entertaine and pay their men.

Not content with a mere reply to the attack, the East India Company ferreted out the author, who, for blaspheming against business, was forthwith lodged in the Fleet, whence he was charitably released on submission to the Privy Council of a written apology for his fault.[91]

---

[91] H. C. Maxwell Lyte (ed.), *Acts of the Privy Council of England, 1615-1616* (London, 1925), pp. 107-8. On April 16, 1615, the Privy Council sent a warrant to the warden of the Fleet for the release of Kayll on his submission of a signed statement admitting his fault. Kayll's statement follows:
"The humble petition of Robert Kaylle.
"Sheweth that whereas it pleased your lordships to comaund the sayd peticioner before you, concerning a late treatise written by him, in answering whereof, for that he nether gave satisfaction to your lordships nor demeaned himselfe as he

The way of publicity once learned, business men of the seventeenth century soon saw to it that the public was supplied with reading matter which carried their ideas. They were not always in agreement, however, and controversies between rival factions or rival theorists found their way into print. Edward Misselden, a Merchant Adventurer, in *Free Trade, or the Means to Make Trade Flourish* (1622), discussed the decay of trade, which he attributed chiefly to excessive consumption of foreign imports and exportation of gold. Gerard Malynes, a member of the Staplers Company, attacked Misselden in *The Maintenance of Free Trade* (1622), in which he found the principal ailments of business in the lack of regulation of foreign exchange. He also declared that the monopolies, such as that held by the Merchants Adventurers, were injurious to business. Misselden retorted in *The Circle of Commerce, or the Ballance of Trade, in Defense of Free Trade* (1623). In these and other pamphlets they argued questions of great interest at the moment to the commercial element in the City. Thomas Mun, wealthy merchant, added a contribution to the literature of business propaganda in *A Discourse of Trade, from England vnto the East Indies* (1621), which defended the East India Company from charges of ruining the country by the exportation of bullion. Some of his statements, questioned by Malynes, resulted in Misselden's defense in *The Circle of Commerce*. About 1630 Mun wrote *Englands Treasure by Forraign Trade*, which was not published until 1668. In this he again defended the balance-of-trade doctrine beneficial to the East India Company—namely, that the export of bullion was not detrimental so long as exports of commodities were in excess of imports. He also expressed regret over the foolish habit of too much smoking (the East India Company at the time having little to do with the tobacco trade) and the encroachment of the Dutch on English fishing (the Dutch being inveterate enemies of the East India Company). He set the stamp of his

---

ought, it pleased your lordships to lay this just correccion upon him. . . . [Pleads his loyalty to the commonwealth.]

"Subscribed, as by the submission it selfe appeareth, the 17 April, 1615.

"The treatise before mencioned is called the Trads Increase.

"ROBERT KAYLL."

Kayll's name is spelled "Keale" in the warrant for his arrest.—P. 99.

approval on a slightly earlier pamphlet concerned with the fishing industry—a pamphlet with a title certain to attract the eye of a tradesman, *Englands Way to Win Wealth* (1614), by Tobias Gentleman.[92]

Tobacco, objected to by Mun, was the subject of propagandic pamphlets, for and against the use of the weed. Henry Buttes, the author of *Dyets Dry Dinner* (1599), like numerous others, maintained the medicinal value of tobacco, though the question was debated in many a pamphlet, both serious and satirical. Tobacco quickly became a theme fit for pamphlets, and there was an outpouring of them at the beginning of the seventeenth century.[93] Importations of tobacco by way of Spain aroused the animosity of Englishmen, especially those looking to Virginia plantations for profit. As early as 1615 one C. T. published *An Advice How To Plant Tobacco In England*, which attacked the Spanish tobacco trade. The fearful results of smoking poisonous Spanish tobacco and the filthy process of manufacture—two arguments of the sort employed today by the Anti-Cigarette League—were emphasized.[94] A little later Edward Bennett published *A treatise . . . touching the inconveniences, that the importation of tobacco out of Spaine, hath brought into this land* [c. 1620].

Out of trade developments and new business undertakings of the early seventeenth century, came a quantity of pamphlet literature to appeal to the citizen. Commercial interests had learned the value of public sentiment. The populace of a city like London was vitally concerned with trading ventures that attracted not only great magnates but also small investors. Hence

---

[92] See *Dictionary of National Biography*, sub Mun.

[93] See *Cambridge History of English Literature*, IV, 530-31.

[94] C. T. warns his readers that ". . . there hath been Tobacco brought out of Spaine, with dissolued sublimate, which euery man knowes to bee poyson, and no way so dangerously ministered without suspition, as by fume."—Sig. A 4ᵛ.

"Now besides these harmefull mixtures, if our English which delight in Indian Tobacco, had seene how the Spanish slaues make it vp, how they dresse their sores, and pockie vlcers, with the same vnwasht hands with which they sluber and annoynt the Tobacco, and call it sauce *Per los perros Luteranos*, for *Lutheran* dogges; they would not so often draw it into their heads and through their noses as they doe : yea many a filthy fauour should they find therein, did not the smell of the hunny maister it ; which smell euery man may plainly perceiue that takes of the blacke role Tabacco, brought from *Orenoque*, *Trinidado*, and else-where."—Sig. B 1.

the bookstalls, which groaned under a fresh burden of trade pamphlets, were certain to lure many a humble artisan and small tradesman to rub shoulders with an alderman as they all, with a common interest, craned their necks to see the latest publicity affecting their investments. The Virginia Company, with its descriptions of the wonderful richness of the new land, and the East India Company, with its insistence on the value of its monopoly to the commonwealth, led the way in the progress of commercial propaganda, which has reached its apotheosis in twentieth-century America.

But since the ephemeral literature written with an eye to the common man was almost as varied as human taste, we need not expect that writings on the mundane theme of commercial expansion were allowed to absorb too much of the citizen's interest, or that complacency over commercial progress should be allowed to develop unchecked.[95] A great mass of moral treatises and indignant satires rebuked the age for its sins, real or fancied. Reformers kept the public supplied with treatises proving the general depravity, an excellent illustration of the type being Philip Stubbes's *The Anatomie of Abuses* (1583), which enjoyed at least four editions by 1595. The preachers were prolific with dour warnings, which often reached the booksellers in pamphlet form,[96] and objectors to particular iniquities voiced their grievances in innumerable tracts. Stephen Gosson's *The School of Abuse* (1579), for example, found in poets and players a subject for alarm. Anglican bishops were the mark of the anonymous pamphleteers of the Martin Marprelate controversy, who kept the lay public snickering at ecclesiastical discomfiture in the late 1580's. The extravagances and weaknesses of women were stock matter for satirists, professional or amateur.[97] Usurers were singled out for condemnation by writers who based their economic theories on the Old Testament.[98] The upstart gentry were ridiculed in such tracts as

---

[95] Useful suggestions regarding popular literary taste will be found in the essays by H. V. Routh, "The Progress of Social Literature in Tudor Times," *Cambridge History of English Literature*, Vol. III, and "London and the Development of Popular Literature," *ibid.*, Vol. IV.

[96] *See* Chap. VIII, *supra*.

[97] *See* Chap. XIII, *infra*.

[98] Cf. the introduction to R. H. Tawney (ed.), *A Discourse Upon Usury . . . by*

Greene's *A Quip for an Upstart Courtier* (1592). Many an industrious tradesman must have laughed at the picture of the despised social-climbing gallant in Dekker's *The Guls Horne-Booke* (1609), and satires like it. The whole pageantry of wickedness furnished the same author with material for *The Seven Deadly Sinnes of London* (1606). Barnabe Rich, in *Faultes Faults, And nothing else but Faultes* (1606), as in other similar tracts, reveled in the shortcomings of his age; yet he would restrain the activities of certain critics and satirists :

I doe not altogither dislike of our *Satyrists* and *Critickes* of these times, that doe chide at vice ; but I cannot allow them so to ayme at any one particularly, nor so to point at anie mans priuate misse, . . .

[Sig. B 2.]

Samuel Rowlands, Richard Brathwaite, George Wither, John Taylor the sculler, and many others found in the London of their day matter for pamphlets in prose and verse satirizing, sometimes gayly, sometimes harshly, the current abuses. John Taylor, laureate of the watermen, waged a warfare of ridicule on hackney coaches and on one occasion revenged himself on his delinquent debtors in a poem.[99] Satirical tracts, humorous and serious, bulked large in the stalls of the booksellers catering to the citizenry.

The satirist who saw in iniquity a theme for laughter, however, was never so popular with the multitude as the purveyor of warnings. Of the warning literature which came from the press in such quantities, that stressing the judgments of God found special favor in the eyes of citizens. John Earle contemptuously sneers at the "pot-poet" who "sitting in a Baudy-house . . .

Thomas Wilson (London, 1924), and A. B. Stonex, "Money Lending and Money-Lenders in England during the 16th and 17th Centuries," *Schelling Anniversary Studies* (New York, 1923), pp. 263-85.

[99] See *The World runnes on wheeles: Or, Oddes betwixt Carts and Coaches* (1623) and *A Kicksey Winsey: Or A Lerry Come-Twang: Wherein Iohn Taylor hath Satyrically suited 800. of his bad debtors that will not pay him for his returne of his Iourney from Scotland* (1619). Perhaps fifty of the debtors were driven to pay, for, in the 1630 folio of Taylor's works, the number in the title was changed to 750.

The productions of Taylor, ranging from pamphlets on journeys made for a wager to a Thumb Bible, provide a cross section of themes treated in the evanescent writings of his day.

writes Gods Iudgements."[100] But the pot-poet knew what would find purchasers among his fellow citizens, who greedily devoured the tales of God's manifest wrath or the doleful predictions of impending disasters. Balladists and pamphleteers, as we have already seen, delighted to find in calamity the evidence of an avenging God.[101] The dire punishments visited by Jehovah upon sinners guilty of Sabbath breaking, disobedience, treason, murder, or some other crime were vividly described in numberless ballads and pamphlets. At length a vast compendium of judgments meted out to all sorts of sinners was brought together by Thomas Beard under the title of *The Theatre of Gods Iudgements: Or, A Collection Of*

---

[100] *Micro-cosmographie* (1628), sigs. F 1v-F 3.

[101] Robert Burton was an industrious collector of popular pamphlets. Typical of the warning pamphlets are the following, preserved in the Burton Collection in the Bodleian Library :

Two Most Strange And notable examples, shewed at Lyshborne the 26. day of Ianuarie now last past. The One By Striking Dumme two of the cheefe of the Holy-house, as they were pronouncing the sentence of death against two English Marriners, . . . The other . . . by burning two Ships of Corne in the Harboure there, which was brought out of France to releeue the King his enimies: An example most wonderfull. A notable warning to such English Marchants, which for their owne benefit, by carrying our victuals away, impouerish our Countrey, and strengthen the enemies of God and our Prince (1591).

The most Rare, Strange and wonderfull Example of Almightie God, shewed in the Citie of Teloune in Prouence, on a cruell Papisticall Bishop (1592).

Gods Warning To His people of England. By The Great Overflowing Of The Waters or Floudes lately hapned in South-wales, and many other places (1607).

Anthony Paint[er] The Blaspheming Caryar. Who sunke into the ground vp to the neck, and there stood two day[s and] two nights, and not to bee drawne out by the strength of Hor[ses] or digged out by the help of man: and there dyed the 3. of Nouember. 1613. Also the punishment of Nicholas Mesle a most wicked blasphemer. Reade and tremble (1614).

The Miracle, of Miracles. As fearefull as euer was seene or heard of in the memorie of Man. Which lately happened at Dichet in Sommersetshire, and sent by diuers credible witnesses to bee published in London. Also a Prophesie reuealed by a poore Countrey Maide, who being dead the first of October last, 24. houres, 1613. reuiued againe, and lay fiue days weeping, and continued prophesying of strange euents to come (1614). The author, T. I., has a preface pointing out that "These and such like examples (good Reader) warneth vs to bee watchfull for the day of the Lord which is at hand."

Gods Handy-worke in Wonders. Miraculously shewen vpon two Women, lately deliuered of two Monsters: with a most strange and terrible Earth-quake (1615). An epistle to the reader calls attention to the mercy of God "in that he forewarneth vs to flie from the wrath to come."

Looke Vp and see Wonders. A miraculous Apparition in the Ayre, lately seene in Barke-shire at Bawlkin Greene neere Hatford. April. 9th 1628. (1628). This is an account of a fall of meteors, but witnesses declared that the phenomenon was accompanied by a battle in the air and the firing of ordnance above. The hand of God in warning is seen in it.

Histories out of Sacred, Ecclesiasticall, and prophane Authours, concerning the admirable Iudgements of God vpon the transgressours of his commandements. Translated Out Of French, And Augmented by more than three hundred Examples (1597). This work classifies the examples of God's visitations under the headings of various sins. Best known of Beard's augmentations is the account of the blasphemous end of Christopher Marlowe. The work was popular. New editions appeared in 1612 and 1631, followed by a folio edition with new examples in 1648.[102]

It remained for a pious merchant of Exeter, one John Reynolds, to take advantage of the taste for both murder stories and accounts of God's vengeance and to bring out what was destined to be one of the most popular bourgeois works of the seventeenth century, *The Triumphs of Gods Revenge Against the crying, and Execrable Sinne of Murther.* The first edition was in three volumes, one each year for 1621, 1622, and 1623. Another quarto edition was published in 1629, followed by a handsome folio edition in 1635. At least ten other editions appeared by the beginning of the eighteenth century, for the work had a long period of popularity. *The Triumphs* had every quality to make it a favorite. The criminal history of the foreign world was drawn on for examples which were presented, as the title-page of 1635 has it, as

Histories which containe great varietie of mournfull and memorable Accidents, Historicall, Morall, and Divine, very necessary to restraine and deterre us from this bloodie Sinne, which in these our dayes makes so ample, and large a Progression.

In his dedication, Reynolds asserts that his purpose is patriotic; he hopes men may be restrained through this "horrour and terrour"; he has chosen his subjects from foreign sources because he does not want to bring shame to his own country and to revive old feuds. Reynolds frankly declares in the advertisement to the edition of 1635 that he writes for a popular audience: "I am not so vaine or presumptuous, to thinke that they deserve to be seene

---

[102] Miss Lily B. Cambell, *Shakespeare's Tragic Heroes, Slaves of Passion* (Cambridge, 1930), pp. 10 ff., calls attention to the popularity of Beard's work and of John Reynolds's *The Triumphs of Gods Revenge*, and the relation of these works to the theme of justice. She asserts that the popularity of Elizabethan revenge plays is in part due to the interest in the meting out of justice through divine instrumentality.—Pp. 23-24.

and read of the more Iudicious ; for my thoughts aspire to nothing unproportionable to my meane abilities." Many of the stories
were raw and sensational, but the moral gloss was intended to
assure the bourgeois reader of a feeling of righteousness as he
read them. Tribute to the value and popularity of this and similar works is piously paid by a later writer in the *genre*, Henry
Burton, who says in the preface to *A Divine Tragedie Lately Acted,
Or, A Collection of sundrie memorable examples of Gods judgements upon
Sabbath-breakers* (1641) :

And as God himself, so holy men of God in all ages, following his example, have carefully observed, and registred to posterity the speciall
most remarkable judgements of God upon obstinate sins and sinners
of all sorts, (with which not onely Ecclesiastical but even prophane
stories are fully fraught) happened in the ages, and the places wherein
they lived : Many whereof *Mr. Jo. Fox in his Acts and Monuments*, near
the end. *Mr. Raynolds* in his *Treatise concerning the miraculous discovery and
punishments of murthers and Murtherers*. Dr. *Thomas Beard in his Theatre of
Gods judgements*, with sundry others, have collected and digested into
intire Tractates, the very reading and serious perusall whereof, would
no doubt daunt the most professed Atheist, and reclaim the most
incorrigible sinner.

The deterrent literature which made such an appeal to the
Renaissance middle class was vast and varied. The Puritan carried
his taste for warning literature to America, where it flourished
on fresh soil with renewed vigor, increasing in gloom and dolorous
commentary as New Englanders pondered the wrath of an avenging deity.[103] Authors and printers tagged their titles with the
"warning" label. The dramatist who named his play *A Warning for
Fair Women* hoped thereby to capture the interest of a public
trained to expect an edifying relation of God's vengeance on
sinners. Journalistically sensational though this literature was, its
pious pretensions, often sincere, elevated it in the minds of its
readers to a position of value and moral worth, the ultimate
standard for the bourgeois critic. The literature concerned with
the judgments of God was deemed so worthy that Nehemiah

---

[103] *See* Ola Elizabeth Winslow, *American Broadside Verse* (New Haven, 1930), and the
leading article, "Broadside Ballads," *Times Literary Supplement*, Jan. 22, 1931,
pp. 49-50.

Wallington, a turner of Eastcheap, spent his leisure compiling examples with a view to publication.[104] One of his manuscripts, now preserved in the British Museum, bears the title "Gods Judgements on Sabbath Breakers." It is significant that Wallington listed among his favorite books Beard's *Theatre of Gods Judgments*. The taste of this pious Eastcheap craftsman was characteristic of his kind.

Though gloom sold well, booksellers kept on hand other works to satisfy gayer moods. Since the tradesmen of Elizabethan England, puritanical though they were, did not all relish solemnity when they bought a pamphlet, jest books, replete with old and often rancid jokes, provided amusement. Although these trivial little books, written for the mere entertainment of the passing reader, were condemned by the serious and the godly, they nevertheless flourished, even if they did have to assert their utility in driving away melancholy.[105] Ancient tales, banal anecdotes, ribald jests, obscene dullness, with an occasional flash of wit which has come down through the ages, made up their subject matter. Year after year, with the regularity of almanacs, some new purveyor of humor brought out a rehash of the old jokes, with a fresh title to catch the eye of the apprentice and the loiterer in Paul's Walk.[106] Certain characters like Sir Thomas More, Dick Tarlton, George Peele, and, a little later, Ben Jonson, began to assume comic proportions. Tricks, quips, and jests were attributed to them, and they lived anew a life of mythical humor. *Tarltons Newes out of Purgatorie* (1590); *Tarltons Jests* (licensed, 1609); the *Merrie Conceited Iests of George Peele* (1607), at least four times printed before 1640; *Pasquils Jests, Mixed with Mother Bunches Merriments* (1604), thrice printed by 1632; and dozens of other books of jests equally famous in their day, preserved the Londoner from melancholy. Thomas Fuller in *The Holy State* (1642), discussing jesting, conceded that

---

[104] R. Webb (ed.), *Historical Notices of Events Occurring Chiefly in the Reign of Charles I. By Nehemiah Wallington*, 2 vols. (London, 1869), I, xxiv-xxv.

[105] *See* Chap. XI, *supra*.

[106] Some of the best examples of the Elizabethan jest books are reprinted in W. C. Hazlitt, *Shakespeare Jest-Books*, 3 vols. (London, 1864). *See also* T. S. Graves, "Jonson in the Jest-Books," *Manly Anniversary Studies in Language and Literature* (Chicago, 1924), pp. 127-39. A short list of jest books will be found in the *Cambridge History of English Literature*, IV, 531-33.

"Harmelesse mirth is the best cordiall against the consumption of the spirits : wherefore Jesting is not unlawfull if it trespasseth not in Quantity, Quality, or Season."[107] Publishers had long used the argument to reassure the readers of the ubiquitous jest books that their time was not being wasted.

The serious intellectual of Elizabethan England, the aristocratic poet, the historian, or the philosopher—all such authors of polite letters as these—were generally convinced that they were writing for all time and made a show of despising popular plaudits. But the rapidly growing army of authors who lived by their wits had few illusions. The Greenes, the Dekkers, the Martin Parkers, and the John Taylors, knowing the taste of the multitude, racked their "sun-burned brains" for subject matter, and the result was as various as the kaleidoscopic life unfolding around them. Between extremes of piety and ribaldry ran a river of penny pamphlets on every subject from original sin to the price of corn. The Elizabethan commoner was omnivorous in his consumption of the products of the printing press, and as the flair for journalism developed in writers for the people, all the concomitants of modern newspaper and periodical subject matter found their way into the infinitely varied broadside and pamphlet literature. The public taste for journalistic *divertissements* was the same as it is today. Only lacking was the mechanical fusion of all the elements into the newspaper and the magazine which today form the intellectual fodder of the average citizen.

---

[107] Bk. III, Chap. II, 155-56. Cf. Chap. XI, *supra.*

XIII

THE POPULAR CONTROVERSY OVER WOMAN

WHILE courtly Platonists and adapters of Petrarchan conventions were glorifying woman in dainty verses, the Elizabethan shopkeeper found a literature on the same theme no less fascinating, albeit the works that interested him had a somewhat different point of view and emphasis from those that delighted the aristocratic audience. For bourgeois authors and readers alike preferred to view the subject a little more realistically than the conventionalized attitudes toward women, often affected in polite letters, usually favored. Hence woman became the theme of many popular poems and pamphlets, which vigorously attacked her weaknesses or with equal vigor defended her virtues. Significantly enough, while aristocratic poets were busy discovering goddesses with whom they might compare their mistresses, burgher writers were arguing about woman's place in society and were setting up some early landmarks in the literature of woman's rights.[1] Not that all citizen-authors defended woman, for it is true that there was no diminution of interest in the age-old controversy, in which priests throughout the Middle Ages had cudgeled their brains for terms evil enough to describe the daughters of Eve. Satires mocking the vanities of women still excited the laughter of the man in the street; and moralistic writers were constantly alarmed at woman's forwardness. Yet, despite the recrudescence of medieval condemnations of the female sex, a new note of respect was creeping into the popular literature, as writers reflecting the trend of middle-class opinion arose to defend woman against her traducers.

---

[1] *See* Chap. VII, *supra.* A brief survey of the feministic literature in this period is provided by Joachim Heinrich, *Die Frauenfrage bei Steele und Addison,* in *Palaestra,* CLXVIII (1930), 1-50.

Elizabethan interest in the controversial literature about women was doubtless stimulated by social changes taking place in England and by a political situation which gave them a queen who realized the power she might wield over popular imagination by reason of her sex. Although some of her subjects might secretly agree with the pessimistic view taken by John Knox in *The Monstruous Regiment of Women* [1558], few dared be so bold as the Scotch preacher. Nevertheless, the unexpressed suspicion of a woman ruler may account for some of the general satire on woman in the early years of her reign, and, by the same token, some of the defenses of women were doubtless inspired by a desire thus to defend indirectly the sex of the sovereign. Moreover, social progress was making for a new interest in discussions of the relations of the sexes, as women of all classes gradually increased their liberties until foreigners observed that England was the paradise of women.[2] In many crafts and trades, women took an increasingly important part, for the Renaissance woman was the able second-in-command to her husband, as many treatises on domestic relations, discussed in an earlier chapter, testify.

But this activity and boldness of women, especially women of the middle class, aroused the ire of conservatives, who vented their displeasure in pulpit and pamphlet, and were answered by staunch defenders of the virtues of the criticized sex. Even stage plays took up the cudgels. For example, in the early seventeenth century the indictment of the extravagance, greed, folly, and lust of tradesmen's wives is a frequent theme of Middleton's comedies, whereas Thomas Heywood's plays—though sometimes dramatizing feminine weakness—offer many a stout passage in the portrayal of their intelligence, spirit, and wisdom. While satirists held forth on the frailties of English wives, eulogists made their virtues a byword. If courtly poets and poetasters busied themselves with verses which praised—and sometimes censured—women, less aristocratic authors were not far behind in their zeal to discuss the eternal theme. If courtiers were witty and graceful, bourgeois writers were diligent to give appraisals—sometimes serious, some-

[2] Fynes Moryson's *Itinerary* (1617): "England in generall is said to be the Hell of Horses, the Purgatory of Servants and the Paradice of Weomen."—Quoted from the edition published by James MacLehose and Sons (Glasgow, 1907-08), III, 462.

times jocular—of woman and her relation to the cosmic scheme of things. These discussions, sometimes reflecting much of burgher ideals and morality, occupied an important place in the literary interest of the substantial middle class.

Popular literature about women came in sporadic outbursts throughout the sixteenth and seventeenth centuries, under the stimulation of some current situation, as in the case of the Overbury murder, or as a result of some provocative publication which demanded replies or begot a progeny of imitations. In the mid-sixteenth century occurred just such a flurry of interest in books attacking and defending women, and printers hastened to supply poems and pamphlets concerned, not with great ladies, but with the average woman, whose freedom was causing alarm to conservative moralists—such alarm, indeed, that a proclamation was issued in 1547 forbidding women to "meet together to babble and talk" and ordering husbands to "keep their wives in their houses."[3] If not every observer of the times would agree with Thomas Underdowne that all manner of vices grow out of the liberty of women to spend their time in gossip until there were never "more ydell women in the whole worlde then is nowe in the small circuit of Englande,"[4] at least one faction among the authors who produced a considerable literature about women in the 1540's would have argued the truth of Underdowne's slightly later statement. These early satires are prevailingly medieval, with infiltrations from French and Italian sources,[5] but underneath the raillery is to be found a new interest in woman as a social factor. Of the several productions that appeared in the 1540's to arouse the partisans of the maligned sex, the best known and most popular was the

---

[3] W. M. Williams, *Annals of the Worshipful Company of Founders of the City of London* (London, 1867), p. 89. In describing the settlement of a dispute between two wives of members of the Company, Williams refers to the proclamation, which the freedom of middle-class wives seems to have precipitated.

[4] In the preface to *Theseus and Ariadne* (1566).—Cited by J. P. Collier, *A Bibliographical and Critical Account of the Rarest Books in the English Language*, 4 vols. (New York, 1866), III, 92.

[5] H. V. Routh, "The Progress of Social Literature in Tudor Times," *Cambridge History of English Literature*, III, 99-102, comments briefly on the early feministic controversy. A short bibliography, pp. 551-54, gives the most significant items about women in the early period. He finds that the *Schole house of women* borrows from *Les quinze joyes de mariage* and *A C. mery Talys*.

Schole house of women, attributed to Edward Gosynhill,[6] a diatribe against the vanity, talkativeness, extravagance, faithlessness, and general frailty of women from Eve to Jezebel. A pious desire to reprehend vice and encourage virtue is the author's asserted intention. The *Schole house of women* immediately provoked replies and imitations, one of the most vigorous retorts being *A Dyalogue defensyue for women, agaynst malycyous detractoures* (1542), attributed to Robert Vaughan,[7] presenting a debate between a falcon and a pye, in which the former defends woman against the prating of the malevolent pye. An early defense of the learning of women is put into the mouth of the falcon, who boasts:

> In our countrey natyue, women thou mayst se
> In both tongues experte, the Latyne and the Greke :
> In Rethorycke and Poetrye, excellent they be
> And with pen to endyte, they be nat to seke
> If women in youth, had suche educacyon
> In knowledge and lernynge, as men vse to haue
> Theyr workes of theyr wyttes, wolde make full probacyon
> And that of men counceyll, they nede nat to craue.　　[Sig. B 2.]

Even the unfairness of the double standard of morality is condemned by the author, who holds that women are not more to blame than men for unchastity, since the latter besiege them with solicitations and exert all their vaunted intelligence to bring about their capitulation.[8] An interesting hint that the attacks on women were being written to please certain "great men" is made by the pye in answer to the falcon's plea that he give over his uncharitable ways:

---

[6] The date of the first edition of the *Schole house* is probably about 1542, though the earliest preserved edition is dated doubtfully 1550 by the *Short Title Catalogue.*

[7] Thomas Corser, *Collectanea Anglo-Poetica,* V, Pt. II (1880), 319-23. Cf. also *ibid.,* IV, Pt. I (1877), 28-35.

In the dedication "To the ryght Worshypfull and his synguler good maystres Arthur Hardberde," Vaughan declares that the manuscript of his poem was given him by a friend to be published under Vaughan's name. Miss Beatrice White, "Three Rare Books about Women," *The Huntington Library Bulletin,* No. 2 (1931), pp. 165-71, has shown that the real author may be Robert Burdet, whose name is concealed in an acrostic in Vaughan's address to the reader.

[8] Sig. B IV.

> I graunt sayde the Pye, but yet adulacyon
> Nedes must I vse, great men to content
> And agaynst women, my cōmon detraction
> These two to contynewe, is my full intent.   [Sig. E 2ᵛ.]

Gosynhill, thus answered by Vaughan's pamphlet, had previously written *The prayse of all women, called Mulierū pean* [1542?], proof of his ability to present both sides of the woman question—proof also of his sense of what the public wanted, for the latter production had two editions, and, of the *Schole house*, four editions are extant.

A burlesque of the books in praise of women, published under the pseudonym of Oliver Oldwanton, bore the title, *A lyttle treatyse called the Image of Idlenesse, conteynynge certeyne matters moued betwene Walter Wedlocke and Bawdin Bacheler. Trāslated out of the Troyane or Cornyshe tounge into Englyshe, by Olyuer Oldwanton, and dedicated to the Lady Lust* [1558?]. Another edition in the British Museum, "Newly corrected and augmented," is dated 1574. While pretending to praise and to advise women, it good-naturedly mocks them in a series of letters concerning marriage, written or received by Bawdin Bacheler—a form which faintly forecasts the epistolary novel, for in Bacheler's matrimonial prospects we discern a semblance of plot. An ironical preface to Lady Lust comments on the prevalence of satires on women :

. . . the iniquitie of tyme is now suche : that the verye graueste and most wyse sort of men (yea and euen they which haue ministration in the common wealth) wyll sometyme soonest laughe and reioyce to here and rede euyll of women : . . . [a state of affairs which] by thoppinion of some doctours, commeth by thinfluence of some disordered planet.

Although most of the controversial works about women in this period seem to have revolved around the position and behavior of middle-class wives, there was a sizable body of such literature that was of general interest to all classes. For example, the learned Sir Thomas Elyot was constrained to make *The Defence of Good women* (1545),[9] a dialogue which cites examples from history and

---

[9] Foster Watson, *Vives and the Renascence Education of Women* (London, 1912), pp. 211 ff., dates the composition of Elyot's dialogue sometime between 1531 and 1538. In calling attention to the books about women, he comments : "There was a considerable literature of women's books in the time of the Renaissance. These books

legend to prove woman's constancy and wisdom. David Clapham with a similar laudable intention made two translations from Cornelius Agrippa, *The Commendation Of Matrimony* (1540) and *A Treatise Of The Nobilitie and excellencye of woman kynde* (1542). A theme so universal in its appeal as woman was not, of course, confined to any class.

The popularity of books about women, gathering momentum for the next decade, led John Kynge, a printer of catchpenny works, to bring out a new edition of the *Schole house of women* in 1560, and to follow it with Edward More's *A Lytle and bryefe treatyse, called the defence of women, and especially of Englyshe women, made agaynst the Schole howse of Women* (1560). In a dedication to his "especyall frende mayster Wyllyam Page, Secretary to Syr Phillip hobdy," dated from Hambleden, July 22, 1557, More expresses his sincere disgust at the "false & forged" *Schole house of women*, which he had recently come upon. He roundly abuses its author, and in irregular fourteeners proves that men are worse than women. To these two works, Kynge now added a third entitled *The proude wyues Pater noster that wolde go gaye and vndyd her husbonde and went her waye*, which he brought out the same year. In riming verses, it burlesques the prayers of women who gaze about at church and envy the gay apparel of other women. After telling the story of an extravagant wife who undid and robbed her husband, the author closes with "the golden Pater noster of deuocyon."

With this trio of works, Kynge sought to capture the market in the 1560's, but he was not the only printer aware of the demand for feministic books. Abraham Vele published, probably in 1560, *The deceyte of women, to the instruction and ensample of all men, yonge and olde, newly corrected*, which supplied, in addition to the text, a pictorial warning to husbands, in a woodcut on the title-page fearsomely presenting a woman astride her spouse, who goes on all fours with a bridle in his mouth as she flogs him with a three-

---

in the praise of women ordinarily were written to secure the patronage of some lady of rank." Many books were dedicated to women, it is true, with the intention of gaining their patronage, and some sought their favor by the choice of flattering subject matter, but undoubtedly most of the popular books were written because of the general interest in the theme.

lashed whip. The prologue maintains that only froward and deceitful women need take offense at the book, which gives a prose account of intriguing females—Eve, Jezebel, Herodias, and many other scriptural women being mingled with modern examples. A conclusion further beseeches "all ye good honest women, and vyrgins be not myscontent" at the matter related. William Copland printed another edition of *The deceyte of women*, apparently in the next year, 1561, and a few years later brought out Robert Copland's *The seuen sorowes that women haue when theyr husbandes be deade* [1568?], a tiresome description in verse of the manner in which a worthy widow conducts herself on the death of her husband. Intrinsically dull as the work is, it nevertheless gives a vivid description of bourgeois literary taste and of the appetite for precisely this sort of thing. In the "Prologue of Robert Copland," a dialogue between Copland and Quidam, the former declares that "we printers" are called upon to publish so much news of everything—pope, emperor, king, great Turk, or Martin Luther —that "maruayle it is, how that our wittes can last." Quidam adds a list of ballads, and Copland laments that "bokes of vertue haue none vtterance," to which the former frankly retorts that he wants no works of "morall wysdome" but prefers to "waste a peny" on "a boke of the wydowe Edith That hath begyled so many with her wordes." He asks if Copland has not seen a "prety geest in ryme Of the seuen sorowes that these women haue," and offers to dictate it to Copland, who hesitates to print anything which will bring "Displeasure of women,"

> And that were I loth, for I haue alway
> Defended them, and wyll to my last day.
>
> . . . .
>
> . . . it is but a fond apetyte
> To geste on women, or a gainst them to wryte.[10]

---

[10] Robert Copland had been industrious in the earlier feministic controversy. To him are attributed *A complaynt of them that ben to late maryed* and *A complaynt of them that be to soone maryed*, doubtfully dated about 1535. He was probably also responsible for *The payne and sorowe of euyll mariage*. These were all translations from the French, according to H. R. Plomer, "Robert Copland," *Transactions of the Bibliographical Society of London*, III (1895-96), 211-25. Miss Beatrice White, "Two Tracts on Marriage by Robert Copland," *The Huntington Library Bulletin*, No. 1 (1931), pp. 205-7, finds acrostics in the first two to prove that they are from Copland's hand. On the popu-

After more conversation, which, incidentally, gives an interesting side light on the printing practices of the time, Copland agrees to publish the book, for

> I care no greatly, so that I nowe and than
> May get a peny as wel as I can.[11]

---

larity of such satires, Plomer comments : "Satire of women was a feature of that age, and Copland, who seems to have been always on the look-out for new matter likely to be popular, and who seems moreover to have received all the latest books from France, very probably put these tracts on the market at the earliest moment."

[11] The dialogue between Copland and Quidam (previously noticed by Plomer, *op. cit.*), which discusses the question of the copy for *The seuen sorowes*, is worth reprinting for the light it throws on the transmission of copy by memory and on printers' motives. Quidam has just assured Copland that the work

<blockquote>

"   .   .   .   is but a mery bourdyng Jeest
without reproufe, dishonesty or shame
That in no wyse can appayre their good name :

Copland.   That is good, but haue ye any copy
That aman myght enprynt it thereby
And when I se it, than I wyll you tell.
If that the matter be ordred yll or well.

Quidam.   I haue no boke, but yet I can you shewe
The matter by herte, and that by wordes fewe
Take your penne, and wryte as I do say
But yet of one thyng, hertely I you praye
Amende the englysh somwhat if ye can
And spel it true, for I shall tel the man
By my soule ye prynters make such englyshe
So yll spelled, so yll poynted, and so peuyshe
That scantly one can rede lynes tow
But to fynde sentence, he hath ynought to do
For in good fayth, yf I should say truthe
In your craft to suffer, it is great ruthe
Suche pochers to medle, and can not skyl
Of that they do, but doth al marre and spyl
I ensure you, your wardeins ben therof to blame
It hyndreth your gayne and hurteth your name

.   .   .   .

Copland.   Wel brother. I can it not a mende
I wyl no man ther of dyscommende
I care no greatly, so that I nowe and than
May get a peny as wel as I can
Howe be it, in our crafte I knowe that there be
Connyng good worke men, and that is to se
In latyn and englysh, which they haue wrought
Whose names appereth, where they be sought
But to our purpose, nowe tourne we a gayne
And let me begyn to wryte a lyne or twayne."

</blockquote>

Likewise reflecting the interest in such works was C. Pyrrye's *The praise and Dispraise of Women, very fruitfull to the well disposed minde, and delectable to the readers thereof. And a fruitfull shorte Dialogue vppon the sentence, know before thou knitte* [*c.* 1569].[12] In his anxiety to deter vice and encourage virtue, as well as to present both sides of the controversy, Pyrrye gives a verse character of the evil woman, followed by examples, and a similar character of the virtuous woman, with corresponding illustrative types.

Proof that books on women were popular with middle-class readers is found in Robert Laneham's account of the library of Captain Cox, the Coventry mason, who possessed *The seuen sorowes that women haue* and *The proude wyues Pater noster*, in addition to such related works as *The wife lapt in a Morels skin*.[13]

The interest in woman is reflected in much of the literature of the later sixteenth century. The satirists of the last quarter of the century found her a source of continual inspiration, and it is their attacks which prompted some of the subsequent defenses. The satirical comments are not merely conventional. Men like Stubbes[14] and Gosson,[15] with the deadly earnestness of Puritans, found in the free conduct of women material for lamentation over the depravity of the times. Undoubtedly the rapid social advancement of women caused serious concern among professional alarmists,[16]

---

[12] Preserved in the Huntington Library.

[13] F. J. Furnivall, *Captain Cox, his Ballads and Books*, Ballad Society (1871), pp. cxiv-cxvi. Of *The seuen sorowes*, Furnivall comments: " 'I am not acquainted with any tract bearing this title,' says Mr. Halliwell, and so say I."

Bound together in the British Museum (C. 20. c. 31) are six of the works popular in the 1560's : *The deceyte of women*, the *Schole house of women*, More's *Defence of women*, *The proude wyues Pater noster*, *The seuen sorowes that women haue*, and a sixth item, *A propre treatyse of a marchauntes wyfe, that afterwarde wente lyke a man and became a grete lorde, and was called Frederyke of Jennen* [1560?], printed by Abraham Vele. Vele seems to have been taking advantage of the popularity of works about women to bring out the Frederick of Jennen story, the first English version of which had been published at Antwerp in 1518.

[14] Philip Stubbes, *The Anatomie of Abuses* (1583). Stubbes's eulogy of his wife, *A Christal Glasse for Christian Women* (1591), points the way for other women to emulate the virtues of a perfect example of her sex.

[15] Stephen Gosson, *Quippes for Vpstart Newfangled Gentlewomen* (1595).

[16] *See* Edward Hake, *Newes out of Powles Churchyarde* (1579), Satire 5. [Ed. by Charles Edmonds (London, 1872).] In the introduction (p. xxi) Edmonds comments on Hake's lost work, which was devoted to a satire of women, *The Slights of Wanton Maydes*, and adds : "On this subject Mr. Payne Collier, in his Bibliographical Cata-

who confused morality and fashions and found in woman's dress the source of social ailments. Extravagance was particularly rebuked by thrifty Puritans bent on maintaining prudential virtues. Not all the bourgeois writers agreed, however, that citizens' wives were totally depraved, even with their gadding and their gossip, their extravagance and their vanity. Thomas Deloney and other ballad writers, though they good-humoredly make fun of woman's foibles, find her glorification a theme worthy of their pens. Most of Deloney's poems in *The Garland of good Will* (licensed, 1593) are concerned with domestic themes favorable to women; one item, for example, is "A Song in praise of Women." Another ballad by Deloney, "Salamons good houswife, in the 31 of his Proverbes,"[17] praises woman for her industry and thrift. Since the bourgeois writer found the sins of unthriftiness and marital instability peculiarly abhorrent, his anti-feministic writing was usually directed at the rebuke of these failings, but he found woman possessed of sufficient good qualities to warrant his defense. Indeed, the ridicule by aristocratic critics of citizens' wives doubtless stimulated many of the encomia. The broadside raillery of the ballad writers, even when satirical of women, was a different thing from the sophisticated cynicism of aristocratic cavalier poets, who developed the attitude that culminated in the Restoration-comedy conception of bourgeois woman as an eager subject for seduction.

---

logue, observes: 'the fact is that "A mery metynge of Maydes in London" had been entered by H. Denham in 1567, and an answer to it, under the title of "A letter sente by the Maydes of London to the vertuous Matrons" was registered in the same year.' "

John Marston, *The Scourge of Villanie*, Satire 7; Edward Guilpin, *Skialethia*, Satire 2; T. M., *Micro-Cynicon*, Satire 3; Samuel Rowlands, *Letting of Humours Blood*, Satire 7; and many others contemporary with them, satirize women's fashions and frailties. George Gascoigne in the epilogue to *The Steele Glas* bitterly arraigns the overdressing of women. Thomas Nashe in *The Anatomie of Absurditie* is equally severe.

[17] F. O. Mann (ed.), *The Works of Thomas Deloney* (Oxford, 1912), pp. 490-92. H. V. Routh, "The Advent of Modern Thought in Popular Literature," *Cambridge History of English Literature*, VII, 380, says of the broadside ballads a little after Deloney (in the first part of the seventeenth century), that they are "frankly goliardic in their cynical invective against marriage or in their satire on female vanity, lust, and caprice." The ballad writers, having an eye on the reading public, frequently managed to give both sides of the problem. Martin Parker, particularly, was skillful in stimulating an interest in controversy and then writing ballads answering himself. *See* Hyder E. Rollins (ed.), *A Pepysian Garland* (Cambridge, 1922), pp. 229 ff., for examples of Parker's ballads about women.

The attacks of the satirists[18] in the last two decades of the sixteenth century aroused other writers, in both the aristocratic and bourgeois traditions, to defend women. Thomas Bentley made the most imposing of all sixteenth-century works for women, in *The Monument Of Matrones: conteining seuen seuerall Lamps of Virginitie* (1582), a pious and beautifully printed work in three quarto volumes. Primarily a devotional treatise, it contains hymns, prayers, and meditations for all occasions, ranging from lamentations over the untimely loss of virginity to praise for the joys of heaven. As proof of woman's nobility and greatness, Bentley provides a great host of examples of worthy women as the converse of his

Mirrour for all sorts of wicked women, as in a cleere glasse with Athalia, Jezabell, Herodias, and such like, perfectlie to see their shamelesse pride, crueltie, idolatrie, and contempt of religion, with Putiphers wife to behold their incontinencie and infidelitie towards their husbands.   [Sig. B 2.]

Although Bentley's work contains much of interest to great ladies as well as to tradesmen's wives, he is concerned that "the simple

---

[18] Barnabe Rich in *The Second Tome of the Trauailes and adventures of Don Simonides* (1584) felt the necessity of defending English women even against the invective in his romance. In an epilogue, he comments: "Ladies and Gentlewomen, hauing brought *Simonides* to *Ciuill*, & hearyng his inuectiue agaynste the femine in generall, bicause he founde *Clarinda* onelie slipper: I altogyther displeased with his preiudicial exclamations, began in hote terms to disalow of his vnsemely vpbraidings, he (poore Gentleman) nothing at all discountenaunced by the memorie of his misfortunes, gaue this answere: It is not the faire damoselles of *England*, my freend, nor the glorie of that nation, which I comprehend wythin these limites of reproofe, but onelie our changelings of *Ciuil*, for suche of your countrie, would God I had eyther loued there, or neuer trauailed hither: O blessed *England*, where Ladies are so learned, Gentlewomen so constant, Virgins so modest, nay all the feminine sexe so honourable: they neuer offend in breache of faith, they neuer looke with vnchaste eies, they neuer burne in vnlawfull lust, they neuer vse to commit abuse: Their beautie hath no staine but of nature, their minds are not alinated with pride, their passions grow not on light loue, they are not carried with euerie light perswasion, they are not subiect to flattering allurementes, they are not faultie in anything that is licencious or light: they are religious not loose, they are comly, yet constant, they are modest, yet mercifull: yea suche they be as their honorable actions do onely make me allowe of their sexe, and wish, that either I might be partaker of their graces or the offals of their good qualities, were bestowed on oure brauest Spanishe Ladies, wythin this countrie. . . . I am readie to auouch it here in *London*, and if hee or I haue erred in anie thing, I referre mee to your owne iudgements, and conclude wyth *Simonides*, that you are the onelie paragones, bothe of *Asia, Africa* and *Europe* . . ."

reader" may understand. The book is fancifully divided into
sections described as "Lamps"; the title to the Seventh Lamp
announces that it contains

the acts & histories, liues, & deaths of all maner of women, good and
bad, mentioned in holy Scripture, as well by name, as without name,
set forth in alphabeticall order, with the signification and interpretation of most of their names: and in some part paraphrastically ex-
planed and enlarged for the better vnderstanding of the story, and
benefite of the simple reader.

The multiplicity of attacks on her sex moved a certain Jane
Anger to the defense in *Iane Anger her protection for Women. To defend
them against the Scandalous Reportes Of a late Surfeiting Louer, and all
other like Venerians that complaine so to bee ouercloyed with womens kindnesse* (1589).[19] "Among the innumerable number of bookes to that
purpose, of late (vnlooked for) the newe surfeit of an olde Louer
(sent abrood to warne those which are of his own kind, from
catching the like disease) came by chance to my handes,"[20] the
author declares. Moved by the impudence of this tract, she is led
to make an old-fashioned recital of man's iniquity and woman's
virtues.

Whatever may have been the allegorical significance of Henry
Willoby's *Willobie His Avisa. Or, The true Picture of a modest Maid, and
of a chast and constant wife* (1594),[21] the reason for the continued
popularity which gave it a fifth edition in 1635 was the fulsome
praise of the honest innkeeping maid, sister in spirit of the heroine
of Thomas Heywood's *Fair Maid of the West*. The poem may be
an allegorical attack on the Earl of Southampton by Raleigh's
faction, as Professor G. B. Harrison and others believe, but outwardly it is a plain poem in praise of middle-class woman and
bourgeois virtue, and it was doubtless interpreted as such by most
of its readers. That it made odious comparisons with the nobility
may account for its having been called in, along with Hall's *Satires*, in 1599. Its own ridicule of the morals of men is obvious, and,
if the "H. W." of the work is Southampton, as Professor Harrison

---

[19] Preserved in the Huntington Library.
[20] Sig. B iv.
[21] Edited by G. B. Harrison (London, 1926).

thinks, the criticism of him as the personification of licentiousness would have been thoroughly applauded. The heroine is precisely the sort to appeal to the bourgeoisie, then and now. Resisting all improper advances of noble suitors, she exemplifies Puritan virtue and provides a warning, patly stated, for other maids.[22] At the end of the poem comes "The resolution of a chast and a constant wife, that minds to continue faithfull vnto her husband." Hadrian Dorrell, who signs the preface, objects to slanders of women by poets:

. . . I must worthely reprehend the enuious rage, both of Heathen Poets, and of some Christian and English writers, which so farre debase the credite and strength of the whole sexe, that they feare not with lying toungs wickedly to publish, that there are none at all that can continue constant, if they be tried.

In an address "To all the constant Ladies & Gentlewomen of England that feare God," Dorrell refers to a promised "Apology" for women, which appeared in later editions of the *Avisa*. He claims to have delayed writing in the hope that some woman would write in her own defense:

. . . I haue long expected that the same should haue beene perfourmed by some of your selues, which I know are well able, if you were but so wellwilling to write in your owne praise, as many men in these dayes (whose tounges are tipt with poyson) are too ready and ouer willing, to speake and write to your disgrace.

Evidence that this vigorous defense of the virtue of middle-class[23] women aroused the antagonism of those who felt that the poem reflected by inference upon those in high places is found in Peter Colse's *Penelopes Complaint: Or, A Mirrour for Wanton Minions. Taken out of Homers Odissea, and written in English Verse* (1596). In a dedication to Lady Edith Horsey, Colse complains against the

---

[22] E.g., *see* the heading of Canto II, "The first triall of Avisa, before she was married, by a Noble man: vnder which is represented a warning to all young maids of euery degree, that they beware of the alluring intisements of great men."

[23] Hadrian Dorrell in the epistle to the reader emphasizes the simple style, likely to appeal to the citizen-reader: "Although hee flye not alofte with the winges of Astrophell, nor dare to compare with the Arcadian shepheard, or any way match with the daintie Fayry Queene; yet shall you find his wordes and phrases, neither Tryuiall nor absurd, . . ."

glorifying of a low-born woman ; a late published "pamplet called *Auisa* (ouerslipping so many praise-worthy matrons) hath registred the meanest."[24] In a preface Colse further rebukes the author of *Avisa* for presuming to praise a tavern maid :

The cause I haue contriued so pithie a matter in so plaine a stile, and short verse, is, that a vaine-glorious *Auisa* (seeking by slaunder of her superiors, to eternize her folly) is in the like verse, (by an vnknowen Authour) described. I follow . . . the same stile and verse, as neither misliking the methode, nor the matter, had it beene applyed to some worthier subiect.

The moral code implied in the sonnet cycles of the last decade of the sixteenth century could have been only an offense to Puritan sensibilities, and much of the amoristic verse throughout the period must have been, in the eyes of bourgeois respectability, a libel upon the honesty of women. Perhaps *Willobie His Avisa*, whatever the purpose of its writing, was interpreted as a protest against some of the chivalric absurdities of the sonneteers.

Harsh and direct were the criticisms heaped upon the middle-class woman by authors of the *fin de siècle* who surveyed her shortcomings and found them manifold. Even if much of the disparagement represented the age-old complaint against feminine vanity, some of it clearly went home to Londoners who daily saw such personages as Mistress Minx, the merchant's wife, described by Nashe as the personification of pride and extravagance,[25] and many must have approved the clergyman bold enough to rebuke their pride.[26] But it remained for Arthur Dent to epitomize the pomp and pride of the female sex in that handbook to eternal felicity, *The Plaine Mans Path-way to Heauen* (1601) :

Yet we see how proud many, especially women, be of such bables : for when they haue spent a good part of the day in tricking and trimming, pricking and pinning, pranking and pouncing, girding and lacing, and brauing vp themselues in most exquisit manner, then out they come

---

[24] Corser, *Collectanea Anglo-Poetica*, II, Pt. II (1869), 421 ff.

[25] *Pierce Penilesse his Supplication to the Diuell* (1592), sig. C 4ᵛ.

[26] An entry in the *Diary of John Manningham* for October 31, 1602, reads : "Dr. Dene made a Sermon against the excessive pride and vanitie of women in apparaile, &c., which vice he said was in their husbands power to correct."—Edited by John Bruce, Camden Society, XCIX (1868), 74.

into the streetes with their Pedlers shop about their backe, and carrie
their crests very high, taking themselues to bee litle Angels : or at least,
somewhat more then other women ; whereupon they do so exceedingly
swell with pride, that it is to be feared, they will burst with it as they
walke in the streetes. And truly wee may thinke the very stones in the
streete, and the beames in the houses do quake, & wonder at their
monstrous, intollerable, and excessiue pride : for it seemeth that they
are altogether a lumpe of pride, a masse of pride, euen altogether made
of pride, and nothing else but pride, pride.   [Pp. 45-46.]

The subject that Dent used for moral observations was likewise
the theme of the satirists, with whom, indeed, the castigation of
women's faults became a conventional fashion.[27]

The attacks on women, whether by preachers or satirists, did
not go unchallenged, and both courtiers and commoners arose
to defend them in terms as emphatic as had been the disparagement. If Anthony Gibson was a courtier, his little book entitled
*A Womans Woorth, defended against all the men in the world. Proouing
them to be more perfect, excellent and absolute in all vertuous actions, then
any man of what qualitie soeuer* (1599)[28] could not have failed to
appeal to women of whatever social position, though he aimed his
effort at the ladies of the Queen's court. After sundry dedications
to ladies, the treatise finally launches into a declaration of the
worth of women "to the end that by the histories of many women,
euery man whatsoeuer may perfectly perceyue, that the gifts and
graces of women are infinite." From the classic philosophers, the
author proves that "the body of a woman is the heauen of humane
perfections, and her soul the treasurie of celestiall and diuine
vertues." From history he cites examples of women great in state-
craft, and of women famous for constancy, courage, and chastity.
Finally, he calls upon men to acknowledge the divinity of woman
and shield her against malevolent cynics :

And this I can assure yee beside, that the most parte of excellent and
vertuous men, haue attributed all tytle of honour to Women, daylie
becomming theyr servantes in hart, yea euen humble in prostration

---

[27] *See* R. M. Alden, *The Rise of Formal Satire in England under Classical Influence* (Philadelphia, 1899), *passim.*

[28] In a dedication to the Lady Elizabeth, Countess of Southampton, Gibson claims
that he is simply editing a friend's translation from the French.

(as it were) to adore them, as if in some sorte they tooke parte with the highest diuinitie.

Then let vs not fayle hencefoorth to looue them hartilye, by examples of our wise and discreete elders, yeelding our selues voluntarily as subiect to them : neuer regarding venemous spightfull tongues, that haue not spared to speake their vttermost against them.

[Sigs. G 10-G 10v.]

In the same year as Gibson's labors, Nicholas Breton answered the critics of women with *The Praise Of vertuous Ladies. An Invectiue against the discourteous discourses of certaine malicious persons, written against Women, whom Nature, Wit, and Wisedome (well considered) would vs rather honour then disgrace* (1599).[29] Breton admits that many women deserve criticism, but he pleads for fair play. Apparently he has in mind the formal satirists, in the opening passage of the treatise, which gives a series of comparisons proving men more wanton and vain than women :

When I peruse and consider of the strange discourses of divers fantasticall fellowes, that haue no grace but in disgracing of women, in invectiues against them, in most despiteful descriptions of their dissimulations, in such shamefull setting out of their sexe ; whereby for a few mad-headed wenches, they seek to bring all, yes, most modest matrons, and almost all women in contempt : surely, methinks, I can terme them by no name fitter for their folly then madde men, that faine would bee authors of somewhat, and knowing not what to take in hand, runne headlong into such absurdities as redounde to their vtter dishonor.[30]

The popularity of the theme of woman is further illustrated in the last year of the century by another treatise which sets out to give both sides of the question, a translation by R. T[ofte?], entitled *Of Mariage and Wiuing. An Excellent, pleasant, and Philosophicall Controuersie, betweene the two famous Tassi now liuing, the one Hercules the Philosopher, the other, Torquato the Poet* (1599). Ercole Tasso's declamation against woman, which the author himself admits was a work of his youth, proves merely a foil for the strong defense from his brother, Torquato.

---

[29] A. B. Grosart (ed.), *The Works in Verse and Prose of Nicholas Breton*, 2 vols., Chertsey Worthies' Library (1879), Vol. II.

[30] *Ibid.*, p. 56.

The early seventeenth century saw a continuation of the controversy over women, with a gradual intensifying of acrimony, a result partly of King James's dislike of women[31] and partly of what seems to have been the actual extravagance and vanity of the sex.[32] Notorious scandals, attracting attention to erring woman, brought a flood of savage attacks in the second decade of the century, and this, in turn, begot a series of defenses. While the bourgeoisie prevailingly upheld women, especially against aristocratic criticism, ballads and pamphlets, expressing the tradesman's point of view and rebuking woman's violations of prudential morality, continued to multiply throughout the century.[33]

The first years of the new reign saw sporadic productions on the theme of the goodness or badness of women, in addition to the numerous references in literature not exclusively devoted to the subject. Barnabe Rich, who earlier had felt that popular good will demanded a vindication of the London woman, now berates her in *Faultes Faults, And nothing else but Faultes* (1606):

. . . they [women] were neuer halfe so detestable in times past, as

[31] *See* Violet A. Wilson, *Society Women of Shakespeare's Time* (London, 1924), pp. 160 ff., and also Myra Reynolds, *The Learned Lady in England, 1650-1760* (Boston and New York, 1920), pp. 23-24.

[32] More than conventional is the criticism of such writers as I. H., the author of *This Worlds Folly. Or A Warning-Peece discharged vpon the Wickednesse thereof* (1615), in which, among other things, he complains of the folly and extravagance of women, especially in dress. Dress is now so much alike for all classes, he asserts, that it is impossible to tell a countess from a courtesan, the chambermaid from her mistress, or a merchant from his factor.—Sig. A 3ᵛ.

[33] *See* Rollins, *Pepysian Garland*, Introduction, p. xiv, and *passim*. W. Parkes in *The Curtaine-Drawer of the Worlde* (1612) is especially hard on women. Arthur Halliarg's *The Cruell Shrow: Or, The Patient Mans Woe* [1610?] condemns the independence and arrogance of women who lord it over their husbands. A popular contribution to the general satire of women was *The Batchelars Banquet* (1603), a translation from *Les quinze joyes de mariage*, long attributed to Thomas Dekker. (For a refutation of the view that Dekker was the translator, *see* F. P. Wilson [ed.], *The Batchelars Banquet* [Oxford, 1929], pp. xxiii ff.) *The Batchelars Banquet* went through at least four editions by 1631. In some of his pamphlets, as in *Newes from Hell*, Dekker pays his satirical respects to women, but his satire is never malicious, and he is often sincerely interested in social problems affecting women. For example, in *The Seven Deadly Sins of London* he inveighs against forced marriage and unequal matches. Samuel Rowlands good-naturedly ridicules the faults of women—and of men—in *A whole crew of kind Gossips, all met to be merry* (1609), in which first the wives and then the husbands reveal the faults of each other. The drama, of course, is full of commentary on women. Jonson and Middleton are severe on women, while Heywood is usually found defending them.

they be at this houre : nay, those women that now would be accounted good, and would be angrie if there should be any exceptions taken to there honesty, are more Courtezan-like (to the shew of the world) than euer was *Lais* of *Corinth,* or *Trine* the famous Curtezan of *Thebes.*

[Sig. G 3.]

Rich inveighs particularly against marriages for money and position. A survey of his pamphlets shows his response to the increasing animosity toward women, which culminated in the outburst in the last half of the second decade of the century—an animosity brought to a head by the scandals in the court, the most notorious of which was the murder of Sir Thomas Overbury in 1613 because of his hostility to the marriage schemes of Frances Howard and Robert Carr. Overbury himself was the author of a poem describing the ideal wife, published after his death as *A Wife Now The Widdow Of Sir Thomas Overburye. Being A most exquisite and singuler Poem of the choice of a Wife* (1614). The sensation caused by his murder at the instigation of Frances Howard through the machinations of Mrs. Turner focused popular interest on his own notions about women.[34]

Such affairs as the Overbury scandal were a stench in the nostrils

---

[34] Overbury's *Wife* enjoyed an enormous popularity, partly, no doubt, because of the morbid interest in the murder. The poem, together with a collection of characters in part by Overbury, went through numerous impressions and editions. A sixteenth impression appeared in 1638. Pamphlets such as *The Just Downfall of Ambition, Adultery and Murder* [1616?] described the crime and reflected upon the insatiate lust of women.

Overbury's notions of the perfect wife express the prevailing opinions of the day. First among the qualities desired are goodness and virtue. Then come intelligence and common sense, but too much curiosity after vain learning must be avoided :

> "A *passiue vnderstanding* to conceiue,
> And Iudgment to discerne, I wish to find,
> Beyond that, all as hazardous I leaue,
> *Learning* and *pregnant wit* in Woman-kind
> What it findes malleable maketh fraile,
> And doth not adde more ballaste, but more saile.
> *Bookes* are a part of mans prerogatiue."—Sig. C 1.

Overbury thinks that "Domesticke Charge doth best that Sex benefit." After intelligence, he demands beauty, for man is to marry "*A Soule,* and *Body,* not a *Soule* alone." He even admits that women may aid nature a little in this respect. The final attribute is modesty. Later, in the character of "A Good Woman," the sensible, modest woman who will not entertain advances unworthy of her is praised. The picture of the undesirable type of woman is given in the character of "A very very Woman" and in the second part of this, called "Her next part."

of respectable London citizens, who saw their wives aping the fashions of court ladies and welcomed the rebukes of writers like Rich, whose *The Honestie Of This Age* (1614), dedicated to the Lord Mayor, laments the increase in fashionable harlotry in an age unable "to iudge of a Harlot, especially if shee be rich." In the preceding year had appeared Rich's *The Excellency of good women* (1613), a threadbare iteration of the deeds of certain noble women of history, praising good women but condemning the current sins of extravagance, pride, and immodesty. Women no longer can cross a street without a coach. Though "nature is sometimes holpen by Arte," much of woman's adornment is costly and shameless. The extravagance of their wives causes the bankruptcy of citizens:

. . . and what is it that doth make so many Cittizens and trades men, so commonly to play Banckrout, but the excessiue pride that is vsed by their wiues.

By this pride of women *Hospitalitie* is eaten vp and good houskeeping is banished out of the country and how many *Items* are still brought in for the bodyes excesse without any consideration of the poore soules nakednes.[35]   [P. 15.]

Modesty and industry are the qualities which should be most sought after.

An effort to take advantage of the wave of interest in books about women is evident in the changed title and the expansion of Rich's earlier *Faults*, which appeared in 1616 as *My Ladies Looking Glasse. Wherein May Be Discerned A Wise Man From A Foole, A Good Woman From A Bad*. Once more he tilts against improper dress—the mannish apparel of women and the effeminate clothes of men. Worse still, women no longer ostracize the harlot, and "the worse a woman liues, the better shee is thought on: if there be any that liues in want, it is *poore chastitie*." Finally, he rebukes the courtier-poet, the writer of amorous verse who will

---

[35] A few years before, Henry Parrot in *The Movs-Trap* (1606) had referred to the satire of merchants' wives:

> "I wonder when our Poets will forebeare,
>   to write gainst Citizens their honest wiues:
> Who (though vnknowne to me) yet durst I sweare,
>   they neuer wronged man in all their liues.
> Put case their husbands pocket (you know what)
> Must they on Stages needs be pointed at?"—Epigram 31, sig. C 2.

hatch out *Rimes*, and learne to indite *amorous* verses in the praise of his mistris (that is many times scarce worth the speaking of) and will borrow colours from *lillies* and *red roses* to beautifie her *cheekes*, her *eyes* shall be *saphires*, her *lippes*, *corall*, her *teeth*, *pearle*, her *breath*, *balme*, a *Pallas* for her wit but he neuer streines so farre as to her *honesty*. [P. 55.]

The type of criticism exemplified in Rich's works was thundered from the pulpit and echoed in poems and pamphlets.[36] A comment at the end of *My Ladies Looking Glasse* expresses Rich's own despair of improving a society deaf to the preachers :

I haue little hope therefore to reforme those by my writing, whom the thundring voyce of Gods word pronounced euery day by the *Preacher* can neither conforme, nor anything at all terrifye.   [P. 74.]

Quickly the friends of women replied, but their efforts were too frequently merely reiterations of the conventional catalogues of worthy women. A certain I. G. managed to make, in pentameter couplets, a fairly spirited description of Eve in *An Apologie For Women-Kinde* (1605),[37] which provided, after the verses on the mother of mankind, a chronicle of famous women who have been acclaimed for either virtue or heroism. Some of I. G.'s observations are worth noting. For example, he would not condemn women more harshly than men for unchastity since men lavish great labor upon their seduction. Among women's notable virtues, he singles out philanthropic generosity :

---

[36] *See* Alden, *op. cit.*, pp. 191 ff. Alden discusses a second wave of formal satire which followed the 1599 outburst, between 1613 and 1625. During this period, satires of women were especially violent. William Goddard, for example, in *A Neaste Of Waspes Latelie Found out and discouered in the Law-countreys* [*sic*] (1615) [facsimile reprint (Oxford, 1921)], ridicules severely the honesty of the "ietting wife" of Crafte the merchant, and heaps coarse invective on women for their painting, their follies of all sorts, and their lack of virtue. Goddard continues the same attack in *A Satirycall Dialogue, Or A Sharplye invectiue conference, betweene Allexander the great and that trulye woman-hater Diogynes* [1616?], a savage castigation of the pride and lust of women. The writers of essays and characters made much capital of women's frailties. Cf. John Stephens' *Essayes and Characters* (1615), reprinted in J. O. Halliwell-Phillipps' *Books of Characters* (London, 1857). Similar items might be multiplied indefinitely.

[37] Preserved in the Huntington Library. Cf. the reference to woman's philanthropy with I. P.'s *A Commemoration of the life and death of the Right Worshipfull and vertuous Ladie; Dame Helen Branch (late Wife to the Right worshipfull Sir Iohn Branch Knight, sometime Lord Maior of the famous Citie of London)* (1594), also in the Huntington Library. Dame Helen is commended particularly for pious contemplation, the reading of good books, and philanthropic deeds.

> How many schooles and Hospitalles are built
> By women's wondrous liberalitie, . . .   [Sig. C 1ᵛ.]

Without the charm of Eve to lighten his pages, Lodowick Lloyd methodically compiled a vast number of good women from biblical and classical history, which he set forth as *The Choyce of Iewels* (1607), a work worthily aiming to force mankind to admit the honorable exploits of women. Occasionally a writer clearly goes out of his way to salve the hurt pride of women, as did Richard Johnson in a passage in *The Pleasant Walkes of Moore-Fields* (1607), praising London citizens and their wives, who are said to "resemble the verie modest Sabine Ladies of Italy."[38] But perhaps the most vigorous and intelligent of the replies to the literary traducers of women was William Heale's *An Apologie For Women. Or An Opposition To Mr. Dr. G. his assertion. Who held in the Act at Oxforde. Anno. 1608. That it was lawfull for husbands to beate their wiues. By W. H. of Ex. in Ox.* (1609),[39] another edition of which appeared as late as 1682, entitled *The Great Advocate and Oratour for Women.* Heale begins his treatise, which is a reasoned plea for women's rights and protection from conjugal tyranny, with a rebuke to the satirical and petty rimers who malign woman. He hopes his own treatise will be well received

after so many Inuectiues framed against them, by their disgracefull adversaries. For although we all know that vnto woman-kinde the world oweth halfe of its life, and man is indebted the whole of his loue, yet it is a custome growne so common to vnder valew their worth, as everie rymer hath a libell to impeach their modestie; everie phantastike a poeme to plaine their vnfaithfulnesse; The Courtier though he weare his Mistresse favour, yet stickes not to sing his Mistresse shame; The Cobler though in himselfe most disgracefull, yet wants hee not a ballade for their disgrace.

He makes a further reply to railing authors who

---

[38] J. P. Collier (ed.), *Illustrations of Early English Popular Literature*, 4 vols. (London, 1864), II, 28.

[39] The dedication to "the Ladie M. H." suggests that it was written to order: "Madam, your commaunde is effected. And this short discourse (the cause of whose being you are) attēds your view." Heale frequently quotes in proof of his statements the *Arcadia* of "our English Worthie," Sir Philip Sidney. Dr. G. is the learned Dr. William Gager.

coniure up [against women] whole catalogues of vices, . . . Avarice, anger, luxury, gluttonie slouthfulnesse, envy . . . First then let mee giue these *Cynickes* to vnderstand, that their trade is not now so good as they could wish it were : for their chiefe ware *detraction* is helde but for childrens rhetoricke. And *Invectiues* are counted the poorest share in learning. They are but the froath of an apish invention : the purge of an idle braine ; the falling sicknes of a giddy wit, flat heresies in true schollership.   [Pp. 38-39.]

Despite Heale's good offices in woman's behalf, the accumulated wrath of a bourgeois writer, a certain Joseph Swetnam, vented itself in 1615 in *The Araignment Of Lewd, Idle, Froward, and vnconstant women: Or the vanitie of them, choose you whether. With a Commendation of wise, vertuous and honest Women. Pleasant for married Men, profitable for young Men, and hurtfull to none,* for more than a hundred years a popular pamphlet, which aroused middle-class writers to a furious controversy and finally reached the stage.[40] The number of editions which, in rapid succession, followed its first printing is proof of its immediate interest : the *Short Title Catalogue* lists ten

[40] The pamphlet by Swetnam is discussed by the Reverend A. B. Grosart in an introduction to the reprint of the satirical play, *Swetnam, the Woman-hater, Arraigned by Women* (1620) (Manchester, 1880). The violence of Swetnam's attack on woman provoked in his editor a passage remarkable among that industrious divine's editorial utterances : "The 'Arraignment' of women by Joseph Swetnam is in every way a sorry production. . . . it is a mendacious attack on Woman *qua* woman, without a spark of wit, or salt of pungency. Somehow the bright, pure, noble Women of Chaucer and Spenser and Shakespeare were (temporarily) forgotten, and it came to be the foolish as malignant *mode* indiscriminately to traduce the female sex. Nicholas Breton and other like-minded contemporaries indeed stood on the 'defensive' for Woman ; but the rage or craze was to hold up Woman to insult and ridicule. . . . Speaking broadly, it may be affirmed that the man who has low thoughts of woman *qua* woman proves himself to be low ; and equally so the woman who has low thoughts of man *qua* man. Whoever recognizes the sanctity of the 'body' as being that 'flesh' assumed by Jesus Christ, and still 'worn' by Him on the Throne of the Universe, and the grandeur of possibilities and destiny for the human 'soul,' must account it treasonous, to utter aught against this human nature of ours. This being so, it is just what we might expect to find the books against Woman, whether earlier or later, to be the productions of (self-evidently) mean, degraded, and impure Writers. It is allowable to touch (if finely and lightly done) on the weaknesses and frivolities and (perhaps) volubilities of the 'weaker Sex,' and only right that the individual bad woman should be portrayed fearlessly and in integrity ; but it is an outrage and an offence for any man to 'rail' and accuse so splendid a piece of God Almighty's workmanship as Woman, whether child ('thing of *beauty*'), maiden ('thing of *joy*'), 'sweetheart' ('all thoughts, all passions, all delights'), wife, mother, sister. Woman is to be reverenced, loved, and transfigured with celestial radiance."—Pp. viii-ix.

printings by 1634.[41] The pamphlet, avowedly written for middle-class readers,[42] rails at sins of extravagance and pride, which ruin and bankrupt even thrifty husbands. Women "degenerate from the vse they were framed vnto, by leading a proud, lazie, and idle life, to the great hinderance of their poore Husbands."[43] Woman is a consuming night crow, who, after wheedling,

makes request for a Gowne of the new fashion stuffe: or for a Petti-cote of the finest stammell: or for a Hat of the newest fashion. Her husband being ouercome by her flattering speech, partly hee yeeldeth to her request, although it be a greefe to him, for that he can hardly spare it out of his stock. . . .   [Sig. C 2ᵛ.]

Extravagant prodigality and idleness ruin many:

For commonly women are the most part of the forenoone painting themselues, and frizling their haires, and prying in their glasse like Apes, to prancke vp themselues in their gawdies, like Poppets, or like the Spider which weaues a fine web to hang the flie. Amongst women she is accounted a slut which goeth not in her silkes: therefore if thou wilt please thy Lady, thou must like and loue, sue and serue, and in spending thou must lay on load; . . . For women will account thee a pinch-penny, if thou be not prodigall. . . .   [Sig. E 2ᵛ.]

If men must marry—and beauty is a snare which they are unable to avoid—then let them choose maids of seventeen, "flexible and bending, obedient and subiect to doe anything." The treatise concludes with a revelation of the vanity of widows.

Swetnam hit upon the grievances that the average citizen,

---

[41] The British Museum Catalogue lists, besides the editions before 1634, later editions in 1690, 1702, 1707, 1733, and 1807. Furthermore, there were two Dutch translations published in Amsterdam in 1641 and 1645.

Numerous references in the literature following the publication of Swetnam's pamphlet indicate that it was much read and that his name became a synonym for a critic of woman. For example, in *Lady Alimony* (pr. 1659), a character describes Timon as "The very profest Smock-satyr, or Woman-hater in all *Europe*. One, had he lived in that State or under that zone, might have compared with any *Swetnam* in all the *Albyon Island*."

[42] Swetnam several times addresses the average reader. He has a prefatory epistle, "Neither To The Best, Nor yet to the worst; but to the common sort of Women." In a further preface to the general reader he says, "neyther to the wisest Clarke, nor yet to the starkest Foole, but vnto the ordinary sort of giddy-headed young men, I send greeting." My quotations are from the edition of 1616.

[43] Sig. B 1.

especially among the Puritans, regarded as the besetting sins of woman. Not since John Kynge and his fellow printers in the 1560's had whipped up anew the woman controversy, had there been so much popular interest in the theme. For the next decade writers busied themselves with one or the other side of the issue.

In the year following Swetnam's diatribe, Daniel Tuvil published a dignified and well-reasoned defense of women entitled *Asylum Veneris, Or A Sanctuary for Ladies. Iustly Protecting Them, their virtues, and sufficiencies from the foule aspersions and forged imputations of traducing Spirits* (1616), which asserted woman's equality with man. Although Tuvil expresses his scorn of the multitude and wishes to make clear that he is no common controversialist, apparently the pressure from printers for works about women was too much for him to resist. If his pamphlet was not an answer to Swetnam, its appearance was timely and its title seems to have been dictated with Swetnam's traducing work in mind.[44]

Several women writers, however, did reply directly to the slanderer of their sex. Rachel Speght, probably a daughter of Thomas Speght, though still under twenty revealed a precocious ability for invective in *A Mouzell For Melastomus, The Cynicall Bayter of, and foule mouthed Barker against Evahs Sex. Or an Apologeticall Answere to that Irreligious and Illiterate Pamphlet made by Io. Sw.* (1617). At the conclusion are "Certaine Quaeres to the bayter of Women. With a Confutation of some part of his Diabolicall Discipline." An abler defense came from a woman writing under the pseudonym of Esther Sowernam, *Ester hath hang'd Haman: Or An Answere To a lewd Pamphlet, entituled, The Arraignment of Women* (1617). In a prefatory address to women, the author says that she proposed to leave the labor of replying to Swetnam to a minister's daughter

---

[44] The *Dictionary of National Biography*, *sub* Swetnam, asserts that Tuvil's treatise was a document in the Swetnam controversy, but Tuvil claims in the preface to his book that it was composed some time before: "But the slight approbation I make of it myselfe, may bee witnessed by my long suppressing it. And but to preuent others, who had gotten from mee some imperfect copies, I would neuer haue published it now."

In a dedication to Lady Alice Colville, Tuvil asserts that criticism awaits a defender of women: "I know this age to be very Stoicall and Criticall, and that many will censure the Author to have seriously busied himself in an idle subiect." He has no interest in the multitude: "Carelesse therefore of all snarling Cynicks & their taxations, with *Horace* I onely court the learned and the good."

(Rachel Speght?), but that finding her efforts too weak, she herself decided to answer the defamer. Just as Swetnam had appealed to young men, so Esther writes a preface "To All Worthy And Hope-full young youths of Great-Brittaine; But respectiuely to the best disposed and worthy Apprentises of London" in which she appeals to their chivalry to right the wrongs of women, reminds them that the chiefest thing they look for is a good wife, asks them to uphold marriage against the attacks of Swetnam, and flatters them by saying:

You my worthy youths are the hope of Man-hoode, the principall poynt of Man-hoode is to defend, and what more man-like defence, then to defend the iust reputation of a woman. I know that you the Apprentises of this Citie are as forward to maintaine the good, as you are vehement to put downe the bad.

After a spirited exposition of the virtues of women and the frailties of men, the treatise closes with a poem, "A Defence Of Women against the Author of the Arraignment of Women," signed "Ioane Sharpe," which expresses sincere indignation at the injustice of criticism by men who seduce women and then rail at their inconstancy, who blame women for pride if they dress well and for sluttishness if they dress ill.

Another writer, apparently also a woman, writing under the pseudonym of Constantia Munda, produced *The Worming of a mad Dogge: Or, A Soppe For Cerberus The Iaylor of Hell. No Confutation But A sharpe Redargution of the bayter of Women* (1617), in which she asserts that she would have gone further "had not Hester hang'd Haman before." The beginning of the pamphlet, which is merely an exposure of the ignorance and malice of Swetnam, throws further light on the abundance of anti-feminist literature. Libels upon women, which litter the bookstalls, have become the theme of every poetaster and stage player, the author declares:

The itching desire of oppressing the presse with many sottish and illit-erate Libels, stuft with all manner of ribaldry, and sordid inuentions, when euery foule-mouthed male-content may disgorge his *Licambaean* poyson in the face of all the world, hath broken out into such a dismall contagion in these our dayes, that euery scandalous tongue and oppro-brious witte, like Italian Mountebankes will aduance their pedling wares of detracting virulence in the publique *Piatza* of euery Stationers shoppe. . . . Yet woman the greatest part of the *lesser world* is generally become the subiect of euery pedanticall goose-quill. Euery fantasticke Poetaster which thinkes he hath lickt the vomit of his *Coripheus* and can but patch a hobling verse together, will striue to represent vnseemely figments imputed to our sex, (as a pleasing theme to the vulgar) on the publique Theatre: teaching the worser sort that are more prone to luxurie, a compendious way to learne to be sinfull.

[Pp. 1-3.]

The stage, of which Constantia Munda complained, became the medium for a renewed satire on Swetnam and a vindication of the female sex in 1620 when *Swetnam, the Woman-hater, Arraigned by Women* was staged[45] and printed. In the play Swetnam is discomfited by his woman antagonist, haled before a tribunal, convicted of abusing women, tortured, and dragged muzzled through the streets until he finally recants. Swetnam's attack and the controversy which it engendered reveal two significant facts: that the average woman was becoming articulate in her own defense and that she was demanding social independence unknown in previous generations.

Reflections of the feministic strife are found in other works contemporary with Swetnam but not directly participating in the feud. The year 1616, immediately following the year of Swetnam's pamphlet, was fruitful of discussions about women. Thomas Gainsford, a spokesman for London's commercial classes, in *The Rich Cabinet Furnished with varietie Of Excellent discriptions* (1616) gives a character of the "Citizen," in which he praises the London tradesman for his civic worth but complains of some of the social changes brought about by wealth, and especially of the extravagance of the citizen's wife, the eternal complaint of the period:

---

[45] Several plays in this period reflect the interest in the feminist controversy—for example, *The Female Rebellion*, and Fletcher's *The Sea-Voyage* describing a commonwealth of women. *See* Felix E. Schelling, *Elizabethan Drama, 1558-1642* (Boston and New York, 1908), II, 237-38. *Swetnam, the Woman-hater* is well written, in the manner of Thomas Heywood. The language, dialogue, and clownery are all patterned after Heywood, and the defense of women is precisely the sort of thing he might have written. It is not improbable that this may be one of the plays in which he had a "main finger." Grosart in the introduction (p. xxxiv) to his reprint makes a suggestion that the play may be by Dekker or Heywood.

Citizens in times past did not marry beyond their degrees, nor would a Gentleman make affinitie with a Burgesse : but wealth hath taught vs now another lesson ; and the Gentleman is glad to make his younger sonne a tradsman, and match his best daughter with a rich Citizen for estate and liuing. . . . A citizen is more troubled with his wife, then his wares : for they are sorted, locked vp, and neuer brought out, but by constraint for the profit of their master ; but his wife is decked, adorned, neatly apparelled, sits for the gaze, goes at her pleasure, and will not be restrained from any sights or delights, or merry-meetings ; where they may shew their beauties, or riches, or recreate themselues.

A Citizen is in great danger of displeasure, if he deny his wife any thing which her meere fancie conceiteth : as shee is in perill of de-spight, if hee would restraine her libertie vpon suspicious iealousie : in both, loue beginneth to breake as ice, which once crakt, runneth further and further.   [Sigs. E 3v-E 4.]

Later, in a character of "Woman," after describing the weaknesses of the sex, which must be borne with by man, he admits that

Woman is indued with the same vertues as man : for there hath beene as valiant, wise, godly, magnanimous, pollitick, iudicious, great spir-ited, and learned women as men.   [Sig. Y 4.]

Nicholas Breton, like most of the character writers, finds in woman material for commentary. In *The Good And The Badde* (1616) he presents favorable pictures of "A Good Wife," "A quiet Woman," and "A Virgin," whom he contrasts with "A wanton Woman" and "An Vnquiet Woman." John Davies of Hereford brought out in 1616 *A Select Second Husband For Sir Thomas Overburies Wife, Now A Matchlesse Widow*, a treatise in verse on domestic relations rather than a controversial tract, but one which reflects the popularity of the theme in the year of its publication. The continued interest in the Overbury case, with its anti-feminist implications, accounts at least for the title[46] of Thomas Tuke's *A Treatise Against Painting and Tincturing of Men And Women: Against Murther and Poysoning: Pride and Ambition: Adulterie and Witchcraft*, which had two issues in 1616. A prejudiced Puritan view, in the manner of William Prynne a little later, it reveals that cosmetics are the devil's own means of seducing women, who lose all sense of shame when they begin to beautify themselves artificially :

---

[46] In a passage on the certainty of murder to out, Tuke mentions by name the Over-bury case.

She hath purchased lips, haire, hands, and beautie more, then nature gaue her, and with these she hopes to purchase loue. For in being beloued consists her life ; . . . To conclude, whosoeuer she be, shee's but a *Guilded Pill*, composde of these two ingredients, *defects* of nature, and an *artificiall seeming* of *supplie*, tempered and made vp by *pride* and *vanitie*, and may wel be reckned among these creatures that God neuer made.   [Pp. 60-62.]

The controversy over women smoldered fitfully during the next few years,[47] to break out with increased fury in 1620, the year of the play attacking Swetnam. Without doubt the prosperity which had brought wealth to tradesmen and frivolous extravagance to their wives was an actual *casus belli*.

King James himself, through the clergy, sought to suppress what

---

[47] The satirists made capital of the situation. A popular pun is illustrated in Henry Fitzgeffrey's *Satyres: And Satyricall Epigrams* (1617) by Epigram 39, "Woman (quasi) Woe-man" :

> "Had I not felt it misery to Woe,
> I had beene *marryed* (certaine) long agoe.
> Had I *not marryed*, straight (Moroso) sayes,
> *I had not once felt* Woe *in all my dayes.*
> *If* after *Woman as* before *comes* Woe,
> *Woe* worth the *Man* with *Woman* hath to doe."

In the *Notes from Black-fryers*, appended to the *Epigrams*, Fitzgeffrey describes the mannish woman, the object of much ridicule in succeeding satires :

> "Now Mars defend vs! seest thou who comes yonder?
> Monstrous! A *Woman* of the *Masculine Gender*."

Arthur Newman brought out in 1619 *Pleasures Vision: With Deserts Complaint, And A Short Dialogue of a Womans Properties, betweene an old Man and a Young*. The old man sets forth the frailties of woman, who is rather weakly defended by the young man. The latter finally admits that women must have their way.

Henry Hutton is bitter against woman in *Follie's Anatomie: Or Satyres And Satyricall Epigrams* (1619). He describes "A Woman creature most insatiate" as proud and overbearing, whose only god is pleasure :

> "Her whole discourse is of *Guy* Warwicks armes
> Of errant Knights, or of blinde *Cupids* charmes.
> Her ciuill gesture, is to faigne a lie
> In decent phrase, in true Ortographie."—Sig. B 6.

W. Fennor(?) satirizes the honesty of merchants' wives in *Pasquils Palinodia, And His progresse to the Taverne* (1619).

Isaac Disraeli, *Amenities of Literature*, 3 vols. (London, 1841), II, 54, mentions the vogue in France of satires on women and cites several works in the year 1617 similar to the controversial matter in England about the same time.

he deemed the arrogance of women. A letter of John Chamberlain, dated January 25, 1620, comments:

Yesterday the bishop of London called together all his clergie about this towne, and told them he had expresse commandment from the King to will them to inveigh vehemently against the insolencie of our women, and theyre wearing of brode brimed hats, pointed dublets, theyre hayre cut short or shorne, and some of them stilettoes or poniards, and such other trinckets of like moment; adding withall that if pulpit admonitions will not reforme them he wold proceed by another course; the truth is the world is very much out of order, but whether this will mende it God knowes.

Again, on February 12, 1620, Chamberlain writes:

Our pulpits ring continually of the insolence and impudence of women, and to helpe the matter forward the players have likewise taken them to taske, and so to the ballades and ballad-singers, so that they can come nowhere but theyre eares tingle; and if all this will not serve, the King threatens to fall upon theyre husbands, parents or frends that have or shold have power over them, and make them pay for it.[48]

Thus in woman's dress[49] the enemies of the sex found the symbol of the evils of the day.

---

[48] Edward Phillips Statham, *A Jacobean Letter-Writer: The Life and Times of John Chamberlain* (London, 1920), pp. 182-83. Criticism of women for masculinity was not confined to England. Critics of the younger generation in Holland objected to women's wearing of the high-crowned hats of men, illustrated particularly in the paintings of W. Buytewech the Elder (before 1640). *See* R. H. Wilenski, *An Introduction to Dutch Art* (London, 1928), p. 200.

[49] The yellow ruffs affected by women were violently condemned by King James, who sent Mrs. Turner to the gallows dressed in the fashion which she was said to have invented.—Wilson, *Society Women of Shakespeare's Time*, p. 205. A further comment on King James's dislike of women and their taste for masculine dress is found in Alexander Niccholes' *A Discourse, Of Marriage And Wiving* (ed. of 1620), in a prefatory poem "In Praise of the Worke" by William Lorte:

> "With poniards, pistols and the rufling yellow,
> The world and hell not parraling their fellow.
> So base iniurious shame of their creation,
> Pleasing hels magistrate to weare his fashion.
> Some reformation hath bin to their shames.
> By his dread Maiesty, thrice honored *Iames*,
> Which in an instant of their choysest glee,
> Vnmask'd their pride to widest infamie."

The pamphlet that aroused the greatest interest among the people was *Hic Mulier: Or, The Man-Woman: Being a Medicine to cure the Coltish Disease of the Staggers in the Masculine-Feminines of our Times* (1620).[50] This pamphlet reads like a journalistic expansion of King James's objections to feminine styles, as revealed in his demand upon the clergy to inveigh against the "insolence" of women. It was replied to immediately in *Haec-Vir: Or The Woman-ish-Man: Being an Answere to a late Booke intituled Hic-Mulier* (1620). The first pamphlet was licensed to John Trundle on February 9, 1620, and the second to the same bookseller on February 16—a speed which suggests that the reply was already in manuscript and that the two were designed as a bookseller's effort to capitalize on popular interest in both sides of the controversy. The title-page of *Hic Mulier* bears a woodcut of two women. One sits in a barber's chair awaiting the snipping shears of the hairdresser, who holds a mirror out to her. The other is being fitted in a man's hat and plume. After praising modest, industrious women, careful of their virtue, the author heaps opprobrium on "you Masculine-women," "that are the gilt durt, which imbroders Playhouses."[51] Short hair, face painting, and extravagance in dress have brought women to perdition :

. . . shee that hath pawned her credit to get a Hat, will sell her Smocke to buy a Feather : Shee that hath giuen kisses to haue her hayre shorne, will giue her honestie to haue her vpper parts put into a French doublet.   [Sig. B 2.]

It is not merely the frivolous and the idle of the aristocracy who indulge in extravagant innovations, but the wives of honest citizens are also given to such excess that they ruin their husbands :

. . . look if this very last edition of disguise . . . this bayt which the Diuel hath layd to catch the soules of wanton Women, be not as fre-

---

[50] A sermon condemning the pride and extravagance of women in 1615 contains the phrase which becomes the title of the pamphlet, and which seems to have been a popular epithet. It is found in Thomas Adams's *Mystical Bedlam. Or The World Of Mad-Men* (1615), p. 50 : "The *proud man?* or rather the *proud woman:* or rather *haec aquila,* both he and shee. For if they had no more euident distinction of sexe, then they haue of shape, they would be all man, or rather all woman : for the *Amazons* beare away the Bell : as one wittily, *Hic Mulier* will shortly bee good latine, if this transmigration hold : For whether on horsebacke, or on foot, there is no great difference : but not discernable out of a Coach."   [51] Sig. A 4.

quent in the demy-Palaces of Burgars and Citizens, as it is either at
Maske, Tryumph, Tilt-yard, or Play-house.   [Sig. C 1.]

After blaming the tailors for fostering wanton extravagance in
dress, the author closes with an exhortation to women to cast off
their deformities.

Haec-Vir, the answer, is a vigorous dialogue, at times eloquent
in the sincere defense of woman's right to personal freedom. A
treatise reflecting the opinion of the more advanced social thinkers
among the bourgeoisie, it is a document whose significance has
been overlooked. In its literary plan, the Womanish-Man, a fop
dressed in new-fangled garments, meets Man-Woman, wearing
bobbed hair and dressed in a man's hat and plume, and berates
her

For a shorne, powdered, borrowed Hayre, a naked, lasciuious, bawdy
Bosome, a *Leaden-Hall* Dagger, a High-way Pistoll, and a mind and
behauiour sutable or exceeding euery repeated deformitie. [Sig. A 4.]

The woman retorts with a fervent plea for freedom from the petty
bondage of foolish custom, citing Virgil, Martial, Du Bartas, and
others in support of change which brings with it progress. To
the charge that she is a slave of novelty, she answers:

What slauery can there be in freedome of election? or what basenesse,
to crowne my delights with those pleasures which are most sutable to
mine affections. Bondage or Slauery, is a restraint from those actions,
which the minde (of its owne accord) doth most willingly desire: . . .
Now for mee to follow change, according to the limitation of mine owne
will and pleasure, there cannot bee a greater freedome. Nor do I in
my delight of change otherwise then as the whole world doth, or as
becommeth a daughter of the world to doe. For what is the world, but
a very shop or warehouse of change? Sometimes Winter, sometimes
Summer; day and night: they hold sometimes Riches, sometimes
Pouertie, sometimes Sicknesse: now Pleasure; presētly Anguish; now
Honour; then contempt; and to conclude, there is nothing but change,
which doth surround and mixe withall our Fortunes. And will you
haue a poore woman such a fixed Starre, that shee shall not so much
as moue or twinkle in her owne Spheare? That were true Slauery indeed, and a Baseness beyond the chaines of the worst seruitude. . . .

To Beasts libertie to chuse their foode, liberty to delight in their food, and liberty to feed and grow fat with their food. The birds haue the ayre to fly in, the waters to bathe in, and the earth to feed on. But to man, both these and all things else, to alter, frame and fashion, according as his will and delight shall rule him. Againe, who will rob the eye of the variety of obiects, the eare of the delight of sounds, the nose of smels, the tong of tasts, & the hand of feeling? & shall only woman, excellent woman ; so much better in that she is something purer, be onely depriued of this benefit? Shall shee bee the Bond slaue of Time, the Hand-maid of opinion, or the strict obseruer of euery frosty or cold benummed imagination? It were a cruelty beyond the Racke or Strapado.   [Sigs. A 4ᵛ-B 1ᵛ.]

The theme of mutability, prevalent in so much Elizabethan literature, appears here in a dignified defense of social progress. Conformity to old and unreasonable custom is foolish and should give way to change :

To ride on Side-Saddles at first was counted heere abominable pride, &c. I might instance in a thousand things that onely Custome and not Reason hath approued. To conclude *Custome* is an Idiot; and whosoeuer dependeth wholely vpon him, without the discourse of Reason, will take from him his pyde coat, and become a slaue indeed to contempt and censure.

But you say wee are barbarous and shameles, and cast off all softnes, to runne wilde through a wildernesse of opinions. In this you expresse more cruelty then in all the rest, because I stand not with my hands on my belly like a baby at *Bartholomew* Fayre, that moue not my whole body when I should, but onely stirre my head like Iacke of the Clocke house which hath no ioynts, that am not dumbe when wantons court mee, as if Asse-like I were ready for all burthens, or because I weep not when iniury gripes me, like a worried Deere in the fangs of many Curres : am I therefore barbarous or shamelesse? He is much iniurious that so baptiz'd vs : we are as free-borne as Men, haue as free election and as free spirits, we are compounded of like parts, and may with like liberty make benefit of our Creations : my countenance shal smile on the worthy, and frowne on the ignoble, I will heare the Wise, and bee deafe to Ideots, giue counsell to my friend, but bee dumbe to flatterers, I haue hands that shall bee liberall to reward desert, feete that shall moue swiftly to do good offices, and thoughts that shall euer accompany freedome and seuerity. If this bee barbarous, let me leaue the Citie, and liue with creatures of like simplicity.[52]   [Sigs. B 2ᵛ-B 3.]

Written with far more dignity and spirit than the usual controversial pamphlet, *Haec-Vir* is the *Areopagitica* of the London woman, a woman who had attained greater freedom than any of her predecessors or than any of her European contemporaries.[53]

Another pamphlet, purporting also to answer *Hic Mulier* and to defend woman, is *Mulde Sacke: Or The Apologie of Hic Mulier: To the late Declamation against her* (1620), but in reality it is a solemn attack on the affectations and vices of the age, supported by learned Latin citations in the margins and the text. Apparently some moralist or hack writer took advantage of the current interest in the *Hic Mulier* controversy to use the name for advertising purposes.[54]

Broadsides and ballads carried on the controversy over women.

---

[52] After this speech, Haec-Vir makes a weak rejoinder that "you shall feede *Ballads*, make rich shops, arme contempt, and onely starue and make poore your selues and your reputations" by overdressing, but the woman has the best of the argument. —Sig. B 4ᵛ.

The attacks on women reached even the cloisters of Oxford and influenced one learned youth, Christopher Newstead, to publish *An Apology For Women: Or, Womens Defence. Pend by C. N. late of Albane Hall in Oxon* (1620). A copy is in the Huntington Library. In a dedication to Lady Mary, Countess of Buckingham, Newstead declares that he has been led to make this defense of women "by the frothy word of many Hyperbolizing selfe-conceitists, who deeme it their greatest grace, to be able to disgrace women." His defense falls back on the ancient roll call of the famous, followed by discussions of their piety, chastity, "dextericall Wits," etc.

[53] For a study of the independence and importance of the wives of tradesmen and craftsmen, see Alice Clark, *Working Life of Women in the Seventeenth Century* (London, 1919), *passim*.

[54] The pamphleteer's satire is directed against pettifogging lawyers, usurers, rentrackers, greedy merchant tailors, unjust justices of the peace, tyrannical bailiffs and jailers, drunkards, flatterers, detractors, Puritans, corrupt churchmen, bribe-taking judges, plotting papists, and countless others. The criticisms and descriptions develop into what almost become characters.

The satire of affected gallants in *Mulde Sacke* has a counterpart in *Haec-Vir*, somewhat like Dekker's famous picture of the playhouse gallant: "To see one of your gender either shew himselfe (in the midst of his pride or riches) at a Play house, or publique assembly how; (before he dare enter) with the *Iacobs*-Staffe of his owne eyes and his Pages, hee takes a full suruay of himselfe, from the highest sprig in his feather, to the lowest spangle that shines in his Shoo-string: how he prunes and picks himselfe like a Hawke set a weathering, cals euery seuerall garment to Auricular confession, making them vtter both their mortall great staines, and their veniall and lesse blemishes, though the moat bee much lesse then an Attome: Then to see him plucke and tugge

Henry Gosson printed in 1620 a broadside, attributed to John Taylor, with the pictures of two strange animals, described by the verse beneath them :

Fill Gut And Pinch Belly : One being Fat with eating good Men, the other Leane for want of good women.
> Now full bellyed Fill gut, so Fat heere in show
> Feeds on our good Men, as Women well know,
> Who flocke in great numbers, all weary of lives
> Heere thus to be eaten, and rid from their Wives.[55]

A broadside print in the British Museum, dated 1620 and entitled *A New Yeeres guift for shrews*, bears this verse :

> Who marieth a Wife vpon a Moneday,
> If she will not be good vppon a Twesday,
> Lett him go to ye wood vppon a Wensday,
> And cutt him a cudgell vpon the Thursday,
> And pay her soundly vppon a Fryday,
> And she mend not, ye Diuil take her a Saterday.
> Then he may eat his meat in peace on the Sunday.[56]

A ballad entitled *The Country Lasse* [*c.* 1620] glorifies the country girl in contrast to the city wanton.[57] Dozens of other ballads, sometimes satirical, sometimes defensive, throughout the 1620's

---

euery thing into the forme of the newest receiued fashion; and by *Durers* rules make his legge answerable to his necke; his thigh proportionable with his middle, his foote with his hand, and a world of such idle disdained foppery : To see him thus patcht vp with Symetry, make himselfe complete, and euen as a circle : and lastly, cast himselfe amongst the eyes of the people (as an obiect of wonder) with more nicenesse, then a Virgin goes to the sheetes of her first Louer, would make patience her selfe mad with anger, and cry with the Poet :

> *O Hominum mores, O gens, O Tempora dura,*
> *Quantus in vrbe Dolor; Quantus in Orbe Dolus!*"—Sigs. C 2-C 2ᵛ.

[55] Robert Lemon, *Catalogue of a Collection of Printed Broadsides in the Possession of the Society of Antiquaries of London* (London, 1866), pp. 52-53. *See* Hyder E. Rollins, "The Black-Letter Broadside Ballad," *Publications of the Modern Language Association*, XXXIV (1919), 273. *See also* Sir Charles H. Firth, "The Ballad History of the Reign of James I," *The Transactions of the Royal Historical Society*, 3d Ser., V (1911), 21-61. He quotes Sir Simonds D'Ewes on "satirical wits" who wrote "libels" on the Overbury murder, and refers to five ballads or broadsides on the subject in the library of the Society of Antiquaries.

[56] F. G. Stephens, *Catalogue of Prints and Drawings in the British Museum. I. Political and Personal Satires* (London, 1870), p. 54.

[57] John Ashton (ed.), *A Century of Ballads* (London, 1887), pp. 36 ff.

and later, treat women as a primary or an incidental theme in their social commentary.[58] A number of allusions in these years testify to the widespread interest attracted by the major works in the controversy. Samuel Rowlands included an epigram called "An Apology for Women" in *The Night-Raven* (1620), in which he refers to Swetnam's terming women night crows :

> Tearm them no more night-Rauens, they are Doues
> True harted Turtles, constant, faithfull, kinde,
> Mylder then men, and of lesse hurtfull minde,
> More pittifull, and more compassionate,
> Lesse enuious and lesse possest with hate,
> And of themselues so rare perfections show,
> Not prouing bad, till bad men make them so.[59]

Thomas Middleton's *The World Tost at Tennis* (1620) refers to the *Hic Mulier* theme as the subject matter of ballads :

. . . one hangs himself today, another drowns himself tomorrow, a sergeant stabbed next day; here a pettifogger a' the pillory, a bawd in the cart's nose, and a pander in the tail : *hic mulier, haec vir,* fashions, fictions, felonies, fooleries.[60]

Dekker in *Dekker his Dreame* (1620), a poem on the horrors of hell, includes a passage describing the tortures of proud, "Gay gawdy women," who spent their lives in extravagant frivolity and expensive dressing. A marginal gloss comments : "Pride of womē (and in that the effeminacy of men in this age) is heere taxed and rewarded." He is particularly scornful of women "Whose Backs

---

[58] Such ballads are : *A most excellent Godly new Ballad: [shew]ing the manifold abuses of this wicked world, the intolerable pride of people, the wantonnesse [of] women* (1624) ; Martin Parker's *A pleasant new Ballad, both merry and witty, That sheweth the humours of the wiues in the city* [1625?] ; *Seldome comes the better: Or, An admonition to all sorts of people, as Husbands, Wiues, Masters, and Seruants, &c. to auoid mutability, and to fix their minds on what they possesse* [1629?] ; *Tis not otherwise: Or: The praise of a married life* [1630?] ; *Halfe a dozen of good Wiues. All for a penny* [1635?]. *See* Hyder E. Rollin s(ed.) : *The Pack of Autolycus* (Cambridge, Mass., 1927), pp. 3 ff. ; *A Pepysian Garland* (Cambridge, 1922), *passim;* and *The Pepys Ballads* (Cambridge, Mass., 1929), Vols. I and II, *passim,* especially II, 169 ff., 174 ff.

[59] *The Complete Works of Samuel Rowlands,* 3 vols., Hunterian Club (Glasgow, 1872-80), II, 7.

[60] Quoted by Rollins, "The Black-Letter Broadside Ballad," *loc. cit.,* p. 266.

wore out more Fashions then their Wit."[61] Robert Aylett, writing
a poem in praise of the heroine so favored by Dutch and Flemish
artists, *Susanna: Or, The Arraignment Of The Two Vniust Elders*
(1622), turns aside to address London women:

> You *females-masculine* that doe pretend,
> You weapons weare your honours to defend,
> If in the Court or City, villany,
> Should be attempted 'gainst your chastity:
> See here this *naked woman* all alone,
> Defends her honour hauing two to one.   [P. 21.]

John Taylor's *Superbiae Flagellum, Or The Whip Of Pride* (1621)
expresses his disgust at the prevailing fashions:

> The Deu'ill laugh'd lately at the stinking stir,
> We had about *Hic Mulier* and *Haec Vir*,
> The Masculine appareld Feminine,
> The Feminine attired Masculine,
> The Woman-man, Man-Woman, chuse you whether,
>
> .   .   .   .
>
> But these things haue so well bin bang'd and firk'd,
> And Epigram'd and Satyr'd, whip'd and Ierk'd,
> Cudgeld and bastinadoed at the Court,
> And Comically stag'de to make men sport,
> Iyg'd, and (with all reason) mock'd in Rime,
> And made the onely scornefull theame of Time;
> And Ballad-mongers had so great a taske,
> (As if their muses all had got the laske.)
> That no more time therein my paines I'le spend,
> But freely leaue them to amend, or end.[62]

A little treatise, not railing with invective, but mournfully sad
and pessimistic over the married state, was *A Discourse Of The
Married And Single Life. Wherein, By Discouering The Misery Of The
one, is plainely declared the felicity of the other* (1621). Cast in the form
of letters addressed by the Philosopher Lindorach to Cultibert,
king of the Indians, it relates "the inconuenience and discommod-

---

[61] Reprinted by A. B. Grosart (ed.), *The Non-Dramatic Works of Thomas Dekker*, 5
vols., Huth Library (1884-86), Vol. III.
[62] In the Spenser Society's reproduction of the 1630 folio of Taylor's works,
pp. 43-44.

ities of the married Life." Stoicism is counseled, for though man may not be "forewarned by wisdome to preuent them [evils of married life], yet he may be forewarned with patience to endure them ; which is the onely drift which herein is aymed at."[63] Woman is the cause of all woes, and whatever she does results in evil. The concluding chapter relates "diuers examples of Women, that haue murdred their husbands," beginning with Clytemnestra. Finally, the anonymous author appends an admonition to "take thy wife as a medicine of Rubarbe" and closes with a prayer to the gods to give the king of the Indians grace to keep from evil, "which thou shalt best do, if thou keepe thee from a wife."

Perhaps in answer to *A Discourse Of The Married And Single Life*, as well as to the other attacks on women, was Richard Ferrers's poem, *The Worth Of Women* (1622), a compilation of the famous women of the Bible and classical history. He ends with extravagant praise of Queen Elizabeth. Doubtless, many in England in the days of James looked back on the previous reign as an age heroic for its women as well as for its men. The prevailing fashion at the moment is to satirize women, Ferrers asserts in an opening passage describing the rage of the critics over his subject matter :

> One cries, a woman is composde of feathers ;
> Another sweares, their faith is like the winde ;
> A third, their zeale is made of frostie weather ;
> A fourth, a chaste one neuer yet could finde.
> A fig for these, since better spirits know,
> Saue ignorance, true knowledge hath no fo.
> Emboldned thus my daring Muse goes on,
> Attir'd with naked Truths vnspotted robe,
> And Eagle-like beholds the dazeling Sunne,
> Euen in the Apogean of his globe,
> To teach these Critics that haue err'd in this
> To know hereafter what a woman is.   [Sig. A 4.]

Ferrers's example was followed by Abraham Darcie in *The Honour Of Ladies: Or, A True Description Of their Noble Perfections* (1622), a prose treatise divided into chapters illustrating the heroism, magnanimity, prudence, wisdom, valor, chastity, learn-

---

[63] Sig. A 8v.

ing, beauty, justice, and piety of women. The material is chiefly examples of these virtues found in classical legend and history.

A definitive encyclopedia of women as a defense against their carping critics was the contribution of Thomas Heywood, who published in 1624 his *Gunaikeion: or, Nine Bookes of Various History Concerninge Women*, a second edition of which appeared in 1657 as *The Generall History of Women*. He warns the reader to

expect not, that I should either enuiously carpe at the particular manners or actions of any liuing, nor iniuriously detract from the Sepulchers of the dead ; the first I could neuer affect, the last I did alwayes detest. I only present thee with a Collection of Histories, which touch the generalitie of Women, such as haue either beene illustrated for their Vertues, and Noble Actions, or contrarily branded for their Vices and baser Conditions.

All women are included, "from the Sceptre in the Court, to the Sheepehooke in the Cottage," in this work, which Heywood maintains has practical utility :

Wiues may reade here of chast Virgins, to patterne their Daughters by, and how to demeane themselues in all Coniugall loue towards their Husbands : Widowes may finde what may best become their solitude, and Matrons those accomplishments that most dignifie their grauitie.[64]

Heywood's later *The Exemplary Lives and memorable Acts of nine the most worthy Women of the World* (1640) contains further praise of the sex. Learned proof that women are as good as men was provided by William Austin's *Haec Homo, Wherein The Excellency of the Creation of Women is described, By way of an Essay* (1637), a work sufficiently popular to warrant further editions in 1638 and 1639. By Scripture and logic, Austin shows that woman is superlatively fine in her origin and in her form and that man's condemnation proceeds only from ignorance ; he even goes so far as to contend that woman is equal with man :

In the *sexe*, is all the difference ; which is but onely in *the body*. For, she hath the *same reasonable soule;* and, in that, there is neither *hees*, nor *shees;* neither *excellencie*, nor *superiority:* she hath the *same soule;* the *same*

---

[64] Preface to the reader.

mind; the *same vnderstanding;* and tends to the *same end* of eternall salvation that *he Doth.* [P. 5.]

Woman is like a stately merchant ship which brings to her husband riches and credit.[65] At length, with help from Spenser's House of Alma, the author allegorically describes woman's body and finds it good.

Although the Puritans looked upon woman with suspicion, as Professor Routh maintains,[66] middle-class writers were not wholly concerned with the reproof of women's faults and, as a matter of fact, a large mass of popular literature in the seventeenth century treats woman sympathetically. Moreover, many bourgeois writers, as we have seen, vigorously defended women against the cynicism of the cavaliers. In the late 1630's a wave of semi-jocular pamphlets concerning woman swept from the presses. Thomas Hey-

---

[65] Austin is probably quoting this figure from a marriage sermon by Robert Wilkinson, published in 1607 as *The Merchant Royal.* Marriage and funeral sermons gave the clergy a chance to make the *amende honorable* for some of the harsh things said about the sex. *See,* e.g., Stephen Geree's *The Ornament of Women. Or, A description of the true excellency of Women. Delivered in a Sermon at the Funerall of M. Elizabeth Machell* (1639). It contains characteristic praise of good women.

Not all the writers agreed that a woman brought to her husband riches and credit. Samuel Rowlands in *Heavens Glory, Seeke It. Earths Vanitie, Flye It. Hells Horror, Fere It* (1628) laments the disasters which come to merchants and other tradesmen through the social climbing of their wives : "Euery man is an eye-witnesse of this vanity, the more is the pittie that it should be so common : your Lady, the Merchants wife, the tradesmans wife, nay, all of all sorts are a degree aboue their estate. Your Gallant is no man, vnlesse his haire be of the womans fashion, dangling and wauing ouer his shoulders ; your woman no body, except (contrary to the modesty of her sexe) shee be halfe (at least) of the mans fashion : shee jets, she cuts, she rides, shee sweares, she games, shee smoakes, shee drinkes, and what not that is euill . . . *O tempora! O mores!*" —*Works,* III, 98-99.

The necessity for answering the critics of women was felt by the author of *The Lanchinge of the Mary or The Seamans honest wyfe* (1633), who put into the mouth of the heroine a comment on the satirists :

> "I know there are a packe of Satyrists
> Malignant Swetnams, drunken poetasters,
> Which farce and bumbast out theyr spurious lines
> With raylinge language 'gaynst our feeble sex."—IV, iv.

Quoted from the MS by F. S. Boas, *Shakespeare and the Universities* (Oxford, 1923), p. 170.

[66] Routh, "The Advent of Modern Thought in Popular Literature," *Cambridge History of English Literature,* VII, 387. *See* his brief bibliography, pp. 513-14.

wood's *A Curtaine Lecture* (1637)[67] is a good example of the popularization of the domestic treatise in a work designed for the
amusement as well as the instruction of the reader, for the pamphlet is really in part a serious discussion of marriage relations from
the middle-class point of view, with certain jests on marital
discords.

John Taylor, the prolific "Water-Poet," who had always one
ear cocked for the commands of his tradesmen-public, took advantage of the interest in these "lectures" to bring out his own
Divers Crab-tree Lectures (1639)[68] and *A Juniper Lecture* (1639). In
the first of these works, the wives of a host of tradesmen and
artisans read their husbands shrewish lessons. Nor is the schooling
exclusively for husbands. A prefatory epistle from "Mary Make-
peace" to all "Sisters of her Female Society" calls upon them to
lament "the course carriage of some of our Sexe," which has
caused a few of the modest sort "(even in Print) [to be] publickly
branded."[69] Mary counsels patience and humility and warns
against such members of the sisterhood as Tabitha Turbulent,
Franks Froward, Bettrisse Bould-face, Ellen Ever-Heard, and
many other abstract vixens. *A Juniper Lecture* is similar in tone,
with somewhat more specific dispraise of women. Taylor, whose
satire is neither violent nor bitter, merely exploits the ancient
husband-wife theme in the spirit of one tradesman jesting with
another.

Richard Brathwaite followed Taylor with *Ar't asleepe Husband?
A Boulster Lecture; Stored With all variety of witty jeasts, merry Tales,
and other pleasant passages* (1640), a small volume of 318 pages,
stored with a large number of short tales and anecdotes, most of
which relate the passions and frailties of the weaker sex. Although
the work pretends to be in praise of women, stories which make
them seem ridiculous predominate. With a canny regard for public favor, Brathwaite salvaged a few of the favorable items from
Ar't asleepe Husband? and included them in *A Ladies Love-Lecture,*

---

[67] *See further* under Chap. VII, *supra*, p. 213, n. 13.

[68] *Divers Crab-tree Lectures. Expressing the severall Languages that shrews read to their
Husbands, either at morning, Noone, or Night. With a pleasant Relation of Shrewes Munday,
and Shrewes Tuesday, and why they were so called. Also a Lecture betweene a Pedler and his
wife in the Canting Language. With a new tricke to tame a Shrew* (1639).

[69] Sig. A 3ᵛ.

printed in the folio volume of *The English Gentleman and the English Gentlewoman* (1641). A preface of the stationer to the reader announces that here "light passages" are omitted that none might be offended by "such affected levitie." Brathwaite now gives a formal defense of women, "Stored With all varietie of ingenious Moralitie," against "Cynick Critics" by setting forth the great part women have played in history. To the critics, he says:

But to answer these prodigies of nature; Tell me, yee *Critick Cavallieres*, who have surely got a stroak over shins with some *French faggot*, or you would never thus inveigh against so exquisite a subject; why were all the *Muses* women; all the *Sibyls* women; those watchfull *Hesperides* women; those *Nine-Worthies*, so lately memoriz'd, women?[70] [P. 442.]

A reply to the lecture pamphlets against women came from a pseudonymous writer, possibly a woman, signing two feminine descriptive names; it bore the title of *The womens sharpe revenge* (1640).[71] Singling out Taylor for a virulent attack, the author heaps calumny upon him, calls him names, rails at his ancestors, accuses him of drunkenness and other vices, and makes him a scapegoat generally for writers who had dared to satirize the opposite sex. Why do not men abjure women, the pamphlet asks, if women are totally bad? The critics of women are those who have had no success in love or have been so unfortunate as to marry shrews. The tract by Mary Tattle-well (and her other self, Ioane Hit-him-home) is not entirely denunciation of the authors of "illfavoured Pamplets . . . called *Lectures*, as the Juniper Lecture, the *Crab-tree Lecture*, & the *Worm-wood Lecture*," and, as a marginal note adds, ". . . a new Lecture called the Bolster Lecture."[72] It protests against the injustice of a double standard of morality and of the poor education of women[73] merely for the comfort and

[70] A reference to Heywood's *The Exemplary Lives*. Brathwaite had displayed an interest in women earlier in his *The Good Wife* (1618) [printed with Patrick Hannay's *A Happy Husband*] and in *The English Gentlewoman* (1631).

[71] *The womens sharpe revenge: Or an answer to Sir Seldome Sober that writ those railing Pamphelets called the Iuniper and Crab-tree Lectures, &c. Being a sound Reply and full confutation of those Bookes: with an Apology in this case for the defence of us women. Performed by Mary Tattle-well, and Ioane Hit-him-home, Spinsters* (1640).

[72] P. 5.

[73] Pp. 40 ff. The author protests that "If wee be taught to read, they confine us within the compasse of our Mothers Tongue, and that limit wee are not suffered to passe."—P. 41.

pleasure of man. Women are not slaves of men:

Man might consider that women were not created to be their slaves or vassalls, for as they had not their Originall out of his head, (thereby to command him;) so it was not out of his foote to be trod upon, but in a (medium) out of his side to be his fellow-feeler, his equal & companion.   [P. 77.]

The controversy over women during the Commonwealth, a subject beyond the scope of the present study, degenerated into coarse invective and ribald satire; typical examples are Henry Neville's *The Ladies Parliament* (1647), a scandalous pamphlet like others which he wrote: *The City-Dames Petition, In The behalfe of the long afflicted but well-affected Cavaliers* (1647), a complaint purporting to come from London citizens' wives that they no longer have the solace of the absent aristocrats, and *The Ladies, A Second Time, Assembled In Parliament* (1647), a conventional satire on the lust and pride of London women. Under stress of prejudice and fanaticism in the Puritan conflict, the medieval distrust of all things giving pleasure found expression. It was but natural that woman should find herself included among things proscribed. For a century preceding the Puritan outburst in the 1640's, woman had been gradually increasing her privileges and position. Her very independence and boldness in the seventeenth century were responsible for the reaction against her by Puritan fanatics.

During the late sixteenth and early seventeenth centuries, middle-class writers debated the position and prerogatives of women, debated the theme of woman's goodness or wickedness, and prevailingly defended her, even while condemning the excesses of pride and extravagance which led to disasters in the citizen's economy. If on occasion they were willing to ridicule the foibles of women, they nevertheless stood ready at other times to attest woman's dignity, intelligence, and nobility of soul. Furthermore, out of the controversial literature about woman came fervent demands from both middle-class and aristocratic writers for the recognition of woman's equality with man. If these demands were few, they were none the less significant of the future. Daniel Tuvil, William Heale, and the unknown author of *Haec-Vir* present the problem with a clarity of logic and a modernity not found in previous writers. Because Puritan zealots of the mid-seventeenth century abused women, it is fallacious to assume that the attitude of the rank and file of the middle class was one of opposition to woman's social progress; the same Puritans objected to the theater, music, and all forms of amusements; yet certainly they did not represent the composite opinion of the class of which, at the moment, they were the most voluble part. In the great mass of popular literature concerning women, we can discern something more than the perennial jests and stories of the frailties or virtues of the sex. A serious undercurrent of intelligent thinking upon woman's status in a new commercial society is evident even in some of the more jocular treatises. Nor was this vital social problem, which became the theme of an increasing number of writers eager to please a public interested in every phase of the relations of men and women, the sole concern of middle-class men of letters, as examples already cited indicate; but it is clear that the taste and opinions of the commercial elements in society had an important influence upon the development of new social ideas as well as upon the literature in which these ideas were reflected. While many a learned and courtly work emphasized in its Platonic philosophy the powerful influence of woman, many other literary efforts in the less learned tradition showed the concern of the average man with practical aspects of the question. If courtly authors who took the trouble to write about women in the seventeenth century frequently became less philosophic and more mundane, the cause is doubtless to be found in the influence of the world of plain men who were buying books and discussing the opinions of their authors. Not the least important of the influences of the literary controversies about woman was the stirring of the public interest in still more discussion of the subject and the creation of an atmosphere favorable to the development of the drama and the novel of domestic relations. Of yet greater consequence were the new trends of thought thus set in motion, which quickened the processes leading to the so-called freedom of woman in modern society.

XIV

THE WONDERS OF TRAVEL

THE lure of the sea, of adventurous voyages in search of gold or shorter routes to Cathay, touched the imaginations of Renaissance Englishmen and acted like a heady drug to spur them to a new interest in the realms beyond the seas. There was created an appetite, insatiable and increasing, for accounts of the strange new worlds that lay beyond horizons suddenly expanding before a people until now satisfied with the narrow circuit of their own coasts. Tales brought home by returning sailors were devoured with avid interest by his lordship in the great hall and the cottager in the village. Small boys, like young Raleigh in the picture by Millais in the Tate Gallery, listened entranced, and determined to grow up into adventuring seamen. Writers felt the stimulus and turned the stuff of romance into song and story. Drayton grew lyrical and sang "To the Virginian Voyage" and Shakespeare wove the witches and spirits of the Bermudas into the magic of the *Tempest*. The tang of the sea permeated a great body of Elizabethan literature and stirred the interest of a public already eager to hear stories of far places.

The appeal of the literature of travel and exploration was confined to no class or group. All England sought out such matter and swallowed the most incredible tales. The travels attributed to the mythical Sir John Mandeville were not too absurd to gain credence[1] nor were they much more bizarre than many stories related as solemn truth. Satirists ridiculed the lies of travelers without diminishing their popularity. In the Royal Exchange and Paul's Walk knots of news-hungry listeners gathered while some

---

[1] Nine preserved editions of Mandeville are recorded in the *Short Title Catalogue*. Despite the tales of wonder, the geographical knowledge set forth in this work was of real value. *See* E. G. R. Taylor, *Tudor Geography, 1485-1583* (London, 1930), p. 5.

sailor or merchant described his adventures in foreign ports. Doubtless they expected a strange story, for, as one critic of the times comments, "Travellers are priuileged to lie, and at their returne, if they doe hitte into a company that neuer trauelled towards the South Pole, beyond *Gads hill*, you shall heare them speake of wonders."[2] Yet despite the skepticism of a few critics, voyagers who brought home stories of distant lands were received with such favor that, as one writer declares, common men "of base descent and lineage, haue thereby not only bin commended to the Honourable; but also their owne experience and triall of occurrents in trauelling, doth procure thus much more than ordinary vnto them, that they are among men vntrauelled as Hesperus among the smaller starres."[3] So eager was the public for accounts of voyages and explorations that printers frequently brought out garbled reports, hurried through the press in advance of authentic relations of returned travelers. The author of *Sir Thomas Smithes Voiage and Entertainment in Rushia* (1605) refers bitterly to the practice of piecing together hasty notes and printing them for gain:

. . . the discourses of this voyage . . . affoorded such pleasure to the hearers, by reason the accidents were strange and Nouell, that many way-laid the News, and were gladde to make any booty of it to delight themselues, by which meanes, that which of it selfe being knit together was beautifull, could not chuse but shew vilde, beeing so torne in peeces. So that the itching fingers of gain laid hold vpon it, and had like to haue sent it into the world lame, and dismembered. Some that picke up the crums of such feasts, had scrapt togither many percels of this Rushian commoditie, so that their heads being gotten with child of a Bastard, there was no remedy but they must be deliuered in *Paules Church-yard*.[4]

Though sheer curiosity accounts for some of the interest in travel literature, other causes prompted the search after facts about distant lands. The national spirit was growing into imperialism, and Englishmen were beginning to think of an empire

---

[2] Barnabe Rich, *Faultes Faults, And nothing else but Faultes* (1606), sig. C 4ᵛ.

[3] Dedication to Sir Henry Sidney, signed "John Stell," of T. Washington's translation from Nicholas de Nicholai, *The Nauigations, peregrinations and Voyages, made into Turkie by Nicholas Nicholay Daulphinois* (1585).

[4] Preface. The author claims to have collected from participants the authentic account of the expedition.

across the seas. News of the vast wealth to be had for the taking had stirred every hearthside. A share in the spoils of rich galleons from Peru was within the range of every sailor's dreams. The very sands of the streams in the New World were said to gleam with jewels and gold, and Raleigh was not alone in seeking a mountain of precious metal in the wilds of America.[5] Even when fine gold was not the direct object of the voyageurs' search, the attainment of wealth lay behind their endeavors. The objective of the voyages in search of the Northwest Passage was a new route to the riches of China and the Indies. The expeditions into the Baltic, into the Mediterranean, and to the coasts of Africa and Asia sought trade, and English factories were soon to stretch from Bantam to Moscow. Cargoes of spices, silks, furs, and other foreign commodities enriched the adventuring merchants of London and Bristol. With each returning ship, interest in the outside world increased. Particularly among the trading classes was the desire keen for knowledge of foreign countries. The search after geographical facts came to be a professional necessity for merchants and seamen.

Credit for a large portion of the geographical and travel literature of Renaissance England must be given to merchants and traders, who were directly responsible for making it available to the public. Progress in nautical and geographical sciences received constant stimulation from the business groups who sought utilitarian helps to further profits and were willing, in pursuit of wealth, to master a new and increasing body of knowledge. The influence of this mercantile interest was enormous. The very form of prose style owes a great deal to the straightforward narratives of practical traders who foreswore unwieldy Ciceronianism and discarded the windy verbiage of Elizabethan polite prose in order that their reports and descriptions might be easily understood by the ordinary layman.

Letters and reports, sometimes official, sometimes personal, were printed in large numbers to inform the public about trading ventures and explorations. Returned merchants were expected to

---

[5] Excitement over the gold of Guiana was intensified by the publication in 1596 of Sir Walter Raleigh's *The Discoverie Of The Large, Rich, And Bewtiful Empire Of Guiana, With a relation of the great and Golden Citie of Manoa (which the spanyards call El Dorado) And the Prouinces of Emeria, Arromaia, Amapaia, and other Countries, with their riuers, adioyning.* The work had three editions in the year of its publication.

write some account of their foreign adventures. The pressure to publish was such that those who shirked it might be accused of the neglect of a duty, asserts Edmund Scott, author of *An Exact Discourse Of the Subtilties, Fashions, Pollicies, Religion, and Ceremonies of the East Indians* (1606).[6] In a dedication to Sir William Romney, "Gouernor of the worshipfull Companie of Marchants trading to the East Indies," Scott comments that it has been usual for officials in the trading companies to publish reports of their foreign activities. Though he has no fine language to display, he has been induced to comply with an established precedent

. . . because heeretofore it hath been a vsuall custome, that those which first haue been resident in other forraine Countries, as Turkey, Persia, and Muscouie, haue registred such matters as haue hapned worthy of note in their times, beeing in those partes of the maine Continent Land; wherefore I hauing been lately Resident for your Worship in the Iland of Iaua maior, toward the East parts of the world; Albeit I am no Scholler to performe it with an eloquent discourse; yet fearing, and withall beeing put in minde by some friendes, that if I neglected it, I should be condemned of slouth: haue thought good to present vnto your Worshippe, these few Lines: the which may certifie you of the great blessings of God, both in preseruing the greatest quantitie of your goods, and our liues; which are come home out of that rude and dangerous Region, into our owne natiue Countrey. Likewise your Worshippe shall vnderstand by this plaine Discourse the situation of the place, and the manners and fashions of the people, with some other strange accidents, which for breuitie sake I did not certifie you of by my Letters sent from thence: but in this small Volume you shall see, from time to time, how euery thing hath been ordered, and performed in your businesse, and other affayres. . . .

A report such as Scott provided was expected to satisfy legitimate curiosity and to encourage possible investors. Though merchants continually sought for news, trade secrets were suppressed and

---

[6] *An Exact Discourse Of the Subtilties, Fashions, Pollicies, Religion, and Ceremonies of the East Indians, as well Chyneses as Iauans, there abyding and dweling. Together with the manner of trading with those people as well by vs English, as by the Hollanders: as also what hath happened to the English Nation at Bantan in the East Indies, since the 2. of February 1602. vntill the 6. of October 1605. Whereunto is added a briefe Description of Iaua Maior. Written by Edmund Scott, resident there, and in other places neere adioyning, the space of three yeeres and a halfe* (1606).

writers are often deliberately vague about important geographical details. James Rosier in *A True Relation of the most prosperous voyage made this present yeere 1605, by Captaine George Waymouth, in the Discouery of the land of Virginia* (1605) declares that the action of certain gentlemen and merchants in promoting a colony in Virginia prompts him to publish his report, though he has hitherto avoided publicity

. . . because some forrein Nation (being fully assured of the fruitful-nesse of the countrie) haue hoped hereby to gaine some knowledge of the place, seeing they could not allure our Captaine or any speciall man of our Company to combine with them for their direction, nor obtaine their purpose, in conueying away our Saluages, which was busily in practise. And this is the cause that I haue neither written of the latitude or variation most exactly obserued of our Captaine with sundrie instruments, which together with his perfect Geographicall Map of the countrey, he entendeth hereafter to set forth. I haue like-wise purposedly omitted here to adde a collection of many words in their language to the number of foure or fiue hundred, as also the names of diuers of their gouernours aswell their friends as their ene-mies. . . .[7]

However, not every explorer shared Rosier's fear of revealing in-formation to foreign competitors, and as voyages increased, the lit-erature produced by participants multiplied. Records of the open-ing of trade relations with India, the East Indies, Russia, the Le-vant, and America are to be found in scores of narratives written by seamen and merchants. Richard Hakluyt and his successor, Samuel Purchas, as we shall see later, busied themselves in the col-lection of notes, letters, reports, and previously published pam-phlets, which went to swell their compilations into vast volumes. The commercial travels of Anthony Jenkinson in Russia, Richard Cocks in Japan, Sir Henry Middleton in Bantam and the Malay islands, Sir Thomas Roe in India, and many others like them, as well as the voyages of Hawkins, Frobisher, Davis, and their contemporaries, were described in journals and reports, which fired the imaginations of Elizabethan tradesmen ; they have been

---

[7] Preface to the reader. Rosier, who signs himself on the title-page, "a Gentleman employed in the voyage," says that he was engaged by Thomas Arundell, Baron of Warder, to make a report of the things seen.

preserved for modern readers in the Hakluyt Society publications.[8] Clergymen who went as chaplains on the voyages served a further useful purpose by writing their experiences. Papers composed by a preacher and several merchants provided the material out of which Theophilus Lavender compiled a remarkably inclusive treatise which recommended itself to the curious under the title of *The Travels Of certaine Englishmen into Africa, Asia, Troy, Bythinia, Thracia, and to the Blacke Sea. And into Syria, Cilicia, Pisidia, Mesopotamia, Damascus, Canaan, Galile, Samaria, Iudea, Palestina, Ierusalem, Iericho, and to the Red Sea: and to sundry other places. . . . Very profitable for the helpe of Trauellers, and no lesse delightfull to all persons who take pleasure to heare of the Manners, Gouernement, Religion, and Customes of Forraine and Heathen Countries* (1609). The documents from which Lavender extracted his material were written to Bezaliel Biddulph by "Master William Biddulph (Preacher to the Company of English Merchants resident in Aleppo), Master Ieffrey Kirbie Merchant, Master Edward Abbot Merchant, Master Iohn Elkin gentleman, and Iasper Tyon Ieweller."[9] Letters from travelers were a regular source for pamphlets that printers were eager to publish,[10] sometimes to the embarrassment of the writers.

[8] *See* the following publications of the Hakluyt Society of London: E. Delmar Morgan and C. H. Coote (eds.), *Early Voyages and Travels to Russia and Persia by Anthony Jenkinson and other Englishmen,* 2 vols. (1886); Edward A. Bond (ed.), *Russia at the Close of the Sixteenth Century* (1856); Edward Maunde Thompson (ed.), *Diary of Richard Cocks, Cape-Merchant in the English Factory in Japan, 1615-1622,* 2 vols. (1883); Bolton Corney (ed.), *The Voyage of Sir Henry Middleton to Bantam and the Maluco Islands; Being the Second Voyage Set Forth by the Governor and Company of Merchants of London Trading into the East Indies* (1855); J. Theodore Bent (ed.), *Early Voyages and Travels in the Levant* (1893); R. H. Major (ed.), *The Historie of Travaile into Virginia Britannia . . . By William Strachey, Gent. The First Secretary of the Colony* (1849); Thomas Rundall (ed.), *Memorials of the Empire of Japan in the 16th and 17th Centuries* (1850); William Foster (ed.), *The Embassy of Sir Thomas Roe to the Court of the Great Mogul, 1615-1619, as Narrated in His Journal and Correspondence,* 2 vols. (1899); Clements R. Markham (ed.), *The Hawkins Voyages during the Reigns of Henry VIII, Queen Elizabeth, and James I* (1878); Richard Collinson (ed.), *The Three Voyages of Martin Frobisher in Search of a Passage to Cathaia and India by the North-West, A. D. 1576-78* (1867); Albert Hastings Markham (ed.), *The Voyages and Works of John Davis, the Navigator* (1880). The latter work has in Appendix A a bibliography of works on navigation, through the Elizabethan age.

[9] Preface, sig. ¶ 4ᵛ.

[10] The interest in foreign news resulted in many ephemeral pamphlets, of which published letters were one form. For further details of this interest, *see* Chap. XII, *supra.* An example of the epistolary form of news, which merchants often furnished, is R. S.'s *The New Prophetical King of Barbary. Or The last newes from thence in a Letter written*

Lavender takes occasion to point out that letters written by Master Henry Tymberley, and printed without his permission, contained many gross errors.

Authors of travel narratives frequently gave a utilitarian reason for their productions, and much publication was directly concerned with spreading the propaganda of expansion. As citizen-authors tasted the joys of publicity, personal vanities also inspired in them an eagerness to be read by the multitude. The dainty reticence affected by poetical courtiers was not found among the literary sea captains and merchants who published the records of their explorations. Royal command, to be sure, was often the excuse for the appearance in print of a captain's journal, but navigators seem to have had as keen a zest for autobiographical authorship as actors displayed in a later period. A good deal of self-advertisement went into the title of *North-West Fox, Or, Fox from the North-west passage . . . By Captaine Luke Foxe of Kingstone vpon Hull, Capt. and Pylot for the Voyage, in his Majesties Pinnace the Charles. Printed by his Majesties Command* (1635). Captain Fox is proud of his plain style, which can be understood of everybody, and warns the reader to "expect not heere any florishing Phrases or Eloquent tearmes, for this Child of mine begot in the North-wests cold Clime, (where they breed no Schollers,) is not able to digest the sweet milke of Rethorick, that's food for them."[11] Beginning with King Arthur, Fox gives an epitome of noteworthy

---

of late from a Merchant there, to a Gentl. not long since imployed into that countrie from his Maiestie (1613). The merchant's letter was prepared for printing by an editor who signed himself I. H. Apparently he was a preacher. A second letter printed with the foregoing is signed G. B. The editor announces that if any further reports come in, he will not withhold them from the public.

[11] Preface. A few years after Fox's treatise Richard Boothby, a merchant, who wrote *A Breife Discovery or Description Of the most Famous Island of Madagascar or St. Laurence in Asia neare vnto East-India* (1646), complained that his style had been one of the reasons for a refusal to license his work. He had hoped to print it two years before but various "lets" prevented, including "the hinderance of a captious licencer, blameing the rudenesse of the stile and my placeing Madagascar in Asia, which he would needs have to be in Affrica, but whether in Asia or Affrica I yet rest unresolved." He was induced to publish his book, by one Francis Lloyd, an East India merchant, who had added some particulars "touching the incouragement for a plantation at Madagascar, and the assured great benefit by trade from thence to all parts of the world, by making or setling there a Magazine or store house for trade into all Christian and heathen Kingdomes."

voyages, culminating in his own, which have added to British maritime glory.

A patriotic obligation had long inspired plain men to chronicle the deeds of English sailors. Pride in England's promise of imperial expansion was not alone the prerogative of aristocratic adventurers in the effervescent court of Elizabeth. The imaginations of commoners, stolid though they were, had been stirred by news of English prowess on the seas. Particularly in the West Country, in the port towns of Devon and Cornwall, tales of the adventures of English sailors were recited in every village tavern. Many an obscure patriot turned out a ballad or pamphlet in praise of English bravery. Among these plain folk was Henry Robarts, a native Devonshireman and a sailor, who later became a London citizen.[12] He was the author of pamphlets that illustrate the working of the new imperial spirit in the common people.

The occasion for Robarts's first effort was Drake's expedition to the West Indies in 1585, an adventure which resulted in the spoil of much Spanish commerce. Shortly after Drake's departure there appeared in London a little pamphlet entitled *A most friendly farewell* "by Henry Robarts of London Citizin."[13] A simple citizen, eager to do the great seaman service because the more erudite had failed to praise his exploits properly, is the description of himself which Robarts gives in a dedicatory statement to Drake. He does not know the names of Drake's colleagues, but his desire to honor them is keen:

. . . seeing none of the learned sort haue vndertaken to write according to custome, I being the vnworthyest, yet the most willing, was lothe good Knight that you should depart our Englishe coastes with-

---

[12] Louis B. Wright, "Henry Robarts: Patriotic Propagandist and Novelist," *Studies in Philology*, XXIX (1932), 176-99.

[13] *A most friendly farewell, Giuen by a welwiller to the right worshipful Sir Frauncis Drake Knight, Generall of her Maiesties Nauy, which be appointed for this his honorable voiage, and the rest of the fleete bound to the Southward, and to all the Gentlemen his followers, and captaines in this exploite, who set sale from Wolwich the xv. day of Iuly, 1585. Wherin Is Briefely Touched his perils passed in his last daungerous voiage, with an Incouragement to all his saylers and souldiers, to be forward in this honourable exploite. Published by Henry Robarts of London Citizen* [1585]. A facsimile reprint has been published by E. M. Blackie (Cambridge, Mass., 1924). In a brief introductory note, Mr. Blackie says of Robarts: "Little is known of him."

out some remembery to be published in prayse both to your worshippe,
and the rest of your Gentlemen followers in this your noble exploit,
who although by name I doe not knowe them as I woulde, whereby
I might giue them their honour due vnto them yet euer as long as my
tongue can speake, or my simple hand holde penne to wryte, I will
euer renowne your worship, and them whose seruice for Country hath
bene such as neuer English gentleman or other yet atchieued but you :
therefore they that haue not giuen you that honor worthie your desartes, haue sought to robbe you of your worthines, a base thing in
schollers and the learned who seeth other countrymen that hath not
vndertaken the one halfe of your troubles to be registred in the mindes
of all men for euer, by their meanes which hath by wryting giuen them
their desartes : as the conquest of the West Indyes can witnesse, wherein
many of theyr names is explained in other wryters also : then Englishmen what dishonour doe you our famous Drake, that you haue left his
name so long vnwritten of, whome fame hath bruited in all the whole
worlde for his most famous enterprises, and hath made him to be admired among his mortall foes for his valour, O noble English heart,
neuer yet daunted, whome the report of any euill newes howe vehement
soeuer they be, can let from thy determinate voyage . . . [Sig. A 2v.]

While lesser persons are being praised by poets, Drake, an unselfish hero, whose deeds are inspired only by love of his country, is
left unsung, Robarts reiterates. Furthermore, he exhorts other
writers to chronicle such heroic achievements, for some among
the ignorant misinterpret the motives of the adventurers. To the
shame of England, authors have neglected the praise of even the
noble Sir Humphrey Gilbert, Robarts complains, but now he proposes to stir them to trumpet abroad the deeds of those who labor
for the nation's good. A little of county pride, he confesses, inspires
his interest in Drake :

. . . the rather haue I vndertaken this because I neuer sawe any to
bid you farewell from Englande, and partly for countries cause being
borne in Deuonshire where your worship was, these causes good Syr
considered, first that by my simple writing it may encourage others to
write that can doe farre better, and then the zeale I beare to my countrey, and to all such as venture for the common weale, . . .
[Sigs. A 4v-B 1.]

For some curious reason, indeed, Drake's voyages did not receive
the literary acclaim which their daring and significance war-

ranted. It is to the credit of Robarts that he realized their value to English prestige.

Robarts practised the doctrine of patriotic propaganda which he preached to other writers. Now lost is *Robertes his Welcome of Good Will to Capt. Candishe*,[14] but other works show the author's continued desire to glorify British seamanship. A description of the valor of English sailors is found in a news-letter, *Our Ladys Retorne to England* (1592).[15] Badly printed, as if it had been set up from a hurriedly scribbled text, it describes the capture by William Grafton of two merchantmen, "loden with fine white Sugars, and dyuers Negros,"[16] which he had brought into the port of Clovelly, where Robarts himself had met him. Like his earlier farewell to Drake, this letter is inspired by pride in the achievement of a fellow citizen for the common good. Robarts remembers that his friend to whom he is writing always wants to hear of

those that for there countries good deserue honorably to be spokē of as your selfe in younger yeares haue many waies ieperted your bodie, in your countries seruice whose scars yet remaine as badges of your forewardnes, . . . [Sig. *2.]

Though the capture of the vessels was a high-handed piece of freebooting, Robarts finds in the deed the providence of God working for the glory of English seamanship, and he recommends to London citizens, in a poem prefatory to the published letter, the noble example of this God-fearing hero. The verses boast that the brave deeds of English citizens, especially Londoners, are known afar, even to the center of the sun.

The next work of Robarts in praise of buccaneers is related to his own career, as are others of his succeeding productions. In this forgotten sailor-author, the spirit of the seagoing commoner,

---

[14] Licensed to John Wolfe on December 3, 1588. See *Dictionary of National Biography*, *sub* Robarts.

[15] *Our Ladys Retorne to England, accompanied with saint Frances and the good Iesus of Viana in Portugall, who comming from Brasell, ariued at Clauelly in Deuonshire, the third of Iune 1592. A wonder of the Lorde most admirable, to note how many Spanish saintes are enforced to come one pilgrimage for Englande. With the most happie fortune of that braue gentill-man William Graftone Cittizen of London, Captaine and oner of our Ladies. Writen by H. R.* (1592). This small quarto, printed by A. I. for William Barley, is preserved in the Huntington Library. It consists of a title-page and three leaves—five pages of printed matter. Clearly, it was a bona fide letter, published for its patriotic value.

[16] Sig. *3v.

of the Elizabethan citizen-adventurer, speaks at first hand. The written accounts of many captains are preserved, but none of these seagoing authors made so strenuous an effort to be man of letters and laureate of sailors as did Robarts. He wrote as eye-witness and participant when he published in 1594 his *Newes from the Levane Seas*.[17] In a none-too-clear narrative, Robarts describes a buccaneering expedition of several ships, headed by Edward Glenham, into the Mediterranean, where they hoped to waylay a coin ship of the Pope's. Robarts maintains the bravery and right-dealing of Glenham, who had become the object of criticism at home for his conduct of the affair. Scornful is the author of cowardly stay-at-homes who criticize their betters and "neglect such service as might therby redound to their owne honor and their countries good, whereof England harboureth too many."[18]

The next year saw a continuation of the praise of English adventurers. Again using Drake as a theme, Robarts blows a blast for British imperialism and foreign expansion with *The Trumpet O[f] Fame* (1595).[19] Once more the author puts into practice his plea for the glorification of the heroes of the sea and of commercial adventure. The ill-fated expedition to the West Indies, which was to meet such disaster in the year following the publication of this verse pamphlet, is the object of Robarts's praise. The sailor-poet

---

[17] *Newes from the Levane Seas. Describing the many perilous events of the most woorthy deserving Gentleman, Edward Glenham, Esquire. His hardy attempts in honorable fights, in great perill. With a relation of his troubles, and indirect dealings of the King of Argere in Barbarie. Also the cause of his imprisonment, and hys challenge of combat against a stranger, mayntaining his Countries honour. Written by H. R.* (1594). Reprinted by J. P. Collier (ed.), *Illustrations of Old English Literature*, 3 vols. (London, 1866), Vol. I. In his introductory note Collier observes that Glenham commanded three ships in this expedition. Perhaps Robarts was master of one of them. Collier mentions a similar expedition in 1591, an account of which was printed by A. J. for William Barley as *The honourable actions of E. Glenham, Esquire against the Spaniards* (1591). The work was anonymous, but it had two seven-line stanzas in commendation of the hero, signed "H. R."

[18] Collier, *op. cit.*, I, 1.

[19] *The Trumpet O[f] Fame: Or Sir Fraunces Drakes and Sir Iohn Hawkins F[are]well: with an encouragement to all Saile[rs] and Souldiers that are minded to go in this woorthie enterprise. With the names of many Ships, and what they h[aue] done against our foes. Written by H. R.* (1595). The unique copy of the quarto, printed by Thomas Creede for William Barley, is preserved in the Huntington Library. The margins have been clipped so that some letters and words have to be supplied. The text begins with sig. A 3, without any dedication or preface. In 1818 Thomas Park published the poem from the Lee Priory Press and emended the mutilated words.

is lavish in commendation of the seamen who have already brought great wealth to England; he applauds the spirit of the merchant, who, like Alderman Wats, fosters so noble an enterprise; he even mentions each individual ship and as many officers as he can list. Wealth and honor are the rewards of daring endeavors for the good of the commonwealth, the author stresses. Drake is compared to Moses, who led his men to a promised land; like Moses also is he in his trust in God. And Robarts interrupts his encomium to instruct the sailors in godly obedience. When the poet has finished with Drake, he paints Hawkins in the same glowing colors. It is Hawkins who has carried the fame of England to India. The Spanish and French, "far and neare," he has vanquished. With such leaders, success is assured.

At length, after paying a tribute to merchants who venture in such enterprises for "London's honor," Robarts closes with a suggestion of the gold and jewels to be reaped from the enterprise —a note which strongly suggests that his work is part of the publicity designed to arouse popular support for the expedition:

> Tis Englands honor that you haue in hand,
> Then thinke thereof, if you do loue our land.
> The gaine is yours, if millions home you bring,
> Then courage take, to gaine so sweete a thing.
> The time calls on, which causeth me to end,
> Wherefore to God, I do you all commend,
> For whom all subiects that do loue our Queene,
> Shall truly pray, to send you safe againe.
> And for my part, I wish you alwaies health,
> With quick returne, and so much store of wealth,
> That Phillips Regions may not be more stord,
> With Pearle, Iewels, and the purest gold.   [Sig. B 3.]

In this appeal to his countrymen, Robarts's motives undoubtedly are mixed, but he was neither the first nor the last thus to mingle God and patriotism and the greed for gold.

In the same year as the poem to Drake and Hawkins, Robarts published another work, *Lancaster his Allarums*,[20] emphasizing the

---

[20] *Lancaster his Allarums, honorable Assaultes, supprising of the Block-houses and Storehouses belonging to Fernand Bucke in Brasill. With his braue attempt in Landing in the mouth of the Ordinaunce there, which were Cannons Culuering, Cannon periall and Sacres of brasse,*

great wealth brought back from the New World by Captain James Lancaster. Perhaps the treatise was also part of the publicity campaign for the Drake and Hawkins expedition. The dedication to Lancaster heaps scorn upon those who envy such men. Robarts apologizes for speaking ill, even of these carpers, but his own profession is the sea, and he must defend its heroes.[21] Furthermore, he makes Lancaster a theme for a prefatory poem, bubbling with class pride, calling on the cavaliers, who have heretofore condemned Londoners, to see what worthy minds these merchants bear. For Lancaster is a tradesman turned adventurer. In him apprentices may find a model:

> If *London-merchants* dare to doe,
>   such actions as hee did:
> Then why should not their acts be tolde,
>   why should his fame be hid.
> Amongst the cheifest *Cauilers*,
>   giue *Lancaster* his place:
> Who by his worthy pollicie,
>   the foe-man hath disgrast.
> He is the man whose courage great,
>   was neuer seene to quaile:
> He is the man that formost was,
>   where wee did foes assaile
> Braue *Lancaster* for woorthines,
>   in this attempt of thine:
> The foeman dooth commend thy worth,
>   whose vertues so dooth shine:
> Then *Caualiers* of highest prize,
>   and Citizens of fame:

---

with other sundry his most resolute and braue attempts in that Country. From whence he laded of their spoyles and rich commodities he there found fifteene good Ships, which was Sinemon, Sugar, Pepper, Cloues, Mace, Calloco-cloth and Brassel-wood with other commodities. With the names of such men of worth hauing charge within this most honorable attempt lost their liues. Published for their eternall Honor. by a Welwiller [1595]. *Quarto, printed by A. I. for W. Barley; in the Huntington Library.*

[21] ". . . of which I humblye craue pardon who intends well vnto all men but especiall bend my deuotion, vnto such skilfull aduentures at sea, for that my profession is such, who am, and euer wilbe readie in all true zealous affection and doe you all the best seruice I can or may, when and where it shall stand with your good pleasure for to commaund mee."

Extoll his prayse which hath deserude,
 and brauely gaind the same :
And gallant Brutes which yet are bound,
 your masters to obay :
When time shall make you free againe,
 think then what I now say.
Learne by this man of woorth to guyde,
 your selues in euerie place :
By land or sea to gaine renowne,
 and enemies to disgrace,
your Countrey then your honor shall,
 for Prince doe seruice good :
and men that see your woorthynes,
 for you will spend their blood.
He is a lamp to light you one,
 Fames pallace to attaine :
wherby your names shall euer liue,
 if *Fame* you seeke to gaine,
Learne by his woorth that valiantly,
 hath ventured life and limme :
To shame of dastard Coward base,
 in place where he hath beene.
His deeds at large doe but peruse,
 and then you all shall say :
an act of more resolue hath not,
 beene complisht at the sea. [Sigs. A 4-A 4ᵛ.]

So patriotic does the consideration of Lancaster's deeds make the eulogist, that he begins his treatise with a pious wish that Englishmen might honor their national heroes as Rome did. "Why," he asks, "should not our thrise famous Cittie of *London* the only wounder of the earth for beautie, gouernment and welth, holde their honor in like account."[22] Clearly, citizens were feeling that their achievements were not sufficiently recognized, and Robarts sets out to rectify the negligence of Fame. He himself again cites the example of Rome, which honored all brave men, regardless of lowly birth, and wishes that England would thus stimulate plain men to deeds of valor :

The Romaines exalted all men of woorth for their vertues not re-

---

[22] Sig. B 1.

garding their parentage, makeing the ignoble and base borne tribunes Senatours and Vice-rois in their territories, honoring them with all titles of nobilitie and honour, and after their victoryes, caused them in tryūphs, to ride throughout their Citties erecting Trophies, in memorie of their actions. Thorough which, they encouraged the noble minded, and moued the most basest groome to aduenture.

Yf such were the manners and conditions, of our minded cuntrymen how florishing an estate might we boast of : But we, forgetting vertue, esteeme wealth, not vallor, (not men) before money, but money farre before men :

Yet are there some of worshippe, Patrones of this famous and most renowned Cittie, who esteeming their Cuntries benifit, haue by their great charge, enriched the Common-welth : And of ther carfull loue to their cuntry, enlarged the Nauy of our Land, by their most bountifull exspences, so that thorough a number of worshipfull Cittizens, our eneimies are weakned, our streingth increased, our eneimies empouerished, and our Land enriched, all for our cuntryes honor, where at they ayme as is dayly seene by the great aduentures they make.

[Sig. B iv.]

He omits the mention of many citizen-heroes, "not doubting but in time, some of good learning, for honor of our Land, will register their names to eternall honor," and hastens to chronicle the deeds of Lancaster, "being a Cittizen of this famous Cittie of London, though by birth of gentillity."[23] A long and circumstantial account of the voyage to the Canaries and thence to "Brassill" follows. The narrative, once under way, is related in the first person as by

---

[23] Not quite all the citizens are omitted from Robarts's chronicle, for, as in *The Trumpet of Fame* to Drake, he mentions Alderman Wats and a few supporters of the expedition, in addition to some of the other officers. E.g. : "In September now last past 1594 these worshipfull graue Citizens, and fathers of London, and most faithfull subiectes to our Prince, and Country, the woorshipfull Iohn Wats, Alderman, master Paul Baning Alderman, Master Sute Salter, master Boreman and others of woorship in this most famous Cittie, desirous for their Cuntries honor and benefit to employ their substance, victuled and equiped for all needfull things to so hard and daungerous a voyage appertaining three good Ships, videl, the Consent of the burthen of 240. tunnes or there about the Salomon of 170. tunnes or there about, and the Virgine 60. tunnes or there abouts, appointing for Commaunders in this voyage Iames Lancaster of London Gentleman, Generall of the Fleete, Mun Barker of London Viz-Admirall, and Iohn Awdley of Popler neer London their Reare-Admirall, hauing in their company Iohn Wats the Sonne of Alderman Wats a proper and forward Gentleman full of resolution. And Symon Boreman sonne of M. Boreman Owner of the Salomon, a toward and likely youth."—Sig. B iv.

an eyewitness, giving such details that it seems obvious that the author took part in the expedition. The book closes, after much emphasis on the captured cargoes and ships—and on the "honor" thereby accruing—with a "Commemoration" of Captain Barker and Captain Cotton, who lost their lives. Like the greater propagandist, Richard Hakluyt, Robarts shows himself in this and the preceding pamphlet consciously trying to arouse public opinion to the support of maritime enterprise. He makes his appeal on a basis of national honor, but in true bourgeois fashion he identifies national honor with the acquisition of wealth and foreign possessions.

Robarts's last work is much like his first, an example of propaganda for English shipping, entitled *A True Relation of a most worthy and notable Fight* [1616?].[24] The pamphlet sets out to present stirring examples of English patriotism, to hearten merchants whose goods are entrusted to such brave spirits—"A patterne worth recording for others to follow, a comfort to Owners, and Marchantes, that commit their Shippes and goods to such mens gouernment, and a ioy to all those that heare their deserued comendations ; . . ."[25] Once more, as in the earlier treatises, the author stresses the necessity of glorifying seamen and merchant-heroes as examples to others of their kind. By comparison with the practice of the Greeks and Romans, he finds the English negligent in recording the deeds of simple men. In classic times, things were different, and the hero, however lowly, was rewarded.

. . . These were the times of true loue and honour. This made the Coward hardy, and the faint-hearted Swaine, to aduance themselues, in hope to gaine, vnto their posterities euerlasting fame. Oh that our Nation would immitate these true tipes of honour, to norish such as aduenture their liues and estates, for welfare of their Country : then there is no doubt, but in time of troubles, when valour should be showne, wee should finde many worthy persons, vnder simple habites,

---

[24] *A True Relation of a most worthy and notable Fight, performed the nineteenth day of Iune now last past, by two small Shippes of the Citie of London: the Vineyard of a hundred and twentie Tunnes; and the Vnicorne of a hundred and fourtie Tunnes, against Six great Gallies of Tunes, hauing in them a thousand and eight hundred men, of the Ile of Way-yorcke in the Straights: Our Shippes hauing in all, Mariners, Merchants, and Passengers, fifty sixe men.* Written by H. R. [1616?]. Quarto, printed for I. White to be sold by T. Langley ; preserved in the Huntington Library.

[25] Dedication to "my esteemed good Friend Mr. Gylbert Robartes."

that would purchase to their country honor, & fame to themselues. But our Countries charity is too cold, to giue Virtue her due in such people, that more it is to be pittyed, that such men as merit either by valour, or other industorous meanes, should not be fostered and well rewarded. But such is the hardnesse of heart in most, now a dayes, that Let a man aduenture their liues and libertie, in neuer so hardie an action for saueguard both of Shippe and good, when they looke for chearfull countenance at their returne, and some reward for their paines, they hardly get either good word, or good deed, (nay scarcely) their wages which God knoweth was neuer so hardly gotten, but with some Braules, and discontent : these doings, is often the cause of much losse to owners and Marchants, where if they nourished the true Labouring hyerling with some small reward, (yea) but sometimes with a good word, it would giue encouragement to men, rather to lose their liues, then part with that is committed to their charge, in any sleight manner. Iudg you that read and know what you read, how many Ships and men of our Nation, hath been taken by these Pyrats, . . .

[Sig. A 3ᵛ.]

Here is set forth the need to build up an *esprit de corps* among the merchant-carriers in the interest of business, if for no other reason, by recognizing the valor of British sailors. The depredations of pirates in the Mediterranean were causing serious inconvenience to English shipping at the moment, and Robarts seized the opportunity of a victory to publish a treatise of praise and encouragement. Perhaps in the employ of naval or commercial shipping interests at the time, he is a deliberate propagandist for public recognition of the British adventurer.

Henry Robarts is significant as a citizen-writer, a seaman himself, who sought to arouse his class to a consciousness of the commoner's destiny in British imperialism. As such he deserves the space accorded him here. He was overshadowed, however, in his efforts to promote a popular interest in maritime expansion, by a propagandist far greater than the plain seaman from Devonshire. Richard Hakluyt, preacher, had a single purpose, and that purpose was the awakening of England to the opportunity of greatness that lay across the seas. The son of a London merchant,[26]

---

[26] For the facts of Hakluyt's life and his relation to the new geography, see the excellent account by G. B. Parks, *Richard Hakluyt and the English Voyages* (New York, 1928).

Hakluyt became an active publicist for the trading companies, notably the East India Company, and with his elder lawyer-cousin, who bore the same name and was adviser to the adventuring merchants, he labored tirelessly for the development of commerce. For the preacher, expansion became a religion. He found his texts in geography and became the evangel of trade and colonization.

Hakluyt worked with the merchants and pilots of his time to increase professional acquaintance with geographical science. He carried on what had been started earlier by practical men. As Hakluyt surveyed the field, he saw that merchants had already been busy in the endeavor to increase their knowledge of geography. Popularization of geography had been slowly going on since the time when John Rastell, printer and explorer, early in the reign of Henry VIII staged *The Nature of the Four Elements* to teach a lesson in cosmography and perhaps to instruct the very merchants who financed his own undertakings. Robert Thorne, a Bristol merchant resident in Seville, in 1527 gathered up what travel and geographical data he could find and compiled a manuscript known as *The Book of Robert Thorne*, which has been described as the earliest English book on the New World;[27] Hakluyt printed it for the first time in his *Divers Voyages* (1582).

Merchants retained the services of learned men to advise them in scientific matters and apparently fostered the publication of technical works. Robert Record, the mathematician and cosmographer, published *The Castle of Knowledge* (1556), in "explication of the sphere," to further the search for a short route to Cathay; Frobisher carried the book as a part of his ship's library.[28] John Dee, strange combination of scientist and charlatan, who as early as 1551 was advising the Cathay merchants, succeeded Record as technical expert.[29] In 1577 he published a part of what promised to be a summation of all he had learned about navigation, *General and rare Memorials pertayning to the Perfect Arte of Navigation*. William Bourne, a gunner, prepared one of the most popular of all treatises on navigation, *A Regiment for the Sea . . . for all Seafaring men and Trauellers* [1574], a work which was repub-

---

[27] *Ibid.*, pp. 12-13.
[28] Taylor, *op. cit.*, p. 24.   [29] *Ibid.*, p. 89.

lished many times. Bourne was avowedly a popularizer. A little later he brought out *A booke called the Treasure for traueilers . . . eyther by Sea or by Lande* (1578), which was the source of the instructions given by William Borough to voyagers of the Muscovy Company in search of the Northwest Passage.[30] The Flemish geographer, Ortelius of Antwerp, advised merchants in the Flanders trade, and it was to him that Richard Hakluyt, the elder, appealed for help in the preparation of a map of a size convenient to be hung in merchants' houses. Hakluyt was collaborating with John Ashley, a London tradesman, in this project.[31]

While English geography was in its infancy, traders had depended on foreign maps, charts, and books. In the second half of the sixteenth century they set about translating and adapting into English such travel narratives and geographies as would benefit them. Richard Eden, who collected materials for a history of the Muscovy Company, translated *A treatyse of the Newe India* (1553) from Sebastian Muenster's *Cosmographia universalis*, and, two years later, *The Decades of the newe worlde* (1555) from Peter Martyr of Anghiera.[32] The latter work omitted some of the original and added facts of Eden's own collection. Upon Eden's *Decades* Richard Willis based *The History of Trauayle in the West and East Indies* (1577), which was prepared as publicity for Frobisher's attempt to find the Northwest Passage.[33] John Frampton, a merchant who had been long in Spain, published a series of translations from the Spanish, *A briefe Description of the portes . . . of the Weast India* (1578), *The most noble and famous trauels of Marcus Paulus* (1579), *A Discourse of Tartaria, Scithia, . . .* (1580), and other works of interest to English explorers. A desire "to animate and encourage the English Marchants" by describing "the infinite treasures . . . which both the Spaniardes, the Portugales, and the Venetians haue seuerally gained by suche nauigations and trauailes"[34] was expressed by John Florio in his translation of Cartier's account of his voyages, which he entitled *A Shorte And*

---

[30] *Ibid.*, p. 160.

[31] Parks, *op. cit.*, p. 55.

[32] *Ibid.*, pp. 23, 270. Parks, pp. 269-77, gives a chronological list of English books on geography and travel to 1600.

[33] *Ibid.*, p. 46.

[34] Dedication to Edward Bray, High Sheriff of Oxford.

*briefe narration of the two Nauigations and Discoueries to the Northweast
partes called Newe Fraunce* (1580). Florio's preface, addressed to
"all Gentlemen, Merchants, and Pilots," is a plea for English
trade and colonization in the New World. Hakluyt, it seems,
prompted Florio to make the translation, which was taken from
Ramusio's Italian version.[35] Florio urges the translation of Ramusio's entire compilation. Such a collection rendered into English would serve the public interest, and by it, "our Sea-men of
England, and others, studious of Geographie, shoulde know many
worthy secrets, whiche hitherto haue beene concealed." The
preface concludes with a pious statement that the Almighty has
stirred men to "seeke Gods glory, the aduancement of their
Countrey, and the happy successe"; it sounds more like the Reverend Richard Hakluyt than the self-styled "Resolute" John
Florio. Hakluyt now became the leading spirit in the promotion
of geographical knowledge. He had received his own stimulation
from his lawyer-cousin and was probably assisted by him in the
collection of narratives. Hakluyt's latest biographer calls him "a
veritable organizer of geographical publishing."[36] It was owing
to his persuasion that Marc-Antonio Pigafetta published the
Itinerario (1585), which described the Italian's journey overland
from Vienna to Constantinople. Hakluyt apparently encouraged
his brother minister, the Reverend Philip Jones of Cirencester, to
translate from Albertus Meierus *Certaine briefe, and speciall Instructions for Gentlemen, merchants, students, souldiers, marriners, &c. Employed in seruices abrode, or anie way occasioned to conuerse in the kingdomes, and gouernementes of forren Princes* (1589).[37] This is precisely
the book that Hakluyt himself might have designed for the
instruction of travelers abroad, for it was not a guidebook but a
syllabus of points to be observed. Its purpose was so to train
observers that, in the country visited, they might study intelli-
gently every characteristic which would be of profit or interest
to their own people.[38] Geographical data were placed first in

---

[35] Parks, *op. cit.*, pp. 64, 119.

[36] *Ibid.*, p. 119.   [37] *Ibid.*, p. 120.

[38] Prefatory to the text is a statement of the twelve divisions of the syllabus, which
gives some idea of its scope:

"1. Cosmographie, or, the description of the worlde.

the list, but minute points about navigation, husbandry, politics, religion, literature, and learning were included. With this syllabus twenty-one pages in length, the traveler was taught what to look for and record. Not only was Hakluyt an organizer of geographical publications; he was a teacher of scientific observation, and the handbook which his friend, Philip Jones, translated was an instrument in that cause. We may be sure that Hakluyt pressed a copy on many a departing merchant, factor, and captain as he urged them to study well its suggestions and to write full reports.

For several years Hakluyt had been gathering material for his own work to promote English maritime glory. In 1582 he published his first compilation, *Divers Voyages touching the discouerie of America and the Ilands adiacent vnto the same, made first of all by our Englishmen and afterwards by the Frenchmen and Britons*, which revealed the utilitarian point of view displayed in all of Hakluyt's later work. Geographical information, maps, and narratives likely to aid future explorers made up the book. He prefaced it with two chronological lists of writers on geography and travel, and he included notes procured from merchants of the Muscovy Company, "not altogether vnfit for some other enterprises of discouerie, hereafter to bee taken in hande."[39] To stir up interest in trade with and colonization of the New World was the purpose of a tabular list giving "The Names Of Certaine Commodities Growing in part of America, not presently inhabited by any

---

2. Astronomie, or, the art of skill, in the course of the starres and planets.
3. Geographie, or, the drawing and proportioning of the earth.
4. Chorographie, or, the demonstration of Cities and Regions.
5. Topographie, or, the portraiture of particular places.
6. Husbandrie.
7. Nauigation.
8. The Politicall State.
9. Ecclesiasticall State.
10. Literature.
11. Histories.
12. Chronicles."

Each section consists of queries and suggestions in tabular form, all designed to remind the observer of things to look for, which he might otherwise neglect.

[39] John Winter Jones (ed.), *Divers Voyages Touching the Discovery of America and the Islands Adjacent*, Hakluyt Society (London, 1850), p. 116.

Christians."[40] Hakluyt's long dedication to Sir Philip Sidney urged colonization as a means of relieving the overpopulation of England and of turning idlers into profitable colonial citizens. It also expressed hope that a lectureship in navigation, which Drake had already promised to aid, would soon be established in London or some convenient place nearby.

The *Divers Voyages* was merely a prelude to what Hakluyt later brought together in a great folio volume as *The Principall Naviga-tions* (1589), a work which he expanded between 1598 and 1600 into three folio volumes.[41] In a dedication of the first edition to Sir Francis Walsingham, Hakluyt describes the acquisition of his own knowledge of geography. At Christ Church, Oxford,

I fell to my intended course, and by degrees read over whatsoever printed or written discoveries and voyages I found extant either in the Greeke, Latine, Italian, Spanish, Portugall, French, or English languages, and in my publike lectures was the first, that produced and shewed both the olde imperfectly composed, and the new lately reformed Mappes, Globes, Spheares, and other instruments of this Art for demonstration in the common schooles, to the singular pleasure, and generall contentment of my auditory. In continuance of time, and by reason principally of my insight in this study, I grew familiarly acquainted with the chiefest Captaines at sea, the greatest Merchants, and the best Mariners of our nation : . . .[42]

Thus, in conference with merchants and seamen, the greatest specialist in England on geographical matters added to the knowl-edge which made possible a work that was more than a mere collection of narratives such as Ramusio had already published in Italian. Hakluyt drew on the archives of the merchant com-panies,[43] on private letters, on formal reports, on information picked up by word of mouth, on every source at his command,

---

[40] *Ibid.*, p. 139.

[41] *The Principall Navigations, Voiages And Discoveries Of The English nation, made by Sea or ouer Land, to the most remote and farthest distant Quarters of the earth at any time within the compasse of these 1500. yeeres: Deuided into three seuerall parts, according to the positions of the Regions whereunto they were directed* (1589). The second edition was reprinted for the Hakluyt Society by James MacLehose and Sons (Glasgow, 1903).

[42] *Ibid.*, I, xviii.

[43] An excellent critique of the *Principall Navigations* is provided by Parks, *op. cit.*, pp. 124-32.

for data that would be useful in furthering English colonization and commerce. More than this, he carefully organized his material, translated passages in foreign tongues, gave statistics and calculations, and in short made the work an encyclopedia of practical utility. And he did it without destroying its interest. Narratives in Hakluyt's *Principall Navigations* are so alive with the romance of the sea that they have fascinated readers from Shakespeare to Coleridge, and even to the present day. While he was giving information to show how colonization and trade would increase the Queen's "dominions, enrich her cofers, and reduce many Pagans to the faith of Christ,"[44] Hakluyt was also stimulating a taste for the direct and matter-of-fact narrations which made up such a large part of his compilation. He marshaled in order the random tales of travelers, winnowed as best he could truth from fiction, and gave to future authors of such materials models to aid them. Furthermore, he aroused the patriotism of England for commercial development. Deliberately, he played on the interests most appealing to middle-class readers, canny business men with money to invest. He emphasized profits and glory; for the religious, he pointed out the heathen souls falling from the Antipodes directly into hell for want of Christian instruction, which English tradesmen might carry to them and return with a profit. He held up the examples of other nations and urged Englishmen not to be insular sluggards asleep over their rights. He drew up papers and memoranda, conferred with an infinite number of officials, merchants, and sailors, sought the establishment of lectures in geography and navigation for the benefit of seamen, and with every means in his power broadcast geographical information and enticing propaganda to rouse Englishmen to go forth and seize their share of the world.

Hakluyt's work is easily available to the modern reader. Its characteristics do not need further discussion here. What is worth emphasizing is Hakluyt's influence on middle-class literary interest. He wove together an epic made up largely of narratives by plain men, directed to plain men for a practical purpose. Wealthy merchants in London, Bristol, and the other port towns kept by

---

[44] Edition of 1903, I, lxvii; dedication of the second volume of the second edition (1599) to Sir Robert Cecil.

them copies of the *Principall Navigations*. It was useful as a reference and textbook; it made pleasing reading; it was not soon exhausted. The work was alluring to both the merchant and his children. To few preachers is it given to be both eloquent in a cause and entertaining.

The printing of the last volume of the expanded version of the *Principall Navigations* in 1600 must have been a relief to the compiler, who had performed an almost superhuman labor in assembling the material, but it brought him no rest from his activities. He plunged into other propaganda for colonization and was apparently engaged in the publicity campaign for the Virginia Company, which was especially active with its propaganda from 1609 to 1611, when both pulpit and press united in behalf of colonization.[45] Narratives of travelers in the New World, with their implied or expressed promises of riches, provided the most appealing forms of propaganda. Hakluyt translated an account of de Soto's expedition, as *Virginia richly valued, By the description of the maine land of Florida, her next neighbor* (1609),[46] and was responsible for Pierre Erondelle's translation from Marc Lescarbot of *Nova Francia, or the description of that part of New France which is one Continent with Virginia* (1609).[47] Both works drew attention to the riches of Virginia and stimulated the popular demand for other accounts of the vast land where citizens were being urged to make investments. Perhaps he was responsible for the publication in English of Michael Lok's complete version of Peter Martyr's *Decades*, which appeared in 1612 as *De Novo Orbe, Or The Historie Of the west Indies*, edited, and in part translated, by Lok, an influential merchant. Lok had long cherished a friendship for Hakluyt, who had himself in 1587 published the *Decades*.[48] The prefaces of many works of travel and geography mention Hakluyt as the

---

[45] Parks, *op. cit.*, pp. 219 ff., discusses this portion of Hakluyt's career as a propagandist. Many documents which throw light on the propaganda for the Virginia colonies at this time are reprinted, as Professor Parks notes, by Alexander Brown, *The Genesis of the United States*, 2 vols. (London, 1890).

[46] Parks, *op. cit.*, p. 220.

[47] *Ibid.*, p. 221.

[48] *Ibid.*, pp. 222-23. The *Decades* had long been useful as propaganda. Both Eden and Willis had found that the work served their needs. Lok used Eden's translation of the first four books.

encourager of the publications. The worthy prebend of Bristol was never averse to using his ecclesiastical connections to push the cause of discovery. For example, he induced the Reverend Abraham Hartwell to translate from Pigafetta *A Report Of The Kingdome of Congo* (1597) and was doubtless pleased when that divine ingeniously hinted that God would bless the conquerors of rude nations :

I thought good thus to make it knowen to my countreymen of *England*, to the end it might be a president for such valiant English, as do earnestly thirst and desire to atchieue the conquest of rude and barbarous Nations, that they doo not attempt those actions for commodity of Gold and Siluer, and for other transitorie or worldly respectes, but that they woulde first seeke the Kingdome of God, & the saluation of many thousand soules, which the common enemie of mankinde still detayneth in ignorance : and then all other thinges shall be put in their mouthes aboundantly, as may bee seene by the Portingalles in this narration.[49]

Business men were already convinced of the manifest destiny of Christians to push into heathen lands, and it was a help to have ecclesiastical assurance that, although God looked askance at the mere greedy search for gold, he was on the side of unselfish pioneers and would, incidentally, grant them wealth.

Hakluyt was a friend of John Davis, the navigator, and perhaps encouraged him to publish *The Worldes Hydrographical Discription* (1595) to prove the possibility of finding the Northwest Passage. Davis's work carries a propaganda that Hakluyt was eager to stress, for it presents a vision of prosperity and relief from the social ills of poverty and unemployment. When the magical passage is discovered, not merely will the merchant grow rich, but the poor artificer will also be recompensed according to his industry and the whole commonwealth will prosper :

For thereby wee shall not onely haue a copious and rich vent for al our naturall and artificiall comodities of England, in short time by safe passage, and without offence of any, but also shall by the first imployment retourne into our Countrey by spedie passage, all Indian commodities in the ripenes of their perfection, whereby her Maiesties Dominions should bee the storehouse of Europe, the nurse of the world,

---

[49] Dedication to the Archbishop of Canterbury.

and the glory of nations, in yelding all forrayne naturall benefites by
an easie rate : In communicating vnto all whatsoeuer God hath vnto
anyone asigned : And by the increase of all nations, through the might-
inesse of trade. Then should the merchant, tradesman, and poor artificer, haue imployment equall to their power and expedition, whereby what notable benefites would growe to her Maiestie, the state, and
communaltie, I refer to your perfect iudgementes.[50]

Of all these things, the public was eager to read. Hakluyt kept
himself and his friends incessantly busy to provide an adequate
supply of appropriate literature.

Partly as a result of Hakluyt's own activities, partly as a result
of the demand of the public, the last decade of the sixteenth
century saw an increasing number of works on travel and geography. They multiplied even more rapidly after the turn of the
century. Behind the interest in such works lay the increasing
pressure of business and trade. England was now thoroughly
aroused to the possibilities of foreign enterprise, and the business
world saw to it that the lay public was informed. The public itself
continued to demand more and more information about distant
lands. Up to this time, geography had been poorly taught—
when taught at all—in the schools.[51] Richard Hakluyt had boasted
that he had been the first to demonstrate the new maps and
globes in the common schools,[52] and he had lectured on geography
at Oxford. His efforts to establish lectureships in geography and
navigation in London we have already noticed. Sir Thomas Smith,
the greatest of Elizabethan promoters, had lectures given at his
own home. Sir Thomas Gresham provided for geographical instruction at Gresham College. A few classical authorities on
geography were in circulation. Thomas Twyne published a translation from Dionysius of Alexandria, *The Surueye of the World, or
Situation of the Earth, so muche as is inhabited* (1572). Arthur Golding
translated *The worke of Pomponius Mela . . . A booke right plesant
and profitable for all sortes of men: but speciallie for Gentlemen, Marchants,*

---

[50] Dedication to the Privy Council. Davis's work was reprinted by Hakluyt in the
Principall Navigations in 1600. It has been given a modern printing by A. H. Markham,
already cited in n. 8.

[51] Foster Watson, *The Beginnings of the Teaching of Modern Subjects in England* (London, 1909), pp. 89-114.

[52] *See* p. 529, *supra.*

Mariners, and Trauellers (1585), which he republished in 1590 with the addition of the "learned worke of Iulius Solinus Polyhistor"; the latter had appeared separately in 1587. Ptolemy's *Compost* had enjoyed some popularity in the first half of the sixteenth century but it was not reprinted again in English until about 1635. Thomas Blundeville published *A Briefe Description Of Vniversal Mappes And Cardes, And Of Their Vse: And Also The Vse Of Ptholemey his Tables. Necessarie for those that Delight in Reading Of Histories: and also for Traueilers by Land or Sea* (1589), a work which Blundeville recommended chiefly as the handmaiden of history; it provided explanations of difficult geographical terms. The virtues of geography studied in relation to history had long been a commonplace of educational theory,[53] but the new scientific geography as understood by Hakluyt and his hard-thinking colleagues was too often only scantily comprehended by the academicians whose books continued to look backward toward Latin and Greek classics rather than toward recent explorers. The works that excited the popular imagination were newer compilations which related to the modern world. And always the suggestions and implications of commerce were conspicuous.

In the excitement over the regions across the seas, Englishmen did not neglect the lands nearer at hand. Thomas Danett was aware that the business interests of the nation would be pleased with a work on the Low Countries; accordingly he extracted material from Guicciardini and produced as a sort of commercial geography, *The Description of the Low countreys and of the Prouinces thereof, gathered into an Epitome out of the Historie of Lodouico Guicchardini* (1593). A more popular and useful book was Robert Johnson's translation from Giovanni Botero, *The Travellers Breviat, Or An historicall description of the most famous kingdomes in the World: Relating their situations, manners, customes, ciuill gouernment, and other memorable matters* (1601). At least five later editions were published in the next quarter of a century. Such condensed descriptions of the world gained in popularity, since they also provided a little history. Archbishop George Abbot was the author of an epitome

---

[53] Watson, *op. cit.*, pp. 91, 99. As Watson points out, geography had been recommended by Erasmus and succeeding writers on education and on the training of the gentleman.

of geography and history, *A Briefe Description Of The whole worlde* (1599), of which there are nine recorded editions by 1636. The Archbishop's summary was used apparently as a textbook. The interest in the outside world had reached such a stage by this time that every intelligent person felt an obligation to have at least a smattering of geography. Both the citizen in the market place and the student found Peter Heylin's *Microcosmus, Or A Little Description Of The Great World* (1621)[54] a helpful as well as an entertaining work. It was, as he describes it, "A discourse in which the long parted Sisters History and Geographie haue shaken hands and kissed each other,"[55] and it gave its information in easily digested portions. After about 1625 more attention seems to have been given to geography in the schools, and textbooks on the subject multiplied.[56] Lest Englishmen forget their native country in the study of foreign lands, John Bill, the King's printer, published in 1626 *The abridgment of Camden's Britañia* in a size to fit the pocket.

Though epitomes and textbooks of geography gradually became more numerous, the populace had learned to look for works with more of the sauce of romance than compilations of dry facts offered. Richard Hakluyt had taught readers that scientific truths could be entertaining. Henceforth, travel narratives, which gave what was believed to be accurate information, combined with descriptions of strange peoples and thrilling adventures, fascinated the public. Samuel Purchas, brother clergyman and successor to Hakluyt, had a journalist's realization of what laymen wanted, and in his own publications he attempted to carry on the work of his master without burdening his volumes with tiresome details. Purchas feared tediousness as an evil genius and continually expresses the hope of avoiding it. For throwing away log-book data, statistics, and calculations, he has been condemned by modern

---

[54] *See* Chap. V, *supra*, pp. 154-55. Watson, *op. cit.*, pp. 125-28, describes the work as a textbook, but undoubtedly it enjoyed a general popularity.

[55] Preface.

[56] Watson, *op. cit.*, pp. 103 ff. Watson gives a brief description of Nathanael Carpenter's *Geography Delineated Forth In Two Bookes. Containing The Sphaericall And Topicall Parts Thereof* (1625), a textbook which illustrates the growing academical interest in geography.

writers on seventeenth-century geography,[57] but Purchas was less a scientist and more a journalist than Hakluyt. He knew that the reading public clamored for accounts of foreign countries and that only navigators and company officials wanted statistical data. Where Hakluyt had been eager to supply statistics, Purchas gave picturesque descriptions and theological musings, which interested most of his readers far more than figures.

Hakluyt and Purchas were both preachers—with a difference. Hakluyt had applied the zeal of a religionist to his propaganda for expansion. Theological concerns did not trouble him. He was a modern, interested in the temporal progress of man and the commonwealth. Purchas was still theologically medieval, as were most of his contemporaries, and he found in geography a subject for sermonizing. The somber shadows of religious discussion and solemn speculations on man's damnation, which grew darker in King James's reign, are evident in Purchas's point of view. Although the average layman of Jacobean England found the fine-spun logic of professional theologians too difficult for his understanding, he was profoundly interested in all things religious, and his curiosity about the religious beliefs of the inhabitants of distant countries was unbounded. Purchas, a man of the people himself, showed an accurate knowledge of what would interest the public when he combined geography and religion in his first large work, *Purchas his Pilgrimage, Or Relations Of The World And The Religions Observed In All Ages And places discouered* (1613).[58] In a folio volume

---

[57] Parks, *op. cit.*, pp. 224 ff. Professor Parks is a trifle hard on Purchas, picturing him as an unctuous Pecksniff, who attempted to carry on Hakluyt's work without much intelligence. Although Purchas lacked Hakluyt's scientific knowledge, he was a man of his age, who seems to have tried to include what would most interest and profit the general reader. Mr. Parks concedes that "the *Pilgrims* is not journalism. Forty per cent of the work is, as I have said, Hakluyt's." He gives Purchas credit for unearthing important items, but adds, "The plan was Hakluyt's, and Purchas is to be praised for carrying it out almost in spite of himself."—Pp. 228-29.

[58] *Purchas his Pilgrimage, Or Relations Of The World And The Religions Observed In All Ages And places discouered, from the Creation vnto this Present. In foure Partes. This First Containeth A Theologicall And Geographicall Historie of Asia, Africa, and America, with the Ilands Adiacent. Declaring the Ancient Religions before the Floud, the Heathenish, Iewish, and Saracenicall in all Ages since, in those parts professed, with their seuerall Opinions, Idols, Oracles, Temples, Priestes, Fasts, Feasts, Sacrifices, and Rites Religious: Their beginnings, Proceedings, Alterations, Sects, Orders and Successions. With briefe Descriptions of the Coun-*

containing 752 pages Purchas presents a theological geography discussing everything from the site of Eden in Mesopotamia, visited by "M. Cartwright, an eye-witness,"[59] to a description of Peru and the practices there of the Spanish Inquisition.[60] The compiler claims to have ransacked the world's literature for his material. After mentioning particularly that "*Ramusius* and M. *Hakluyt*, in their Bookes of Voyages, haue beene two Libraries vnto me of many Nauigations and Discoueries," Purchas gives a six-page list of authors and boasts that he might have added "some hundreds more."[61] Despite its great size, the work was immediately popular. New editions were published in 1614, 1617, and 1627. The last edition was expanded to 967 pages.[62] From king to cottager, the book was read for its information about the manners and customs of the heathen world. The vast encyclopedia of curious lore with its garnish of theological observation and conjecture was a delight to King James, who reveled in its very pedantry. Purchas was emboldened to dedicate the fourth edition to King Charles and, in an additional dedication to the Archbishop of Canterbury, to mention

the testimonie of our late deceased Soueraine of happie memorie (the King of literature also) King Iames, who shewing me it by him in his Bed-chamber, said, that he had read it seuen times : Whereto if I should adde his iudicious questions of diuers particulars therein, his ready and milde satisfaction, his ample commendation, copious discourse, pierc-

---

tries, Nations, States, Discoueries, Priuate and Publike Customes, and the most Remarkable Rarities of Nature, or Humane Industrie, in the same (1613).

[59] Edition of 1613, p. 15.

[60] *Ibid.*, p. 751.

[61] Sig. A 4. In the dedicatory letter to the Archbishop of Canterbury in the edition of 1627, Purchas claims to have used "aboue thirteene hundred Authors of one or other kind, in I know not how many hundreths of their Epistles, Treatises and Relations."

[62] It also contained three additional treatises which, Purchas observes in the dedicatory letter to the Archbishop, would have "found fitter place with my Pilgrimes, had they then comme to my hands : but their rarities merit a place, yea a welcome, in what place soeuer." The first two treatises are by William Methold, *Two Relations, One Of The Northerneasterne Parts, Extracted Out Of Sir Ierome Horsey Knight . . . The Other, Of The Southeasterne Parts, viz. Golchonda, and other adiacent Kingdomes within the Bay of Bengala.* The third treatise is *The Saracenical Historie*, translated and abridged by Purchas.

ing wit, admirable memory, gentle affabilitie, I might seeme to some emulous carpers to magnifie my self, . . .[63]

King James and Purchas, putting their heads together over the religions of the Indians, symbolize the change that had taken place since Elizabeth, a greater sovereign, had shown a more practical interest in the New World. But the age of James, taking its cue from the royal pedant, drank deep of theological infusions. Purchas gave the public a work full of religion, travel, and romantic strangeness, a combination which made the popularity of his production inevitable. Even yet the book has its fascination. It was over the *Pilgrimage* that Coleridge fell asleep to dream the exotic vision of "Kubla Khan,"[64] and delvers into forgotten lore still find its pages alluring. Pious tradesmen of Jacobean London found in it ample reasons why they ought to send colonists to people the new lands and convert the heathen.

Purchas's second labor also showed his knowledge of popular interest, for in it he turned to the eternal problem of man's relation to the universe. Although only indirectly related to travel literature, *Purchas his Pilgrim. Microcosmus, Or The Historie Of Man* (1619) reflects man's concern, in an expanding world, over his relation to the scheme of things. Man and cosmography were important subjects in the seventeenth century, and Purchas imagined himself a philosopher-scientist as he set forth the relation of the Microcosm to the Macrocosm. The public applauded and ministers preached from his work.

The crowning glory of the cleric who became the King's chaplain was *Purchas His Pilgrimes* (1625).[65] Building on the edifice left by Hakluyt, and using materials obtained from him, Purchas produced four folio volumes containing the five sections that made up his compilation of travels, from the voyages of King Solomon's navy to the latest expeditions of his own day. Like Hakluyt before

---

[63] In the dedication to King Charles, Purchas describes his personal presentation of his *Pilgrimes* to the late King, who questioned him about the difference between it and the *Pilgrimage*, which the King had read seven times. "No lesse [Purchas adds] did hee promise touching the *Pilgrimes*, which he made his Nightly taske, till God called him by fatall sicknesse to a better Pilgrimage . . ."

[64] J. L. Lowes, *The Road to Xanadu* (Boston and New York, 1927), pp. 356 ff.

[65] Reprinted by James MacLehose and Sons for the Hakluyt Society. 20 vols. (Glasgow, 1905).

him, Purchas drew on the accounts written by merchants and seamen, but he unhesitatingly abbreviated and epitomized when authors lapsed into the tediousness so feared by the parson. Like Hakluyt he professed a patriotic purpose, but he was less inspired by zeal for English expansion than desire for English godliness. Without the title "Preacher," which Hakluyt proudly signed, one would hardly suspect his profession. But the clergyman shines through all of Purchas's editorial utterances. Yet the populace liked to contemplate the wonders of God in the new discoveries, and Purchas pleased them with his application of divinity to geography. The inclusion of an enormous amount of curious lore was a point of professional theory with Purchas, who was eager to show from the study of strange countries the marvelous handiwork of God. Of things to be studied Purchas writes:

Naturall things are the more proper Obiect, namely the ordinary Workes of God in the Creatures, preseruing and disposing by Prouidence that which his Goodnesse and Power had created, and dispersed in the diuers parts of the World, as so many members of this great Bodie. Such is the History of Men in their diuersified hewes and colours, quantities and proportions; of Beasts, Fishes, Fowles, Trees, Shrubs, Herbs, Minerals, Seas, Lands, Meteors, Heauens, Starres, with their naturall affections: . . .

It is true, that as euery member of the bodie hath somewhat eminent, whereby it is seruiceable to the whole; so euery Region excelleth all others in some peculiar Raritie. . . .

My *Genius* delights rather in by-wayes then high-wayes, and hath therein by Tracts and Tractates of Trauellers made Causies and Highwayes, euery where disposing these Pilgrime-Guides, that men without feare may trauell to and ouer the most vncouth Countries of the World: and there be shewed with others Eyes, the Rarities of Nature, and of such things also as are not against Nature, but either aboue it, as Miracles, or beside the ordinarie course of it, in the extraordinary Wonders, which Gods Prouidence hath therein effected according to his good and iust pleasure. And thus much for the workes of God.

Things humane, are such as Men are, or haue, or haue done or suffered in the World. Here therefore the various Nations, Persons, Shapes, Colours, Habits, Rites, Religions, Complexions, Conditions, Politike and Oeconomike Customes, Languages, Letters, Arts, Merchandises, Wares, and other remarkeable Varieties of Men and humane Affaires are by Eye-witnesses related more amply and certainly then any Collector euer hath done, or perhaps without these helpes could doe. And thus we haue shewed the scope of the Author, and profitable vse of the Worke: which could not but be voluminous, hauing a World for the subiect, and a World of Witnesses for the Euidence: and yet (except where the Author or Worke it selfe permitte not) these vast Volumes are contracted, and Epitomised, that the nicer Reader might not be cloyed. Here also both Elephants may swimme in deepe voluminous Seas, and such as want either lust or leisure, may single out, as in a Library of Bookes, what Author or Voyage shall best fit to his profit or pleasure. . . .[66]

Purchas is as good as his word. His compilation is a vast encyclopedia of information about the lands and peoples across the seas. Though it was too expensive for every citizen to possess, it was a work that well-to-do merchants owned and used. Preachers found in it subjects for sermons, and it became a work of popular reference.

With Purchas, the compilation of travels into huge anthologies reached its culmination. The first half of the seventeenth century saw in England no further undertakings of similar scope. But the public interest in travel literature was even greater than before.[67] Professional travelers and explorers continued to publish their adventures in books, great and small, which enjoyed the widest circulation.

The popularity of the writings of Captain John Smith is an illustration of the reception given travel narratives. The fortunes of the colonies in the New World were the intimate concern of substantial citizens who had invested in the undertakings. John Smith, one-time merchant's apprentice, who had fought the Turks and tried to govern the unruly colonists of Virginia, was precisely the person to write a colorful story to appeal to the London citizen. He had first come to the notice of the public with *A True Relation of such occurrences and accidents of noate as hath hapned in Virginia since the first planting of that Collony, which is now resident in the South part thereof, till the last returne from thence* (1608), which he

---

[66] Preface to the first volume, edition of 1625.

[67] For general discussions of travel literature in this period, see *Cambridge History of English Literature*, Vol. IV, Chaps. III, IV, and V; and *Cambridge History of American Literature*, Vol. I, Chaps. I and II.

followed in 1612 with *A Map Of Virginia. With A Description Of The Countrey, The Commodities, People, Government and Religion*. After 1615 he lived in London and devoted himself to turning out accounts of the new land.

A defense of his own record appeared in *A Description of New England* (1616), heavily laden, fore and aft, with verses in commendation of the author. In an address to the adventurers of London, Bristol, Exeter, Plymouth, Dartmouth, Barnstaple, Totness, and other towns that had furnished investors in the voyages, Smith complains that he has been unfairly blamed for failure because he did not return with riches, but he emphasizes the value of the products of the New World, from which profits can be realized when the country is properly colonized.[68] In 1624 Smith produced a folio volume giving *The Generall Historie Of Virginia, New-England, and the Summer Isles: with the names of the Adventurers, Planters, and Governours from their first beginning Anº: 1584. to this present 1624*. Resplendent with engravings showing the rescue of the author by Pocahontas, personal encounters of the doughty captain with the Indians, war dances, and numerous scenes of Indian life, the volume was destined to excite an enormous interest. Furthermore, long lists of the names of the subscribers to the colonial ventures created a personal appeal to London tradesmen, who could here see their names immortalized in print. Michael Sparke, the stationer for whom the book was printed, seems to have anticipated a heavy demand and had a large

---

[68] The hope of wealth through the development of colonies and the stimulation of trade, instead of the discovery of gold, was gaining ground. Richard Whitbourne, a merchant and ship captain, in 1620 published *A Discourse And Discouery Of New-Found-Land, With many reasons to prooue how worthy and beneficiall a Plantation may there be made, after a far better manner than now it is*. The British Museum copy has attached a broadside sheet, signed by the Bishop of London, authorizing the collection of funds to advance the distribution of the treatise. A command from the King to the Archbishops of York and Canterbury to order collections for the same purpose is also printed in the preface. Whitbourne insists upon the importance of colonies as a source of trade. In 1622 he published *A Discourse Containing A Loving Invitation both Honourable, and profitable to all such as shall be Aduenturers, either in person, or purse, for the aduancement of his Maiesties most hopefull Plantation in the New-Found-Land, lately vndertaken*. Again he insists upon the trade likely to develop in the new colony. Not gold mines but trade will bring prosperity, he points out, and calls attention to the Dutch by "whose wealth and strength gotten in a few yeeres only by fishing, are good testimonies." (P. 22.) This point of view is found in much of the travel literature in the seventeenth century.

edition prepared. New issues with fresh title-pages appeared in 1625, 1626, and 1627, and another issue with the imprint of the stationer J. Dawson was brought out in 1632. Smith knew that the work would attract the attention of London tradesmen. In the Huntington Library there is preserved a copy[69] with a note written on a flyleaf in Smith's own hand presenting the book to "The Worshipfull the Master Wardens & Societie of the Cordwayners of ye Cittie of London." Though Smith now proudly signs himself "Admirall of New England," he is still mindful of the friendship of his brother-tradesmen : "Not only in regard of your Courtisie & Loue, Butt also of ye Continuall vse I haue had of your Labours, & the hope you may make some vse of mine, I salute you with this Cronologicall discourse, . . ." And he prays the Cordwainers to give his work "Lodging in your Hall freelie to be perused for euer, in memorie of your Noblenesse towards mee, . . . " For professional reasons, the Cordwainers should read his book and encourage colonies in a region where the oyster beds have been destructive of shoes, the author hints, reminding them of "how many thousand of shooes hath bin transported to these plantations, . . . what vent your Commodities haue had & still haue, . . ."

In plan, Smith fell back on the previous compilers. He drew from other explorers such material as fitted into his work and embroidered upon it his own tales and observations. Purchas encouraged him and composed a prefatory page of execrable verse in commendation "of his friend Captaine Iohn Smith," who was likewise commended by John Donne, George Wither, and numerous others less well known. The Admiral of New England had now arrived at the port of popular literature.

The labor of compilation which Hakluyt and Purchas exerted to furnish forth travel narratives for the edification of their countrymen was too great for Smith. If he proposed to follow in his predecessors' footsteps, as the plan of the *History of Virginia* suggests, his resolution weakened. The personal narrative of his own exploits suited him better, and probably was more entertaining to the casual reader. In 1630 he published in a thin

---

[69] Press mark 69,259.

folio *The True Travels, Adventures, And Observations Of Captaine Iohn Smith, In Europe, Asia, Affrica, and America, from Anno Domini 1593. to 1629,* in which he refers to critics who already accuse him of writing too much and doing too little. As usual he prefaces his work with many verses which commend him for his labors, literary, military, and maritime, especially his *Sea Grammar* (1627), a handbook for sailors. Smith claims that his exploits have been so talked about that "they have acted my fatall Tragedies upon the Stage, and racked my Relations at their pleasure."[70] Certainly his narratives furnished the average reader with colorful romance. And despite the Captain's bluster, the career of the self-made hero, who started life an apprentice "with ten shillings and three pence,"[71] must have excited the admiration of tradesmen who had long ago learned to glory in the deeds of apprentice-heroes.

Although travels and voyages in the New World were a never failing source of popular fascination, the early seventeenth century saw a renewal of interest in the out-of-the-way places of Europe and the Near East. The activity of the Levant merchants undoubtedly had much to do with the curiosity about the regions which they touched. Romantic narratives of personal adventures of several noted travelers stimulated the public imagination. As John Smith had realized, the Great Turk was still a personage worthy to adorn a tale, and accounts relating experiences in Turkish territory were certain to attract attention. The most famous of the Near Eastern travelers were the brothers Sherley. Their adventures are chronicled in several pamphlets; they were the subject of a stage play;[72] and for the multitude they became

[70] In a dedication to the Earls of Pembroke, Lindsey, and Dover, Smith says: "Sir *Robert Cotton*, that most learned Treasurer of Antiquitie, having by perusall of my Generall Historie, and others, found that I had likewise undergone divers other as hard hazards in the other parts of the world, requested me to fix the whole course of my passages in a booke by it selfe, whose noble desire I could not but in part satisfie; the rather, because they have acted my fatall Tragedies upon the Stage, and racked my Relations at their pleasure. To prevent therefore all future misprisions, I have compiled this true discourse. Envie hath taxed me to have writ too much, and done too little; but that such should know, how little I esteeme them, I have writ this, more for the satisfaction of my friends, and all generous and well disposed Readers: . . ."

[71] See the opening chapter of *The True Travels.*

[72] *The Travailes of The three English Brothers* (1607), by John Day, William Rowley, and George Wilkins, was founded on Nixon's pamphlet. (See note 74.) It was acted by the Queen's Men.

the symbol of romantic adventure in the Near East. The books
about them center around Sir Anthony, a soldier of fortune, who
led a party of twenty-five Englishmen to Italy and in 1599 became
an unofficial ambassador to the Shah of Persia. Sherley was
financed by English merchants in Constantinople and Aleppo,
and managed to obtain trade concessions from the Shah, whom
he later represented in embassies seeking an alliance of Christian
powers with Persia against the Turks.[73] The first account of his
journey, published in 1600, was suppressed, but in 1601 William
Parry, one of the adventurers, brought out *A new and large discourse
of the Trauels of sir Anthony Sherley Knight, by Sea, and ouer Land, to the
Persian Empire.* A little later, Anthony Nixon, author of popular
pamphlets, published *The Three English Brothers* (1607),[74] followed
by Ro. C.'s *A True Historicall discourse of Muley Hamets rising to the
three Kingdomes of Moruecos, Fes, and Sus* (1609),[75] which drew
material from the travels of the Sherleys. John Cartwright, chaplain to English merchants in the Levant, found cause for rejoicing
in the work of the Sherleys. Even an indifferent reader, he suggests
in the dedication of *The Preachers Travels* (1611), ought to get
satisfaction from his description of

how two of the most mightie and most warlike Princes among the
Barbarians, the great Turke and the Persian, are now in armes one
against the other; stirred vp thereunto by two of our Countrey-men,
Sir Anthonie Sherley, and Master *Robert Sherley* his brother. A warre not
onely like to be long and bloudie, but also very commodious and of
great oportunitie to the Christian Commonweale: for that it doth
graunt and giue leasure to diuers parts of Christendome to refresh
themselues, and to increase their forces, much weakned, both by the
Great Turkes warres; and most of all by their ciuill dissentions at
home.

[73] *Dictionary of National Biography, sub* Anthony Sherley.

[74] *The Three English Brothers. Sir Thomas Sherley his Trauels, with his three yeares imprisonment in Turkie: his Inlargement by his Maiesties Letters to the great Turke: and lastly,
his safe return into England this present yeare, 1607. Sir Anthony Sherley his Embassage to the
Christian Princes. Maister Robert Sherley his wars against the Turkes, with his marriage to
the Emperour of Persia his Neece* (1607).

[75] *A True Historicall discourse of Muley Hamets rising to the three Kingdomes of Moruecos,
Fes, and Sus. The dis-vnion of the three Kingdomes, by ciuill warre, kindled amongst his three
ambitious Sonnes, Muley Sheck, Muley Boferes, and Muley Sidan. The Religion and Policie of
the More, or Barbarian. The aduentures of Sir Anthony Sherley, and diuer other English Gentlemen, in those Countries. With other Nouelties* (1609).

Finally, in 1613, was published an authorized account, *Sir Anthony Sherley His Relation Of His Travels Into Persia*, written by Sir Anthony himself, who was persuaded to publish it, so the preface claims, by a gentleman who wanted the true information, "whereof he had formerly heard, and read some incoherent and fabulous reports."

Most Englishmen had heard reports, fabulous or otherwise, about Sir Anthony and his two brothers, and they were eager to learn more about the Persians, the Turks, and other peoples of the East. This curiosity about the East was stimulated by other books which appeared in increasing numbers throughout the early seventeenth century. One of the ablest of the accounts of such travels was George Sandys's *A Relation of a Iourney begun An: Dom: 1610. Foure Bookes. Containing a description of the Turkish Empire, of Aegypt, of the Holy Land, of the Remote parts of Italy, and Ilands adioyning* (1615), of which new editions appeared in 1621, 1627, 1632, and 1637. Learned without pedantry, Sandys gives a vivid account of his observations in the countries bordering the Mediterranean. The book is alive with human interest. Marriage and funeral customs, the dress, food, amusements, monuments, religion, and the personal qualities of the people observed—all these are described in vigorous clear English. Pictures of a Turkish beauty, the Egyptian pyramids and sphinx, the Chapel of the Nativity at Bethlehem, and numerous other engravings illustrate the text. Written with urbanity and discrimination, here was a book which could gain the respect of scholars and fascinate the crowd. Most preserved copies are well worn, as if they had seen hard usage. And even yet, the old book tempts the investigator to linger over its pages. Sandys was an author who deserves better of modern readers than he has received.

Seventeenth-century Englishmen were fascinated with the wonder of their world, and this wonder increased in its intelligence until it embraced an inquiry into the ways of peoples nearer home. Buffoon though he was, Thomas Coryate served a useful purpose by informing his countrymen about European countries which few of them ever saw. After clowning his way from Odcombe in Somerset through central Europe, he returned to England to become the jest of literary London and the author of

Coryats Crudities, Hastily gobled vp in fiue Moneths trauells in France, Sauoy, Italy, Rhetia comonly called the Grisons country, Heluetia alias Switzerland, some parts of high Germany, and the Netherlands (1611), which was published with a multitude of burlesque encomia by the wits of London. Despite his buffoonery, Coryate provided a great deal of accurate observation and his work was popular for its serious information. He continued to travel and to write, but his letters from India were chiefly foolery directed to the wits who had made him their clown.[76]

Other travelers soon succeeded Coryate in popular favor. William Lithgow, son of a Scottish merchant, wandered farther and wrote longer. His first travel narrative was published in 1614 as *A Most Delectable, And True Discourse, of an admired and painefull peregrination from Scotland, to the most famous Kingdomes in Europe, Asia and Affricke.* Manners and customs of people occupy much space in his pages. Like the more scholarly Sandys, he finds the Turks a subject to his liking. Everything, from their manner of sitting cross-legged to the multitude of their concubines, is described. So it is with the other peoples whom he observes. Like the picaresque heroes of fiction, Lithgow wandered in strange places, seeing curious sights and undergoing adventures that fascinated his readers. In Rome he sees a "Librarie of the aun. cient *Romanes*"[77] and is horrified at the worship of the "Idol" of St. Peter, "erected of pure Brasse, and sitting on a brasen Chaire." In the Greek islands, he is shown the tomb of Homer, "but whether it was this Toombe or not, I do not know, but this they related."[78] The beastliness of the Armenians offends even his sensibilities, and he despises his fellow pilgrims in the Holy Land. In Jerusalem he sees all the sights, from the place where Christ stood when Pilate said "Ecce Homo," to the house where "Diues the rich glutton dwelt."[79] Finally, after viewing the pyramids of

---

[76] Cf. *Thomas Coriate Traueller for the English Wits: Greeting. From the Court of the Great Mogul, Resident at the Towne of Asmere, in Easterne India* (1616), which contains (sigs. F 3 ff.) a letter addressed "To The High Seneschall of the right Worshipfull Fraternitie of Sireniacal Gentlemen, that meet the first Fridaie of euery Moneth, at the signe of the Mere-Maide in Bread-streete in London, giue these: From the Court of the great Mogul, resident at the Towne of Asmere, in the Easterne India."

[77] Edition of 1614; sig. B 2v.

[78] *Ibid.*, sig. G 2.   [79] *Ibid.*, sig. O 4v.

Egypt and a spot on the banks of the Nile where was killed a crocodile which had eaten forty-six men and women, he finds his way home by way of Italy, and concludes the account of his travels with "A Sonet Made By The Author vpon Helen when hee pitched at Argo and Mycene in Sparta whence she was rauished." British readers found Lithgow entertaining. He continued to travel and to amplify his narratives, which had five printings by 1640; as late as 1814 a "twelfth edition" appeared. Lithgow himself was a picturesque figure, less of a clown than Coryate, but holding for his readers the fascination of a Calvinistic Jack Wilton.

The narrative of European and Near Eastern travels reached its culmination in this period with *An Itinerary Written By Fynes Moryson Gent.* (1617),[80] a great folio encyclopedia of information collected at first hand by a conscientious traveler. Useful undoubtedly it was, but it was too costly a volume to have the popularity which favored the cheaper and more colorful narratives of Coryate and Lithgow.

The explorations and travels of the sixteenth and seventeenth centuries for the first time brought the ordinary Englishman in contact with other peoples. The average citizen's horizon was enormously widened. No longer was travel confined to the wealthy gentleman, with his train of followers, who made the circuit of Europe and absorbed the decadent iniquities of Italy. Humble folk like Coryate and Lithgow were now going on the grand tour, which had extended its sweep to include the Far Mediterranean countries. Merchants, mariners, and apprentices were sailing the seven seas, pushing into unknown countries, and coming back to tell their brethren of the marvels of the great world. Furthermore, these plain men turned authors and composed a literature which was greedily read by their own kind. Incalculably influential in the awakening of the middle class was travel; but much of the travel that molded Englishmen's thinking was vicarious, done through

---

[80] *An Itinerary Written By Fynes Moryson Gent. First in the Latine Tongue, And Then Translated By him into English: Containing His Ten Yeeres Travell Through The Twelve Dominions Of Germany, Bohmerland, Sweitzerland, Netherland, Denmarke, Poland, Italy, Turky, France, England, Scotland, and Ireland* (1617).

the pages of Hakluyt, Purchas, Sandys, Coryate, Lithgow, or some other of the infinite multitude who made it possible for tradesmen to see through the mind's eye the wonders of the Indies, the glamor of Cathay, or the power of the Great Turk. The common man found in the narratives of travel not only a romantic literature more fascinating than fiction, but a call to personal adventure. These were the stories, not of King Arthur or of fabulous knights, but of men who lived and had their being in Elizabethan England. To any apprentice might come adventures that would have dazzled even Guy of Warwick, as Captain John Smith himself had witnessed. Nor was rhetorical decoration needed to adorn these tales. The sober narratives were sufficiently vivid without adornment. No one has yet appraised the influence on modern English prose of the matter-of-fact relations of the voyageurs; but merely as evidences of the development toward verbal simplicity many of these works deserve the study of literary historians. Out of utilitarian works on geography and the homespun accounts of merchants and seamen, grew a vast literature, perhaps more completely than any other inspired by and appealing to the middle class.

XV

THE STRANGE WORLD OF SCIENCE

AS man's perception of the universe was suddenly magnified in the Renaissance, revealing a world of undreamed wonders in which the infinite seemed possible, his curiosity about things hitherto forbidden, his spirit of inquiry, and his zeal to know were intensified until even the man in the street partook a little of the spirit of Faustus, who was willing to mortgage his immortal soul for supreme knowledge. If Faustus' insatiable thirst for knowledge, his inquisitive search after the mysteries of God's universe, his traffic with black magic, which made possible the attainment of his ambition, were not the experience of every Elizabethan, some, at least, of Faustus' enthusiasm for hidden learning penetrated into the average consciousness. Despite the pall of theology, ignorance, and prejudice which still enveloped the populace, the stirrings of the Renaissance spirit of inquiry were felt in all ranks of society. Not merely were a few great minds making investigations that were to become the foundations of modern science, but the rank and file of the citizenry were displaying a curiosity about the natural world that was to prove a seed ground favorable to the growth of a popular interest in things scientific. The Elizabethan's contemplation even of himself was intimately bound up with a knowledge of the universe, for he saw himself as a small reflection of the macrocosm, containing within his microscosm all the elements of the greater universe. Fascinated with this miracle, he pondered his relation to the rest of nature more earnestly than ever before and began new explorations into the hidden recesses of worldly knowledge for light which might illuminate himself. As his interest broadened, the fascination of the natural world increased until he was eagerly searching new and old books for descriptions and explanations of the

[549]

phenomena of nature. With an appetite for natural philosophy acutely stimulated, the Elizabethan consumed voraciously all the literature on the subject within his reach, leaving to later generations more queasy than his the acceptance and rejection of morsels. If Sir Thomas Browne questioned the facts of Pliny's natural history, the generations that immediately preceded him reveled in the strange information found in the Roman's pages, without bothering to question too skeptically its accuracy. Although the average reader showed little of the skepticism that is the basis of scientific inquiry, he was vastly interested in the raw material from which a study of the natural sciences grows. If a part of this interest of the general public in scientific matters was utilitarian— as, for example, the almost universal knowledge of elementary medicine—there was nevertheless a remarkable interest in the elements of natural philosophy for its own sake. The beginning of the literature of "popular science," a type that occupies such an important place in the average man's reading at the present time, is evident in many Elizabethan works which attempted to explain the wonders of the world to simple readers.

The Elizabethan inherited from the past a body of knowledge which, for want of a better term, we may describe as scientific.[1] Available to him was a hodgepodge of classical and scholastic learning, the backbone of which was the teachings of Aristotle, overlaid with scholastic interpretations. From classical and medieval sources he inherited his scientific vocabulary, his established notions, and his method of approach. Aristotle, Galen, Ptolemy, Pliny, and the church fathers had all contributed to the heritage. From the schools and from popular books a fairly conventional body of knowledge about moral and natural philosophy percolated into the mass consciousness. Alchemists, astrologers, travelers, physicians, and quacks of one sort and another spread the

---

[1] It is not my purpose to attempt any survey of the history of science in Elizabethan England. I merely wish to point out evidences of an interest among middle-class Englishmen in scientific subject matter. The sources of Elizabethan scientific knowledge are also outside the scope of this study. Professor Hardin Craig is now preparing a work on Elizabethan school learning, which will treat the latter subject.

I am indebted to Dr. Sanford V. Larkey for the use of his manuscript of the bibliography of Elizabethan science, prepared by him for the new volume of bibliographies in the *Cambridge History of English Literature*.

information about "science" which the ordinary citizen picked up. From the Middle Ages, encyclopedic works had preserved a large amount of miscellaneous information which was absorbed into the common stock of learning and reappeared in Elizabethan outlines of knowledge. The essence of Renaissance learning was its universality. Although the law, medicine, and theology had marked out definite boundaries, every citizen felt it his privilege and his necessity to know something about even the learned professions. When every householder might be his own doctor, medicine could not be an exclusive mystery. Although such esoteric studies as alchemy and astrology were regarded with a good deal of popular suspicion, even here the details were sufficiently well known to enable the ordinary person to follow the elaborate jargon of Ben Jonson's *Alchemist*. Since learning had not yet become departmentalized, every intelligent person felt it his prerogative to participate in the common stock of knowledge, scientific and otherwise, with the result that the average citizen of Tudor and Stuart England was probably better informed about the accepted facts of contemporary science than is the same type of person today; furthermore, the literature of popular science perhaps approximated more closely what was received as truth in academic circles than does similar modern literature. The citizen, therefore, who had never been within sight of a university could gather from countless outlines and handbooks a great store of information concerning the natural sciences and could talk as learnedly as some of his more academic contemporaries.

The relation to daily life of the natural sciences known to the Elizabethan gave vitality to his interest and provided a utilitarian reason for much of the citizen's curiosity. From natural history he learned about the curative properties of many drugs, vegetable, animal, and mineral. From astronomy he might learn much of profit to a traveler, and from its variant, astrology, he gathered a deal of lore concerning astral influences. Physiology helped him to understand himself and to account for his moods and mental states. When all other reasons failed, there was always the value of seeing the glory of God in his handiwork. Thus the citizen was adequately supplied with reasons to justify his curiosity.

Encyclopedic works inherited from the Middle Ages, filled with miscellaneous information about the natural world, were among the works published in the vernacular by the earliest English printers. Caxton, for instance, translated from the French and published *The myrrour of the worlde* [1481], an encyclopedia compiled from various medieval authorities, incorrectly attributed to Vincent of Beauvais. It provided in compendious form a survey of medieval scientific knowledge, beginning with a discussion of the nature of God, which precedes the account of the creation, and ending with an exposition of the system of the universe. From this time on, the unlearned citizen found available to him summaries of knowledge in a language that he could understand. Caxton's contemporaries and successors followed his lead in printing in the vernacular encyclopedic works designed, not for the learned scholar, who might read the Latin texts, but for the unlatined reader, the tradesman of London, who was already inquiring after more knowledge than the grammar school or the apprenticeship had taught him. The most influential of all the medieval encyclopedias was *De Proprietatibus Rerum* of Bartholomaeus Anglicus, first printed, in Trevisa's translation, by Wynkyn de Worde in 1495. It was the basis of an Elizabethan encyclopedia, compiled by Stephen Batman as *Batman vppon Bartholome, his Booke De Proprietatibus Rerum* (1582).[2] This was a storehouse of curious learning from which Shakespeare and his contemporaries garnered much of their scientific knowledge.[3] The orders and ways of angels, the properties of the soul, man's body with its parts and qualities, diseases with their causes and cures, the heavens, the earth (with all its minerals, plants, and creatures), colors, odors, liquids, numbers, music, and divers other themes made up the subject matter of this folio volume, wherein the scientific

---

[2] *Batman vppon Bartholome, his Booke De Proprietatibus Rerum, Newly corrected, enlarged and amended: with such Additions as are requisite, vnto every seuerall Booke: Taken foorth of the most approued Authors, the like heretofore not translated in English, Profitable for all estates, as well for the benefite of the Mind as the Bodie* (1582).

[3] For Shakespeare's acquaintance with such learning as is found in this encyclopedia, see Lily B. Campbell, *Shakespeare's Tragic Heroes, Slaves of Passion* (Cambridge, 1930), and Ruth Lelia Anderson, *Elizabethan Psychology and Shakespeare's Plays*, University of Iowa Humanistic Studies, III (1927). Both of these studies emphasize the ethical and psychological material utilized by Shakespeare. For other material which Shakespeare drew from *De Proprietatibus Rerum* and similar compilations, see H. W. Seager, *Natural History in Shakespeare's Time* (London, 1896).

learning of the past had been distilled. Batman in a preface speaks with pride of his labors in bringing the work up to date. Upon Bartholomaeus' foundation, as prepared by the learned translators and editors who preceded him, Batman declares that he has

added so much as hath bene brought to light by the trauaile of others, as Conradus Gesner of Tygure, Phisition, writing of the nature of beasts, birds, fishes, & Serpents, Fuchsius, Mathiolus, Theophrastus, Paracelsus, and Dodoneus, these wrote of the natures, operations and effects of Hearbs, Plants, Trees, Fruit, Seeds, Metalls and Mineralls. Sebastian Munster, Henry Cornelius Agrippa, and others of Astronomie and Cosmographie. Abraham Ortelius of Antwarpe for maps & discriptions : all which woorkes hath done great good in diuerse and sundrie Common wealths. I haue therefore as an imitator of the learned, for the good will I bare to my countrie, collected forth of these aforesaid Authors, the like deuises, which they in times past gathered of their elders, and so renuing the whole booke, as is apparant by additions, is brought home, the Master, the Pilot, and the profit thereto belonging, . . .

In spite of this claim Batman did little more than modernize the text and add a few scattered observations from later writers. His version was essentially the same as the earlier editions, but it made more accessible and readable a standard work which profoundly influenced popular thinking.

An encyclopedic digest of natural history, avowedly for the unlearned, was prepared by John Maplet and published under the pleasant title of *A greene Forest, or a naturall Historie* (1567).[4] Inspired by the desire to simplify university learning and make it available to the multitude, Maplet put his knowledge into compendious form and set forth a work in three parts treating of plants, minerals, and animals. The information is of the briefest kind, but from such books came whatever acquaintance the citizen might have with the facts of nature. Usually not more than a short

---

[4] *A greene Forest, or a naturall Historie, Wherein may bee seene first the most sufferaigne Vertues in all the whole kinde of Stones & Mettals: next of Plants, as of Herbes, Trees, & Shrubs, Lastly of Brute Beastes, Foules, Fishes, creeping wormes & Serpents, and that Alphabetically: so that a Table shall not neede. Compiled by John Maplet, M. of Arte, and student in Cambridge: entending hereby yt God might especially be glorified: and the people furdered* (1567). A modern reprint, edited by W. H. Davies, has been published by the Hesperides Press (London, 1930). My quotations are from the original edition.

paragraph is devoted to any one object.[5] Scanty as are the facts
of natural history, Maplet provides each section of his book with
a learned preface in which he mentions great authorities that give
his work an air of erudition. Such names as Aristotle, Pliny, Theophrastus, Dioscorides, Cardan, and many others are frequently
cited. But mere pedantic parade of learning is not the ultimate
aim of the author. The text is reduced to the understanding of
plain men. His purpose is

not to teach or shew the learned, howe in this point Nature hath
wrought (for that were as the prouerb is, ye Sow to Minerua :) But to
record & repeate in maner of Storie, with the residue of men simple &
plaine : And I cannot tell how it may somewhat helpe those that be
learned also, If they shall espie and consider but the effect and proofe
of these. I therefore desire a Reader not learned, but vnskilfull : yet
rather learned then immoderate.[6]

With Maplet's little octavo volume, the busy man might learn
many of the secrets locked away in recondite Latin treatises. A
later handbook of astronomy completed Maplet's outline of scientific knowledge for unlettered readers.[7]

Moralistic purposefulness often garbed the popular literature
of natural science. The allegorical interpretations and the moral
lessons of the medieval bestiaries and lapidaries continually reappeared in Elizabethan treatises and accentuated their vogue with
a public always ready to see in the simplest phenomena the man-

---

[5] For example, all the knowledge of the rhinoceros is summarized into four sentences :
"Rhinoceros in Greeke is interpreted horned beast or *Monoceron*, and is englished
the *Vnicorne*. Plinie in his .viii. booke saith, that his Horne is set aboue his nostrils. His
continuall strife is with the Elephant, & vseth to defend himself thus. Whē he seeith
his enimie come, he whetteth his Horne against sharpe stones, & then setteth on : and
in his fight wardeth and foyneth at the Elephant his bellye, the most tender part that
he hath, and so riddeth him."—Fol. 101.

[6] Preface to the first book.

[7] Maplet entitled his astronomical treatise *The Diall Of Destiny. A Booke Very Delectable And Pleasaunt: wherein may be seene the continuall and customab[le co]urse, disposition,
qualities, effec[tes and] influence of the Seuen Planet[s . . .] kyndes of Creatures here bel[onging
to] the seuerall and sundry situation of Countryes and Kingdomes. Compiled and discussed Briefly,
aswell Astrologically, as Poetically, and Philosophically* (1581). The title-page of the British
Museum copy, which I have used, is defective. Maplet discusses celestial phenomena
and what they signify. Although he treats of the influence of the stars on men and animals, his book is a popularizing of astronomy rather than primarily an astrological
work.

ifestations of the supernatural. Compilers of encyclopedias assured their readers that a study of the physical world and of man
in his mental and physical aspects revealed profitable lessons of
God's will. Thus what we should today call psychology, physiology, and natural history found a pious excuse, in addition to
the newer appeal of an aroused curiosity. English translators
combed foreign literatures for works of natural history illustrating
the divine hand. Natural history, divinity, and domestic economy
were often hopelessly confused, but writings of this sort entertained
and edified Elizabethan readers. Such a treatise was John Alday's
translation from Pierre Boaistuau, *Theatrum Mundi, The Theatre or
rule of the world* [1566?], a little moralized encyclopedia of strange,
wonderful, and useful information ranging from a description of
the habits of wild beasts to advice on the management of children.
New editions appeared in 1574 and 1581. The conduct of animals
in comparison with that of man was the theme of I. B.'s rendering
from Pierre Viret of *The Schoole of Beastes, Intituled, the good Hous-
holder, or the Oeconomickes* (1585).

The desirability of studying natural philosophy was conclusively
asserted in Thomas Twyne's translation from Lambertus Danaeus
of *The Wonderfull Woorkmanship Of The World: wherin is conteined
an excellent discourse of Christian naturall Philosophie, concernyng the
fourme, knowledge, and vse of all thinges created* (1578). The study of
the natural universe, the author maintains, is not to furnish idle
entertainment or mere profane instruction for man, but to prove
the glory of God, who by his will created a world perfect in all
its parts. That man may the better see God's wisdom, the work
explains such profundities as the nature of the light which God
created, why there was darkness on the face of the void, why the
universe was created in parts and not all at once, and many other
hidden matters. If Danaeus seemed extremely diligent in the
refutation of the new astromony, his readers were not concerned,
for they were satisfied with his traditional explanations.

Popular treatises on natural philosophy throughout the sixteenth and early seventeenth centuries were closely linked with
divinity. The strong theological influence is prominent in such
an important encyclopedia of diverse learning as Pierre de La
Primaudaye's *The French Academie*, the first section of which was

translated and published by T. B. in 1586. Beginning with the
new portions of the third edition in 1594, natural philosophy
takes a prominent place in the work. The second part of the
Academie is concerned with "a naturall historie of the bodie and
soule of man."[8] The Elizabethan could find here explanations of
his physiological and psychological conditions, with just the requisite amount of good morality to make it pleasing to him. Having explained man, the *Academie* in its third part turns its attention
to the rest of the physical universe by providing

a notable description of the whole world, and of all the principall parts
and contents thereof: As namely, of Angels both good and euill: of
the Celestiall spheres, their order and number: of the fixed stars and
planets; their light, motion, and influence: Of the fower elements,
and all things in them, or of them consisting: and first of firie, airie,
and watrie meteors or impressions of comets, thunders, lightnings,
raines, snow, haile, rainebowes, windes, dewes, frosts, earthquakes,
&c. ingendred aboue, in, and vnder the middle or cloudie region of
the aire. And likewise of fowles, fishes, beasts, serpents, trees with their
fruits and gum; shrubs, herbes, spices, drugs, minerals, precious stones,
and other particulars most worthie of all men to be knowen and considered.[9]

In a readable form, La Primaudaye gives an outline of the natural
sciences of his time. When the sixth edition was printed in 1618,
it was concluded with a theological and devotional section, which
would have saved the work from any taint of worldliness even had
the author not persistently moralized elsewhere.

One cannot emphasize too strongly that in general the reading
public of Elizabethan England was not concerned about scientific
method. The average reader never is, whatever the age. The literate populace, however, was profoundly interested in religion,
in itself, and in the strange creations of the universe. Any book,
therefore, that combined materials in these three fields was certain of popularity. A work with this appeal was Du Bartas's encyclopedic religious poem, which Joshua Sylvester began to translate early in the 1590's and published in a collected edition in 1605
as *Bartas: His Deuine weekes and workes*. For the next half century Du

---

[8] Title-page of "The Second Part" of the edition of 1594.
[9] Title-page of the third volume of the fourth edition, printed 1601.

Bartas provided Puritan readers with information about their universe. So pertinent a subject as the creation was the place for a discussion of man, plants, and animals, and the world in which they live. Du Bartas omitted nothing. Explanations are many and curious. Readers long familiar with the heathen Pliny could now in a Christian poet see the wonders of the universe, properly moralized. Good lessons come in unexpected places. A description of the fishes leads the poet to recommend to wives the example of the virtuous and faithful mullet:

> But, for her Loue, the Mullet hath no Peere;
> For if the Fisher haue surpriz'd her Pheere,
> As mad with woe, to shoare she followeth,
> Prest to consort him, both in life and death:
> As yerst those famous, louing *Thracian Dames*
> That leapt aliue into the funerall flames
> Of their dead Husbands, who deceast and gone,
> Those loyall Wiues hated to liue alone.[10]

Before the eager eyes of Du Bartas's readers passes the whole array of created things, from the fish of the sea to the lights in the heavens. He explains the seasons, the weather, the plants, the heavenly bodies, the marvelous care in the devising of man in mind and body. The pious reader was wonderfully pleased with a religious poem which at the same time informed him about the intricacies of human anatomy, as in the passage descriptive of the work of the stomach and liver:

> Or, shall I rip the Stomaches hollownes,
> That readie Cooke, concocting euerie Messe,
> Which in short time it cunningly conuerts
> Into pure Liquor fit to feed the parts;
> And then, the same doth faithfully deliuer
> Into the *Port-Vaine* passing to the Liuer,
> Who turnes it soone to Blood, and thence againe
> Through branching pipes of the great *Hollow vaine*
> Through all the members doth it duly scatter.[11]

Finally, the course of man's history leads the poet from the creation and the flood to the discovery of the New World, with

[10] Edition of 1605, p. 152.   [11] *Ibid.*, p. 215.

the lessons in geography and astronomy which that event suggests. The whole is a vast digest of information which was accepted in its own day by most people as authentic. Harvey might discover the circulation of the blood, Galileo might prove the Copernican theory, and Bacon might propound a new method of scientific approach, but the lay public got its information from such popular works as that of Du Bartas. In the encyclopedia of miscellaneous learning Elizabethans found answers to their questionings about natural philosophy, with all that that term embraces. In Du Bartas the general reader had an "outline of science." So popular was it that new editions continued to appear throughout the first half of the seventeenth century. Thomas Lodge, who had given up romance and drama for medicine, translated from the French *A Learned Summary Upon the famous Poeme of William of Saluste Lord of Bartas* (1621),[12] a synopsis of the learned matters in Du Bartas, which was three times reprinted by 1638. Thus did Dr. Lodge advance the cause of popular science in his age.

The influence of Du Bartas is evident in some of the encyclopedias of miscellaneous scientific lore, which continued to appear in the seventeenth century.[13] John Swan published in 1635 *Speculum Mundi Or A Glasse Representing The Face Of The World.*[14] A "second Edition enlarged" appeared in 1643. In this encyclopedia Swan follows the plan suggested by Du Bartas in arranging the wonders of the universe according to the days of creation. Thus, for example, Chapter VII "concerneth the fourth day, together with such things as are pertinent to the work done in it; namely the

---

[12] *A Learned Summary Upon the famous Poeme of William of Saluste Lord of Bartas. Wherin are discovered all the excellent secretts in Metaphysicall, Physicall, Morall, and Historicall knowledge. Fitt for the learned to refresh theire memories, and for younger students to abreviat and further theire studies: Wherin nature is discovered, art disclosed, and history layd open* (1621). See N. Burton Paradise, *Thomas Lodge, the History of an Elizabethan* (New Haven, 1931), pp. 172-73, 242-43.

[13] A discussion of Du Bartas's influence, especially on seventeenth-century literature, is to be found in a manuscript dissertation by W. R. Abbot, "The Influence of Du Bartas in English Literature" (University of North Carolina, 1931).

[14] *Speculum Mundi Or A Glasse Representing The Face Of The World; Shewing both that it did begin, and must also end: The manner How, and time When, being largely examined. Whereunto Is Joyned an Hexameron, or a serious discourse of the causes, continuance, and qualities of things in Nature; occasioned as matter pertinent to the work done in the six dayes of the Worlds creation* (1635.) For comment on Swan and some of his views, see Foster Watson, *The Beginnings of the Teaching of Modern Subjects in England* (London, 1909), pp. 192 ff., 369.

Matter, Names, Natures, Motions, and Offices of the Starres."
Chapter VIII deals with "the creatures made in the fifth day of
the world ; viz. Fish, and Fowl." Chapter IX ends the book with
a consideration of the creatures made on the sixth day, and concludes with a discussion of man. Swan was no slavish follower of
Du Bartas ; from many writers about natural things he gleaned
information, which he garnished with a theological commentary
delightful to Puritan readers. The facts of natural history are
even more curious than those Du Bartas had given. One learns,
for example, about the shrewd ways of the fox, even to this animal's method of drowning his fleas.[15] Swan frequently becomes so
absorbed in his natural history that he goes several pages without
drawing a moral application ; then he remembers his duty and
hastens to correct the error, as in concluding his description of the
habits of the fox whose whelps "when they can finde no more
milk in the paps of their damme, will bite them with their teeth,
and rend and teare them, reputing them as strangers. So have I
seen fraudulent friends, who will love no longer then you feed
them."[16] Not content with merely the classical natural history
found in Pliny and the early writers, Swan describes creatures
indigenous to the New World. From his pages, Englishmen who
may have missed the description in Purchas first read of the
'possum : "In Virginia there is a beast called *Ovassom*, which hath
a head like a Swine, a tail like a Rat, as big as a Cat, and hath
under his belly a bag, wherein they carrie their young. *Purch.*"[17]

Much information, useful to his age, is crowded into Swan's
pages. His descriptions of plants lead him to mention the curative
herbs. The passages on minerals and chemicals were likewise designed for practical utility. In his pages the reader might acquire a liberal education in the knowledge of that age in astronomy, botany, zoölogy, mineralogy, and kindred sciences. Mixed
with his lessons in astronomy are discussions of the correct interpretations to be drawn from comets and meteors, which may be
the warnings of Almighty God. Comets, or "New starres," particularly disturb the encyclopedists :

Now here I must confesse that I know not what to write : for how they

---

[15] Edition of 1635, p. 450.   [16] *Ibid.*, p. 451.   [17] *Ibid.*, pp. 446-47.

are generated, or what they signifie, is a most intricate question. Noble *Tycho*, that Phenix of Astronomie, and after him *Longomontanus*, with certain others, have been perswaded that they were more then Comets, and generated farre otherwise, or of other matter than fierie Meteors are; being first set awork so to think by the sight of that strange and admirable New starre which was seen in the constellation of *Cassiopea;* seen from the ninth of November in the yeare 1572, untill the last of March in the yeare 1574.[18]

Though Swan is inclined to regard the new star as a harbinger of wars and plagues and to find in it some relation to the Massacre of St. Bartholomew's Day, he is uncertain and turns for guidance again to Tycho Brahe, who had asserted "that the effects were to be declared by succeeding events."[19] It is useful to man to know such things and to interpret them rightly: "Eclipses, conjunctions, prodigious sights, flashings, comets, new starres, what are they but the Oracles of God?"[20] Though Swan believes in certain aspects of astrology, he warns vigorously against overfaith in the stars and the interpretations of quacks:

Onely beware that more be not attributed to the heavens, then to him that made the heavens; not more to the servants then to the Master, as they did who made them gods; or they who trust and rely upon them, not daring to take a journey, or begin a work, or speak with a friend about any businesse, without a needlesse consultation. Also know that the observing of these signes must not be mixed with magicall spells, as charmers do, when instead of using, they come to abusing of herbs: . . .[21]

As the newspapers of the present time bandy about the names of scientists and offer interpretations suitable to the understanding of the public, so did Swan mention the great names in science and discuss their merits as he saw them. Tycho Brahe is often quoted; Kepler is occasionally mentioned; Copernicus is cited and refuted. But withal, Swan's cosmography is confused. He has a chapter on the motions of the heavenly bodies, in which he mentions the theories of Tycho and Kepler and gives a diagram showing "Tycho's demonstration"[22] of the planets, but he does not commit himself conclusively. In a passage discussing the causes of tides, he

---

[18] *Ibid.*, p. 107.   [19] *Ibid.*, p. 108.   [20] *Ibid.*, p. 351.
[21] *Ibid.*, pp. 351-52.   [22] *Ibid.*, p. 317.

denies that the earth has any circular motion, and completely refutes the notion that "there is a daily motion of the earth round about the heavens, which it performeth in 24 houres"—an "opinion [which] came first from the *Pythagoreans*, and is defended by the Copernicanians."[23] Finally, after advancing many reasons to disprove the Copernican belief in the motion of the earth, Swan clinches the argument with a question which is still valid with thousands of bourgeois readers who combat scientific advance with the same weapon :

Last of all, let me demand how the earths motion and heavens rest can agree with holy Scripture. It is true indeed (as they alledge) that the grounds of Astronomie are not taught us in Gods book : yet when I heare the voice of the everlasting and sacred Spirit say thus, *Sun stand thou still, and thou Moon in the valley of Ajalon*, I cannot be persuaded either to think, teach, or write, that the earth stood still : but the sunne stood, and the moon stayed, untill the people had avenged themselves on their enemies.[24]

In Swan's *Speculum Mundi* the popular outline of science in this period reached its culmination. From it many a Puritan tradesman must have acquired an acquaintance with the heretical beliefs of Copernicus and learned the names of such modern scientists as Kepler and Tycho Brahe. Swan was a popularizer, and like most popularizers he was content with the facts as set forth in the established authorities. Many names lent weight to the compilation : Aristotle, Plato, Galen, Pliny, Aelianus, Virgil, Ovid, Lucretius, Thomas Aquinas, Du Bartas, Gerard, Conrad Gesner, Topsell, and a score of others less well known were called upon to witness the accuracy of Swan's scientific observations. His public was satisfied with his teachings. Though the tradesman of London may never have heard lectures in the university upon the learned works of Aristotle, academic knowledge was simplified, translated, and passed on to him in digestible portions through the medium of such outlines of science as Swan provided in his encyclopedia.

Many other works of encyclopedic proportions catered to the popular taste for information about the wonders of the world.

[23] *Ibid.*, pp. 210-11.   [24] *Ibid.*, pp. 213-14.

Not all were so thorough or so inclusive as Swan's. Many were merely hodgepodges of natural curiosities, like penny museums, appealing to the perennial interest in strange wonders. Innumerable pamphlets describing outlandish marvels littered the bookstalls. Thomas Johnson, an apothecary and citizen of London, published a potpourri of such material in *Cornucopiae, Or diuers secrets* (1595).[25] In short-sentence form, Johnson packs an array of miscellaneous information about natural things, with which he mixes scraps of history and odds and ends of learning. In the popular consciousness there is a faith in the value of information, however curious and heterogeneous, to increase man's knowledge and wisdom. The Elizabethans were particularly tolerant of undigested compilations that provided them with what they accepted as facts. Although the exact purport of the information was often not clear, the reader naïvely believed that it would turn to some good once he had mastered it, and if it had a dash of morality, that was sufficient to assure the utility of any work. Since a book like Johnson's informed the reader in the briefest manner about some of the strange things rapidly coming to every man's attention, those who did not have the time or inclination to pore over longer works might be saved from ignorance of natural philosophy by such an epitome.

Many books of "secrets" were mixtures of medical recipes, household hints, and stray bits of information. Such an assortment was found in an extraordinarily popular collection attributed to Albertus Magnus. The first editions of this book began to appear about the middle of the sixteenth century, and continued to be reprinted for the next hundred years. An edition of 1637 is entitled *The Secrets of Albertus Magnus*.[26]

The credulity of the age was great enough to warrant two editions of Ferdinand Walker's translation from Antonio de Torque-

---

[25] *Cornucopiae, Or diuers secrets: Wherein is contained the rare secrets in Man, Beasts, Foules, Fishes, Trees, Plantes, Stones, and such like, most pleasant and profitable, and not before committed to bee printed in English. Newlie drawen out of diuers Latine Authors into English by Thomas Iohnson* (1595).

[26] *The Secrets of Albertus Magnus. Of the vertues of Herbes, Stones, and certaine Beasts. Wherunto is newly added, a short discourse of the seven Planets governing the Nativities of Children. Also a Booke of the same Author, of the marveilous things of the world, and of certaine things caused of certaine Beasts* (1637).

mada, *The Spanish Mandeuile of Miracles* (1600).[27] Spectacular and alluring tales from travelers, authors of natural histories, and divers other sources went into this encyclopedia of vulgar errors; the table of contents promises "many thinges woorthy of admiration, which Nature hath wrought and daily worketh in men, contrarie to her common and ordinary course of operation, with other curiosities strange and delightfull." These delightful wonders consist of descriptions of the "properties & vertues of Springs, Riuers, and Lakes, with some opinions touching terrestriall Paradise"; discourses on "Visions, Fancies, Spirits, Ghosts, Hags, Enchaunters, Witches, and Familiars"; conjectures on "Fortune & Chaunce" and "what the influence of the heauenly Bodyes import"; and finally, an exposition on the "Septentrionall Countries, which are neere and vnder the North-pole" with the "sundry wonderfull things that are in the Septrionall Regions, worthy of admiration." Among the marvels is an account of a woman, shipwrecked on the coast of Africa, who mated with an ape and brought forth two sons. Although the author makes some effort to rationalize the more preposterous tales, most of them are related as facts of natural philosophy. Such was the pabulum on which the lover of popular science might feed.

The travels and discoveries in the New World had intensified interest in the physical geography, the flora, and the fauna of strange lands. The absurdities of Torquemada merely put into encyclopedic form the most curious of the descriptions found bountifully in many books of travel. The compilations of Hakluyt and Purchas as well as the accounts of individual writers devoted much space to observations of natural objects. A systematic discussion of the natural history of the newly discovered regions was made available to Englishmen in E. G.'s translation from Joseph de Acosta of *The Naturall and Morall Historie of the East and West Indies. Intreating of the remarkeable things of Heaven, of the Elements, Mettalls, Plants and Beasts which are proper to that Country: Together with the Manners, Ceremonies, Lawes, Governements,*

---

[27] *The Spanish Mandeuile of Miracles. Or The Garden of curious Flowers. Wherin are handled sundry points of Humanity, Philosophy, Diuinitie, and Geography, beautified with many strange and pleasant histories. First written in Spanish, by Anthonio De Torquemada, and out of that tongue translated into English* (1600). Another edition was published in 1618.

and Warres of the Indians (1604).[28] Shrewdly the Jesuit reconciles
the roundness of the earth with scriptural statements to the contrary, explains St. Augustine's denial of the antipodes, examines
Aristotle's and Pliny's theories, and asserts that Plato knew nothing about the Indies when he wrote of Atlantis. After a survey
of ancient scientific knowledge, the author launches into a careful exposition of the physical geography and the natural history
of the new-found lands, particularly of Peru and Mexico, the
subject matter of the first four of the seven books which make
up the work. Everything, from the heavens as seen from the
southern continent to the tricks of monkeys and the virtues of the
bezoar stone in the treatment of disease, finds its way into this
compendium, from which Englishmen of the early seventeenth
century added to their knowledge of natural science.

Important as were encyclopedic works in disseminating knowledge of natural science to laymen, cheaper books on separate
fields of knowledge were more available and therefore even more
important in the edification of the citizenry. The earliest English
printers realized the popular demand for inexpensive treatises on
scientific themes; Caxton, Wynkyn de Worde, Pynson, Copland,
Wyer, and their contemporaries turned out large numbers of
cheap books in English, dealing with medicine, astrology, botany,
and kindred subjects. By the middle of the sixteenth century there
was already an established tradition of popular literature of a
scientific nature. The later sixteenth and early seventeenth centuries saw merely the extension to still larger audiences of the
type of literature that plain citizens had learned to seek out.

The average reader's knowledge of scientific things was vague
and unsystematized. To him Aristotle was a great name symboliz-
ing classic authority of an academic sort. The tradesman, who may
never have been within sound of university lecturers, knew that
Aristotle was an omniscient Greek, who pronounced upon all
things—the soul, the body, nature, and what not. For the tradesmen, for the unlatined and unlectured, popular writers filtered
the school learning and made it available in little books full of
utility, erudition, and morality. For those who did not have some

---

[28] Edited by Clements R. Markham for the Hakluyt Society, 2 vols. (London, 1880).

encyclopedia containing outlines of all learning, smaller books of specialized knowledge were purchasable. The productions of Thomas Hill are typical of the less comprehensive guides to popular science, through which non-academic readers might acquire the truths of Aristotle, Galen, Pliny, Ptolemy, and even later writers upon the broad theme of nature. Hill was a citizen who proudly signed himself "Londoner." If any muse inspires the makers of handbooks, she must have chosen to shower upon him an unusual zeal for the revelation of all esoteric matters and to inspire him to turn out treatises which explained nature, both theoretically and practically, so that simple Londoners might learn and profit. Beginning his career with a work on physiognomy and an almanac, Hill was soon busy with other books, giving information about everything from gardening to the stars. His writings make no extravagant claims for his own scientific knowledge, but they always enumerate a host of authorities, from whom the author claims to have extracted his information. At the end of *The proffitable Arte of Gardening, now the third tyme set fourth* (1568),[29] Hill appended an advertisement of his works, both published and projected, which shows that he had become a professional popularizer of what may be described as the applied science or pseudo-science of his day. Explanations of physiognomy, astrology, astronomy, gardening, palmistry, botany, bee culture, Hippocratic medicine, chemistry, animal husbandry, and countless other revelations, which Hill is fond of alluding to as "secrets," find their way into his little treatises,[30] some of which were frequently reprinted. Had this

---

[29] The first edition seems to have been in 1563. I have quoted from the third edition in the Huntington Library. The *Short Title Catalogue* lists eight editions by 1608.

City dwellers must have read with considerable interest the books on agriculture and related subjects. Many works on farming, gardening, horse training, beekeeping, and similar themes were published in the sixteenth and seventeenth centuries. The writings of Fitzherbert, Tusser, and Markham long remained popular and were printed so often that one can be reasonably sure that many a London merchant, having made his money in trade and invested in a country place, was buying the books which described methods of leading successfully a rural life. One of the stock complaints against London tradesmen was that they were buying up country lands. Undoubtedly there was much armchair gardening and farming. *See* the *Cambridge History of English Literature*, IV, 364-77.

[30] The advertisement of Hill's works, appended to *The proffitable Arte of Gardening*, gives such a clear indication of the diversity of material of this nature appealing to the popular audience that it deserves quotation in full:

industrious compiler been living today he would have been editor of one of the magazines devoted to popular science. He appeals frankly to the unlettered reader. A projected treatise on urinalysis is set forth in English to profit young practitioners and those "that lacke the Lattine Tungue." He emphasizes his labors in searching

"The bookes and Treatises, all readie Printed be these.

"1 A briefe Epitome of the whole arte of Physiognomie, imprinted by Iohn Wayland, Anno. 1556.

"2 A pleasaunt Almanacke seruinge for thre yeres, as. 1560. 1561. 1562. teachinge not only worthie lessons in the letting of bloud, and taking of purgacions, but extraordinarie rules for the weather, matter profittable for the meaner people & husbandmen to know, & imprinted by Thomas Marshe, dwellyng neare to S. Dunstones churche. 1560.

"3 A pleasannt Treatise of the interpretacion of sundrie dreames gathered part out of the woorcke of the Learned Phylosopher Ponzettus, and part out of Artemidorus, & imprinted by Thomas Marshe. Anno. 1563.

"4 A briefe Treatyse of Gardeninge teaching the apt dressing, sowinge, and setting of a Garden, with the remedies against such beastes, wormes, flyes &c. that commonly annoye Gardens, encreased by me ye seconde tyme, & imprinted by Thomas marsh. Anno. 1563.

"5 A pleasaunt Treatise intytuled Naturall & Artificial conclusions. &c. and imprinted by William Copland dwelling in Lothburie in the yeare. 1567.

"6 A proper Treatyse, of the marualouse wunders seene in the ayer, wyth the straunge and rare secreetes of the Laekes and wells, and prodygiouse effectes of the lightninges, imprinted by the sayd Copland, the sixt day of May, & in the said yere 1567.

"7 A litle Treatise of the interpretacion of dreames, fathered on Iosephe that godly parson, vnto which is annexed (in the beginning of it) certaine pleasaunt Probleames agreing to the matter, and imprinted by the said Copland, the fyfte day of March. Anno. 1567.

"8 An apt historye and discourse of the art of Gardening now the thyrde time increased, in which is not only taught a number of pleasant secretes, but the Physicke helpes which the herbes sarue vnto, & that easie to be prepared, and imprinted by Thomas Marshe. 1568.

"The bookes of mine, now in a readynesse to be imprinted and the most of them with the Printers.

"1 First a large historie, and discourse of the whole art Physiognomie, nowe the second time encreased, vnto whiche is annexed sundrie rare Examples, of dyuers forreine Princes, that came to straunge happes, accordinge to the fore tellinge of the Phisiognomer Cocles, which notes do not a lytle healpe to the furtherance of the arte, with other rare Secretes adioyned, not the lyke extante in the Latine Tungue, whiche worcke loke for at the handes of Edward Suttone stacioner, dwellinge in Lumbarde strete.

"2 A pleasaunt Treatise, intituled the Pathe way to knowledge, teaching all such principles, as necessarilie sarue to the better vnderstanding of the arte of Astronomie, and Astrologie, with other pleasaunte rules besydes annexed, and that right proffitable, the which looke for at the handes of the sayd Suttone.

"3 Also a proper Treatyse, intytuled the Myrroure of Tyme, contayning manye

strange languages, ancient and modern, for the learning that he makes available for the plain Englishman. By scanning his pages, the casual reader might gain an acquaintance with many learned names, from Aristotle to the modern writers. Even so brief a treatise as his discussion of bees is "gathered oute of, Plynie,

---

woorthye maters, and predictions ryghte necessarie to bee vnderstanded, which also is in the handes, of the foresayd Suttone.

"4 A proper Treatise intytuled, certaine pleasaunt probleames, with their apt answers, gathered out of the Greekes Arabians, and auncient Phisitions in Latyne, by a learned Philosopher named Ponzettus, in which are taught manye Physicke pointes, for the preseruation of health, with other matters besydes right pleasant to reade, and this in a readynes with the Printer Thomas Marshe.

"Certaine husbandly coniectures of the state of eache yeare, in the forme of an euerlasting Prognostication, with rules as proffitable for the commoditie of Cattell, as also saruing to the benefyte of health, vnto which is adioyned a very proper Treatyse, settynge furthe the maruelouse Gouermente and vsage of the honnye Bees, with the great commodityes both of the honnye and waxe (whyche they Cunninglye make) and applyed after the distillinge to the vse of Physicke and Surgerie, as the Treatyse it selfe more at large vttereth, and this to be loked for at the handes of the sayd printer Thomas Marshe.

"The Bookes which remaine wyth mee fullye ended, halfe done, and part begunne of them.

"1 And first, a most fruitfull Treatyse of the Sphere, righte profitable for Mariners, and seafaringe men, gathered part oute of the large Commentarie of Stoeflerus vpon the Sphere of Proclus, and parte of others, and this in a readynesse to the printing.

"2 A profitable Treatyse of Physicke, conteyninge manye woorthye Lessons and Secretes, in the drawyne Oyles of the seuen Mettalls, and other Simples, saruing to ye vse of Phtsicke, matter not ye like vnderstäded in ye English tunge and gathered out of the best practisioners, whiche heatherto haue wryten of the same, and this halfe writen, in sundrye papers.

"3 A briefe Herbal very profitable, for the rare pointes of physicke taught in ye same, wryten first by a singuler Phylosopher and skylful practisioner of Bolognia in Italye, and part, begunne of the same.

"4 A necessarie Treatyse of the Iudgement of vrines, much helpinge young practisioners of Phisicke, and that lacke the Lattine Tungue, vnto whyche is annexed sundrie pleasaunte Cautells, healpinge greatlye the furtheraunce in iudgement, and this in a maner readie to the printing.

"5 The greate woorcke, of the arte of Paulmestrie, dyuided into two bookes, the fyrste prouynge it by solempne argumentes, alledged oute of the aunciente Phylosophers and worthye Physitions, as Hermes, Ptholomeus Paruus, Petrus Apponesis, Helenus Priami, Iulianus, Albertus Magnus Hypocrates, and others, that the same too be an arte found oute, of longe experience, & this so reasoned of, in dyologue forme.

"And the other proueth it by apt demonstrations, accordyng to the instructions of the art and by sundrie examples here and there placed, whyche not a lytle further and healpe the confirminge of the former, and besydes added to (such number of handes) as maye gyue an Euydente lyghte, and vnderstandynge to the arte. All whyche by great dyligence of the Phisiognomer, and Paulmester, gathered and penned out of

Albertus, Varro, Columella, Palladius, Aristotle, Theophrastus, Cardanus, Guilhelmus de Conchis, Agrippa, and diuerse other singuler Authours."[31] The more extensive works bore longer lists of authorities. London citizens found in Hill's interpretations enough of Aristotle, Pliny, Galen, Cardan, and "sundry others" to give them the pleasant feeling of enlightenment still so gratifying to middle-class intelligences, which are satisfied with innumerable outlines.

The satisfaction that comes from a work both informative and practically useful was found in books like Hill's. Even a treatise on gardening had wider value than the subject matter seems to promise. As Hill himself points out to his fellow Londoners, the craft of gardening "bringeth moste necessarie commodities, both to Citties and Townes," and the study of it is recommended to all intelligent citizens, for though some may think it inferior to certain arts, yet it is as "profitable, & altogither as necessary as the others are : forsomuch as this is so linked and chained to the noble artes, both of Phisicke and Surgerie."[32] He managed to pack into his treatises both curious learning and practical help, and thereby insured the widest popularity for his books. A compilation of odds and ends, entertaining and practical, makes up *A Briefe and pleas-*

---

the most Authours that euer wrought, eyther in auncient tyme or of Late yeares, and broughte nowe into one solempne and parfyt worke, the lyke not extante in the common shoppes, and this in a maner fynished by me.

"6 A proper Treatyse intytuled the Ecclesiasticall counte, in the whyche is conteyned muche necessarie matter, for all soortes of people to reade, and thys in a readynesse to the pryntynge.

"7 The last parte of Alexis Piemont. not yet extant in the Englishe tungue, as the same shall euidentlye appeare at the comming furth of the Booke, vnto which I haue annexed (here and there) in the Booke, sundrie newe inuentions about the drawing of costly Oyles, and waters, saruing not onlye for inwarde meanes in the presaruation of healthe, but outwardly to be applyed, for ye liuely Garnishing of the face, and colouring of the heare of the head, eyther yelow, or flaxine of Coloure, wyth other matters besydes, as these more euidentlye shall appeare, at the cōming furth of ye booke.

"8 A proper Treatyse of the daungerous tymes of the sicke, according to ye mones course throughe the twelue Signes, wryten by that auncient Physition Hypocrates, & this in a readynesse to the printynge."

[31] From the heading to p. 1 of *A pleasaunt Instruction of the parfit orderinge of Bees* (1568), bound with *The proffitable Arte of Gardening* in the Huntington Library copy.

[32] Quoted from the dedication to Sir Henry Seamer of *The Arte of Gardening*, edition of 1608.

aunt treatise, entituled, Naturall and Artificiall Conclusions (1581).[33] Here one finds such diverse material as the qualities of the adamant stone, the secret properties of eggs, "A proper practice to make a Capon bring vp yong Chickens," "How to turne water into wine, a proper secret," and finally, in conclusion, a brief recipe "To ease thy feete for going." In expounding the secrets of astronomy, Hill is likewise mindful of the utility of his teaching, as he proves in *A Contemplation of Mysteries: contayning the rare effectes and significations of certayne Comets, and a briefe rehersall of sundrie Hystoricall examples . . . with matter delectable both for the Sayler, and Husbandman, yea and all traueylers by Sea and lande* [1571], a work appropriately dedicated to Hill's "singuler friend mayster Henrie French Marchant."[34] More learned but equally useful for practical students was *The Schoole Of Skil: Containing two Bookes: The first, of the Sphere, of heauen, of the Starres, of their Orbes, and of the Earth, &c. The second, of the Sphericall Elements, of the celestiall Circles, and of their vses, &c.* (1599), published after Hill's death by William Jaggard, who wrote a preface praising the forwardness of his age in arts and sciences.[35] Helps to the improvement of both the mind and soul might be found in Hill's treatise on applied psychology and physiology, *The Contemplation of Mankinde, contayn-*

---

[33] *A Briefe and pleasaunt treatise, entituled, Naturall and Artificiall Conclusions: Written first by sundrie scholers of the Uniuersitie of Padua In Italie, at the instant request of one Bartholemew a Tuscane: And now Englished by Thomas Hill Londoner, as well for the commoditie of sundrie Artificers, as for the matters of pleasure to recreate wittes at vacant tymes* (1581). Preserved in Huntington Library.

[34] General utility, particularly to the merchant class, was the purpose of *The Arte of vulgar arithmeticke . . . A knowledge pleasant for Gentlemen, commendable for Capteines and Soldiers, profitable for Merchants, and generally necessarie for all estates and degrees* (1600). This work has many tables useful for merchants engaged in foreign trade.

[35] Preface "To the Reader" : "Diuers haue writtē of sundry matters in former Ages, to the intent to benefit these our later times, wherin a man can name no kind of Art or Science, liberall or mechanicall, but there are as rare wits to bee found as euer liued since lerning florished. The reason is good that it should be so. For first, we haue come to our handes, vse and iudgement, whatsoeuer either antique or moderne Authors haue left behinde. Secondly, the gouernment (God be blessed) hath a long time (now these 40. yeares) bin so peaceable, that Students had neuer more libertie to looke into learning of any profession, for the inlarging of their vnderstanding. Lastly, the meanes otherwise, aswell out of the vniuersities, as in them, haue been and are so many and so good, to attaine to all knowledge, that I dare be bold to say, England may compare with any Nation for number of lerned men, and for variety in professions."

*ing a singuler discourse after the Art of Phisiognomie, on all the members
and partes of man, as from the heade to the foote, in a more ample maner
than hytherto hath beene published of any* (1571), a new edition of which
was brought out by Jaggard in 1613. The treatise is lavish in its
citations of Aristotle's authority. The revelations of physiognomy,
even when they prove unpleasant, may be of advantage to the
individual, who can strive to correct the faults that an analysis of
his character reveals, Hill points out; from Aristotle, he quotes
the story of Philemon's analysis of Socrates' weaknesses, which the
latter confessed but claimed to have subdued. "By this a man may
conclude," Hill comments, "that our will to be subiect vnder the
gouernement of reason and grace : and that through these we may
bridle nature in vs, turning the prouocations of them vnto goodnesse."[36] Through a close study of this illustrated book, any reader
might become an adept in the judgment of character, the value
of which was clear, even without the commendations from Aristotle. In business and politics and in the schools,[37] physiognomy
might be extremely useful, Hill insists. The thickness of the eye-
brows, the brightness of the eyes, the carriage of the body, the
shape of the head, all indicated certain qualities worth recognition. For example, "The bearing of the heades of the shoulder
pointes verie farre out : doe denote foolishnesse to consist in that
creature : which maner, Aristotle reporteth vnto king Alexander :
to be a note of rygorousnesse, and vnfaythfulnesse to dwell in that
person."[38] For the Elizabethan, such works on physiognomy took

---

[36] Preface to the reader, edition of 1571.

[37] In a comment in the epistle addressed to the Duke of Norfolk, Hill anticipates the
application of psychological tests to school children : "Further, this Art procureth no
smal commoditie and profite to Schoolemaysters, in searching out & knowing the apt-
nesse and pregnancie of their scholers vnto learning. For if they deale like honest and
faythfull tutors, they ought to receyue none into their schoole to be instructed in learning and Arts, contrary to their capacitie, but rather followe the example of Apollonius
Alabandensis, that deuine and rare Schoolemayster, of whom Cicero writeth in his
booke De Oratore. This man (sayth he) although he customablye reade and taught
schollers for a stipende and gayne, yet would he suffer none vnder him, to lose their
tyme, if hee perceyued their wittes vnapt to attayne Oratorye : but rather wylled them
to leaue of and cease that study, and to follow that skill and Arte that he knew and saw
them inclyned vnto. Which example if our schoolemaysters and tutors would indeuor to
practyse and followe, we shoulde then enioy and haue many more excellent scholers, in all laudable studies & Artes, than at these daies are knowne to be."

[38] *Ibid.*, sig. X 8ᵛ.

the place of popular treatments of psychoanalysis, written to appeal to middle-class intelligences of the present time. Thomas Hill was "painful with his pen whiles he liued," as Jaggard said of him,[39] to make the manifold secrets of the sciences that he knew available to laymen. His books are typical of an enormous literature supplying middle-class readers with information similar to that purveyed by modern magazines that traffic in science and pseudo-science.

Not every compiler of treatises for the populace possessed Hill's versatility and range of interests. Few could come so near compassing all scientific knowledge, but innumerable writers turned out works expounding varied phases of natural philosophy.

As the consideration of the encyclopedic works has already made clear, few fields of scientific knowledge made a stronger appeal than the study of natural history. The element of wonder in the contemplation of the natural world was ingrained in the Elizabethan consciousness. The citizen who had seen wild Indians, new plants, and strange beasts brought home from overseas was not inclined to be skeptical about the marvels of nature. With the naïveté of the modern who believes that anything is possible through science, the Elizabethan believed that the world might somewhere harbor unicorns and basilisks. He had been brought up on the natural history of Pliny and the traditional lore of the bestiaries. The ancient writers were learned men ; and all things were possible in God's universe. Strange as Pliny's relations might be, it did not behoove a simple citizen to question such things.

Pliny was a familiar name on every tongue. Any unlatined reader might quickly digest the little epitome, translated from the French by I. A., *A Summarie of the Antiquities, and wonders of the worlde, abstracted out of the sixtene first bookes of the excellente Historiographer Plinie, wherein may be seene the wonderfull workes of God in his creatures* [1566], which had three editions before it was superseded in 1601 by Philemon Holland's enormous folio edition of the complete Pliny in English, which had a second edition in 1634. To assure the reader who might be troubled by the unusual descriptions in Pliny, I. A. prefaces his summary with a comforting assurance :

---

[39] Preface, *The Schoole Of Skil.*

For asmuch (gentle Reader) as the works of God are maruelous, not onelye in vs his creatures, whom he hath fashioned and formed like to his similitude, but also in others, as beastes, foules, fishes, trees, plantes, & such like, whose miraculous works, although vnto vs some things seeme uncredible : yet if we did consider ye omnipotencie of God, vnto whom nothing is vnpossible, doubtlesse we should not runne into so many daungers of sinne as we daily do.[40]

Thus it was made clear to the reader that it was a deed of piety to study the natural historians and contemplate the marvels of God's power.

Whatever the cause, the interest in natural history reached such a height that in the 1570's and 1580's writers of prose and poetry found in the habits of animals and the qualities of plants and stones material from which literary style might be enriched. How far the similitudes from unnatural natural history helped to stimulate a further inquiry into nature no one knows. Perhaps euphuistic style increased the desire of some people to read in the herbals about the persistence of the camomile or in the zoölogies about the weeping habits of the crocodile.

Zoölogical information reached its culmination for the early seventeenth century in the massive folios of Edward Topsell, in which were united zoölogy and morality to the complete satisfaction of Puritan readers. The first volume was *The Historie Of Foure-Footed Beastes* (1607).[41] Topsell was chaplain of the church of St. Botolph, Aldgate, and his profession made him eminently successful in compiling a zoölogy that would please morality-devouring Londoners. No opportunity is missed for making an application of zoölogy to the problems of human conduct. The harmony which beasts show among themselves, for example, is an argument against murder. After a long moral disquisition, Topsell comments :

---

[40] "The Translator to the Reader," edition of 1566.

[41] *The Historie Of Foure-Footed Beastes. Describing the true and liuely figure of euery Beast, with a discourse of their seuerall Names, Conditions, Kindes, Vertues (both naturall and medicinall) Countries of their breed, their loue and hate to Mankinde, and the wonderfull worke of God in their Creation, Preseruation, and Destruction. Necessary for all Diuines and Students, because the story of euery Beast is amplified with Narrations out of Scriptures, Fathers, Phylosophers, Physitians, and Poets: wherein are declared diuers Hyerogliphicks, Emblems, Epigrams, and other good Histories, Collected out of all the Volumes of Conradus Gesner, and all other Writers to this present day* (1607).

How great is the loue and faithfulnesse of Dogges, the meeknesse of Elephants, the modesty or shamefastnesse of the adulterous Lyonesse, the neatnesse and politure of the Cat and Peacocke, the iustice of the Bee which gathereth from all flowers that which serueth their turne, and yet destroyeth not the flower. The care of the Nightingale to make her voice pleasant, the chastity of the Turtle, the Canonicall voice and watchfulnesse of a Cocke, and to conclude the vtility of a Sheepe.[42]

The descriptions are detailed and bristle with classical authorities : Aristotle, Pliny, Aelianus, and many others. Twenty-one pages are devoted to the elephant, for "There is no creature among al the Beasts of the world which hath so great and ample demonstration of the power and wisedome of almighty God as the Elephant."[43] Not least instructive are the engravings that illustrate the text. Here one may actually see the images of such mythical creatures as the sphinx and the unicorn, as well as more plausible beasts like the ape and the elephant. So successful was *The Historie Of Foure-Footed Beastes* that Topsell followed it the next year with *The Historie Of Serpents. Or, The second Booke of liuing Creatures* (1608). The compiler points out that since Christ commanded men to be as wise as serpents, they deserve careful study. So eager had been unlearned readers to garner every morsel of truth in the first volume, that some had criticized Topsell for not translating Latin quotations—a fault which he corrected in the sequel.[44] Mixed with the descriptions of the lives and habits of serpents, including all crawling things from earthworms to dragons, are antidotes for snake-bite and allegorical lessons derived from the behavior of certain snakes. In 1658 an inclusive edition was published, with Thomas Moffett's description of insects to complete it.[45] Even from insects, Puritans extracted mo-

[42] Dedication to Dr. Richard Neile, dean of Westminster.

[43] P. 190.

[44] In the preface to the reader, Topsell apologizes for errors in printing his previous volume, and adds : "The second exception taken against the former Treatise, was the not englishing or translating of the Latine verses, which thing I purposed to haue done if I had not beene ouerhastened in the businesse ; for it had beene to the worke an ornament, and to the History a more ample declaration. This faulte I haue now amended in the setting forth of this second Booke of *Liuing Creatures*."

[45] *The History Of Four-footed Beasts And Serpents . . . Whereunto is now Added, The Theater of Insects; or Lesser living Creatures: As Bees, Flies, Caterpillars, Spiders, Worms, &c. A most Elaborate Work: By T. Muffet, Dr. of Physick. The whole Revised, Corrected, and*

rality and piety. One reason for studying these lesser creatures was the fact that John the Baptist had lived on locusts and the Saviour had once eaten a piece of honeycomb.

Fascinating as was the animal kingdom, the vegetable world attracted even more attention. As Thomas Hill asserted, plants were so closely linked to medicine and surgery that no Elizabethan could afford to neglect the study of so vital a subject as botany. The Elizabethan housewife, who included in her multifarious duties the compounding and prescribing of remedies, studied her herbal with a diligence accorded only to the Bible and printed sermons. Throughout the sixteenth and seventeenth centuries herbals were household books, more necessary in the family economy than even cookbooks. The Elizabethan herbals combined descriptions of plants with discussions of their cultivation and use, and included many proper recipes. Herbals, great and small, expensive and cheap, were on the market.[46] The man of wealth might procure a folio illustrated in colors, but always available were less pretentious books to fit the purse of the small tradesman and artisan. The *Grete Herball* and the treatise described as *Banckes' Herbal*, both constantly reprinted during the first half of the sixteenth century, were household books. The latter was sometimes called the *Little Herbal* to distinguish it from its bulkier rival. Both works, perpetuating the traditional lore found in the encyclopedias and in the manuscript herbals,[47] had as their chief purpose the explanation of the uses of common plants available in the physic garden. The herbal and the medical book often blended into one, as in the case of *Bulleins Bulwarke of defēce againste all Sicknes, Sornes, and woundes, that dooe daily assaulte mankind* (1562), by Dr. William Bullein. In an age when disease rode ruthlessly through the land and every man was often by necessity his own doctor, no further incentive was needed to stimulate interest in

---

Inlarged with the Addition of Two useful Physical Tables, by J. R. M.D. (1658). The dedication to the Marquis of Dorchester is signed John Rowland.

[46] Discussions of the sixteenth- and seventeenth-century herbals will be found in E. S. Rohde, *The Old English Herbals* (London, 1922), Agnes Arber, *Herbals, Their Origin and Evolution* (Cambridge, 1912), and R. W. T. Gunther, *Early British Botanists and Their Gardens* (Oxford, 1922).

[47] Rohde, *op. cit.*, pp. 55 ff.

these herbals, which were little more than compilations of folk-lore, traditional commentary on plants, and folk medicine.

Accurately scientific observation of plants, however, began with the studies of William Turner, a tanner's son, who became dean of Wells and also a learned physician. Turner's observations were embodied in *A new Herball* (1551), which showed a great advance over previous works on botany, though it repeated many of the traditional notions about plants.[48] The esteem in which the author was held as a physician gave great prestige to a work that not only advanced the scientific study of botany, but also helped in the further dissemination of popular knowledge of botanical lore. After him came a number of translators who searched out the best works of the Flemish, Swiss, and other foreign herbalists, and gave them an English dress.

For the benefit of plain citizens who could not read foreign languages and who might not be rich enough to afford the expert advice of physicians, Henry Lyte translated from the French *A Niewe Herball, Or Historie Of Plantes: . . . First set foorth in the Doutche or Almaigne tongue, by that learned D. Rembert Dodoens, Physition to the Emperour* (1578).[49] The volume, carefully illustrated, was immediately popular. By 1619 four editions had appeared. In 1606 William Ram based upon Lyte's translation his own epitome of plant and medicinal information, which he entitled *Rams little*

---

[48] *Ibid.*, pp. 75 ff.

[49] In the preface to the reader, Lyte comments : "Seing then yt my translation shall make this good & profitable historie (which hitherto hath lien hid from many of my Countriemen, vnder the vayle of an vnknowen language) familiar and knowen vnto them : and if it be good (as no good man wil denie) to enlarge a good thing, and to make many partakers thereof : then can there not lacke iust cause to be alleaged of this my doyng : neither thinke I, that any will mislike or repine thereat, except such, as either enuie the Weale of others whom they accompt simpler then them selues, and therfore recken vnworthy to be in their owne language made partakers therof : or els are so studious of their owne priuate gaine, that they feare, least by this meanes some parte therof may be lessened : whyles others vnderstanding the nature and vertues of Plantes and herbes, shalbe the lesse beholding to their scrupulous skill. But the good and vertuous Phisition, whose purpose is rather the health of many, then the wealth of him selfe, will not (I hope) mislike this my enterprise, whiche to this purpose specially tendeth, that euen the meanest of my Countriemen (whose skill is not so profounde that they can fetche this knowledge out of strange tongues, nor their habilitie so wealthy, as to entertaine a learned Phisition) may yet in time of their necessitie, haue some helpes in their owne, or their neighbours fieldes and gardens at home."

Dodoen. A briefe Epitome of the New Herbal, or History of Plants.[50] Ram's work is chiefly a collection of recipes. Like Lyte before him, his avowed purpose is to make available to the ordinary citizen the practical information so eagerly sought. Even Lyte's work, for all his good intentions, had apparently been too expensive for some purses, and Ram had set out to supply something cheaper,

so as where the great booke at large is not to be had but at a great price, which cannot be procured by the poorer sort, my endevor herein hath bin chiefly to make the benefit of so good, necessary and profitable a worke to be brought within the reach and compasse as well of you my poore countrymen and women whose lives, healths, ease and welfare is to be regarded with the rest, at a smaller price than the great volume is.[51]

Though Ram's epitome was less costly, the reading public preferred Lyte's translation, which gave more botany along with its remedies and recipes. Only one edition of Ram's book seems to have been published.

Expensive as the large herbals were, the interest of the public was such that many a citizen who would have begrudged a few pence for any lesser book, parted with the price of one of the huge illustrated folios which became popular in the late years of the sixteenth century. John Gerard, practical gardener and botanist, produced the most massive botanical work in English up to his time, in *The Herball Or Generall Historie of Plantes* (1597), a folio containing 1,392 pages of text and illustrations.[52] Even this was not sufficiently inclusive, and Thomas Johnson brought out a new edition in 1633, "Very much Enlarged and Amended." The enlargements brought the volume to 1,631 pages. Still another edition was published in 1636. These great volumes did not hold the botanical stage alone, for they had rivals in both foreign and native works. From Crispin de Passe was translated *A Garden Of*

---

[50] Title quoted from Rohde, *op. cit.*, p. 212. I have not examined this herbal at first hand.

[51] *Ibid.*, pp. 96-97. Ram's words are taken from his preface to "my poore and loving countrymen."

[52] For an account of Gerard's place in English botanical history, see Rohde, *op. cit.*, pp. 98 ff.

Flowers (1615),[53] a work resplendent in gorgeously colored plates showing the plants as they appeared in the natural state. A little later, John Parkinson, apothecary and the King's herbalist, compiled two books of importance in the study of botany. The first was *Paradisi In Sole Paradisus Terrestris* (1629).[54] Though this purports to be merely a practical treatise on the growing of plants, its 612 folio pages are filled with information of a scientific as well as a useful nature, and Parkinson displays the interest that was to culminate in the bulkiest of all the herbals, the *Theatrum Botanicum: The Theater Of Plants* (1640),[55] whose 1,755 pages provided a complete compendium of botanical information known to that day. From the best European botanists Parkinson gleaned the material that he laboriously assimilated into the book that was to rival Gerard's *Herbal* as expanded by Johnson.[56] Somewhat sarcastic is Parkinson in comparing his own research with "Master Iohnsons agility"[57] in the preparation of herbals. Though the expense of such works must have seemed excessive to the purchasers, the number of herbals in folio indicates that the demand was great. The price evidently impressed some of the buyers, for the original owner of the Huntington Library copy of Johnson's 1633 edition of Gerard's *Herbal* carefully noted on a flyleaf that he had paid to Mims, the bookseller in Little Britain, two pounds, eight shillings for the volume on September 1, 1654.[58] Compila-

---

[53] *A Garden Of Flowers, Wherein Very Lively Is Contained A True And Perfect Discription Of Al The Flowers Contained In These Foure Followinge Bookes. . . . Faithfully And Truely Translated Out Of The Netherlandish originall into English for the common benifite of those that vnderstand no other languages, and also for the benifite of others newly printed both in the Latine and French tongues all at the Charges of the Author* (Utrecht, 1615).

[54] *Paradisi In Sole Paradisus Terrestris. or A Garden of all sorts of pleasant flowers which our English ayre will permitt to be noursed vp: with A Kitchen garden of all manner of herbes, rootes, & fruites, for meate or sause vsed with vs, and An Orchard of all sorte of fruitbearing Trees and shrubbes fit for our Land together With the right orderinge planting & preseruing of them, and their vses & vertues* (1629).

[55] *Theatrum Botanicum: The Theater Of Plants. Or, An Herball Of A Large Extent . . . Shewing withall the many errors, differences, and oversights of sundry Authors that have formerly written of them . . . Published by the Kings Maiestyes especiall priviledge* (1640).

[56] Rohde, *op. cit.*, pp. 142 ff.

[57] Preface to *Theatrum Botanicum*.

[58] Press mark, 59,936. The Huntington Library copy of Parkinson's *Paradisi In Sole* [press mark, 14,065] bears on a flyleaf, in what looks like a seventeenth-century hand, "Pretium 20 s."

tions of this sort were essential for the doctor and apothecary, and were regarded as important to health and happiness by every citizen able to buy them.

One of the boasts which Parkinson made for his *Theatrum Botanicum* was that it described many plants found in the New World. To America Englishmen looked not only for riches but for rare new herbs of untold power in the cure of disease. Tobacco was first looked upon as a boon to the medical profession, and even the potato was believed to have the qualities of a drug.[59] Much space was devoted by travelers to descriptions of plant life in the recently discovered regions, and Hakluyt[60] and Purchas printed a great deal of botanical information. It remained for an English merchant, John Frampton, to translate from the Spanish of Nicholas Monardes the standard work of the sixteenth century on the medicinal plants of America, which he published in 1577 as *Joyfull Newes Out Of The Newe Founde Worlde*.[61] So popular was Frampton's translation that it had three editions and a separate issue by 1596.[62] The edition of 1580 added three more books,

---

[59] The potato was regarded as an aphrodisiac, and allusions to this quality are a commonplace in Elizabethan literature.

[60] Museums of rare plants and animals, collected by interested students of natural history, are mentioned by Hakluyt in the preface to the *Principall Navigations* (1589) : "And whereas in the course of this history often mention is made of many beastes, birds, fishes, serpents, plants, fruits, hearbes, rootes, apparell, armour, boates, and such other rare and strange curiosities, which wise men take great pleasure to reade of, but much more contentment to see : herein I my selfe to my singuler delight have bene as it were ravished in beholding all the premisses gathered together with no small cost, and preserved with no litle diligence, in the excellent Cabinets of my very worshipfull and learned friends M. Richard Garthe, one of the Clearkes of the pettie Bags, and M. William Cope Gentleman Ussier to the right Honourable and most prudent Counseller (the Seneca of our common wealth,) the Lord Burleigh, high Treasourer of England."—MacLehose edition (Glasgow, 1903), I, xxx. A little later John Tradescant, the botanist, made a collection, at Lambeth, which became known as Tradescant's ark.

[61] *Joyfull Newes Out Of The Newe Founde Worlde Wherein Is Declared The Rare And Singuler Vertues Of Diverse And Sundrie Hearbes, Trees, Oyles, Plantes, And Stones, With Their Aplications, Aswell For Phisicke as Chirurgerie, The Saied Beyng Well Applied Bryngeth Suche Present Remedie For All Deseases, As Maie Seme Altogether Incredible: Notwithstandyng By Practize Founde Out, To Bee True: Also The Portrature Of The Saied Hearbes, Very Aptly Discribed* (1577). Reprinted, 2 vols., with an introduction by Stephen Gaselee, in The Tudor Translations (London, 1925).

[62] Apparently herbs and drugs from the New World were revolutionizing the European pharmacopoeia. Frampton in the dedication to Edward Dyer comments : "And

which treated of the virtues of the bezoar stone. Frampton's translation was published in quarto and was within the reach of most readers. It must have been read not only by those bent on finding out new physic but by many others who were merely curious about the flora—and to some extent, the fauna—of the New World. In this book one might learn of the remarkable qualities of tobacco, sassafras, wild lettuce, and countless other plants, including a "Tree That Doth Showe If One Shall Live Or Die."[63] Clearly this was a useful work for both doctor and layman.

To an age that looked upon the Bible as the ultimate explanation of the secrets of life, every aid to a better understanding of the sacred writings was a boon. Biblical botany might have been an obscure field of speculation but for the industry of Thomas Newton, who translated from the Latin of Levinus Lemnius *An Herbal For The Bible. Containing A Plaine And Familiar Exposition of such Similitudes, Parables, and Metaphors, both in the olde Testament and the Newe, as are borrowed and taken from Herbs, Plants, Trees, Fruits and Simples, by obseruation of their Vertues, qualities, natures, properties, operations, and effects* (1587). Beginning with a learned discussion of the mandrake, desired by Rachel of her sister Leah, the treatise proceeds in leisurely and pleasant fashion to a concluding chapter discussing the metaphors and similes,

since the afore saied Medicines mentioned in the same worke of Doctour Monardes, are now by Marchauntes and others, brought out of the West Indias into Spaine, and from Spain hether into Englande, by suche as dooeth daiely trafficke thether, and that the excellencie of these Hearbes, Trees, Oyles, Plantes, and stones, etc. hath been knowen to bee so precious a remedie for all maner of deseases, and hurtes, that maie happe unto Man, Woman, or Childe, thet have fledde verie muche from the olde order and maner of Phisicke, which was used before, that this was knowen, as thynges not so healthfull as these are, and by greate experience thereof in Spaine, and other Countries, throughly and effectuously proved, to dooe the effectes which is contained in this booke."—*Tudor Translations* reprint, I, 4-5.

Nationalistic zeal seems to have prompted Timothy Bright to publish *A Treatise: wherein is declared the sufficiencie of English Medicines, for cure of all diseases, cured with Medicine* (1580). (Copy in the Huntington Library.) A new edition was brought out in 1615, "Whereunto is added a collection of Medicines growing (for the most part) within our English Climat, approoued and experimented against the Iaundise, Dropsie, Stone, Falling-sicknesse, Pestilence." The idea that disease and remedy are found together was an old one.

[63] *Ibid.*, II, 21.

from the vegetable world, used by the prophets. The information is both practical and curious. We learn that turpentine is a remedy useful in healing wounds, that Aaron's rod was an almond sprig, that cloths dipped in mulberry juice infuriated King Antiochus' elephants—for "Elephants cannot abide the sight of red colour"—[64] that no venomous thing will approach a plane tree—in short, an endless variety of matter discovered in the study of the Scriptures. For the ordinary citizen of Elizabethan England, the wonders of the natural world were an adjunct of religious contemplation. For him, the warfare of science and religion would have been unthinkable.

As the necessity of knowing the curative powers of herbs prompted a widespread interest in botany, so the dictates of health likewise made it the duty of every literate man to familiarize himself with works on medicine and allied subjects. Medicine had not yet become so restricted a mystery that the average man could not understand and apply its theories, and although the minutiae of the science were understood best by the initiate, a layman might even write medical treatises in the interest of public health. Few households were without one or two medical books which answered the requirements of ordinary ailments; in time of plague, specific remedies were sometimes printed and circulated in London by order of the authorities. Most of the popular works expounded age-old theories, and even though medical theory made great strides in the sixteenth and seventeenth centuries, ordinary practice still followed traditional methods established by long usage.[65] The average citizen contemporary with William Harvey died blissfully ignorant of the new theory of the circulation of the blood, but he did have a fair familiarity with Galen's doctrine of the four humors, the aphorisms of Hippocrates, and the remedies of the Arabian physicians. Popular medicine for the Elizabethans meant Greek and Arabian medicine tinctured with medieval folk superstitions and beliefs. The encompassing of medical knowl-

---

[64] P. 181.

[65] For the development of medical theory and practice, see Sir William Osler, *The Evolution of Modern Medicine* (New Haven, 1923) ; Charles Greene Cumston, *An Introduction to the History of Medicine* (New York, 1926) ; Fielding H. Garrison, *An Introduction to the History of Medicine* (4th ed., Philadelphia and London, 1929) ; Charles Singer, *A Short History of Medicine* (Oxford, 1928).

edge, such as it had become, was limited for the average citizen only by his diligence, for he had at hand an extensive literature designed to lay open for him the secrets of health.

The general reader's knowledge of anatomy and physiology was, of course, vague, as indeed was the knowledge of most physicians. Physiological information often came from such unreliable sources as *The Problems of Aristotle*, a question-and-answer book erroneously attributed to the Greek philosopher and first published in Latin in 1583. The Widow Orwin, scenting a book that would appeal to the multitude, published an English translation in 1595, and the book has been constantly in print ever since.[66] But the desire for knowledge about the composition and functions of the body sometimes demanded more accurate information than was contained in books of this type, or even in the treatises on medicine and health, which often gave brief anatomical and physiological descriptions. The most widely known work on anatomy was Thomas Vicary's *A profitable Treatise of the Anatomie of mans body* first printed in 1548 and "revived" in 1577, the date of the earliest extant edition. Subsequent editions bore the promising title of *The Englishemans Treasure, Or Treasor For Englishmen: With the True Anatomye of Mans Body*.[67] This thin little quarto, though it provided only scanty and often inaccurate descriptions of the parts of the body, served laymen and all but a few exceptional physicians until the middle of the seventeenth century. Interest in the rudiments of physiology, however, was widespread and manifested itself occasionally even in the poets, Spenser's allegory of the body being the best known poetical treatment of the subject, though Phineas Fletcher's *Purple Island* (1633) was noted in its time. Another example of the poetical description of the body is Robert Vaughan's *The Little World. Or, A Liuely Description of all the partes and properties of Man. For Inuention Wittie, for Iudgement Learned, and for Practise Necessarie* (1612).[68] Vaughan, who describes himself as a bachelor of divinity, is soon led into theology,

---

[66] *See* Sir D'Arcy Power, *The Foundations of Medical History* (Baltimore, 1931), p. 150. So late as 1930, according to this authority, *The Problems of Aristotle* was reprinted and circulated as a sex book.

[67] This title is quoted from the edition of 1586. The last edition listed in the *Short Title Catalogue*, that of 1633, is described as "Now eighthly augmented."

[68] Title quoted from the copy in the Huntington Library.

however, and ends his description with an account of the body's iniquities.

The beliefs of folk medicine still prevailed in obstetrics, though the doubtful benefits of professional advice were available in a treatise compiled in Germany about 1513 by Eucharius Röslin[69] and translated into English in 1540 by R. Jonas as *The byrth of Mankynde*. Thomas Raynald in 1545 brought out a fuller edition as *The Birth Of Man-Kinde; Otherwise Named, The Womans Booke*,[70] which was often reprinted until 1634 and throughout the period was a standard work on obstetrics and ailments peculiar to women. It was designed for midwives and non-professional readers rather than for physicians.

One of the accepted treatises of popular medicine in the sixteenth century was Sir Thomas Elyot's *The Castel Of Helthe*.[71] This work, first published in 1534, was many times reprinted until 1610, the date of the last edition recorded in the *Short Title Catalogue*, which lists fifteen extant editions. Criticized by physicians for having invaded their field by writing on medicine, Elyot in the edition of 1541 wrote a prefatory defense to prove his own proficiency. Incidentally, it summarizes admirably the sources of the medical knowledge utilized by him and his contemporaries :

. . . whan I wrote fyrste this boke, I was not all ignorante in phisycke. fore before that I was .xx. yeres olde, a worshipfull phisition, and one of the moste renoumed at that tyme in England, perceyuyng me by nature inclined to knowledge, rad vnto me the workes of Galene of temperamentes, natural faculties, the Introduction of Iohãnicius, with some of ye Aphorismes of Hippocrates. And afterwarde by mine owne study, I radde ouer in order the more parte of the warkes of Hippocrates, Galen, Oribasius, Paulus Celius, Alexander Trallianus, Celsus, Plinius ye one and the other, with Dioscorydes. Nor I dyd ommit to reade the longe Canones of Auicena, ye Commentaries of Auerrois, ye practisis of Isake, Halyabbas, Rasys, Mesue, and also of the more part of them which were their aggregatours and folowers. And all thoughe

---

[69] Garrison, *op. cit.*, p. 198.

[70] Title quoted from the edition of 1634.

[71] *The Castel Of Helthe. Gathered, and made by syr Thomas Elyot knight, out of the chief authors of Phisyke, whereby euery man may knowe the state of his owne body, the preseruation of helthe, and how to instruct well his phisition in sicknes, that he be not deceyued.* Title quoted from the edition of 1539.

I haue neuer ben at Mōtpellier, Padua, nor Salern, yet haue I foūd some thynge in phisycke, whereby I haue taken no litle profyte concernynge myne owne helthe.

For the good of the commonwealth, Elyot presents in plain English a statement of the theory and practice of medicine. From a general account of physiological principles according to Galen, including such fundamentals as a discussion of the humors, Elyot proceeds to observations on diet, hygiene, and simple pathology, with recommended remedies. In plan, purpose, and presentation the treatise is sensible and enlightened, according to the standards of the age, and deserved the popular reputation which it had for nearly a century. Many books written by doctors showed far less professional learning.

Popular medical knowledge had profited even earlier than Elyot's treatise by the translation of the famous *Regimen sanitatis Salerni*, which Thomas Paynell rendered into English in 1528. The medical school at Salerno, near Naples, had been influential since the eleventh century, and the *Regimen*, a collection of verse precepts on diet and hygiene, with additional commentary in prose, all bearing the authority of the great school, circulated for centuries throughout Europe.[72] Paynell's prose translation, which reappeared at intervals until 1634, was prepared for the benefit of the citizenry, or, as he says, "for the welthe of vnlerned persones."[73] Its suggestions are sensible and it became a standard text for household medicine. In 1607 Sir John Harington, who had already labored in the cause of health with a ribald treatise on sanitation, translated the *Regimen* into verse with the title of *The Englishmans Doctor. Or, The Schoole of Salerne. Or, Physicall Obseruations for the perfect Preseruing of the body of Man in continuall health*, which required five editions by 1624 to meet the demand. As in every other field of knowledge, Tudor and Stuart Englishmen relished their medical learning in aphoristic form. The *Regimen* happily suited their tastes and helped, as they believed, their health.

---

[72] Garrison, *op. cit.*, p. 150 : "It passed through some 240 separate editions, including Irish, Bohemian, Provençal, and Hebrew."

[73] Dedication to the Earl of Oxford, quoted from the edition of 1530 in the Huntington Library.

Innumerable other medical works were printed for non-professional readers, but few made any marked advance over Elyot's treatise or the *Regimen*. The most popular books gave a general description of man's physical make-up, based on Galen, and proceeded from generalities to discuss definite ailments and their cures. Some were merely compilations of remedies. Some dealt with specific maladies, like the plague,[74] which concerned everyone. Some taught the relation of the stars to health. A few books, frequently reprinted, were prepared to serve as the "poor man's doctor" and were designed to make the individual his own physician. Though practically everyone was vitally interested in treatises on health, the advances in medical science made by men like Vesalius and Harvey[75] did not affect the popular consciousness. The public continued to believe old theories and to consume old remedies, augmented, it is true, by herbs from the New World and chemicals developed by Paracelsus and his successors, but popular medicine remained essentially empirical. Folk medicine kept a strong hold on medical practice, both professional and amateur.

An example of the mixture of astrology, surgery, pharmacy, and folk beliefs in a single treatise that enjoyed a long popularity is found in Thomas Moulton's little book entitled *This is the Myrrour or Glass of Healthe*,[76] which had at least fourteen printings between about 1539 and 1580. Not only to surgeons and physicians was the book useful, but to all men, for therein one might "know when it is good to begyn manye dyuers thinges & when it is not good."[77] In addition to providing astrological information, it gives remedies for ailments and injuries likely to befall one.

---

[74] Many of the medical books on the plague are cited by F. P. Wilson, *The Plague in Shakespeare's London* (Oxford, 1927), *passim*.

[75] It is traditionally stated, indeed, that Harvey's practice fell off immediately after the publication of his discovery of the circulation of the blood. Cf. Garrison, *op. cit.*, p. 249.

[76] *This is the Myrrour or Glass of Healthe Necessary and nedefull for euery person to loke in, that will kepe theyr bodye from the syckenesse of the Pestylence, and it sheweth howe the Planettes do reygne in euery houre of the day and night, with the natures and exposicions of the xii. sygnes, deuyded by the .xii. Monethes of the yeare, and shewed the Remedyes for dyuers Infyrmyties and diseases that hurtethe the bodye of Man.* Title quoted from the edition of 1565(?) in the Huntington Library.

[77] Quoted from the "Prologue" which introduces the treatise.

Most of the extant copies are dogeared, dirty, and marked with the indications of long use.

Some households, of course, depended on almanacs for their astrological guidance in medicine, but special treatises were available for those who wanted them. In 1598 a new edition of an astrological treatise by Claudius Dariot was published, with a supplement on medicine, as *A Briefe and most easie Introduction to the Astrologicall Iudgement of the Starres*.[78] Equipped with the tables and diagrams that this work provided, any person might treat himself according to the most careful dictates of astrology, which was accepted by many of the foremost physicians of the time as important in all concerns of disease and health.

A type of popular treatise on health, savoring more of good sense, was supplied by Thomas Cogan in *The Haven Of Health* (1584), which seems to have had at least six separate printings by 1636.[79] Basing his work on Hippocrates, Cogan set forth a rationale of living, prepared, as he states, for the guidance of students, but apparently so useful that it was widely read. Cogan gives a professional dress to a doctrine reflected in much Renaissance literature, philosophic and otherwise—the philosophy of temperance. In a readable book he describes a regimen of living based on temperateness in all things. Like many of his contemporaries he still looked upon Elyot's *Castle of Health* and the *Schola Salerni* as sources of the highest wisdom, where health was concerned.[80]

---

[78] *A Briefe and most easie Introduction to the Astrologicall Iudgement of the Starres. . . . Also hereunto is added a briefe Treatise of Mathematicall Phisicke, entreating very exactly and compendiously of the Natures and Qualities of all diseases incident to humane bodies by the naturall Influences of the Coelestiall motions. Neuer before handled in this our natiue language. Written by the sayd G. C. practicioner in Phisicke.*

[79] *The Haven Of Health: Chiefely gathered for the comfort of Students, and consequently of all those that haue a care of their health, amplified vpon fiue words of Hippocrates, written Epid. 6. Labor, Cibus, Potio, Somnus, Venus* (1584). The sixth edition listed by the *Short Title Catalogue* is self-described as the "fourth."

[80] In the preface to the reader, edition of 1584, Cogan states: "Yet one thing I desire of all them that shall reade this booke: If they finde whole sentences taken out of Maister *Eliote* his Castle of Health, or out of *Schola Salerni*, or anie other author whatsoeuer, that they will not condemne me of vaine glorie, by the olde Prouerbe (*Caluus Comatus*) as if I meant to set foorth for mine owne workes that which other men haue deuised, for I confesse that I haue taken *Verbatim* out of others where it serued for my purpose, and especiallie out of *Schola Salerni:* but I haue so enterlaced it with mine

To serve the needs of people who could not afford to employ expensive physicians was the purpose of one A. T., who prepared *A Rich Store-house or Treasury for the Diseased* (1596), which had an edition in 1630 "Now seventhly augmented." In dedicating the treatise to Thomas Skinner, the lord mayor, Ralph Blower, the printer, recommends the book as valuable to "poore peoples profit and good, both in health and wealth."[81] Following an introductory section of rules for physic and surgery, with advice on such subjects as bloodletting, the book presents the usual variety of remedies and treatments for ailments.

The path of the popularizer of medicine, then as now, was beset with the thorns of professional jealousy. Yet in spite of the hostility of physicians, medical books for laymen, much nearer the best professional knowledge of the day than some such works of the present time, were published in large numbers. One of the fullest and most widely read of these compilations was Philip Barrough's *The Method Of Phisick*,[82] an eighth edition of which was published in 1639. Barrough realized that physicians would attack him for discovering the mysteries of medicine for every citizen to read in English, and in the preface he anticipates their criticism :

---

owne, that (as I thinke) it may bee the better perceiued. And therefore seeing all my trauaile tendeth to common commoditie, I trust euerie man will interprete all to the best."

[81] *A Rich Store-house or Treasury for the Diseased. Wherein, are many approued Medicines for diuers and sundry Diseases, which haue been long hidden, and not come to light before this time. Now set foorth for the great benefit and comfort of the poorer sort of people that are not of abillitie to go to the Physitions* (1596).

Adequate medical attention for the poorer citizens was a problem in the sixteenth century. Cf. Garrison, *op. cit.*, p. 239 : "In 1542-3, on account of the greed of surgeons 'minding their own lucres,' and disdaining to help the poor, Acts 34 and 35, Henry VIII, cap. 8, were enacted, permitting common persons having knowledge of herbal and folk-medicine to minister to the indigent, thus affording a loophole for unqualified practitioners, like the *Kurierfreiheit* of modern Germany."

[82] *The Method Of Phisick, Containing The Causes, Signes, And Cures Of Inward Diseases In Mans Body From the Head To The Foote. Whereunto is added, the forme and rule of making remedies and medicines, which our Physitions commonly vse at this day, with the proportion, quantitie, and names of each medicine.* Title quoted from the third edition of 1596 in the Huntington Library. The first edition was published in 1583. Although the edition of 1639 was described as the eighth, the *Short Title Catalogue* records nine extant editions.

. . . I haue (good Reader) for thy benefit, collected out of sundry Authors, as it were a breuiary or abridgement of physick, & together with those deductions, I haue interlaced experiments of mine own, which by long vse & practise I haue obserued to be true. Throughout the whole booke I haue bin more curious in prescribing the sundrie curations & waies to helpe the diseases, then in explaning the nature of them : my reason was, because if my books should come to the hands of the vnlearned a litle would suffice (the former being more necessarie.) Againe I knew, that the learned would not be contented or satisfied with it, though it had bene neuer so great : and yet I haue not omitted any necessarie signe, that the disease may appeare easily to any capable braine. I shall seeme boldly to haue aduentured the edition of this labour, seeing that I shall runne into the babble of our countrey Physitions, who thinke their Arte to be discredited, when it is published in a base tongue, and againe, are loth to haue the secrets of their science reuealed to euerie man. Indeed I know that vnder some colour they may obiect somwhat, but yet they may vnderstand, that I haue followed the example of many learned Phisitions both of our Englishmen and other countrymen also, who published their practises in their mother tong, . . .   [Sig. A 7.]

Since Barrough described the symptoms of diseases, outlined the procedure in treatment, and prescribed remedies, his treatise was easily followed by the amateur, and was long a standard handbook for the medicining of the sick. It was part of the equipment which the Virginia and New England colonists brought with them to the New World, and its remedies passed into the traditional pharmocopoeia of early America.[83]

Guides to good health had a necessary place among the supplies deemed essential for the colonists sent out by the London companies. It was for the benefit of the Newfoundland settlers[84] that William Vaughan compiled *Directions for Health, both Naturall and*

---

[83] Edward Eggleston, *The Transit of Civilization from England to America in the Seventeenth Century* (New York, 1901), pp. 54, 169.

[84] Dedication to Sir Francis Bacon in the fifth edition (1617): ". . . so it will please you likewise to illustrate with your Countenance the rising Fortunes of our Plantation in Newfound-land, whereby Iustice may shine in that incompassed Climate, and consequently our Nauigation increase by the industry of our Merchants, for whose sakes partly, I haue reuiewed these my former labours, hoping with the fauour of God, sometime or other in person there to partake of their Westerne Ayre."

Artificiall (1600),[85] a treatise which proved so popular that by 1633 it had gone through seven editions. Using a question-and-answer method, Vaughan gives injunctions for proper diet, exercise, and medication. He even includes a section on mental hygiene, beginning with the explanation of the four humors and ending with a revelation of the passions of the soul. The relation of the body to the soul, which included all that we would describe as the mind, was the object of Vaughan's effort in another curious little book, *The Newlanders Cure* (1630), in which he urged strict adherence to temperance in diet and anticipated the vegetarians in his warning against too much meat.

The state of the mind was a subject of almost as much interest to the ordinary Elizabethan as the welfare of the body. In addition to material in the encyclopedias and medical books on the humors and temperament that influenced the passions of the soul and hence controlled the mental state, several works definitely devoted to studies of mental conditions enjoyed widespread popularity. The Elizabethan citizen talked as glibly in the jargon of the psychology of his time as does the modern man who alludes to complexes and neuroses without understanding clearly what the terms mean. Elizabethan literature is filled with allusions to the psychological beliefs of the day. Shakespeare enriched his character studies and Jonson enlivened his satires with motivations and situations growing out of the application of contemporary theoretical psychology.[86] Physicians explained mental derangements in the terminology of the physiological psychology which had been made popular in the encyclopedias of Bartholomew and La Primaudaye. Further dissemination of knowledge about the mind came in Timothy Bright's learned dissertation on abnormal

---

[85] *Directions for Health, both Naturall and Artificiall: Approued and deriued from the best Physitians, as well moderne as auncient. Teaching how euery Man should keepe his body and minde in health: and sicke, how hee may safely restore it himselfe.* Title quoted from the fifth edition, 1617.

[86] For the reflection of psychological theory in Shakespeare, see Campbell, *op. cit.*, *passim*, and Anderson, *op. cit.*, *passim.* An unpublished dissertation by Harry K. Russell, "Certain Doctrines of Natural and Moral Philosophy as an Approach to the Study of Elizabethan Drama; with an Appendix Containing Illustrative Material from the Plays of Ben Jonson" (University of North Carolina, 1931), throws further light on the dramatists' use of theoretical psychology.

psychology, *A Treatise Of Melancholie* (1586),[87] a work which was drawn upon by Robert Burton in his more famous *Anatomy Of Melancholy* (1621). Bright's book had two editions in the first year of its publication and was reprinted in 1613. Burton's *Anatomy* was five times printed by 1638. The application of psychology to the ordinary concerns of life was one of the aims of Thomas Wright in *The Passions of the Minde* (1601), which had five editions by 1628. The Latin races, Wright observes,[88] have a reputation for shrewdness and policy, whereas Englishmen often seem naïve and unsophisticated. To protect his countrymen against the wiles of the nimbler-witted Italians and French, Wright offers his book as an aid in analyzing the conduct of other men.

Wherefore I thought good to trie if a little direction would helpe our contrimen to counterpose their natiue warinesse, and open the way not to become crafty and deceitfull, which is, vitious, but how to discouer other mens passions, and how to behaue our selues when such affections extraordinarily possesse vs, the which is the chiefest poynt of prudence, and fittest meane to attaine vnto religious, ciuill, and gentlemanlike conuersation, which is vertuous. Whereunto especially this discourse of Affections aymeth, albeit for more complete doctrine I haue handled (almost) all those questions, which concerne the Passions in generall.

But for all this, I would not haue any man to thinke that I am of opinion, that all Italians and Spaniards go beyond all Englishmen in subtiltie and warinesse, for I haue found diuers of our Nation, whom I beleeue, neither Italian, nor Spaniard could ouer-reach, in what negotiation soeuer: but only I meane that for the most part, those Nations surpasse ours in certaine politique craftinesse, the which Nature first bred in them, Education perfited, Vertue amendeth, and Art discouereth; the which I haue endeuoured first of all (as I thinke) to drawe into forme and method, according to the principles of Sciences, hoping that some other will heereby take occasion, either to perfite mine, or to attempt a better; my desire is, the good of my Country, the effect, euery mans prudent carriage, the last end, the glorie of God, . . .

---

[87] *A Treatise Of Melancholie. Containing The Causes thereof, & reasons of the strange effects it worketh in our minds and bodies: with the phisicke cure, and spirituall consolation for such as haue thereto adioyned an afflicted conscience* (1586).

[88] Preface, edition of 1601.

From the physical bases of the passions, and the interaction of the humors and the passions, Wright passes on to such practical problems as "How the Passions may be well directed and made profitable,"[89] and at length comes to matters of conduct where the reader might learn to put into practice the theories of psychology in which he has been instructed.[90]

A desire to enlighten the multitude prompted Thomas Walkington to publish *The Optick Glasse of Humors* (1607),[91] three times printed by 1638. Walkington's aim is to ground the reader in the physical bases of mental conditions by explaining in much detail the theory of humors. Significantly his opening chapter is headed "Of Selfe knowledge" and stresses the importance of introspective examination.

I wish therefore in conclusion the meanest, if possible, to haue an insight into their bodily estate (as chiefly they ought of the soule) whereby they may shun such things as any waies may bee offensiue to the good of that estate, and may so consequently (being vexed with none, no not the least maladie) be more fit not onely to liue, but to liue well: . . .[92]

Practical utility was one of the appeals made by R. C.'s translation of Huarte's *Examen de Ingenios. The Examination of mens Wits* (1594),[93] which soon went through four editions. Like other con-

---

[89] *Ibid.*, p. 27.

[90] Cf. *ibid.*, pp. 216 ff., the discussion of praise and flattery, in which Wright gives some sage advice on how to praise judiciously without committing oneself too far: "Wherefore it were wisedome to vse superlatiues very rarely, and say, such a man is vertuous, but not most vertuous. So, therefore praise goodmen, that thou reserue a caueat for their errours. Besides, commonly prowd men can not abide their equalls should much be commended, for the praise of the one obscureth the glorie of the other; and as I haue obserued by experience, they eyther openly, or secretly will seeke to disgrace him and discouer some defects, the which impeacheth more his credite than your commendation aduaunceth his reputation, because that men bee more prone to conceiue ill, than good of others, . . ."

[91] *The Optic Glasse of Humors. Or The touchstone of a golden temperature, or the Philosophers stone to make a golden temper, Wherein the foure complections Sanguine, Cholericke, Phlegmaticke, Melancholicke are succinctly painted forth, and their externall intimates laide open to the purblinde eye of ignorance it selfe, by which euery one may iudge, of what complection he is, and answerably learne what is most sutable to his nature* (1607).

[92] Edition of 1607, p. 17.

[93] *Examen de Ingenios. The Examination of mens Wits. In which, by discouering the varietie of natures, is shewed for what profession each one is apt, and how far he shall profit therein* (1594).

temporary works on physiological psychology, this treatise not only discusses the physical processes which determine the state of the wits, but it goes further and applies its theories to such practical matters as vocational guidance. More than this, it even provides directions for begetting intelligent children. Modern utilitarian psychology dares not promise so much.

Learned like Huarte's work was Pierre Charron's *Of Wisdome*, translated by Sampson Lennard and published about 1612 with a dedication to Prince Henry; again like its Spanish contemporary, this French work, which combined psychology and ethics, was not confined exclusively to academic readers. The demand for Lennard's translation was sufficient to warrant three editions within a year, with later editions in 1630 and 1640. Emphasizing the dictum, "Know thy self," Charron offered a guide to man's understanding of his mental and moral states. From Charron the student of human conduct might learn of the relation of the body to the mind and soul, the motives stimulating human conduct, the place of the passions in human behavior and the means of controlling them—in short, the physical and mental bases of all ethics. It is a readable treatise which furnished much incidental learning and material for contemplation. Many a London citizen, chained to his duties in the city, must have read wistfully Charron's praise of the virtues of the country over the city, in the elevation of the human spirit:

In the fields the spirit is more free and to it selfe : in Cities, the persons, the affaires, both their owne and other mens, the contentions, visitations, discourses, entertainments, how much time doe they steale from vs? . . . How many troubles bring they with them, auocations, allurements to wickednesses? Cities are prisons to the spirits of men, no otherwise than cages to birds and beasts. This celestiall fire that is in vs, will not be shut vp, it loueth the aire, the fields ; and therefore *Columella* saith, that the country-life is the cousen of wisdome, . . . Againe, the country life is more neat, innocent and simple ; In cities vices are hid in the rout, and are not perceiued, they passe and insinuate themselues pell-mell, the vse, the aspect, the encounter so frequent and contagious, is the cause. As for pleasure and health, the whole heauens lie open to the view, the sun, the aire, the waters, and all the elements are free, exposed and open in all parts, alwayes sustaining vs, the earth discouereth it selfe, the fruits thereof are before our eyes ; and none of all this is in cities in the throng of houses : so that to liue in cities is to be banished in the world, and shut from the world. Againe, the country life is wholly in exercise, in action, which sharpeneth the appetite, maintaineth health, hardeneth and fortifieth the bodie. That which is to be commended in cities, is commoditie either priuate, as of merchants and artificers, or publike, to the managing whereof few are called, and in ancient times heretofore they were chosen from the country life, who returned hauing performed their charge.[94]

A philosophy of conduct based upon what the seventeenth century believed to be scientific truth is found in Charron's treatise. Clarity is the aim of the author, who is more concerned over being understood than with exhibiting his erudition ; hence he handles "this matter, not Scholarlike or Pedantically, nor with enlarged discourse, and furniture of Eloquence or other Art . . . but rudely, openly, and ingenuously." Despite his efforts to simplify his language, he still fears that the exposition will be difficult for unlearned readers, "too harsh and briefe, too rude and difficult for the simpler sort." Therefore many things he has "for the loue of them explicated, enlightened and sweetned in this third Edition, reviewed, and much augmented."[95]

If the Elizabethan erred through a failure to understand himself, it was not for want of scientific works to explain his behavior. When the melancholy Jaques and the gloomy Hamlet viewed themselves introspectively, they were abundantly supplied with theories to account for their reactions. As the modern reader glibly interprets human conduct in terms of Freud, Jung, or whoever may be his pet theorist, so the Tudor and Stuart citizen found satisfactory explanations in Bright, Walkington, Huarte, Charron, and other writers who elucidated the always interesting question of the reasons for man's behavior.

The sciences with which the average citizen gained the greatest familiarity were those that affected his welfare, like medicine and its related subjects, or those that were descriptively comprehensible, such as natural history with its revelations of the wonders

---

[94] Edition of 1612, p. 217 ; from Chap. LVI, "The comparison of the country-life with the Citizens."

[95] The preface.

of the created universe. Some of the pseudo-sciences like alchemy and the more abstruse phases of astrology were mysteries into which only the specialist might penetrate. Both alchemy and astrology were associated in the popular consciousness with magic, and it was not for the layman to inquire too deeply into their mysterious procedures. Especially was alchemy a mystery subtly bound up with the smoke and soot of hell. Although the belief in the power of the alchemist to transmute base metal into gold was well-nigh universal,[96] the nature of the subject led to efforts to keep its processes secret, and there was no literature explaining alchemy to the multitude as there was a literature simplifying medicine and natural history. Yet so numerous were alchemists in Elizabethan London that the public was familiar with the generalities of the subject, and many apothecaries, physicians, and dabblers in the occult sought the philosopher's stone by which the transmutations might be made. The knowledge of alchemy was spread by the innumerable quacks who plied their trade among gullible seekers after easily acquired wealth. Alchemy being an esoteric subject, the bulk of its literature, however, was couched in Latin or foreign tongues, and little thought was given to making the written materials available to lay readers until Elias Ashmole compiled his *Theatrum Chemicum Britannicum* in 1652. Alchemical frauds had been ridiculed since Chaucer, and not only Jonson, but Lyly, Greene, Nashe, and other Elizabethan satirists paid their respects to the trickeries of the quacks who preyed on the credulities of the age. In spite of the satirists' jibes at the poor success of the multipliers of gold, so learned a man as Dr. John Dee committed himself to alchemical charlatanries and Queen Elizabeth interested herself in the search for the philosopher's stone. Alchemy was a subject about which every Elizabethan knew, and in which most Elizabethans believed, but the public was more interested in the results than in the procedure, and willingly left the technicalities to specialized practitioners of an

---

[96] For a discussion of alchemy in Elizabethan England, see the introduction by Charles Montgomery Hathaway, Jr. (ed.), *The Alchemist by Ben Jonson*, Yale Studies in English, XVII (New York, 1903). Other material may be found in H. D. Traill and J. S. Mann (eds.), *Social England*, 6 vols. (London, 1902-04), III, 446-53; IV, 118-22.

art that somehow always smelled strangely of sulphur and damnation.

Astrology was almost as esoteric as alchemy, but being concerned with the stars instead of evil-smelling fumes, was less damnable. Astrologers, it is true, were frequently accused of malicious conjurations and were suspected of leagues with the devil,[97] but some portions of astrological belief and practice were so generally accepted in everyday life that astrology did not share the popular odium that frequently befell alchemy. Judicial astrology, with its forecasts of future events, was principally responsible for the disasters that overtook the practicers of this branch of learning. The public was almost unanimous in believing that the stars had some effect on human affairs, and the casting of horoscopes was a routine task for men like Dee, and even for so serious an astronomer as Tycho Brahe. Had the astrologers stopped here they would have saved themselves much grief, but many of them were voluble fortune tellers, and some were accused of meddling with black magic. The excesses of the astrologers, rather than the fundamental beliefs on which their art was founded, were the targets of satirists who exposed their weaknesses, as did W. P. in *Foure Great Lyers, Striuing who shall win the siluer Whetstone. Also, A Resolution to the countri-man, prouing it vtterly vnlawfull to buye or vse our yeerly Prognostications* [1585?]. The astrological information necessary for the ordinary man was provided in almanacs and medical works, some of which have already been noted, but even unprofessional readers might dip deeper into astrology than was possible in alchemy. Popular instruction in the rudiments of astrology was provided for nearly three-quarters of a century by an often-printed treatise attributed to a pseudonymous astrologer Arcandum.[98] The general reader, however, probably contented

---

[97] *See* G. L. Kittredge, *Witchcraft in Old and New England* (Cambridge, Mass., 1929) pp. 226 ff.

[98] *The Most Excellent Profitable, and pleasaunt Booke of the famous Doctor and expert Astrologian Arcandum, or Aleandrin, to find the Fatall destiny, constellation, complexion, & naturall inclination of euery man and childe, by his birth. With an addition of Phisiognomy, very pleasā to read. Now tourned out of French into our vulgar tongue,* by William Warde (1578). The first edition recorded in the *Short Title Catalogue* is dated doubtfully 1562. Seven editions by 1637 are recorded.

Because the common people were being misled by works on judicial astrology and kindred subjects, Henry Howard published a refutation, the full title of which makes

himself with learning a few "signs" which were useful to him in determining lucky and unlucky days.

In addition to other scientific interests, the Elizabethan public shows, toward the end of the sixteenth century, an unusual curiosity about inventions. Mechanical skill was developing and ingenious minds were striving to perfect useful devices. Cyprian Lucar published in 1590 *A Treatise named Lucar Solace*, which had one section devoted to the description of useful inventions, including, among other things, a fire engine in the form of "a kinde of squirt made to holde an hoggeshed of water."[99] His treatise also taught mensuration and geometry. Sir Hugh Platt, son of a wealthy London brewer, was one of the most energetic of the writers who turned a hand to describing new inventions. *The Jewell House of Art and Nature* (1594)[100] is the most comprehensive of Platt's several works on practical devices and useful contrivances. A patriotic desire to set forth something of profit to the commonwealth inspires his effort, Platt assures the public, whom he begs to encourage those "choice wits" who can so enrich England with inventions that she need have no fear of the power of Spain.[101] Scientific learning should find some practical outlet, he believes, and he vigorously attacks pedantic scientists who wrap their learning in too much Latin, or merely write of vague theories spun out of their studies and not from their practice. Particularly is

---

the point of view plain : *A defensatiue against the poyson of supposed Prophesies: Not hitherto confuted by the penne of any man, which being grounded, eyther vppon the warrant and authority of olde paynted bookes, expositions of Dreames, Oracles, Reuelations, Inuocations of damned spirites, Iudicialles of Astrologie, or any other kinde of pretended knowledge whatsoeuer, De futuris contingentibus: haue beene causes of great disorder in the common wealth, and cheefely among the simple and vnlearned people: very needefull to be published at this time, considering the late offence which grew by most palpable and grosse errours in Astrology* (1583).

[99] See *Dictionary of National Biography, sub* Lucar.

[100] *The Jewell House of Art and Nature. Conteining diuers rare and profitable Inuentions, together with sundry new experimentes in the Art of Husbandry, Distillation, and Moulding. Faithfully and familiarly set downe, according to the Authors owne experience* (1594).

[101] John Napier, who published his famous treatise on logarithms in 1614, was stimulated by fear of Spain to exert himself to make some practical inventions "proffitabill & necessary in theis dayes for the defence of this Iland & withstanding of strangers enemies of Gods truth & relegion." The results were a burning mirror for the destruction of ships, and an armored chariot.—W. T. Sedgwick and H. W. Tyler, *A Short History of Science* (New York, 1929), p. 242.

Platt critical of writers about chemical discoveries, who make a vast mystery of simple matters :

But the best and most approoued Authors of the rest, haue written al their learned experiments so figuratiuelie, and wrapped them vp in such clouds of skill (and that maketh them so often to tel vs, Scribimus nobis & Philosophis, scribimus filijs artis, calling their minerals by the name of aurum nostrum, mercurius noster, stibium noster, &c.) as that no man, without a manuel maister that may euen lead him by the hand thorough al their riddles, is able either to make the sweete oile of Antimonie, or to dulcifie Mercurie as it ought to be, or to bring any mettal to be medicinable by making it irreducible to it selfe.
[Preface.]

Platt's zeal for applied science is obvious in his book, which teaches a curious variety of things : how to keep meats from spoiling, how to keep fresh water from putrefaction, how to use secret ink, how to make a wind vane which will register in the merchant's room in order that he may know at any hour whether winds are favorable, how to stain new walnut like old, how to cement broken glass, and scores of other useful processes. He describes a pistol two feet long which will shoot accurately at "eight skore." To discourage gaming, as he ingeniously insists, he reveals "A perspectiue Ring that wil discouer all the Cards that are neere him that weareth it on his finger." He even gives an easy way to learn the A B C's and describes an "Art of memorie which master Dickson the Scot did teach of late yeres in England, and whereof he hath written a figuratiue and obscure treatise, set downe briefly and in plaine termes according to his owne demonstration, with the especiall vses thereof."[102] Platt was the author of several other treatises that simplified his own studies for the profit of the general reader. Ten editions of his *Delightes for Ladies*, printed between 1602 and 1636, are preserved. This work is a collection of useful recipes for cooking, remedies, and cosmetics. His agricultural studies won him widespread acclaim, and his invention of a briquet of powdered coal was of considerable practical utility. King James knighted him for his services to the commonwealth.[103]

---

[102] P. 81.

[103] *Dictionary of National Biography, sub* Platt.

Many of the books of so-called inventions were in fact merely collections of recipes for the manufacture of useful or curious articles and products. W. P.'s *A Booke Of Secrets* (1596), for example, provided recipes for making various colored inks and preserving wines. Typical of the collections of miscellaneous information about useful devices and processes was Thomas Johnson's *A new Booke of new Conceits, with a number of Nouelties annexed thereunto. Whereof some be profitable, some necessary, some strange, none hurtful, and all delectable* (1630), which taught such diverse things as a signal system to be used by prisoners of war, a conceit to make white roses red, a way to rid gardens of worms, a rule of the Chaldees to know whether a man or his wife will die first, a means of telling what disease a man has, and a method of cutting glass. Having discovered the fascination of simple experiments in mechanics and chemistry, the public turned to these, as a source of new entertainment, with the zest of a child who discovers the attractions of a mechanical toy. Johnson realized the general interest in such things and prepared another little pamphlet whose title is sufficient indication of its nature, *Dainty Conceits, with a number of rare and witty inuentions, neuer before printed. Made and inuented for honest recreation, to passe away idle houres* (1630). When the student of Johnson's book of inventions tired of making gunpowder, according to the recipe provided, he might try the inventions for growing fruit without a core, for keeping ale from souring in summer, and for detecting blindfolded the four aces in a deck of cards.

One of the most complete treatises on inventions was published by John Bate, the mechanician,[104] as *The Mysteryes Of Nature, And Art* (1634).[105] A second edition was called for in the following year.

---

[104] The contribution of unlettered artisans to mechanical advancement excited the admiration of Gabriel Harvey, who wrote in 1593: "He that remembereth Humphrey Cole a Mathematicall Mechanician, Matthew Baker, a shipwright, John Shute an architect, Robert Norman a Navigator, William Bourne, a gunner, John Hester, a Chymist or any like cunning and subtile empirique, is a prowd man, if he contemn expert artisans, or any sensible industrious practitioners, howsoever unlectured in Schooles or unlettered in books."—Quoted by E. G. R. Taylor, *Tudor Geography, 1485-1583* (London, 1930), p. 161.

[105] *The Mysteryes Of Nature, And Art: Conteined in foure severall Tretises, The first of water workes, The Second of Fyer workes, The third of Drawing, Colouring, Painting, and Engrauing,*

Bate's care "to write in plaine termes, that in regard of the easinesse thereof it might suit with the meanest capacity,"[106] may
have helped the popularity of a work which described many
useful appliances as well as some curious experiments merely for
amusement.[107] Bate's little book is utilitarian in purpose and attempts to lay before the unlearned reader the advantages of useful
inventions and discoveries. The descriptions of pumps, for instance, are especially valuable.

Tudor and Stuart England eagerly pursued new inventions and
new manufacturing processes as a means of increasing its wealth.
The State Papers contain many references to applications for
patents for new methods of draining the fens, pumping out mines,
utilizing coal, and making dyes, glass, steel, clocks, military supplies, and innumerable other products.[108] The literature on the
subject is a manifestation of the general interest of a public awak-
ing to the fascination of scientific discovery and mechanical development. The beginnings of the spirit of the mechanical age can
be discerned in the eager interest of the Elizabethans in new
gadgets that might enrich or amuse them.

Great as were the scientific developments in the sixteenth and
seventeenth centuries, it would be too much to claim, even for
that alert age, that the rank and file of the citizenry participated
in the advanced thinking of men like William Gilbert, William
Harvey, John Napier, and other contributors to scientific advancement. But so widespread had become the spirit of inquiry and so
insistent was the questioning about natural causes that theological
writers in alarm warned the public that God would resent meddling in his secret affairs. A work on earthquakes, translated by
Abraham Fleming as *A Bright Burning Beacon* (1580), opposed too
much exploration into natural phenomena.

---

*The fourth of divers Experiments, as wel serviceable as delightful: partly Collected, and partly of
the Authors Peculiar Practice and Invention* (1634).

[106] Preface.

[107] Another work published in the year of the second edition of Bate's book gives
evidence of the popular interest in fireworks. It was *Pyrotechnia Or, A Discourse Of
Artificiall Fire-Workes: . . . Whereunto is annexed a short Treatise of Geometrie . . . Written
by John Babington Gunner, and Student in the Mathematicks* (1635).

[108] T. F. Ordish, "Early English Inventions," *The Antiquary*, XII (1885), 1-6, 61-65,
113-18.

any thing chaunce contrarie to common course and order, *vp starts
ne or other wisard, and he by his knowledge will be busie to bolt out
ιe mysterie which God hath reserued to his owne secrete counsell.
'his commeth to passe (sayth one) of such and such a cause : the rea-
ɔn thereof notwithstanding vnknowne to them : and yet because their
lind coniectures haue in them some probabilities, the ruder sort of
eople are readie to giue credit: & thus betweene both, the forewarn-
ιgs of Gods heauie iudgement are neglected, . . .   [Sig. C 3.]
  * The presumption of man in seking after the secret counsels of God.

ven William Vaughan, who had considerable scientific interest
imself, violently condemned the persistence of common men in
:rreting out the mysteries reserved to God. In something of the
ιme spirit that Milton later displayed in Raphael's rebuke of
ιdam's questioning, Vaughan in *The Spirit Of Detraction* (1611)
epeatedly voices his displeasure over "Mans curiosity in prying
ιto Gods nature,"[109] "intermedling with Gods secrets,"[110] "curious
raines [who] will not leaue off plodding and practizing of pro-
ɔund problems."[111] If, however, the theologically minded railed
t the public for the spirit of inquiry, popular interest in scientific
hemes nevertheless increased rather than diminished. It is re-
.ected in such an odd place as a question-and-answer book pre-
·ared as an aid to conversation, Robert Basset's *Curiosities: Or
The Cabinet of Nature* (1637), which furnishes bits like the following
ɔr the edification of those who would talk well :

2. Wherefore is it, that sometimes we seeme to see the Starres fall?
ι. Those are not Stars, but Meteors caused of exhalations, which
·eing not great in quantity, and drawne up to the lower Regions of
he Ayre, taking fire, fall in the likenesse of a Starre.[112]

Though the London citizen might know no more about Galileo's
liscoveries than his modern descendant knows about Einstein's
heories, the ferment of science was in the air. What the great
ɔnes did, the lesser prattled of, and gradually down to the com-
ɲon understanding spread the desire to know more about sub-
ects that had once been the exclusive prerogatives of academi-
ians. Even the shopkeeper in Cheapside might listen to lectures
ɔn astronomy and other scientific subjects at Gresham College,

[109] P. 6.   [110] P. 64.   [111] P. 65.   [112] P. 79.

and plain seamen, learning enough of astronomy and mathematics to be good navigators, doubtless heard of strange new theories which they passed on to their friends. With the zest of middle-class culture-seekers of the present time, London citizens pursued lecture courses that would instruct them in the elements of natural science, until by the early seventeenth century, indeed, attending scientific lectures was a hobby cultivated by many citizens. The advantages of these popular lectures are described in an extraordinarily interesting but little known book by Thomas Nash, self-styled "Philopolites," *Quaternio Or A Fourefoll Way To A Happie Life; set forth in a Dialogue betweene a Countryman and a Citizen, a Divine and a Lawyer* (1633). The citizen is stressing the cultural advantages of London over the country:

Againe when I considered how we haue divers other Lectures [in addition to sermons], Anatomie, Astronomy, Geometry, whereby we reape much good which you haue not. Sometimes wee heare a learned Physitian reade vpon all the parts both Homogenean and Heterogenean of the dead Corps of a malefactor, one while of the head, shewing how from the *braine the nerves haue their essence and being*, and that from thence a power to the eye is given to see; . . . [short epitome of the anatomy lecture] . . . These things and many more are we taught out of these Lectures. Sometimes againe, we betake our selues to the Astronomie Lecture, where we learne how the Spheres are placed in degree one aboue another; and how one starre differs from another in greatnesse and glory. Sometimes againe to the Geometry Lecture, where we are taught the vsefull art of Surveying; how to measure out the circle of the Earth, to know what Compasse it beareth about, and what distance is betweene the Center and the Circumference. Sometimes to the Arithmeticke-Lecture, where we learne to better our knowledge in the casting vp of our reckonings and accounts, by being taught the rules of Addition, of Subtraction, of Multiplication, Division, Reduction, and the golden-Rule. Sometimes to the Physicke & naturall Philosophy-Lecture, where we learned the naturall causes of the foure seasons of the yeare, of Summer and Winter, Spring and Autumne, of the winds and earthquakes, of the Comets and Meteors, of thunder and lightning, hayle and snow, & how it commeth to passe that the *Lightning should kill the childe in the wombe, yet never hurt the mother:* how the Springs do mount to the tops of hils, and are more cold in Summer than Winter: how the *Seas never exceede their bounds, though all the Chanels of the earth doe emptie themselues into them:* how the Clouds composed of heavie materials, doe hang in the middle Region of the ayre; and why the earth is by many degrees more cold than the water. The naturall causes of these effects there we learne. Sometimes to the Musicke Lecture, where I never come but admire, that out of the greatest discords, should arise the sweetest harmony & concord, that a Base and Treble, Tenor and Counter-tenor, high and low, should cause a Diapason. In these, I say, which doe better our best part, our knowledge and vnderstanding, doe wee out-strip and goe beyond you likewise; . . .   [Pp. 44-46.]

Thus did the citizen find instruction in lectures that revealed the mystery of science in a language that he could understand. If few citizens bothered to read Gilbert's scholarly treatise, *De Magnete* (1600), they could at least learn something about his scientific discoveries, in an appendix to Thomas Blundeville's *The Theoriques of the seuen Planets* (1602), a work designed to make astronomy understandable to sailors. Even if the revolutionary discoveries of sixteenth- and seventeenth-century science seemed slow in making an impression on popular thinking, the mind of the public was absorbing a great deal of traditional information and enough of the newer theories to stimulate a desire for more. When scholars failed to make their erudition available to the populace, men less learned sometimes felt it their duty to interpret scientific knowledge for the benefit of their countrymen. For instance, William Bourne, who described himself as "a poore Gunner," adapted material from Henry Billingsley's translation of Euclid[113] and published *A booke called the Treasure for trau-*

---

[113] In this connection, Billingsley's own statement about scientific knowledge may be worth quoting from the preface, "The Translator to the Reader," of *The Elements Of Geometrie* (1570): "There is (gentle Reader) nothing (the word of God onely set apart) which so much beautifieth and adorneth the soule and minde of mā, as doth the knowledge of good artes and sciences: as the knowledge of naturall and morall philosophie. The one setteth before our eyes, the creatures of God, both in the heauens aboue, and in the earth beneath: in which as in a glasse, we beholde the exceding maiestie and wisedome of God, in adorning and beautifying them as we see: in geuing vnto them such wonderfull and manifolde proprieties, and naturall workinges, and that so diuersely and in such varietie: farther in maintaining and conseruing them continually, whereby to praise and adore him, as by S. Paule we are taught. The other teacheth vs rules and preceptes of vertue, how, in common life amongest men, we ought to walke vprightly: what dueties pertaine to our selues, what pertaine to the gouernment or good order both of an housholde, and also of a citie or commonwealth."

eilers (1578), a manual of practical geometry, with a supplement on geology. Scholars frequently find fault when others attempt such labors, Bourne observes in his preface, but since they too often neglect the duty of giving explanations understandable by common men, he has prepared his book "to instruct them that are simple and vnlearned." If some scholars were loth to popularize their knowledge, as Bourne implies, others succeeded in writing books which the lay public could profitably use, and from the encyclopedias, from little guides to the separate divisions of scientific learning (like those turned out by Thomas Hill), from the works on the plant and animal world, from the medical books, and from treatises on the body, mind, and soul, came the multifarious information that further stimulated in plain citizens a taste for a wider acquaintance with the facts of what we call natural science. The efforts of Elizabethan writers to satisfy the demand of the non-academic public for enlightenment about the substance of natural philosophy laid the foundations for the vast literature of popular science which has ever since entertained and instructed the public.[114]

---

[114] The entertaining quality of scientific material was not unknown to Elizabethan journalists. Thomas Dekker, for instance, utilized it in *A Strange Horse Race* (1613), described by the *Cambridge History of English Literature*, IV, 356, as a sort of "popular encyclopedia, in which the knowledge of the day is vulgarised under the attractive conceit of a race. Astronomy is taught under the guise of races of the heavenly bodies, and physiology as the races in a man's body, earth, water, air, and fire all competing."

XVI

THE STAGE AND DRAMA

MONG all the forms of entertainment that amused the public of Elizabethan England, none flourished with greater vigor than the drama, and none appealed more generally to all classes. Stage plays furnished diversion for the courtier and the shopkeeper alike, and, though there came a differentiation of taste in the seventeenth century, the taste of the Court and that of the City were not far apart until very late in the sixteenth century.[1] Robust drama, full of clownery, dancing, song, and an infinite variety of spectacular elements, beguiled a public which developed the habit of playgoing so strongly that theatrical ventures became a profitable business.

Whatever city aldermen or Puritan preachers might say about the undesirability of stage plays and the actors thereof, the rank and file of the citizens gave to the drama their enthusiastic support throughout the sixteenth and first half of the seventeenth centuries. So ingrained was the love of dramatic spectacle that neither the power of Puritanism with its proof of the iniquity of stage plays, nor the cogent reasoning of municipal authorities against the waste and dangers of idle amusements could prevent the drama from gaining a great hold on the mass of citizens, however much they might reprehend certain evils obvious enough to any godly spectator. But the very tradesman-groups who furnished recruits to the cause of Puritanism had long nourished the production of plays. Even in Shakespeare's lifetime, the memory of the mystery drama, produced by the trade guilds, was still fresh, and plays were still a part of the entertainment at feasts in the guild halls. Among other amusements, Henry Machyn mentions that at the Barber-Surgeons' feast on the tenth of August,

---

[1] Charles J. Sisson, *Le goût public et le théâtre Élisabéthain* (Dijon, 1922), pp. 42, 49-50.

1562, there was "good syngyng . . . and after diner a play";[2] a play after the "cony-feast," held in Christmas week by the Cutlers Company of London, was traditional;[3] the Company of Pewterers of London still collected small fees from the membership "towards the play";[4] and in all phases of civic festivities, from the installation of a mayor to the annual celebrations of the worshipful companies, Londoners and citizens of provincial towns were accustomed to see a show, a pageant, or a play. Performances were sometimes by amateurs, but frequently the records show payments to professional players. Even if the despised actors were classed with rogues and vagabonds and were regarded as too lewd to be buried in holy ground, tradesmen, from time too dimly distant to be remembered, had found use for them and had been entertained by their world of make-believe. And citizens refused to be stinted of their amusement, in spite of the admitted evils of playhouses and the malice that authors and actors often displayed.

Opposition from the commercial classes, it is true, was encountered by play producers, but the loose assertion sometimes made that the middle class hated theaters and aimed at their destruction is hardly consistent with the citizens' patronage, upon which some of the theaters depended almost solely for support. With greater tact, theater managers might have avoided much of the hostility to their activities; indeed, a few dramatists and actors, notably Thomas Heywood, appreciated the sensibilities of the commercial groups and made strenuous efforts to placate public opinion, but their efforts were counteracted by their more satirical contemporaries, who delighted in portraying what they represented as the weaknesses of citizens.

In a large measure the players and dramatists brought upon themselves whatever wrath was aroused. While Puritan preachers found in the church fathers precedents for condemning plays and were fortified from the same source by arguments of their evils,[5]

---

[2] J. G. Nichols (ed.), *The Diary of Henry Machyn*, Camden Society, XLII (1848), 290.

[3] Charles Welch, *History of the Cutlers' Company of London*, 2 vols. (London, 1923), I, 151, 177.

[4] *Idem, The History of the Worshipful Company of Pewterers of the City of London*, 2 vols. (London, 1902), I, 201, 234.

[5] A detailed study of the opposition to the stage is provided by E. N. S. Thompson, *The Controversy between the Puritans and the Stage*, Yale Studies in English, XX (New

the lay brethren were excited to resentment by being insulted
in plays that injured their vanity and flouted their most cherished ideals. With disdain of the commonalty, the greater dramatists sought the favor of the highborn, with little regard for the
feelings of the middle class; careless of any hostility which their
jibes might produce, they were sure that clownery would be
enough to hold the crowd. But London tradesmen grew weary
of seeing themselves pictured as grasping usurers, easily tricked
by some witty gallant; the satire of their social ambitions touched
them too nearly; and they resented the cuckoldry which their
stage counterparts invariably suffered from aristocratic dandies,
for whom, if the playwrights were to be believed, city wives in-
ordinately lusted. Moreover, plays frequently implied a loose
morality displeasing to bourgeois audiences. Spendthrifts and
wasters became heroes; witty rogues tricked their masters; sons
and daughters resisted their parents; extravagance became a
virtue and thrift a weakness to be mocked; and adultery, instead
of being damned in awful sentences, was a subject of merriment.
The players themselves set bad examples by their dissolute lives.
On the stage they taught bawdry and swore bloodcurdling oaths,
until, indeed, King James objected; and they desecrated the
Sabbath by playing in church time until the authorities with
difficulty restrained them. It was even said that Tarlton, most
famous of clowns, advised his hearers "to pull downe the Church,
and set vp the Ale-house."[6] Players made sport of constituted
authority, ridiculed the city magistrates, and represented upon
the common stages affairs of state in which they had no business
to meddle.[7] Furthermore, stage playing brought down upon the

York, 1903). See also J. D. Wilson, "The Puritan Attack on the Stage," Cambridge History
of English Literature, VI, 373-409; C. Cullen, "Puritanism and the Stage," Proceedings
of the Royal Philosophical Society of Glasgow, XLIII (1911-12), 153-81; and T. S. Graves,
"Notes on Puritanism and the Stage," Studies in Philology, XVIII (1921), 141-69.

[6] Preface to Barnabe Rich's Faultes Faults, And nothing else but Faultes (1606).

[7] A common charge against the players was that they railed at authority and made
grave citizens ridiculous. Their activities in the time of the Martin Marprelate controversy in behalf of the episcopal party did nothing to endear them to the people
(cf. Thompson, op. cit., p. 115), and the presumption of players in meddling in such
matters was generally condemned by public opinion. The dramatists who write for
the stage are responsible for the libels upon persons in authority, declares I. H. in
This Worlds Folly (1615), which describes them as "mercenary Squitter-wits miscalled

city that most fearful of calamities, the plague, by reason of God's wrath at the blasphemy of the actors and because of the crowds who flocked in a disorderly rout to the playhouses. Worst of all, from the sober tradesman's point of view, stage plays demoralized apprentices and encouraged idleness and unthriftiness.[8] Yet in

---

Poets, whose illiterate and picke-pocket Inuentions, can *Emungere plebes argento,* slily nip the bunges of the baser troopes, and cut the reputations throat of the more eminent rank of Cittizens with corroding scandals : these are they, who by dipping their Goose quils in the puddle of mischiefe, with wilde and vncollected spirites make them desperately drunke, to strike at the head of *Nobility, Authority,* and high-*seated Greatnesse.*"—Sig. B 3. William Prynne in *Histrio-Mastix* (1633) inveighs against the evils of personal satire which encourages disrespect for the law : "Not to particularize those late new scandalous invectiue Playes, wherein *sundry persons* of place and eminence haue beene particularly personated, jeared, abused in a grosse and scurrilous manner ; the *frequent scoffes, reproaches, scandals, Satyrs, and disgracefull passages that are darted out in Stageplayes against Ministers, Lawyers, Courteours, Phisitions, Marchants, Citizens, Tradesmen* of all sorts ; against *Iudges, Iustices, Maiors,* and such like Officers ; but especially against all zealous practicall professors of Religion, *who seldome scape the Players lash.*"—P. 124. The literature antagonistic to the stage throughout the period is filled with similar complaints.

[8] The practical objection that plays lure apprentices from work and cause the poor to waste money is frequently met with. The Common Council on December 6, 1574, passed an ordinance condemning stage plays not only because they spread the plague, induce God's wrath, and seduce into evil ways, but also because they cause "unthrifty waste of the money of the poor and fond persons."—J. Q. Adams, *Shakespearean Playhouses* (Boston and New York, 1917), p. 23. One of the chief grievances cited by the Privy Council in an order dated June 22, 1600, is that plays draw people from their toil and encourage idleness. Playhouses are "the dayly occasion of the ydle, ryoutous and dissolute living of great nombers of people, that leavinge all such honest and painefull course of life as they should followe, doe meete and assemble here."— J. R. Dasent (ed.), *Acts of the Privy Council,* n.s., XXX (London, 1905), 395-98.

Thomas Nashe gives an insight into the propaganda of business men against the theater, in a passage in *Pierce Penilesse* (1592) in which he attributes a part of the campaign against playhouses to a desire of the keepers of alehouses and ordinaries to suppress competition for the spending money of apprentices : "Whereas some Petitioners of the Counsaile against them obiect, they [plays] corrupt the youth of the Cittie, and withdrawe Prentises from theyr worke ; they heartily wishe they might bee troubled with none of their youth nor their prentises ; for some of them (I meane the ruder handicrafts seruants) neuer come abroade, but they are in danger of vndoing : and as for corrupting them when they come, thats false ; for no Play they haue, encourageth any man to tumults or rebellion, but layes before such the halter and the gallowes ; or praiseth or approoueth pride, lust, whoredome, prodigalitie, or drunkennes, but beates them downe vtterly. As for the hindrance of Trades and Traders of the Citie by them, that is an Article foysted in by the Vintners, Alewiues, and Victuallers, who surmise if there were no Playes, they should haue all the companie that resort to them, lye bowzing and beere-bathing in their houses euery after-noone. Nor so, nor so, good brother bottle-ale, fore there are other places besides where money

spite of these manifold reasons why the citizenry should have cast out the drama, it continued to have for them a fascination which the Long Parliament in 1642 could not absolutely destroy.

The reasons for the hold which the drama had upon all classes, even upon prudent burghers who had ample excuse for deploring it, are found in the infinite variety and robust vigor of a stage that had not yet narrowed its appeal to a particular class, as the Restoration stage was later to pander exclusively to a libidinous courtier group. Though the beginning of such a class distinction in the theaters was forecast and became clearer with the passage of every year in the seventeenth century, the very nature of Elizabethan drama gave it a universal quality. Themes as kaleidoscopic as the life of the times went into its composition. Wild romance which took the Londoner to the Indies or the courts of Eastern potentates; dramatized history which re-created the past and magnified the deeds of English heroes; plays which glorified plain folk and homespun virtues; dramatic journalism which brought to the stage the latest murder or domestic triangle, properly moralized; clownery, boisterous and crude, which entertained playgoers not too critical—these ingredients created a drama which the general public found irresistible, even if it did at times smack of damnation. As a matter of fact, however, dramatists frequently exerted themselves to provide a didacticism

can bestow it selfe : the signe of the smock will wipe your mouth cleane; and yet I haue heard yee haue made her a tenant to your tap-houses. But what shall hee doo that hath spent himselfe? where shall hee haunt? Faith, when Dice, Lust, and Drunkennesse, and all haue dealt vpon him, if there be neuer a Playe for him to goe too for his pennie, he sits melancholie in his Chamber, deuising vpon felonie or treason, and howe he may best exalt himselfe by mischiefe."—Edited by G. B. Harrison (London, 1924), pp. 89-90.

The municipal authorities and the city companies at various times attempted to regulate the attendance of apprentices at plays. In 1582, for example, the Lord Mayor of London issued an order to the city companies forbidding them "at annye tyme hereafter [to] suffer any of ther sarvants, apprentices, journemen, or children, to repare or goe to annye playes, peices, or enterludes" either in the suburbs or the city.—John Nicholl, *Some Account of the Worshipful Company of Ironmongers* (London, 1851), p. 141. Clearly the appeal of the theaters exerted a demoralizing influence upon apprentices and upon business.—*See* Thompson, *op. cit.*, p. 124. Many persons who did not condemn plays, as such, thought they were a bad influence for the lower classes. Lady Bacon, for example, objected to her son Anthony's residence in Bishopsgate Street for fear his servants would be corrupted by plays at the Bull Tavern nearby.—Adams, *op. cit.*, p. 15.

that further pleased audiences whose appetite for instruction could scarcely be satisfied. Just as New England later received *Othello* as a "moral lecture" against the sin of jealousy, so Elizabethan playgoers comforted their consciences with the good lessons that the drama extracted for them from the doleful ends of traitors, faithless wives, and other sinners whose dying speeches were filled with repentance and advice. The convention of didacticism was so strong that apologists for the stage could justify it on grounds of its moral teachings. Even though many plays were wicked in the eyes of the puritanically minded, the qualities of popular appeal were too many for the citizenry to forfeit their interest in the drama. Although the commercial classes found fault with the morality of plays which mocked their ideals, not until the fanaticism of 1642 would public sentiment permit a prohibition of stage plays, and then only half-heartedly.[9]

Elizabethan drama flourished too luxuriantly to be restricted to any class, and in the sixteenth century the dramatic taste of the aristocrat was so nearly like that of the commoner that innumerable plays did duty both at court and in the public playhouses. Gradually, however, as class consciousness increased, certain types of plays began to appeal more and more strictly to the élite, while, by the same token, other plays were pitched to the level of ordinary commoners. The preferences of James I and his court helped to accentuate the growth of a social differentiation in the drama, which continued to develop until ultimately in the Restoration it resulted in driving the citizen from the theater. But conditions were different in the earlier period, and the citizen who disliked plays written to please the courtiers attending the fashionable theaters, could betake himself to another playhouse, where the drama was to his liking.

From the time of the establishment of regular playing places in London, before much class distinction can be seen in the drama itself, the social differences in the playhouses are discernible. The inns at which plays were acted, like the Bull in Bishopsgate Street,

---

[9] Proof of the unwillingness of the public to give up theatrical entertainments is provided by Leslie Hotson, *The Commonwealth and Restoration Stage* (Cambridge, Mass., 1928), *passim*.

and the Bell and Cross Keys in Gracious Street, were naturally sought out by nondescript audiences; whereas the stages occupied by the choir boys of Windsor, the Chapel Royal, or St. Paul's attracted courtiers and gentlemen. The so-called private theaters, from the establishment of Richard Farrant's first Blackfriars stage about 1576, attempted to win the patronage of aristocratic audiences who would be willing to pay larger fees than those charged by the public theaters.[10] The first and second Blackfriars, the small theater at St. Paul's, the Whitefriars, the Salisbury Court playhouse, and, at first, the Cockpit in Drury Lane, were fashionable resorts where the lesser citizenry, even if they had been willing to pay the higher admission charges, would have felt ill at ease. On the other hand, the theaters north of the city were popular from the first with the multitude, who long had been accustomed to use Finsbury Fields for a recreation ground, and found the Theatre and the Curtain convenient resorts.[11] Though the nearby Fortune started with a proud flourish, it also was soon catering to the masses, and the Red Bull in St. John's Street was, from the beginning, frankly a plain man's playhouse, where clownery, clamor, and spectacle vied with subject matter flattering to the vanity of tradesmen. In the opinion of reputable burghers, the Curtain, the Fortune, and the Red Bull[12] were preferable even to the Bank-

---

[10] Adams, *op. cit.*, p. 94, and *passim*. Speaking of the audiences to whom the children's companies appealed, Professor Adams comments (p. 112): "The Children, indeed, catered to a very select public. Persons who went thither were gentle by birth and by behavior as well; and the playwrights, we are told, could always feel sure there of the 'calm attention of a choice audience.'" Later he quotes a passage from *Jack Drum's Entertainment* which indicates that the rabble stayed away from the entertainment offered by the child actors (p. 115):

> "*Plan.* S'faith, I like the audience that frequenteth there
> With much applause. A man shall not be choak't
> With the stench of garlic, nor be pasted
> To the barmy jacket of a beer-brewer.
> *Bra. Ju.* 'T is a good, gentle audience; and I hope the Boys
> Will come one day into the Court of Requests."

The author of *The Actors Remonstrance or Complaint* (1643) boasts of the Blackfriars, the Cockpit, and Salisbury Court, all "private" theaters, that "none use to come but the best of the Nobility and Gentry."—Hotson, *op. cit.*, p. 8.

[11] In addition to the historical details provided by Adams, see T. F. Ordish, *Early London Theatres (In the Fields)* (London, 1899), pp. 35-36, 54, and *passim*.

[12] Adams, *op. cit.*, pp. 289, 303.

side playhouses, for the latter shared to some extent the odium of the extensive public stews in their vicinity. Although the attractions of the Swan, the Rose, and the Globe found interested spectators in all classes, the Bankside audiences contained a larger percentage of the sporting group than attended the theaters north of the city walls. Indeed, of all the public theaters, the Globe was the most favored by fashionable theatergoers and well-bred dandies. Attending a play at the Globe or Blackfriars was the smart thing for a social-climbing gallant, who, after dining at a fashionable tavern, "must venture beyond sea, that is, in a choice pair of noblemen's oars, to the Bankside, where he must sit out the breaking-up of a comedy, or the first cut of a tragedy; or rather, if his humour so serve him, to call in at the Blackfriars, where he should see a nest of boys able to ravish a man."[13] When the Cockpit became less fashionable, it was deserted by the gallant, for "now vpon the Fryers stage hee'll sit" until at length he is bankrupt and

> His silken garments, and his sattin robe
> That hath so often visited the Globe,
> And all his spangled rare perfum'd attires,
> Which once so glistred in the Torchy Fryers,
> Must to the Broakers to compound his debt.[14]

It was the Globe which a reveling gentleman remembered first:

> Speake Gentlemen, what shall we do today?
> Drinke some braue health vpon the Dutch carouse?
> Or shall we go to the Globe and see a play?[15]

As the Globe and the Blackfriars[16] came more and more to be the

---

[13] Thomas Middleton, *Father Hubburds Tales* (1604), in A. H. Bullen (ed.), *The Works of Thomas Middleton*, 8 vols. (London, 1885), VIII, 77.

[14] Francis Lenton, *The Young Gallants Whirligigg* (1629), p. 16.

[15] Samuel Rowlands, *The Letting Of Humours Blood In The Head-Vaine* (1600), in *The Complete Works of Samuel Rowlands*, 3 vols., Hunterian Club (Glasgow, 1872-80), I, 13.

[16] The Blackfriars Theatre was a nuisance to the citizens who lived or had their businesses in its vicinity, because of the concourse of carriages of its fashionable patrons. Adams, *op. cit.*, pp. 228-32, cites a petition of shopkeepers in 1631 to have the theater suppressed because of the hindrance to their business by the congestion of traffic. Tradesmen in that area kept up their complaints about the injury to business by reason of the coaches—an agitation which, as Professor Adams points out, "implies a fashionable and wealthy patronage of the Blackfriars."

theaters of fashionable London, their plays increasingly sneered
at citizens, who sought the more hospitable stages of the Fortune
and the Red Bull. Particularly was the Red Bull favored of apprentices and small tradesmen, for there they might sit on the
stage with the air of grandeur affected by the gallants who patron-
ized the more stylish theaters.[17] Established about 1605, the Red
Bull flourished throughout the first half of the seventeenth century
and helped to preserve the dramatic tradition during the Commonwealth.[18] To take care of the crowds who came to its plays,
it had to be enlarged about 1625. Both the Red Bull and the
Fortune had a reputation for providing the spectator with his
money's worth of varied entertainment. A thrifty citizen in the
prologue to *The Careless Shepherdess*, acted at Salisbury Court
Playhouse after 1629, is made to comment on the cheapness of
these common playhouses in comparison with the more stylish
private theater :

> And I will hasten to the money Box,
> And take my shilling out again, for now
> I have considered that it is too much ;
> I'le go to th'Bull, or Fortune, and there see
> A Play for two pense, with a Jig to boot.[19]

As the popularity of the Red Bull and Fortune increased, they
were almost deserted by aristocratic patrons. James Wright in
Historia Histrionica (1699) declares that these theaters were
"mostly frequented by citizens and the meaner sort of people."[20]

As might be expected, the entertainment paralleled the quality
of the audiences, and we have numerous references to the boister-

---

[17] *Ibid.*, p. 300. In April, 1622, a felt-maker's apprentice, one John Gill, while sitting on the stage of the Red Bull Theatre, was accidentally injured by a sword-thrust
from one of the actors. Gill called upon his brother apprentices to help him collect
damages, and precipitated a riot.

[18] Hotson, *op. cit.*, p. 8.

[19] C. R. Baskervill, *The Elizabethan Jig and Related Song Drama* (Chicago, 1929),
p. 115.

[20] Adams, *op. cit.*, p. 303. A jibe at the quality of persons who made up the Red Bull
and Fortune audiences is implied in *Albumazar*, acted before King James at Trinity
College, Cambridge, in 1614. A clownish farmer, Trincalo, is made to say : "O 'tis
Armellina: now if she haue the wit to begin, as I meane she should, then will I con-
found her with complements drawn from the Plaies I see at the Fortune, and Red
Bull, where I learne all the words I speake and vnderstand not."—III, i.

ous "tear-throat" acting, the liking for jigs,[21] the emphasis on clownery and the excellence of the fools,[22] the robustious plots, the spectacle, and the noise with which audiences at the Red Bull, the Fortune, and the old Curtain were regaled. No idle tricks of love but manly plays, full of vigor, were to be seen at the Red Bull if we may believe a passage from *Turners dish of Lentten stuffe* (1612):

> That's the fat foole of the Curtin,
>   and the leane foole of the Bull:
> Since *Shanke* did leaue to sing his rimes,
>   he is counted but a gull.
> The players of the Banke side
>   the round Globe and the Swan,
> Will teach you idle trickes of loue,
>   but the Bull will play the man.[23]

Plays of action, the noisier the better, were beloved by apprentices, artisans, and tradesmen, who frequented the theaters north of the city, asserts Edmund Gayton in *Pleasant Notes upon Don Quixot* (1654) in a vivid passage describing the reception of plays, especially on holidays:

I have heard, that the Poets of the Fortune and red Bull, had alwayes a mouth-measure for their Actors (who were terrible teare-throats) and made their lines proportionable to their compasse, which were *sesquipedales*, a foot and a halfe. . . . men come not to study at a Playhouse, but love such expressions and passages, which with ease insinuate themselves into their capacities. . . . To them bring *Jack Drumm's* entertainment, *Greens tu quoque*, the *Devill of Edmunton*, and the like; or if it be on Holy dayes, when Saylers, Watermen, Shoomakers, Butchers and Apprentices are at leisure, then it is good policy to amaze those violent spirits with some tearing Tragoedy full of fights and skirmishes: as the *Guelphs* and *Guiblins*, *Greeks* and *Trojans*, or the three [*sic*] *London Apprentises*, which commonly ends in six acts, the spectators frequently mounting the stage, and making a more bloody Catastrophe amongst

---

[21] Baskervill, *op. cit.*, p. 115: "Among the public theatres it is noticeable that the only houses mentioned by name in connection with the jig are those to the north of the city—the Curtain, the Fortune, and the Red Bull."

[22] T. S. Graves, "Some References to Elizabethan Theatres," *Studies in Philology*, XIX (1922), 317-27. Thomas Greene, leader of the Queen's Men, who were playing at the Red Bull in 1609, was the best known clown since Tarleton and Kemp.

[23] Hyder E. Rollins (ed.), *A Pepysian Garland* (Cambridge, 1922), p. 35.

themselves, then the Players did. I have known upon one of these *Festivals*, but especially at *Shrove-tide*, where the Players have been appointed, notwithstanding their bils to the contrary, to act what the major part of the company had a mind to ; sometimes *Tamerlane*, sometimes *Jugurth*, sometimes the Jew of *Malta*, and sometimes parts of all these, and at last, none of the three taking, they were forc'd to undresse and put off their Tragick habits, and conclude the day with the merry milk-maides. And unlesse this were done, and the popular humour satisfied, as sometimes it so fortun'd, that the Players were refractory ; the Benches, the tiles, the laths, the stones, Oranges, Apples, Nuts, flew about most liberally, and as there were Mechanicks of all professions, who fell every one to his owne trade, and dissolved a house in an instant, and made a ruine of a stately Fabrick. It was not then the most mimicall nor fighting man, *Fowler*, nor *Andrew Cane* could pacifie ; Prologues nor Epilogues would prevaile ; the Devill and the fool were quite out of favour.[24]

Not every performance could have been as riotous as the one described by Gayton, but the plays mentioned as favorites of the crowd give an index to the taste of commoners.[25]

Although it is patently impossible to parcel out all Elizabethan plays into neat piles with labels certifying that this pile contains plays for commoners, and that, plays for courtiers, it is nevertheless possible to ascertain within broad divisions certain types of plays which were particularly favored or disliked by each class. But since much of the drama, especially that written before 1603, made such a widespread appeal that it could win the favor of apprentice and courtier alike, generalizations about class distinctions are hazardous. The plays of Shakespeare, to cite the best known illustration, were applauded by all classes, and the King's Men had trouble preventing other players from pirating the plays

[24] Quoted by Hotson, *op. cit.*, p. 45.

[25] *Jack Drum's Entertainment* (1600), *The Merry Devil of Edmonton* (c. 1603), and *Greene's Tu Quoque* (1611) had enough clownery to make them popular ; *The Guelphs and the Ghibbelines, The Greeks and the Trojans*, and *Jugurtha*, all of which are now lost, doubtless were pseudo-historical plays of violent action with some of the sensationalism which gave *Tamburlaine* (c. 1587) and *The Jew of Malta* (c. 1589) an unholy fascination ; *The Four Prentices of London* (c. 1592), with its extravagant praise of the valor of tradesmen, was one of Thomas Heywood's best liked plays ; and *The Two Merry Milkmaids* (before 1620) so mixed magic and necromancy with a romantic love story that it was sure to gain a favorable hearing.

of their own great dramatist. For example, John Heminges, in behalf of the King's Men, was willing in 1627 to pay £5 to Sir Henry Herbert, Master of the Revels, to restrain the Red Bull Company from playing Shakespeare.[26] Though Shakespeare betrays little sympathy with the ambitions of plain citizens and doubtless wrote with an eye to courtly approval, most of his plays touch interests common to all groups. Like Shakespeare, other dramatists, especially during the vigorous period, between 1590 and 1610, in which the drama reached its highest development, wrote plays pleasing to every class. Nevertheless, by the end of the sixteenth century professional drama was beginning to show a cleavage along class lines, and this cleavage grows distinct as a few dramatists, like Thomas Heywood, became the protagonists of middle-class ideals, and others, like Beaumont and Fletcher, concentrate their effort upon courtly plays designed to please aristocratic taste.

Before the social cleavage in the drama was apparent, however, the general public, as distinguished from courtly audiences, had begun to regard as favorites certain types of plays that were to continue to amuse unsophisticated audiences until the end of the period. Among the earliest of these favored plays were those founded upon knightly adventures, long familiar in the romances entertaining to plain citizens, who were delighted to see enacted on the stage the deeds of traditional heroes. To the modern reader, some of these romantic plays are unbelievably dull, but to the Elizabethan they were as fascinating as the unrealities of cinema adventures are to present-day shop girls. Whether in London or in the provinces, in the last quarter of the sixteenth century or in the fourth decade of the seventeenth, the plays on old romantic themes continued to find favor with the public.

Two of the early dramas of this type, which still show traces of the morality plays, were *Common Conditions* (before 1570)[27] and *Sir Clyomon and Sir Clamydes* (1570-84), plays which enjoyed a long life of popular esteem. *Sir Clyomon* was perhaps still being

---

[26] J. Q. Adams (ed.), *The Dramatic Records of Sir Henry Herbert* (New Haven, 1917) p. 64.

[27] In this section, dates are those of acting. Play titles have been shortened and given in modernized spelling.

performed in the second decade of the seventeenth century by English actors in Germany.[28] Both plays present the extravagant deeds of knight errantry, with singing and buffoonery in such a combination that it could not fail to please. In the former play, which recounts the wanderings of Lamphedon in pursuit of his truelove, Clarisia, through Arabia, Phrygia, Thrace, and the Isle of Marofus, the audience is further amused by encounters with pirates, the songs of three musical but thievish tinkers of Arabia, and the trickeries of Common Conditions, the clown. In the latter play, the plot is somewhat similar, with the inclusion of an enchanter, Bryan Sansfoy, who, in the Forest of Marvels, keeps a dragon which has to be slain by Sir Clamydes before he can claim the love of the Danish princess, Juliana. Such plays, with many others known only by name,[29] delighted naïve spectators as heartily as they excited the scornful comment of Sir Philip Sidney.[30] Not merely in the formative years of Elizabethan dramatic development were romantic plays favored, but throughout the period audiences in the public theaters reveled in the impossible valor of their old heroes in the strangest of fabulous lands. Greene's *Orlando Furioso* (*c.* 1591), presenting an account of Orlando's mad love for Angelica, has all the conventions of the older romantic plays, and includes among its characters an enchanter, potentates from Cuba, Egypt, and Mexico, and the Twelve Peers of France. The very absurdities of this play made it a valuable addition to the repertory of a traveling company,[31] and its attractions were sufficient to enable Greene to sell it to the Admiral's Men in the summer of 1591 when the Queen's Men, the original purchasers, were in the country.[32] Thomas Heywood's *The Four*

---

[28] E. K. Chambers, *The Elizabethan Stage*, 4 vols. (Oxford, 1923), II, 286.

[29] Felix E. Schelling, *Elizabethan Drama, 1558-1642*, 2 vols. (Boston and New York, 1908), I, 198-99, and H. S. Murch (ed.), *The Knight of the Burning Pestle*, Yale Studies in English, XXXIII (New York, 1908), lxxxi-lxxxii.

[30] G. Gregory Smith (ed.), *Elizabethan Critical Essays*, 2 vols. (Oxford, 1904), I, 197.

[31] W. W. Greg, *Two Elizabethan Stage Abridgements: The Battle of Alcazar and Orlando Furioso*, Malone Society (London, 1922), pp. 134, 354. Dr. Greg suggests that the play was a failure on first production (p. 128), but elsewhere deduces evidence to show that it was repeatedly acted (p. 134). His implication that the vulgarization of the play would have appealed only to provincial audiences is hardly consistent with what we know of the taste of Londoners.

[32] Chambers, *The Elizabethan Stage*, II, 112.

Prentices of London, only one of many contemporary plays utilizing themes of absurd romance,[33] was nevertheless the favorite of its type with unsophisticated commoners. If, as Dryden commented about his own work, it was "bad enough to please,"[34] the predominant virtue in the eyes of tradesmen was its portrayal of their own heroism. Even if the four apprentices were descended from a mythical Earl of Bulloigne, they learned their valor in the marts of London, and went about the world displaying the prowess of plain citizens and mouthing speeches in praise of their fellow tradesmen, all of which was flattering to the listeners.

Nor did the caustic sallies of aristocratic critics in any whit affect the popuarity of such plays. Even dramatic travesties of the type of Peele's *The Old Wives' Tale* (c. 1590) and Beaumont's *The Knight of the Burning Pestle* (1607-08) fell on deaf ears. It is significant that the latter play, satirizing the dramatic taste of citizens and burlesquing productions like Heywood's *The Four Prentices of London,* was a stage failure, while Heywood's play, as the title-page of the 1615 quarto boasts, was "diuerse times Acted, at the Red Bull" and elsewhere.

The ridicule in *The Knight of the Burning Pestle,* however, gives an interesting insight into the drama which the grocer, his wife, and his apprentice preferred. The burlesque opens with the grocer's protest over the announced play:

This seven yeares there hath beene playes at this house, I have observed it, you have still girds at citizens; and now you call your play *The London Marchant.* Downe with your title, boy! downe with your title![35]

Having suffered enough from the insults of players, he refuses to see another satire:

. . . what need you study for new subjects, purposely to abuse your betters? Why could not you be contented, as well as others, with *The Legend of Whittington,* or *The Life and Death of Thomas Gresham, with the Building of the Royal Exchange?* or *The Story of Queene Elenor, with the Rearing of London Bridge upon Wool-sackes?*

---

[33] *See* Schelling, *op. cit.,* I, 200-208.

[34] R. M. Alden (ed.), *The Knight of the Burning Pestle* (Boston, 1910), Introduction, p. xxxviii.

[35] *Ibid.,* Induction, pp. 7-10.

The grocer's wife has not had so much experience at plays, but she has been promised a sight of *Jane Shore* and *The Bold Beauchamps*. When at length Ralph, the apprentice, is permitted to take a rôle in a play pleasing to citizens, the wife comments that he "hath playd before, my husband sayes, *Musidorus*, before the wardens of our Company," and, the husband adds, "hee should have played *Jeronimo* with a shooemaker, for a wager."[36] Ralph also demonstrates that he had learned at least Hotspur's speech about drowned honor from *Henry IV*, Part I. Among other plays with which the grocer shows an acquaintance is *The Travels of the Three English Brothers* (1607), recounting the adventures of the Sherley brothers in Italy, Russia, and Persia.[37] But it is *The Four Prentices of London* which furnishes the citizen-critic with the most fertile suggestions for improving the play in which his boy Ralph will bear the honor of captain of the trained bands in Mile End Road and at length make a dramatic end crying, "I die! flie, flie, my soule, to Grocers' Hall."[38]

Long after *The Knight of the Burning Pestle* had disappeared from the city stages, plays based on the fantastic romances which it satirizes continued to amuse and edify citizens, though a new type of romantic play, derived from the Italian *novelle*, competed for favor. Guy of Warwick, born of common parents, whose adventures were even more wondrous than those of Ralph, the grocer's boy, had a long stage career. In October, 1618, the Earl of Derby's

---

[36] *See ibid.*, p. 139. These were all plays whose themes would make them popular with citizens. A play on Dick Whittington, the apprentice who became thrice Lord Mayor of London, was entered in the *Stationers' Register* in 1604 but is no longer extant. The story of Gresham's philanthropy was related in Heywood's *If You Know Not Me, You Know Nobody* (1604-05). *The Story of Queen Eleanor* is unknown unless it refers to *Edward I*. Jane Shore's life furnished the dramatic material for Heywood's *Edward IV* (1593-94). A lost play called *The Bold Beauchamps* may have been written by Heywood. *Mucedorus* (before 1598), a mixture of romance and pastoral, in which the hero wins the princess by slaying a bear and a cannibalistic wild man, enjoyed enormous popularity for four decades and went through more than fifteen printings. It was the comedy of *Mucedorus* which a group of countrymen were acting at Witney in 1652 when the room collapsed, killing many and prompting John Rowe to write a dolorous pamphlet against plays. *See* T. S. Graves, "Notes on Puritanism and the Stage," *loc. cit.*, pp. 149 ff. *Jeronimo* may refer to *The Spanish Tragedy* (c. 1589) or to *The First Part of Jeronimo* (c. 1604).

[37] Alden, *op. cit.*, pp. 97, 147. (IV, i.)

[38] *Ibid.*, p. 134. (V, iii.)

Men performed at Islington a play now lost, *The Life and Death of Guy of Warwick*.[39] Twelve years later it was still being acted. In 1639 appeared another version entitled *The Tragical History, Admirable Achievements, and Various Events of Guy Earl of Warwick. A Tragedy*, attributed to B. J.[40] Though the clown, Philip Sparrow, burlesques the main action at times, the play is in no sense a travesty of the Guy legend, which is treated as a patriotic story of a national hero. St. George of England, of course, is the hero of John Kirke's *The Seven Champions of Christendom* (1634), which the author printed with a dedicatory epistle solemnly avouching the historical nature of the work.[41] The play undoubtedly delighted audiences at the Cockpit and the Red Bull, with its compound of "combats, witches, ghosts, hobgoblins, deeds of enchantment, thunder and lightning, heavy-witted clownery, uproarious song,"[42] and it provided the maximum amount of thrilling adventure as English George overthrew the other champions, saved them from an enchantment, rescued a damsel in distress, and performed other miracles. Not even a Shrove Tuesday crowd of unruly apprentices could have found such a play tame. Kirke, who possibly later deserted the stage for the career of a tradesman,[43] knew the taste of his kind and fed them to satiety.[44]

Even Italianate plays of love and intrigue, which all theatergoers took to their hearts, never completely superseded in bourgeois

---

[39] R. S. Crane, "The Vogue of *Guy of Warwick* from the Close of the Middle Ages to the Romantic Revival," *Publications of the Modern Language Association*, XXX (1915), 125-94.

[40] No copy of the first edition appears to be extant. This title is quoted from an edition of 1661, the title-page of which says the play was "Acted very Frequently with great Applause."

[41] In the dedication, Kirke comments on the possibilities for entertainment in a "history" of this sort: ". . . the Nature of the *Worke*, being History; it consists of many parts, not walking in one direct path, of *Comedy*, or *Tragedy*, but hauing a larger field to trace, which me thinks should yeeld more pleasure to the Reader, *Novelty* and *Variety* being the only Objects these our *Times* are taken with: the *Tragedy* may be too dull and solid, the *Comedy* too sharpe and bitter; but a well mixt portion of either, doubtlesse would make the sweetest *harmony*."

[42] W. J. Lawrence, "John Kirke, the Caroline Actor-Dramatist," *Studies in Philology*, XXI (1924), 586-93.

[43] *Ibid*., p. 592.

[44] Kirke's play is available in a modern reprint edited by Giles Edwin Dawson in the Western Reserve University *Bulletin*, N.S., No. 32 (1929).

favor the drama influenced by traditional romance. The fact that the common people continued to read the older romances throughout the seventeenth century may have influenced their liking for dramatic renderings of familiar stories or plots following well known patterns, but one must always remember that it was an age of adventure, when the draper in his shop could hear tales of veritable heroes as wondrous as the accounts of the Seven Champions of Christendom. The impossibilities and absurdities of the incidents did not offend audiences who had seen the doings of such swashbuckling contemporaries as Captain Thomas Stukeley[45] staged before them as actual truth. Outside of set conventions, naïve tastes do not ask for realism and credibility, as is evident from current motion-picture plays which exploit afresh the bourgeois interest in bizarre adventure. The zest for romantic otherworldliness persists more strongly than elsewhere in the appetites of those who practise in life the humdrum routine of getting and spending. Shopkeeping spectators who today gasp over the dashing heroics of a cinema actor as D'Artagnan or as a wanderer in Bali are spiritually akin to their predecessors who reveled in the acting of some Elizabethan favorite in the rôle of Guy of Warwick or the Blue Knight.

The attractions of the strange and the wonderful, though confined to no class, made a peculiarly strong appeal to the Elizabethan commonalty. As the pressure increased for plays which would transport their spectators to pleasing opera lands of unreality, the resources of mythology, history, geography, travels, and even folk-lore were ransacked to furnish forth the stage. Settings might bear indifferently the labels of the Kingdom of Fess, the steppes of Asia, the courts of Charlemagne or Pluto, but the conventions of adventurous action were the same. Such plays as *The Travels of the Three English Brothers*, which Beaumont's grocer had seen, had the additional fascination of timely journalism without sacrificing any of the trappings of romance. With the development of Levantine trade came a new interest in the Turks and

---

[45] The play of *Stukeley* was acted about 1596; it dealt with the deeds of that notorious, though doubtless secretly admired, soldier of fortune, in England, Ireland, Spain, Rome, and Africa.

their wars, and in the piracy incidental to that trade.[46] Robert Daborne's *A Christian Turned Turk* (1609-12) wove apostacy, piracy, and the atmosphere of the sea into a play dramatizing the lives of two pirates about whom the populace had already read in penny pamphlets. The very titles of Heywood's *Fortune by Land and Sea* (c. 1607) and *The Fair Maid of the West, or a Girl Worth Gold* (c. 1617) were enough to attract the apprentice in search of vicarious adventure, which was spiced in the latter play with a dashing barmaid fearless alike in the clutches of villainous Turkish bashaw and amorous Italian duke. The anonymous *Dick of Devonshire* (1625), in which a lusty Englishman with a simple quarterstaff proves his ability to trounce three fully armed Spaniards, must have thrilled to emulation the youths who saw the play. The audience who witnessed the deeds of Hercules and as many of his mythical contemporaries as Heywood could crowd upon the Red Bull stage in the noisy *Age* plays made no distinction between the doings of gods, demigods, and men. Adventurous action was what the spectators wanted and was what the dramatist furnished, whether the scene was Olympus, Cadiz, or the islands beyond the seas.

Tragedies of rant and blood, filled as they were with heroics, clashing arms, vengeful ghosts, retributive death, and high-flown oratory—often bearing implications of good morality—could not fail to please the general run of Elizabethans. Tamburlaine, roaring his way through two plays to a bloody destiny, was the delight of groundlings as well as of courtly listeners to Marlowe's mighty line as delivered by the rafter-rocking Edward Alleyn. *The Spanish Tragedy* (c. 1589) with its murders, madness, and mutilations curdled the blood of playgoers for a generation and spawned a school of drama that carried on its conventional horrors. Rowdy audiences whose appetites for gore had been whetted by *The Spanish Tragedy* and *Titus Andronicus* (1594) found even *Hamlet* (1601?) merely another sensational play, and English actors in search of something obvious enough to entertain German audiences who understood little of their language added it to their repertory. *The Jew of Malta*, with the villain in the title rôle

---

[46] For the vogue of plays on the Turks, see J. Q. Adams (ed.), *John Mason's The Turke*, in *Materialien*, Vol. XXXVII (1913), Introduction.

setting the lovers of Abigail to murder each other in a thrilling stage duel, poisoning the nuns, and at length falling into a pot of boiling oil, was a popular success. Of the traffic of Faustus with the devil, of his compacts in blood, and of the buffoonery of the magician with the Pope and the friars, spectators could never have enough. Witches, called up from the nethermost depths, or brought upon the stage from a contemporary witch-hunt, as in Heywood and Brome's *The Late Lancashire Witches* (1633), were an ingredient certain to thrill a public who believed implicitly in their machinations. Not only tradesmen but courtiers enjoyed such spectacles, as Shakespeare well knew when he wrote *Macbeth*. A dramatic prescription which produced an orgy of horrors, relieved with incongruous clownery, delighted the audiences in the popular theaters throughout the period.

Plays based on history, native and foreign, made up a large part of the dramatic fare acceptable to all types of audiences, aristocratic and plebeian. Even to a Puritan it was more difficult to find fault with a play that preached a propaganda of patriotism, and citizens whose consciences plagued them about idle and wanton shows felt a satisfaction in learning from the stage the past grandeur of their country. Better even than plays on biblical themes were those derived from chronicle-histories, for the former might smack of blasphemy, whereas the latter could offend only when they meddled with contemporary affairs of state and brought grave personages into ridicule.[47] As the hysterical fervor of nationalism, set aflame in 1588, swept on, the stage kept pace with current thought by dramatizing from English history episodes which glorified national virtues and idealized heroes of the past. So great was the demand for history plays that for nearly two decades after the Spanish Armada, one play in five was drawn from English history, and approximately two hundred and twenty of the total number of plays acted before 1642 were derived from

---

[47] For the interest in general historical literature, see Chap. IX, *supra*.

Nashe in *Pierce Penilesse*, edited by Harrison, pp. 86-88, called attention to the value of chronicle plays, "wherein our forefathers valiant acts (that haue line long buried in rustie brasse, and worme-eaten bookes) are reuiued, and they themselues raised from the Graue of Obliuion, and brought to pleade their aged Honours in open presence: than which, what can be a sharper reproofe to these degenerate effeminate dayes of ours."

historical sources.[48] Few dramatists were so shrewdly careful to capitalize upon popular interest as William Shakespeare, and it was not mere chance that made him found more than a third of his plays on the English chronicles. With a public eager for dramatized history, few playwrights neglected the *genre*, which brought upon the stage every sovereign from Edward the Confessor to King James, besides such shadowy monarchs as Arthur, Lear, and Cymbeline.

In the history plays more clearly than anywhere else one finds reflected the popular conceptions of the state and of kingship, for though the dramatists were consistently royalists, so were the masses of the citizenry throughout the reigns of Elizabeth and James, and even in the early years of Charles. Nothing pleased the groundlings better than a royal king, and all were ready to approve sentiments expressing the subject's obligations of loyalty. In the portrayal of wicked and tyrannical kings, dramatists were careful to imply, and sometimes baldly to state, the contrast with the magnanimity of the reigning house. Plays about traitors, from *The Life and Death of Jack Straw* (1587) to Ford's *Perkin Warbeck*[49] (1633), gave an opportunity for object lessons heartily approved by citizens, for nothing was so objectionable to tradesmen as the disruptions of civil strife. Strong kings were the favorites of the multitude. Thus it was not merely the clownery of Richard Tarlton in *The Famous Victories of Henry V* (c. 1586-88) which gave that play its popularity and paved the way for the long stage life of Shakespeare's great trilogy on Henry IV and Henry V. The glory of the Plantagenets was felt to forecast and parallel Tudor greatness. The Wars of the Roses, likewise important for stage purposes, represented to the Elizabethan the chaos which the strong hands of Henry Tudor and his successors had modeled into the state of their own time. Richard III with his

---

[48] Schelling, *op. cit.*, I, 251-52. Cf. the same author's *The English Chronicle Play* (New York, 1902), *passim*.

[49] That the play of *Perkin Warbeck* provided valuable lessons against treason for those who could not read is attested by Thomas Gainsford in *The True Exemplary, And Remarkable History of the Earle of Tirone* (1619) : "How *Perkin Warbeck*, for all his exhaled vapourings, went forward assisted by the Scottish policie, Flemmish credulitie, and inueterat malice of the Duches of *Burgundy*, against the house of *Lancaster*, our stages of *London*, haue instructed those which cannot read."—Sig. B 1ᵛ.

crooked back and sinister record made an admirable stage foil for the noble founder of the House of Tudor, for whom the populace had an affection which made them never weary of plays magnifying Tudor grandeur. The type of flag-waving and nationalistic rant still so conspicuous today in our newspapers and political oratory, found vent in Elizabethan history plays which excited the admiration of super-patriotic citizens. No play was utterly bad if it afforded a few speeches reminding Englishmen of their valor at Agincourt, or recalled the splendors of their island girdled by a silver sea, or boasted that they were chosen of God to smite the Spaniards and inherit, not only the earth, but heaven as well. Through the mouths of oratorical players, the effervescent nationalism, bubbling in the breast of every citizen, found utterance.

Historical and pseudo-historical plays in which plain Englishmen were portrayed in romantic fashion enjoyed unusual popularity with middle-class audiences. Honest artisans and tradesmen who by their frankness, bravery, and loyalty won the praise of kings became conventional characters in plays which frequently sacrificed history to romantic fiction, as in the case of *George a Greene, the Pinner of Wakefield* (c. 1593), an excellent example of the type. Exalting the virtue of English wives and the heroism of plain yeomen and citizens, the play had every element to arouse the enthusiasm of commoners, including a scene much favored by such plays, in which royalty in disguise mingles with the subjects in bluff good fellowship. The title-page of the 1600 quarto of Heywood's *Edward IV* (1593-94) emphasizes features which the printer thought would appeal to citizen-purchasers, for besides odd bits of history from Edward's reign, the play also relates "His mery pastime with the Tanner of Tamworth, as also his loue to faire Mistrisse Shoare, her great promotion, fall and miserie, and lastly the lamentable death of both her and her husband. Likewise the besieging of London, by Bastard Falconbridge, and the valiant defence of the same by the Lord Maior and the Citizens." Similar ingredients dilute the historical material of the same author's *If You Know Not Me, You Know Nobody* (1604-05) which provides, along with a dramatization of the early years of Elizabeth and the later Armada victory, scenes in which Sir

Thomas Gresham is held up as the peerless merchant, and Old Hobson, the humorous shopkeeper, blusters his way to the hearts of the listeners. Most applauded, perhaps, were those scenes in Samuel Rowley's play about Henry VIII, *When You See Me You Know Me* (1603-05), in which the King in disguise is arrested by the watch, like any common citizen, for beating with a broadsword a rascal whom he encounters during a night adventure in London.[50] Obvious appeals to the prejudices of the citizenry are found in such plays as *Sir Thomas More* (c. 1596) and *The Life and Death of Thomas, Lord Cromwell* (c. 1592). The former stresses More's affection for the common people and devotes considerable space to dramatizing the anti-alien sentiment which was breaking out afresh when the play was being acted. In the life of Cromwell, the dramatist found material for extolling qualities admired by the commonalty. In him the people saw, as Professor Schelling has said, "the very apotheosis of citizen virtue. It is Cromwell's honorable thrift and capacity in trade, his temperance, piety, and staunch Protestantism which are dwelt on and extolled. He befriends the broken debtor and outwits the wrong-doer. He is mindful of others' favors to him, forgetful of his own. When humble intimates of his youth claim the notice of his lordship, he acknowledges them with gracious candor and bestows largesses on them, and he kneels in his chancellor's robes to receive the blessing of his aged blacksmith father."[51] If not every play could flatter the multitude with so apt an example of their own kind, scores at least presented upon the stage worthy citizens to excite the emulation and stimulate the patronage of plain Englishmen. Plays based on history and legend offered many opportunities for situations pleasing to bourgeois vanity.

Historical plays occasionally were used to further propaganda favored by the citizenry. Dekker's *The Whore of Babylon* (c. 1605) was an arrant piece of dramatic allegory directed against Spaniards and Catholics and was apparently prepared to take advantage of a flare of popular sentiment against Rome and the traditional enemy of England. It "doubtless represents faithfully enough the popular contemporary attitude of the lower classes,"[52]

---

[50] Schelling, *The English Chronicle Play*, p. 243.
[51] *Ibid.*, p. 217.   [52] *Ibid.*, p. 240.

and if the Gunpowder Plot did not help to inspire the play, few dramatists have been so fortunate in the timing of a production whose success depended upon popular prejudice. Of slightly different color was Wentworth Smith's *The Hector of Germany, or the Palsgrave, Prime Elector* (*c.* 1615), which was acted "at the Red-Bull, and at the Curtayne, by a Company of Young men of this Citie."[53] The dramatization of a heroic German prince was intended as an expression of the enthusiasm of the citizens of London over the marriage of the Princess Elizabeth to the Protestant Elector of the Palatinate. Though the prologue denies that the play has any relation to recent events,[54] the disavowal only

---

[53] From the title-page of the quarto of 1615. The play has been edited by L. W. Payne, Jr., in the Publications of the University of Pennsylvania (Philadelphia, 1906).

[54] "Our Author for himselfe, this bad me say,
  Although the Palsgraue be the name of th' Play,
  Tis not that Prince, which in this Kingdome late,
  Marryed the Mayden-glory of our state:
  What Pen dares be so bold in this strict age,
  To bring him while he liues vpon the Stage?
  And though he would, Authorities sterne brow
  Such a presumptuous deede will not allow:
  And he must not offend Authoritie,
  Tis of a Palsgraue generous and high,
  Of an vndaunted heart, an Hectors spirit,
  For his great valour, worthy royall merite;
  Whose fayre achieuements, and victorious glory,
  Is the mayne subiect of our warlike Story.
  Mars gouerns here, his influence rules the day,
  And should by right be Prologue to the Play:
  But that besides the subiect, Mercury
  Sent me to excuse our insufficiencie.
  If you should aske vs, being men of Trade,
  Wherefore the Players facultie we inuade?
  Our answere is, No ambition to compare
  With any, in that qualitie held rare;
  Nor with a thought for any grace you giue
  To our weake action, by their course to liue:
  But as in Camps, and Nurseries of Art,
  Learning and valour haue assum'd a part,
  In a Cathurnall Sceane their wits to try,
  Such is our purpose in this History.
  Emperours haue playd, and their Associates to,
  Souldiers and Schollers; tis to speake and do.
  If Citizens come short of their high fame,
  Let Citizens beare with vs for the name.

strengthens the impression that the "men of trade" who performed the play took this means of paying a compliment to the couple whom Protestant Londoners, especially, regarded as protagonists of the ideals for which they were at that moment ready to fight. The play was a success—the certain destiny of any stage piece which could so completely express current prejudices by glorifying English and German prowess and deriding Spaniards and Frenchmen. A hint is given by Smith in the dedication to Sir John Swinnerton, the lord mayor, that he proposes to honor citizens in other plays:

. . . this Play, intuled [entitled] The Palsgraue, beeing made for Citizens, who acted it well; I deemde it fitte to bee Patronizde by a Citizen. And not knowing any so worthy thereof as your selfe, I made choyce of your Wor : to be my Mecoenas : The kinde acceptance whereof, will make me proceede farther in your praise. And as I haue begun in a former Play, called the Freemans Honour, acted by the Nowseruants of the Kings Maiestie, to dignifie the worthy Companie of the Marchantaylors, whereof you are a principall Ornament, I shall ere long, make a choyce of some subiect to equall it.[55]

Judged by the plays that Smith wrote,[56] the promised productions might be expected to derive from history and legend and to voice ideals that citizens favored.

Some of the most charming, as well as most popular, of Elizabethan plays presented idealized pictures of citizen life. No Londoner could complain that Dekker failed to give a noble description of the gentle craft in *The Shoemaker's Holiday* (1599), with its vivid characterization of Simon Eyre, the jolly shoemaker, whose virtues made him lord mayor of London. Shoemakers, indeed, were useful persons to writers who wished to draw a

---

And Gentlemen, we hope what is well meant,
Will grace the weake deede for the good intent.
Our best we promise with a dauntlesse cheeke ;
And so we gayne your loue, tis all we seeke."

[55] In contrast to this compliment to Sir John Swinnerton was Robert Tailor's *The Hog Hath Lost His Pearl* (1613), acted by apprentices "divers times" at Whitefriars, in which the real or fancied satire of the Lord Mayor was so clear that several of the apprentice-actors were arrested and lodged in Bridewell. *See* Schelling, *Elizabethan Drama*, I, 521-22.

[56] In addition to the extant *Hector of Germany*, see the list of lost plays in Chambers, *op. cit.*, III, 493-94.

sympathetic picture of the world of craftsmen, for by tradition they were merry souls full of whimsies but possessing, albeit, hearts of gold.[57] William Rowley's *A Shoemaker a Gentleman* (c. 1608), "sundry Times Acted at the Red Bull and other Theaters,"[58] was pillaged from the same source as Dekker's play on the cobblers (namely, Deloney's *The Gentle Craft*), and must have delighted London tradesmen with its scenes showing the sons of an ancient British king practising the honorable trade of the shoemaker. Crude but vigorous clownery, filled with the salty idiom of London streets, added to the entertainment offered by these plays. Deloney, scoffed at by more aristocratic writers as a mere "balleting silk-weaver," furnished material for other plays idealizing craftsmen ; but now lost are Haughton's *Six Yeomen of the West* (1601), and a second part by Hathway and Wentworth Smith, *The Six Clothiers of the West* (1601-02).[59] Not only was the average spectator fascinated by stage representations of fancied worlds in regions beyond the seas, but he also enjoyed the dramatization of the world he knew. Scores of plays depended for their popularity on their fidelity to scenes from ordinary English life, and, if one balances idealized pictures against biased satires, a reasonably accurate transcript of contemporary middle-class life can be recreated from the drama alone.

Though not completely eschewed by middle-class audiences, the satirical drama of London life made less of a popular appeal than the drama that painted a favorable picture of the bourgeois milieu. Some of the stage satires which lashed the follies and vices of contemporary London were popular successes, for human nature is such that the individual rarely applies the jibes of the satirist to himself. Undoubtedly many a usurer who witnessed the discomfiture of Sir Giles Overreach saw in him the outlines of some rival extortioner. Theatrical satire of commercial dishonesty, sharp practice, and conventional follies and iniquities found citizens

---

[57] A compilation of some of the craftsmen in the drama and elsewhere is provided by C. W. Camp, *The Artisan in Elizabethan Literature* (New York, 1924), *passim*.

[58] From the title-page of the quarto of 1638. In the dedicatory address by the printer, the statement is made that "it is a Play that is often acted ; and when others fade and are out of date, yet this doth endure to the Last." Cf. Alexis F. Lange (ed.), *The Gentlecraft*, in *Palaestra*, XVIII (1903), xlii-xliii.

[59] Schelling, *The English Chronicle Play*, p. 221.

ready to applaud, for each saw in the stage caricature, not himself but some neighbor at whom he was perfectly willing to laugh. Animosity was aroused, however, when dramatists began to single out the commercial groups for general scorn. What the worthy grocer in *The Knight of the Burning Pestle* resented was an apparent effort to make citizens ridiculous. The tendency among dramatists to condemn burghers as a class increased in the seventeenth century as class consciousness became more acute and as the citizen became identified in the minds of playwrights with the unpleasant aspects of Puritan narrowness.[60] As the hostility between bourgeoisie and aristocracy increased in the early seventeenth century, the drama became more definitely differentiated into types appealing to one or the other social group. The more popular of the public playhouses continued to offer plays which could not fail to please the multitude, while such a fashionable public playhouse as the Globe and the more expensive private theaters produced innumerable plays in which citizens were held up to derision.[61] Beaumont and Fletcher, Middleton, Richard Brome,[62] and others delighted in stressing the tradesman's greed, hypocrisy, dishonesty, and cowardice. As the comedy of manners developed, the citizen, too often for his comfort, found himself at a play in which the dramatist's choice jests were to him merely an insult. Naturally he showed no enthusiasm for such plays and gave his patronage to other types. The comedy of manners, therefore, found little favor with the middle class, who expressed a decided preference for older types of drama. Even if the citizen had not been the butt of the jests in the comedy of manners, it is doubtful whether the multitude would have shown much more enthusiasm than they did because such plays required sophisticated tastes for proper appreciation.

Nevertheless, the popular reception of a few of Ben Jonson's comedies shows that citizens were able to laugh at a satirical lashing of their follies; the failure of other comedies by Jonson

---

[60] Wilhelm Creizenach, *The English Drama in the Age of Shakespeare* (Philadelphia and London, 1916), p. 144.

[61] Cf. the ridicule of the citizen in such a play as the anonymous *An Alarm for London* (1600) and in Beaumont and Fletcher's *The Woman Hater* (c. 1606).

[62] C. E. Andrews, *Richard Brome*, Yale Studies in English, XLVI (New York, 1913), 106, 129.

indicates that the populace resented his bludgeon of scorn. Though Jonson gave an immense stimulus to the drama of London life, he was no such idol of the multitude as was Thomas Heywood, and he[63] had no sympathy with the aspirations of the middle class. His dramatic reputation was chiefly with the intellectual and aristocratic groups, as was natural, since most of his plays were produced at the more expensive private theaters. A few of his comedies, however, which later critics have regarded as his best— *Volpone* (1606), *The Alchemist* (1610), and *Bartholomew Fair* (1614) —were acted at the public theaters "with great applause."[64] It is significant that these plays satirize shortcomings which the average individual would condemn, and the last two, presenting a great gallery of rogues from the London that everyone knew, were certain to produce laughter from all men familiar with the trickeries of the alchemists, projectors, cheats, and fakirs with which the metropolis swarmed, in fair time and out. Even the damning caricatures of the Puritans in the panoramic *Bartholomew Fair*, most popular of all the comedies, did not prevent its amusing many whose common sense rebelled at much of Puritan fanaticism and who must have appreciated the comic aspects of Jonson's stage representations of Puritan weaknesses.[65] The patronage accorded such plays indicates that citizens could see humor in their own foibles if the satire was not intended to make them ridiculous as a class.

If Jonson had shown more sympathy with the middle class and had put less vitriol into his satires, his comedies would have won far more general favor. Yet curiously the dramatist who was most violently scornful of the ambitions of tradesmen[66] col-

---

[63] C. H. Herford and Percy Simpson (eds.), *Ben Jonson*, 10 vols. (Oxford, 1925), II, 33.

[64] *Volpone* and *The Alchemist* were Globe plays; *Bartholomew Fair* was acted at the Hope.—*Ibid.*, II, 49, 87 ff., 131.

[65] The darkening controversy, however, forced the withdrawal of the play about 1620 because of its attacks on the Puritans.—*Ibid.*, II, 131.

[66] The latest editors of Jonson suggest that his appointment to the office of city chronologer was calculated to silence the ridicule that he had heaped on citizens. "And, in effect, Jonson's remaining plays show a remarkable abstention from topics offensive to the City."—*Ibid.*, I, 93. Perhaps the authorities had found by experience with Thomas Middleton, predecessor of Jonson in office, that the bribe of a municipal post went far toward softening dramatic attacks.

laborated with Marston and Chapman in *Eastward Ho!* (1605), one of the best dramatic expressions of bourgeois ideals.[67] Though *Eastward Ho!* finally enjoyed a career in the public theaters under the aegis of Henslowe,[68] it was not originally designed to tickle the ears of the multitude. Instead, it was first performed at the Blackfriars Theatre, where few defenses of the city were ever heard, and was a reply to *Westward Ho!* (1604), prepared by Dekker and Webster for the rival theater of St. Paul's, which catered to a select and aristocratic audience. *Westward Ho!* represents a new fashion in plays about the city, a fashion evident in the contemptuous satires of Thomas Middleton, whose influence might have been responsible for Dekker's giving over the older type of play like *The Shoemaker's Holiday* in favor of the new comedy, which sentimentalized vice and mocked the virtues of respectable citizens.[69] Jonson and his colleagues must have been irked by their rivals' success with the claptrap appeal of *Westward Ho!*, which set forth as a realistic picture a London in which city-wives dallied with court gallants in an atmosphere totally devoid of moral integrity. The opposite picture appears in *Eastward Ho!*, which reveals an ideal of morality approved by citizens. Master Touchstone, the goldsmith, the very personification of success resulting from industry, frugality, and honesty, sets such an example to his apprentice, Goulding, that the latter by applying the master's lessons marries his daughter, rises to distinction, and becomes an honored municipal official. In contrast, the idle Quicksilver pursues a prodigal's course leading to debt and prison. Touchstone's two daughters present a similar contrast. The vapid Gertrude, sensual and extravagant, desires above all else to match with a knight and be called a lady, whereas Mildred remembers her position and is content to make a good wife to a thrifty apprentice. In Touchstone, Goulding, and Mildred the virtues that common-

---

[67] To emphasize the bourgeois quality of this play, Creizenach (*op. cit.*, p. 144) observes—with surprising inaccuracy: "There is only one play among those surviving from the Shakespearean period in which the newly conceived middle-class views are expressed. This play is *Eastward Ho!* . . ."

[68] Julia Hamlet Harris (ed.), *Eastward Hoe*, Yale Studies in English, LXXIII (New Haven, 1926), lv-lvi.

[69] Thomas Marc Parrott (ed.), *The Plays and Poems of George Chapman: The Comedies* (London, 1914), pp. 839-40.

ers regarded as the keystones of society were glorified rather than derided as in the rival play, *Westward Ho!*, and its successor, *Northward Ho!* With the incidental satire of the ambitions of foolish and vain daughters, eager for social promotion, the average sturdy burgher was in hearty accord.

It is not my contention that the dramatists who wrote *Eastward Ho!* deliberately set out to be the protagonists of middle-class ideals. But Jonson, Chapman, and Marston all possessed a strong moral streak, and what they were doing was to protest against the twisted and false ethics of a play with which their rivals were winning plaudits. From the Blackfriars stage, a play presenting a favorable picture of bourgeois conduct must have been something of a *tour de force*; indeed, it is perfectly possible that the complacence and self-righteousness of Touchstone and Goulding were so burlesqued in the acting as to make such tradesmen ridiculous. The underlying morality of the play, however, was sound, and if it was acted straight, as it must have been when Henslowe later produced it, undoubtedly it attracted the favorable attention of the mass of playgoers, who resented the new style of realism ridiculing their prudential virtues.

The non-satirical play dealing with domestic situations, based on the lives of ordinary people, found in the average citizen an eager spectator. While it is unnecessary to seek a reason for an interest perennially fresh, the consumption of treatises and printed sermons about family relations shows the trend of much Elizabethan social thinking.[70] The tragic relations of husband, wife, and illicit lover provided a vehicle for a theatrical sensation capable of running the gamut of sentimentality or pandering to the grosser appetites of the multitude, while, at the same time, it preached a sermon against the crying sins of adultery and murder. In place of the tabloid newspaper, the Elizabethan had his ballad, pamphlet, and stage play presenting journalistically the latest crime, with all the gory details, which the modern reader is accustomed to demand. Philip Henslowe, with a canniness which brought that unlettered producer financial success, made much use of the triangle play, both comic and tragic. In comedy, a good example

---

[70] *See* Chap. VII, *supra*.

is Henry Porter's *The Two Angry Women of Abington* (1598) with its scolding wives and embarrassed husbands. As if the boisterous wrath of the angry women were not enough, the play also emphasizes "the humorous mirthe of Dicke Coomes and Nicholas Prouerbes, two Seruingmen." The favorite domestic plays, however, were devoted to more serious themes, and murder, actual or intended, usually added its grim fascination to the piece. Naturally the interest generally focuses upon the conduct of the wife. In *Patient Grissil* (1598), in *How a Man May Choose a Good Wife from a Bad* (1602), and in *The London Prodigal* (1605), the dramatists stress the virtues of the faithful wife in the face of extraordinary provocation. A variation on the theme is presented by Heywood's *A Woman Killed with Kindness* (1603), in which the husband forbears to wreak the usual blood vengeance on his wife and her lover. The use of the stage as a platform for the promotion of a definite domestic propaganda reached its culmination in George Wilkins's *The Miseries of Enforced Marriage* (1607). This play relates the marital infelicities of a certain Walter Calverly, whose misfortunes were attributed to a marriage into which a scheming uncle had forced him. It was the same Calverly, who, by slaying his wife, had provided the theme for *The Yorkshire Tragedy* (c. 1606).

The horrors of murder, especially when there were domestic complications, delighted many an audience who were also eager readers of ballads and pamphlets on the same theme. A typical example of the *genre* is *Arden of Feversham* (c. 1592), which tells of the violent death of a Kentish man, "most wickedlye murdered, by the meanes of his disloyall and wanton wyfe, who for the love she bare to one Mosbie, hyred two desperat ruffins Blackwill and Shakbag, to kill him. Wherein is shewed the great mallice and discimulation of a wicked woman, the vnsatiable desire of filthie lust and the shamefull end of all murderers."[71] Surely the terrors of retributive justice promised here must have been sufficient for any Puritan. Most of the murder plays were more timely than this Kentish tragedy, dating from the reign of Edward VI. Presumably the more recent the crime, the more fascinating was the play. Robert Yarington found in the slaying of one Beech, a Thames Street

---

[71] Title-page of quarto of 1592, quoted by Chambers, *op. cit.*, IV, 3.

chandler, in 1594, material for half of his *Two Lamentable Tragedies* (1594-1601); the other half he filled out with a darker version of the story of the Babes in the Wood. The Beech murder, which Londoners seemed unwilling to forget, was the theme of a lost play by Day and Haughton in 1599. A tragedy involving a merchant in the year 1573 was the subject of *A Warning for Fair Women* (before 1599), "Containing, The most tragicall and lamentable murther of Master George Sanders of London Marchant, nigh Shooters hill. Consented vnto By his owne wife, acted by M. Browne, Mistris Drewry and Trusty Roger agents therin : with their seuerall ends."[72] A passage in the play emphasizes the utility of plays about murders, by relating the case of a Norfolk woman who was moved to the confession of her crime by seeing a play similar to *A Warning for Fair Women*. Heywood later used this incident in *An Apology for Actors* (1612).[73] Occasionally the domestic drama so accurately described a contemporary event that it created a scandal, as was true of a lost play, *The Late Murder in Whitechapel, or Keep the Widow Waking*, by Dekker, William Rowley, Ford, and Webster, an arrant piece of scandal-mongering acted at the Red Bull in 1624.[74] The ingenious authors put into one play the separate elements of a local murder and the forced marriage of an old widow who lived almost within earshot of the Red Bull. Undoubtedly plays of murder and domestic misadventure found favor in the sight of the multitude, who extracted therefrom sufficient good lessons to atone for the enjoyment of such sensations.[75] Only when the playwrights overstepped all

---

[72] Title-page of quarto of 1599, quoted *ibid.*, IV, 52.

[73] John Payne Collier, *The History of English Dramatic Poetry to the Time of Shakespeare, and Annals of the Stage to the Restoration*, 3 vols. (London, 1831), II, 438.

[74] Charles J. Sisson, "Keep the Widow Waking, a Lost Play by Dekker," *The Library*, 4th Ser., VIII (1927-28), 39-57, 233-59. Professor Sisson has made a skillful reconstruction of the play from legal records.

[75] For mention of other murder plays, see Schelling, *Elizabethan Drama*, I, 343-48. *See also* Sidney Lee, "The Topical Side of the Elizabethan Drama," *Transactions* of the New Shakespeare Society (1887), pp. 1-35. Speaking of *Arden of Feversham* and *A Warning for Fair Women* the author says : "Viewed from a purely historical standpoint the plays are very accurate though not very striking descriptions of middle-class society in London in the sixteenth century. There are everywhere plain hints of the dangers incurred by the presence of a large class of riotous idlers, discharged soldiers, and sailors over whom the police exercised little control." Somewhat similar in interest to the murder plays were the journalistic witch plays.

bounds of decency, as in the foregoing play by Dekker and his colleagues, did London citizens find fault with this type of drama.

Stage representations of events concerned with the foreign ventures of London tradesmen indicate that business men of the day were not behind those of our own in utilizing the stage for purposes of commercial propaganda. Such plays made a natural appeal to the general public, for there was scarcely a tradesman who did not expect the activities of the trading companies to affect his business, and a large proportion of the commercial class made investments in the foreign enterprises. Whether *The Conquest of the West Indies* (1601), a lost play by Day, Haughton, and Smith, recounted the adventures of English buccaneers, we have no way of knowing, but we may be sure that *A Tragedy of the Plantation of Virginia*, licensed for performance at the Curtain in 1623 on condition that the profaneness be left out, attracted a throng of Londoners who had a personal interest in that undertaking. And we may also be reasonably certain that the authorities did not permit the actors to censure the management of that colonial project. Though an unknown playwright was quick to see the dramatic and the propagandic possibilities of the massacre by the Dutch of the East India Company's trading post at Amboyna in 1623, the Privy Council forbade the performance of the play, which perished. The best extant example of a play designed to further business propaganda is *The Launching of the Mary, or the Seaman's Honest Wife*, licensed by Sir Henry Herbert in 1633, provided that "all Oathes, prophaness, and publick Ribaldry" be omitted.[76] The preserved manuscript, which bears the censor's deletions, shows that all political allusions, even the decade-old Amboyna affair, were still frowned upon. The author was Walter Mountfort, an official of the East India Company, who apparently wrote the play to restore himself to favor after having been charged with minor peculations. The drama, an elaborate apologia for the company, is essentially a dramatization of Thomas Mun's prose defense, *The Discourse of Trade from England vnto the East Indies* (1621). Since

---

The 1658 title-page of *The Witch of Edmonton, a Known True Story* (1621), by Dekker, William Rowley, and Ford, indicates the appeal of the journalistic quality in such plays.

[76] A complete account of the play is given in F. S. Boas, *Shakespeare and the Universities* (Oxford, 1923), pp. 167-238.

disasters to ships, the high prices of some of the imported commodities, and jealousy of the power of the East India Company had created considerable talk, no doubt the play was highly acceptable to company officials, for it denies charges of profiteering, of flooding the country with unnecessary luxuries, of losing ships and men in large numbers, and of neglecting the widows and orphans of its sailors.[77] On the contrary, the play maintains, the company fosters the export trade by which the country flourishes; it trains sailors for use in times of national necessity; and it even helps farmers by buying corn and food supplies at home. How successful the play was, we do not know, but, with considerable skill, it put into dramatic form matter of widespread concern. It is another indication that the commercial classes were aware of the potency of the stage as a means of influencing public opinion.

The use of dramatic entertainment as a vehicle for mercantile ideas and even definite propaganda was not a completely new discovery of seventeenth-century playwrights. Not only in many of the preceding plays had middle-class ideals been consciously set forth, but in the annual pageants given on Lord Mayor's Day, the satisfaction that citizens felt in the contemplation of their own glory reached the zenith of dramatic expression. In the hands of city-poets like Munday, Dekker, Webster, Heywood, or even the usually contemptuous Middleton,[78] the pageants were wondrous creations presenting an allegory which emphasized the dignity of citizens and the importance of the particular company from whose membership came the lord mayor for that year. Past heroes were called from the records of the company to parade before an admiring populace and proclaim the glory of London tradesmen. Nor was the opportunity lost to drive home the value of simple virtues, which business men regarded as fundamental; and doubtless many an apprentice, witnessing the passing spec-

---

[77] *Ibid.*, pp. 200 ff.

[78] *See* J. G. Nichols, *London Pageants* (London, 1837), pp. 97-98, for a brief account of the city-poets. The same author also gives a list of the lord mayors' pageants. The subject is also treated with considerable detail by F. W. Fairholt, *Lord Mayors' Pageants*, Percy Society, X (1843), and by Robert Withington, *English Pageantry*, 2 vols. (Cambridge, Mass., 1918-20), II, 3-119. Cf. also George Unwin, *The Gilds and Companies of London* (London, 1908), pp. 267-92, and R. C. Bald, "Middleton's Civic Employments," *Modern Philology*, XXXI (1933-34), 65-78.

tacle from crowded Cheapside, went back to his shop, determined
to be industrious and thrifty so that some day he might ride to
the Guild Hall amid such splendors as were prepared by Munday
for Sir John Leman and the Fishmongers in 1616, or by Webster for Sir John Gore and the Merchant Taylors in 1624, or by any
of the other makers of pageants, for each tried to outdo the other
in extravagant praise of the dignity of trade.[79] In Webster's pageant, fighting Sir John Hawkwood accompanies the scholarly and
beneficent Sir Thomas White, as the great merchant tailors of the
past are revived to inspire their later brethren. In addition to the
historical personages, there are allegorical figures who teach lessons profitable to young tradesmen. Edward III appears to tell of
eight kings who were proud to be of the fellowship of merchant
tailors; and when Prince Henry is figured forth in a bit of allegory, lessons useful to both prince and apprentice are stressed,
not least of which is diligence, taught by the thrifty ant.[80] Middleton's pageant in 1617 for Sir George Bowles and the Grocers'
Company, entitled *The Triumphs of Honor and Industry*, contains
an allegorical figure of Industry "holding a golden ball in her
hand, upon which stands a cupid, signifying that industry gets
both wealth and love."[81] In all the pageants the virtues responsible
for the glory of tradesmen find exemplification.

The importance of dramatic productions as a means for the
expression of bourgeois ideas and ideals in Tudor and Stuart
England has not been sufficiently realized. The playhouse, which
under the later Stuarts was to alienate middle-class support, remained throughout the first four decades of the seventeenth century the recreational resort of employer and apprentice; and, as
we have seen, though Puritan criticism asserts the contrary, the
stage was often the instrument for the inculcation of middle-class
virtues. Of all the dramatists who drew material from the life

---

[79] Spendall, a thriftless apprentice in John Cooke's *Greene's Tu Quoque* (1611), exclaims: "By this light, I do not think but to be Lord Mayor of London before I die,
and have three pageants carried before me, besides a ship and an unicorn."—Quoted
by Fairholt, *op. cit.*, p. 1.

[80] W. C. Hazlitt (ed.), *The Dramatic Works of John Webster*, 4 vols. (London, 1897),
III, 225-47. The title of Webster's pageant is *Monuments of Honor*.

[81] Fairholt, *op. cit.*, p. 43.

around them, Thomas Heywood was the most significant of the
stage spokesmen of burgher ethics and ideas, for he best expresses
those prudential qualities which were the basis of middle-class
solidarity and strength of character. Consciously and unconsciously he sets forth a doctrine of thrift, industry, and fair play.
Long before Poor Richard, Heywood proclaimed from a London
stage that honesty is the best policy.[82] Always Heywood insists
upon the paying quality of moral goodness. Drunkenness, gambling, and riotous living are represented as wasteful and ruinous.
In Heywood all the virtues extolled by Addison and Steele in the
eighteenth century find voice. And invariably, as with the eighteenth-century Whigs, the mercantile rewards of right living are
held up. I have no intention of ascribing to Heywood the zeal of
a reformer or the fervor of altruistic moral purpose; he was simply a spokesman, and at times the propagandist, of concepts common to the middle class.

In no other dramatist, unless occasionally in Dekker, is London
life of the substantial bourgeoisie so well and so favorably mir-
rored as in Heywood. Not even Dekker so completely under-
stands as many different types of tradesfolk. Merchants, traders,
innkeepers (both male and female), sea captains, tanners, goldsmiths, artisans of all descriptions, apprentices in any number of
trades, all find theatrical articulation in Heywood. Always these
persons of the drama speak the sentiments which their class spoke
in Elizabethan England and are still speaking the world over.
Since Heywood was not only the chief, but one of the earliest
stage heralds of bourgeois virtues—an author who boasted that
he had had a whole hand or a main finger in two hundred and
twenty plays, which (to judge from extant examples) continually
repeated themes pleasing to the London citizenry—the point of
view expressed in his plays deserves a somewhat detailed consideration, because these plays present an illuminating picture of
middle-class intelligence and help to explain why the citizenry

---

[82] Mr. Mowbray Velte in *The Bourgeois Elements in the Dramas of Thomas Heywood*
(Princeton dissertation, 1922) makes only general observations about Heywood's
middle-class ideals. He fails to stress what seems to me one of the most significant of
Heywood's bourgeois qualities: his dramatic expression of those sentiments and beliefs which were crystallizing into the pragmatic code of mercantile life.

found some virtues in the stage despite Puritan objections.

The growing class consciousness and the prejudices and ideals that colored all middle-class thinking find expression in Heywood's plays. Certain notes of democracy are evident; frequent scorn is heaped on court flatterers and sycophants;[83] independence is praised; the importance of the laboring and trading groups as the backbone of the nation is emphasized; the dignity of work is upheld. Gresham, laying the corner stone of the Royal Exchange, puts down a gold piece and exclaims, "The gold we lay due to the workmen is."[84] Trade and tradesmen are exalted. Phillis, heroine of *The Fair Maid of the Exchange* (*c.* 1602),[85] keeper of a dress-goods shop, is pictured as the sum of all the virtues—thrifty, beautiful, spritely, chaste. Heywood loses no opportunity of courting the favor of apprentices and of extolling their merits. Indirectly, he seeks to inculcate proper notions and ideals in young tradesmen. The Lord Mayor in *Edward IV*, Part 1 (before 1599), exhorts the 'prentices to resist the rebels:

> And, prentices, stick to your officers,
> For you may come to be as we are now.[86]

The clown in *The Royal King and Loyal Subject* (1602?) drops a moral hint to the apprentices: ". . . I scorne to fellow to any that will leave their Masters in adversity."[87] Frequently, in the

---

[83] Cf. the words of the merchant who praises "the honest parts" of Young Forrest in *Fortune by Land and Sea* (III, i) and adds:

> "Indeed I flatter not, none flatter those
> They do not mean to gain by, 'tis the guise
> Of siccophants, such great men to adore
> By whom they mean to rise, disdain the poor."

Cf. also *The Royal King and Loyal Subject*, IV, i.

[84] *If You Know Not Me, You Know Nobody*, Pt. 2. John Pearson (ed.), *The Dramatic Works of Thomas Heywood*, 6 vols. (London, 1874), I, 290. Hereafter, in plays of Heywood having no act and scene divisions, page references will be made to the Pearson reprint.

Cf. the situation in *Fortune by Land and Sea* (II, i) in which Phillip and his wife Susan serve the former's father as manservant and dairymaid.

[85] Heywood's authorship of this play is in doubt. *See* Chambers, *op. cit.*, IV, 13.

[86] *Works*, I, 17. Several tributes to the bravery and loyalty of apprentices occur in this play. *See* pp. 18, 20. Heywood's authorship of this play is disputed.

[87] IV, i. The praise of apprentices in *The Four Prentices of London* is, of course, familiar. One should observe particularly the introductory epistle "To the Honest and

midst of his praise of the commoner, Heywood puts in a word of advice.[88] He is prompt to point out the value of industry and benevolence. He always upholds an ideal of loyalty to the established order. Democratic he is, but his democracy takes the form of pride and self-satisfaction in the progress of the middle classes. He insists that apprentices ought to be faithful to their masters, children to their parents, and subjects to their rulers.[89] Characteristically, Heywood is never iconoclastic and rarely even speculative. His characters are respectful of royal authority and full of praise for the benignity of the lord mayor and aldermen.[90]

Heywood is little concerned with theoretical problems of absolute morality, but he does show an unusual interest in practical problems of conduct and human relationships. Keenly conscious of the pragmatic value of right conduct, he sprinkles his plays plentifully with sentiments expressive of this belief. His admonitions may be roughly divided into two main divisions, deal-

---

High-spirited Prentices, the Readers" and the Earl of Bulloigne's speech to his four sons apprenticed to trades (*Works*, II, 169 ff.). Son Godfrey replies :

> "I prayse that Citty which made Princes Trades-men :
> Where that man, noble or ignoble borne,
> That would not practice some mechanicke skill,
> Which might support his state in penury,
> Should die the death ; not sufferd like a drone,
> To sucke the honey from the publicke Hiue.
> I hold it no disparage to my birth,
> Though I be borne an Earle, to haue the skill
> And the full knowledge of the *Mercers* Trade."

[88] Cf. the general moralistic tone of the lord mayors' shows written by Heywood. *A Woman Killed with Kindness* emphasizes chastity, forgiveness, loyalty to friends, payment of debts, thrift, and Christianity. The same ideas recur in *Edward IV*, together with those of benevolence, love of country, independence, and sympathy for the distressed. *The Four Prentices* is full of moral and pious tags for the edification of spectator-apprentices.

[89] *Fortune by Land and Sea* (I, iii) : Phillip continues loyally to love his father despite mistreatment. The lesson in *The Royal King and Loyal Subject* is obvious. In *Edward IV*, Pt. 2 (*Works*, I, 170) Master Aire berates Mistress Blage for treachery to her friend Jane Shore.

[90] In *Edward IV*, Pt. 2, the King expresses pride in knighting the lord mayor, the recorder, and other London burghers for their loyalty. In this play, the lord mayor is cast in a conspicuous and heroic rôle as defender of the city against the usurpers. In *London's Gate to Piety*, a lord mayor's show, Heywood calls attention to the fame of many lord mayors for their support of hospitals, almshouses, chapels, colleges, and other civic and charitable institutions.

ing on the one hand with moral virtues and on the other with more strictly business virtues.

The standards of conduct insuring a stable family life and an orderly system of society are set forth as right and desirable. With the definiteness of an Old Testament prophet, Heywood shows the rewards of virtue and the punishment of vice. That it pays to be good is his constant reminder. The deep-dyed villain Stroza in *A Maidenhead Well Lost* (before 1633) remarks after his own repentance in the last scene, in which everyone is forgiven :

> Who would striue
> To bee a villaine, when the good thus thriue?   [P. 164.]

That heaven rewards the honest is the lesson deduced from Phillip's conduct in *Fortune by Land and Sea*. His stepmother, Anne, remarks after he has come into his estate :

> Heaven being just could not deal longer roughly
> With one so virtuous and compleatly honest.[91]

The cash value of a good turn is further illustrated in the same play, as the merchant who befriended Young Forrest is made to share in a rich prize because of his earlier generosity. Anne, who also was kind to Forrest, gets two thousand pounds by reason of her benevolence. This play ends with a masque-like entry of all of Phillip's dissolute and ruined brothers, who receive from him a sermon on the evil that brought about their plight.

Heywood's plays are full of sermonizing and pious talk. Between deeds of valor, the Crusaders in *The Four Prentices* supply religious moralizing. Old Geraldine in *The English Traveller* (printed, 1633) advises his son :

> You are growne perfect man, and now you float
> Like to a well built Vessell ; 'Tweene two Currents,
> Vertue and Vice ; Take this, you steere to harbour
> Take that, to eminent shipwracke.[92]

He then suggests that the son marry a girl who has "immediate means."

Heywood is fond of moralizing tags. In *The Royal King and*

---

[91] IV, i.   [92] III, i.

Loyal Subject, for example, Lady Mary concludes a speech piously :

> Vertue will last when wealth flyes, and is gone :
> Let me drinke *Nectar* though in earth or stone.[93]

In the next act, Isabel in the presence of the King utters this brief sermon :

> . . . . . Princes still
> Should be the Lords of their owne appetites
> And cherish vertue.[94]

A word of advice to Noncomformists is apparent in the good Abbot's description of the aims of a true religious order in *The Captives* (1624) :

> . . . . Unity,
> Due conformation, and fraternall love;
> Devotion, hott zeale, and obediens ; these
> Are vertues that become a cloyster best.[95]

Earlier he had warned of the clergy's necessity of watching its deeds,

> Least we that are profest religious
> Be in the least defective.

Extended and fulsome praise of the English Bible, spoken by Queen Elizabeth, concludes the first part of *If You Know Not Me, You Know Nobody*, in which good Queen Bess preaches a sermon on the Bible, exhorting the populace to

> Lay hand vpon this Anchor euery soule,
> Your names shall be in an eternall scroll.

An anticipation of the repentances of the eighteenth-century villains in the drama of sensibility may be found in Heywood.

---

[93] II, ii.

[94] Such examples are numerous. In *The Iron Age*, Pt. 2 (V, i), Helen, soliloquizing before strangling herself, says :

> "Here's that, my soule and body must divide
> The guerdon of Adultery, Lust, and Pride."

Act I of *Love's Mistress* concludes with an explanation that the masque scenes that have preceded are a moral allegory in which lust is condemned and true love is exalted.

[95] I, ii. Edited by A. C. Judson (New Haven, 1921).

41

Young Chartley, a London Don Juan in *The Wise Woman of Hogs-don* (printed, 1638),[96] after his deceptions are revealed before his lovers, expresses sorrow over his philandering, promises reform, and cleaves to his first love, who retains faith in him. Young Lionel in *The English Traveller* is contrite over all his riotous living, puts aside his old companions, and duly reforms.[97] In the same play, the wife, pictured as a weak woman, faithless to both Wincott and Geraldine, is humbly sorrowful in the end and dies of grief and remorse. Even Dalavill is sorrowful over his sin.[98] The outstanding example of repentance, of course, comes in *A Woman Killed with Kindness*. Anne, discovered in her guilt, becomes violently repentant and addresses a message to womankind :

> O women, women, you that yet haue kept
> Your holy Matrimoniall Vow vnstain'd,
> Make me your instance, when you tred awry,
> Your sinnes like mine will on your conscience ly.[99]

Sir Charles, the unfortunate murderer in the subplot, laments his reckless crime and is glad to lead the simple life of a farmer. Jane Shore in *Edward IV*, Part 2, like Frankford's wife in *A Woman Killed with Kindness*, draws a moral from her plight, for the benefit of other London citizens' wives :

> . . . my guests repentant thoughts
> That whoso knew me and doth see me now,
> May shun by me the breach of wedlocks vow.[100]

---

[96] V, i. *Ibid.*   [97] IV, i.   [98] V, i.

[99] *Works*, II, 141. A new note in domestic tragedy occurs in this play. Frankford (pp. 137 ff.) prays for Christian forbearance and restraint in punishing his erring wife. Later he says :

> "But that I would not damme two precious soules
> Bought with my Sauiors blood, and send them laden
> With all their scarlet sinnes vpon their backes,
> Vnto a fearfull iudgement, their two liues
> Had met vpon my rapier."—P. 138.

It is worthy of note that Christianity is made the reason for failure to achieve a conventional revenge.

Very similar to eighteenth-century dramas of sensibility is the conquest of vice by virtue in the subplot of this play. Sir Charles Mountford's desperate plan to pay Sir Francis Acton with his sister's honor, and her own unselfish offer of sacrifice, so impress Acton that he repents his former ways and marries the girl.

[100] *Works*, I, 166.

Since one of the strongholds of middle-class solidarity rests upon the integrity of the family, Heywood is peculiarly sensitive to its importance and to the wickedness of any attacks upon it. Old Hobs in *Edward IV*, Part 1, berates his neighbor, Harry Grudgen, for a stinginess that results in his keeping "two ploughs going, and nere a cradle rocking."[101] Heywood is always careful to present the sanctity of the marital relation. Even in the tricking of the lustful Bashaw and his wife in *The Fair Maid of the West*, he shows a respect for the accepted canons of morality and is careful to indicate that the relations of Bess and Spencer are strictly regular. Middle-class regard for the sanctity of the home accounts for much of the insistence on chastity throughout Heywood's plays. Emphasis on virtue in woman, to be sure, is conventional, but Heywood makes his characters preach far too vigorously against sexual irregularity to warrant dismissing the subject with a word. Unstintingly he praises chastity and condemns license. He uses *The Captives* to set forth a doctrine of loyalty to virtue and chastity, and of repentance of sins. The two maids, Palestra and Scribonia, are exalted because they have lived without defilement in the midst of bawdry. The friar who seeks the illicit love of his benefactor's wife is punished with death. The bawd, Mildew, is ridiculed and vilified mercilessly until he repents and talks "lyke a convertite." In *The Wise Woman of Hogsdon*, Luce, keeper of her father's shop, comments, upon refusing the advances of a lover:

> . . . might I have my wish,
> I would seeme faire but onely in his eye
> That should possesse mee in a Nuptiall tye.[102]

Phillip, in *Fortune by Land and Sea*, is content to have no other dower or inheritance than the virtue of his bride, because "when all else fails us that alone shall last."[103] *The Rape of Lucrece* (1603-08) is twisted until there is an obvious preachment against violent love, to serve as a sort of "moral" to that miserable play. Helena,

---

[101] *Ibid.*, p. 71. Love of home and kin is frequently reflected in Heywood. In *A Woman Killed with Kindness* (*ibid.*, II, 101), Charles and Susan refuse to dispose of their small patrimony because it represents home. In *If You Know Not Me*, Pt. 1 (*ibid.*, I, 209 ff.), the three soldiers cannot understand Mary's unkind treatment of Elizabeth, her own sister.

[102] I, ii.   [103] *Ibid.*

the heroine of *A Challenge for Beauty* (1635), whose birth is "not high degree'd," has beauty and chastity to rival the Spanish Queen's.[104] In spite of what is apparently a hopelessly immoral situation in *A Maidenhead Well Lost*, Heywood manages to provide a moral gloss. Lauretta, who supplies the bed of Julia, does so not for money but for love of the Prince of Florence. Through her, the villainy of Stroza is revealed and the tangled situation is cleared. Eventually she marries the Prince quite regularly and Julia regains her own Prince of Parma. Heywood felt some hesitation about the theme, for in an address to the reader, he excuses the means on the ground of the worthy end attained. Susan, in *A Woman Killed with Kindness*, scornfully rejects the money with which Sir Francis Acton attempts to seduce her: "My honour neuer shall for gaine be sold."[105] In the same play, Anne, about to repeat her sin with Wendoll, moralizes, with an eye on London wives:

> That which for want of wit I granted erst,
> I now must yeelde through feare. Come, come, lets in,
> Once ore shooes, we are straight ore head in sinne.[105a]

The cripple in *The Fair Maid of the Exchange* is vigorous in his actual and spoken defense of virtuous maidens against "damn'd villains." *Edward IV* is full of sermonizing on virtue and warnings to wives. Jane Shore and her husband both preach of the value of chastity; indeed, Matthew Shore almost forgets his rôle, in addressing the audience on the subject:

> See what dishonour breach of wedlock brings,
> Which is not safe, euen in the arms of kings.[106]

In all the plays of Heywood the necessity of a strict standard of conduct between the sexes is emphasized.[107]

---

[104] V, i.

[105] *Works*, II, 126.

[105a] *Ibid.*, p. 135.

[106] Pt. 2 (*ibid.*, I, 126).

[107] The dramatist voices disapproval of bawdy plays, in the prologue to *A Challenge for Beauty*, lamenting that

> ". . . now the common argument intreats
> Of puling Lovers, craftie Bawdes or cheates."

Another ideal for which Heywood is a conscious propagandist is that of generosity and benevolence. He is lavish in his praise of the lord mayors who have left foundations for schools, hospitals, and other public charities. Such philanthropy is a major theme in *If You Know Not Me, You Know Nobody*, Part 2. Gresham, having observed the benefactions of wealthy citizens before him, determines to emulate or even to exceed them:

> Why should not all of vs being wealthy men
> And by Gods blessing onely raisd, but
> Cast in our minds how we might them exceed
> In godly workes, helping of them that need.[108]

In a fashion quite modern, the liberality of Gresham is used to spur on other citizens to greater giving. In the same play, Hobson is presented as another charitable citizen, who relieves the wants of needy soldiers and provides small doweries for poor maidens. Master Generous is portrayed in *The Late Lancashire Witches* as a benevolent character. Old Lionel in *The English Traveller* is so blest by a fortunate voyage that he exhorts all not to "prooue niggards in our store."[109] The Lord Mayor in *Edward IV*, Part 1, recounts his humble origin and is glad that he has remembered to share his wealth with the needy by contributing to a hospital and founding a poorhouse.[110] The will of Bess Bridges in *The Fair Maid of the West*, Part 1, is significant. She allots £1,000 "To set up yong beginners in their trade," £500 to relieve those who have had loss at sea, and sums for maimed soldiers and for "every maid that's married out of Foy." The Alderman commends this munificence with a pointed moral:

Even a soldier is made to deliver a moral lecture in *The Royal King and Loyal Subject* in the captain's rebuke to a whore (III, i) for spreading disease. Characteristically for Heywood, the reason for righteousness here is prudential. The captain says:

> "I came to schoole you Whoore,
> Not to corrupt you . . .
> . . . . observe
> This rule from me, where there is lodg'd a Whore,
> Thinke the Plagues crosse is set upon that doore."

[108] *Works*, I, 278. [109] II, i.
[110] *Works*, I, 57.

> Let never such despaire,
> As dying rich, shall make the poore their heyre.[111]

Heywood reveals an even more definite middle-class heritage in his commendation of those qualities which insure business success and worldly prosperity. The strictly moral virtues praised are those which make for social stability, a primary concern of the substantial bourgeoisie. The other traits of character which he chiefly emphasizes are those most beneficial to temporal success. Indeed, he frequently represents the accumulation of wealth as the outstanding *raison d'être* for good conduct. He insists upon truthfulness because it establishes credit. Drunkenness, gambling, and riotous living, he condemns because they are ruinous to business. He is always a spokesman for peace so that trade may flourish.

The ideals of commercial life found a dramatic personification in Sir Thomas Gresham, hero of *If You Know Not Me, You Know Nobody*, Part 2. He is the prototype of the hero of Big Business, so familiar on the modern American stage. He is generous, daring, and ready to take a risk. Undaunted by mischance, he accepts the loss of £30,000 on a Barbary sugar monopoly without a qualm and sets about recouping his fortune. Upon this hero, Heywood lavishes much sympathetic detail and holds him up as a model for young men,[112] for the author is fond of portraying worldly prosperity. Even Bess Bridges, romantic heroine of a romantic play, is withal the shrewd, successful proprietor of the Wind Mill Inn.

All the conservatism characteristic of the mercantile class finds expression in Heywood's plays. Above everything, his tradesmen abhor internal strife. The Lord Mayor of *Edward IV*, Part 1, exhorts the forces battling against the rebels,

> Either to vanquish this rebellious rout,

---

[111] IV, i. The calamities that come to those who oppress the unfortunate are pointed out in *Fortune by Land and Sea* in the discomfiture of Phillip's grasping brothers (IV, i).

[112] Gresham himself admires shrewd business acumen. He is more pleased than otherwise over his nephew's trick to gain £100 from him (*Works*, I, 282):

> "And, afore-god, it hath done my heart more good,
> The knaue had wit to do so mad a tricke,
> Then if he had profited me twice so much."

Preserue our goods, our children, and our wiues,
Or seale our resolution with our liues.[113]

The Third Lord in *If You Know Not Me, You Know Nobody*, Part 2, praises Elizabeth because "The peace we haue is by her government."[114] *Londini Status Pacatus, or London's Peaceable Estate* (1639), the very name of which is significant, was prepared as a lord mayor's show for the drapers; it is an encomium on the blessedness of peace and freedom from civil strife.[115] Love of order and respect for law find numerous expressions. Bess Bridges threatens rowdy customers with arrest.[116] Old Harding, in *Fortune by Land and Sea*, acknowledges the right of Young Forrest in the fatal encounter with Rainsford but tells his wife that "Law must have his course."[117] So great is his respect for authority that, without a protest, Master Generous in *The Late Lancashire Witches* gives over his witch-wife to trial and punishment.

That sobriety is necessary to thrift is one of the preachments of Heywood's philosophy. "Much ale, little thrift," is the warning of the clown in *The Rape of Lucrece*.[118] Old Forrest in *Fortune by Land and Sea* regards drinking parties, of all practices, "the most ill."[119] Cynical Thersites in *The Iron Age*, Part 1 (*c.* 1613?), comments, in the tone of a temperance lecturer:

'Tis better liue in fire, then dye in wine:
That burnes but earth, this drownes a thing diuine.
I'le scald my soul no more.[120]

---

[113] *Ibid.*, p. 14.

[114] *Ibid.*, p. 322.

[115] *Ibid.*, V, 371 ff. The author, in a discussion of war, says: "War is of two sorts, Civill, or Forraigne. Domesticke War is the over-throw and ruine of all Estates and Monarchies, and the incendiary of whatsoeuer is most execrable," etc.

In a somewhat similar plea for peace, the Abbot in *The Captives* (I, ii) reprimands the quarreling friars:

"I will complayne to th' fownder of your loosenes,
  Your riotts, and disorders, and petition
  That you, as sowers of seditions heare
  And sole disturbers of our comon peace,
  Maye bee excluded this society."

[116] *The Fair Maid of the West*, Pt. 1 (II, i).

[117] *Works*, VI, 391 (II, i).

[118] *Ibid.*, V, 183.

[119] I, i.   [120] I, i.

The honest servant Robin in *The English Traveller* mourns his master's riotous living and drunken surfeits, which waste "all that masse of wealth Got by my Masters sweat and thrifty care."[121] *Love's Mistress* (1634)[122] is made to teach an even more obvious lesson in frugality and sobriety. Apuleius introduces a prodigal ass :

> A fellow hee,
> Who riots that, which most penuriously
> His father hoorded, in drabs, drinke and play ;
> Wearing fantastick habitts, and gay clothes,
> Till hee hath quite exhausted all his gold,
> And for a Prodigall Asse may bee enroul'd.[123]

The English Traveller is full of moralizing on the merit of saving. From a soliloquy of Young Lionel we gather that the whole of a young man's training was designed to teach this virtue. Only against love is "The thrift with which our fathers tiled our Roofes" powerless.[124] Frankford, in *A Woman Killed with Kindness*, reproves his servant, Nick, for unthriftiness :

---

[121] I, ii.

[122] Cf. the sermon on thrift delivered by Phillip to his riotous brothers in *Fortune by Land and Sea* (IV, i) :

> "Spend but in compass, rioting eschew,
> Waste not, but seek to encrease your patrimony,
> Beware of dice and women ; company
> With men of best desert and qualitie ;
> Lay but these words in your hearts inrold
> You'l find them better then these bags of gold."

Earlier in the play (I, i), Old Forrest had reprimanded his profligate son in the same manner for his extravagant life.

[123] *Works*, V, 105.

[124] I, ii. Cf. Lionel's remarks, upon the entrance of a whore :

> "Oh heer's that Haile, Shower, Tempest, Storme, and Gust,
> That shatter'd hath this building ; Let in Lust,
> Intemperance, appetite to Vice ; withall,
> Neglect of euery Goodnesse ; Thus I see
> How I am sincking in mine owne disease."

Old Lionel, who is later incorrectly informed that his son has made a profitable purchase, cannot rest until he has opportunity to "much commend his Thrift."—III, i.

> . . . Now Nicklas you want money;
> And vnthrift-like would eate into your wages
> Ere you haue earn'd it.[125]

The same ideal is frequently expressed by Hobs, the Tanner of Tamworth in *Edward IV*, who is pleased to see the celebration in honor of the king's visit but is glad that such expense is infrequent, for "euery day would begger vs." In a moment of disgust, exclaiming that "its a crooked world, and an vnthrifty,"[126] he determines to have nothing to do with the court but to confine himself to his cowhides. In *If You Know Not Me, You Know Nobody*, Part 2, Gresham counsels economy and industry in his nephew. Hobson likewise warns his apprentices against their spendthrift ways.

The importance of money looms large in Heywood's plays. *The Wise Woman of Hogsdon* is concerned with the exposure of the charlatanry by which London "wise women" were swindling the credulous out of hard-earned savings. Hobson's dread of the expense of courts and lawyers is characteristic of middle-class frugality and conservatism.[127] Likewise, Heywood's characters frequently express a healthy distaste for usurers, who are condemned in more than conventional language for oppressing the poor and unfortunate.[128] The prompt payment of debt as a goal to be sought

---

[125] *Works*, II, 118. In the same play (p. 126), Tydy attributes Charles's troubles to "roysting" and "swagg'ring"; the comment then follows: "I am no cosen vnto them that borrow."

The close-fisted Berry in *The Fair Maid of the Exchange* (*ibid.*, p. 28) berates his debtors for their thriftlessness:

> "A crew of unthrifts, carelesse dissolutes,
> Licentious prodigals, vilde taverne-tracers.
> Night watching money-wasters, what shall I call yee?"

He insists that

> ". . . . . 'tis no charity
> To favour you that live like libertines."

The Cripple (p. 31) rejoices that he is not in debt and decides to be even more provident:

> ". . . ile to my shop
> And fall to work."

[126] Pt. 1 (*ibid.*, I, 39).

[127] *If You Know Not Me, You Know Nobody*, Pt. 2 (*Works*, I, 262).

[128] Cf. *Love's Mistress* (I, i); *A Woman Killed with Kindness* (*Works*, II, 127-28); and *The Fair Maid of the Exchange* (*ibid.*, II, 87).

is pointed out in several plays. The general's wife in *A Maidenhead Well Lost* is anxious to pay her husband's soldiers with her remaining gold and jewels. After dispensing her property to the troops, she says with satisfaction : "Nothing we owe, my Husbands debts are payd."[129]

In all the plays of Heywood there breathes a spirit of sturdy independence and patriotism. Indeed, the patriotic spirit quite naturally at times lapses into an insularity evidenced by panegyrics over English qualities and disparagement of all things foreign. Spaniards, Italians, and the French are held up to ridicule, while English prowess is glorified.[130] Bess Bridges, the entrancing keeper of the Wind Mill Inn, must have voiced the heroic independence typical of the best ideals of the English common people in her plea for her lover before the King of Fess :

> . . . . Stood I ingag'd to death,
> I'de scorne for life to bend a servile knee.[131]

It is not my purpose to read Heywood's own personality into all his characters, but it is impossible to believe that many of these frequently repeated ideas are not part of his thinking. On the basis of his preserved plays, he remains the greatest theatrical spokesman of the bourgeois ideals of his age. His plays have in them a greater moral purposefulness than is attained by any other middle-class dramatist. Conscious of his own learning, Heywood had a sense of responsibility to the public, a sense of "service" —an idea now much worshipped by the bourgeoisie. Homer, the presenter in *The Silver Age* (before 1612), announces in the opening of the play that he comes to spread knowledge among the

---

[129] I, i. Heywood shows in *A Woman Killed with Kindness* to what extremes a man may be brought by the desire to pay a debt. Charles Mountford, deeply grieved, but about to offer his sister's honor in satisfaction of his debt, asks her :

> "Dost loue me Sister? wouldst thou see mee liue
> A Bankrupt begger in the worlds disgrace
> And die indebted to my enemies?"—*Works*, II, 143.

One reason the Marshal offers for refusing the King's dower in *The Royal King and Loyal Subject* (V, i) is that he does not want to be indebted to his sovereign.

[130] Cf. *The Fair Maid of the West*, Pt. 1 (IV, i) ; Pt. 2 (IV, i) ; *Edward IV*, Pt. 2 (*Works*, I, 103) ; *The Captives* (III, ii, ll. 88 ff.).

[131] *The Fair Maid of the West*, Pt. 2 (III, i).

less learned.[132] Coarse sometimes is Heywood's humor, but not even the bitterest Puritan could say that he made sin seductive or failed to drive home some pragmatic moral. In *An Apology for Actors* he defends the stage against Puritan attack by showing the moral purpose of drama and its value to a commercial society.[133] Not before the rise of the eighteenth-century middle class did bourgeois ideals have a sturdier voice than Heywood's.

---

[132] I, i. :

> ". . . . . *Homer* old and blinde,
> Of eld, by the best iudgements tearm'd diuine,
> That in his former labours found you kinde,
> Is come the ruder censures to refine :
> And to vnlocke the Casket long time shut,
> Of which none but the learned keepe the key,
> Where the rich Iewell (*Poesie*) was put.
> She that first search't the Heauens, Earth, Ayre, and Sea.
> We therefore begge, that since so many eyes,
> And seuerall iudging wits must taste our stile,
> The learn'd will grace, the ruder not despise :
> Since what we do, we for their vse compile
> Why should not *Homer*, he that taught in *Greece*,
> Vnto this iudging nation lend like skill."

[133] It is possible that Heywood was induced by his fellow actors to pen a vindication of the stage in a period of relative calm because, of all the playwrights of the period, he could give his arguments a tone of sincerity which would have been lacking in a defense by almost any of his theatrical contemporaries. A justification of the stage on a basis of moral function would come more fittingly from Heywood than from others and would meet the Puritans on their own ground. As a matter of fact, Heywood went further than this and showed, in addition to the ethical value of drama, its political and economic benefits, urging its advantages to business. Though not new, his reasons were summarized with skill and presented in a way to appeal to middle-class intelligence. Heywood was one to whom even the Puritans would have given the most favorable hearing. He had held them up to no such ridicule as had Jonson, Marston, and others. The satire which does occur in his plays is leveled at eccentric types rather than at any class. In the *Apology* he is careful not to specify the Puritans as a group but declares that he has been moved by "many seditious sectists." Apparently he wishes to implicate merely the extremists among the Puritan opponents of the stage. No bitter words are hurled at the Puritans, but throughout the work the tone is mild, and the worst antagonist of the stage is described as a hypocrite who merely uses his religion and his attack on the theater as a cloak for his iniquities. The author evidently hoped to arouse no prejudice and to convert by reason all who were amenable to common sense. Evidently he succeeded, for when at length, after three years, a certain I. G. replied with *A Refutation of the Apology for Actors*, he complained of the seductive quality of his opponent's pamphlet : "I considered, that thereby too too many credilous people might be seduced, and therefore a matter (in some sort) worth the answering."

In vivid contrast to the tone of Heywood's plays is Thomas Middleton's dramatic satire. Clever in the exploitation of realistic London life, he betrays not the slightest sympathy with the middle class in the plays which he wrote alone. Already is evident the Restoration contempt for the citizen, who becomes in Middleton and the later Stuart dramatists merely an object for ridicule and ribald merriment. For Middleton, the citizen's ambitions were material for mockery.[134] While Heywood praises thrift, Middleton, the Cambridge graduate and a gentleman born, discovers the ugliness of greed. Although the upper classes do not entirely escape his ridicule, the London middle class bore the brunt of his satirical onslaught. Lacking the moral wrath and indignation of Jonson, Middleton was content to regard his world of fools and knaves with a contemptuous amusement. And his point of view is reflected in other dramatists whom he influenced, noticeably in Dekker's later plays.

Space forbids an extended discussion of Middleton's work, but a few examples will show why his plays paved the way for the middle-class rejection of the drama after the Restoration. The avarice and greed of citizens, the trickery of lawyers and their go-betweens, the dishonesty and rapacity of guardians, the cringing servility of creditors toward a man of wealth, the blood-thirsty hounding of bankrupt victims, the immodesty of women— these are the themes with which *A Trick to Catch the Old One* (1604–06?) is concerned. The play is a galaxy of mean and low-minded characters without a single noble person. If Middleton in conclusion bows to convention and permits sentimental reform among his sinners, the "moral" quality is only superficial. The London of which its citizens were proud inspired in Middleton only scoffing and cynical amusement at its total depravity and utterly despicable inhabitants.

London citizens are objects of ridicule in *The Family of Love* (1604–07?), which plays on the dishonesty of tradesmen's wives, the knavery of doctors and apothecaries, the lechery of gallants, the hypocrisy and narrowness of the Puritans, and the unpleasant qualities of citizens generally. One of the cleverest and most

---

[134] Cf. Kathleen M. Lynch, *The Social Mode of Restoration Comedy*, University of Michigan Publications in Language and Literature, III (New York, 1926), pp. 25 ff.

sardonic of Middleton's comedies is *A Chaste Maid in Cheapside* (1611). Tired of inventing conventional repentances and punishments for his villains, the author here permits them to reap the rewards of their wit. Yellowhammer and his wife reveal those ambitions of tradesmen which Middleton continually derides. Eager for gold and influential family connections, they are ready to force their daughter, Moll, into a marriage with Sir Walter Whorehound because he is rich and has a title, and they encourage Tim, their foolish son, ill-crammed with Latin and logic at Cambridge, to wed a woman who is reported to own mountains and cattle in Wales, but who in reality is a courtesan. But the best of Middleton's wit is lavished on Allwit, the supreme cuckold in pre-Restoration drama, who finds contentment in cuckoldry, and in defense of it offers a philosophy unanswerable in its cynical logic. Almost invariably Middleton's tradesmen are willing to barter honor for profit. If gallants kiss the wives of citizens, what do husbands lose by that, asks Purge in *The Family of Love*, for "they that will thrive must utter their wares as they can and wink at small faults."[135] The relations between tradesmen and the gentry find significant expression in Quomodo, the woolen-draper in *Michaelmas Term* (1606?), who comments, "They're busy 'bout our wives, we 'bout their lands."[136] In practically all of Middleton's plays, only unpleasant qualities are attributed to citizens, and the conventional dishonesty of their wives and their own contented cuckoldry become merely symbols for the despicable nature of the whole middle class.

The sharp differentiation in tone and sympathies between Heywood and Middleton is typical of the break along social lines which is discernible with increasing clearness in the drama, as elsewhere, as the seventeenth century moves toward the upheaval of the Puritan revolution. The drama was still vital enough to divide into a sufficiently large number of types to attract diverse social groups. Though citizens saw many disadvantages in the playhouse, it is a mistake to believe that the rank and file condemned drama as a whole. Up to the very day in 1642 when the Long Parliament decreed that henceforth stage playing should be for-

---

[135] II, i.   [136] I, i.

borne, the popular theaters produced old-fashioned plays in which the citizenry delighted, for the love of drama was deep-seated in public taste, and so long as robust plays were offered at the Red Bull or the Fortune, citizens were there to attend. It is just as true that the comedy of manners, which had been developing as a form particularly favored by aristocratic audiences at the private theaters, offered little to delight the middle class. Not even the theatrical effects found in the romantic drama of Beaumont and Fletcher, past masters though they were in the creation of clever plays, could counteract the insults that citizens observed in the more sophisticated productions. Gradually the apprentice and his master drifted to one group of theaters, while the noble and the gallant sought out others, where plays to the liking of each could be found. After the interregnum, when actors returned to their professions in 1660, the citizenry had lost the habit of theater-going. The old playhouses had decayed, and the new theaters were controlled by aristocrats for aristocrats, who delighted in heaping fresh insults upon the group responsible for their troubles. The theater, totally abandoned by the middle class, became in the popular consciousness a sink of sin, where bawdry and all wickedness were taught—a conception reflected in the theoretical prohibition of theatergoing by certain evangelical sects of the present day. Only with the invention of the motion-picture play has there come a renewal of the interest of the middle class in the theater that approaches the support given by citizens to their favorite playhouses in the London of Elizabeth and James, before fierce controversy and class hatred had divorced the theater from the amenities of middle-class life.

XVII

CONCLUSION

ASURVEY of the intellectual interests of the commercial classes in England of the sixteenth and seventeenth centuries shows that the great awakening of the Renaissance was not confined to the learned and the courtly elements in society. On the contrary, the intellectual ferment was particularly active among the groups that were already laying the foundations for a commercial and industrial structure later to have an importance beyond the dreams of any contemporary thinker. Without an understanding of the scope of the intellectual awakening of the preceding era, one cannot account for the rapid rise of the middle class in the eighteenth century, a rise which was the result of far more than merely favorable economic factors, essential though these were. The mental preparation throughout the long years of Elizabeth and the first two Stuarts was necessary to the development that followed. For in the seventeenth century the middle class first came of age and reached the maturity which gave it assurance and enabled it to take a place by the beginning of the eighteenth as an emphatic element in the body politic. This development was not a sudden and phenomenal growth, beginning in the reign of William and Mary and coming to full strength in the age of Queen Anne, as it is sometimes glibly inferred; instead, a long sequence of events—social, political, and intellectual—had made inevitable the predominance of a commercial society.

For a hundred years preceding the upheaval of the mid-seventeenth century, the seeds of change had been ripening and the minds of the intelligent middle group in society had been prepared to cope with the new ideas which that era reflects. The period of the Civil War and the Commonwealth was profoundly

influential in the further education of the middle class and contributed largely toward bringing about that intellectual maturity
which the end of the century witnessed. Social and political
changes reacted powerfully upon the burgher mind. No citizen
could remain unconscious of the stir around him when the traditional world was tumbling about his ears and old conventions and
old ideals were being replaced by new. Citizens whose thinking
had previously been confined to the beaten paths of a narrow
world suddenly found themselves facing the broad highways of a
new social dispensation. Since the rebellion of the 1640's was a
bourgeois rather than a proletarian revolt, the burden of responsibility for the Commonwealth government fell upon the shoulders
of the middle class, who learned that government could be administered by the sons of tradesmen as well as by heaven-appointed
kings. Even though Cromwell ruled as a military dictator, the
seeds of democratic government were sown in the movement that
made him the head of the state. While the tattered banners of
divine right were to be flaunted again under the last Stuart kings,
the awful respect for the ruler as the viceroy of God had passed.
Henceforth men of trade would have an increasing voice in the
government, and kings—if they were wise—would listen to the
counsel of citizens.

The social ideals that were to dominate English life for generations to come—ideals which had been slowly taking shape for
several generations—crystallized in the emergence of the middle
class as an economic and political power in the seventeenth century. For example, the gospel of work, one of the most significant
articles of the bourgeois dogma, was promulgated with great
earnestness during the period of Puritan supremacy[1] and paved
the way for the later apotheosis of business, which has colored the
entire outlook of the modern world. However much the stern
Puritans of Cromwell's government might be interested in intricate reasoning about predestination, they were equally concerned
over problems of trade and finance. These pious children of the
Lord had long since completed their economic novitiate and were
now establishing the mercantile system that was to prevail over

---

[1] See Margaret James, Social Problems and Policy during the Puritan Revolution, 1640-1660
(London, 1930), pp. 344-45.

two continents for more than two centuries to come. Nor did the Restoration, with its reaction against the citizenry, seriously curb the economic progress of the middle class. Instead, it gave them further opportunities, for shrewd business men of London soon had the gallant but spendthrift courtiers at their mercy, and many a nobleman lost his lands to some lowborn money lender who laid the foundations for his own social rise upon his newly acquired landed property. Though the middle class suffered political reverses, their economic progress went steadily and consistently onward, to reach its fruition in the era of trade in the eighteenth century, when the great merchant was a power indeed and any humble tradesman might look forward to acquiring riches and, presently, to becoming a gentleman.

The record of the subtle changes going on in the minds of the middle class is preserved in part in the literature paralleling their rise to greatness. Just as a vast literature of the period before 1640 shows the development of the bourgeois point of view, so a great deal of the literature of the later seventeenth century is filled with the expression of the realization of their ideals. If one wished to pick a single author in whom the intellectual coming-of-age of the middle class is best expressed, that author would be Daniel Defoe. His works concentrate into a sort of essence all the burgher philosophy that had been gathering force for the preceding century and a half. Moreover, his own ambitions for riches and social distinction, as well as many incidents in his life, are typical of the desires of his class.

Born plain Daniel Foe, the son of a Baptist butcher, just at the end of the interregnum, educated in a dissenting academy by a schoolmaster later to become vice-president of Harvard College, apprenticed to a merchant, and subsequently established for himself as a hosier in Cornhill, the tradesman at length turned to authorship and politics and signed himself grandly, Daniel De Foe. Like Samuel Pepys, another bourgeois spirit before him, Defoe yearned for the glory of social distinction. Unhappily, a bankruptcy ruined him, but Defoe rose from the wreckage of his fortune to greater heights by means of political activities, the details of which are even yet shrouded in obscurity. Although the vicissitudes of fortune made Defoe at one time a confidant of

42

King William and at another a prisoner, he managed to spend most of his last days in comfort and to be written down a gentleman in the burial register of St. Giles. Surely there could be no better apprenticeship for the writing of works reflecting the life of the middle class than the full experiences of this tradesman-politician.

From the variety of Defoe's published works, one might think that he had sought to supply all the types of literature appealing to the citizen. As a journalist, he mixed partisan politics with human-interest features that would be the envy of a modern editor. As a novelist, he made *Robinson Crusoe* and *Moll Flanders* preach prudential morality without destroying their interest for his own or succeeding ages. As a sociologist and economist, he published, in addition to many other treatises, *An Essay upon Projects*, setting forth the views of a practical business man upon education, chain banking, good roads, prison reform, and numerous other matters of public concern. As a social philosopher, Defoe wrote *The Complete English Tradesman* and *The Complete English Gentleman*. In the last two works, the London business man epitomized the whole philosophy of the middle class. Defoe's "complete tradesman" is, first of all, a success in business, shrewd, clever, prudent, and lucky—qualities which the author would have desired for the ideal Defoe.[2] The morality of the perfect tradesman is one of business expediency in which the ends justify the means. Since the successful tradesman accumulates wealth, he may become the founder of a line in the new aristocracy derived from trade, described by Defoe in his treatise on the gentleman, in which the author ridicules the gross ignorance of the sons of the gentry and suggests, with certain reservations, that wealth and education are proper bases of gentility.[3] In fact, the modern

---

[2] Paul Dottin, *The Life and Strange and Surprising Adventures of Daniel Defoe*, translated by Louise Ragan (New York, 1929), pp. 257-58

[3] Karl D. Bülbring (ed.), *The Compleat English Gentleman, by Daniel Defoe* (London, 1890), p. 268. In a passage describing the entrance into the ranks of the gentry of the sons of wealthy commercial families, Defoe comments:

"It comes of course now to enquire into the usuall education of the eldest sons of these familyes; and first I am to tell you they generally out-do the born gentlemen all over the Kingdom, I mean in education.

"I can assure you they are not thought to be above educacion. Their parents never think learning or going to schoole a disgrace to them or below their quallity.

conception of the aristocracy of wealth is forecast in *The Complete English Gentleman.*

Defoe writes with the assurance and sophistication of the well informed man of affairs, in a tone that is often amazingly modern. Yet he is a connecting link between the middle class of the Renaissance and the middle class of the modern world. He reaches back in literary kinship to Deloney, Dekker, Heywood, and innumerable other bourgeois writers of the sixteenth and early seventeenth centuries, and at the same time he expresses the Whig prejudices of Addison and Steele and the prudential morality of Samuel Richardson. His works sum up middle-class culture as developed in the preceding generations and look forward to the time when the middle classes would become the predominant social factors on both sides of the Atlantic.

Indeed, Defoe is a sort of intellectual herald of Benjamin Franklin, perhaps the greatest spokesman of bourgeois philosophy. Both were intensely interested in the practical and the utilitarian. Both expressed the accumulated prudential wisdom of the age. Each in his day epitomized middle-class thought and ideals.

The trends of modern commercial civilization were fixed in the sixteenth and seventeenth centuries, when the foundations were laid for the later supremacy of the middle class. Therefore the intellectual development of the commercial classes profoundly influenced the culture of their descendants. As the bourgeois civilization, which had firmly established itself on the ruins of the medieval world, gathered strength, its powers of growth and its intellectual capacities increased ; and upon transplantation to the New World, it acquired even greater virility. Hence, in America middle-class culture has been supreme—whether for good or for evil, it is not for the historian to determine. If it is desirable to trace the pedigree of the popular culture of modern America, it

---

"And thus I am brought down to the terms of admission, as I may call them, vpon which the modern families of our gentry rank with the antient ; and I think they are very fairly reduc'd to two heads :—1. Great estates, whether rais'd by trade or any of the usuall improvements of the meaner people, supposing them onely to be without a blot of scandal, which I may explain in its turn. 2. A remove or two from the first hand or, as 'twas call'd above, the workman that built the house. These, and these onely, are the *postulata* requir'd, or at least that I insist upon as necessary."

is possible to find most of its ideology implicit in the middle-class thought of Elizabethan England. The historian of American culture must look back to the Renaissance and read widely in the forgotten literature of tradesmen.

BIBLIOGRAPHY

The following books and articles represent a selected list of secondary works, and certain edited texts which are useful because of their notes and introductory material. Limitations of space forbid the repetition of all titles of original sources, which may be found in the text by means of the Index.

Abbott, W. R. "The Influence of Du Bartas in English Literature," University of North Carolina unpublished dissertation, 1931.

Adams, J. Q. *Shakespearean Playhouses*. Boston and New York, 1917.

———— (ed.). *The Dramatic Records of Sir Henry Herbert*. New Haven, 1917.

————. *John Mason's The Turke*, in *Materialien*, Vol. XXXVII (1913).

Adamson, J. W. "The Extent of Literacy in England in the Fifteenth and Sixteenth Centuries : Notes and Conjectures," *The Library*, 4th Ser., X (1929-30), 163-93.

————. *Pioneers of Modern Education, 1600-1700*. Cambridge, 1905.

————. *A Short History of Education*. Cambridge, 1922.

Alden, R. M. *The Rise of Formal Satire in England under Classical Influence*. Philadelphia, 1899.

———— (ed.). *The Knight of the Burning Pestle, . . . by Francis Beaumont*. Boston, 1910.

Amos, Flora Ross. *Early Theories of Translation*. New York, 1920.

Anderson, Ruth Leila. *Elizabethan Psychology and Shakespeare's Plays*, "University of Iowa Humanistic Studies," Vol. III (1927).

Andrews, C. E. *Richard Brome*, "Yale Studies in English," Vol. XLVI. New York, 1913.

Arber, Agnes. *Herbals, Their Origin and Evolution*. Cambridge, 1912.

Arber, Edward (ed.). *A Transcript of the Registers of the Company of Stationers of London; 1554-1640*, 5 vols. London, 1875-77.

Aronstein, Philipp. "Der sozialogische Charakter des englischen Renaissance-Dramas," *Germanish-Romanische Monatsschrift*, XII (1924), 222 ff.

Aydelotte, Frank. *Elizabethan Rogues and Vagabonds*, "Oxford Historical and Literary Studies," Vol. I. Oxford, 1913.

Baddeley, John J. *The Aldermen of Cripplegate Ward from A.D. 1276 to A.D. 1900*. London, 1900.

Bailey, J. E. "Bishop Lewis Bayly and his 'Practice of Piety,'" *Manchester Quarterly*, VII (1883), 201-19.

Baker, Ernest A. *The History of the English Novel*, 4 vols. London, 1924-30.

Ballard, George. *Memoirs Of Several Ladies Of Great Britain Who Have Been Celebrated For Their Writings Or Skill In The Learned Languages, Arts And Sciences*. Oxford, 1752.

Bang, W. (ed.). *Materialien zur Kunde des Älteren Englischen Dramas*, 44 vols. Louvain, 1902-14.

Baskervill, C. R. *The Elizabethan Jig and Related Song Drama*. Chicago, 1929.

————. "Taverner's *Garden of Wisdom* and the *Apophthegmata* of Erasmus," *Studies in Philology*, XXIX (1932), 149-59.

Beaven, Alfred B. *The Aldermen of the City of London temp. Henry III-1908*, 2 vols. London, 1908-13.

Bent, J. Theodore (ed.). *Early Voyages and Travels in the Levant*. Hakluyt Society, London, 1893.

Boas, F. S. *Shakespeare and the Universities*. Oxford, 1923.

————, and Reed, A. W. (eds.). *Fulgens and Lucres . . . by Henry Medwall*. Oxford, 1926.

Bond, Edward A. (ed.). *Russia at the Close of the Sixteenth Century*. Hakluyt Society, London, 1856.

Bosanquet, Eustace F. *English Printed Almanacks and Prognostications; a Bibliographical History to the Year 1600*. London, 1917.

————. "English Seventeenth-Century Almanacks," *The Library*, 4th Ser., X (1929-30), 361-97.

"Broadside Ballads" (anon.). *Times Literary Supplement*, Jan. 22, 1931, pp. 49-50.

Brown, Alexander. *The Genesis of the United States*, 2 vols. London, 1890.

Bruce, John (ed.). *Diary of John Manningham*, 1602, Camden Society, XCIX (1868).

Bruce, P. A. *Institutional History of Virginia in the Seventeenth Century*, 2 vols. New York, 1910.

Bülbring, Karl D. (ed.). *The Compleat English Gentleman, by Daniel Defoe*. London, 1890.

Burgon, John W. *The Life and Times of Sir Thomas Gresham*, 2 vols. London, 1839.

Cambridge History of American Literature, The, Vol. I. New York, 1917.

Cambridge History of English Literature, The, Vols. III-VII. Cambridge, 1909-11.

Camden, Carroll, Jr. "Elizabethan Almanacs and Prognostications," *The Library,* 4th Ser., XII (1931-32), 83-108, 194-207.

Camp, Charles W. *The Artisan in Elizabethan Literature.* New York, 1924.

Campbell, Killis. "A Study of the Romance of the Seven Sages with Speciall Reference to the Middle English Versions," *Publications of the Modern Language Association,* XIV (1899), 1-107.

Campbell, Lily B. *Shakespeare's Tragic Heroes, Slaves of Passion.* Cambridge, 1930.

Carlisle, Nicholas. *A Concise Description of the Endowed Grammar Schools in England and Wales,* 2 vols. London, 1818.

Chambers, E. K. *The Elizabethan Stage,* 4 vols. Oxford, 1923.

Chandler, Frank W. *The Literature of Roguery,* 2 vols. London, 1907.

Chappell, William, and Ebsworth, J. W. (eds.). *The Roxburghe Ballads,* 10 vols. The Ballad Society, Hertford, 1871-99.

Chevalley, Abel. *Thomas Deloney. Le Roman des métiers au temps de Shakespeare.* Paris, 1926.

Cheyney, Edward Potts. *A History of England, from the Defeat of the Armada to the Death of Elizabeth,* 2 vols. London, 1926.

Clark, Alice. *Working Life of Women in the Seventeenth Century.* London, 1919.

Clark, Andrew (ed.). *The Shirburn Ballads, 1585-1616.* Oxford, 1907.

Clark, G. N. "Edward Grimeston, the Translator," *English Historical Review,* XLIII (1928), 585-98.

Clode, Charles Mathew. *The Early History of the Guild of Merchant Taylors,* 2 vols. London, 1888-89.

————. *Memorials of the Guild of Merchant Taylors.* London, 1875.

Cokayne, G. E. *Some Account of the Lord Mayors and Sheriffs of the City of London during the First Quarter of the Seventeenth Century.* London, 1897.

Collier, J. P. *The History of English Dramatic Poetry to the Time of Shakespeare, and Annals of the Stage to the Restoration,* 3 vols. London, 1831.

———— (ed.). *A Bibliographical and Critical Account of the Rarest Books in the English Language,* 4 vols. London, 1865.

———— (ed.). *Broadside Black-Letter Ballads.* London, 1868.

———— (ed.). *Illustrations of Early English Popular Literature,* 4 vols. London, 1864.

———— (ed.). *Illustrations of Old English Literature,* 3 vols. London, 1866.

Collinson, Richard (ed.). *The Three Voyages of Martin Frobisher in Search of a Passage to Cathaia and India by the North-West, A.D. 1576-78.* Hakluyt Society, London, 1867.

Comper, Frances M. M. (ed.). *The Book of the Craft of Dying, and Other Early English Tracts concerning Death.* London, 1917.

Conley, Carey H. *The First English Translators of the Classics.* New Haven, 1927.

Corney, Bolton (ed.). *The Voyage of Sir Henry Middleton to Bantam and the Maluco Islands; . . .* Hakluyt Society, London, 1855.

Corser, Thomas. *Collectanea Anglo-Poetica,* 5 vols. Chetham Society, Manchester, 1860-83.

Craig, Hardin. "A Contribution to the Theory of the English Renaissance," *Philological Quarterly,* VII (1928), 321-33.

Crane, R. S. "The Vogue of *Guy of Warwick* from the Close of the Middle Ages to the Romantic Revival," *Publications of the Modern Language Association,* XXX (1915), 125-94.

———. *The Vogue of Medieval Chivalric Romance during the English Renaissance.* Menasha, Wis., 1919.

Creizenach, Wilhelm. *The English Drama in the Age of Shakespeare.* Philadelphia and London, 1916.

Cullen, C. "Puritanism and the Stage," *Proceedings of the Royal Philosophical Society of Glasgow,* XLIII (1911-12), 153-81.

Cumston, Charles Greene. *An Introduction to the History of Medicine.* New York, 1926.

Cust, Lionel. "Foreign Artists of the Reformed Religion Working in London from about 1560 to 1660," *Proceedings of the Huguenot Society of London,* VII (1901-04), 45-82.

———. "Painting, Sculpture, and Engraving," *Shakespeare's England,* Vol. II. Oxford, 1916.

Dasent, John R. (ed.). *Acts of the Privy Council.* London, 1890-.

Davies, Godfrey. *Bibliography of British History, Stuart Period, 1603-1714.* Oxford, 1928.

Dawson, Giles Edwin (ed.). *The Seven Champions of Christendom, by John Kirke,* 1634, Western Reserve University *Bulletin,* N.S., No. 32 (1929).

Disraeli, Isaac. *Amenities of Literature,* 3 vols. London, 1841.

Dottin, Paul. *The Life and Strange and Surprising Adventures of Daniel Defoe,* translated by Louise Ragan. New York, 1929.

Douce, Francis (ed.). *The Customs of London, Otherwise Called Arnold's Chronicle.* London, 1811.

Edwards, Edward. *Memoirs of Libraries,* 2 vols. London, 1859.

Eggleston, Edward. *The Beginners of a Nation*. London, 1897.

————. *The Transit of Civilization from England to America in the Seventeenth Century*. New York, 1901.

Ellis, Henry (ed.). *The New Chronicles of England and France, by Robert Fabyan, 1516*. London, 1811.

———— (ed.). *Original Letters of Eminent Literary Men of the Sixteenth, Seventeenth, and Eighteenth Centuries*, Camden Society, XXIII (1843).

Ernle, Rowland Edmund. *The Light Reading of Our Ancestors*. New York, 1927.

Esdaile, Arundell J. K. *A List of English Tales and Prose Romances Printed before 1740*, The Bibliographical Society. London, 1912.

Fairholt, Frederick W. *Lord Mayors' Pageants*, Percy Society, X (1843).

Ferguson, Professor. "Books of Secrets," *Transactions of the Bibliographical Society of London*, XII (1911-13), 145-76.

Firth, Charles H. "Ballads and Broadsides," *Shakespeare's England*, Vol. II. Oxford, 1916.

————. "The Ballad History of the Reigns of Henry VII and Henry VIII," *Transactions of the Royal Historical Society*, 3d Ser., II (1908), 21-50.

————. "The Ballad History of the Reigns of the Later Tudors," *Transactions of the Royal Historical Society*, 3d Ser., III (1909), 51-124.

————. "The Ballad History of the Reign of James I," *Transactions of the Royal Historical Society*, 3d Ser., V (1911), 21-61.

————. "The Reign of Charles I," *Transactions of the Royal Historical Society*, 3d Ser., VI (1912), 19-64.

———— (ed.). *An American Garland*. Oxford, 1915.

Fischer, Julius (ed.). *Das "Interlude of the Four Elements,"* in *Marburger Studien zur englischen Philologie*, Hft. 5 (1903), pp. 41 ff.

Fletcher, William Y. *English Book Collectors*. London, 1902.

Fordham, Herbert George. *The Road-Books and Itineraries of Great Britain, 1570 to 1850*. Cambridge, 1924.

Foster, William (ed.). *The Embassy of Sir Thomas Roe to the Court of the Great Mogul, 1615-1619, as Narrated in His Journal and Correspondence*, 2 vols. Hakluyt Society, London, 1899.

Fox, Evelyn. "The Diary of an Elizabethan Gentlewoman," *Transactions of the Royal Historical Society*, 3d Ser., II (1908), 153-74.

Frere, Walter H. *The English Church in the Reigns of Elizabeth and James I*. London, 1911.

Funke, Otto. *Zum Weltsprachenproblem in England im 17. Jahrhundert*. Anglistische Forschungen, Heidelberg, 1929.

Furnivall, F. J. *Captain Cox, his Ballads and Books*, Ballad Society, 1871.

────── (ed.). *The Babees Book*, Early English Text Society, Orig. Ser., XXXII (London, 1868).

────── (ed.). *The Passionate Morrice*, 1593, New Shakespeare Society, Ser. 6, II (1876).

────── (ed.). *Robert Laneham's Letter*, New Shakespeare Society, Ser. 6, XIV (1890).

────── (ed.). *Tell-Trothes New-yeares Gift, 1593*, New Shakespeare Society, Ser. 6, II (1876).

────── (ed.). *Tom of all Trades, Or The Plaine Path-way To Preferment*, by Thomas Powell, 1631, New Shakespeare Society (1876).

────── (ed.). *Harrison's Description of England*, Pts. I-III, New Shakespeare Society, Ser. 6, I, V, VIII (1877-81) ; Pt. IV, The Shakespeare Library (1908).

Gairdner, James (ed.). *The Historical Collections of a Citizen of London in the Fifteenth Century*, Camden Society, N.S., XVII (1876).

Gardiner, Dorothy. *English Girlhood at School*. Oxford, 1929.

Garrison, Fielding H. *An Introduction to the History of Medicine*, 4th ed. Philadelphia and London, 1929.

Gaselee, Stephen (ed.). *Joyfull Newes Out Of The Newe Founde Worlde*, in *The Tudor Translations*, 2 vols. London, 1925.

Gee, Henry, and Hardy, William J. (eds.). *Documents Illustrative of English Church History*. London, 1896.

Gooch, G. P. *English Democratic Ideas in the Seventeenth Century*, 2d ed. Cambridge, 1927.

Graves, T. S. "Jonson in the Jest-Books," *Manly Anniversary Studies in Language and Literature*. Chicago, 1924.

──────. "Notes on Puritanism and the Stage," *Studies in Philology*, XVIII (1921), 141-69.

──────. "Some References to Elizabethan Theatres," *Studies in Philology*, XIX (1922), 317-27.

Greg, W. W. *Two Elizabethan Stage Abridgements: The Battle of Alcazar and Orlando Furioso*. Malone Society, London, 1922.

Gretton, R. H. *The English Middle Class*. London, 1919.

Grosart, A. B. (ed.). *The Life and Complete Works in Prose and Verse of Robert Greene*, 15 vols., Huth Library (1881-86).

────── (ed.). *The Complete Works of Joshuah Sylvester*, 2 vols., Chertsey Worthies' Library, Edinburgh, 1880.

────── (ed.). *Miscellanies of the Fuller Worthies' Library* (1870).

———— (ed.). *The Non-Dramatic Works of Thomas Dekker*, 5 vols., Huth Library (1884-86).

———— (ed.). *The Works in Verse and Prose of Nicholas Breton*, 2 vols., Chertsey Worthies' Library, Edinburgh, 1879.

———— (ed.). *Swetnam, the Woman-hater, Arraigned by Women, 1620.* Manchester, 1880.

Gunther, R. W. T. *Early British Botanists and Their Gardens.* Oxford, 1922.

Hard, Frederick. "Spenser's 'Clothes of Arras and of Toure,'" *Studies in Philology*, XXVII (1930), 162-85.

Harleian Miscellany, The, 12 vols. London, 1808-11.

Harris, Julia Hamlet (ed.). *Eastward Hoe*, "Yale Studies in English," Vol. LXXIII. New Haven, 1926.

Harrison, G. B. "Books and Readers, 1599-1603," *The Library*, XIV (1933-34), 1-33.

———— (ed.). *The Bodley Head Quartos*, Vols. I-XV. London, 1923-26.

———— (ed.). *Willobie His Avisa, 1594.* London, 1926.

Hartley, Dorothy (ed.). *Thomas Tusser.* London, 1931.

Hatcher, O. L. "Aims and Methods of Elizabethan Translators," *Englische Studien*, XLIV (1912), 174-92.

Hathaway, Charles M., Jr. (ed.). *The Alchemist, by Ben Jonson*, "Yale Studies in English," Vol. XVII. New York, 1903.

Haweis, John O. W. *Sketches of the Reformation and Elizabethan Age, Taken from the Contemporary Pulpit.* London, 1844.

Hayes, Gerald R. "Anthony Munday's Romances of Chivalry," *The Library*, 4th Ser., VI (1925-26), 57-81.

Hazlitt, W. C. *A Roll of Honour.* London, 1908.

————. *Schools, School-Books, and Schoolmasters.* London, 1888.

———— (ed.). *Old English Jest-Books*, 3 vols. London, 1864.

Headley, Alfred H. *London in Literature.* London, 1920.

Hebel, J. W., and Hudson, Hoyt H. (eds.). *Poetry of the English Renaissance, 1509-1660.* New York, 1929.

Heinrich, Joachim. *Die Frauenfrage bei Steele und Addison*, in *Palaestra*, CLXVIII (1930), 1-50.

Herbert, William. *The History of the Twelve Great Livery Companies of London*, 2 vols. London, 1836-37.

Herford, C. H., and Simpson, Percy (eds.). *Ben Jonson*, 10 vols. Oxford, 1925-.

Hewins, William A. S. *English Trade and Finance Chiefly in the Seventeenth Century.* London, 1892.

Horstmann, Carl (ed.). *Richard Rolle of Hampole . . . and His Followers*, 2 vols. Yorkshire Writers, London, 1895-96.

Hotchkiss, George B. (ed.). *A Treatise of Commerce, by John Wheeler, 1601.* New York, 1931.

Hotson, Leslie. *The Commonwealth and Restoration Stage.* Cambridge, Mass., 1928.

Hume, Martin A. S. *The Great Lord Burghley.* London, 1898.

Hunt, Mary Leland. *Thomas Dekker: A Study.* New York, 1911.

Hutchinson, F. E. "The English Pulpit from Fisher to Donne," *Cambridge History of English Literature*, IV, 257 ff.

James, Margaret. *Social Problems and Policy during the Puritan Revolution, 1640-1660.* London, 1930.

Johnson, Arthur H. *The History of the Worshipful Company of the Drapers of London*, 5 vols. Oxford, 1914-22.

Jones, John W. (ed.). *Divers Voyages Touching the Discovery of America and the Islands Adjacent*, by Richard Hakluyt, 1582. Hakluyt Society, London, 1850.

Jordan, J. C. *Robert Greene.* New York, 1915.

Judges, Arthur V. *The Elizabethan Underworld.* London, 1930.

Jupp, Edward B. *Genealogical Memoranda Relating to Richard Wyatt.* London, 1870?.

————. *An Historical Account of the Worshipful Company of Carpenters of the City of London.* London, 1848.

Jusserand, J. J. *The English Novel in the Time of Shakespeare.* London, 1899.

Kelso, Ruth. *The Doctrine of the English Gentleman in the Sixteenth Century*, "University of Illinois Studies in Language and Literature," Vol. XIV. Urbana, 1929.

Kennedy, Arthur G. *A Bibliography of Writings on the English Language from the Beginning of Printing to the End of 1922.* Cambridge and New Haven, 1927.

Kingsford, Charles L. (ed.). *Chronicles of London.* Oxford, 1905.

———— (ed.). *A Survey of London by John Stow*, 2 vols. Oxford, 1908.

———— (ed.). *Two London Chronicles*, Camden Miscellany, 3d Ser., XVIII (1910).

Kittredge, George L. *Witchcraft in Old and New England.* Cambridge, Mass., 1929.

Lake, Cuthbert. *Notes on the Will of Henry Cloker, 1573.* London, 1924.

Lambley, Kathleen. *The Teaching and Cultivation of the French Language in England during Tudor and Stuart Times.* Manchester, 1920.

Lamond, Elizabeth (ed.). *A Discourse of the Common Weal of This Realm of England* [*c.* 1549]. Cambridge, 1893.

Lange, Alexis (ed.). *The Gentlecraft, by Thomas Deloney,* in *Palaestra,* XVIII (1903).

Larkey, Sanford V. "The Vesalian Compendium of Geminus and Nicholas Udall's Translation: Their Relation to Vesalius, Caius, Vicary, and De Mondeville," *The Library,* 4th Ser., XIV (1932-33), 367-94.

Lawrence, W. J. "John Kirke, the Caroline Actor-Dramatist," *Studies in Philology,* XXI (1924), 586-93.

Leach, Arthur F. *Educational Charters and Documents, 598 to 1909.* Cambridge, 1911.

————. *English Schools at the Reformation, 1546-8.* London, 1896.

————. *The Schools of Medieval England.* London, 1915.

Lee, Sidney. "The Topical Side of the Elizabethan Drama," *Transactions* of the New Shakespeare Society (1887), pp. 1-35.

Lemon, Robert. *Catalogue of a Collection of Printed Broadsides in the Possession of the Society of Antiquaries of London.* London, 1866.

Lomas, S. C. (ed.). *Letters and Speeches of Oliver Cromwell,* 3 vols. London, 1904.

London, William. *A Catalogue Of The most vendible Books in England* (1657).

Lynch, Kathleen M. *The Social Mode of Restoration Comedy,* "University of Michigan Publications in Language and Literature," Vol. III. New York, 1926.

McIlwain, Charles Howard (ed.). *The Political Works of James I.* Cambridge, Mass., 1918.

Mackay, Charles (ed.). *A Collection of Songs and Ballads Relative to the London Prentices and Trades,* Percy Society, Vol. I (1841).

McKerrow, R. B. (ed.). *The Works of Thomas Nashe,* 5 vols. London, 1904-10.

Major, Richard H. (ed.). *The Historie of Travaile into Virginia Britannia . . . By William Strachey, Gent. . . .* Hakluyt Society, London, 1849.

Mann, Francis O. (ed.). *The Works of Thomas Deloney.* Oxford, 1912.

Mark, Harry T. *An Outline of the History of Educational Theories in England.* London, 1899.

Markham, Albert H. (ed.). *The Voyages and Works of John Davis the Navigator,* 2 vols. Hakluyt Society, London, 1880.

Markham, Clements R. (ed.). *The Hawkins Voyages during the Reigns of Henry VIII, Queen Elizabeth, and James I.* Hakluyt Society, London, 1878.

————— (ed.). *The Natural and Moral history of the Indies, by Father Joseph de Acosta, 1604*, 2 vols. Hakluyt Society, London, 1880.

Matthiessen, Francis O. *Translation, An Elizabethan Art.* Cambridge, Mass., 1931.

Meads, Dorothy M. (ed.). *Diary of Lady Margaret Hoby, 1599-1605.* Boston and New York, 1930.

Meissner, Paul. *Der Bauer in der englischen Literatur*, Bonner Studien zur englischen Philologie, Heft XV. Bonn, 1922.

Mitchell, W. Fraser. *English Pulpit Oratory from Andrewes to Tillotson.* Society for Promoting Christian Knowledge, London, 1932.

Montmorency, J. E. G. de. *The Progress of Education in England.* London, 1906.

—————. *State Intervention in English Education.* Cambridge, 1902.

Moore, J. L. *Tudor-Stuart Views on the Growth, Status, and Destiny of the English Language*, Studien zur englischen Philologie, Hft. 41. Halle a. S., 1910.

Morgan, E. Delmar, and Coote, C. H. (eds.). *Early Voyages and Travels to Russia and Persia, by Anthony Jenkinson and other Englishmen*, 2 vols. Hakluyt Society, London, 1886.

Mullinger, James B. *The University of Cambridge from the Royal Injunctions of 1535 to the Accession of Charles the First.* Cambridge, 1884.

Murch, H. S. (ed.). *The Knight of the Burning Pestle, by Beaumont and Fletcher*, "Yale Studies in English," Vol. XXXIII. New York, 1908.

Murray, James A. H. *The Evolution of English Lexicography.* Oxford, 1900.

Nicholl, John. *Some Account of the Worshipful Company of Ironmongers.* London, 1851.

Nichols, John G. *London Pageants.* London, 1831.

————— (ed.). *The Diary of Henry Machyn*, Camden Society, XLII (1848).

—————, and Bruce, John (eds.). *Wills from Doctors' Commons*, Camden Society, LXXXIII (1863).

Ordish, T. F. "Early English Inventions," *The Antiquary*, XII (1885), 1-6, 61-65, 113-18.

—————. *Early London Theatres (In the Fields).* London, 1899.

Osler, William. *The Evolution of Modern Medicine.* New Haven, 1923.

Overall, W. H. and H. C. *Analytical Index to the Series of Records Known as the Remembrancia.* London, 1878.

Owst, Gerald R. *Preaching in Medieval England.* Cambridge, 1926.

—————. *Literature and Pulpit in Medieval England.* Cambridge, 1933.

Page, William (ed.). *The Victoria History of the County of Gloucester*. London, 1907.

Palmer, Henrietta R. *List of English Editions and Translations of Greek and Latin Classics Printed before 1641*. Bibliographical Society, London, 1911.

Paradise, N. Burton. *Thomas Lodge; the History of an Elizabethan*. New Haven, 1931.

Parrott, Thomas Marc (ed.). *The Plays and Poems of George Chapman: The Comedies*. London, 1914.

Payne, L. W., Jr. (ed.). *The Hector of Germanie, or the Palsgrave Prime Elector*, by Wentworth Smith, *c.* 1616. Publications of the University of Pennsylvania, Philadelphia, 1906.

Pearce, Ernest H. *Annals of Christ's Hospital*, 2d ed. London, 1908.

Pearson, A. F. Scott. *Thomas Cartwright and Elizabethan Puritanism, 1535-1603*. Cambridge, 1925.

————. *Church and State: Political Aspects of Sixteenth Century Puritanism*. Cambridge, 1928.

Plomer, H. R. "Books Mentioned in Wills," *Transactions of the Bibliographical Society of London*, VII (1902-04), 99-121.

————. *A Dictionary of the Printers and Booksellers . . . 1668-1725*, edited by Arundell Esdaile. Bibliographical Society, Oxford, 1922.

————. "Robert Copland," *Transactions of the Bibliographical Society of London*, III (1895-96), 211-25.

Pollard, A. F. "The Advent of the Middle Class," *Factors in Modern History*. London, 1907.

————, and Redgrave, G. R. (eds.). *A Short Title Catalogue of Books Printed in England, Scotland, and Ireland and of English Books Printed Abroad, 1475-1640*. The Bibliographical Society, London, 1926.

Pollard, A. W. "The Unity of John Norden: Surveyor and Religious Writer," *The Library*, 4th Ser., VII (1926-27), 233-52.

Ponsonby, Arthur. *More English Diaries*. London, 1927.

Powell, Chilton. *English Domestic Relations, 1487-1653*. New York, 1917.

Power, D'Arcy. *The Foundations of Medical History*. Baltimore, 1931.

Prideaux, W. S. *Memorials of the Goldsmiths' Company*, 2 vols. London, 1896.

Proctor, Francis, and Frere, Walter Howard. *A New History of the Book of Common Prayer*. London, 1914.

Quick, Robert H. (ed.). *Positions of Richard Mulcaster*. London, 1888.

Raleigh, Walter. *The English Novel*. London, 1894.

————— (ed.). *The Book of the Courtier*, by Baldassare Castiglione, translated by Sir Thomas Hoby, 1561, *The Tudor Translations*. London, 1900.

Read, Conyers. *Bibliography of British History, Tudor Period, 1485-1603*. Oxford, 1933.

—————. *Mr. Secretary Walsingham and the Policy of Queen Elizabeth*, 3 vols. Oxford, 1925.

Reed, Arthur W. *Early Tudor Drama*. London, 1926.

Reynolds, Myra. *The Learned Lady in England, 1650-1760*. Boston and New York, 1920.

Roberts, J. H. "Samuel Daniels' Relation to the Histories and Historical Poetry of the Sixteenth Century," *Abstracts of Theses* (University of Chicago Press, 1923-24), pp. 402-3.

Robertson, H. M. "Sir Bevis Bulmer, A Large-Scale Speculator of Elizabethan and Jacobean Times," *Journal of Economic and Business History*, IV (1931), 99-120.

Rohde, Eleanor S. *The Old English Herbals*. London, 1922.

Rollins, Hyder E. *An Analytical Index to the Ballad-Entries (1557-1709) in the Registers of the Company of Stationers of London*. Chapel Hill, N.C., 1924.

—————. "The Black-Letter Broadside Ballad," *Publications of the Modern Language Association*, XXXIV (1919), 258-339.

—————. "Martin Parker," *Modern Philology*, XVI (1918-19), 449-74.

—————. "William Elderton: Elizabethan Actor and Ballad Writer," *Studies in Philology*, XVII (1920), 199-245.

————— (ed.). *Old English Ballads, 1553-1625*. Cambridge, 1920.

————— (ed.). *The Pack of Autolycus*. Cambridge, Mass., 1927.

————— (ed.). *The Pepys Ballads*, 8 vols. Cambridge, Mass., 1929-32.

————— (ed.). *A Pepysian Garland*. Cambridge, 1922.

Routh, H. V. "The Advent of Modern Thought in Popular Literature," *Cambridge History of English Literature*, Vol. VII.

—————. "London and the Development of Popular Literature," *Cambridge History of English Literature*, Vol. IV.

—————. "The Progress of Social Literature in Tudor Times," *Cambridge History of English Literature*, Vol. III.

Rundall, Thomas (ed.). *Memorials of the Empire of Japan in the 16th and 17th Centuries*. Hakluyt Society, London, 1850.

Rushworth, John. *Historical Collections*, 8 vols. (1680-1701).

Russell, Harry K. "Certain Doctrines of Natural and Moral Philosophy as an Approach to the Study of Elizabethan Drama ; with an Appendix Containing Illustrative Material from the Plays of Ben Jonson," University of North Carolina unpublished dissertation (1931).

————. "Elizabethan Dramatic Poetry in the Light of Natural and Moral Philosophy," *Philological Quarterly*, XII (1933), 187-95.

Sandys, John Edwin. "Education," *Shakespeare's England*, Vol. I. Oxford, 1916.

Schelling, Felix. *Elizabethan Drama, 1558-1642*, 2 vols. Boston and New York, 1908.

————. *The English Chronicle Play.* New York, 1902.

Schoell, F. L. *Études sur l'humanisme continental en Angleterre à la fin de la Renaissance.* Paris, 1926.

————. "G. Chapman's 'Commonplace Book,' " *Modern Philology*, XVII (1919-20), 199-218.

Schücking, Levin L. *Die Familie im Puritanismus.* Leipzig and Berlin, 1929.

Scott, E. J. L. (ed.). *Letter Book of Gabriel Harvey, A.D. 1573-1580.* Camden Society, n.s., XXXIII (1884).

Scott, Mary Augusta. *Elizabethan Translations from the Italian.* Boston and New York, 1916.

Scudder, Vida D. *Social Ideals in English Letters.* Boston and New York, 1923.

Seager, Herbert W. *Natural History in Shakespeare's Time.* London, 1896.

Sedgwick, William T., and Tyler, Harry W. *A Short History of Science.* New York, 1929.

Shaaber, Matthias A. *Some Forerunners of the Newspaper in England, 1476-1622.* Philadelphia, 1929.

Sharpe, Reginald R. *London and the Kingdom*, 3 vols. London, 1894.

————. *Calendar of Wills . . . in the Court of Husting*, 2 vols. London, 1889-90.

Sherwell, John W. *A Descriptive and Historical Account of the Guild of Saddlers of the City of London*, 2 vols. London, 1889.

Singer, Charles. *A Short History of Medicine.* Oxford, 1928.

Sisson, Charles J. *Le gout public et le théâtre élisabéthain.* Dijon, 1922.

————. "Keep the Widow Waking, a Lost Play by Dekker," *The Library*, 4th Ser., VIII (1927-28), 39-57, 233-59.

Smith, G. C. Moore. *Gabriel Harvey's Marginalia.* Stratford-upon-Avon, 1913.

Smith, G. Gregory (ed.). *Elizabethan Critical Essays*, 2 vols. Oxford, 1904.

Sombart, Werner. *The Quintessence of Capitalism*, translated and edited from Sombart's *Der Bourgeois*, 1913, by M. Epstein. New York, 1915.

Spedding, James. *The Letters and the Life of Francis Bacon*, 7 vols. London, 1861-72.

Spingarn, Joel E. (ed.). *Critical Essays of the Seventeenth Century*, 3 vols. Oxford, 1908-09.

Starnes, D. T. "Purpose in the Writing of History," *Modern Philology*, XX (1922-23), 281-300.

————. *Sir Thomas Elyot and the "Sayings of the Philosophers,"* "University of Texas Studies in English," Vol. XIII (1933).

Statham, Edward P. *A Jacobean Letter-Writer: The Life and Times of John Chamberlain*. London, 1920.

Stauffer, Donald A. *English Biography before 1700*. Cambridge, Mass., 1930.

Stephen, Leslie, and Lee, Sidney (eds.). *Dictionary of National Biography*, 22 vols. New York, 1908-09.

Stephens, F. G. *Catalogue of Prints and Drawings in the British Museum. I. Political and Personal Satires*. London, 1870.

Stone, Wilbur Macy. *The Thumb Bible of John Taylor*. Brookline, Mass., 1928.

Stonex, A. B. "Money-Lending and Money-Lenders in England during the 16th and 17th Centuries," *Schelling Anniversary Studies*. New York, 1923.

Surrey Wills. Surrey Record Society, London, 1920.

Symonds, E. M. "The Diary of John Greene, 1635-1657," *English Historical Review*, XLIII (1928), 385-94.

Tanner, J. R. *Tudor Constitutional Documents*. Cambridge, 1922.

Tawney, R. H. *The Agrarian Problem in the Sixteenth Century*. London, 1912.

————. *Religion and the Rise of Capitalism*. London, 1929.

————. "Studies in Bibliography. II. Modern Capitalism," *The Economic History Review*, IV (1933), 336-56.

———— (ed.). *A Discourse Upon Usury*, by Thomas Wilson. London, 1925.

Taylor, Eva G. R. *Tudor Geography, 1485-1583*. London, 1930.

Thomas, Henry. "The Palmerin Romances," *Transactions of the Bibliographical Society of London*, XIII (1913-15), 98-144.

————. "The Romance of Amadis of Gaul," *Sociedade portuguesa de estudas historicos* (Porto, 1916).

————. *Spanish and Portuguese Romances of Chivalry*. Cambridge, 1920.

Thompson, Edward M. (ed.). *Diary of Richard Cocks, Cape-Merchant in the English Factory in Japan, 1615-1622*, 2 vols. Hakluyt Society, London, 1883.

Thompson, Elbert N. S. *The Controversy between the Puritans and the Stage*, "Yale Studies in English," Vol. XX. New York, 1903.

————. *Literary Bypaths of the Renaissance*. New Haven, 1924.

Thompson, Guy A. *Elizabethan Criticism of Poetry*. Menasha, Wis., 1914.

Thorp, Margaret Farrand. "Shakespeare and the Fine Arts," *Publications of the Modern Language Association*, XLVI (1931), 672-93.

Thorp, Willard. *The Triumph of Realism in Elizabethan Drama*. Princeton, 1928.

Tilley, Morris P. *Elizabethan Proverb Lore in Lyly's Euphues and in Pettie's Petite Pallace, with Parallels from Shakespeare*, "University of Michigan Publications, Language and Literature," Vol. II (1926).

Traill, Henry D., and Mann, J. S. (eds.). *Social England*, 6 vols. London and New York, 1902-04.

Tymms, Samuel (ed.). *Wills and Inventories from the Registers of the Commissary of Bury St. Edmunds and the Archdeacon of Sudbury*, Camden Society, Vol. XLIX (1850).

Underhill, John G. *Spanish Literature in the England of the Tudors*. New York, 1899.

Unwin, George. "Commerce and Coinage," *Shakespeare's England*, Vol. I. Oxford, 1916.

————. *The Gilds and Companies of London*. London, 1908.

————. "Medieval Gilds and Education," *Studies in Economic History: The Collected Papers of George Unwin*. London, 1927.

Usher, Abbott P. *An Introduction to the Industrial History of England*. Boston and New York, 1920.

Ustick, W. L. "Advice to a Son : A Type of Seventeenth-Century Conduct Book," *Studies in Philology*, XXIX (1932), 409-41.

————. "Changing Ideals of Aristocratic Character and Conduct in Seventeenth Century England," *Modern Philology*, XXX (1932-33), 147-66.

————. "The English Gentleman in the Sixteenth and Early Seventeenth Century," Harvard University unpublished dissertation (1931).

Velte, Friedrich Mowbray. *The Bourgeois Elements in the Dramas of Thomas Heywood*. Princeton, 1922.

Verney, Margaret M. *Memoirs of the Verney Family, during the Commonwealth, 1650 to 1660.* 4 vols. London, 1892-99.

Wadmore, James F. *Some Account of the Worshipful Company of Skinners of London.* London, 1902.

Wallace, Malcolm W. *The Life of Sir Philip Sidney.* Cambridge, 1915.

Watson, Foster. *The Beginnings of the Teaching of Modern Subjects in England.* London, 1909.

————. "The Curriculum and Text-Books of English Schools in the First Half of the Seventeenth Century," *Transactions of the Bibliographical Society*, VI (London, 1900-02), 159-267.

————. *The English Grammar Schools to 1660: Their Curriculum and Practice.* Cambridge, 1908.

————. "George Snell and Right Teaching," *Educational Review* (London), Jan., 1896, pp. 408-14.

————. *The Old Grammar Schools.* Cambridge, 1916.

————. *Richard Hakluyt.* London, 1924.

————. "Richard Mulcaster and his 'Elementarie,'" *Educational Times*, Jan., 1893.

————. *Vives and the Renascence Education of Women.* London, 1912.

Webb, R. (ed.). *Historical Notices of Events Occurring Chiefly in the Reign of Charles I., by Nehemiah Wallington*, 2 vols. London, 1869.

Weber, Max. *The Protestant Ethic and the Spirit of Capitalism*, translated by Talcott Parsons. New York, 1930.

Weigall, Rachel. "An Elizabethan Gentlewoman," *Quarterly Review*, CCXV (1911), 119-38.

Welch, Charles. *History of the Worshipful Company of Pewterers of the City of London*, 2 vols. London, 1902.

————. *History of the Cutlers' Company of London*, 2 vols. London, 1923.

Wertenbaker, Thomas J. *The First Americans, 1607-1690.* New York, 1927.

Wheatley, Henry B. "Notes on Some English Heterographers," *Transactions of the Philological Society* (1865), pp. 13-59.

White, Beatrice. "Three Rare Books about Women," *The Huntington Library Bulletin*, No. 2 (1931), pp. 165-71.

————. "Two Tracts on Marriage by Robert Copland," *The Huntington Library Bulletin*, No. 1 (1931), pp. 205-7.

White, Helen C. *English Devotional Literature [Prose], 1600-1640*, "University of Wisconsin Studies in Language and Literature," Madison, 1931.

Wilenski, R. H. *An Introduction to Dutch Art.* London, 1928.

Williams, William M. *Annals of the Worshipful Company of Founders of the City of London*. London, 1867.

Williamson, George C. *Lady Anne Clifford*. London, 1922.

Willkom, H. W. *Über Richard Johnsons Seven Champions of Christendome*. Berlin, 1911.

Wilson, F. P. *The Plague in Shakespeare's London*. Oxford, 1927.

———— (ed.). *The Batchelars Banquet*. Oxford, 1929.

———— (ed.). *Foure Birds Of Noahs Arke, by Thomas Dekker*. Oxford, 1924.

———— (ed.). *The Plague Pamphlets of Thomas Dekker*. Oxford, 1925.

Wilson, H. B. *The History of Merchant-Taylors' School*, 2 vols. London, 1812-14.

Wilson, J. D. "The Puritan Attack on the Stage," *Cambridge History of English Literature*, Vol. VI.

Wilson, Violet A. *Society Women of Shakespeare's Time*. London, 1924.

Winslow, Ola Elizabeth. *American Broadside Verse*. New Haven, 1930.

Withington, Robert. *English Pageantry*, 2 vols. Cambridge, Mass., 1918-20.

Wolff, Samuel L. *The Greek Romances in Elizabethan Prose Fiction*. New York, 1912.

Wood, Norman. *The Reformation and English Education*. London, 1931.

Woodward, W. H. "English Universities, Schools, and Scholarship in the Sixteenth Century," *Cambridge History of English Literature*, Vol. III.

————. *Studies in Education during the Age of the Renaissance, 1400-1600*. Cambridge, 1906.

Wright, Arnold. *Early English Adventurers in the East*. London, 1917.

Wright, Louis B. "Henry Robarts : Patriotic Propagandist and Novelist," *Studies in Philology*, XXIX (1932), 176-99.

————. "Heywood and the Popularizing of History," *Modern Language Notes*, XLIII (1928), 287-93.

————. "The Reading of Renaissance English Women," *Studies in Philology*, XXVIII (1931), 671-88.

————. "The Scriptures and the Elizabethan Stage," *Modern Philology*, XXVI (1928), 47-56.

————. "William Painter and the Vogue of Chaucer as a Moral Teacher," *Modern Philology*, XXXI (1933-34), 165-74.

Wright, Thomas G. *Literary Culture in Early New England, 1620-1730*. New Haven, 1920.

INDEX

A., I., tr. *See* Pliny, *A Summarie of the Antiquities.*

A., L., tr. *See* Ortuñez, *The Mirrour of Princely deedes, The Seuenth Booke.*

Abbot, George, *A Briefe Description of the whole worlde,* 535.

Abbot, Morris, alderman, 162 n.

Abbot, W. R., "The Influence of Du Bartas," 558 n.

Abbott, John, 45 n.

Abridgment of Camden's Britaña, The. See Camden, W.

Abridgement of the Booke of Acts and Monumentes, An. See Foxe, J.

Abridgement of the Chronicles of England, An. See Grafton, R.

Abridgment of the Histories of Trogus Pompeius, The. See Justine.

Abridgements. *See* Epitomes.

Academiarum Examen. See Webster, J.

Academy of Complements, The. See Philomusus.

Achademy of Eloquence, The, 146 n.

Accidence, An. See Smith, J.

Acosta, Joseph de, *The Naturall and Morall Historie,* tr. by E. G., 563.

Actors Remonstrance, The, 609.

Acts and Monuments. See Foxe, J.

Acts of the Privy Council. See Lyte, H. C. M.; *see* Dasent, J. R.

Adagia. See Erasmus, D.

Adams, J. Q., 609-10, 620; *Shakespearean Playhouses,* 606; ed. *See* Herbert, H., *The Dramatic Records;* ed. *See* Mason, J., *The Turke.*

Adams, Thomas, *Mystical Bedlam,* 494 n.

Adamson, J. W., "The Extent of Literacy in England," 44 n., 103-4; *Pioneers of Modern Education,* 67 n., 104 n.; *A Short History of Education,* 45 n.; tr. *See* Comenius, *Reformation of Schooles.*

Addison, Joseph, 225, 637, 659.

Admiral's Men, 615.

Advancement of Learning. See Bacon, F.

"Advent of Modern Thought in Popular Literature, The." *See* Routh, H. V.

Advice How to Plant Tobacco, An. See T., C.

Advice of W. P. to Mr. Samuel Hartlib, The. See Petty, W.

Advice to a Son. See Osborn, F.

Aelianus, 561, 573.

Æsop, 79, 231, 400.

Æthopian Historie, An. See Heliodorus.

Africa, 510, 563.

Age plays of Thomas Heywood, 620.

Agincourt, 623.

Agnus Dei, An. See Weever, J.

Agrarian Problem in the Sixteenth Century. See Tawney, R. H.

Agrippa, Cornelius, *The Commendation of Matrimony,* tr. by D. Clapham, 470; *A Treatise of the Nobilitie . . . of woman kynde,* tr. by D. Clapham, 470.

"Aims and Methods of Elizabethan Translators." *See* Hatcher, O. L.

Akers, Thomas, 58.

Alarm for London, An, 628 n.

Allarme to England. See Rich, B.

Albions England. See Warner, W.

Albumazar, 611 n.

Alchemist, The. See Jonson, B.

Alchemy, 551, 593.

Alday, John. *See* Boaistuau, P., *Theatrum Mundi.*

Alde, John, 360, 376.

Alden, R. M., 616, 617; *The Rise of Formal Satire,* 479 n., 484; ed. *See* Beaumont, F., *The Knight of the Burning Pestle.*

Aldermen of Cripplegate Ward. See Baddeley, J. J.

Aldermen of the City of London, The. See Beaven, A. B.

Aleman, Mateo, *The Rogue,* tr. by J. Mabbe, 409.

Aleppo, 365, 544.

Alexis Piemont, The last parte of. See Hill, T.

Allegory, moralized, 228, 294; religious, 395 ff.; economic, 399; of the body, 581.

Allen, William, alderman, 356.

Alleyn, Edward, actor, 61, 620.

Allot, Robert, *Wits Theater of the little World,* 151, 300.

Allwit (character in *A Chaste Maid in Cheapside*), 653.

Almanacs, 85, 90, 565, 566 n., 567 n., 585, 594; contain handbook information, 168-69; burlesque, 169, 450; popularity of, 450.

Amadis of Gaul, 375, 378.

tellectual development, 16-17; literary interest, 18; pride, 19 ff.; rivalry with aristocracy, 20, 32; learning, 43 ff.; influence of learning on religion, 55; influence upon utilitarian learning, 66 ff.; faith in learning, 78; quest for education, 80; literary taste, 81 ff., 87 ff., 100; catholicity of literary taste, 83, 85; lists of books bought by, 89; writers, 93; sneered at by Nashe, 93; ridiculed in literature, 95; favorite writers and works, 97; taste for pious works, 101; diversity of literary taste, 103; education of women, 104, 107; literary taste of women, 107 ff.; women read romances, 115 ff.; desire handbooks, 114 ff., 128, 169; ideals influenced by conduct books, 124; helped to gentility by courtesy books, 128-30; aided by conversation manuals, 132 ff.; letter-writing manuals for, 139 ff.; letter expresses bourgeois ideas, 143-44; wisdom literature for, 146 ff.; cultural training from history, 153 ff.; desire for factual information, 155; technical handbooks for merchants, 160 ff.; guidebooks for, 163 ff.; epitomes of prudential wisdom for, 165 ff.; piety taught, 167 ff.; belief in diligence and thrift, 170 ff,; worship of prudential morality, 185 ff.; faith in business success, 199-200; theory of domestic relations, 201 ff.; position of women, 201, 218; marriage and divorce, 206 ff., 213-14; parents' duties in choice of mates, 208 ff.; pamphlets discuss domestic relations, 209 ff.; marriages with upper class, 211, 213 n.; ideals of domestic relations reduced to a code, 226; influence of books on domestic relations, 227; taste for pious works, 228 ff.; not interested in theology, 228, 240; buy religious books, 229; read Bible, 236; need concordances, 237; find practical guidance in Bible and devotional works, 237-38, 240, 241 ff.; independent of clergy, 240-41, 295; in conflict with established church, 241; hate idleness, 256; ideal of life and religion, 258; religion maintains established order, 266; prosperity taught by devotional books, 268; influenced by preachers, 269 ff.; sermons appeal to prejudices, 272 ff.; 288, 291; suited by mild Calvinism, 279; prefer conservative sermons, 291-92; taste for history, 297 ff.; consider history perfect literature, 301; praised by Stow, 311 ff.; glorification ridiculed, 312-14; read verse histories, 326 ff.; popularity of Foxe's work on martyrs, 333 ff.; effect of history upon intellectual development, 337 ff.; intellectual background, 339; interest in languages, 339; obligations of translators to, 341 ff., 345; want utilitarian translations, 353 ff.; study modern languages, 357 ff., 371-72; realize value of English language, 367 ff., 371; stories to amuse and edify, 375 ff.; delight in romances, 376, 377 ff.; read Euphues, 383; Greene's romances, 384 ff.; Richard Johnson's works, 391 ff.; taste for stories increases, 393 ff., 417; religious allegories for, 395 ff.; interest in journalistic ballads and pamphlets, 418 ff.; write ballads, 420 ff.; heroes of ballads, 422; satirized in ballads, 426; praised in ballads, 429-31; interested in news, 433, domestic problems, 435; pamphlets to satisfy, 436 ff., 445; read of plague and death, 446-50; commercial propaganda, 431 ff., 435 ff., 450 ff.; interest in judgments of God, 460-63; read jest books, 463-64; interest in books about women, 465, 471, 473, 487 ff., 503 ff.; position of women, 466 ff., 506-7; vanity of women condemned, 478 ff., 503 n.; extravagance of citizens' wives, 490-91, 494-95; interested in travel literature, 508 ff., 547-48; commercial interest in travel, 510 ff.; merchants and mariners write of travels, 510 ff., 547-48; popularity of sailors' adventure stories, 515 ff.; pride of, 520; Henry Robarts, citizen-writer, 524; geographical interest, 525 ff.; Hakluyt appeals to prejudice of, 530; belief in godliness of expansion into heathen countries, 532; popularity of John Smith's writings, 540 ff.; interest in travels in Near East, 543 ff., in Europe, 545 ff.; develop spirit of inquiry, 549-50, 598; acquaintance with scientific knowledge, 551, 599 ff.; aided by encyclopedias, 551-54; not interested in scientific method, 556; interpreted science religiously, 554 ff.; natural history popular, 554 ff., 571 ff.; vagueness of scientific knowledge, 564; scientific lectures for, 599 ff.; acquire scientific lore, 601-2; find botany useful, 574 ff.; medical knowledge of, 580 ff.; favorite sciences, 592-93; interested in inventions, 595 ff.; pleasure in plays, 603 ff., 607-8, 636-37, 653-54; drama opposed on some grounds, 604 ff.; theaters catering to, 609 ff., 654; pleased with varied entertainment, 611-13; dramatic taste of, 612-

DATE DUE

DEC 13 2003	
JAN 27 2009	